Surfing Eu

Chris Nelson and Demi Taylor

“”

Surfing throughout Europe to me is always best done in a campervan so that you can be on the spot for those frequent wind changes and swell pulses that can happen sometimes more than once a day. Being able to surf Hossegor in the morning until it’s too big then head off down to Mundaka in the afternoon for the all-time wave is something I will always remember.

Al Hunt, Association Surfing Professionals (ASP) Contest Director

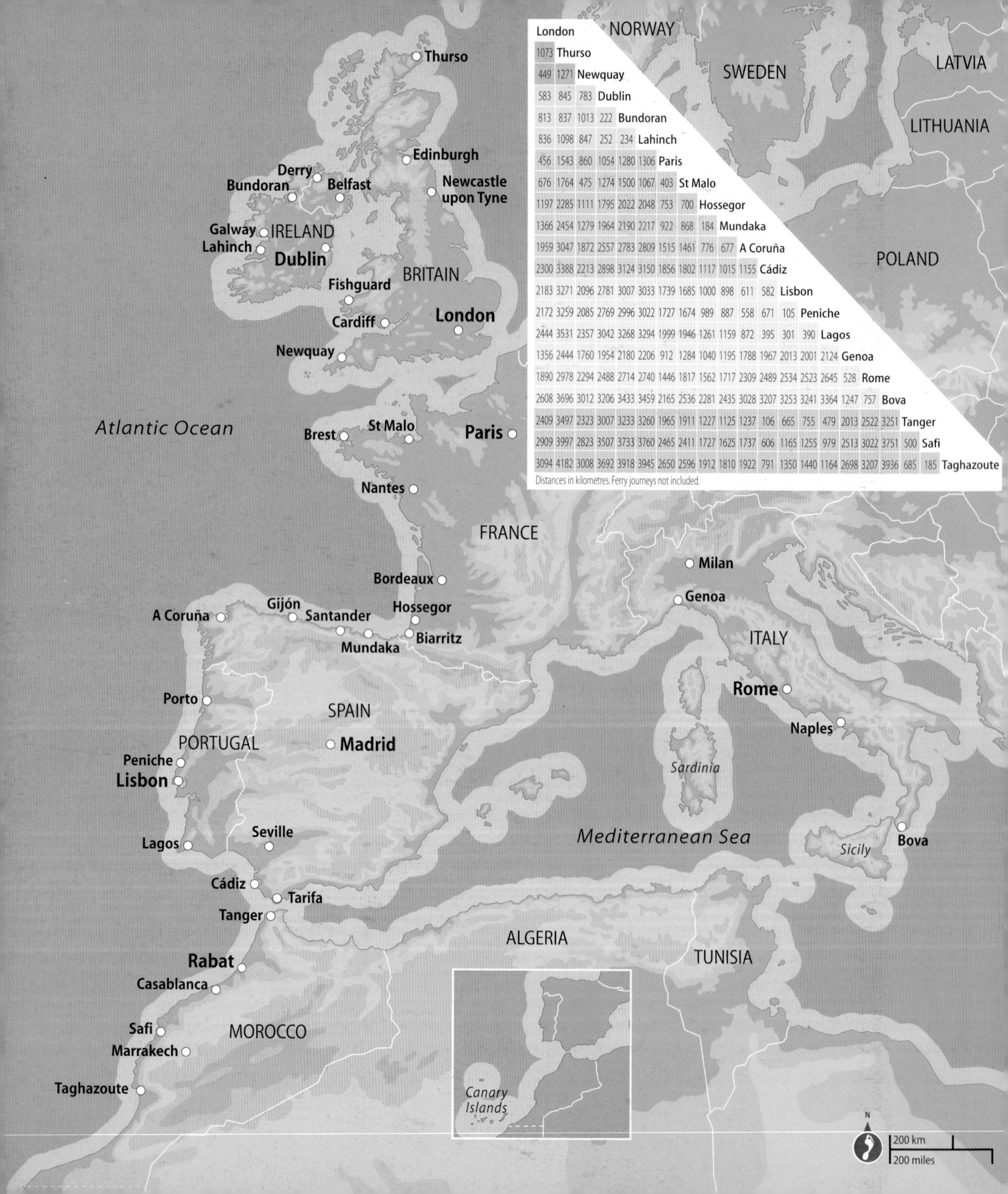

	London	Thurso	Newquay	Dublin	Bundoran	Lahinch	Paris	St Malo	Hossegor	Mundaka	A Coruña	Cádiz	Lisbon	Peniche	Lagos	Genoa	Rome	Bova	Tanger	Safi
Thurso	1073																			
Newquay	449	1271																		
Dublin	583	845	783																	
Bundoran	813	837	1013	222																
Lahinch	836	1098	847	252	234															
Paris	456	1543	860	1054	1280	1306														
St Malo	676	1764	475	1274	1500	1067	403													
Hossegor	1197	2285	1111	1795	2022	2048	753	700												
Mundaka	1366	2454	1279	1964	2190	2217	922	868	184											
A Coruña	1959	3047	1872	2557	2783	2809	1515	1461	776	677										
Cádiz	2300	3388	2213	2898	3124	3150	1856	1802	1117	1015	1155									
Lisbon	2183	3271	2096	2781	3007	3033	1739	1685	1000	898	611	582								
Peniche	2172	3259	2085	2769	2996	3022	1727	1674	989	887	558	671	105							
Lagos	2444	3531	2357	3042	3268	3294	1999	1946	1261	1159	872	395	301	390						
Genoa	1356	2444	1760	1954	2180	2206	912	1284	1040	1195	1788	1967	2013	2001	2124					
Rome	1890	2978	2294	2488	2714	2740	1446	1817	1562	1717	2309	2489	2534	2523	2645	528				
Bova	2608	3696	3012	3206	3433	3459	2165	2536	2281	2435	3028	3207	3253	3241	3364	1247	757			
Tanger	2409	3497	2323	3007	3233	3260	1965	1911	1227	1125	1237	106	665	755	479	2013	2522	3251		
Safi	2909	3997	2823	3507	3733	3760	2465	2411	1727	1625	1737	606	1165	1255	979	2513	3022	3751	500	
Taghazoute	3094	4182	3008	3692	3918	3945	2650	2596	1912	1810	1922	791	1350	1440	1164	2698	3207	3936	685	185

Distances in kilometres. Ferry journeys not included.

DAMIEN POULLENOT

Outside perspective

Perspective. We all know that a wave viewed from the shore looks very different when seen from the line-up. Similarly, the jostling pack of surfers bobbing way outside seems distant when separated from the land by fizzing lines of white water. They become a different entity when viewed from the paddle out – that last duck-dive bringing you into a whole new realm.

Although our lifestyle has undergone a massive shift over the last ten years, surfing itself has still managed to remain fundamentally detached from everyday convention. We are not sitting on the margins, watching from a safe distance, but nor are we cut adrift, floating aimlessly. Surfing positions itself 'outside', just close enough to the mainstream to ride the odd wave of benefit, but not close enough so we end up stranded on the shore. Our line-up will always be dynamic, somewhere between the blue-black of the deep ocean and the white sand of the beach – where the magic happens, where the two worlds collide. Being a surfer is still about riding waves, just as it was back in the fifties when Europe first walked the board and just as it was when the original Waikiki beach boys rode those Hawaiian south shore peelers in the early 20th century. Surfers are still an outside set. For a surfer, waveriding is all about perspective, and the best view is always from outback.

Contents

Essentials

Britain

Ireland

France

Spain

Contents

Portugal

Italy

Morocco

Cover image
Fergal Smith, Ireland
by Sharpy

Title page image
by Laurent Masurel

About the book

Change. It is at the very heart of surfing. As surfers we are attuned to the constantly changing elements, diverse weather patterns and endlessly shifting sandbars. We have also developed a strong appreciation of the history and nostalgia ingrained within our lifestyle. Special moments captured, unique times that will never again be repeated – like a perfect swell where every wave is savoured and then locked away in the memory to be relived sometime in the future.

This second edition of Surfing Europe reflects the changes that have occurred in European surfing over the last three or four years. Although the book started life as an update of the original, it soon became apparent that the very dynamic of our shifting lifestyle warranted a complete rewrite and revision. When you see how many changes have occurred across this continent, it helps you realise just how fluid our lifestyle is. Yes, shops open and close and new accommodation options spring up, but in the line-up we have seen a continued growth in crowds and a change in the composition of the crew outback. Shifting demographics, a change in the balance of the sexes and different experience levels have coincided with a rise in the profile of new surf locations and new styles of surfing.

With the increase in crowd levels has come an increased appreciation of the concept of the secret spot or semi-secret spot. Some are world class, but most are simply places to get away from the crowds, perhaps no better than the breaks nearby. In this book we have not set out to map the entire coastline of Europe. It is important to leave plenty of scope for exploration and to preserve those hidden gems. Surfing is all the richer by having breaks that offer a few quiet waves to those who are willing to search them out, or to know that there are spots left that we can stumble upon while exploring. Many surfers now worry that this is under threat from a new breed of Internet sites that seem to revel in the posting of secret spots, lacking any form of editorial control. You will not find secret spots within this book.

What you will find is knowledge and advice pooled from the surfers across this vast continent, from WCT pros to underground heroes and local chargers, from magazine editors to surf shop owners, and from surf explorers to environmentalists including Surfers Against Sewage, Surfrider Europe and Save the Waves. Surf photography has undergone a seismic shift which you will see reflected in the quality of the new selection of images contributed by the world's leading lensmen. For each region featured in Surfing Europe we have included board recommendations. We wanted to work with the world's leading authority, and through their extensive network of leading shapers from Al Merrick through Rusty Presiendorfer to Wayne Lynch, Surftech were our natural choice. We have also incorporated the feedback from the first edition and mixed it all with over 20 years' experience scouring the European coastline for waves. For those who sent through feedback on the first edition, many thanks. Remember, there's a huge continent out there with waves still going unridden. Go explore.

About the authors

Chris Nelson and Demi Taylor are two of Europe's leading surf travel writers with a combined surf travel experience of over 30 years. They have written five books on surfing and contribute regularly to the surf media across the globe, as well as national magazines and newspapers on surf travel issues. Chris started surfing in the mid eighties on the frigid reefs of England's northeast coast. He founded and edited *Asylum* and *Freeride,* two of the UK's most influential boardsports magazines. Demi caught her first wave in '92 and has been hooked ever since. Before becoming established as a freelance photojournalist, she managed the UK communications for the world's largest surf brand.

Having dreamt up the idea of Surfing Europe on a long road trip, they packed in their 'desk jobs', packed up their van and undertook a year of intensive on the road research – surfing, exploring and documenting the whole of Europe's Atlantic coastline. The resulting groundbreaking first edition was published by Footprint in 2004 to critical acclaim. They have also written the best selling *Surfing Britain* and *Surfing the World* and live in Cornwall overlooking the sea. www.halfnelson.co.uk.

Acknowledgements

We'd like to say a thank you to all those who contributed their time, tales, thoughts, wisdom, images and support during this mammoth undertaking and the original Surfing Europe project. We would especially like to thank: The Gill for his slightly random, but massively in-depth filing cabinet memory; Nik Zanella editor of Surfnews for his priceless Italian knowledge; Andy Hill for his insight into surfing in Northern Ireland; Duke Brouwer of Surftech for coordinating the board selection for each region and our lovely sponsors Gravis for ensuring that whether we're flip-flopping through the jungles of Central America or clambering down to a soggy Scottish point, they've got our feet covered – cheers Dan.

A big thank you goes to Tony Butt, Save the Waves Coalition founder Will Henry, Mike Fordham, Den Tolley, Roger Sharp, John S Callahan, Andy Marr, Thierry Organoff and Surfer's Against Sewage Campaign Officer Andy Cummins who all brought a unique personal insight into this wave-rich continent through their surfer's tales. Many thanks also to Chops Lascelles, Chris 'Guts' Griffiths, Mark Lumsden, Sam Christopherson, Pat Keiran, Chris Noble, Andrew Harrison, Ben Pepler, Nick Noble, Gary Rogers, Tommo, Roger Povey, Will Boex, Minzie, James Hendy, Nick Lavery, Derek McCloud, Tim Nunn editor *Wavelength*, Vince Medeiros editor *Huck*, Jesse Davies, Louise Searle Surf Girl, Fergal Smith, Riche Fitzgerald, Graham Collins, Paul McCarthy, Ben Farr, Roy Kilfeather, Bertrand Portrat editor *Trip Surf*, Fred Robin, Phil Grace, Nick Gammon, Franck Lacaze, Surfrider Foundation, Fred Papageorgiou, Damien Poullenot, Kristen Pelou, Nick Lavery, Ian Cairns, Dani Garcia, Fernando Munoz editor *Surfer Rule*, Willy Uribe, Dan Harris, Joao da Camara Valente editor *Surf Portugal*, Nick Urrichio, Laurent Miramon, Dominique Kent, Marcus Waters, Toby Milliage, Shayne MacIntyre, Emilano Cataldi, Dan Malloy, CJ and Damien Hobgood, Marcus Sanders editor *Surfline*, Lars Jacobsen editor *Surfers*, and ASP Contest Director Al Hunt.

Special thanks to Maisie, David, Bron and Richard for helping to get us here and to Sarah and Damian Tate, Claire King and Bryony Claxton for technical and moral support.

Huge appreciation goes, as always, to the whole Footprint crew on our fourth project together. They epitomise the real spirit of surf travel – they've had their van stolen in Sydney, crashed motorbikes in Nam, caught Dengue Fever in Venezuela, been robbed by banditos in Costa Rica, arrested in Laos and shot in a hold-up in Mexico, all in the name of research. Special thanks go to Alan 'Silver Murpher' Murphy, Pat Dawson, Andy Riddle, Rob Lunn, Sarah Sorensen and Angus Dawson.

Photography

Damien Poullenot, Laurent Masurel, Alex Laurel, Demi Taylor, The Gill, Sharpy, Tim Nunn, Scott Wicking, Stu Norton, John S Callahan, Greg Martin, Ester Spears, Andy Hill, Kristen Pelou, Thierry Organoff, Tony Plant, Roger Powley, Ben Selway, Paudie Scanlon, Mickey Smith, Yannick Le Toquin, Jakue Andikotxea, Juan Fernandez, Willy Uribe, Jordan Weeks, O'Neill, Josh Sward, Joao Maya, Carla Tome, JS Callahan, Will Henry, Hilton Dawe, Krisha Sowinski, Marcus Waters, Lucia Griggi, Den Tolley, Rocco Cartisano, Emiliano Cataldi, Emiliano Mazzoni, Alessandro Dini, Davide Sacchetti, Riccardo Ghilardi, Al MacKinnon, Achille Piotrowicz, ghiglio.com, Salomon, Giuseppe Arioni, Stefano Viola, Antonio Muglia, Elena Gramolelli.

Chris Nelson and Demi Taylor, on the road research.

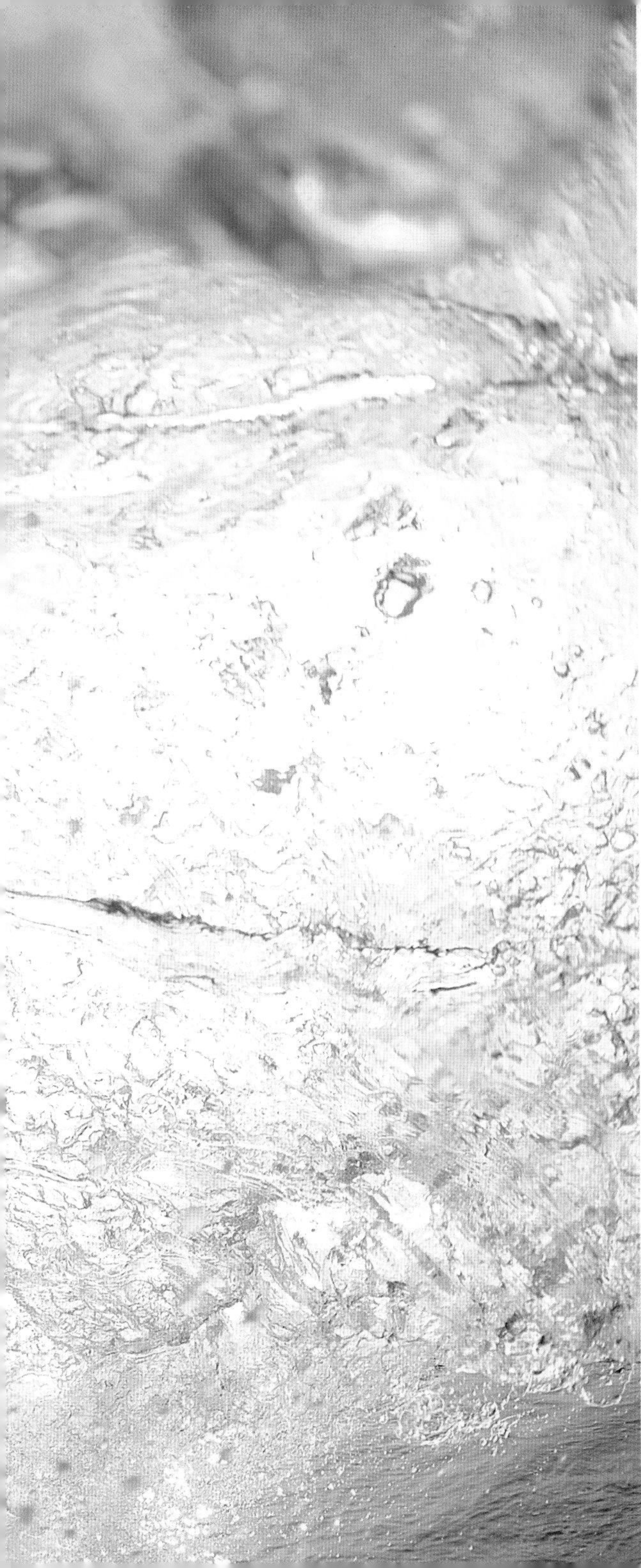
SHARPY

Essentials

Sam Lamiroy explores the innermost limits of pure fun, European style.

Surfing Europe

"Is there any better place to live on earth than in Europe? If you ask me, I would say no! So much culture, so much history, such a variety of waves. Each time I come back from a far away place, I recognise again how happy we should be to live here. You can travel 1000 km and cross five different countries, all with their specific culture, language, traditions and lifestyles. From the crowded, fun, summer beach-breaks in Hossegor, to the forgotten hollow reef-breaks in northern Scotland, the quality of our waves are perfect. I'm fascinated that there is still so much to discover, so many waves we have probably never heard about. There are still perfect waves out there, which never appear in any surfing media. So let's do it like our ancestors, set the sails, go out and discover our beautiful coastlines! It's worth it!" *Lars Jacobsen, editor* Surfers Magazine

Europe. A simple word whose true meaning can never be captured in something as concise as a mere dictionary definition. Its utterance elicits a rainbow of emotional responses. To certain politicians it is more than a word – it's a concept that raises their hackles. To some football fans, it whispers the tantilizing promise of finals played on warm nights in far off stadiums with the burden of history weighing heavily on the outcome. For others it liberates memories of damp camping holidays that define their frustrating pre-teen years. To the surfer, it opens the door to a world of exploration and adventure – so near and yet so far. So familiar and yet so exotic. This splendid continent is a wondrous place, not only to be a surfer but to be a surf traveller.

LAURENT MASUREL

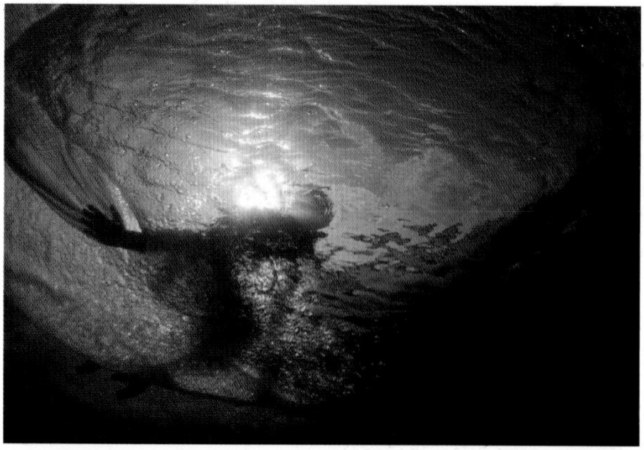

KRISTEN PELOU

> The best thing about surfing in Europe for Americans is not only how good the waves get and how cool the culture is, but also how damn stoked most European surfers are. It's much more fun to surf with grinning Euros than with scowling, bitter California dudes, for sure.
>
> *Marcus Sanders, editor* Surfline

For practitioners of the glide, the most basic European map surveyed with even a cursory glance transforms from green and blue hues to reveal the mind-blowing potential offered up by Europe's undulating coastline. The two dimensional cartography teases the imagination; no longer just a myriad of tiny CMYK dots, it's instantly transformed – over here into jagged limestone reefs around the western coast of Ireland, over there granite cliff-lined bays are gouged out of the fringes of Kernow. Boulder points erupt from the turbulent waters churning around Brittany and heat haze dances above endless golden sands that are the very backbone of Les Landes. We are transported to the smoke-filled bars of San Sebastián where the staccato tune of an excitingly new and vibrant language fills the air. Europe offers not just the seemingly endless geographical and geological variation, but also a rich mix of cultures and experiences.

To the travelling surfer, borders are a fluid concept. You can swiftly cross from France to Portugal via Spain in the time it takes the sun to traverse the deep blue Iberian sky, driven ever onwards by a sea lust, transported on the shimmering tarmac of coldly efficient autoroutes. You can cruise back in time from Spain to Morocco in just 14 km of crowded, white-capped waterways via modern high-speed ferry. And every region of every country can boast its very own world-class waves for the traveller to experience – even those less renowned surfing destinations. Italy may not proffer the consistency of her Atlantic cousins, but this merely allows all the more time to savour Europe's richest culture and finest food. And when the swells do kick in, you'll be surprised at just how long the points can be and by how powerful the reefs are.

THIERRY ORGANOFF

Left: Cotillo reflections. Bottom left: Splitting the peak, Cap Frehel. Above: Mundaka madness.

Yes, Europe offers you the opportunity to sample a smorgasbord of glassy beaches, reeling rivermouths, heaving reefs and endless points – even Hawaiian size big waves. And it's not just the waves that are world class. European surfers are now among the best on the planet. Tiago Pires, Micky Picon, Russell Winter and Eneko Acero are all up there with the top Aussies and Americans when the heat sheets are posted. And it's not just at competition level – at any major break you'll find inspirational surfing, sometimes in the smallest packages. This great continent offers plenty of opportunities to get away from the crowds – in even the busiest regions. Just be prepared to get your head down and do a bit of research.

So, as a surfer, when you look at the maps in this second edition of Surfing Europe, let your mind drink in the possibilities that lie out there. When you read, let your imagination transport you to the line-up – to the cool, clear waters of an offshore morning anywhere along this wondrous coastline. Then get out your planner, get yourself on the road and enjoy the reality – for it is there, easily within your grasp. We're not talking about getting yourself all the way to the Mentawais for a boat trip – but you can experience boat trip quality if you read the charts right. Load your beaten-up van and get on the road. That's the beauty of Europe. It's all just there, right on your doorstep.

Climate and Surf Seasons

The majority of Europe has a temperate continental climate. Detailed water and air temperatures are given in each regional chapter, but in general summers are warm (average highs in Paris 25°C and Lisbon 28°C) and winters can be chilly (average lows in Paris 1°C and Lisbon 8°C). The UK and Ireland has a more complex climate, affected by weather systems from continental Europe as well as maritime systems coming in off the Atlantic and down from the Arctic (average highs of 20°C in the summer and average lows of 2°C in the winter). The southern reaches of Europe are much warmer and have a Mediterranean climate. During hot summers, temperatures in Rome have hit 40°C, but average high is 30°C and in the winter, the average low tends to be about 5°C.

For the European surfer, Autumn is the golden season. Air and water temperatures remain high and the Atlantic low pressure

Cold 'n' delicious Scotland.

systems usually start to deliver a consistent stream of swell after the small summer surf. Winter can see big surf bombarding the coasts. It's a time when sheltered spots come alive, waves are there for the taking for those who brave the cold water and harsh weather. Winter is a great season for regions like the Algarve, which boasts consistent swells and warm weather. It is also a great time to hit the Atlantic coastline of Morocco. Here long distance groundswell combines with hot sunny days and mild nights. Spring is a turbulent time with changeable conditions. Coastal regions can be especially rainy, but classic days do crop up. Keep an eye on those charts because spring swells can be epic and the crowd factor low.

Localism and etiquette

Over the last five or six years, the popularity of surfing has undergone another boom. Numbers in the line-up keep increasing year on year, and with these pressures comes increased tensions and competition. Modern surfing was founded on bedrock of unwritten and loosely enforced rules. People mostly got on with riding waves and having fun. Today, it's increasingly important to know about wave priorities, ensuring there's no dropping in and making sure we travel and surf respectfully. If you want to surf a break where there have been localism issues, try to stay friendly and relaxed. Vibing out the locals will gain few friends. If travelling surfers come to our break and are respectful, we should try to treat them the same. All surfers have one thing in common: we are all travellers.

Europe and the environment

Europe has an incredible and diverse coastline. There are areas of stunning natural beauty – virgin territory and crystal-clear waters. On the flip side, there are regions blighted by heavy industry, waters darkened by pollution, beaches soiled with domestic waste, potato crisp packets floating on the breeze. There are organizations out there run by surfers who aim to maintain and improve the quality of our marine environment. The two most prominent in Europe are Surfers Against Sewage and Surfrider Foundation Europe who have provided some information about their organizations – check out the box on page 20 and their websites to find out what you can do to help.

Surfers' tales

A fridge too far by The Gill

We all take getting to the surf for granted, but sometimes you've got to put a bit more than a few hard miles in to get a classic session in return. This is a story told to Chris Nelson by UK surf legend Paul 'The Gill' Gill, photographer, shaper, discoverer of Thurso East and wielder of the finest porn moustache in surf history.

It was the late summer of 1978 and four British surfers where whiling away their last few days in sunny Biarritz before heading south to the warmer climes of Portugal. The Gill and his future wife, Sarah, Fast Eddie and his girlfriend had no time limit and no worries. Their camper van had been a permanent feature in the car park at 'La Barre', Europe's premier surf break, which attracted the likes of Gerry Lopez & Co to come and strut there stuff in front of the awestruck travellers at this Pipeline-esque beach break. Psychedelic Super-8 surf films of the seventies portrayed these demi-gods casually cruising inside these cavernous tubes breaking powerfully along this perfect sand bar into the river Adour. All this was before the jetty was built. Today La Barre is no more: a groyne of huge concrete blocks cuts straight through the line-up, disrupting the currents and the sand deposition. "It was one of the truly classic waves of the truly classic era," says The Gill.

Every surf trip should have a guy called Fast Eddie along – it's a guarantee that things will happen. "The Aussies all new him as 'Fast", you could see why as his girl, the dark-haired Welsh version of Brigitte Bardot, could hold her own in a bikini on any beach in Europe. We were in my metallic green VW combi – the bay window, not the split screen," remembers Gill. "It had a 1700 cc twin carb engine and was the envy of the car park."

It was now late September and Paul, who'd been studying the charts in the local French papers with an almost religious tenacity, could see a trademark low winding up north of the Bay of Biscay. "A big swell and southerly winds was on the 'plate d'asure', 'Mundacca' (that was the way we spelt it then) would be reeling off perfect left-hand barrels by low tide (without crowds)." This semi-secret rivermouth was then, and still is, one of the best surf spots on the planet, and La Barre to Mundaka should be an easy drive of three hours.

The Basque region is split between southwest France and northeast Spain. It has a unique language and culture and many of the population would like to see their region as an autonomous or independent state. Back in the seventies, the Spanish Basques were much more radical than their French counterparts. Under the Franco dictatorship, their culture, their language and their identity had been suppressed and the Basque separatist terror group ETA actively bombed targets within Spain and their homelands. Little did Paul and Fast Eddie realise that their trip south of the border would involve a journey through an uprising.

"The weather was beautiful and we crossed the border at lunchtime after the usual strip search and grilling, knowing we had to get to Mundaka for low. At high tide, the estuary and its sand bar is swamped by the incoming ocean so the waves don't break, but at low tide the sand bar is exposed to the full force of the swell, creating long, peeling lefts. We were making good time and to save money we decided to avoid the new toll motorway. In the distance we could see smoke billowing from left to right. Now heading due east, I turned to Fast Eddie and said 'It's offshore!' It never occurred to me to think where all the smoke was coming from."

The Basque region is a green and fertile land sandwiched between a backdrop of the rugged Pyrenees and the jagged coastline of the Bay of Biscay. Skirting along the back roads they first hit the crowds at a town called Renteria. "You've got to remember a place with a name like Renteria, as it sat along a stinking grey brown river that looked like everyone's rear had some part to play in its colour," says Paul. "Suddenly it was like being back at Anfield running into a mob of mad football fans funnelling out of a stadium. There was a throng of people all around the van. We assumed we'd driven into the middle of a fiesta but there were police everywhere." The midday sun beat down and the tension in the air was suffocating. The atmosphere screamed that something was going to go down. Then there was a banging on the van. Paul wound down the window and a police officer stuck his head into the cab of the VW, "You must turn round and get out of here! This is a riot!" His eyes were wild and he had to scream to be heard over the roar of the crowd. "I told him this was impossible, that the swell pumping and we had to get to Mundaka for low tide. He looked puzzled, perhaps my Spanish wasn't quite up to scratch and, as I grappled for the dictionary beneath the dashboard, he shouted, 'No, you must go back now!'" But Paul had sampled its perfection once before and was not going to be denied his low-tide wave fest. "We decided to circle around the town, sneak through to San Sebastián and onwards to Mundaka."

The metallic green bus waded through a sea of people,

heading up to the motorway slip road. "I knew it was probably starting to break on the outgoing tide," recalls Paul. "If we pressed on we could still make it for low." Then they reached a police roadblock. "Wait here," said an officer. "A tanker is blocking the motorway. It's not safe. You cannot turn back; the border is closed. You must stay here." "We were surrounded by huge tower blocks," says Paul. "Great! Just like being stuck on Scotland Road in Liverpool again with the Orange Lodge marching. Keep your windows up!" People were chucking stuff out of the windows and it was raining onto the motorway ahead. There was shouting and smoke from the burning tanker. A group of people were heaving something up onto the railing of the bridge. It fell in slow motion and impacted onto the tarmac below. "It was a fridge. They were throwing fridges off the bridges!"

"I could see the police were becoming edgy. This was ETA heartland and things were turning nasty," says Paul. Suddenly shots rang out, splitting the background shouts like a cracking whip. Luckily for the surfers, the snipers were aiming at the cluster of policemen. Unluckily for the travellers, those policemen were clustered around the green camper van. Fast Eddie hit the van floor quicker than the fridge off a motorway bridge and his girlfriend piled on top of him. The police took up defensive positions using the VW as cover. "Sarah and I sat bolt upright in the front seats, frozen, while the uniformed shadows returned fire from behind our van. I looked out of the huge windscreen to see a policeman sprawled around the front shooting up at a highrise block. We could see bullets strafing the concrete tower." The shots from the sniper snapped around the stationary bus. "I just sat there, staring out, for what seemed like an eternity," says Paul. "I could see us missing the surf".

Gradually the police seemed to zero in on the sniper's position. "It sounded like firecrackers were going off all around." Then everything went quiet. Suddenly the silence was punctuated by a policeman hammering on the window shouting 'Go, go, go!' and pointing down the motorway. Paul didn't need to be asked twice. "My foot hit the floor and we tore off down the slip road, the 1700 cc twin carb came into its own. As I slipped her into top at about 70 mph, Eddie came up for air." They entered a crazy, post-apocalyptic world. Wreckage and the carcasses of various domestic appliance littered the way ahead. The trusty VW weaved along the deserted motorway for about a mile until they were confronted by the burning tanker, suddenly visible, straddling the carriageways. Billowing black smoke, the wreckage glowed

THE GILL

white-hot, halting any progress. "It looked as if it could blow at any moment," says Paul. "I hit reverse and charged backwards at about 30 miles an hour until we screamed up another slip road, (I'd do anything to avoid tolls in those days). It was like a scene out of '*Mad Max*' but all I could think was we're gonna miss Mundaka if we don't get a move on".

Once off the motorway they managed to navigate through the deserted back roads in the hills beyond San Sebastian and then on into Gernika. Here again they were met by surging crowds – this was obviously a co-ordinated day of mass unrest. "I don't think I got out of first gear."

Picasso's famous painting '*Guernica*' is a dark mixture of angled, fractured greys and blacks. Contorted people and animals – a woman holding a dead child, a bird with a broken wing. It represents the bombing of the town, on 26 April, 1937, by the Luftwaffe. Franco, the Spanish leader, ordered an air strike on the unsuspecting civilians shopping in the packed marketplace in a clumsy attempt to crush Basque resistance during the Civil War. "Wars end," said Picasso. "Hostilities go on forever."

Here hostilities were still ongoing, spilled onto the streets of the holiest of Basque towns, the place where kings were crowned. This was the scene which now confronted the travellers. "I thought we'd have to give up, turn around," says Paul. "There were no police and the sea of faces had engulfed our small van. But miraculously they waved us through and we crawled along and out the other side. That place needs a bypass, but we were on the home straight to Mundaka".

"We pulled up by the harbour and looked out on beautiful

6-8-ft sets reeling along the sandbank. Perfect Mundaka and only just off low. The waves were so big you could fit our VW camper inside the barrel, and still have room to put the roof up. I jumped into my shortie." Fast Eddie peeped up from the back, groaned, then dropped back to the floor again. Gill jumped into the river and paddled out into the awesome surf. Pipeline-like barrels were grinding mechanically along the sandbank. He reached the peak and there were only a few locals out. Alfonso and one of the González brothers were sitting at the head of the pack and smiled as he stopped paddling and sat up on his board. "I think they knew the hell I'd been through to get there," says Paul. "'The next set shall be yours', one of them said to me. Back then the town was still off the beaten track for most travelling surfers, but even so this was an unusual moment in such a competitive line-up. I looked at the approaching monster set. I was tired. I'd been shot at and had yet to get my bearings. I knew if I took off on one of those I could get sucked over the falls and pounded into the sandbank, probably breaking my board, my neck and losing all face. After the day I'd had I casually replied, 'No, after you.' They smiled back, 'Please, after you.' 'I insist' I said, paddling for the horizon."

Paul turned to see the last surfer disappearing under the lip into another massive barrel. He, on the other hand, was looking for a smaller wave to get going. A 6-ft set approached and he paddled into position. He angled his take off and was popping to his feet as he felt the wave lift him. Suddenly he was pitched forward, like a matador being thrown at a bullfight. Only this wave was meaner than a mere rampaging bull. He looked down at the swirling, waist-deep, white water that churned below him. Propelled headfirst, momentum took over, twisting him as he free-fell two storeys. "I hit the bottom on my back and the force of the landing knocked all the air out of me. It was like being inside a huge blender – I had no idea which way was up or down. I was thrown around like a household appliance being hurled off a motorway bridge." Paul hit the bottom again and was ground along the compacted sand.

"Just when I thought my lungs would burst it released me and I broke the surface, gulping down air. To my surprise my board was floating next to me and just as my brain was pondering how it had survived the beating in one piece, the second wave unleashed on my head. It was like being hit by a mortar round." Paul had been deposited in the impact zone and was now a mere passenger as a series of waves pounded him as he drifted along parallel with the beach. "Each pounding was gradually wearing me down. Eventually I reached the point where the locals would have been tucking into their third barrel of the wave and a break in the onslaught meant I could regain my board and my dignity and paddle back out towards the line-up." Luckily all this misery had been hidden from the locals' view by the backs of breakers. For all they knew Paul had just experienced a classic Mundaka barrel as opposed to a classic Mundaka beating. "I smiled as I reached the line–up and they smiled back. 'Is good, eh?' one of them said. 'Oh, yes,' I replied as water dribbled from my nose."

"The board I was riding was a 'Tris pintail' shaped by Chops and when I bought it he said 'This board was made for barrels – you'll get plenty on this baby.' I raced a few across the estuary, chased by the barrel. Then came the moment that had so far eluded me – the tube ride. I stood bolt upright on a sucking double overhead wall, just like I'd seen Lopez do at La Barre, and glanced up to see the lip throwing out over my head. I was completely enveloped, looking out from inside the barrel onto the open face and getting deeper, I felt like John Holmes. One second passed, two seconds passed, three seconds passed – then suddenly I was experiencing weightlessness and I felt like Major Tom. As if in slow motion I had been sucked up the face, my legs were too straight, too late to bend the knees, I was now upside down and in full orbit, still standing on my board, looking out of the barrel, knowing I was about to get pile driven into the sandbar. The last thing I saw were a couple of surfers scratching over the shoulder smiling, I just smiled back and was driven into the bottom again. Langland reef hadn't prepared me for this."

Fast Eddie had kept his head down again during the whole of that session enjoying a long siesta with his squeeze and bought himself a little more time. "Sadly, he died recently, still a young man," says the Gill. "You have to take your chances in life as they come at you, otherwise you may end up with just stories of dreams or dreams of stories. I climbed out of the water that day in old-style Spain and Sarah handed me a towel and a cold San Miguel. She asked if I'd had a good time and hoped that it had all been worth it. After being caught up in a riot, shot at, nearly drowned, battered, bruised and had sand wedged into every orifice, I said it had been great. And it had. I married her that next year and we went back again together for more. We are still together today".

Europe Essentials

European Union (EU)

The EU is an economic, political and judicial collective of countries with certain shared goals and objectives. This 'private members club' of European states initially consisted of six countries: Belgium, Germany, France, Italy, Luxembourg and the Netherlands. In 1973 the group expanded when Denmark, Ireland and the United Kingdom (UK) joined. The number of nations has gradually increased with the entry of Greece in 1981, Spain and Portugal in 1986 and Austria, Finland and Sweden in 1995. A huge enlargement took place in 2004 with ten new countries joining from Eastern Europe and the former communist bloc. The EU has become much more than a trade association. Member countries have agreements and treaties covering security, law, residency and border controls.

The Euro (€)

In 1992 the Treaty of Maastricht agreed the principle of the single European currency but it took another ten years for the euro to come into being in January 2002. It is now the common currency for over 300 million Europeans in 12 countries. You can use the euro in any of the 12 states including Ireland, France, Spain and Portugal. Britain has not yet joined the Eurozone – the Queen's head still adorns its currency. (Note that Northern Ireland is part of Britain and is therefore outside the Eurozone.)

Red tape

Schengen is a small town on the border of Luxembourg where a treaty was signed to remove all border controls from participating states and to introduce a common visa policy. In terms of the regions covered within this guide, France, Spain, Italy and Portugal are Schengen States between which you can happily travel with no restrictions. Britain and Ireland are not Schengen States, which means that a valid passport is required for travel to and from the UK and Ireland, or an ID card if you are an EU national.

Airlines

It is worth shopping around for flights as prices can vary widely season to season. For the best deals, avoid July and August, school half-term and the Christmas period. But if you can find a spare week during the rest of the year, there is a plethora of budget airlines servicing the continent once you are actually in Europe. From outside Europe, budget travel specialists **Trailfinders**, www.trailfinders.com, or student travel specialists **STA**, www.statravel.com, can be an excellent first port of call.

Airline policies towards surfboard carriage are a minefield (see table opposite). While some take the pragmatic approach that if you have spent your hard-earned cash on a flight to surf-central, you should therefore be allowed to take whatever luggage you want within your quota, others are less accommodating and see surfboards as a quick way to make a fast buck. While **Virgin** come out as the surfer's choice, at the time of going to press **BA** has stopped accepting surfboards on their flights, and **Iberia** will leave you with just enough spending money for one straw donkey between five of you. Airlines are fickle and their policies regarding surfboard carriage are subject to change so make sure you double check terms and conditions before you book your flight.

GREG MARTIN/FINDYOURWAVE

TONY PLANT/SURFTWISTED

Top: Southern Portugal, uncrowded. **Above**: Mole, 'Leven. **Right**: Cornish cream.

Visas and passports

Visa regulations are subject to change. Everyone entering the EU and Morocco requires a passport that is valid for the duration of their visit.

Britain Citizens of Australia, NZ, Canada, SA and US do not need a visa. The duration of stay can be up to six months, but sufficient

SHARPY

funds for the visit must be demonstrated, as well as a booked return ticket. Those wishing to stay longer must contact the Home Office, T020-8686 0688. If you are unsure of entry requirements to the UK, check out www.fco.gov.uk.

Europe For the other European countries, EU citizens and those from the Schengen countries can move freely between states and have no limit to the length of their stay. Citizens of Australia, NZ, US and Canada can enter without a visa for up to 90 days. Other foreign nationals will require a visa for the country they are visiting, which can be obtained from the relevant embassy in their home country. Check that this visa will allow travel to other states if required.

Morocco is outside the EU and Schengen agreements. A valid passport is required but citizens of Britain, US, Canada, Australia and NZ, as well as most EU countries, do not need a visa. If in any doubt check with the Moroccan Embassy. Entry is valid for three months, after which an extension must be applied for at the Bureau des Etrangers in larger towns and cities (see page 363).

Health and insurance

Europe is a fairly trouble-free zone when it comes to health but to be on the safe side, check with your healthcare clinic before leaving. Make sure your tetanus is up to date and avoid getting bitten by a rabid animal. For Morocco, check that your polio, tetanus and typhoid are up to date while Hepatitis A and B are also advised.

Britain, Ireland, France, Spain, Italy and Portugal are all governed by EU health standards. EU citizen should carry a European Health Insurance Card (EHIC) which replaces the old E111 form. In the UK these are available through the Post Office (or online at ehic.orh.uk). Wherever you are travelling, good travel insurance is recommended, covering healthcare, flights and personal effects. Check that your policy covers you for surfing as well as snowboarding if you are planning to hit the hills. Also check that your insurance extends down to Morocco as well as Europe.

Best Airlines

AIRLINE	BOARD CARRIAGE POLICY	
Aer Lingus aerlingus.com	Transatlantic: permitted as part of normal free baggage allowance (2 bags combined weight up to 36 kg). All other: Additional charge per item of €25 pre-booked on line or €30 at airport.	★★★★
Alitalia alitalia.com	Book in advance via Alitalia. **Note**: No carriage on ATR42/72 small aircraft. Between US and Europe: €150 per item. Within Europe: €50 per item up to 250 cm, (over 250 cm €100 per item).	★★★
Air Canada aircanada.com	Board length must be less than 203 cm. Fixed charge all flights: CAD/USD$50.	★★★
Air France airfrance.com	Sum of all dimensions must be less than 300 cm. Between US and Europe: €150 per item. Within Europe: €40 per item. Within France: €20 per item.	★★★
Air New Zealand airnewzealand.com	Permitted to carry 1 board and 1 piece luggage as part of free baggage allowance (up to 23 kg per bag).	★★★★
Air Portugal flytap.com	Permitted as part of free baggage allowance provided board length below 150 cm or the following fees apply: Between US and Europe: (allowance: 2 bags up to 23 kg each) €100 per item. Within Europe: (allowance 2 bags combined weight 20 kg) €50.	★★★
Air Southwest airsouthwest.com	Fixed charge: €25/ £17.	★★★
Altas Blue atlas-blue.com	Fixed charge: €25.	★★★
BMI flybmi.com	Business/premium passengers: permitted as part of free baggage allowance, above which charges apply. Economy fixed charge: £15 (per max 20 kg item) and subject to space in hold.	★★★
BMI Baby bmibaby.com	Fixed charge: £15 board booked on website, £20 if board booked at airport.	★★★
British Airways britishairways.com	**NO SURFBOARDS ARE PERMITTED ON ANY BA ROUTES** They advise you to 'contact your local freight company to arrange carriage for any items that exceed the permitted weight and size.' **We advise you to take your business to an airline that values surfers as customers.**	
Continental Airlines continental.com	Fixed charge on item up to 32 kg and 292 cm length (203 cm on Continental Express/ Continental Connection). Board bag with up to 2 boards US$95, up to 3 boards US$380, up to 4 boards US$665.	★★★
EasyJet easyjet.com	Fixed charge: £15 (plus excess baggage fee of £6/kg if over 20 kg baggage allowance).	★★★
Flybe flybe.com	Fixed charge: £20 on a standby basis subject to hold space **Note**: Bombardier aircraft can carry boards up to 4.5ft only.	★★★
Iberia iberia.com	Boards are heavily charged as excess baggage in 2 ways : Between US and Europe: via piece system – 2 charges made. Within Europe: via weight system – flat 20 kgs charge.	★
KLM klm.com	Board space must be reserved in advance via KLM. Between US and Europe: €150 per item. Within Europe/Morocco: €40 per item.	★★★
Lufthansa lufthansa.com	Fixed charge on item up to 200 cm length (over 200 cm fees double): Intercontinental: €80 (weight system) or 50% excess fee (piece system) Within Europe €40.	★★★★
Qantas qantas.com.au	Permitted as part of 20 kg free baggage allowance, above which charges apply.	★★★★
Royal Air Maroc royalairmaroc.com	Permitted as part of free baggage allowance, above which charges apply.	★★★★
Ryanair ryanair.com	Fixed charge: £15.50 on website, £20.50 at airport/ via call centre.	★★★
United Airlines united.com	Charged at 50% excess baggage rate, must be under 23 kg and 277 cm.	★★★
Virgin Atlantic virgin-atlantic.com	**★★★ SURFERS CHOICE ★★★** **Permitted to carry 1 surfboard up to 32 kg for free in addition to free baggage allowance.**	★★★★★

Surfers' tales

Surfers Against Sewage by Andy Cummins

Surfers Against Sewage (SAS) is a UK-based non profit-making organization campaigning for clean, safe recreational waters, free from sewage effluents, toxic chemicals, marine litter and nuclear waste. That's what we do!

We have been doing this since 1990 when a group of surfers, who were literally 'sick of getting sick', formed a local group and set about taking grassroots action to stop the sewage pollution at local surf breaks in Cornwall.

We were swiftly joined by like-minded water users from around the UK and created what has now become a highly successful national campaign that gives recreational water users a voice on building a clean and safe water environment. Our core objective is to ensure that anyone who wishes to enjoy the water environment, whether as a year-round surfer or a summertime beach-user, can do so without fear of sickness or long-term illness.

Wetsuits, gas masks and a 6-ft inflatable turd have been the essential tools of the trade for us. Unusual (often humorous) and photogenic media-friendly tactics have ensured that the campaign message of pollution-free recreational waters has reached a wide audience, whilst persistence and perseverance are turning the SAS 'pipedreams' into reality.

The SAS campaign has already had a considerable impact on the whole sewage debate and the UK has now started to clean up its act in reducing the amount of sewage pollution. As a result of this campaign, SAS have become respected eco-campaigners and are now putting skills learnt to good use in campaigning vigorously on a broader range of water issues that can impact both on the health of the water user and that of the water environment.

We are doing our bit, but we need everyone to step up and help with these problems. As with many environmental issues, the problems are often so huge that the solution appears out of our grasp as individuals. However, as the Chinese proverb goes, many hands make light work. So what can you do? Loads! We all have an impact on the environment, but we can all look to reduce our impact. Make the decisions everyday that will reduce your impact!

Sewage and Sickness

If you surfed in the UK in the early '90s then you will know we have achieved wonders already. However, there are still certain brown spots around the UK that need to clean up their act. Guernsey, Brighton and Northern Ireland to name but a few. The obscene amounts of untreated sewage these places pump out pose a serious health risk to recreational water users. After a wipeout, if you come into contact with the harmful bacteria or viruses present in sewage you can suffer from eye, nose or ear infections, or find yourself huddled over the toilet for a week. And it can be much worse: Ecoli 0157, Hepatitis A and Meningitis can be contracted from using polluted waters. We all need to be aware that water quality around the UK, even at surf spots that benefit from full sewage treatment, can drop dramatically after heavy rain. Combined Sewage and Stormwater Overflow drains (CSOs) pump raw sewage into our rivers and seas after heavy rain, and this is predicted to become more frequent as climate change affects us. This presents a huge threat to water quality and is the focus of our campaigning for the next water industry review in 2010.

What can you do?

You can stop flushing plastics down the toilet! Sanitary items cause blockages in sewage treatment works, which can result in CSOs discharging raw sewage.

Climate Change

This is the biggest challenge facing humans. Surfers in particular will see a reduction in water quality as heavy rain drowns our sewerage system, forcing raw sewage out through CSOs. Sea level rises are predicted, low tide breaks might not work as well, some classic breaks might be lost altogether. Just flick through this book and you will have some idea of what's at risk! Further afield, more CO_2 in the atmosphere will result in more CO_2 in the oceans, making them more acidic. This could devastate coral reefs, over which we often find perfect waves.

What can you do?

How often do you and your mates turn up at the same beach in separate cars? Car share! Turn off the TV at the plug after watching it; the same goes for the radio, computer, phone charger etc. Use low energy light bulbs, turn the heating down by 1°C, shut windows and so on. There are libraries of information out there to help you save energy, which not only cuts CO_2 emissions but also saves you money. Who would you prefer gets your money, your energy supplier or you? You can change energy suppliers so they produce the electricity you use from renewable sources. As a consumer you have a lot of power. As surfers we could also look a little closer to home in planning a surf trip. Why not switch your trip from Indo for a trip to Europe. Go by boat to France or get on a train explore Scotland. We have cranking waves on our doorstep, we don't need to get on a plane every time to score perfect points, gnarly slabs or sucky beach breaks.

No To Toxics

This sounds like common sense, but every time we go shopping we are confronted with everyday household cleaning products that are crammed with hormone-disrupting chemicals instead of low impact alternatives. What do you choose? Do you know what's in your washing powder, shampoo or paint stripper? Do you care? You should. Hormone-disrupting chemicals, or gender bender chemicals as we call them, are already turning boy fish into girl fish, as scientists tell us. We are concerned about the possible effect on water users and have called on the government to undertake a full study. This is going to take years, but you don't have to wait for this report; you are the solution. Buy the low impact cleaning products, they work and they are on the shelves today. The more we use low impact products, the less gender bender chemicals we will have in the sea.

Marine litter

This will affect every break in this book and every beach in the world. Only the oldest surfers will be able to remember what a beach looks like without plastic on it, a memory that will soon be lost for generations. Plastics cause havoc with marine wildlife, killing whales, dolphins and turtles amongst others. Plastics take hundreds of years to break down and carcinogenic chemicals from some plastics can get into the food chain and affect humans. Remember, our beaches are just like any other playgrounds, so it's important we keep them help to keep them clean. So firstly, NEVER drop litter. Cigarette butts, surf wax wrappers, junk food packaging, disposable BBQs and sun block should all be taken off the beach and disposed of responsibly, recycling it whenever possible. We also try and persuade surfers to pick up one piece of litter for every good wave they have surfed. If they have had a killer surf, they should grab handfuls of litter! This helps clean your beach and hopefully builds up their good karma for your next surf. If you find any identifiable litter you can download the return to offender campaign message from the SAS website and send it off with the litter to the litter manufacturers calling for them to do more to keep their trash off your beach.

We have become quite effective in spreading our message. This book, TV and newspaper articles, websites and education talks all carry our campaign messages to the masses. But we need you to do the same. We need you to protect your surf spots, we need you to tell your mates. Jump in my car today, don't drop that fag end, turn the telly off, try a 'green' washing up liquid and so on. You are our best method of getting the message across because you want clean and safe surf as much as we do. www.sas.org.uk.

Surfrider Foundation

by Nathalie Williams

Surfrider Foundation EUROPE

For water users, the main environmental challenge is fighting bacteriological pollution with city beaches the areas of greatest concern. Avoid going in the sea after heavy rains as run-off and overflows from water treatment works may cause health problems!

Since 1997, Surfrider Foundation Europe has worked to improve water treatment systems. For the past 6 years we as an NGO have handed out 'black flags' to the most polluted beaches in France. Subsequently, Surfrider has opened laboratories to monitor water quality, these are based on the Basque Coast and Marseille and future plans will hopefully see this extended to Brittany, Spain and Portugal. These independent laboratories allow for the year round monitoring of water quality, an essential programme that incredibly is still not carried by any European Ministry of either tourism or the environment. This is why Surfrider Foundation Europe continues to lobby – to urge the European Institutions to take into account recreational water users health by monitoring water all year long on bacteriological and also chemical criteria. Litter is still not considered 'pollution'. To highlight the issue, Surfrider Europe organises a huge, annual European beach clean-up called Ocean Initiatives that is held every spring. The collected debris is sorted into categories and the data is fed to an independent 'Observatory of Waste'.

Surfrider also has an important education programme: an interactive travelling exhibition called 'Waves and Coastline' which combines a teaching kit for schools with public speeches. Thanks to the 20 chapters through Europe, we are spreading the message!

If you are concerned about water pollution and want to support these initiatives, you should become a member! www.surfrider-europe.org

SHARPY

Britain

It's a bit grey and dull in Britain. You probably wouldn't enjoy it here. Much.

Star breaks

1. **Thurso East** If you sat down and designed a perfect right-hand reef, you could do no better than this. Flat, slate reef, dry hair paddle out and long, hollow waves ▸▸ *p41.*

2. **Lynmouth** Long, long walling left-hand point in stunning north Devon ▸▸ *p74.*

3. **Fistral Beach** Just because it's well known, doesn't mean it isn't a fantastic beach break ▸▸ *p79.*

4. **Porthleven** This is a world-class reef that offers heavy, powerful barrels to only the best surfers ▸▸ *p83.*

5. **Crab Island** Quality right-hand reef in the Welsh heartland ▸▸ *p97.*

Russel Mullins wrapping himself up for a Scottish winter.

The undulating, storm-lashed coastline of the British Isles is blessed with some of the world's most picture-perfect surfing environments. Whether it's a flat slate reef peeling in the shadow of a once proud Scottish castle, the golden shifting sands of a Cornish beach below the tumbledown ruins of a once thriving cliff-top mine workings or the dark silhouette of a fallen battlement, built by hand from the rumbling, polished cobbles of the Northumbrian point break it watches over. The clear blue waters and white spray are home to a passing pod of dolphins or the hulking presence of a cruising basking shark. Here, the day-to-day grind is soon left behind, whether via a quick bike ride to the beach, or crawling along the crowded M5 on a long weekend away from the urban sprawl. In Britain, like nowhere else in Europe, quality surf is accessible to all; no city is more than two hours from the coast. The British are taking to the water in record numbers: salt water is in the blood, after all. This is an island nation, with a strong seafaring tradition. Captain Cook was the first explorer to stumble across the 'Sport of Kings' back in the 1770s at a time when Britain really did rule the waves. Today, although surf shops line every high street and line-ups are creaking under the strain of numbers, it is not too difficult to get away and enjoy a quiet few waves in a beautiful location. Just embrace the spirit of Captain Cook, get out there and do a bit of exploring. Don't fight tradition. After all, it's part of the surfing gene.

Surfing Britain

"Britain is both a frustrating and exhilarating place to be a surfer. We have a north, east, south and west coast that is dotted with quality surf spots which all receive swell, but we also have our changeable weather meaning that we usually only get fleeting glimpses of perfection at spots before they get blown out or go flat. Still it keeps you on you toes and if you're dedicated enough you will get good waves." Tim Nunn, Editor, *Wavelength*

When surfing first came to Europe in the late 1950s and early 1960s, it found enthusiastic and hardy converts already playing in the chill whitewater of the British Isles. Short wooden belly boards ridden by beachgoers decked out in colourful bathing hats had been a summer staple for decades. Something this fun...? Well, the cold was just a slight obstacle that had to be tolerated.

From the mid-1960s, pioneering brands like Bilbo, Tiki, and Gul sprang up in southwest England, delivering boards and wetsuits to a primed audience with typical British enthusiasm, while an influx of Aussie and American equipment, build techniques and surfing styles were readily absorbed by the expanding scene, keen for the hottest designs and latest moves. Surfers like Rodney Sumpter, Nigel Semmens and Ted Deerhurst were the best in Europe and helped the UK scene fast become the most cutting edge on the whole continent. From its humble beginnings in the southwest, the waveriding lifestyle quickly swelled to become a national scene. Bilbo expanded into Wales and soon other shapers and brands were springing up across the country. By 1975 a young Paul Gill, still sporting a full head of hair, was looking out over the amazing potential of Thurso reef, while a hardy band of surfers in northeast England were already braving the North Sea with little more than an iron will. *Atlantic Surfer* magazine gave a voice to the growing counter-culture, kick-starting Britain's ongoing hunger for home-grown surf publications. Today, despite the often harsh conditions, the UK has the second largest surfing community in Europe, numbering some 250,000. The standard of surfing is equally high with Newquay's Russell Winter showing true 'Bulldog' spirit to become the first European to make the exclusive World Championship Tour, gaining recognition as one of the world's top 44 surfers, while Jersey's Ben Skinner's silver medal at the World Surfing Games showed him to be one of the longboard elite. Britain is also embracing the "surfuture", becoming the first European nation to construct an artificial surf reef. Yes, UK surfing

GREG MARTIN/FINDYOURWAVE

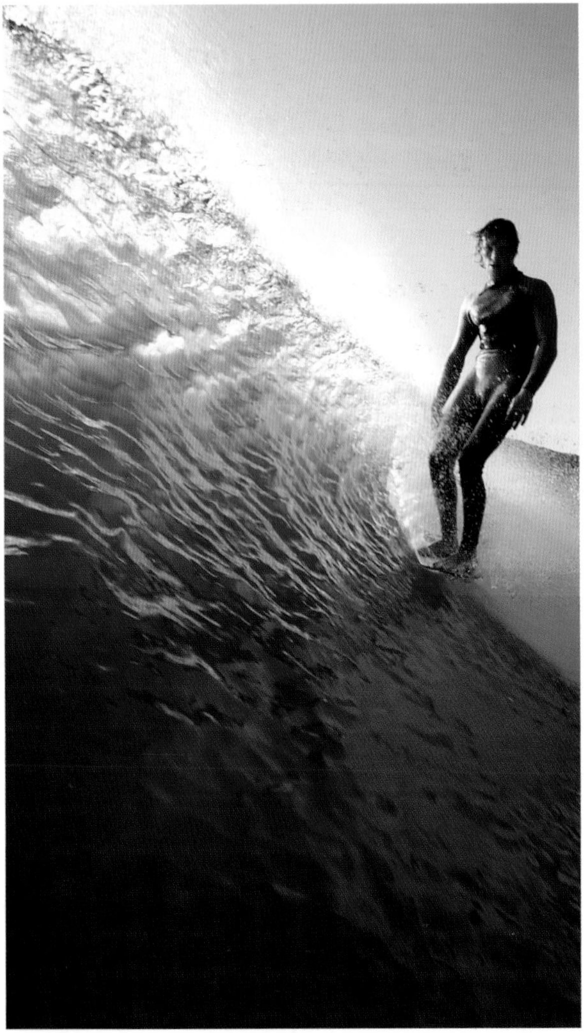

Pros

- Warm summers with cool water.
- Regions have distinct geographical and surf characteristics.
- Still potential to explore quieter regions.
- Extensive surfing infrastructure.
- High standard of living – ok food but good nightlife.
- No sharks!

Cons

- Inconsistent summer swells.
- Main breaks are crowded.
- Expensive food and accommodation.
- Cold winters.

TONY PLANT/SURFTWISTED

Above: Mitch Corbett connecting with south coast Cornwall.
Opposite page: Ben Skinner – high lines of summer.

has come a long way since the days of bellyboards and swimming caps. Mind you, the Brits never forget their roots. If you really want to go 'old skool', check out the annual World Bellyboarding Championships in Chapel Porth, Cornwall. Now that is retro.

Climate

When it comes to climate and weather, Britain is world class. The British are a people obsessed with weather because they have so much of it – as an island sitting off the coast of continental Europe, it is exposed to maritime, continental and arctic weather systems, which roll across the country at regular intervals. Maritime systems ferry wet weather in off the oceans, continental weather systems filter in from mainland Europe and bring dry weather, while freezing arctic systems can push down cold northerly winds bringing overnight snow and ice.

There are a mixture of benefits and drawbacks to this. Outside the summer season there is a fairly consistent stream of low pressures feeding swell to the Atlantic or North Sea coasts, but accompanying wind and weather can be less than favourable. Cornwall picks up loads of swell, but with dominant trade winds from the southwest, can suffer from onshores. The northeast has predominantly offshore winds, but is less consistent. Scotland, with an undulating, wave-rich coastline, usually has somewhere to surf, but in the winter the lack of daylight and cold temperatures make surfing an activity only for the seriously committed.

Best seasons to go

In the **summer**, Britain can be surprisingly warm and pleasant. Devon and Cornwall can have long sunny days with water temperatures high enough for shorties or 3/2-mm spring suits. There can even be years when a consistent stream of lows filter through a steady supply of small, summer waves. Summer also sees the WQS circus roll into Newquay, and the beaches become jammed with beginners and holidaymakers. Scotland and Wales receive less swell in the summer, but can still have regular waves. The north coast of Scotland has the added bonus of virtually constant daylight in June, allowing maximum use of any summer swells on offer. Unfortunately for east coast England, the low pressures tend to dry up, and long flat spells can drive the local surf community to the edge of insanity. Luckily for them, autumn is always just around the corner.

Autumn is the golden season. The days are still long, the water is still relatively warm, the peak swell season kicks in and the tourists go home. In September and October daytime temperatures can still be in the high teens or low 20s, the water is a mild 15-18°C. The high pressures sitting over Europe force the low pressures to the north, funnelling well travelled groundswells into the Atlantic coastlines. The lows tracking past Iceland send the north shore of Scotland into overdrive, and as soon as the depression passes across the top of the North Sea, the legendary reefs of the northeast reawaken. For many British surfers, in the autumn season, there's nowhere else they'd rather be.

The **winter** and **spring** seasons can be harsh times that hold rewards for the willing. Swells pump through the cold months, but

Low Pressure Chart for Britain

In all instances we assume the depressions are deep enough to produce classic swells (say 986 to 992mb). **L1** is a low pressure tracking in an easterly direction from Iceland that has stalled just off the coast of Norway. This normally lasts for just a day or two but when followed by another low, can produce days of classic swell for the east coast. **L2** tracking just south of Iceland delivers northwesterly swell to the Hebrides and the north shore as well as westerly swell to the Orkneys. Will continue to push swell into the north coast as it tracks east. **L3**, a big low sitting in the Atlantic, delivers to south Wales, the southwest and the Channel surfers. Will either move northeast to position **L2** or in over the UK bringing unsettled weather. West Wales and the south coast of Devon and Cornwall come alive with the southwesterly swell delivered from an **L4** low in Biscay.

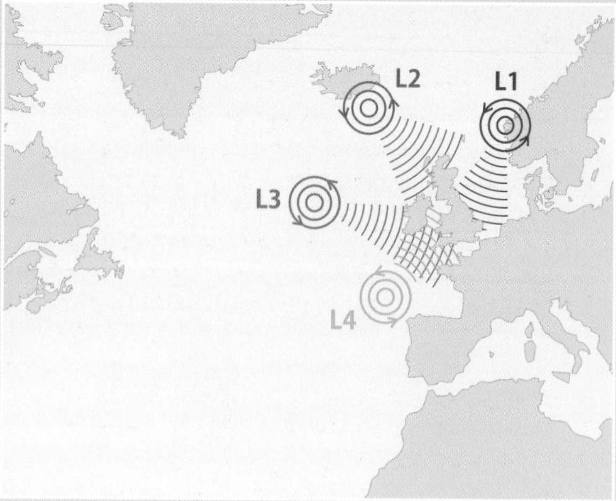

water temperatures plummet and air temperatures can regularly dip below freezing making it a time to break out 6-mm suits, hoods, gloves and booties. Serious improvements in wetsuit technology have extended the surf window for many, resulting in greater numbers seeking out sheltered spots throughout the storms. Although the surf may be classic, few travelling surfers ever venture here to see it and many British surfers seek winter waves in warmer climes.

One thing the British climate has given to local surfers is a great sense of appreciation. During good swells, the British will cram in as many sessions as possible, and when travelling, they appreciate any good waves they come across, never taking their next session for granted.

Boards

In Britain, the surf can be just about as varied as it can get, ranging from 2-ft slop to stand-up barrels, so when it comes to boards, flexibility is the name of the game. As the majority of the surf falls into the 3-4 ft category, a good small wave board is a must. Either a fish or a thruster with a bit of extra volume. A good second board would be a flexible performance thruster for when the swells kick in and the waves pick up.

Geography and the breaks

Cornwall is a jagged mix of cliff and sandy beaches. Exposed to the pounding of the Atlantic, the slate, granite and sandstone has eroded in a disjointed way to produce a complex coastline dotted with tiny coves and open bays predominantly home to quality beachies with the odd hidden reef. Devon has a less rugged coastline and here, where the forest covered cliffs fall into the sea, sit a couple of excellent points. The beaches are powerful and consistent but the reefs are few and always busy.

The northeast coastline of England is one of the most interesting. Here fingers of flat slate produce some very high quality reef breaks and long, winding points. Its orientation is such that in the predominant northerly swells it produces mainly left-hand breaks. Winter and spring can see the odd southeasterly swell sneak up the North Sea and awaken sleeping rights. The beaches can be powerful and punchy and the fine sediments ensure the water resembles anything from a weak cup of tea to a pint of Newcastle Brown Ale.

The coastline of Wales offers great diversity. The undulating shore encompasses polluted urban breaks, classic rocky points, huge open sandy beaches, and stunningly beautiful, deserted coves. But for sheer surf potential, it is difficult to beat the north shore of Scotland. The sheltered harbours of Caithness once shipped the local slabstone around the world, paving streets as far away as Buenos Aires and Sydney. Today, that same slate geography creates the quality reefs and points for which the region is so famous. Neighbouring Sutherland has a completely different coastal landscape, one where deserted bays with golden sand and crystal-clear waters are punctuated by imposing cliffs and peat-brown rivermouths.

Surfing and environment

Britain is a collection of very diverse coastal environments. While there are vast regions, such as Northumbria, northwest Scotland and southwest Wales, that enjoy relatively unspoilt line-ups, some of the most popular breaks sit in polluted waters. Areas of the northeast, like the Gare in Teeside, and parts of south Wales around Aberavon, suffer badly from industrial discharge. Other spots, such as St Agnes in Cornwall, have suffered due to sewage infrastructure badly in need of updating. In northeast Scotland, Dounreay Nuclear Power Station casts a shadow over the nearby surf spots such as Sandside Bay, where radioactive particles have been found.

It is, however, a country where surfers have been at the forefront of

> “”
>
> What makes the surfing life so special in these islands? Lonely dawn escapes to sheltered headlands with the sun low in the February sky; high summer evening sessions, your shoulders aching from the paddle for that last ten o'clock wave; Cornish beaches, Devonian points, Welsh reef and constant swell from the great arc of the Atlantic, distinctly flavoured surf within easy grasp.
>
> *Michael Fordham, Creative Director,* September

the campaign to clean up the oceans and protect areas under threat. Founded in 1990, Surfers Against Sewage (SAS) is a UK-based non profit-making organization campaigning for clean, safe recreational waters, free from sewage effluents, toxic chemicals, marine litter and nuclear waste. Campaigns Officer Andy Cummins highlights the main issues facing surfers in the UK:

"Water quality around the UK varies from the most pristine, to the most disgusting depending on where you surf. In all corners of the UK you can find crystal-clear water and gorgeous green waves, but even these surf spots will suffer from a reduction in water quality after heavy rain. The heavy rain overpowers sewerage works resulting in raw sewage polluting seas and rivers all around the UK. The heavy rain can also cause diffuse pollution, topsoil and animal waste from farmland washed into rivers and the sea. These periods of heavy downpours will become increasingly common as climate change affects us. Surf spots around the UK suffer from various sources of pollution – chemicals from household products, risk of shipping accidents, nuclear waste, marine litter are but a few. These different types of pollution can ruin your surf and groups like Surfers Against Sewage are campaigning to bring a stop to them all.

Surfer's research surf spots, what swell and wind direction it works best on, what stage of tide and size. Surfer's should research possible sources of pollution and use this information to make an informed decision - it might not be worth exposing yourself to these pollutants for 2-ft dribble. Good starting points include The Good Beach Guide (see below), The Environment Agency (www.environment-agency.gov.uk) and the local authorities' Environmental Health Departments. The information is out there for you to make up your own mind."

To find out more visit www.sas.org.uk. The Marine Conservation Society (MCS) is the UK's national charity that has been campaigning for the protection of the marine environment and wildlife since 1977. Among their campaigns and projects is The Good Beach Guide (www.goodbeachguide.co.uk), an independent survey of the UK's bathing waters whose aim is to stop the dumping of raw sewage at sea by promoting beaches with good water quality. To find out more check out www.mcsuk.org.

The Surf Community

Overall the British are an honest people, polite to strangers and quick to warm to those with whom they have a common bond. With travelling surfers there is a tendency to give the benefit of the doubt to new arrivals in the line-up – if no rules are broken and respect is shown, there are rarely any problems.

There are few spots where the mere presence of a stranger in the line-up is enough to spark acts of localism. 'The Badlands' around St Agnes in Cornwall developed a reputation for heavy localism in the 1970s and 1980s, and the label has stuck. These beaches have very tight-knit, competitive line-ups of high calibre surfers, but aggressive acts of localism are rare these days. Other breaks where tight-knit line-ups dominate include Crab Island on the Gower, Porthleven in south Cornwall, Fraserburgh in Scotland and the Cove in the northeast.

Resources

Britain supports four main surf magazines including *Wavelength, Carve, Surf Girl, Pitpilot* and *The Surfer's Path*, plus pan-European titles *Cooler, Surf Europe* and *Huck*. There are hundreds of online surf resources including: **www.A1surf.com** news, reviews, forecasting, charts, webcams and tide tables; **www.britsurf.co.uk** BSA news, competitions and approved surf schools; **www.goodbeachguide.co.uk** independent survey of UK bathing waters; **www.magicseaweed.co.uk** reports and forecasting including charts, webcams, tide tables, wavebuoys; **www.sas.org.uk** Surfers Against Sewage, campaigning for clean seas; **www.surfcore.co.uk** forecasting.

Britain: a brief surf history

1770s → Captain Cook experienced Britain's first brush with surfing while exploring the South Pacific. **1920s** → Surfing becomes the sport of kings with Edward Prince of Wales giving surfing a go in Hawaii. **1930s** → Newquay's Pip Staffien builds and rides one of the first boards in Britain. **1937** → The Countess of Sutherland on a trip to Hawaii wins a trophy in a local surf contest. **1965** → Bilbo, the first British surf company, is established in Newquay by surfers and shapers Bob Head and Bill Bailey. **1969** → The UK's first surf magazine *British Surfer* is founded. **1978** → The British surf team are invited to tea at Buckingham Palace and Prince Charles becomes patron of the BSA. **1978** → British surfer, Viscount Ted Deerhurst, becomes Europe's first professional surfer. **1981** → *Wavelength* magazine launches. **1980s-1990s** → The British surf scene continues to expand and Britain dominates in the European surfing stakes with top surfers including Carwyn Williams, Grishka Roberts, Spencer Hargreaves, Gabe Davies and Russell Winter. **1990** → Surfers Against Sewage (SAS) formed in St Agnes, Cornwall. **1998** → Newquay surfer Russell Winter becomes the first European to take part in the prestigious WCT. **Today** → Britain boasts four surf magazines, a booming surf industry and many of the continent's top riders.

Surfers' tales
Death of a secret spot

How the death of the secret spot in Britain is threatening the end of an era in surf travel and pushing previously friendly surf communities into more militant action to protect their few remaining refuges.

"There were a group of us sitting in the line-up enjoying a quiet surf when we noticed these two guys making the long paddle out. Suddenly someone shouted 'Piss-off, this is a locals' spot. Go surf somewhere else.'" It was a cathartic moment. This surf community had watched their best waves, once a closely guarded secret, become overrun by surfers from across the country. Every time the web foretold the arrival of clean lines, the long travelled panel vans and estate cars were soon to follow. So now this out of the way spot has become their haven, an escape from the crowds. It's hard to find, nestled away along this inhospitable coastline, and it is theirs. With that one outburst, a line had been drawn. "Suddenly we all joined in. And we mean it. That's our spot. It's where we go to get away from the crowds. There are plenty of other breaks to go surf in the area. We've seen all our other secret spots lost, we're not losing this one!"

This is a long established surf community that has never been known for any acts of localism before. What has triggered this sudden change? Why would once accommodating surfers decide enough is enough?

"When spot X was first discovered it was a closely guarded secret," says one of the wave's pioneers. "We kept it to just a few local crew. But more and more people found out, it cropped up on the internet and one year it just blew up. Now I only really surf it on classic days when the crowds thin out."

"I've been going to this spot since the '80s and I'd usually come with one, or maybe two people – usually the same people," says The Gill. "In the water we're always respectful. Don't paddle round the locals. We're friendly. The locals also know I have some great photos locked away of other local spots that I've never released and never will." Losing one excellent spot is pretty bad, but losing another pushes the frustration levels even higher. "We have a break that doesn't work very often, is out of the way, and just a few locals surf there," says another local surfer. "A few guys from the next area used to come and surf every now and again, but it was all very relaxed and low key. Then one day someone stumbled across it and a few days later it was splashed across an internet site. Why? Why does someone feel the need to go and tell everyone when they don't even surf there?"

So, are there any secret spots left? The Gill has amassed a pretty encyclopaedic knowledge of Britain's waves, and although many secret spots have been blown over the years there are still some that have stayed beneath the radar. "The spots that are still pretty secret tend to be those that don't work very often. Consistent breaks get surfed and then someone spots bodies in the water or someone brags to the wrong person and before you know it the secrets out. No, most of the breaks that are still underground are either really out of the way or need very specific conditions to fire." But there are still a few breaks out there waiting to be discovered. During our travels through Europe over the years, we have been lucky enough to discover more than a handful of unsurfed spots, so they are out there.

If you are lucky enough to track down a new break, the hard part is making sure you don't find it overrun the next time you visit. But just how do you keep that secret spot secret? The first rule is "Don't tell anyone!" This is the golden rule and the hardest to keep. As surfers we tend to have a natural disposition towards openness and sharing stories – it's part of our culture. Imagine you've just scored classic eight foot, Indo-like lefts at the secret reef and you're in the pub afterwards chatting to some other surfers – how hard is it not to say anything when they ask why you weren't at the beach?

One of the joys of discovering and surfing a new break is getting to christen it. However, this name is of vital importance. Never call it after it's location or a prominent feature nearby. Calling a secret spot after the village or a landmark is a sure way to guarantee you can't even talk about the place without blowing it. "There's a few secret spots I go to in Ireland, one very good one in particular, and I say to the local guys 'You can't expect that just calling it after it's Gaelic name will keep it secret.' If you know the Gaelic name, it doesn't take much detective work to find the break."

"If you are lucky enough to track down a new break, the hard part is making sure you don't find it overrun the next time you visit."

SCOTT WICKING

"The third rule is be careful with the pictures you take. Framing that huge red and white lighthouse in the background isn't going to keep your spot underground for long."

The third rule is be careful with the pictures you take. Framing that huge red and white lighthouse in the background isn't going to keep your spot underground for long. Another classic mistake is parking your surf sticker covered car, with an empty board bag in it, by that coastal path down to the break. Surfers are like the forensic scientists from CSI. 'Oh, what's this then. Lets have a little wonder down here and check it out.' "To tell you the truth, that's how I found F*******," confesses The Gill. "When you're looking for new breaks, you gotta keep your eye's open." Luckily for the locals this particular surf photographer knows how to keep a secret. Next time they might be reading about it on the Internet.

'Ah, but this is a surf guide' some of you might be saying. We'll, responsible surf guides have a policy of not naming secret and semi-secret breaks. It's not like we get on the phone to each other, more that we realise a mutual obligation not to pull back the curtain too far. Some of you may notice that there are a few waves that have been featured in videos or on the Internet whose location can't be found within the pages of Surfing Europe. Secret spots are part of surfing culture and part of surfing lore. Ultimately waves are a limited resource, there are only so many underground breaks out there. Once the last is blown, an era will be over, and surf travel will never be the same. Surf exploration is a central motivation for the travelling surfer and it's in all of our interests to keep that dream alive. We should all do our bit.

Chris Nelson got a taste for surf exploration scouring the northeast coast of England in the late 1980's, with a well-worn Ordinance Survey map in hand. In frequent trips along the Scottish coastline and around continental Europe he has discovered numerous new breaks.

Essentials

Position

The island of Britain encompasses England, Wales and Scotland. To the west, the force of the Atlantic Ocean is muted only by the presence of Ireland and the Irish Sea, but continues north through Scotland. To the east, the North Sea dominates while the south coast is hemmed in by the English Channel. Neither Northern Ireland or the Channel Islands are part of Britain – they form part of the United Kingdom and British Isles respectively

Language

English, in a variety of accents and guises, is the official language spoken nationwide. In Wales, road signs are written in both English and Welsh – keeping the Celtic language alive. In Scotland, Gaelic is fairly uncommon except in the Hebrides where it is still used and features on road signs.

Crime/safety

Britain is a generally safe place to travel. However, as with anywhere, it pays not leave valuables on display in cars/vans and to be more vigilant in urban/city environments. Cornwall and the south coast have recently suffered a spate of summer car thefts/break-ins resulting from surfers stashing their keys in wheel arches/exhausts. In terms of beach safety, RNLI Beach Lifeguards seasonally patrol selected beaches www.rnli.org.uk. In an emergency, alert the coastguard T999/112.

Health

Visitors from outside the EU/reciprocal agreement are entitled to receive free emergency treatment only in most **National Health Service** (NHS) hospitals' Accident and Emergency departments. Chemists are a good first port of call for non-emergencies but can only sell basics over the counter such as painkillers. Antibiotics etc. require a doctor's prescription. Recreational drugs are illegal in the UK.

GREG MARTIN/FINDYOURWAVE

Porthmeor Peak.

Fact file

Capital: → London
Time zone: → GMT
Currency: → Pound sterling (£)
Coastline: → 11,075 miles
Emergency Numbers:
→ General Emergency: 999/112
→ International Operator: 155
Country code: → +44
Electricity: 240v, 3 square pronged adaptor
Visa: None required for citizens of EU countries, or tourists from the US, Canada, Australia and New Zealand. For all up to date info check: www.ukvisas.gov.uk
Tourist Board: www.visitbritain.com plus www.visitscotland.com, www.enjoyengland.com, www.visitwales.com

Opening hours

General hours of opening are 0900-1730 Monday to Saturday with limited opening on Sundays for shops and supermarkets.

Sleeping

Accommodation in Britain is relatively expensive. **Hotels** are not usually the best option unless you can afford to go 'haute couture' (£200+ per night) but the occasional gem can be found: www.laterooms.com, is worth a punt as excellent deals can be found on hotels nationwide. **Bed & Breakfast (B&Bs)** are practically a British institution providing a bedroom in a private house and a full English breakfast (see below). What you get – from boxy affairs to sprawling country estates – isn't always reflected by the price – from £35-100+ for a double. Prices vary seasonally and deals can sometimes be struck if you're staying for more than one night. There is a good network of **hostels** across Britain – independents, **YHA** (www.yha.org.uk) and **SYHA hostels** (www.syha.org.uk) with beds around £15 per night. **Camping** in general isn't as cheap as on the continent with some sites charging £20+ peak season for a van and two people. Groups may find camping options limited with many sites only accepting families or couples. Check out www.ukcampsite.co.uk, for sites and reviews. If

SHARPY

A bit of a bore in Wales.

you plan to do a lot of camping, it can be cheaper to join the **Caravan Club**, www.caravanclub.co.uk, or **Camping and Caravanning Club**, www.campingandcaravanningclub.co.uk, who, alongside plush sites, offer very basic options from £3 a night. Free-camping is not really an option in Britain.

Eating and drinking

When it comes to food, Britain has a bad rep - but this is not technically fair. The country is a melting pot of cultures and Britain's culinary tastes reflect this. It is as much the home of bangers 'n' mash (sausages and mashed potatoes) and fish 'n' chips as it is the home of excellent Asian, Indian, modern European and Middle Eastern cooking. The **full English breakfast** – eggs, bacon, sausage, mushrooms, tomato/baked beans plus toast and a pot of tea or coffee – is a cheap, filling 'greasy spoon' or café staple and great post-surf warmer-upper - a session at Thurso East followed by a fry-up at Somerfield's is practically a tradition. **Pub grub** can be a cheap eating option with quality varying from filled jacket potatoes to gourmet snacks ranging from £5-10. Dinner is the most popular meal of the day except on Sundays when **Sunday lunch** (roast lamb, beef, chicken or pork with vegetables and roast potatoes) rules. Vegetarians are generally well catered for. The major drawback is the eating hours, which are often inflexible – lunch 1200-1400, dinner 1700-2100. The Brits are drinkers and enjoy a pot of tea almost as much as they enjoy a pint down the pub while no trip to Scotland would be complete without sampling the satisfaction of single malt whisky.

Getting there

Road Although an island, Britain is connected to continental Europe via the **Eurotunnel Shuttle Service**, a freight train transporting you and your vehicle between Calais (France) and Folkestone (England) in about 35 minutes, 365 days a year. Singles from about £135 per vehicle – book in advance for better deals, T08705-353535, www.eurotunnel.com.

Rail Hop on the **Eurostar**, T08705-186186, www.eurostar.com, as a foot passenger from Paris, Brussels or Lille and arrive in London in less than 3 hrs, or around 6 hrs from Avignon. Return fares from Paris start at around £60 but can be a lot more so book in advance and look out for special offers. Their route map shows connecting journeys for more than 100 European destinations with a booking facility. The downside is no item longer than 2 m can be taken on the train and surfboards under this size will attract a £20 Registered Baggage Charge – T08705-750750 for info. **Rail Europe**, www.raileurope, also has a useful interactive route map and booking facility for journeys right across Europe.

Air The major international airports for the UK are London-based Heathrow and Gatwick, with limited international services direct to Glasgow in Scotland, Birmingham in the Midlands and Manchester in the North. Flights from the east coast of **America** take about 6½ hours and off-season cost around US$300 – New York is usually cheapest. Flights from the west coast take 9-10 hours and cost around $400 to $600, with LA your best bet for a cheap deal. From Canada, journey times are around 9-10 hours with flights from Toronto usually the cheapest from around CAN$400. For deals compare prices on **www.flightcentre.com and www.flightcentre.ca**, for students try **STA Travel**, www.statravel.com.

Flights from **Australia** and **New Zealand** are serious business, taking 20+ hours and costing from A$1400-1800 off-season. The cheapest routes are usually via Asia, serviced by **Garuda Air** plus pricier **Singapore Airlines**, **Quantas**, and **Air New Zealand**. Try **Trailfinders**, www.trailfinders.com.au, and **Flight Centre**, www.flightcentre.com.au, ww.flightcentre.co.nz, for cheap flights from Australia and New Zealand or **Usit Beyond**, www.usitbeyond.co.nz, for good youth fares from New Zealand.

Travel from **Europe** to a wide range of British destinations – including London Heathrow, Gatwick, Luton, City and Stansted; Bristol, Newquay and Plymouth in southwest England, Birmingham in the Midlands; Leeds, Liverpool, Manchester and Newcastle in the north; Cardiff in Wales; as well as Edinburgh, Glasgow and Aberdeen in Scotland – well serviced by the budget airline sector including, www.ryanair.com, www.flybe.com, www.easyjet.com, www.flybmi.com. Fares can range between €10 and €250. On top, most budget airlines do charge for board carriage, which usually needs to be booked on when reserving your flight.

Sea The main ports providing links with **France** and **Spain** are based on the south coast of England with Calais to Dover the shortest and cheapest route - the 90 minutes crossing costs from around £140 for a van and two people with **P&O**. Ferries from northern France and Bilbao also run to Portsmouth, a popular entry point. Plymouth and Poole also offer access from France and Northern Spain. From **Ireland**, ferries run to Scotland, with **P&O Irish Sea** operating some of the cheapest routes, from Larne to Troon or Cairnryan from around £78 for a van and two people; or to Wales – **Stena Line** run between Rosslare and Fishguard from about £125 for a van and 2 people. Book crossings on Mondays-Thursdays and at least 28 days in advance for best rates. For crossings to England, Dublin-Liverpool takes about 7½ hours with P&O Irish Sea and costs from around £95 for a van and two passengers. From **Northern Europe** ferries take 12-plus hours with a price tag to match. From Norway and Denmark try **DFDS Seaways** with routes to Newcastle. From Holland check out Stena Line who run services to Harwich. For full listings of routes check out the main carriers **Brittany Ferries**, www.brittany-ferries.com, **P&O**, www.poferries.com, **Stena Line**, www.stenaline.co.uk, **Irish Ferries**, www.irishferries.com, **DFDS Seaways**, www.dfdsseaways.com.

Getting around

Driving (left-hand side) Distances and speed limits indicated in miles. A full driving licence or International Driving Permit is required plus adequate insurance. A good network of motorways (M) and primary roads cover the country, all but a couple of which are toll free. Traffic levels however often result in delays and even gridlock – especially around cities and during rush hour on the capital's M25 and the north's M62 motorways. Summer and long weekends can see the M4 and M5 motorways to the southwest become clogged making travelling at non-peak times preferable. Speed limits are enforced (resulting in fines) with much of the road network peppered with speed cameras. A fee is now levied for anyone driving in or through London's congestion charging zone between 0700 and 1800, Mon-Fri. For more information check out www.cclondon.com.

Motorways **Speed limit 70 mph (about 110 kph).** With an average of 3 or 4 lanes, these super highways connect the main body of Britain and are signed in blue. Major routes from London: M1/A1(M) to Newcastle (northeast England); M4 to Swansea (Wales); M4-M5 to Exeter (southwest England); M40-M6-A74(M) to Glasgow (Scotland).
Other roads **Speed limit 70 mph dual carriage, 60 mph single carriage, 30 mph urban areas** (unless otherwise indicated). **Primary route A** roads take over where motorways leave off and are usually good quality, fast routes with a mixture of single and dual carriageway Green on road maps. Other single/dual carriageway **A** roads are marked red on road maps. **B** road single/dual carriageway are yellow on maps. These secondary roads are of varying standards and often less direct.

Car hire There are plenty of choices but can be expensive – from £150 a week for a small car. Fly/drives may offer better deals. All the multinationals operate here but better deals can often be found with local companies if you're prepared to hunt around. You need to be over 21, have held a licence for more than a year and usually have to pay by credit card.

The Lowdown

"Bring a decent wetty, a good waterproof coat, a range of boards, a good attitude and an open mind. You'll be amazed at the quality of the waves lurking around our little island. Of course, if it's not happening we'll be in the pub."
Roger Sharp, photographer

"An outstanding combination of country pub decadence and powerful beachbreak surf makes Newquay a totally unique destination – a boozy beach party in the summer; a serious wave-riding experience once September comes round."
Vince Medeiros, Editor Huck

"The outer reaches of West Wales hold many a cherished secret. Take particular note of the vagaries of tide and you'll discover bouldery points, jagged slabs and a few endless, slanted slides that conceal themselves to the impatient."
Michael Fordham, Creative Director, September

"It's easy to moan about the surf in Britain but despite having to put up with the cold, the onshore winds, clampers, the gutless surf, crowds and loser pervs in the car parks, Britain has an amazing variety of surf spots from mellow beach breaks to challenging reefs. So get out there and have fun!"
Louise Searle, Carve, Surf Girl

Public transport **Coach** travel although cheap is not a viable proposition for a surfer with a board - the largest UK operator **National Express** does not allow board carriage. **Rail** networks cover the majority of Britain but tickets can be very pricey unless booked well in advance. Most companies try to accommodate boards in the guard's van (some, like **South West Trains**, for a fee of £5 each way). For details try **National Rail Enquiries**, T0845-7484950, or www.nationalrail.co.uk. London is well serviced by the underground train service – the Tube, www.thetube.com. It can be like a mosh pit during peak times when it's best to avoid travelling with your kit. With a good network of airports across Britain, **flying** is a real option and with a bit of pre-planning can sometimes be the most affordable option. Try Air Southwest www.airsouthwest.com (including 4 flights daily Gatwick-Newquay), FlyBe, www.flybe.com (including Exeter-Aberdeen and Newcastle) and Ryanair, www.ryanair.com (Stanstead-Newquay). Most budget airlines do charge for boards – usually around £15 per journey.

adventure
CORNWALL
>>>
The online adventure sports magazine
> Surfing
> Adventure Activities
> Extreme Sports
Visit the website to plan your surf break or adventure trip.
www.adventure-cornwall.co.uk

Northern Scotland

Overview

The 'Norse Shore' holds an allure for British surfers and it's easy to see why. We spend so much of our time caught up in crowded beach breaks, fighting the rips, the long paddle-outs, searching for those elusive gems among the close-outs. The flat tapering reefs of Scotland's northern fringe however offers us the chance to take on machine-perfect barrels without the need to board a plane bound for Indo or Hawaii. The cold water, long drive and temperamental weather patterns are becoming increasingly smaller issues, once the sheer quality of waves are factored into the equation. The undulating mountain-lined A9 is today one of surfing's great pilgrim routes.

The purple moorland of northern Scotland stretches like a taught canvas over the rolling landscape until the hills finally give way to the dramatic jagged fringe of the north coast, broken and torn rocky fringes softened by the occasional crescent of dune backed sand. In the far northeast, Caithness was once world renowned, producing and exporting quality flagstones to as far away as Australia and Argentina. In the mid-19th century, ships docked in the solid stone harbours of Ham and Harrow. Today the harbours are gone, destroyed by the pounding waves of the north Atlantic, just as the waves of modernization destroyed the trade on which they were dependent. The flat, slate coastline remains, providing an almost computer generated surfers playground – a perfect foil for the clean arctic swells that relentlessly bombard the region. A crest in the coastal road west and the coastline of Sutherland comes into view, the succession of gently curving sandy bays serving up rivermouths and sandbanks overlooked by grazing sheep and wind-buffeted crofters cottages. Out of season there will be few surfers checking the many wave-riding possibilities that pepper this coastline. It's a place where another face in the line-up may actually be a welcome addition.

The surfing capital of north Scotland is the hardy town of Thurso, regional hub and base for countless northshore surf adventures. The seafront campsite and the cosy rooms of Sandra's Backpackers are as much a part of local surf folklore as the fabled right-hand reef. The town has been home to a small and hardcore community of chargers since Pat Kieran set up home here in 1977 and moved into a house overlooking Thurso reef. "I lived in a farmhouse cottage

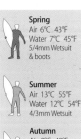

Spring
Air 6°C 43°F
Water 7°C 45°F
5/4mm Wetsuit & boots

Summer
Air 13°C 55°F
Water 12°C 54°F
4/3mm Wetsuit

Autumn
Air 9°C 48°F
Water 12°C 54°F
4/3mm Wetsuit & boots

Winter
Air 3°C 37°F
Water 6°C 43°F
6mm Wetsuit, boots, gloves & hood

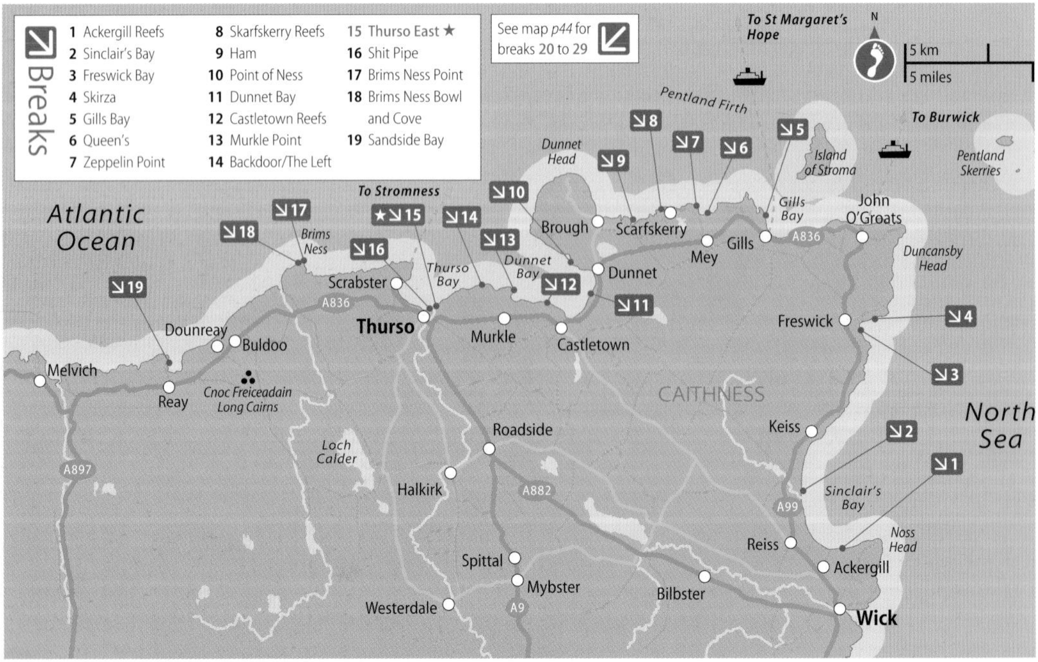

6'1" Byrne HP

Shaper: Phil Byrne

6'1" x 18³⁄₈" x 2⁵⁄₁₆"

Built with Surftech's proven TUFLITE construction.

High-performance shortboard that'll work well in the Scottish beach breaks and smaller reefs.

Single to double concave with FCS fins.

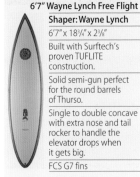

6'7" Wayne Lynch Free Flight

Shaper: Wayne Lynch

6'7" x 18³⁄₄" x 2³⁄₈"

Built with Surftech's proven TUFLITE construction.

Solid semi-gun perfect for the round barrels of Thurso.

Single to double concave with extra nose and tail rocker to handle the elevator drops when it gets big.

FCS G7 fins

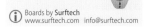

Boards by **Surftech**
www.surftech.com info@surftech.com

"Scotland has it all. There's the amazing scenery, the pristine beaches, and the clean, clear waters. You can really get away from the crowds of Devon and Cornwall plus the Gulf Stream means that the water is actually quite mild during the summer and autumn. Scotland offers consistent surf in a beautiful setting – what more could you want?"

Mark Lumsden, Lewis Surf Trek

overlooking the surf," says Pat. "It was a brilliant spot. I was a single bloke surfing and shaping boards in the barn and the bedroom next door. Surfers from all over the country used to drop in and stay, even when I wasn't home. I never used to lock my door. When I moved out a few years later, I picked up the key to hand it back to the landlord and it left a key-shaped hole in the dust." Today the steady stream of visitors has today grown to a level where there is enough footfall to help sustain a harbour-side surf shop – the only one you'll find along the long northern coast.

Coastline

Heading west from Duncansby Head, the Caithness coastline unfolds into series of flat slabstone reefs, which eventually run into the towering cliffs of Dunnet Head, the mainland's most northerly point. From the shelter of Dunnet Bay the coastline opens out into flat slate again. Reef after reef leads into the rivermouth at Thurso and on to the natural harbour at Scrabster. It is from here that ferries depart for Orkney (see page 57) and Shetland. Sandside Bay is last of the Caithness breaks before the bays and rivermouths of Sutherland offer isolated beauty, crystal-clear waters and dune-backed seclusion.

Local environment by Surfers Against Sewage

"This coastline hosts the horrid Dounreay Nuclear Reactor. Fragments of irradiated nuclear fuel were released from this reactor into the sea. There are thought to be thousands on the seabed, however, they don't just stay there. Particles have been found on the Dounreay foreshore, on the beach at Sandside and a single particle the size of a thumbnail has been found on Dunnet beach. Limited surveying has been done, so we just don't know where else they might be. Diffuse pollution around agricultural land is also a problem." Andy Cummins (www.sas.org.uk).

While **Pat Kieran** helped pioneer surfing in the region, if you see a guy snagging the lion's share of the barrels at Thurso, chances are it's local charger Chris Noble. Despite the WQS O'Neill Highland Pro showing the world just how good the waves can be here at Thurso, the crowd factor, although defi140 nitely growing, hasn't reached the level the locals worried it would. The reef is still the main draw of the area, leaving the breaks around Sutherland largely overlooked and under explored. It's not a safe region for beginners to strike out on their own. The isolated beaches are appealing but it's best to learn the ropes under supervision.

Getting around

The roads up here are of very good quality and rarely busy, even in the height of the tourist season. It's quick and easy to get around by car as the A836 follows the coast and access roads run off it to most of the breaks. The road changes to single track for small stretches in Sutherland. Some spots are only accessible via farms or over fields. Remember to be respectful and, if in doubt, ask permission first.

SHARPY

18 It seems unjust that Brims has been labelled a fall-back option.

Breaks

RIGHT REEF BREAK

↘1 Ackergill Reefs

- **Conditions** Medium N or SE swells, offshore in W or SW winds
- **Hazards/tips** Good waves in spectacular location
- **Sleeping** John O'Groats » p46

Situated at the southern end of the open expanse of Sinclair Bay are two right-hand reef breaks. These waves are set in a spectacular location, overlooked by the dark shadow of ruined battlements, and come to life when northeasterly or big southeasterly swells roll through the North Sea. Offshore with winds from the west. Access is via Ackergill off the A99. Park near the jetty.

BEACH BREAK

↘2 Sinclair's Bay

- **Conditions** Medium to big NE to SE swells, offshore in W winds
- **Hazards/tips** Quiet spot, rarely surfed
- **Sleeping** John O'Groats » p46

Sinclair's Bay is vast and crescent shaped, backed by a huge expanse of sand dunes.

THE GILL

There are set access points on this east facing beach break and in a big northeasterly or easterly swell you'll struggle to find any other surfers along this great stretch. Good quality but rarely surfed. Access is at the northern end of the bay at Stain or via the dune paths.

BEACH BREAK

↘3 Freswick Bay

- **Conditions** Medium to big NE to SE swells, offshore in W winds
- **Hazards/tips** Quiet spot, pronounced 'Fresik'
- **Sleeping** John O'Groats » p46

Freswick is a small picturesque bay with sand and rocks forming lefts and rights in big northeasterly swells. Works through all tides. Great break but not really suitable for beginners.

LEFT POINT BREAK

↘4 Skirza

- **Conditions** Big to huge NE swells, offshore in NW winds
- **Hazards/tips** Rocky, fast, heavy waves
- **Sleeping** John O'Groats » p46

This long, peeling, classic, left-hand point is a Scottish legend. Waves reel along a rocky headland in only the biggest north or northeasterly swells when rides become etched on the memory forever. Epic in the right conditions producing leg-numbing rides that barrel along the cobblestones towards the quay. Worth checking when the north shore is maxed out. Access from the A99 signposted Skirza. Follow road to harbour and park respectfully.

LEFT POINT BREAK

↘5 Gills Bay

- **Conditions** Big to huge N or NW swells, offshore in SW winds
- **Hazards/tips** Big, heavy wave for experts.
- **Sleeping** John O'Groats/Dunnet Bay » p46

In a big northwesterly swell, this long point comes to life and can produce huge, heavy barrelling waves that break over a slate and rock reef. Holding waves of over 10 ft, it is one of the north shore's true quality waves. Can be checked from the pier at Gills Bay harbour, where the ferry departs for the Orkneys. Described as "a Scottish G-Land", this is a wave for experienced surfers only. Size is misleading from a distance - the walk out to the point is further than you think and rips can be strong.

DEMI TAYLOR

Above: 5 Classic Gills – not for the inexperienced. **Top: 4** Skirza: a rare sighting.

LEFT REEF BREAK

↘6 Queen's

- **Conditions** Small to medium NW swells, offshore in S winds
- **Hazards/tips** Overlooked by royal Castle of Mey
- **Sleeping** John O'Groats/Dunnet Bay ›› *p46*

A low to mid tide slate reef that produces walling lefthanders in clean northwesterly swells. Intermediate and experienced surfers. Access is via left at crossroads after Mey village.

LEFT POINT BREAK

↘7 Zeppelin Point

- **Conditions** Medium NW swell, offshore in S winds
- **Hazards/tips** Shallow and rocky.
- **Sleeping** John O'Groats/Dunnet Bay ›› *p46*

Quality, slate reef point break that produces long, shallow left hand walls. Works best at mid tide. Walk north along the point from parking at Harrow Pier, which bizarrely, was officially opened by rock god Jimmy Page.

REEF BREAK

↘8 Skarfskerry Reefs

- **Conditions** Small to medium NW swells, offshore in S or SE winds
- **Hazards/tips** Rocky reefs, rarely surfed.
- **Sleeping** Dunnet Bay ›› *p46*

Check these reefs from the coast road through Skarfskerry. These breaks need a clean northwesterly swell and south or southeasterly wind. Rarely surfed reefs but worth checking.

LEFT REEK BREAK

↘9 Ham

- **Conditions** Big W swells, offshore in W winds
- **Hazards/tips** Shallow boulder reef, breaks in storms.
- **Sleeping** Dunnet Bay ›› *p46*

This sheltered left reef can be the only wave working on the north shore in big, stormy surf and westerly winds. Swell wraps around the headland and into the sheltered bay, breaking in front of the carcass of a massive, 200-year-old stone harbour destroyed by violent storms. Best from low to three quarter tide. Not an epic wave but a decent, if shallow, walling left. There is also a heavy, shallow left further out on the point definitely for experienced surfers only.

RIGHT POINT BREAK

↘10 Point of Ness

- **Conditions** Medium NW swell, offshore in SE wind
- **Hazards/tips** Fun but rocky point
- **Sleeping** Dunnet Bay ›› *p46*

This is a walling, quality right point that peels over a crescent shaped slate and boulder reef. It needs a decent, clean northwesterly swell to work and is offshore in a southeasterly wind. Works best around mid tide. Parking available at Dwarwick Pier. Jump-off point from the rocks.

BEACH BREAK

↘11 Dunnet Bay

- **Conditions** Small swells, offshore in SE winds
- **Hazards/tips** Closes out in swells over 4 ft, flatters to deceive
- **Sleeping** Dunnet Bay ›› *p46*

Despite its ability to Hoover up northwesterly swells, this is generally a disappointing beach break. Can be good fun on small, summer days but the lack of defined banks means it tends to close out when the swell picks up. Works on all tides. The middle of the bay by the stream picks up the most swell and has the best chance of banks. Perfect for (supervised) beginners.

REEF BREAK

↘12 Castletown Reefs

- **Conditions** Medium to big NW swells, offshore in S or SW winds
- **Hazards/tips** Difficult access on foot, rarely surfed
- **Sleeping** Dunnet Bay/Murkle Point ›› *p46*

These reefs are visible from the main A836 Thurso road as a series of white water outcrops fringing the southwestern edge of

THE GILL

10 Point of Ness.

Dunnet Bay. However, few make the effort to discover the true potential of these slate reefs. Starting in the corner of Dunnet Bay with a sheltered A frame reef, they run out to the west becoming more exposed. Now that region is becoming busier, might be worth checking them out to escape the crowds.

LEFT POINT BREAK

↘13 Murkle Point

- **Conditions** Medium to big NW swells, offshore in S or SW winds
- **Hazards/tips** Exposed spot with rips and rocks
- **Sleeping** Murkle Point » *p46*

One of the most visible breaks in Caithness yet probably the least surfed. This pinwheel left point wraps around the 'Spur' at the southern mouth of Dunnet Bay, where it can produce excellent lefts but which is also exposed. Needs light winds from a southerly direction. Access is via farm tracks so park with respect.

RIGHT REEF BREAK

↘14 Backdoor/The Left

- **Conditions** Small to medium NW swells, offshore in S winds
- **Hazards/tips** Shallow, heavy, experienced surfers only.
- **Sleeping** Murkle Point/Thurso » *p46*

Shallow, hollow right-hander that sucks onto a shallow ledge. It sits opposite a nice, tapering left in an exposed spot that picks up loads of swell. Other challenging spots nearby, including a grunting slab charged by the pros during the O'Neill Highland Pro. Needs southerly winds. Access via farm tracks.

RIGHT REEF BREAK

↘16 Shit Pipe

- **Conditions** Medium to big N or NW swells, offshore in S winds
- **Hazards/tips** Excellent wave overshadowed by Thurso East
- **Sleeping** Thurso » *p46*

This is an excellent quality, right-hand slabstone reef that breaks in front of the pier to the west of Thurso rivermouth. Picks up less swell than Thurso East but is a class act when it's on. Fast, walling waves with occasional barrels peel in southerly winds. Works on all tides except high. The peaty river run-off can make the waves brown and drops the water temperature in the winter. A good wave that is often overlooked due to its proximity to Thurso East. Car park on seafront.

THE GILL

THE GILL

Top: Oli Adams plays the bagpipe. **Above:** East of Eden.

Right reef break

↘15 Thurso East

- **Swell** Huge W, big NW or any N swell
- **Wind** SE
- **Tide** All tides, best quarter to three-quarter tide on the push
- **Size** 3-12 ft
- **Length** 50-100 m
- **Bottom** Kelp covered slabstone reef
- **Ability level** Intermediate to advanced
- **Best months** Sep-Dec, Apr-Jun
- **Board** Performance thruster/semi-gun
- **Access** Off the rocks, or via the river in big swells
- **Hazards/tips** Rocky bottom, can be heavy when big
- **Sleeping** Thurso » *p46*

SHARPY

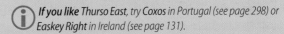

15 Sunny, swell just kicking in and not too many people out – that's the sight you want greeting you after the long drive .

Of all the waves in the UK, the one that has undergone the biggest change in profile over the last five years is Thurso East. It held a pretty unique position being one of the planet's few world-class waves where you could still score uncrowded perfection. Now, however, it's on the way to joining the elite list of surfing Meccas that draw waveriders from across the globe. Blame improved wetsuit technology, blame media exposure, blame contests, blame the surf boom, but whatever the reason, rock up at Thurso East on a good chart, and even in the middle of the dark chill of a Scottish winter you can pretty much guarantee other pilgrims will already be slaking their thirst. Yet, having said that, the concept of a crowd is a relative thing. At Malibu it might be counted in the hundreds, in Cornwall it might be in three figures, here it will probably still be under 20. For a spot that has been called anything from 'a cold water Nias' to 'the best right reef in the UK', it still offers the potential of a pretty chilled world-class session. The WQS O'Neill Highland Pro events bring a flurry of the world's best to the line-up, but it doesn't take long for the status quo to return. As local charger Andy Bain says, "We all thought we'd get swamped after the WQS event, but to be honest, it's still a heck of a drive. Yeah, it's busier, but not as bad as we thought."

Thurso East is a point style reef set up, where big arctic swells wrap enticingly along a perfect, flat, slabstone reef. Access to the peak is pretty straightforward, the rip from the river depositing surfers in the line-up on even the biggest days, and adding a distinctive peaty brown marbling to the waves. In the winter, this influx of cold water also drops the temperature, testing even the hardiest surfer. Swell lines roll into the deep-water bay and begin to feather as they feel the bottom at the fringe of the reef, before peaking and throwing out the trademark reeling rights. In a northerly swell these tend to be more walling, in a nor'westerly the angle of attack means they are more hollow. The take off zone is pretty tight, so a friendly and relaxed attitude is essential. On a good day the crew will take it in turns, so paddling around the locals will make you few friends. Swells can reach an epic size in the winter months, but the autumn is prime Thurso hunting season. "When I was there in December one year it was pretty much as big as I'd want to surf it," says Chris Griffiths, former world number 5. "The only thing I could compare it to was on the North Shore of Hawaii when we surfed Haleiwa at 15 ft. You've got to put it up there with the world's best."

With the popularity of today's internet forecasting sites and the increasing ease with which we all seem to be able to wangle that week away, Thurso has become a big draw for British surfers, but the thing to remember on a North Shore trip is that there are many options on this stretch of coastline, and even a few classic secret spots out there for the adventurous. If Thurso is cranking, so will many other spots. Sometimes it pays to explore.

Thurso was first surfed by shaper/photographer Paul Gill, back in 1975 and he has made many trip here since. Pat Kieran set up home here in 1977 and helped pioneer the spot, shaping boards and acting as host to visiting surfers from across the country. Today local charger Chris Noble lives in the same row of cottages and rules the line-up, even when the most esteemed of company is in town.

If you like Thurso East, try Coxos in Portugal (see page 298) or Easkey Right in Ireland (see page 131).

LEFT POINT BREAK

↘17 Brims Ness Point

- **Conditions** All W, NW and N swells, offshore in S winds
- **Hazards/tips** Heavy wave, dangerous rips, experts only
- **Sleeping** Thurso » p46

This left point peels along a flat slate reef producing excellent, long walls but it is an exposed spot and while this is a blessing in small swells, it can easily get pretty big. Also the direction of the wind is key. Light winds are essential as there's no shelter - preferably southerlies. Check it from low up to three-quarter tide but remember it has shallow sections. Surf is visible from the A836 but as it is a couple of miles away, any sign of white water means that there are waves. Access is via a farm track with respectful parking in the farmer's yard. Remember that you are on private land at the farmer's discretion and access has been withdrawn in the past.

O'NEILL

18 Russell Winter, O'Neill Highland Pro, Brims Ness.

RIGHT REEF BREAK

↘18 Brims Ness Bowl and Cove

- **Conditions** Small to medium W, NW, N swells, offshore in S winds
- **Hazards/tips** Shallow, powerful and consistent
- **Sleeping** Thurso » p46

These two right-hand reef breaks have salvaged many a trip to the north shore, as they Hoover up any swell available. The **Cove** is to the west of the Point and is a short, hollow right-hand wave breaking onto a kelp-covered, slanting shelf. It is also offshore in a southerly wind and surges onto a finger of reef offering a short cover-up or wall before petering out into a deep inlet. The **Bowl** is a fast, hollow, shallow, barreling right that lunges out of deep water onto a slate shelf. The Bowl can be 4 ft when Thurso is flat. It is best left to experienced surfers as any mistake will be met by the barnacle-encrusted reef (regulars wear helmets!). Works from quarter to three- quarter tide and is offshore in southerly winds. Access is the same as the **Point**. This is an exposed spot so wind is important. These breaks can get surprisingly busy in the summer, when they may be the only surfable spot. Watch out for dive-bombing terns in the June nesting season.

LEFT REEF BREAK

↘19 Sandside Bay

- **Conditions** Medium to big W, NW and N swells, offshore in SW winds
- **Hazards/tips** Quality break overshadowed by Dounreay
- **Sleeping** Thurso » p46

This is a quality, walling or barreling left that breaks over a shallow reef in front of a picturesque slate harbour. Works best when the tide has pushed in a bit, so from mid to high. Although it is offshore in a southwesterly wind, it can handle wind from the west. It needs a big westerly swell or a medium northerly to work. Sandside is a pretty bay but the backdrop is the Dounreay nuclear power plant, a facility with a less than unblemished safety record. Signs warn of radioactive particles on the beach. It warns children not to play in the sand and advises owners not to let their dogs dig - so how safe is it to surf there?

> “”
> I surfed Thurso in 1993 during the Euro titles held in Scotland. It was several months after I discovered J-Bay in South Africa. I couldn't believe the similarity of these two waves, except Thurso was unknown at that time and hardly ever surfed by "foreigners". I guess things have changed since, but I'm definitely going back there some day.
>
> *Franck Lacaze, former Editor,* Trip Surf Magazine

RIVERMOUTH BREAK

↘20 Melvich

- **Conditions** Small to medium NW or N swells, offshore in S winds
- **Hazards/tips** Rips when big
- **Sleeping** Melvich » p48

The brown, peaty river at the eastern end of the bay is usually home to an excellent rivermouth sandbar. Lefts and rights work best in smaller swells through the tides. Rights are longer. Access from the village to a car park above the dunes, or at the eastern end near the Big House. Not suitable for unsupervised beginners due to rips and isolation. Good water quality.

BEACH BREAK

↘21 Strathy

- **Conditions** Big W, all NW and N swells, offshore in S winds
- **Hazards/tips** Beautiful spot, stunning location
- **Sleeping** Melvich » *p48*

Walling lefts peel from the rivermouth at the western end of this beautiful bay. The sheltering effect of Strathy Point means that although this spot picks up less swell in northwesterly and westerly swells, it can be a surfable heaven in westerly winds. The beach produces lefts and rights, working on all tides. Park by the graveyard and walk down to the beach through the dunes. This is a wonderful spot that has increased in popularity. Suitable for beginners, as long as they are supervised by more experienced surfers.

BEACH BREAK

↘22 Armadale

- **Conditions** Medium NW and N swells, offshore in a S wind
- **Hazards/tips** Quiet beach
- **Sleeping** Melvich/Bettyhill » *p48*

Quiet, north facing beach set back from the north coast road. Beach break peaks work well up to head high and through all tides but is rarely surfed. Can be checked from the hill west of the bay on the A836.

AL MACKINNON

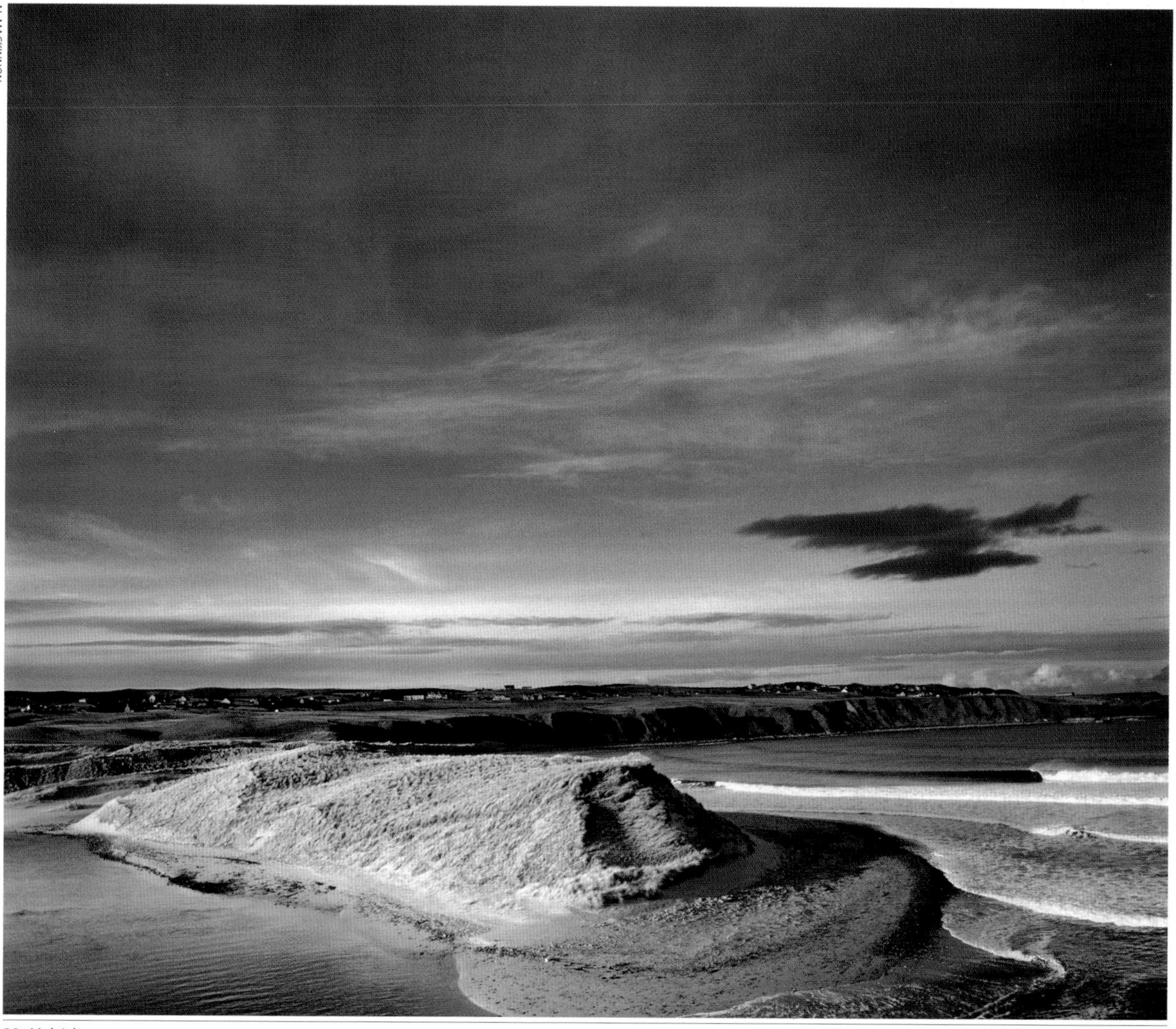

20 Melvich.

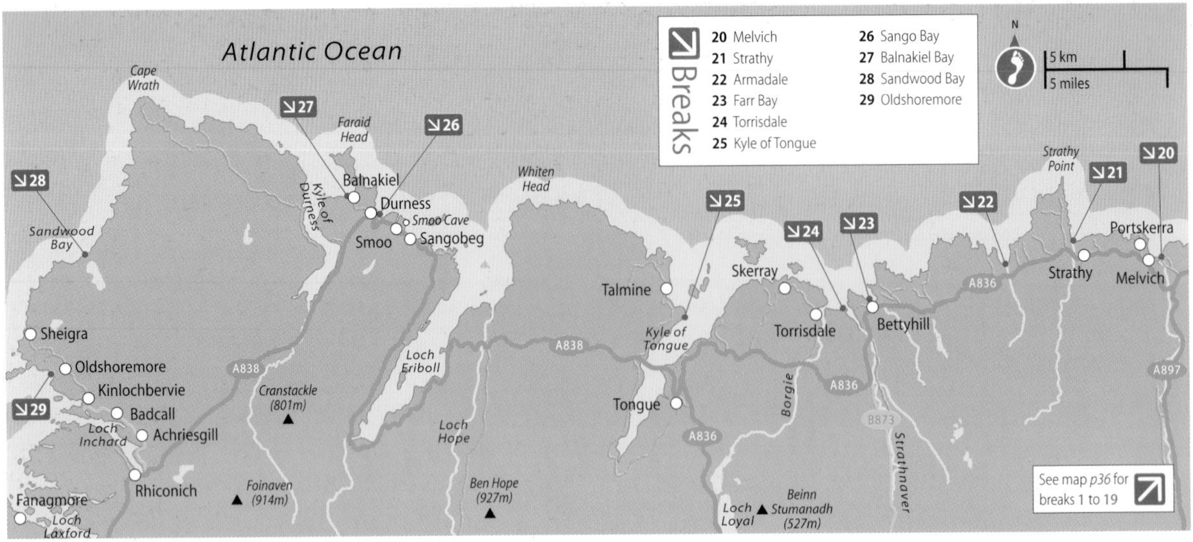

BEACH BREAK

23 Farr Bay

Conditions Medium NW swells, offshore in a SE wind
Hazards/tips Closes out in big swells
Sleeping Bettyhill » p48

This small bay picks up more swell than Armadale and Strathy due to its northwesterly orientation, but the shifting banks tends to close out in bigger swells. Access is via a path from Bettyhill, where parking is available.

BEACH AND RIVERMOUTH BREAK

24 Torrisdale

Conditions All W, NW and N swells, offshore in S winds
Hazards/tips Isolated spot with rips in big swells
Sleeping Bettyhill » p48

A big bay that really feels part of the big country. Depending on how the rivermouth sandbar is working, Torrisdale can produce some epic waves. When the bank is at its best, it produces long, hollow rights that peel away from the river at the eastern end of the bay and long hollow lefts peel towards it. This is a very flexible spot as it works in small swells as well as over head-high and from low to three-quarter tide. There are many peaks along the beach and there is another rivermouth at the western end that generally picks up less swell, but can also have some great waves. A track from Bettyhill leads down to the rivermouth at the eastern end but the only access from here is to paddle across the river. For the western end keep on the A836, then turn right to Torrisdale village. Can have big rips but the river can be useful for getting out back in big swells. Experienced surfers only.

BEACH BREAK

25 Kyle of Tongue

Conditions Big N swells, offshore in S winds
Hazards/tips Rips
Sleeping Tongue » p48

Legend has it that on very big, clean, northerly swells there are long, reeling waves on each side of the bay. Definitely a place to check, but watch out for rips on big tides. Check from the road either side of the inlet.

DEMI TAYLOR

24 The river at Torrisdale lays down a triangular sandbar serving up generous helpings of rights and lefts.

BEACH BREAK

26 Sango Bay

Conditions Medium NW or N swells, offshore in SW winds
Hazards/tips Pretty beach with average waves
Sleeping Durness » p49

Sango is a very dramatic, picturesque beach that sits below the village of Durness. It works on all tides and although it faces northeast, it does pick up plenty of swell. Not a renowned surfing beach but does have some OK waves. You can also visit Smoo Caves.

BEACH BREAK

↘27 Balnakiel Bay

- **Conditions** Medium NW swells, offshore in SE or E winds
- **Hazards/tips** Very flexible spot
- **Sleeping** Durness » *p49*

An amazing, big U-shaped bay at the mouth of the Kyle of Durness that picks up northwesterly swell but is sheltered from northerly winds. Works through all tides and is best in an easterly wind. Follow road from Durness to Balnakeil. Watch out for rips – not for inexperienced surfers.

BEACH BREAK

↘28 Sandwood Bay

- **Conditions** Small to medium W or NW swells, offshore in SE or E winds
- **Hazards/tips** Very isolated spot, rips, no road access
- **Sleeping** Kinlochbervie » *p49*

This is a long, sandy beach set in a stunning location but definitely not one for the beginner. The beach is very remote and picks up the most swell in northern Scotland. If it's flat here, it's flat everywhere. The surf can be excellent with many peaks and a couple of reefs to chose from. Works on all tides. The only access to this bay is on foot so come prepared. It's a wonderful hike in and a great place to camp up for a few days. Check the chart before you make the trek as the last thing you want is to be pounded by a 20-ft swell closing out the beach – which does happen, or get drenched by days of endless rain – which is also a Scottish speciality.

BEACH BREAK

↘29 Oldshoremore

- **Conditions** Medium to big W swells, offshore in NE winds
- **Hazards/tips** Sheltered break with great views
- **Sleeping** Kinlochbervie » *p49*

A small, southwesterly-facing bay at Oldshoremore that works on all states of tide. Needs a good westerly or northwesterly swell to wrap in around the offshore island. Parking overlooking the break. Stunning location looking across to Lewis.

SCOTT WICKING

24 Reading between the lines.

Practicalities

John O'Groats

On the northeast edge of Scotland, this is a fairly joyless 'tourist attraction' complete with tat shops competing to be the first or last on the mainland. Best bet? Take your picture by the famous milemarker sign, take in the views over the notorious Pentland Firth and take off!

Sleeping

££ **John O'Groats Hostel**, T0870-0041129, Apr-Sep, is actually to the west, in the village of Canisbay on the A836. As part of the SYHA, there are curfews.

Camping John O'Groats Caravan and Camping Site, T01955-611329, Apr-Sep, is basic and fairly exposed to the elements but you can often see dolphins swimming just off the coast.

THE GILL

14 Royden Bryson at Backdoor.

Dunnet Bay

Although John O'Groats takes all the glory, unspoilt Dunnet Head is actually the most northerly point on the British mainland. The awesome 300-ft cliffs give way to Dunnet Bay – a 3-km sweep of golden sands.

Sleeping

£ **Dunnet Head Self Catering**, T01847-851774, www.iberacal.com. Easter-Oct is a quaint, 2-double room, converted croft on the B855 to Dunnet Head at Brough and a good option for small groups. They also offer reasonably priced B&B. Opposite is the useful Dunnet Head Info centre with internet access.

Camping Dunnet Bay Campsite, T01847-821319, Apr-Sep is beautifully located in the dunes overlooking the eastern edge of the 2-mile crescent. As a Caravan Club site, if you're planning a long stay, it may be worth joining for the discounts.

Murkle

Murkle was the scene of a great battle where the Celts rose up to defend their land, driving the marauding Vikings back into the sea. Murkle, from Morte Hill or 'hill of death', certainly lives up to its name, with the local farmers still ploughing up the odd Viking skeleton or two.

Sleeping

Camping West Murkle, T01847-896405, for spectacular seclusion plus your own private access to a firing point and a sandy bay, it's woth joining the Caravan Club just to stay at the lovely yet basic certified site with running water for about £3 a night.

Thurso

The most northerly town on the mainland (and in fact it is the only one on this coastline), Thurso's Viking roots are revealed through its name - Norse for Thor's River. It has been a regular staging post for legendary north shore surf trips since the 70s as well as more recently a high money stop on the WQS. Although a little basic, it is no longer as bleak as it once was and even has a surf shop - it's well stocked and is the only one on the north shore. Thurso also acts as a good jumping off spot for trips to Orkney with ferries leaving from Scrabster, a fishing port to the west (see page 57).

Sleeping

£££ **Royal Hotel**, on Traill St, T01874-893191, is comfortable and the best of the bunch. If you're after a quiet-ish night get a room at the back. Off season, you may be able to strike a deal for long stays.

££ **Central Hotel**, on Traill St, has rooms above the legendary bar ensuring the sounds and smells from the weekend travel up to you.

££ **Station Hotel**, Princess St, T01847-892003, has clean rooms as well as 1 and 2 bed 'apartments' complete with microwaves.

£ **Sandra's Backpackers**, Princes St, T01847-894575, is the popular and

Flat spells

Sutherland

Fishing Game fishing is big news in this part of the world. Buy permits for trout and salmon fishing at Kinlochbervie Hotel or Rhiconich Hotel and catch your own supper.

Golf is the other Scottish staple. Get a round in at the 18-hole course at **Reay**, T01847-11288. Further west **Durness GC**, T01971-511364, to the west of the town has a 9-hole course.

Riding **Torrisdale Pony Trekking**, based at the Ferry House, Invernarver, just inland from Bettyhill, T01641-521472, offers a number of treks including one along the sands at Torrisdale.

Sights For **Cape Wrath**, take the 15-min ferry ride (May-Sep) across the Kyle of Durness from Keodale, just south of Durness, T01971-11376. From here the minibus, T01971-511287, bumps down the 12 miles of rough road to the Cape and lighthouse which watches over the most northwesterly point of the mainland, and one of the most dramatic. Despite the number of ships claimed by this coastline, the cape takes its name from the Norse for 'turning place' - the Vikings used the cliffs as a navigation point during their raids on the Highlands. Park up at Blairmore and make the 4-mile trek to the magnificent, secluded white-sand **Sandwood Bay**. Make sure you've got good footwear as the track follows an old peat road across exposed and often damp moorland. It's a crofting estate with grazing, so no dogs are allowed on the track. The awesome **Smoo Cave** (www.smoocave.org), just east of Durness, is the area's biggest draw. The 200-ft long limestone chambers are home to a massive 'waterfall' which bursts through the cave's roof, 80 ft above.

Caithness

Bowling and cinema The **All Star Factory**, on Ormlie Rd, Thurso, T01847-89080, has a 2-screen cinema complex. It is also home to the 10-pin bowling arena, the **Viking Bowl**, T01847-8905050, which is also a bar-cum-nightspot-cum-sports-screening venue with eating options.

Sights **Cnoc Freiceadain Long Cairns**, overlooking the Dounreay Nuclear Power Station. Signposted from the A836 heading west, these Neolithic ceremonial cairns are worth a visit and provide excellent views along the coast. There are other cairns in the area, the best is the partially reconstructed **Grey Cairns of Camster**, accessed via the A99 south of Wick.

Golf Following the B870 out of town, Thurso's 18-hole golf course is just southwest of the town, T01847-893807, green fees £15.

recommended choice for surfers on a budget offering good hostel accommodation, (dorms or private rooms), which includes a free continental breakfast and no curfews. Open year round, it has free hot showers and cooking facilities as well as internet access and a lock-up for bikes. If a decent swell is predicted, book in advance. If they're full try £ **Thurso Hostel**, Ormlie Lodge, on Ormlie Rd, T01847-896888.
Camping **Campbell Caravan Hire**, T01847-893524, Apr-Sep is just off the main road into Thurso, providing prime views towards the reef. With up to 6-berth statics to rent, it's a good bet for groups as it can be one of the cheapest options around. It is also within stumbling distance of the town. Opening times vary so call ahead.

Eating and drinking

Le Bistro, opposite the Central, is moderately priced and a good bet for an evening meal that isn't fish 'n' chips. It also does good cakes and coffee.
The Central, has had a facelift and opened a bar upstairs, **Top Joes**, which serves real ale, as well as a cafe next door **Central Café** which does a good line in coffee and cake plus toasted sandwiches.
At the harbour **Tempest Surf**, has a café next to the shop open Tue-Sun dishing up decent post-surf fare from all day breakies to soups and sandwiches.
Somerfield, supermaket has a café - it may not be glamorous but you can get an all day breakfast and pot of tea for less than a fiver on your way back from the reef.
If you're hankering after a 'with chips' combo **Sandra's** (which offers 10% discount to guests) and **Robin's** sit opposite each other on Princes St and do a roaring trade.
In Scrabster, head to the mid range **The Upper Deck** (at the Ferry Inn). Andy Bain swears it's "the best steak in Scotland" and their seafood including Thurso salmon or Dunnet Bay bass is pretty good too.

Directory

Surf Shops **Tempest Surf**, T01847-892500, www.tempestsurf.co.uk, at Thurso Harbour is well stocked with boards, wetties and all the essentials. **Internet** **Sandra's**, Olrig St. The guest facility is better than the café – a tiny booth in a greasy spoon.
Banks In town. **Chemists** Traill St.
Hospital Ormlie Rd, Thurso, T01847-893263. **Police** Olrig St, just down from the campsite. **Post office** Grove Lane.

Tourist information T01847-892371, Apr-Oct, Riverside Rd.

Melvich

Crossing into Sutherland from Caithness via the A836, Melvich is an unassuming entrance.

Sleeping

£££ **Melvich Hotel**, T01641-531206, on the headland doesn't quite live up to the price but it overlooks the bay complete with bar, pool table and eating options.
££ **Sharvedda**, at Strathy Point, T01641-541311. As well as a B&B, it's a working croft so no dogs but it does have the bonus of good breakfasts and a storage area for boards or bikes. Stunning location.
Halladale Inn Chalet & Caravan Park, T01641-531282, is a small site offering basic camping facilities with good showers as well as reasonably priced 4 person chalets available to rent Jul-Oct. It's only a short walk to Melvich Bay and a stroll next door to the **Halladale Inn** where you can grab a pint and a bit to eat.
Pick up provisions at the **West End Store**, Portskerra.

Bettyhill

Continuing along the A836, the road narrows to stretches of single track with designated passing places. Bettyhill, named after Elizabeth, Duchess of Sutherland, was created following the clearances of the 19th century. The Duchess evicted her tenants managing smallholdings in the valley of Strathnaver to make way for a much more profitable option – sheep.

Sleeping

££ **Bettyhill Hotel**, T01641-521352, www.bettyhill.info, open year round, has a 'local' bar, restaurant and a range of rooms catering to different budgets offering B&B as well as negotiable rates for longer stays. Can be chilly in winter.
£££ **Dunveaden House B&B**, T01641-521273, also manage the **Craig'dhu Caravan Camping Site**, Apr-Oct – a pretty average place just off the A836.

Eating and drinking

Bettyhill Hotel, does a range of food from a good all-day breakfast to bar snacks and full 3-course meals.
Elizabeth's Café, on the main road, overlooking Farr Bay, sells cheap, basic grub such as burgers, pizzas and fish 'n' chips to eat in/take away. Formerly the village jail, they also serve afternoon tea. Open Nov-Mar Fri and Sat only 1700-2000, rest of the year 1200-2000.

Directory

Internet Teleservice Centre, has internet access as well as a mobile bank service (Fri 1000-1200). **Tourist information** Available seasonally at Elizabeth's Café.

Tongue

Sleeping

££ **Strathtongue Old Manse B&B**, T01847-611252, is a beautiful old house set in lovely gardens, 3 miles east of Tongue on the road from Thurso. They have a drying and storage area and great breakfasts using local ingredients where possible including their own free-range eggs.
££ **Rhian Guest House**, T01847-611257, from Tongue, head south on the picturesque, single track route towards Ben

DEMI TAYLOR

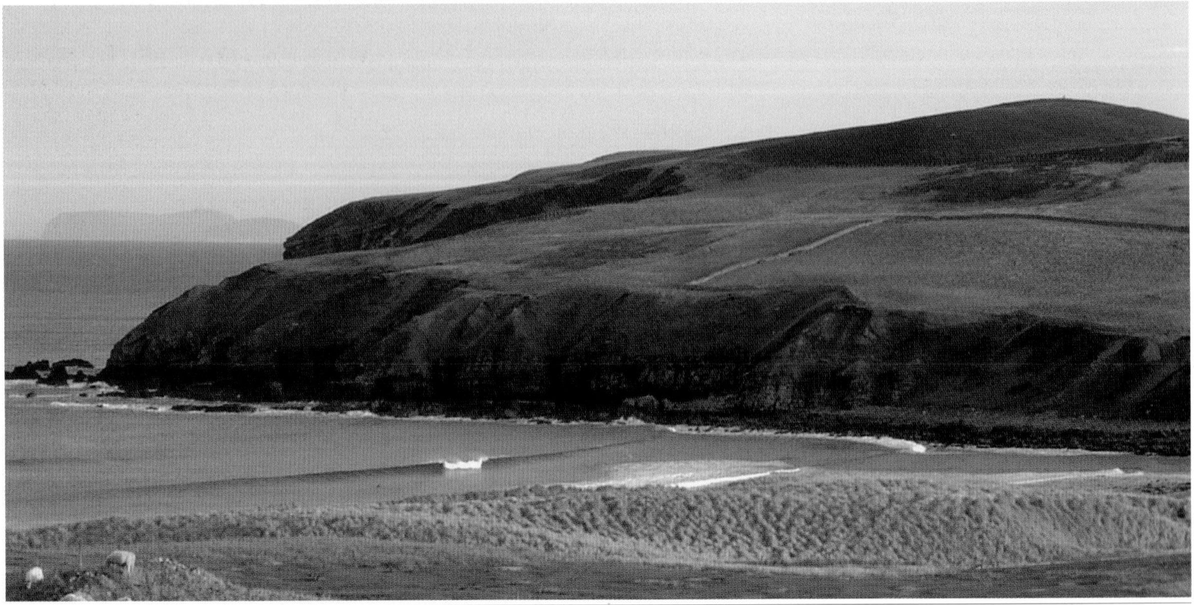

20 Travelling west, the geography of Sutherland creates a whole new range of set-ups and opportunities.

Hope for this pretty, former gamekeeper's cottage. They have internet access, storage for boards/bikes and can even organize packed lunches.
Camping Just south of the village, **Kincraig Camping & Caravan Site**, T01847-55218, is open Apr-Oct.

Durness

Continuing west, the A838 is a mixture of dual and single track road with passing places. Durness is the most northwesterly village on the mainland, spectacularly located, nestling between coves of blindingly white sand and awesome limestone cliffs. Be aware, they have around 200 days of rain a year.

Sleeping

As a popular spot for green tourism, there are plenty of sleeping options.
£££ **Mackay's**, T01971-511202, Easter-Oct. The 7-ensuite rooms here are well done and have a contemporary, luxurious feel. Breakfast is included in the price, they also have a restaurant on site for evening meals.
££ **Foinaen**, T01971-511726, is a reasonably priced B&B option.
£ **The Lazy Crofter Bunkhouse**, T01971-511209, is a good budget bet. It only has dorm beds but on the plus side has kitchen facilities, is close to the village store, has bike/board storage, a drying room, dehumidifier and no curfew.
Camping Try **Sango Sands Oasis Campsite**, T01971-511726/222, on the road into Durness which offers statics as well as having a bar and restaurant.
Self-catering A good option for groups is one of the **Norsehaven Cottages**, T01732-882320, www.norsehaven.com. A short walk from Sango Bay, the reasonably priced cottages sleep 4 or 8 people.

Eating and drinking

Mackay's, in Durness is a good dinner option and focuses on using local seafood and meats. Just north, **Balnakeil**, is home to a hippy craft village with a couple of cafés.

LUCIA GRIGGI

The Caithness coastline is riddled with reefs and once-unrideable slabs.

Loch Croispol Bookshop & Restaurant, is a bizarre looking yet licensed affair, serving up good food year among the book shelves round until 2030 (summer), 1730 (winter).

Directory

Tourist information Just off the A383, T01971-511259, www.visithighlands.com, open year round.

Kinlochbervie

On the northwest coast of Sutherland sits the large fishing port and small village of Kinlochbervie. It's not particularly pretty but is a handy place to stop off before making the trek to Sandwood Bay.

Sleeping

££ **The Old School Restaurant & Roms**, T01971-521383, Apr-Oct is a B&B on the B801 between Rhiconich and Kinlochbrevie. The restaurant is good, reasonably priced and open in the evenings delivering, ironically, quite old school fare including prawn cocktail and lasagne alongside local beef. Last orders 2000.
Camping **Sheigra Rough Camping**, overlooks the beach and has no facilities except a water tap.
Self Catering **Clashview Cottage**, T07788-441977, in Kinlochbervie sleeps 9 comfortably in a well maintained modern cottage with very reasonable prices (between £300-600 per week). 800 yds from the beach at Oldshoremore **Oldshoremore Lodge**, T01971-521224, also sleeps up to around 10 but is about double the price.

Eating and drinking

Kinlochbervie Hotel, has a bar and does reasonable bistro-style meals as well as a restaurant serving up fresh fish suppers.
Fisherman's Mission, on the harbour front, is mainly there for the fleet but the canteen welcomes visitors and does a mean fish 'n' chips.

Directory

London Stores, just south in Badcall, sells all the basics but if you want to pick up some fish get down to the port in the evening. The **mobile bank** visits Mon and Thu.

Overview

The Scottish Isles have a true frontier feel to them. Pull onto the forecourt of the village store-cum-petrol station and the ping of a bell summons a friendly, if slightly gruff attendant to top up your tank while you venture inside to pick up a copy of *The Orcadian* and a few snacks – fuel for bodies still chilled from their immersion in the freezing North Atlantic. The yellow butterfly valve, clearly visible, spins hypnotically in the glass bubble that crowns the pump as the life giving petrol is mainlined into the waiting van. It doesn't pay to run too low out here – of either type of fuel.

> As you come down the road to Bru, the coastline opens out in front of you. You don't have to confuse the issue with break names. The points – the best of them are of Peruvian quality, 500-600 yards long – are walling when small, but a real challenge when the surf hits 6-8ft…
>
> *Derek Macleod, Hebridean Surf*

At nearby Skara Brae, a pathway winds from the visitor centre to the beachside Neolithic village nestled in the wind-scoured sand dunes nearly 200 m away. Subtle plaques mark time as you journey back through the ages. Within a few steps you are past the discovery of the 'New World', the Dark Ages arrive all too quickly and at the halfway mark the pyramids are being built by one of the world's greatest civilizations. Yet, still 100 m away, sits a village of warm, stone-built residences, a sewage system running under paths and stone sideboards decorated with precious ornaments. Within this short journey 5000 years have melted away and you find yourself transported to an ancient place. On this timescale, surfing would only have arrived at the points of Skaill Bay within a few millimetres of the start of the walk. Closer than the width of a fin, maybe even the depth of wax on your deck…

If there is an overwhelming feeling in these islands, it is the relentless pressure of time, weighing heavy on the landscape and the relics of lost civilizations. If you look up from the archaeological site at Skara Brae, you will see that the landscape has conspired with the elements to produce two perfect point breaks, unnoticed by the eminent scientists and legions of birdwatchers drawn to these shores. The varied breaks of the Scottish Islands are some of the most unspoilt and pristine in the whole of Britain, and surfing has made no impact here. No surf centres or board hire on these beaches. Against the roaring ocean, the wild landscape and the weathered monuments it is an insignificant presence. Here, surfing is still as refreshing as a crisp offshore breeze.

Coastline

The **Hebrides**, composed of grey Lewisian Gneiss, some of the oldest exposed rock in the world, sit off the far northwestern corner of mainland Britain. Their exposed position means that the rock and boulder reefs and quality beach breaks pick up

Spring
Air 6°C 43°F
Water 8°C 46°F
5/4mm Wetsuit, boots & gloves

Summer
Air 13°C 55°F
Water 12°C 54°F
4/3mm Wetsuit

Autumn
Air 9°C 48°F
Water 12°C 54°F
4/3mm Wetsuit & boots

Winter
Air 4°C 39°F
Water 7°C 45°F
6mm Wetsuit, boots, gloves & hood

GREG MARTIN/FINDYOURWAVE

11 Valtos.

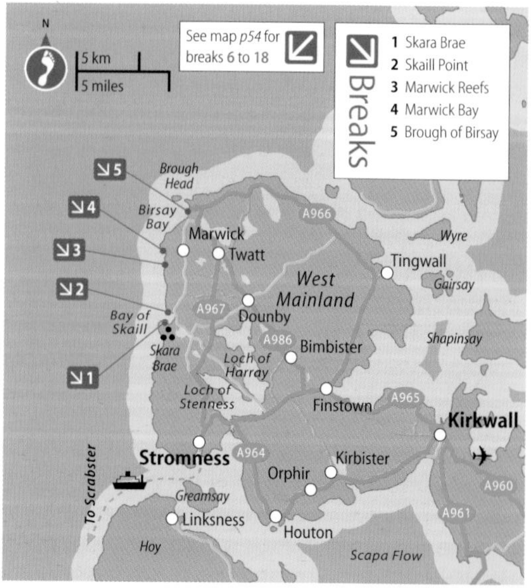

GREG MARTIN/FINDYOURWAVE

10 Bus Stops.

swell from virtually every low pressure system out in the Atlantic. The islands are home to every conceivable type of surf, from firing rocky point breaks to sheltered white-sand beaches that produce Hossegor-type waves. The rugged coastline and winding roads mean that a week-long trip won't even begin to open up the potential of this magical place. The islands are also renowned for the storms that come lashing through and for the severe, unforgiving winter winds. The east coast of the islands can offer some wonderfully sheltered little gems when the westerlies kick in.

Lying off the northeastern tip of Britain are the **Orkney Isles**, an extension of the wonderful slabstone geography of the Caithness region and an offshore account of fairly low-interest reefs and points. Add to this the fact that the islands pick up more swell than the mainland and you have a place of amazing surf potential. If it's beaches you are after, just look at the potential of Sanday.

Local Environment by Surfers Against Sewage

"Because of where these islands sit, they get ocean currents and predominant winds pushing marine litter onto their beaches from far away. Debris litters the high tide line on the most remote surf spots. Also, tertiary treated sewage (the highest level of treatment) is rare in these areas. It is common practice for small communities to dump their raw sewage into rivers and the sea." Andy Cummins www.sas.org.uk

The waves here are powerful and the rips can be dangerous, so if you are in any doubt about your ability, stay well within your safety zone. Beginners should stick with the local surf schools. The Hebrides has a growing number of committed surfers, with the local community pioneered by former fisherman **Derek Macleod** (see page 58) whose **Hebridean Surf Camp** was founded in 1996 and Mark Lumsden who runs Lewis Surf Trek. Orkney now boasts a handful of hardy surfers.

Getting around

The road networks on Orkney and the Hebrides are of pretty good quality but are mostly single-track and winding, and can get clogged with tourists in the summer, especially coaches on Orkney. Always allow way more time than you think.

6'2" Surftech UFO

Shaper: Randy French

6'2" x $19\frac{1}{4}$" x $2\frac{1}{8}$"

Surftech's lively, responsive TL2 composite technology.

Super light to respond quickly whether carving, sliding or throwing down airs. Flat entry rocker, flat bottom, hard edge in tail insures incredible speed through even flattest sections. Ideal for small summer surf but can handle overhead with bigger fins.

FCS M5 fins.

6'8" JC Peter Mel Machine

Shaper: John Carper

6'8" x $19\frac{1}{2}$" x $2\frac{7}{16}$"

Built with Surftech's proven TUFLITE construction.

Designed for big wave charger Peter Mel, blends wider nose and tail with medium entry rocker to get into waves early with speed to fly down the line yet loose enough for big power gouges in the pocket. The 6'8" PMM is a high performance step-up board for a bigger surfer.

FCS fins.

Boards by **Surftech**
www.surftech.com info@surftech.com

Breaks

Orkney

LEFT POINT BREAK

↘1 Skara Brae

- **Conditions** All W and NW swells, offshore in E winds
- **Hazards/tips** Shallow when small, very quiet spot
- **Sleeping** West Mainland » *p58*

This is a wonderful, pinwheel, left-hand point that breaks over a shallow boulder reef into the calm waters of Skaill Bay. The point provides an awesome backdrop to the beachfront Neolithic site at Skara Brae and one look at the postcard selection will show you how consistent this point is. Works in any northwesterly or westerly swell but the wind needs to be from an easterly direction.

RIGHT POINT BREAK

↘2 Skaill Point

- **Swell** Medium NW and W swells
- **Wind** Easterly
- **Tide** Mid to low tide
- **Size** 3-10 ft
- **Length** 50-200 m
- **Bottom** Flat reef
- **Access** Off the rocks
- **Ability** Intermediate to Advanced
- **Best months** Sep-Nov, Apr-Jun
- **Board** Performance thruster
- **Hazards/tips** Long walls breaking over rocky reef
- **Sleeping** West Mainland » *p58*

Skaill Point is hard to miss when it's on. Just look to the northern edge of this west-facing crescent shaped bay to find a perfect long, walling right-hand point. In ideal conditions, swell unloads onto the outside fringe of the flat slabstone reef. Lines wrap beneath the grassy headland, sending waves reeling through to the beach. The clear green walls can fold into hollow sections on the outside, slowing slightly as they hit the inside before lining up into long, long walls, perfect for carving turns and cutbacks.

In big swells with little wind, this place transforms into an empty, crystal paradise, the kind of location that is getting increasingly rare to find these days. At a time when the remotest corners of the globe have surfers scrambling over them, the Orkneys must be one of the few areas where quality surf really does go unridden.

There are good reasons of course. The coastline around Thurso, where the ferry leaves for the Orkneys, is wave rich and relatively uncrowded, meaning there has always been little incentive to splash out on the expensive ferry tickets to the islands. Also conditions in Scotland are notoriously fickle. It really is the land of 'four seasons in one day' and a chart that looks perfect for the Orkneys can quickly change into a week of onshore rain. For the perfect Orkney chart means a deep low pressure system, tracking just to the south of Iceland, the kind of chart that will turn Thurso into reeling perfection. Just how easy is it to board the ferry and steam out of the bay while just to your right there are classic barrels for the taking?

However, Skaill Bay is a consistent swell catcher. Get it with light easterly winds and you should be treated to the sight of two quality point breaks reeling at each side of this wonderful bay, home to a world famous 5,000-year old Neolithic settlement. Skara Brae is probably the only break in the world where surfers are outnumbered by archaeologists.

DEMI TAYLOR

2 Skaill Point.

*If you like **Skaill Point**, try **Lafitenia** in France (see page 194), **Anchor Point** in Morocco (see page 387) or **Ribeira d'Ilhas** in Portugal (see page 299).*

REEF BREAK

↘3 Marwick Reefs

- **Conditions** Small to medium NW and W swells, offshore in E winds
- **Hazards/tips** Shallow, very quiet bay, experienced surfers only
- **Sleeping** West Mainland » *p58*

A series of reefs to the south of the bay for experienced surfers only. Waves come out of deep water and break onto a series of shallow, flat slab reefs through the tides. Those who have surfed Brims Ness (see page 42) will know exactly what to expect. These reefs throw up fast, powerful, barrelling waves even in small swells.

RIGHT REEF BREAK

↘4 Marwick Bay

- **Conditions** Small to medium W to NW swells, offshore in E winds
- **Hazards/tips** Quiet bay, boulder reef
- **Sleeping** West Mainland » *p58*

Wander the dark, boulder strewn low tide mark at Marwick and you'll find the scattered detritus of numerous decades of shipwrecks littering the rockpools, testament to the raw power of the ocean here. On sunny autumn days birdwatchers scan the heavens, missing the reeling mid tide right-hand reef that breaks over boulders in the middle of the bay. It throws up a quality, walling right that can produce the occasional barrel. Best in small to medium swells. Bigger swells stimulate a right that comes to life under the cliffs at the northern end of the bay. Rarely surfed spot, so not ideal for inexperienced surfers.

DEMI TAYLOR

RIGHT REEF BREAK

↘5 Brough of Birsay

- **Conditions** Medium to big W to NW swells
- **Hazards/tips** Rocks, access, shallow, big colony of seals
- **Sleeping** West Mainland » *p58*

The Brough (pronounced Brock) of Birsay is a small offshore island attached to the mainland by a low-tide causeway. There are a number of reefs in Birsay Bay that break at different tides and in different swell sizes. Offshore in easterly and southeasterly winds.

Above: 4 Marwick Point. **Below:** 3 Marwick Reefs.

DEMI TAYLOR

Outer Hebrides

BEACH BREAK

↘6 Tolsta

Conditions Medium N swells, offshore in SW winds
Hazards/tips Powerful, hollow waves
Sleeping Stornoway » p58

A mile-long stretch of beach that picks up northerly swell. Tolsta has some quality sandbanks that produce hollow peaks. Faces northeast and works through all the tides. Follow the B895 from Stornoway.

BEACH BREAK

↘7 Port of Ness (Port Nis)

Conditions Small and medium N to NE swells, offshore in SW winds
Hazards/tips Small bay with some rocks
Sleeping Stornoway/W Coast » p58

Port Nis is a sandy bay with rocks that has some excellent low tide rights. There are rocks at mid tide in the middle of the bay and a right breaking at the southern end, which picks up the most swell. There is also a left peeling off the broken pier. Be aware, it can have bad rips.

BEACH BREAK

↘8 Europie (Eòropaidh)

Conditions All N to W swells, offshore in SE winds
Hazards/tips Quality beach break, big rips
Sleeping Stornoway/W Coast » p58

Europie is the best-known break on the Hebrides and an excellent quality beach with hollow, powerful sandbanks. There can be big right-hand barrels peeling along the northern end of the beach while the middle of the beach can be home to barrelling rights which break into a channel and work best from low to near high tide. At the southern end there is a sand-covered rocky bank that has some great, hollow waves at low tide. As this beach gets lashed by huge swells, the formation of banks can change from week to week. "Europie is a challenging, A-grade beach break and the most northwesterly break in Britain," says Derek McCloud. "It's very powerful - like big Hossegor. It's board breaking and neck breaking." Parking available near the cemetery.

BEACH BREAK

↘9 Swain Bost Sands

Conditions Small to medium NW swells, offshore in SE winds
Hazards/tips Rocks and rips
Sleeping Stornoway/W Coast » p58

Part of the same stretch of beach as Europie. Low tide rocky sandbanks that lie in a double bay, divided by a rocky reef. **Gunshots** is a massive, heavy left-hand tube for the hard-core. Breaks like Teahupoo when big and is a big paddle.

REEF AND POINT BREAK

↘10 Barvas (Barabhas)

Conditions All swells, offshore in SE to SW winds
Hazards/tips A selection of excellent breaks, popular spots
Sleeping Stornoway/W Coast » p58

Barvas is a big, right-hand boulder reef that can hold swells up to 10 ft. Works like a reverse Easkey Left (see page 132), breaking through the tides and on all swell sizes. It produces long walling quality rides and has

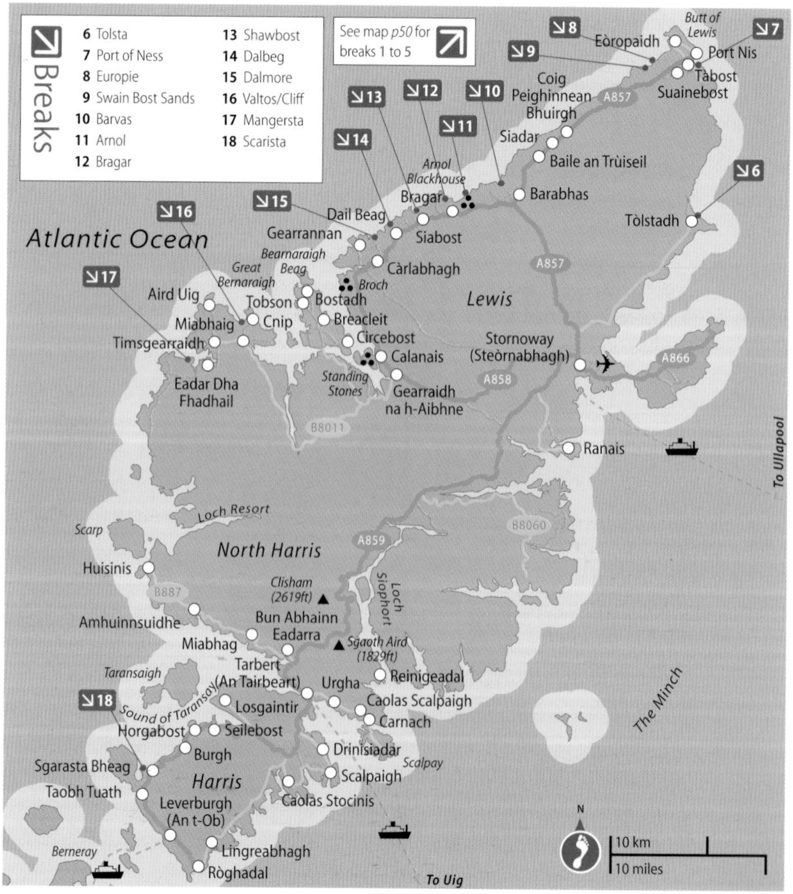

sections that can combine in the right swell. A south or southeasterly wind is offshore.

Bru is a long left-hand point that has quality walling waves breaking over boulders. Best in a southerly or southwesterly wind. It is one of the island's most recognizable waves due to the large green bus, hence the name **Bus Stops**. Long, walling waves. According to Derek McCloud, "Bru is like a Peruvian point break that can peel for 500 yds on its day. When it gets big it is very heavy and challenging with big hold-downs and a hard reef."

Outer Lefts is a left point at the western end of the rocks. It is a rock and boulder reef that is always bigger than the other breaks and can hold a big swell up to 10 ft. Offshore in southerly/southwesterly winds. "Follow the road to Bru and you'll see all the breaks open out in front of you," says Derek.

REEF BREAK

↘11 Arnol

- **Conditions** Big swells, offshore in SW winds
- **Hazards/tips** Big wave spot for experienced surfers
- **Sleeping** Stornoway/W Coast ›› *p58*

This is a big wave peak that breaks over a boulder and rock reef in the middle of the bay. It is best at low tide when it breaks up to 15 ft plus and there are strong rips. For hellmen only.

ROCKY LEFT POINT BREAK

↘12 Bragar

- **Conditions** Medium NW swells, offshore in W or SW winds
- **Hazards/tips** Difficult exit from water in big swells
- **Sleeping** Stornoway/W Coast ›› *p58*

A long, left-hand point break that fires along a rocky, bouldery reef. The tide depends on the swell size but in the right conditions rides of up to 300 yds are possible on good quality walling waves. Entry and exit from the water can be difficult over boulders and rocks.

GREG MARTIN/FINDYOURWAVE

GREG MARTIN/FINDYOURWAVE

Above: Glen Hall smacks a Hebridean lip. **Below**: 11 Valtos keg.

ROCKY LEFT POINT BREAK

↘13 Shawbost (Siabost)

- **Conditions** Big NW swell, offshore in W or SW winds
- **Hazards/tips** Rocky wave, difficult access
- **Sleeping** Stornoway/W Coast ›› *p58*

This point needs a big southwesterly swell to get going due to the rocky nature of the line-up. Best at about 6-8 ft, access can be tricky due to boulders and rocks.

BEACH BREAK

↘14 Dalbeg

- **Conditions** Small to medium NW swells, offshore in SE wind
- **Hazards/tips** Powerful, hollow lefts
- **Sleeping** Stornoway/W Coast ›› *p58*

This beach has a low tide left breaking off a quality sandbank. Dalbeg is a small, sheltered bay with a strong rip at the right end. The wave here is powerful and hollow but closes out on the end section.

BEACH BREAK

↘15 Dalmore

- **Conditions** Small to medium NW swells, offshore in SE winds
- **Hazards/tips** Powerful peak
- **Sleeping** Stornoway/W Coast ›› *p58*

The next bay to Dalbeg, this spot has a low tide hollow peak, which produces punchy lefts and rights. As the swell picks up there is

15 Cornwall's Spencer Hargreaves making the Celtic connection at Dalmore.

a dredging left-hand point. Once you step in , you have to be committed due to the powerful nature of the waves and the rips.

BEACH BREAK

↘16 Valtos (Bhaltos) /Cliff

- **Conditions** Medium N or NW swells, offshore in SE winds
- **Hazards/tips** Rips
- **Sleeping** Stornoway/W Coast » *p58*

An hour's drive inland and along the B8011 brings you to the small bay at Valtos. There are two peaks, both producing excellent hollow and powerful waves. The break works on all tides, but better at low to mid. There is parking overlooking the break. "Every year people get into trouble on the western breaks due to the powerful rips," says Derek McCloud, "and there are no lifeguards here. We have to bail them out ourselves."

BEACH BREAK

↘17 Mangersta

- **Conditions** Small NW swells, offshore in SE winds.
- **Hazards/tips** Beautiful, white sand bay
- **Sleeping** Stornoway/W Coast » *p58*

Crystal-clear water and white sand make this pretty beach an excellent destination. It just so happens that it also has an excellent low tide peak producing hollow lefts and rights. Best in small swells when it produces great barrels. Gets nasty when the swell picks up and is exposed to the wind.

BEACH BREAK

↘18 Scarista

- **Conditions** All NW swells, offshore in SE winds
- **Hazards/tips** Beautiful, exposed spot
- **Sleeping** Tarbert » *p58*

This is a big stretch of beach exposed to the wind. There are peaks along the length, with powerful waves from northwesterly and southwesterly swells. A beautiful spot that looks across to Taransay, home of the original reality TV show, *Castaway*. A wonderful quiet spot worth checking if the northwest coast is too big and the wind is from the southeast. Quite a long but beautiful drive from Stornoway.

Practicalities

Orkney

The low lying Orkney Islands are lapped by the Gulf Stream and take their name from the orcas (killer whales) that make their migratory journey through the archipelago's surrounding waters. There are about 70 islands in all, the largest of which is Mainland. Although only a short hop across the water from John O'Groats, Orkney is a world apart, with its Neotlithic village, burial mounds, stone circles and Viking graffiti.

Transport

Air **British Airways**, T0870-8509850, operates direct flights to Kirkwall Airport T01856-872421, 3 miles southeast of the town, from Aberdeen, Edinburgh, Glasgow and Inverness through Loganair. Connections from London, Manchester, Dublin and Belfast. Flights are pricey; ring ahead to ensure your board will be allowed on, especially during busy summer months.

Ferries **Pentland Ferries**, T01856-831226, www.pentlandferries.co.uk, operate the cheapest and quickest service between Gills Bay west of John O'Groats on the A836, and St Margaret's Hope on South Ronaldsay. Foot passengers from £24 return, vans from £56 return. **Northlink Ferries**, T0845-6000449, www.northlinkferries.co.uk, runs between Scrabster, near Thurso, and Stromness. Taking in the breathtaking 450-ft sea stacks of the Old Man of Hoy, the journey takes about 1½ hrs. Return from £26 foot passenger and £82 van. Northlink also operate ferries year round from Aberdeen, on Scotland's east coast, to Stromness. Taking 8 hrs, it costs about double the Scrabster service.

Stromness

This pretty fishing town is complete with cobbled streets and a strong seafaring tradition. Many of the Atlantic's whaling crews set out from here.

Sleeping

££ **Sincalir's B&B**, John St, T01856-850949, within walking distance of the harbour.
£ **Browns Hostel**, Victoria St, T01856-850661, independent, popular, open year round with internet access and well placed for the town. Dorms and private rooms, beds from about £11.
£ **Mrs Worthington's B&B**, South End, T01856-850215, Apr-Oct, has views over Scapa Flow and easy access to the town.
Self-catering Plenty of options which can work out as a cheaper option for groups. Traditional stone house on Dundas St overlooking the harbour, sleeps up to 6 from £200 per week: contact **Mr and Mrs Seater**, T01856-850415. For full listings check out (www.visitorkney.com).
Camping Responsible free-camping is permitted but ask the landowner's permission first.
Point of Ness Caravan and Camping, T01856-850262, May-Sep, short walk from town with great views across the water to neighbouring Hoy (can be a bit windy).

Eating and drinking

Julia's café, opposite the ferry terminal, does a good range of reasonably priced lunch staples.The **Ferry Inn**, near the terminal, is a popular spot and does reasonably priced pub grub for lunch and dinner. If you feel like splashing out head to the **Hamnavoe Restaurant**, on Graham Pl, T01856-850606, Apr-Sep, and eat the catch of the day, straight off the boats.

Directory

Internet **Julia's Café**, opposite the ferry terminal. **Tourist information** Scrabster ferry port, T01856-850716, www.visitorkney.com. **Car Hire** **Stromness Car Hire**, North End Rd, T01856-850850, www.stromnesscarhire.co.uk, is within walking distance of the ferry at the Blue Star Filling Station.

Kirkwall

The capital, Kirkwall, is a busy working town that lacks the natural charm of Stromness. However, its redeeming feature is that it does offer basic amenities, from chemists to banks to supermarkets.

Sleeping

££ **Berstane House B&B**, St Ola, T01856-876277, is a grand looking house and a quiet getaway, set in 8 acres of woodland and just 2 miles into town. Also has self-catering house for up to 4.
£ **Peedie Hostel**, Ayre Rd, by the seafront, T01856-875477, is pretty basic and not particularly spacious with beds from £10.
£ **SYHA**, Old Skapa Rd, T0870-1553255, Apr-Oct, is basic, about a 15-min walk into town, with a midnight curfew.
Camping The **Pickaquoy Centre**, T01856-879900, offers basic camping facilities, Apr-Sep, with pay showers (get a good haul of £0.20s).
Self-catering **Mrs Sinclair's**, house and flat on Tankerness, T01856-872035, are about as central as you can get. The house sleeps up to 7 people with prices around £350 per week.

Eating and drinking

The **Bothy Bar**, at the Albert Hotel, Mounthoolie La, is pretty lively, occasionally has live bands and serves a full range of real ales including the local Dark Island as well as reasonable bar food. **Ayre Hotel**, on the harbour-front offers reasonably priced staples such as fish 'n' chips and steak and ale pie. The **St Magnus Café**, at the community centre is a good and cheap place to grab a sandwich and a cup of tea, as is the **Mustard Seed**, on Victoria St, which also does home baking.

For a night out, head to **Fusion**, on Ayre St which, along with the **Fire Lounge**, are the most stylish places hosting regular DJ and live music nights on the island.

Directory

Internet Free at the library on Junction Rd. **Chemist** Albert St. **Hospital** Balfour Hospital, New Scapa Rd (running south out of town), T01856-888000. **Police** Buttquoy Cres. **Tourist information** Broad St, T0185-872856. **Car Hire** **WR Tullock**, Castle St, T01856-875500, www.orkneycarrental.Co.uk. Also at the airport.

West Mainland

The west coast is home to the major breaks on Orkney and is a good base for those wanting to escape the tourists. **Sandwick** is a short hop to Skaill Bay with its two point breaks. Heading north from Skaill is **Marwick Bay** in Birsay, with some excellent reefs and a good point.

Sleeping

Sandwick ££ **Netherstove**, a working farm 15 mins' walk from Skaill Bay, T01856-841625, offers B&B May-Oct and year-round self-catering accommodation in chalets on the premises.

££ **Hyval Farm**, a family-run beef farm near Skaill Bay, T01856-841522, B&B Apr-Oct.

Birsay ££ **Primrose Cottage**, T01856-721384, views over Marwick Bay, comfortable B&B.

££ **Linkshouse**, T01856-721221, is a lovely Edwardian guesthouse which also overlooks Marwick and does good breakfasts.

There are plenty of self-catering facilities here including **Bryameadow Caravan**, T01856-841803, in Dounby. The modern caravan available to let sleeps 4 people from £140 per week.

Eating and drinking

Smithfield Hotel, in Dounby does a very reasonable lunch and evening meal.

Outer Hebrides

This 130-mile long chain of islands, 30 miles off the coast of Scotland is home to Britain's most northwesterly beach, Europie, as well as puffins, golden eagles, dolphins, whales and basking sharks. Tradition has a strong foothold on the islands where Gaelic is still spoken and Sundays really are a day of rest.

Transport

Air **BMI** (www.flybmi.com) operate daily flights between Stornoway and Edinburgh. There are also limited flights with **Highland Airways** (www.highlandairways.co.uk) and **Eastern Airways** (www.easternairways.com). **Ferries** **CalMac**, T08705-650000, www.calmac.co.uk, run regular services year round between Ullapool and Stornoway (not Sun), 2-3 times daily, around 2 hrs 40 mins. From £175 return for a camper and 2 passengers. Also inter-island crossings.

Stornoway (Steòrnabhagh)

Lewis is the largest of the Outer Hebrides and makes up the top two-thirds of the most northerly island in the chain. Stornoway on the east coast is the focal point for island life and the only major town servicing the islands with full facilities.

Sleeping

££ **Westwind B&B**, Newton St, T01851-703408. Basic but handy bolthole within walking distance of ferry.

£ **Stornoway Surf House**, Keith St, www.hebrideansurf.co.uk, T01851-705862. Run by former fisherman and hardy surfer, Derek McCloud, who knows this coastline well. £10 will buy you a bed in a dorm and access to a self-catering kitchen, twins and doubles also available.

££ **Lewis Surf Trek**, T07939 194880, www.lewissurftrek.com. Run by Mark Lumsden who offers instruction and guided trips across the islands in a fully kitted out expedition vehicle for up to 5 surfers, complete with DVD player, bunks, toilet and a separate 'wetroom' for boards and wetties.

£ **Laxdale Holiday Park**, T01851-706966, www.laxdaleholidaypark.com. 1½ miles outside Stornoway with camping facilities as well as caravans and a bungalow for hire Apr-Oct. Their bunkhouse is open year round with beds from £12 per night.

Eating and drinking

Sunsets Restaurant, near the surf camp, serves tasty and healthy meals using local produce and fresh fish straight off the boats. The **Crown Hotel**, on Castle St, is a nice place to grab a pint and a bite to eat but there are also plenty of other pubs around the quay. The **Thai Café**, on Church St, is surprisingly good – and good value. **Digby Chick**, Bank St, does a good line in fresh local produce. **Heb**, is the nightclub for the islands, so get down there Thu-Sat nights, but remember Sat nights finish before 2400.

Directory

Surf Shop Derek McCloud runs a fully stocked surf shop off Keith St. **Internet** Get online at the local library on Cromwell St or try Captions on Church St. **Bank** opposite TIC. **Chemist** Cromwell St. **Post office** Francis St. **Tourist information** Cromwell St, www.visithebrides.co.uk, year round.

West coast

Sleeping

Port Nis (Ness) At the northwest tip of the Butt of Lewis, 45-min drive from Stornoway.

££ **Galson Farm Guest House**, 8 miles south of Port Nis off the A857, T01851-850492, 18th-century converted farmhouse in a Gaelic crofting village offers traditional B&B and can even organize packed lunches. Also has a bunkhouse with 8 beds plus self-catering kitchen for around £10.

Barabhas (Barvas) At the junction with A857 and A858.

££ **Rockvilla B&B**, T01851-840286, well placed for coastal access.

Siabost (Shawbost)/Carlabhagh (Carloway) ££ **Airigh**, B&B in South Siabost, T01851-710478.

£ **Garenin Gatliff Hostel** (non-profit), is south along the A858 to Carlabhagh, then down a back road towards the coast, in the old crofting village of Garenin. Open year round with beds in a restored blackhouse from £8. You can't book ahead and it is heated by coal fire but it is a great place to stay and well located for Dalbeg and Dalmore Bays. Try the **Copper Kettle** at Dalbeg Bay for cheap and good lunchtime snacks and jacket potatoes.
Camping **Eilean Fraoich Campsite**, T01851-710504, www.eileanfraoich.co.uk, May-Oct.

Tarbert (An Tairbeart)

Harris is joined to Lewis to the north. The port of Tarbert, lying in a sheltered bay, is the main settlement on the island and joins north and south Harris.

Sleeping

££ **MacLeod Motel**, near the ferry pier, T01859-502364, offers rooms as well as cottages for 4-6 people to rent.
£ **Rockview Bunkhouse**, Main St, T01859-502626, is a touch 'intimate' but a cheap, well placed option with kitchen facilities and games room.
£ **Drinishader Hostel**, about 5 miles south of Tarbert, T01859-511255, has a roaring coal fire.

Eating and drinking

The **Harris Hotel** near the ferry terminal does good value bar food plus dinner menu and serves on Sun. **First Fruits** teahouse, Harbour St Apr-Sep, is a cosy place to enjoy some traditional home cooking. There are also a few pubs on Harbour St.

Directory

Banks Harbour St. **Chemists** Bannockburn Building on Barmore Rd. **Post office** Campbeltown Rd. **Police** School Rd. **Tourist information** Harbour St, Apr-Oct

An T-ob (Leverburgh)

Continuing south along the A859, Leverburgh has a shop and a few basic facilities including the £ **Am Bothan Bunkhouse**, on Ferry Rd, T01859-520251. An ordinary exterior gives way to a great interior, warmed along by the peat fire and central heating plus it has a drying room and allows camping.

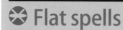

Flat spells

Orkney

Bike Hire **Orkney Cycle Hire**, Dundas St, Stromness, T01856-850255; **Cycle Orkney**, Tankerness La, Kirkwall, T01856-875777.

Cinema **Pickaquoy Centre**, Pickaquoy Rd, Kirkwall, T01856-879900, is home to the **New Phoenix Cinema**. Also here is a fitness studio with sauna, jacuzzi and steam room plus a café and bar with pool tables and Sky TV.

Golf **Orkney GC**, just west of Kirkwall on Grainbank, T01856-872457, has an 18-hole course, fees from £15.

Sights If you only see one thing while you're here, it should be **Skara Brae**, a 5,000-year-old village and world heritage site. It's 2,000 years older than the Pyramids, predates Stonehenge, and yet features a sewage system and individual dwellings boasting a course of damp-proofing, stone sideboards for displaying treasures, and even cool boxes. Open year round with an excellent visitors' centre, entry £6.50. Access via the B9056. **Maeshowe** may look like a hill from the outside but is one of the most impressive chambered tombs in Western Europe, made even more interesting by the fact it was raided by the Vikings in the 12th century. The plundering Norsemen carved runic graffiti into the walls boasting of their conquests in battle and with women. The **Stones of Stenness** and the bigger **Ring of Brodgar** are both spectacular ceremonial stone circles dating from the time of Skara Brae. You're allowed to walk freely and actually touch the stones. Accessed via the B9055 running northwesterly off the A965, the circles and nearby standing stones run along powerful lay lines.

Outer Hebrides

Bike Hire **Alex Dan's Cycle Centre**, Kenneth St, Stornoway, T01851-704025, hire by the hour, day or week.

Golf **Stornoway G C**, Lady Lever Park, just east of Stornoway, T01851-702249, 18-hole course in the grounds of Lews Castle. On Harris the 9-hole **Scarista Golf Club**, T01859-502331, except Sun.

Kitesurfing **Western Isles Kite Company**, West View, Aird Uig, Lewis T01851-672771. If the wind doesn't give up, give in and give power kiting or kite surfing a go.

Sights **Calanais (Callanish) standing stones**, forming a Celtic cross and overlooking Loch Roag, are the most spectacular Neolithic monument on the island. **Clach an Truiseil**, near Barabhas, standing 20-ft tall it is the largest monolith in Europe. The east coast of Harris is worth exploring for the bizarre lunar-style landscape of the so-called 'Golden Road'.

DEMI TAYLOR

Scara Brae overlooks the classic points of Skaill Bay.

Northeast England

Overview

The northeast has had time to mature as a surfing destination. It is no longer a novelty to think of surfers charging in the cold depths of winter on ice-fringed reefs. Like Californian wine, the novelty factor has worn off, its reputation is established and the region has developed a sense of identity as well as a fiercely loyal following. It may not have the open ocean fetch of the Pacific or the regular tracking depressions of the Atlantic, but any aficionado will look north to the vast Arctic Ocean and see a swell generator capable of producing corduroy lines to the horizon when a suitable low tracks past the North of Scotland. Luckily, the geography is perfectly suited to these clean, well-spaced swells, allowing the regions waveriders to become connoisseurs of the many points and reefs that line the undulating coastline. Brown, ruler-edged barrels can angle flawlessly along a geometrically precise reef, the opaque waters folding into Indo-like perfection. This is the home of a wave universally recognized as the country's premium left-hander and a place where top surfers can truly test their skills. The brown, cold water and stark industrial backdrops of the manufacturing heartlands of Teeside, Wearside and Tyneside offer some of the most dramatic backdrops in the UK but head north on the A1 and they soon melt into the memory as the pristine clear waters of Northumbria with its white sandy beaches and dark, brooding castles come into view. A land where a crowd can be counted on one hand and where a tidal causeway to a holy island may also lead to the ultimate in surfing isolation.

But this region is not all surfing perfection and empty line-ups. The surfing population of Yorkshire and the urban northeast has exploded over the last decade as the boom in surfing has led to increased numbers of locals. Line-ups are swollen by a host of inland raiders offered easy access via the good road links and short distances from many of central England's major cities. The fickle weather patterns of the east coast means flat summers can stretch into weeks and winter water temperatures of 4°C can test the hardiest locals. However, during the gravy days of autumn the northeasterly swells can be replaced by the occasional southeasterly firing the wrong way up the North Sea. This is when local knowledge comes to the fore as reefs and points that slumber for the majority of the year come to life and the locals beat the crowds and enjoy those golden days that live in the memory forever, lingering like a fine wine on the palate.

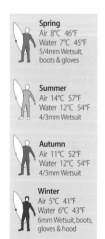

Spring
Air 8°C 46°F
Water 7°C 45°F
5/4mm Wetsuit, boots & gloves

Summer
Air 14°C 57°F
Water 12°C 54°F
4/3mm Wetsuit

Autumn
Air 11°C 52°F
Water 12°C 54°F
4/3mm Wetsuit

Winter
Air 5°C 41°F
Water 6°C 43°F
6mm Wetsuit, boots, gloves & hood

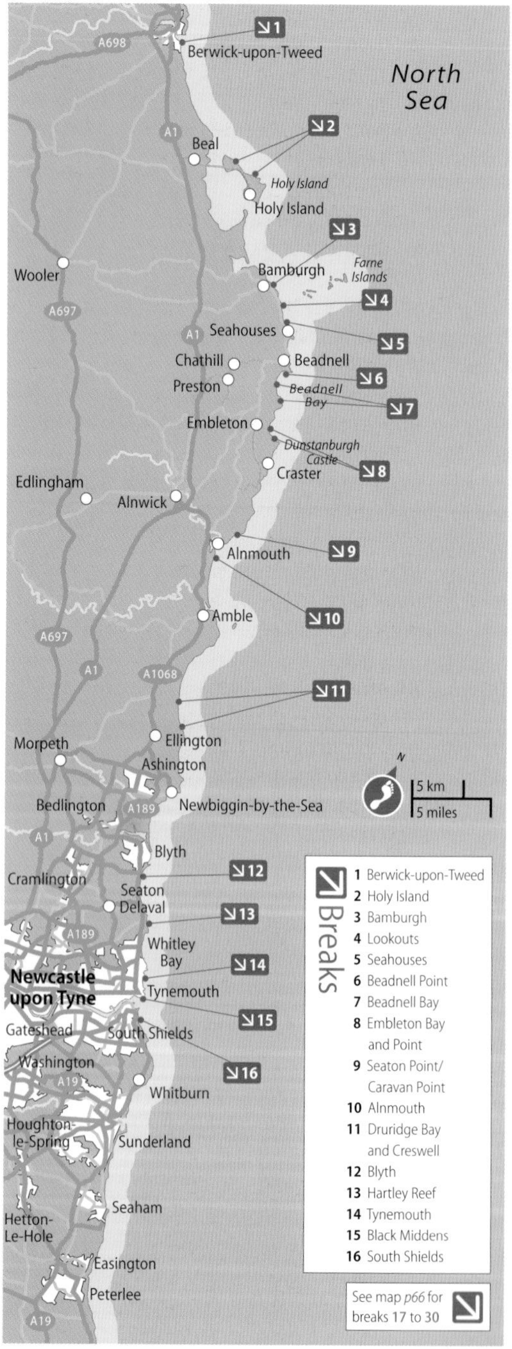

Coastline

The coastline from Scarborough to the Scottish border has England's best surfing terrain. From flat, slate reefs and long, rocky points to heavy, hollow beach breaks, this area has it all. Northumbria has miles of white sand beaches interspersed with point breaks, whereas Yorkshire has an amazing slate geology that not only attracts fossil hunters from all over the world, but also provides the perfect base for producing quality reef breaks.

A trademark of these northern waves is the brown colour of the coastal waters. This is not down to pollution, but more to the silty composition of the soil and coastal sediments. However, north of Newcastle the sea clears, the line-ups clear, and crystalline waves peel in front of the silhouettes of once great castles.

Local Environment by Surfers Against Sewage

"This region has some of the best and worse water quality in the UK. Heavily industrialized areas and large populations result in some extremely poor water quality. One of the left-hand jewels on the coastline is consistently failing the bathing water standards and one of the better rights has a nuclear power station, a steelworks, a chemical plant and sewage outfall from Middlesbrough and Redcar discharging into the line up." Andy Cummins (www.sas.org.uk).

Despite the sharp rise in popularity, the line-ups here are still quite tight-knit. They are, however, generally relaxed, and respectful surfers can expect few problems. The region has produced many top surfers from the late **Nigel Veitch** through to **Sam Lamiroy** and **Gabe Davies**.

Getting around

The road network in the northeast is very good. Northumbria and Newcastle are serviced by the A1, Saltburn via the A19, while the A64 feeds the Yorkshire coastline. Access to breaks is excellent from the coast road. Check parking as many coastal villages have strictly enforced no parking areas.

SCOTT WICKING

What lies beneath the sea in this region conspires to create epic reef breaks. But where it is, we're not telling.

STU NORTON

Jesse Davies, cold comforts.

> **“”**
>
> With a vast array of bombing slate reefs and off-the-highway points, the Northeast is one of the surfing world's best-kept secrets. Powered by numbing Arctic swells, commitment here is key - but the rewards are sure to keep you coming back for more.
>
> *Vince Medeiros, Editor,* Huck

5'10" Xanadu Rocky Model

Shaper: Xanadu

5'10" x $19\frac{3}{4}$" x $2\frac{1}{16}$"

Built with Surftech's proven TUFLITE construction.

Flatter entry rocker, "wider nose, wider tail" make up for shorter length. Should be ridden 6" shorter than performance shortboard. Flatter deck makes rails fuller for more buoyancy and better performance in smaller waves. Can be ridden as tri-fin, twin fin, or with small trailer fin, so adaptable to all conditions.

FCS YU fins.

6'3" Channel Islands K-Board

Shaper: Al Merrick

6'3" x $18\frac{5}{8}$" x $2\frac{5}{16}$"

Built with Surftech's proven TUFLITE construction.

Single concave, low entry rocker – What the winningest competitive surfer of all time rides when the waves start pumping!

FCS K 2.1 fins.

Breaks

BEACH BREAK

↘1 Berwick-upon-Tweed

Conditions Medium NE swells, offshore in SW winds
Hazards/tips Beware of rips from the river, not for inexperienced surfers
Sleeping Beadnell » *p69*

Peeling along a sandbar near the rivermouth is a left-hander that needs a good clean northeasterly swell but can produce excellent, long walls. Quiet line-up.

BEACH BREAK

↘2 Holy Island

Conditions Medium NE swells, offshore in SW winds
Hazards/tips Quiet spot, access via low tide causeway
Sleeping Beadnell » *p69*

A low tide left-hander breaks towards the northern end of the island. Rarely surfed but can be classic. Needs a good, clean north or northeasterly swell. Park in the car park and walk to the northeast corner of the island. There can also be a left point off the southern tip of the island in big swells. Access to Lindisfarne is only possible at low tide via a causeway that is submerged at high. Make sure you have your tide times or you may find your visit extended longer than you planned.

DEMI TAYLOR

4 Looking out to the Farne Islands.

BEACH BREAK

↘3 Bamburgh

Conditions Small to medium NE swells, offshore in SW winds.
Hazards/tips Overlooked by Bamburgh Castle
Sleeping Beadnell » *p69*

Good quality, popular beach break that picks up loads of swell coming out of the northeast. In a big southeasterly the southern end of the beach picks up the most swell. Near the castle end of beach there is a carpark behind the dunes, as well as roadside parking further south. A rocky finger of reef extends towards the Farne Islands and can produce a right-hander of variable quality.

RIGHT POINT BREAK

↘4 Lookouts

Conditions Big SE swell, offshore in SW wind
Hazards/tips Can have longshore rips in a big swell pushing north, clean water
Sleeping Beadnell » *p69*

A concrete watch tower stands guard over this quality, sand-covered rocky point that works in a big, clean, southeasterly or easterly swells. Works through the tides but is best from low to mid. In a good swell, long, walling rights peel along the reef. Just to the north, a sandbar peak offers good lefts and rights. Park on the road near the lifeguard tower.

RIGHT-HAND BEACH AND REEF BREAKS

↘5 Seahouses

Conditions Medium to big NE to SE swells, offshore in SW winds
Hazards/tips Ledge is shallow and heavy. Experienced surfers only
Sleeping Beadnell » *p69*

A stretch of beach leads into a series of reefs, in front of the houses on the coast road that heads north towards Bamburgh. Big southeasterly swells produce right-handers where as lefts predominate in northeasterly swells. There is a dredging right-hander near the harbour mouth called the Ledge. Parking on seafront and in car park near harbour.

LEFT-HAND POINT BREAK

↘6 Beadnell Point

Conditions Big to huge N to NE swells, offshore in N to NW winds
Hazards/tips Check in winter storms. Park near the sailing club
Sleeping Beadnell » *p69*

This sheltered rocky point needs huge northerly or big northeasterly swell to do its thing going. The left walls peel along in front of the old lime kiln at Beadnell Harbour and round to the sheltered beach. The point is offshore in northwesterly or northerly winds due to the fact that the swell has to wrap nearly 180 degrees, but this makes it the place to check when everywhere else is maxed out.

BEACH BREAK

↘7 Beadnell Bay

Conditions Medium to big NE swells, offshore in W winds.
Hazards/tips Flexible spot, very quiet
Sleeping Beadnell » *p69*

Beadnell is a really flexible spot. The huge, crescent-shaped bay picks up swells from the south, east and north and can produce nice waves through the tides. It is a nice open beach with sand dunes. Parking at northern and southern (Newton) ends. At the southern end is a small bay called **Football Hole** which is worth checking for its sheltered right.

BEACH BREAK AND ROCKY POINT

↘8 Embleton Bay and Point

- **Conditions** All NE to SE swells, offshore in W winds
- **Hazards/tips** Shallow rocky point, rips when big
- **Sleeping** Beadnell » p69

Probably one of the most beautiful surfing locations in the UK, Embleton is overlooked by the haunting ruins of Dunstanburgh Castle. The most consistent and popular beach-break on this coastline, this is one of the few spots you'll find fellow surfers. In 3-6 ft foot swells there'll be excellent walls and a few barrels in the offing. Works through the tides and southwesterly or westerly winds are offshore. The point at the southern castle end reels in good southeasterly swells producing quality rights at mid to high tide. Park and walk across the golf course.

LEFT-HAND POINT BREAK

↘9 Seaton Point/Caravan Point

- **Conditions** Big to huge NE swells, offshore in N winds
- **Hazards/tips** Shallow, rocky, experienced surfers
- **Sleeping** Alnwick/Alnmouth » p69

Another break to head for in huge winter storms, this left produces nice long walls, even in northerly winds. Best tackled at low to mid tide but this rocky spot is best left to experienced surfers. The more sheltered beach breaks through the tides but the waves can be a bit weak as the banks aren't great. Park by the holiday chalets that overlook the break.

RIVERMOUTH AND BEACH BREAK

↘10 Alnmouth

- **Conditions** All NE to SE swells, offshore in W winds
- **Hazards/tips** Strong rips by the river
- **Sleeping** Alnwick/Alnmouth » p69

DEMI TAYLOR

DEMI TAYLOR

Top: 7 He looks, he finds, he scores. **Right: 8** Embleton Point watched over by Dunstanburgh Castle.

Alnmouth rivermouth is always worth checking when the big, clean swells kick in. The banks are distributed by the river and can have long lefts and rights. Inexperienced surfers should avoid this section of beach. To the north of the river the beach is sheltered and offshore in northwesterly winds and accessed via the seafront car park through the golf club. The main beach, to the south of the river, is accessed through the dunes and can have good waves in everything from northeasterly to southeasterly swells. Isolated and quiet.

BEACH BREAK

↘11 Druridge Bay and Creswell

- **Conditions** Medium NE swells, offshore in W winds
- **Hazards/tips** Suitable for all surfers
- **Sleeping** Alnwick/Alnmouth » p69

Picturesque, dune-backed bay reminiscent of Les Landes in France (see page 180). Facing east, this crescent-shaped bay picks up lots of swell, the northern end best in southeasterly swells and the southern end best in swells from the north. Works on all tides and has great potential. Worth checking the reef at Creswell on the southern end of the bay. This is where the Northumberland Heritage Coastline ends so from here south the water quality deteriorates. Ellington Colliery marks the start of the industrial Northeast. Coast road to Creswell liable to flooding.

BEACH BREAK

↘12 Blyth

- **Conditions** Medium NE swells, offshore in SW winds
- **Hazards/tips** Rips in big swells
- **Sleeping** Alnmouth/Tynemouth » p69

This long, crescent-shaped, sandy bay is quite a consistent spot that is home to both lefts

> Tynemouth and surrounding area has plenty of people in the water. Most people new to surfing around here would probably have more fun and catch more waves surfing the beaches.
>
> *Jesse Davies, local charger and owner Rise Surf School*

 and rights. Again, works in the more common northeasterly swells as well as the occasional spring southeasterly. Quite a consistent spot with the southern part of the beach being the best. Safe for supervised beginners. Access via the A193. Parking at the beach.

REEF BREAK

↘13 Hartley Reef

- **Conditions** Medium to big NE swells, offshore in SW winds
- **Hazards/tips** Crowds
- **Sleeping** Tynemouth » p70

The proving ground for a generation of the northeast's best rippers, Hartley is a flat reef that can produce excellent quality lefts as well as some good rights. This mid to high tide break can hold decent sized swell, breaking up to 8 ft. The long, walling waves can produce hollow sections as they race along the reef towards the cliff. Easy parking overlooking the break. Gets crowded when good. Access off the A193 at roundabout with B1325.

BEACH BREAK

↘14 Tynemouth

- **Conditions** All NE swells, offshore in W to SW winds
- **Hazards/tips** Road parking near the beach
- **Sleeping** Tynemouth » p70

Longsands is Tyneside's most famous break and has been the site of the British Surfing Championships in recent years. Home for Newcastle surfers, this spot offers a range of waves during the fairly consistent northeasterly swells. There are beginner friendly peelers as well as challenging peaks working on all tides. Nearby **Eddies** (King Edwards Bay) is also worth checking at low to mid tide.

RIVERMOUTH REEF BREAK

↘15 Black Middens

- **Conditions** Big E swells, offshore in W winds
- **Hazards/tips** Parking near Collingwood's Monument
- **Sleeping** Tynemouth » p70

Truly a hardcore wave and northeast legend, this left-hand reef break can produce excellent hollow waves in a big easterly swell. The drawback is that it peels inside the breakwaters at the mouth of the industrial River Tyne. Dire water quality means this is a wave for those superheroes with a natural immunity to toxicity.

Below: Despite its proximity to the urban sprawl of Newcastle, Northumbria's peaks remain relatively quiet. **Bottom: 15** Black Middens and the mouth of the River Tyne.

DEMI TAYLOR

STU NORTON

BEACH BREAK

↘16 South Shields

- **Conditions** Medium NE to SE swells, offshore in SW winds
- **Hazards/tips** Beachfront parking
- **Sleeping** Tynemouth » p70

A stretch of good quality beach, with nice peaks along its length and fairly clean water. It works on all tides. Good for all surfers. Check to the south where you may find a couple of hidden spots.

BEACH BREAK

↘17 The Pier, Hartlepool

- **Conditions** Small to medium NE swells, offshore in SW winds
- **Hazards/tips** Polluted water, bad rips near houses on the seafront, not for beginners
- **Sleeping** Saltburn » p70

Stunning location, though not in a classical way. Huge, empty beach overlooked by the shells of once mighty northern engineering plants. This massive industrial pier helps to sculpt sandbars on either side that produce heavy waves in clean swells on all tides. Can produce epic dark water waves with hollow, powerful lefts and rights. A unique break which, despite, (or because of) the bleak derelict factories watching over the brown

North Sea, is quite beautiful. Park on Old Cemetery Road or on the seafront at Hartlepool and walk. Watch out for the groynes.

BEACH BREAK

↘18 Seaton Carew

- **Conditions** Big NE swells, offshore in SW winds
- **Hazards/tips** Pollution
- **Sleeping** Saltburn » p70

Sheltered beach with harbour at the north end and a groyne with sandbar. Doesn't pick up as much swell as other beaches in the area. Rarely surfed.

RIGHT-HAND POINT BREAK

↘19 The Gare

- **Swell** Big E or SE swells
- **Wind** From the S or SW
- **Tide** Works on all tides
- **Size** 3-10 ft
- **Length** 50-150 m
- **Bottom** Small, sharp, hard boulders
- **Access** Off rocks at inside of the break
- **Ability** Advanced
- **Best months** Dec-Apr
- **Board** Fast, gunny shortboard
- **Hazards/tips** Bad pollution, heavy wave, long hold downs, cold water
- **Sleeping** Saltburn » p70

The Gare is the northeast's best right-hander, a wave that can be pretty much world-class on it's day. In big easterly and southeasterly swells, the man-made breakwater that delineates and protects the mouth of the River Tees provides shelter for this amazing break. The wave actually breaks inside the mouth of the river where a bleak boulder bank is transformed into a brown Jeffrey's Bay. On a few choice days every year, long fast, hollow waves reel along the sharp boulders. This is a heavy wave best left to experienced surfers as the point holds swells up to 10 ft. Even at 6-8 ft surfers have had two wave hold-downs in cold mirky waters.

STU NORTON

SCOTT WICKING

Above: 20 The Gare. **Top: 16** The South Shields yield.

Water quality has been diabolical with sewage and petrochemical outflows, but this is *supposed* to be slowly improving. The white water fizzes and has a strong aftershave/chemical smell.

The Gare needs very specific conditions to work – galeforce southeasterly winds blowing for over 24 hours. This means it usually breaks only a handful of times a year, usually in the depths of winter or during spring squalls – one of the reasons why there are never photos that show the true quality of the wave. Bring a thermos flask, warm clothes and don't swallow the water.

*If you like **The Gare**, try **Immessouane** in Morocco (see page 378) or **Coxos** in Portugal (see page 298).*

BEACH BREAK

20 Saltburn

- **Conditions** All NE swells, offshore in SW winds
- **Hazards/tips** Good beach for all surfers
- **Sleeping** Saltburn » p70

Fairly good quality beach break with the best waves near the pier. Very popular spot due to parking access and surf hire on the beach. Great place for beginners. To the south under the cliffs, the Point is a quality wave that comes to life at low tide in big, clean swells when hollow right-handers reel off the flat reef. In the corner, **Penny Hole** is a low tide peak with short rights and long lefts, which can be excellent.

This beach has been one of the central hubs of northeast surfing due to the beachfront Saltburn Surf Shop first opened by Gary Rogers and Nick Noble back in 1987, one of the first surf shops in the Northeast. Pollution was always a problem here but things seem to have improved with a new treatment works.

REEF BREAK

21 Runswick Bay

- **Conditions** Medium to big NE swells, offshore in SW to W winds
- **Hazards/tips** Dangerous rips, beach disappears at high tide
- **Sleeping** Saltburn/Whitby » p70

Drop down the amazingly steep road into Runswick Bay and a large cliff lined, northeasterly facing bay opens up to your right. It's home to three quality right-hand reefs sitting side by side on southern side of the crescent. Slabs of flat slate form excellent kelp covered reefs where fast, walling right-handers break from low through to mid tide. The inner reef is the most sheltered and it needs the most swell to get going; the middle reef is the most popular. Watch out for rips to the middle of the bay, which can be strong. **Cobbledump** is a left-hand reef breaking over rocks, on the north side of the

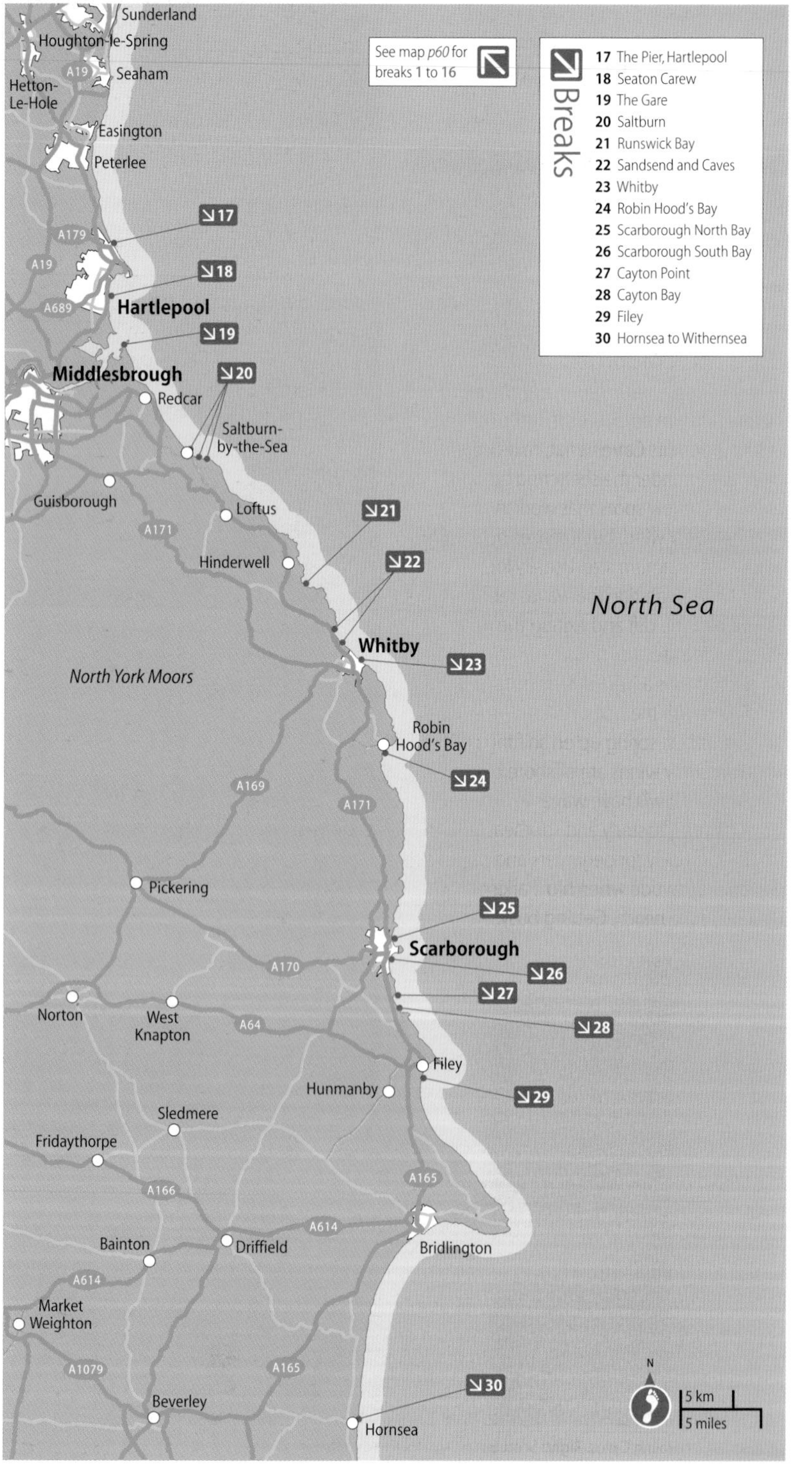

bay near the village. Runswick is slightly sheltered and so is traditionally surfed when big swells max out the more exposed beaches.

BEACH AND REEF BREAK

↘22 Sandsend and Caves

- **Conditions** Small to medium NE to SE swells, offshore in SW winds
- **Hazards/tips** Heavy beach break with dangerous rips, can be crowded
- **Sleeping** Whitby »p71

At the northern end of this huge, straight sandy beach sits **Caves** a flat, mid tide reef that nestles under the sheltering headland. It is one of the few spots that work in a northwesterly wind, but it maxes out easily – 3-4 ft is its optimum size. Usually looks better than it is. At high tide the waves rebound off the base of the cliff and exiting the water is difficult. Beware.

Sandsend is a high quality beach that works through the tides. Hollow, powerful lefts and rights spring up on shifting banks. Southwesterly winds are offshore but this flexible beach will have waves in northeasterly, easterly and southeasterly swells. Not really for beginners and packs a punch at high tide when big. Parking alongside the beach. Getting busy.

BEACH BREAK

↘23 Whitby

- **Conditions** Small to medium NE swells, offshore in SW winds
- **Hazards/tips** Parking on cliff top
- **Sleeping** Whitby »p71

This section of beach is just north of Whitby Abbey, one time haunt of Count Dracula. Popular with grommets in small swells and one of the few spots sheltered in a southeasterly wind due to the harbour wall. Works best on low to mid tide near the harbour. Has a longstanding surf community.

REEF BREAK

↘24 Robin Hood's Bay

- **Conditions** Medium to big NE swells, offshore in W or SW winds
- **Hazards/tips** Rips, rocks, shallow, big tidal range
- **Sleeping** Whitby »p71

There are a number of flat slate reefs in the bay that work on big northeasterly swells. Best from low to thee-quarter tide as beach disappears. Quiet spot. The point can be good in big swells. Not a good spot for inexperienced surfers. There is a car park in town. Long walk to breaks.

SCOTT WICKING

Above: 22 Potholing Caves. **Right**: Scott Eastwood, northern exposure.

BEACH BREAK

↘25 Scarborough North Bay

- **Conditions** All NE to E swells, offshore in SW winds
- **Hazards/tips** Beachfront parking on Marine Drive overlooking the surf
- **Sleeping** Scarborough »p71

Scarborough Castle overlooks two bays, the northeasterly facing North Bay and the sheltered, southeasterly facing South Bay. The most consistent is North Bay, where good quality banks can form in conjunction with flat rocky outcrops to produce both lefts and rights. It's one of the regions most reliable spots picking up plenty of swell and works in north, northeasterly and easterly swells. A huge, concave sea wall backs the beach meaning it's surfable only from low to mid tide. Plenty of pay parking on Marine Drive overlooking the surf.

BEACH BREAK

↘26 Scarborough South Bay

- **Conditions** Big NE swell, offshore in N to NW winds
- **Hazards/tips** Crowds, average waves
- **Sleeping** Scarborough »p71

To be honest this is a pretty poor quality, flat beach that needs a really big northeasterly to work. During huge winter gales this is a popular spot as it is one of the few sheltered breaks in the area. The best peaks are found in front of the Spa, from low to three-quarter tide, and there is limited parking here. The waves to the north of the Spa in front of the amusements and fish and chip shops are short

THE GILL

SCOTT WICKING

SCOTT WICKING

Top: Yorkshire point. **Above:** 28 Pumphouse, Cayton Bay.

and pretty weak but good for beginners. Better waves to the south between the Spa and the headland in medium swells.

LEFT POINT BREAK

↘27 Cayton Point

- **Conditions** Medium to big NE swells, offshore in SW winds
- **Hazards/tips** Access, crowds, heavy wave, rocks, experienced surfers
- **Sleeping** Scarborough » *p71*

Breaking over a boulder bottom, this is a powerful and heavy left-hand point. Can and does produce grinding lefts between 4 and 10 ft, wrapping around the point at the northern end into the sheltered bay. Too shallow at low, it's best surfed from quarter tide up to high. Needs a good northeasterly swell to get going. Definitely a wave for experienced surfers.

Access is difficult. Check from the A165 where the point is visible through the trees. There is an path through the woods.

BEACH BREAK

↘28 Cayton Bay

- **Conditions** Small to medium NE swells, offshore in SW winds
- **Hazards/tips** Busy spot, suitable for all surfers
- **Sleeping** Scarborough » *p71*

Bunkers is the most popular and consistent spot with lefts and rights breaking off the sandbanks formed in front of Second World War concrete bunkers. Best from mid to high tide and with a southwesterly wind. There is also the fickle **Pumphouse**, that produces lefts and rights in front of the pumping station, but needs a much rarer southeasterly swell. Pay parking available above the bay. Popular break with Scarborough surfers but also attracts visitors from as far as Manchester due to the good road links.

BEACH BREAK

↘29 Filey

- **Conditions** Big to huge NE swells, offshore in SW winds
- **Hazards/tips** Rips in big swells, parking on the seafront
- **Sleeping** Scarborough » *p71*

Filey has a long, flat crescent-shaped beach, the northern end of which is sheltered by Filey Brigg, a rocky headland, which helps provide protection in big, storm surf. The southern end of the bay picks up the most swell. Not renowned for the quality of its waves, but worth checking if everywhere else is maxed out.

BEACH BREAK

↘30 Hornsea to Withernsea

- **Conditions** Medium to big NE swells, offshore in W winds
- **Hazards/tips** Dangerous longshore drift in big swells
- **Sleeping** Scarborough » *p71*

These are not really a surfer's first choice but are worth checking in a clean northeasterly or easterly swell if you're in the area. As the groynes show, when the surf picks up there is a longshore drift from the north, so keep a beach marker in view. Better on low to mid tide. Not many surfers here, so not really a good spot for the inexperienced.

Practicalities

Beadnell

Beadnell village makes for a good base from which to access Northumbria's northern breaks. Just off the B1340 on a sheltered point break, it has great winter surf potential as well as a pretty 18th-century harbour at the head of a 3-mile stretch of beach.

Sleeping

££ **Low Dover**, Harbour Rd, T01665-720291, 30 seconds from the harbour, is a quiet, family-run B&B with self-catering caravan onsite.

£ **Joiners Shop Bunkhouse**, slightly inland at Preston, Chathill, T01665-589245, www.bunkhousenorthumberland.co.uk. Good for groups, with kitchen facilities, board storage, cosy communal area and beds from £10 per night.

Camping There are several sites in the area.

Beadnell Camping and Caravanning Club, on the coast road at the edge of the village, T01665-720586, Apr-Oct, is pretty basic and exposed.

Dunstan Hill, inland from Embleton, T01665-576310, open Mar-Oct is only 20 mins' walk from the beach, plus visitors receive 10% off golf at nearby Embleton.

Newton Hall, T01665-576239, www.newtonholidays.co.uk, Apr-Oct sits to the southern end of Beadnell Bay in the grounds of Newton Hall.

Seafield Caravan Park, a couple of miles up the coast in Seahouses, T01665-720628, open Feb-Dec, offers statics and touring pitches with views across to the Farne Islands. Includes entry to the Ocean Club pool and spa.

Eating and drinking

There are 2 good pubs in the village.

The **Towers** has a nice bar and fairly expensive but good restaurant.

The nearby **Craster Arms** is well known for its home cooking.

The **Village Pantry**, opposite the church, has a selection of provisions as well as coffee and sandwiches.

Directory

Beadnell has limited facilities. Nearby Seahouses has a full complement of amenities and a glut of Fish 'n' Chip shops **Surf Shops** **Ledge Surf Shop**, T01665-721257, is actually a corner of an arcade, opposite the Olde Ship Hotel in Seahouses, but sells all the basics including wax and a limited range of wetsuits and boots. **Internet** **Village Pantry**, Beadnell. **Banks** Main St, Seahouses. **Tourist information** At Seahouses car park, www.northumberland.gov.uk.

Alnwick

A pretty walled town just inland from Alnmouth, Alnwick (pronounced 'Annick'), is perhaps the best base for Northumberland trips, with easy access from the A1, close proximity to the breaks and a good choice of amenities.

Sleeping

££ **The Georgian Guesthouse**, Hotspur St, T01665-602398, is relaxed, with a bike store and internet access and is one of many B&B options.

Camping Bizarrely you can camp at the **Alnwick Rugby Club** in Greensfield Park, T01665-510109, Apr-Oct.

Proctors Steads Caravan and Camping Park, Craster, T01665-576613, Mar-Oct, is a mile from the sea, just north of Alnwick. They also have reasonably priced self-catering cottages to rent sleeping 4 or 6, Feb-Oct.

Eating and drinking

On the square in Bondgate Within is the **Gate Bistro** where you can get a 3-course, candlelit meal.

The **Grape Vine** offers basic, good value lunches and evening food on the same square while up the road you can grab a cheap takeaway pizza or a curry.

Just to the north **The Craster Inn** in Dunstan Village T01665 576658 (near Proctor Steads) do a wide selection good quality pub grub and decent Sunday Carvery.

STU NORTON

What's the story northern glory?

STU NORTON

Ice-cream headaches, Seaburn.

DEMI TAYLOR

War of the Worlds – Gare Backdrop.

Directory

Internet Barter Books on Bondgate Without, www.barterbooks.co.uk (while browsing the excellent second-hand book selection). **Banks** A selection with cashpoints in the town square on Bondgate Within. **Chemist** On Bondgate Within. **Tourist information** The Shambles, Market Place, T01665-510665, www.visitalnwick.org.

Alnmouth

This is a quiet little coastal village with a couple of pricey B&Bs, hotels and a choice of golf courses.

££ **Beaches**, on Northumberland St, T01665-830006, offers cosy accommodation and also has the best food in town in their restaurant downstairs - local fish, meat and game.

££ **Hope & Anchor**, Northumberland St, T01665-830363. The pub is the heart of the village so pumps the night away. The rooms are en suite, clean and attractive. If you ask nicely they may even stash your boards for you …

Eating and drinking

Tea Cosy Tea Room, offers typical café fare such as jacket potatoes and fairly average sandwiches.

Tynemouth

At the mouth of the Tyne, this workaday town is a good base for exploring the Newcastle area without having to venture into the city.

Sleeping

£££ **Park Hotel**, Grand Parade, T0191-257106, separated from Longsands by the road, they have en suites with beach views.

££ **No 61 Guesthouse**, Front St, T0191-2573687, is fairly quaint with a tea room downstairs plus a secure garage where they may store your board for you.

Camping **The Whitley Bay Holiday Park**, North at Whitley Bay, T0191 2531216, Mar-Nov, old school holiday camp taking mixed groups/families only. Statics available.

Directory

Surf Shops **Tynemouth Surf Co**, Grand Parade, T0191-2582496, overlooks Longsands and has been servicing the region's hardy surf community since 1995 with hardware, equipment hire, surf school, ding repair services and now a surf report hot line: T09058-200177.

Saltburn

Traditional Victorian resort town complete with a water-balance cliff tram ferrying people to and from the seafront and the pier.

Sleeping

There are a couple of hotels and plenty of B&B options on the Victorian terraces running down to the cliffs including ££ **Spa Hotel**, above the beach, T01287-622544.

Camping **Serenity Touring Caravan Park**, on the A174 in Hinderwell, T01947-841122, open Mar-Oct, is well located but doesn't cater for children.

Flat spells

Golf There is a plethora of courses on this stretch of coast including **Alnmouth GC**, T01665-850231, an 18-hole course and one of the oldest in England. Handicap certificate needed. **Alnmouth Village GC**, Marine Rd, T01665-830370, is a 9-hole course. **Dunstanburgh Castle GC**, Embleton Bay, T01665-576562, is a lovely 18-hole links course. **Saltburn by Sea GC**, Hob Hill, Guisborough, T01287-622812. **Seahouses GC**, south of Seahouses, T01665-720794, is another 18-hole links. **Whitby GC**, Sandsend Rd, T01947-600660, is a dramatic 18-hole cliff-top course overlooking the sea.

Sights This is also officially castle country, built for defence as well as a show of strength. **Bamburgh Castle**, www.bamburghcastle.com, Apr-Oct, dominates the skyline and overlooks an amazing beach from its basalt outcrop. It's impressive on the approach, but not quite so nice up close though, so save your pennies. **Dunstanburgh Castle** is a spectacular ruin overlooking Embleton Bay - like a backdrop to a horror film. Entry around £2.50. **Scarborough Castle** has a commanding position overlooking North and South bay. Worth a visit for the spectacular views **Whitby Abbey** was the inspiration for Bram Stoker's *Dracula*. Climb the hill for great views over Whitby Bay. **Holy Island** – or Lindisfarne – is separated from the mainland by a tidal causeway. Famous for its monastery, founded in AD 634, it is well worth a visit but check the tides as it is cut off for about 5 hrs a day. **Flamborough Head** is a 7-mile chalky promontory between Filey and Bridlington, Yorkshire. This is the 'Land's End of the East Coast' - minus the tat and parking piracy of course. You may be surprised at what you find.

Skating **R-Kade Skate Park**, Majuba Rd, Redcar, T01642-483520, is an excellent indoor wooden park with everything you could want. Entry from £4. **Scarborough North Bay Skate Park** - metal banks, ¼ pipes and rails - is free, overlooks the sea and floodlit until around 2200.

Eating and drinking

Gary Rogers of Saltburn Surf shop recommends **Virgos** on Dundas St as a good bet for lunch.
A lot of the local crew drink in the **Victoria**, again on Dundas St.
SAS man and former local Andy Cummins recommends **Windsor's** for a beer and **Signals** for a bite to eat.

Directory

Surf Shops **Saltburn Surf Shop**, T01287-625321, opened in 1986 and run by Gary Rogers, open year round, stocks hardware and clothing. Handily located on the seafront car park by the pier, also the site of a changing and shower facility. **Saltburn Surf Hire**, in the same location, T01287-209959, owned by Nick Noble who also runs the BSA surf school from the base. For a surf update, ring his check line on T09068-545543. **Tourist information** In the railway station, T01287-622422.

Whitby

One of Yorkshire's seaside gems, this town is now as famous for its Gothic connection with *Dracula* (it hosts an annual Goth Weekend over Halloween) as it is for its picturesque harbour with cobbled streets and excellent seafood.

Sleeping

£££-££ **Sander's Yard**, Church St, T01947-820228, has a central location with pretty (if slightly hit and miss) rooms set around a courtyard with café/restaurant attached.
There are also a vast number of average B&Bs to choose from on West Cliff.
£ **Whitby Backpackers Hostel**, Hudson St, T01947-601794, has bunks and private rooms and is the only backpackers in the area with no curfew.
Sandfield House Caravan Site, Sandsend Rd, T01947-602660, Mar-Oct. Overlooks the sea north of Whitby, has lovely free hot showers but unfortunately doesn't take tents.

Eating and drinking

The **Magpie Café** has a reputation for serving up the best fish 'n' chips and seafood. Expect big queues during peak times of the year, but it is worth it!
Java, café on Flowergate serving light, cheap snacks and with internet access.
The Whitby Tandoori, Station Sq, T01947-820871, is a quality Indian restaurant and recommended.
The Moon and Sixpence, on Marine Parade, T01947-604416, is recommended by Ben at Zero Gravity for good food and atmosphere.
The Greedy Pig, at the bottom end of Flowergate, is the place for a mega roast pork, crackling and apple sauce lunchtime bap – takeaway and devour in privacy.
The **Shambles** on Market Place is a popular and busy spot that also has a restaurant selling snacks (jackets and sandwiches).
Duke of York, at the end of Church St, for cheap pub grub.
Elsinore is a busy pub and popular with visiting Goths.

Directory

Surf Shops **Zero Gravity Surf Shop**, Flowergate, T01947-820660, was opened by shaper Andrew Harrison in 1995 and sells the full range of hardware and clothing. **Banks** On Baxtergate. **Tourist information** Near the train station on New Quay Rd, T01947-602674.

Scarborough

A real Jekyll-and-Hyde resort. Neon-signed amusements line South Bay, yet if you scratch the surface and explore the medieval ginnels it becomes clear that Scarborough hides its real light under a bushel.

Sleeping

££ **Rockside Hotel**, Blenheim Terr, overlooking North Bay, T01723-374747, is run by well-known local surfer, Del.
££ **Hotel Helaina**, also Blenheim Terr, T01723-375191, is a beautifully run, recommended B&B.
£ **Scarborough YHA**, on Burniston Rd, 2 miles north out of town, T0870-7706022.
Camping **Scalby Close Park**, on Burniston Rd, T01723-365908, Mar-Oct, offers camping and van pitches.
Self-catering A good option is **Brompton Holiday Flats**, Castle Rd, T01723-364964, Mar-Oct, overlooking North Bay.

Eating and drinking

Scarborough Tandoori on Thomas St, T01723-352393, is fantastic – great Indian food at very reasonable prices.
Mother Hubbard's, on Westborough, has the best fish 'n' chips in town, eat in or take away.
Florio's, on Aberdeen Walk off Westborough, does good Italian food in a central location.
Café Italia, on St Nicholas Cliff near the **Grand** is a great place to grab a coffee and pastry.

Directory

Surf Shops **Secret Spot Surf Shop**, Somerset Terr, T01723-500467, is Scarborough's oldest surf shop and stocks hardware and clothing on their large premises. Started by Roger Povey in '89, it is now owned by Tommo who is happy to offer advice to travelling surfers and give an update on surf conditions. **Cayton Bay Surf Shop**, Killerby Cliff, T01723-585585, is something of an institution. They stock hardware, own the car park next door (£2!) and take no prisoners. They do however have free hot showers. **Tourist information** Pavilion House, Valley Bridge Rd, T01723-373333.

SCOTT WICKING

23 Take the drop.

Overview

GREG MARTIN/FINDYOURWAVE

The jagged, fractured cliffs look down over the sandy bay, its boulder-strewn margins a testament to the power of the ocean here. The rugged windswept land a blend of heath and gorse. This place has a very Celtic feel and Kernow could, in places, be a very good double for much of the fringes of Scotland, Ireland or Wales. However, the crumbling mine workings stamp this land with a unique silhouette, like some ancient Arthurian watchtowers awaiting the return of the Knights of the Round Table. To the north, the landscapes are more lush, clothed in a green blanket. Here the Tamar River delineates the start of Devon, a county where narrow hedge-lined lanes link broad sandy, beaches with dark boulder points or continue hugging the coastline, eventually winding down to sheltered reefs. While Cornwall has it's raw edginess, Devon has a much smoother feel. Almost creamier…

Both counties have a long and proud association with the 'Sport of Kings'. Surfing took root here as soon as the seeds arrived in the late fifties, and both have developed their cultural epicentres. For Devon it's the picture-book village of Croyde, thatched cottages and narrow thoroughfares that throng with visitors during the summer months, swelling the numbers in the surf shops and in the bustling line-up. Devon's surf capital is home to a classic and powerful beachie, legendary low tide barrels and heaving crowds. On warm evenings drinkers spill into the street from the Thatch, enjoying a cool beer after another sunny day at the beach. Somehow the place manages to retain its charm and feel.

Newquay, on the other hand, would have been very happy to live on as a kind of Torquay of the northern Cornish coast, but what happened in the 1960s changed all that. The seeds were sown long before, due to the town's coastal geography, but the advent of Bilbo surfboards and advances in wetsuits made by Gul meant that surfing had gained a foothold in the

Spring
Air 10°C 50°F
Water 11°C 52°F
4/3mm Wetsuit & boots

Summer
Air 17°C 63°F
Water 15°C 59°F
3/2mm Wetsuit

Autumn
Air 13°C 55°F
Water 13°C 55°F
4/3mm Wetsuit

Winter
Air 7°C 45°F
Water 9°C 48°F
5/4mm Wetsuit, boots, gloves & hood

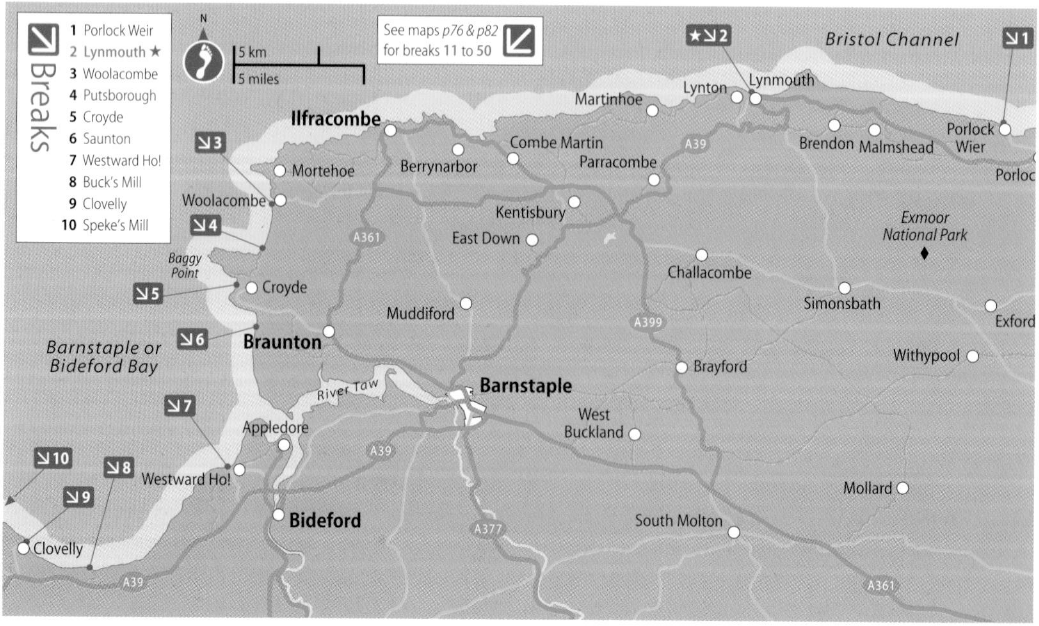

5'6" Xanadu Rocket Fish

Shaper: Xanadu

5'6" x $21\frac{3}{16}$" x $2\frac{1}{4}$"

Built with Surftech's proven TUFLITE construction.

Flatter entry rocker, "wider nose, wider tail" to make up for the shorter length.

Should be ridden 8" shorter than a performance board. Flatter deck makes the rails fuller for more buoyancy and better performance in smaller waves. Flat vee to double concave for quick projection down the line.

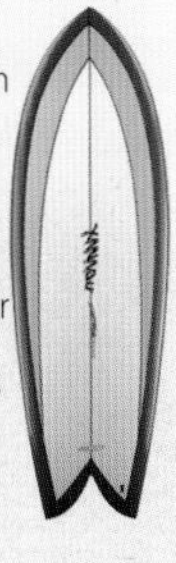

6'6" Bushman Pancho Sullivan Model

Shaper: Jeff Bushman

6'6" x $19\frac{3}{8}$" x $2\frac{1}{2}$"

Built with Surftech's proven TUFLITE construction.

Designed with North Shore power surfer Pancho Sullivan, for big winter reefbreaks like Porthleven. Medium entry rocker to help negotiate late drops and single to double concave for down the line speed make this the board of choice when the waves are firing!

FCS G7000 fins.

Boards by **Surftech**
www.surftech.com info@surftech.com

town and it has stubbornly refused to let go. Today, Newquay has grown to become one of the surf capitals of Europe. Surfing is big business with the number of surf shops and shapers still expanding year on year, while the annual Rip Curl Boardmasters continues to attract over 100,000 spectators.

The southwest excels in the fact that it offers an environment to suit everyone's surfing needs. There's the hustle and bustle of Newquay, the relaxed rollers of Saunton, the dredging low tide boardbreakers of Croyde, yet it still dangles the chance to get off the beaten track and score some quiet, clean waves. It's just about getting out there and looking beyond the next bend in the road.

Coastline

It was along this rocky shores of Kernow that wreckers lured unsuspecting ships onto the rocks and the myriad tiny coves have, for centuries, been a smugglers' haven. Today it is the tourists who are lured to the Cornish coastline and although the beaches do reach bursting point during the months of July and August, for those who are willing to explore, there are still a few places off the beaten track. Most surfers stay north and only head south in particular conditions, usually in the winter. The coastline of North Devon can be as spectacular as any in Britain. Forest-shrouded sea cliffs drop off into the Atlantic and small villages like Lynmouth take shelter where stream-eroded valleys meet the sea. Between Ilfracombe and Westward Ho! sit the county's main tourist and surfing beaches. These westerly facing stretches of sand are a heaving mass in the summer months, but in the spring and autumn are home to quality waves. And in the biggest winter storms, sheltered points spring to life, allowing waves to be ridden on even the biggest Atlantic swells.

Local Environment by Surfers Against Sewage

"Heavy rain results in poor water quality in the South West. The large amounts of water are overflowing sewerage treatment plants resulting in raw sewage and rainwater being pumped out

GREG MARTIN/FINDYOURWAVE

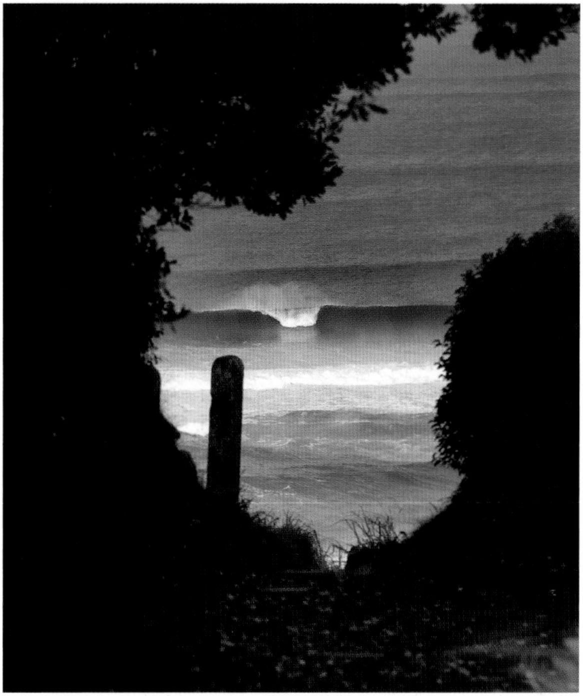

Above: 32 Gwenver. **Opposite:** Alan Stokes, deep inside the West Country.

into rivers and the Atlantic. The heavy rain also produces diffuse pollution, the rain washes pollutants off agricultural land. Sewerage infrastructure often can't cope with the large influx of tourists in the summer resulting in more pollution problems." Andy Cummins, www.sas.org.uk

There is no doubt that a lot of breaks in the southwest are already very crowded and every summer seems to bring a new influx of people into the water. This can lead to tension in the water. With this in mind, if you are visiting the area, try to be honest about your ability and the types of waves you want to be surfing. Rather than small, tight-knit spots it's probably best to head for the bigger open beaches where there is more room to spread out and less tension in the water. Breaks like Perran Sands and Godrevy/Gwithian in Cornwall and Putsborough and Saunton in Devon offer a more mellow vibe and more space. If you're heading to the Newquay area, Watergate tolerates more of a crowd.

Getting around

The road network in Cornwall is pretty good. The A30 acts as a main artery and access to breaks by car is pretty straightforward. During the peak summer season, especially around the last two weeks in August, the roads can become very congested. Devon looks great on a map, but in reality it can be a bit of a nightmare. The so-called Atlantic Highway (A39) can be surprisingly narrow in places and frustratingly slow in summer traffic.

Breaks

Devon

LEFT REEF

↘1 Porlock Weir

- **Conditions** Big to huge W swells, offshore in S or SW winds
- **Hazards/tips** Crowds
- **Sleeping** Woolacombe » *p85*

Sitting in the heart of Exmoor National Park, Porlock is actually just over the Devon border in Somerset and has a notoriously steep hill. It is a spot that is surfed on big swells two hours before or after high tide. There is a toll road on the way in, parking above the break.

LEFT POINT BREAK

↘2 Lynmouth

- **Swell** Large NW or W
- **Wind** Light S or SE
- **Tide** Through the tides, best at low
- **Size** 3-8 ft
- **Length** 300 m plus
- **Bottom** Boulders
- **Access** Off the rocks
- **Ability** Intermediate/Advanced
- **Best months** Sep-Apr
- **Board** Squashtail Thruster or longboard
- **Hazards/tips** Crowds, rips, rocks
- **Sleeping** Woolacombe » *p85*

In a country that's not really renowned for its point breaks, Lynmouth is a real gem. When big swells hit Devon, you'll find many of the regions surfers heading for the 300 m walls that can be found peeling at the edge of this quaint village. Lynmouth works through all states of the tide, although it is generally better at low. The exposed nature of the break means it needs light winds.

When it is on it will generally be crowded, especially at weekends or where big swells have been forecast well in advance. Parking is available on the headland pay and display carpark.

GREG MARTIN/FINDYOURWAVE

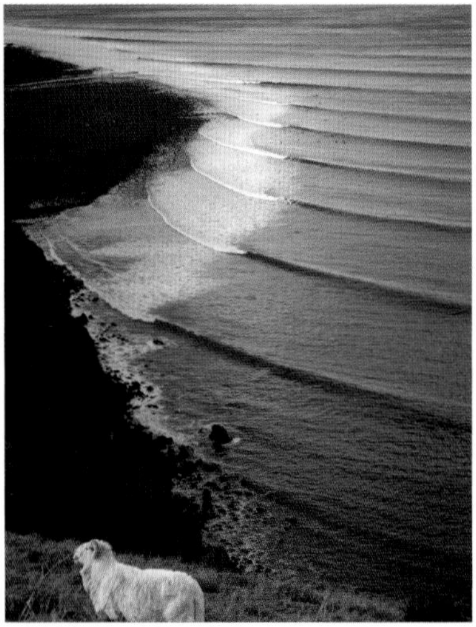

2 Lynmouth lines.

The long walls, bad rips, boulders and crowds make this a break for experienced surfers. The inside section can see pitching lips reeling along the shallow boulders. A great wave for all surfers, whether you prefer longboards, fish or shortboards.

ⓘ ***If you like** Lynmouth, try **La Fortaleza** in Spain (see page 225) or **Gills Bay** in Scotland (see page 38).*

BEACH BREAK

↘3 Woolacombe

- **Conditions** All NW to SW swells, offshore in E winds
- **Hazards/tips** Big beach, good place to escape crowds
- **Sleeping** Woolacombe » *p85*

A two mile stretch of beach with peaks and a high tide right at the northern end. Various peaks work at different states of tide. Can be a good place to escape the crowds at Croyde and ideal for beginners. Parking above the beach.

BEACH BREAK

↘4 Putsborough

- **Conditions** Medium NW or W swells, offshore in E winds
- **Hazards/tips** Rips when big
- **Sleeping** Woolacombe/Croyde » *p85*

The southern end of Woolacombe beach is protected from southerly winds by Baggy Point, so can be the place to check when Croyde and Saunton are blown out. Works at

ROGER POWLEY

5 Croyde Inner limits.

all states of tide. The waves here can be good, but it's usually smaller so it's worth checking if Croyde is packed as the beach can throw up good banks. Popular with beginners but watch out for rips near the point in larger swells. The road down to the beach is narrow and windy if you are in a van. Parking and toilets above the beach.

BEACH AND REEF BREAKS

↘5 Croyde

Conditions All NW and W swells, offshore in E winds
Hazards/tips One of the UK's most crowded beaches
Sleeping Croyde » *p85*

Devon's own 'surf city' attracts surfers from Bristol, Birmingham and across the UK due to the access from the M5. Add these surfers of mixed abilities to a hungry core of locals and the water can get pretty crowded. Keep your eyes open and don't drop in. The banks here can produce powerful, hollow waves, especially at low tide. If you're not an experienced surfer then it may be better to check out another spot. Croyde was crowded even before the recent surf boom.

The **beach** has some excellent banks, is offshore in an easterly wind. The quality of waves and consistency makes it a regular contest venue. Croyde has the distinction of being privately owned and there are a number of car parks near the beach. Low tide can be a board snapping experience. "Croyde low tide on its day can look like Hossegor – people getting pitted everywhere," says James Stentiford, Croyde local and one of Europe's top pro snowboarders. "Above four foot it's heavy and fast but it needs the right swell direction and good banks to fire."

At the north end of the beach Baggy Point has a right-hand reef, **Baggy End Reef**, which works best on a spring high tide. It gets busy but doesn't really handle crowds well. The reef breaks in bigger swells up to three-quarter tide and is for experienced surfers only.

At the south end of the beach, **Downend Point** is probably the most surfed reef. It doesn't really work below 4 ft and is best from low to mid tide on neap tides. It's also a good spot when it gets too big for the beach. It can be a bit of a cut-back wave but on it's day it can produce a few barrels. It does get crowded but can handle a crowd pretty well. The reefs are shallow and rocky and are popular with locals when they are on.

BEACH BREAK

↘6 Saunton

Conditions Medium NW to W swell, offshore in E winds
Hazards/tips Very mellow, popular longboard wave
Sleeping Croyde/Braunton » *p85*

This long stretch of sand is a very gently sloping beach not renowned for the quality of its sandbanks. It runs from the headland south to the mouth of the River Taw so there is plenty of room to spread out. It's fairly consistent and works at all states of tides. It's a great place for beginners and longboarders as the waves peel pretty gently and lack much punch. The paddle out can be a chore in bigger swells. Backed by miles of sand dunes. It's a pretty safe beach, with lifeguards in the summer. Car park off the main road.

BEACH AND REEFS

↘7 Westward Ho!

Conditions Small to medium NW and W swells, offshore in E winds
Hazards/tips Good spot to escape the crowds
Sleeping Westward Ho! » *p86*

Westward Ho! is the only town in Britain named after a book. It would make for a great review if we could say that the break was a fairy tale, but it's a pretty average spot that can have its good days. The beach works through the tidal range and is much less busy than the breaks north of the Taw. It's a good spot for beginners and inexperienced surfers and those looking to escape the crowds. Easy parking at beach. Laid-back line-ups.

DEMI TAYLOR

4 Putsborough Peak.

LEFT REEF BREAK

↘8 Buck's Mill

Conditions Big SW, W and NW swells, offshore in S winds
Hazards/tips Not a wave for the inexperienced
Sleeping Westward Ho! » *p86*

When massive swells hit the West Country, local surfers head for sheltered breaks where quality waves come alive in locations that are usually as flat as a pond. In southwesterly gales and huge swells, Buck's Mill has a long left that breaks along a man-made boulder groyne. It's a low tide break and can be crowded due to the quality of wave produced here. Park respectfully in the village.

LEFT POINT BREAK

↘9 Clovelly

Conditions Huge NW to SW swells, offshore in SE winds
Hazards/tips Very fickle
Sleeping Westward Ho! » *p86*

Clovelly is a picturesque village sheltering in the lee of a huge wooded point. It is this protection that ensures this fickle point break is very hard to catch when it's on. Works at low tide on a massive swell, when long, walling lefts peel along a boulder-fringed sandy point. It's a really long walk down to the break from the expensive car park. Also sheltered from strong southwesterly to easterly winds. The wave breaks down the point towards the harbour. Access off the boulder beach or harbour if it gets big (once a decade).

A FRAME REEF BREAK

↘10 Speke's Mill

- **Conditions** Small to medium NW and W swells, offshore in E winds
- **Hazards/tips** Respect locals, difficult to find
- **Sleeping** Westward Ho! » *p86*

Speke's is a shallow, rocky reef, which gets crowded, so not for the inexperienced. It has always been a popular spot with Devon surfers as it Hoovers up swell on small days. Difficult to find the reef (we haven't shown it on the map) so you'll need to do some exploring. Respect the locals if it's on and if it's already busy, head south to Cornwall's Sandy Mouth.

North Cornwall coast

BEACH BREAK

↘11 Duckpool

- **Conditions** Small to medium NW to SW swells, offshore in E winds
- **Hazards/tips** Not really suitable for beginners due to rocks and rips
- **Sleeping** Bude » *p86*

A sandy cove flanked by rocky outcrops that works best from low to mid, on an incoming tide. Less busy than the breaks to the south, this spot can have some good waves at low tide, but needs easterly winds to work properly. Picks up plenty of swell. Easy access off the A39 with parking above the break.

BEACH BREAK

↘12 Sandy Mouth

- **Conditions** Small to medium NW to SW swells, offshore in E winds
- **Hazards/tips** Watch out for rips and submerged rocks
- **Sleeping** Bude » *p86*

This cliff-backed beach can produce high quality lefts and rights when the banks have formed well. Although an extension of the sandy bay leading to Bude, this is a better bet for escaping the crowds. Best from low to mid on a pushing tide – access limited at high tide. National Trust car park plus toilets near the break.

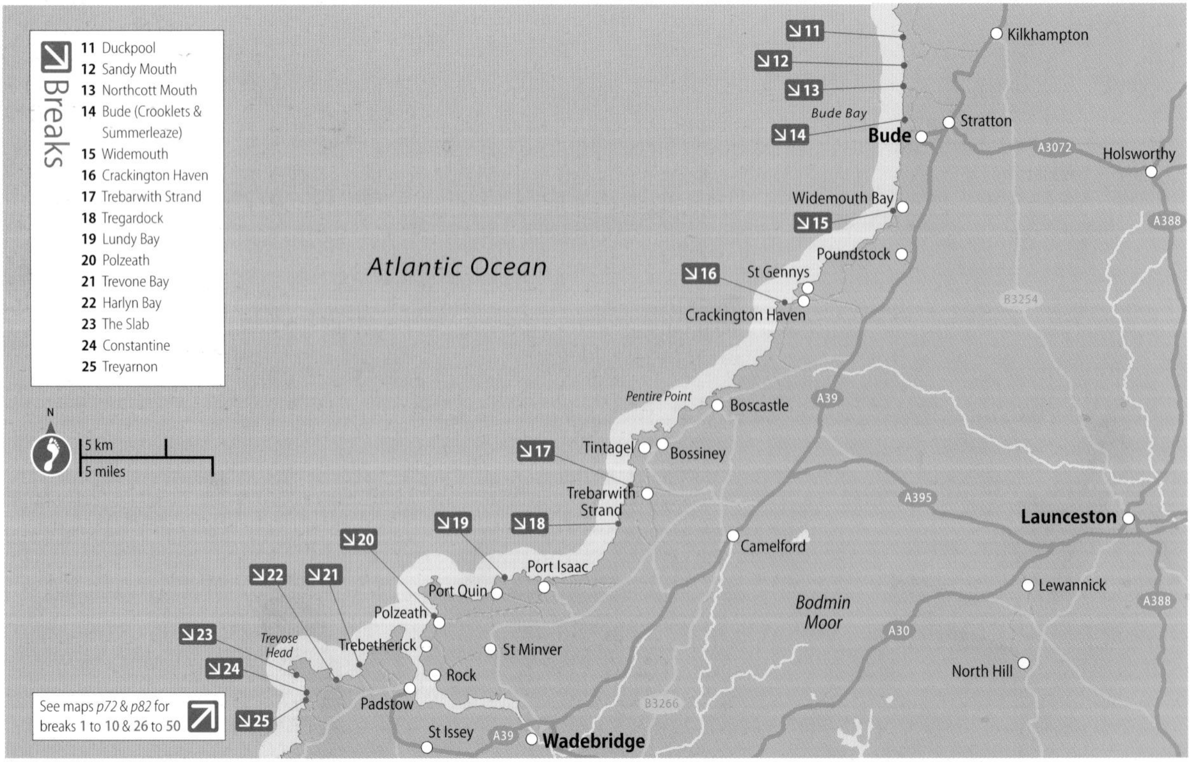

BEACH BREAK

↘13 Northcott Mouth

- **Conditions** Small to medium NW to SW swells, offshore in E winds
- **Hazards/tips** Watch out for rips when big
- **Sleeping** Bude » *p86*

Good quality beach break that can produce powerful and hollow waves, best from low to mid tide. At high tide the beach can disappear so beginners should bear this in mind. Beach parking.

BEACH BREAK

↘14 Bude (Crooklets and Summerleaze)

- **Conditions** Small to medium NW to SW swells, offshore in E winds
- **Hazards/tips** Crowds, rips, rocks
- **Sleeping** Bude » *p86*

Summerleaze has a number of waves that work in bigger swells. There is a quality left at low tide and a right at high tide near the swimming pool. There are also various sandbanks on the beach which change with the swells. **Crooklets** has a number of waves including sandbank peaks and a good right to the northern end and a left to the south. Watch out for rocky outcrops at high tide. Bude gets busy during the summer and during good swells. Suitable for beginners but watch out for rips near the river.

BEACH BREAK

↘15 Widemouth

- **Conditions** Small to medium NW and W swells, offshore in E and SE winds
- **Hazards/tips** Crowds, rocks
- **Sleeping** Bude » *p86*

This beach runs for almost a mile and the shifting sandbars can produce some quality waves. There can be lefts, rights and peaks depending on the banks and, as a result, is popular. There are also a couple of good reefs

BEN SELWAY

4 Bude.

worth checking. Easy access off the A39 with a large car park overlooking the break. Beginners should watch out for rocky outcrops.

BEACH AND POINT BREAK

↘16 Crackington Haven

- **Conditions** Big NW and W swells, offshore in E winds
- **Hazards/tips** Rips, rocks
- **Sleeping** Bude » *p86*

This sheltered bay sits at the mouth of a lush valley, overlooked by 400-ft cliffs of limestone, sandstone and shale. The left-hand point break is surfable in even the biggest surf, with the right winds, hence the name 'Unmaxables'. Tends to work in big winter storms but there is a café in the car park for hot tea and food.

BEACH BREAK

↘17 Trebarwith Strand

- **Conditions** Small to medium swells, offshore in an easterly/southeasterly wind.
- **Hazards/tips** Beach disappears at high.
- **Sleeping** Tintagel/Polzeath » *p86*

A north Cornwall gem that can have quality lefts and rights, depending on the sandbars. Best surfed from low to mid tide as the beach is covered at high. Suitable for surfers of all abilities. Parking available at the beach. A great place to escape the summer crowds when the tide is out.

BEACH BREAK

↘18 Tregardock

- **Conditions** Small to medium NW to W swells, offshore in E to SE winds.
- **Hazards/tips** Good place to escape the crowds
- **Sleeping** Tintagel/Polzeath » *p86*

Remote stretch of beach with good peaks from low to mid tide. Access on foot from Treligga. Not suitable for beginners.

BEACH BREAK

↘19 Lundy Bay

- **Conditions** Medium to big NW to W swells, offshore in S to SW winds.
- **Hazards/tips** Worth checking when other spots are blown out
- **Sleeping** Polzeath » *p86*

This sheltered north-facing bay works best at low to mid tide and needs a big swell to work. No car park near the beach. Follow footpath.

BEACH BREAK

↘20 Polzeath

- **Conditions** Medium to big W to NW swells, offshore in E to SE winds
- **Hazards/tips** Pentire Point provides some shelter in light northwesterlies
- **Sleeping** Polzeath » *p86*

Polzeath has a series of lefts and rights that work on all tides. There are peaks in the middle of the bay, with lefts to the south and rights at the northern end by the point. This is a popular and flexible break with parking by the beach. Suitable for surfers of all abilities.

BEACH BREAK

↘21 Trevone Bay

- **Conditions** Big NW to SW swell, SE winds are offshore.
- **Hazards/tips** Small bay with good peaks
- **Sleeping** Polzeath » *p86*

Small and sheltered bay that faces northwest and needs a decent swell to wrap into it. Produces peaks that are best from low to mid tide. Signposted from the B3276.

BEACH BREAK

22 Harlyn Bay

- **Conditions** Big NW, W or SW swells, offshore in S winds
- **Hazards/tips** Busy when it breaks, popular spot in winter storm surf
- **Sleeping** Polzeath/Watergate » *p86*

The northerly facing aspect makes this a popular winter beach. This means that it works in southwesterly winds with a big swell. Works best from low to three-quarter tide on the push. Parking by the beach. One of the few breaks that works in these conditions so can get crowded.

RIGHT REEF BREAK

23 The Slab

- **Conditions** Medium NW to SW swells, offshore in E to SE winds
- **Hazards/tips** Rips, rocks, crowds.
- **Sleeping** Polzeath/Watergate » *p86*

This low tide reef needs a good swell to turn on but the crowds and rips make it a spot best left to experienced surfers. Access to Booby's Bay is on foot from Constantine Bay.

REEF AND BEACH BREAK

24 Constantine

- **Conditions** All NW to SW swells, offshore in E winds
- **Hazards/tips** Crowds, rips when big
- **Sleeping** Polzeath/Watergate » *p86*

At low tide the beach here opens out into half a mile of golden sand and the south of the bay is home to a left-hand reef break that can produce long, walling rides. This is a consistent beach with some excellent banks. Gets busy due to the quality of the waves and its reliability. Easterly winds are offshore. Good spot for surfers of all abilities and has lifeguards in the summer, but beginners should beware of rips. Parking by the beach.

BEACH BREAK

25 Treyarnon

- **Conditions** Small to medium NW to SW swells, offshore in E to SE winds
- **Hazards/tips** Parking near the beach
- **Sleeping** Polzeath/Watergate » *p86*

A series of peaks along this stretch of sand break from low to high tide. There are also a couple of low tide sand-covered reefs worth checking. A popular spot with quality waves.

BEACH BREAK

26 Mawgan Porth

- **Conditions** Small to medium NW to SW swells, offshore in E to SE winds
- **Hazards/tips** Popular, rips when big
- **Sleeping** Watergate » *p87*

This bay can produce fast, walling lefts and rights through all tides. There can also be an excellent left into the rivermouth. Parking off the B3276. It's also worth checking **Beacon Cove** to the south.

BEACH BREAK

27 Watergate Bay

- **Conditions** Small to medium NW to SW swells, offshore in SE to E winds
- **Hazards/tips** Crowds, popular spot, good spot for beginners
- **Sleeping** Watergate » *p87*

The open sandy beach at Watergate is a less crowded option to the bustling peaks of Fistral, especially in the summer. Busy in the middle of the beach near the entrance, but low tide sees the beach open out to the north and south. As the tide pushes in towards high the beach shrinks, compressing the crowds. In a good swell there can be excellent, punchy waves here. Watergate is a popular contest site for British and English surfing championships. It's suitable for all abilities and home to the Extreme Academy and Jamie Oliver's 15.

BEACH BREAKS

28 Newquay Beaches

- **Conditions** All NW and W swells, offshore in S to E winds
- **Hazards/tips** Crowded beaches, surf schools, flexible beaches
- **Sleeping** Newquay » *p87*

When it comes to the European surfing capital, Newquay probably rivals anywhere on the entire continent. Although Hossegor (see page 183) has the cafés and beach culture and Biarritz (page 196) certainly has the edge when it comes to surf chic, Newquay has more surf shops and shapers per mile than probably anywhere on the planet, and each year more seem to pop up. However, what it lacks in boutiques and pastry shops, it makes up for in pasty shops and nightclubs. **Lusty Glaze** is a privately owned, cliff-lined cove with some good waves in smaller swells at low to mid tides. Gets narrow near high. Site of the Fat Face night surfing competition and home to The Adventure Centre. The **Town Beaches** (Tolcarne, Great Western, Towan) face north and are more sheltered. They work through all tides and need a much bigger swell to get going. There is a left near the harbour wall on Towan and assorted peaks heading east. Round the headland and just north of Fistral lies the **Cribbar**, a rocky point in front of the Headland Hotel. This infamous big-wave spot comes alive in huge clean swells and has become increasingly popular with British big wave riders. Expect to see tow-in action when it's booming.

GREG

30 Crantock.

BEACH BREAK

↘29 Fistral Beach

- **Swell** NW to SW
- **Wind** E to SE
- **Tide** All tides
- **Size** 2-8 ft
- **Length** 10-100 m
- **Bottom** Sand
- **Access** From the beach
- **Ability** All
- **Best months** Sep-Dec
- **Board** Performance thruster
- **Hazards/tips** Crowds, heaps of beginners, rocks at Little Fistral
- **Sleeping** Newquay ›› *p87*

Sitting at the heart of Newquay, Fistral is Britain's most famous surfing beach. It has remained at the heart of British surfing since the sixties, and although often maligned, it is actually a very high quality spot that can produce hollow and powerful waves.

Little Fistral is a low tide spot to the north that can produce excellent waves with long walls and barrels. It breaks in front of rocks so is not a good place for beginners.

The main beach works through all tides and the waves vary with the quality of the sandbanks. Although very busy in the summer, the autumn and winter sees the crowd drop off, but it is rarely quiet here. South Fistral offers some shelter in southwesterly winds. The beach has been home to a generation of world class UK surfers including Russell Winter, Lee Bartlett, Alan Stokes, Spencer Hargreaves, Ben Baird – even ex-world champ Martin Potter had a spell here. The National Surfing Centre overlooks the beach and every year the Rip Curl Boardmasters surf contest attracts some of the best surfers in the world. Watch out for the over-zealous clamping in the beach front car park.

If you like Fistral, try Santa Cruz in Portugal (see page 298) or Praia Reinante in Spain (see page 247)

TONY PLANT/SURFTWISTED

TONY PLANT/SURFTWISTED

Above: 19 A grom tucks into an icy Little Fistral barrel. **Top:** Russell Mullins, north Cornwall.

RIVERMOUTH AND BEACH BREAK

↘30 Crantock

- **Conditions** Medium NW to W swells, offshore in SE winds
- **Hazards/tips** Worth checking as a less crowded alternative to Fistral
- **Sleeping** Newquay ›› *p87*

This northwesterly facing beach has a rivermouth sandbank that can produce some excellent rights. It needs a decent swell to get going and works best from low to mid tide. The south end of the beach can produce good lefts.

BEN SELWAY

Fistral.

BEACH BREAK

↘31 Holywell Bay

- **Conditions** Small to medium NW to SW swells, offshore in SE winds
- **Hazards/tips** Less crowded than Newquay
- **Sleeping** Newquay/Perranporth ›› *p87*

Used to be the home of a conrete skate bowl, now the site of go-karting and golf. The bay faces northwest and works on all states of tide, producing some good quality lefts and rights. Always worth checking as it can produce excellent waves. Take turning off the A3075 Newquay road.

BEACH BREAK

↘32 Penhale Corner and Perran Sands

- **Conditions** Small to medium NW to SW swells, offshore in E winds
- **Hazards/tips** Rips when big, OK for beginners when small
- **Sleeping** Perranporth ›› *p88*

This huge, golden beach, stretches from Penhale Corner corner south to Droskyn Head. An endless line-up of lefts, rights and peaks, varying in quality from mellow peelers to reeling, hollow barrels. Works through all tides. A good spot for beginners with summer lifeguards. Travelling surfers who want to escape the crowded and competitive line-ups should check this beach with its more chilled-out atmosphere. Drive through the holiday camp to the pay and display car park overlooking the beach.

BEACH BREAK

↘33 Perranporth and Droskyn

- **Conditions** Small to medium NW to SW swells, offshore in E winds
- **Hazards/tips** Crowds in summer, good for beginners.
- **Sleeping** Perranporth ›› *p88*

Droskyn head offers a great spot to check the surf. Waves break in front of the cliffs at the southern end of the beach. Best at low through to mid tide when lefts are predominant, backwash makes the waves bumpy and unpredictable as the tides gets higher. From here a huge expanse of westerly facing sand stretches out north joining up with Perran Sands and Penhale. The Perranporth beach works on all tides but doesn't handle big swells. Parking on the cliff top at Droskyn or in Perranporth. Chilled line-ups so a good spot for holidaying and travelling surfers.

BEACH BREAK

↘34 Trevaunance Cove, St Agnes

- **Conditions** Medium to big SW to W swells, offshore in SE winds
- **Hazards/tips** Very busy, localism, rips, rocks
- **Sleeping** St Agnes ›› *p88*

Aggie is one of the few spots that works in big southwesterly storm surf. Works through to three-quarter tide but best at mid, the small line-up gets crowded. Can hold a good size swell but above head high gets very powerful. A strong rip to the left of the bay and crowds makes this a spot for experienced surfers only. The heart of the large Badlands surfing community, so rarely uncrowded. Parking near the Driftwood Spa pub. The birthplace of SAS and still polluted.

BEACH BREAK

↘35 Chapel Porth

- **Conditions** Small to medium NW to SW swells, offshore in SE to E winds
- **Hazards/tips** Crowds, localism
- **Sleeping** St Agnes/Porthtowan ›› *p88*

Fast, powerful and hollow rights and lefts break in northwesterly or southwesterly swells. Chapel is a small beach that works from low to mid and has a big local crew. The standard of surfing is extremely high here and it is not a place for beginners. Visiting surfers may struggle to get a wave and there have been incidents of localism. Limited parking by the beach in small National Trust car park. Excellent café.

BEACH BREAK

↘36 Porthtowan

- **Conditions** Small to medium NW to SW swells, offshore in SE winds
- **Hazards/tips** Crowds, dangerous rips, powerful waves
- **Sleeping** Porthtowan ›› *p88*

Heavy, punchy break that works through all tides, opening out at low to reveal Lushingtons to the south. Offshore in southeasterly or easterly wind, but at high the cliffs provide some shelter from light southerlies. So crowded now that village parking full in summer. Powerful waves, rocks and strong rips are a real danger so in anything but small surf it is best left to competent surfers. Not for the inexperienced.

BEACH BREAK AND REEF

↘37 Portreath

- **Conditions** Medium to big NW to SW swells, offshore in SE winds
- **Hazards/tips** Sheltered bay
- **Sleeping** Porthtowan » *p88*

Portreath is usually about half the size of Porthtowan, but can be more sheltered from the wind. The right-hand reef that breaks off the rocks in front of the harbour wall is popular with bodyboarders and experienced surfers. The beach break is usually a short, fast right that can easily become a close-out. Works best from low to near high. Car park overlooking break. Can get crowded in the summer.

BEACH BREAK

↘38 Godrevy and Gwithian

- **Conditions** All SW to NW swells, offshore in SE winds
- **Hazards/tips** Relaxed line-up, popular spot
- **Sleeping** Gwithian » *p88*

This 4 mile stretch of sand heads south from Godrevy to Hayle Rivermouth, only broken by the occasional cluster of high tide rocks. This exposed beach can be fickle but Godrevy, the headland at the northern end of the bay, picks up the most swell and can produce some quality waves. Easy access here from the National Trust car park. Although it does get busy in the summer, there are plenty of peaks to escape the crowds and the atmosphere here is pretty chilled. Good café in the car park. River can be polluted after heavy rains.

GREG MARTIN/FINDYOURWAVE

40 Hawks Point.

RIVERMOUTH BREAK

↘39 Hayle Rivermouth

- **Conditions** Medium NW to big SW swells, offshore in S or SE winds
- **Hazards/tips** Crowds, rips
- **Sleeping** Gwithian » *p88*

Needs a decent swell to get going but can provide good quality waves around the rivermouth. Can get crowded when good. Watch out for rips and pollution after heavy rains.

BEACH BREAK

↘40 Hawks Point

- **Conditions** Big SW swells, offshore in SW winds
- **Hazards/tips** Crowded, difficult access
- **Sleeping** Gwithian » *p88*

A good left breaking off the western end of Carbis Bay. Needs a really big swell to get going so it's a great place to check during a big southwesterly storm surf. Works best low to mid but if it's on, it will be packed. Parking and access are also difficult.

BEACH BREAK

↘41 Porthmeor, St Ives

- **Conditions** Medium NW to big SW swells, offshore in S winds
- **Hazards/tips** Crowds, parking
- **Sleeping** Gwithian » *p88*

Porthmeor is a sheltered beach that faces north and needs a decent swell to get going. Popular winter break that gets busy in the summer when parking can be a problem. Overlooked by the St Ives Tate Gallery.

BEACH BREAK AND POINT

↘42 Gwynver

- **Conditions** Small to medium NW to SW swells, offshore in E winds
- **Hazards/tips** Punchy waves, access on foot
- **Sleeping** Sennen » *p89*

Gwynver is a quality beach break that joins up with Sennen at low tide. It picks up more swell than Sennen and in a good northwesterly swell, right-handers peel off the point at the north end of the beach over a rocky/sandy bottom. Also has a punchy shore break. Works best from low to near high. Watch out for rips. Access is from parking off the A30 and a 20-minute walk down the cliffs.

BEACH BREAK

↘43 Sennen Cove

- **Conditions** Small to medium NW to SW swells, offshore in E winds
- **Hazards/tips** Rips in front of car park in bigger swells
- **Sleeping** Sennen ▸ p89

Of any beach in Cornwall, Sennen probably has the best chance of a wave during the small summer conditions. Low down on the toe of the county, this west-facing bay works well from low through to near high. Suitable for all surfers, but watch out for rips and rocks towards the southern end of the beach in front of the car park. A popular, year-round spot. Surf shop and toilets in car park.

34 Low tide Aggie

Breaks

26 Mawgan Porth	38 Godrevy/Gwithian
27 Watergate Bay	39 Hayle Rivermouth
28 Newquay Beaches	40 Hawks Point
29 Fistral Beach ★	41 Porthmeor, St Ives
30 Crantock	42 Gwynver
31 Holywell Bay	43 Sennen Cove
32 Penhale/Perran Sands	44 Porthcurno
33 Perranporth/Droskyn	45 Perranuthanoe
34 Trevaunance Cove,	46 Praa Sands
St Agnes	47 Porthleven ★
35 Chapel Porth	48 Church Cove
36 Porthtowan	49 Kennack Sands
37 Portreath	50 Falmouth Beaches

See maps p72 & p76 for breaks 1 to 25

Atlantic Ocean

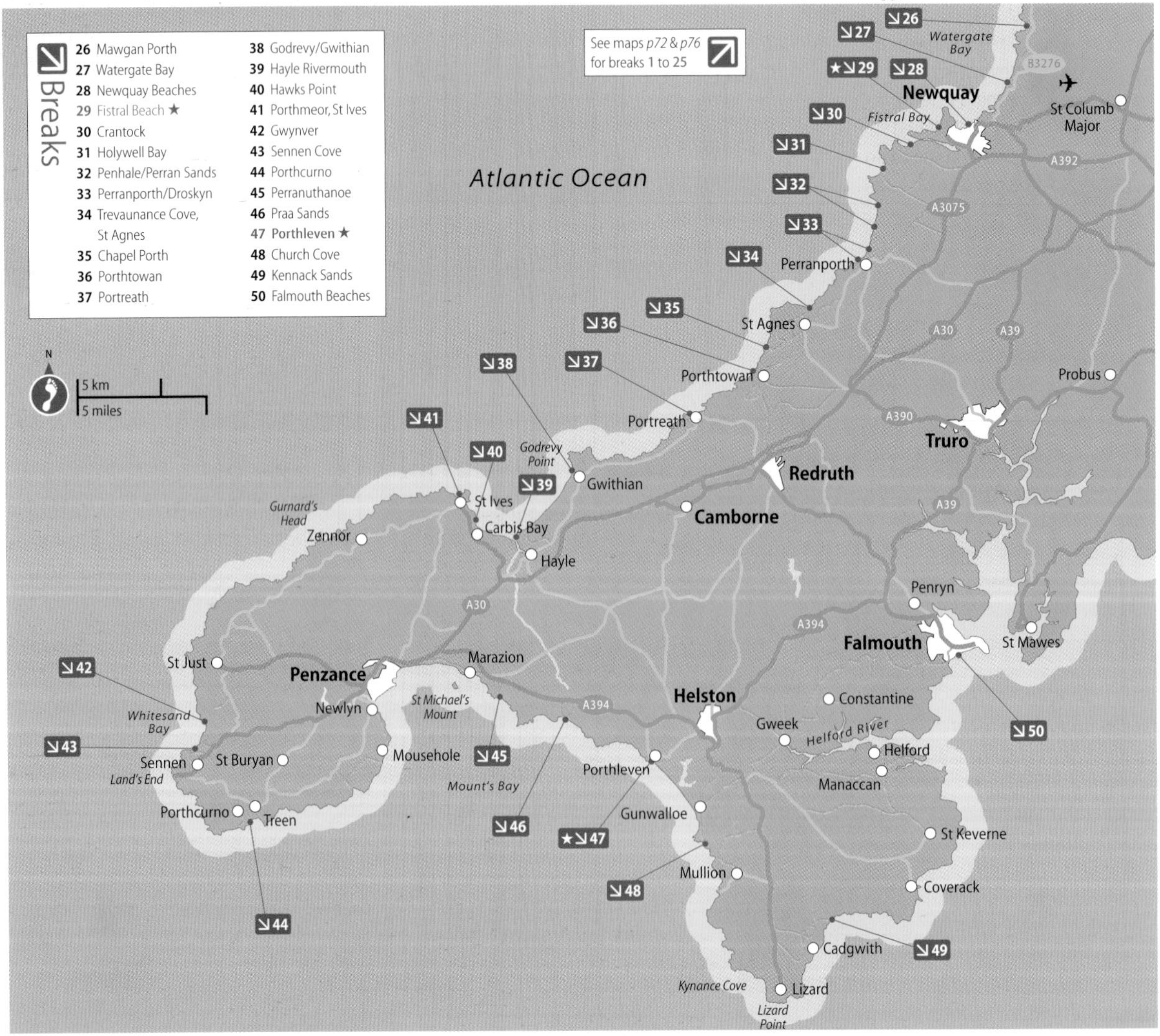

South Cornwall coast

BEACH BREAK

↘44 Porthcurno

- **Conditions** Medium SW to big W swells, offshore in N winds
- **Hazards/tips** Beautiful spot, not too crowded
- **Sleeping** Sennen » p89

Cocooned by granite cliffs, at high tide this narrow bay almost disappears and turns into a shore dump. At low the bay opens up with lefts and rights in the emerging bay to the east. Needs a southwesterly swell or a big northwesterly wrapping in to work. With crystal-clear water, this sheltered spot is a great place to see basking sharks on calm, flat summer days. The open air Minack Theatre overlooks the bay.

BEACH BREAK

↘45 Perranuthanoe

- **Conditions** Medium SW to big W swells, offshore in NE wind
- **Hazards/tips** Busy spot
- **Sleeping** Sennen » p89

Underestimated bay with a good right breaking off the rocks at the west. In the middle are peaks of variable quality. Works best from low to three-quarter tide as high tide sees the bay virtually disappear. It's usually a couple of feet smaller than Praa Sands. Parking near the beach. Used to be very quiet but as Praa has got busier, this spot has taken the overspill. With a more relaxed vibe, it is popular with beginners, intermediate surfers and longboarders. There is an A-frame reef, **Cabbage Patch**, which breaks over boulders nearby.

GREG MARTIN/FINDYOURWAVE

Kernow, south coast.

BEACH BREAK

↘46 Praa Sands

- **Conditions** Medium SW to big W swells, offshore in NE winds
- **Hazards/tips** Very crowded, can be heavy, rips
- **Sleeping** Sennen » p89

Praa is the most popular beach break on the south coast. Works in southwesterly or big northwesterly swells to produce powerful, punchy waves that are offshore in northerly or northeasterly winds. Draws a big crowd in the winter because when Praa is on, the north coast is usually blown out. Gets packed at weekends on good swells. Works on all tides but at high can become a shore dump. Parking overlooking the break.

GREG MARTIN/FINDYOURWAVE

Porthleven

RIGHT REEF BREAK

↘47 Porthleven

- **Swell** SW swells
- **Wind** NE winds
- **Tide** Three-quarters to just off low
- **Size** 3 – 10 ft
- **Length** 50 – 75 m
- **Bottom** Rock reef
- **Access** Off the rocks
- **Ability** Intermediate to advanced
- **Best months** Sep-Dec
- **Board** Performance gunny thruster
- **Hazards/tips** Shallow near low, crowds, crowds and more crowds!
- **Sleeping** Sennen » p89

Cornwall isn't exactly famed for its classic reef breaks. The geology of the region, a complex mix of granite, sandstone and slate, is too fractured and angular to provide a consistent base for reef formation. Porthleven, however, is one of the exceptions to the rule. The wave breaks onto a rocky slab situated just to the west of the entrance to Porthleven harbour and the hollow and powerful waves here have established a fanatical following. It quickly became the most respected reef break in the south of England and, as such, attracts a large crew every time it breaks. 'Leven is famed for its fast, hollow rights, which have a board-snapping ferocity, but has the added bonus of throwing up some juicy lefts just to keep the goofy footers happy. Best at mid-tide, low gets pretty shallow and high suffers a bit from backwash.

"Due to the shape of the reef, 'Leven forms one of the heaviest waves in the UK," says local surfer Will Boex. "Unfortunately it's no longer an the all local line-up from yesteryear but when Leven is on, it's certainly a privilege to surf." The biggest factor in surfing here is the crowds. Most of Cornwall's best surfers will be in the line-up when it's firing and if you watch you will see that no waves go through unridden. The UK's most competitive line-up is no place for the faint-hearted. Porthleven regular James Hendy says, "The thing about 'Leven is that when it's good, it's so competitive that there's only a handful of guys actually getting waves. Some people just paddle out to say they were in." The rocks provide a great vantage point to watch all the action.

"'Leven can be a real board eater," recalls Minzie. "I remember one session where I'd just snapped my board and I was scooting in on what was left of it and I saw Chops paddling out. He saw me and started laughing. Luckily I had a spare board with me so I grabbed it, put my leash on and jumped back off the rocks. I'm paddling out and guess who I meet coming in on the remains of his board?"

If you like Porthleven, try Thurso East in Scotland (see page 40) or La Sauzaie in France (see page 171).

GREG MARTIN/FINDYOURWAVE

TONY PLANT/SURFTWISTED

Top: 38 Gwithian. **Above**: Dan 'Mole' Joel at Porthleven.

BEACH BREAK

48 Church Cove

- **Conditions** Small to medium W to SW swells, offshore in NE to E winds
- **Hazards/tips** Crowds
- **Sleeping** Sennen ▸▸ p89

Bay facing southwest on the Lizard Peninsula that can produce some quality waves in southwesterly or big northwesterly swells. Works best from low to three-quarter tide. Winds from the northeast or easterly direction are preferable. Popular break in the winter.

BEACH BREAK

49 Kennack Sands

- **Conditions** Big W to SW swells, offshore in NW to W winds
- **Hazards/tips** Crowds
- **Sleeping** Sennen ▸▸ p89

Beach facing southeast on the eastern side of the Lizard. There are two beaches separated by a large rocky mass known as the Caerverracks. A good place to check in winter storms. At low tide the beach opens out with a long stretch to the east and a small section to the west. Can have lefts and rights. Gets busy when working. Parking by the beach.

BEACH AND REEF BREAKS

50 Falmouth Beaches

- **Conditions** Big SW swells, offshore in N to NW winds
- **Hazards/tips** Crowds
- **Sleeping** Sennen ▸▸ p89

The three beaches closest to Falmouth – Maenporth, Swanpool and Gyllyngvase – can break in big southwesterly swells and the occasional easterly in the channel. Between Swanpool and Gyllyngvase lies Falmouth Reef. Busy when working.

Practicalities

Devon

Woolacombe

Just south of Morte Point sits Woolacombe and the 3-mile stretch of sand leading down to Putsborough.

Sleeping

££ **Surf View Guesthouse**, Beach Rd, T01271-870448, is a family B&B, 10 mins walk to the beach (near to the Woolacombe Sands Holiday Parc). They offer board storage and wetsuit drying facilities.
Self Catering **Westbeach Accommodation**, Beach Rd, T01271- 870634, www.westbeach accommodation.co.uk, have well placed, clean, modern studios and flats to let with board storage facilities. Studio for 4 from around £250-550 per week.
Camping There are plenty of campsites in the area – the majority do not cater to groups.
Europa Park, Beach Rd, T01271-871425, is open year round, takes groups and caters for tents and vans as well as renting out "surf cabins" and lodges with beds and fridges – comfortable camping!
Damage Barton, T01271-870502, Mar-Nov, between Lee Bay and Bull Point is a working farm and quiet campsite.
North Morte Farm, T01271-870381, about a mile north of Woolacombe at Mortehoe, Mar-Oct, statics also available (couples and families only).
Woolacombe Bay Holiday Parcs, T01271-870343, have 4 family oriented sites to choose from, with **Golden Coast** open year round (no groups under 25 yrs).
Woolacombe Sands Holiday Park, Beach Rd, T01271-870569, a 15-min walk to beach. Open Easter-Oct, no groups.

Eating and drinking

The **Red Barn**, just back from the beach is a local staple. Enjoy a post-surf beer and affordable, filling food with a view.
West Beach, Beach Rd, bar and restaurant, is a great place to enjoy mainly seasonal, organic produce and fresh, local seafood all with beach views. Mains can be pricey but the Bar menu has some good affordable alternatives.

Directory

Surf Shops/facilities There are plenty of surf shops here including **Bay Surf Shop**, Barton Court, **Gulf Stream Surfboards**, 12 South St, T01271-870831 (shop and factory). **Hunter**, West Rd, T01271-870872, are a north Devon brand with several shops, selling hardware and hiring equipment.
Banks Rosalie Terr.
Pharmacy Medi-scene, West Rd. **Post office** As with most things here, head to the main West Rd. **Tourist information** Year round on the Esplanade.

Croyde

Croyde, with its thatched roofs and little streets, has retained its chocolate-box feel despite being a summer tourist Mecca. The village, named after the Norse raider Crydda who landed here, also has a large population of surfers who generally rip.

Sleeping

£££ **The Thatch**, Hobbs Hill, , T01271-890349. This central pub is the focus of village life with rooms over the pub or a (slightly) quieter option, over the road.
££ **Crowborough Farm**, in Georgeham between Croyde and Putsborough, T01271-891005, is a quieter option with a lovely garden as well as an outside tap for rinsing suits.
Other surf-friendly choices offering board storage include:
££ **Moorsands House**, Moor Lane, T01271-890781, between the village and beach.
££ **Oamaru**, Down End, T01271-890765.
££ **Sandy Hollow**, Sandy Way, T01271-890556. Also available to rent entirely as a self-catering bungalow Jul-Aug.
££ **Thistledoo**, Bonnicott Lane, T01271-890245.
Self-catering ££ **Croyde Bay Holiday Village** at Down End have chalets to rent, T01271-890890.
Camping There are loads of campsites but Croyde is not a particularly cheap option and many places will not take groups.
Bay View Farm, T01271-890501, has easy access to both the beach and village as well as statics for hire.
Surfers Paradise Campsite, Sandy La, T01271-890477, Jul-Aug, happy to accommodate groups.
Ruda Campsite is the older brother of Surfers Paradise and is open to families and couples only.

Eating and drinking

The **Thatch** on Hobbs Hill is top spot with good food at reasonable prices. It's always packed out, especially in the summer, so be prepared to wait for your post-surf pint. **Billy Budd's** just up the road is another popular spot. Local lensman, Ester Spears, recommends **Blue Groove**, Hobbs Hill, a great café run by a couple of surfers.

Directory

Surf shops **Little Pink Shop**, T01271-890453, in the centre of the village sells all the surfing essentials and does full equipment hire. **Redwood**, Hobbs Hill, T01271-890999, stocks all the gear as well offering equipment hire. **Surfing Croyde Bay**, Hobbs Hill, is part pasty shop, part surf shop but does have a range of hardware.

Braunton

Off the A361, Braunton is a fair sized market town with most amenities including banks, a supermarket and a good campsite.

Sleeping

££ **The Firs**, Higher Park Rd, T01271-814358, a mile from the village, 2 miles from the beach with board and bike storage.
Lobb Fields Caravan and Camping Park, Saunton Rd, T01271-812090, Mar-Oct.

Westward Ho!

The only town in England to be punctuated by an exclamation mark!

Sleeping

Plenty of B&B options on Atlantic Way.
£ **Elmscott Youth Hostel**, T01237 441367, Mar-Sep, is about half a mile inland, heading southwest on the A39 to Hartland.
Self-catering **The Old Granary** in Pusehill, T01237-421128, sleeps up to 6 people for £175-425 per week.
Camping **Dyke Green Farm Camp Site** Higher Clovelly, T01237 431279, Apr-Oct. **Pusehill Farm Camp Site**, in Pusehill, T01237-474295. **Surf Bay Holiday Park**, Golf Links Rd, T01237-471833, Apr-Oct, walking distance to beach, statics for up to 6 people for around £500 per week.

North Cornwall Coast

Bude

The northernmost town in Cornwall, Bude is accessed off the A39 or the optimistically named 'Atlantic Highway' (more byway than highway). Built around a 19th-century canal and a stretch of golden beaches, Bude is a pretty town with a relaxed attitude. Accommodation gets booked up in Aug during annual **Jazz festival**.

Sleeping

£££ **Trevigue**, Crackington Haven T01840-230418, www.trevigue.co.uk. Beautiful B&B option set in the courtyard of a 16th-century working farm, serving excellent farmhouse breakfasts. A short walk from the sea this is ideally suited for a weekend of loving and surfing. They also have 3 upmarket self-catering cottages to rent nearby, and there's a seasonal restaurant on site.
££ **Elements Surf Hotel** , Marine Dr, Widemouth Bay, T01288-352386, has been set up with surfers in mind, there's board storage and a drying room, a gym and sauna plus the bedrooms have PS2. There's also a restaurant on site.
££ **Widemouth Manor** , overlooks Widemouth Bay, T01288-361263, www.widemouthmanor.co.uk, and has a pub down stairs with B&B rooms upstairs.
££ **Bay View Inn**, overlooking Widemouth, T01288-361273. Contemporary B&B and restaurant with reasonably priced bar food and restaurant menu.
£ **North Shore Backpackers**, T01288-354256, www.northshorebude.com, have reasonably priced dorms and doubles with beds from around £14.
Camping Plenty of choices but many sites do not take single sex groups so call before you rock up with a van load of 20 mates. **Cornish Coasts**, Poundstock about 2 miles south of Widemouth on the A39, T01288-361380. Open Easter-Oct, with statics are a friendly site, about the cheapest and one of the best options.
Redpost Inn & Holiday Park, 4 miles inland from Bude in Launcells, T01288-381305, is a small with an on-site Inn, open year round with the option of statics.
Upper Lynstone Caravan & Camping Park, just south of Bude on the road to Widemouth, T01288-352017, www.upper lynstone.co.uk, has cabins, is open Easter–Oct to couples and families only.
Budemeadows Touring Park, T01288-361646, open year round; **Bude Holiday Park**, T01288-355980,summer only; and **Sandymouth Holiday Park**, T01288-352563, Apr-Oct, are very family orientated and don't take same sex groups.

Eating and drinking

The Bencoolen Inn, Bencoolen Rd, popular spot for a pint and a spot of pub grub.
Next door, is something a bit special, **El Barco** on Bencoolen Rd is recommended by Surf Spot owner Jay Squire, for the 'best steaks in Bude, cooked by a Spanish chef with 30 years' experience'.
Overlooking Summerleaze, **Life's A Beach** is a popular and chilled bistro/bar to grab a bite and watch the sun go down.
Carriers Inn overlooking the River Neet is another good place for a sundowner beer.
At Crackington Haven, the **Cabin** on the beach serves a full range of snacks from pizza to cream teas and operates a BYO booze system for eating in.

Directory

Surf Shops There are several in Bude including **Surf Spot**, Belle Vue, www.surfspot.co.uk and **Zuma Jays**, also on Belle Vue, www.zumajays.co.uk.
Internet **Coffee Pot**, Morwena Terr – grab a coffee while checking the charts.
Banks most of the main banks are on Lansdown Rd by the river. **Chemist** Bellle Vue, including a **Boots** chemist. **Post office** on Morwena Terr. **Tourist information** Crescent car park, www.visitbude.info, year round opening.

Tintagel

The castle here may or may not be the birthplace of the legendary King Arthur, but the castle ruins clinging to the 'island' are certainly worth exploring. There are plenty of tat shops in the one-street town touting myths and magic to the willing.

Sleeping

£ **YHA Hostel**, Dunderhole Point, T0870 7706068, Mar-30 Oct, with fantastic views along the coast.
Camping **The Headland**, Atlantic Rd, T01840-770239, Easter-Oct, or the small **Bossiney Farm**, T01840-770481, Apr-Oct just north at Bossiney, with statics also available.

Polzeath

In the lea of Pentire Point nestles the upmarket seaside resort of Polzeath – popular with middle England's guitar-toting, school-leaving population.

Sleeping

££ **Surf's Up Surf School**, just up from the beach, T01208 862003, www.surfsupsurfschool.com, have very comfortable, surf friendly accommodation (predominantly for pupils of their surf school). However, it is worth contacting them (especially off-season) for B&B rooms.
££ **Pentire View**, by beach, T01208-862484.
Camping If you're not in a couple or with a family, camping in Polzeath is going to prove difficult – **The Valley Caravan Park**, T01208-862391, and **Tristram Camping Park** overlooking the bay, T01208-862215, Easter-Oct, is one of the most expensive sites in the area and does not accommodate groups. **Trenant Steading**, T01208-869091.

Eating and drinking

On the beach there are a number of places serving snacks. Just up from the beach sits the **Oyster Catcher**, a lively spot for an evening drink.

Directory

Surf Shops **Ann's Cottage**, T01208-863317, stock a full range of gear. **TJ**'s on Polzeath beach has a full range of hardware and goodies. **Shapers** **Fluid Juice**, Old Airfield, St Merryn Padstow, T01841 520928. **Local Hero**, Brook Rd, Wadebridge, T01208-814282 – both bring more than 20 years experience to their boards.

Watergate

Watergate Beach is somewhere you can escape the crowds and mayhem of nearby Newquay. There isn't a lot here and that's the point.

Sleeping

£££ **Watergate Bay Hotel**, T01637-860543, www.watergatebay.co.uk, overlooks the bay combining well-thought-out contemporary design with beach living and creature comforts. Bar, Brasserie and restaurant on site. They also have a more affordable B&B option ££ **The Coach House**, just behind the hotel but without views.

DEMI TAYLOR

46 Evening session at Praa Sands.

££ **Pendoric**, 5 mins inland at St Magwan, T01637 860043, www.pendoric.co.uk. Eco-minded, comfortable B&B with board storage, also yoga and massage on site.
Self Catering There are several good options from cottages to modern apartments by the beach. See www.beachretreats.co.uk, T01637 861005, for more details.

Eating and drinking

The premier eating destination here is the beachfront **Fifteen Cornwall**, T01637-861000, brainchild of celebrity chef, Jamie Oliver. Top end, innovative menus utilizing seasonal, local produce are served in cool surroundings with picture window and views across the bay. Breakfast is the affordable '15' meal. Aside from the hotel, **The Beach Hut** does good, reasonably priced, post surf fare from soup and sandwiches to Nachos, burgers and steaks, also with far reaching views.

Directory

The Extreme Academy, on the beach front provides tuition in everything from surfing to kitebuggying and hires equipment.

Newquay

Newquay is Europe's self-styled surf capital and deserves the title. There are surf shops on every corner and shapers galore as well as a WQS event rolling into town every summer. It even has good surfing beaches – with crowds to match. It's also a real party town: summer nights can be a throng of stag nights, hen parties and a rainbow spectrum of football shirts.

Sleeping

Newquay is awash with hotels, B&Bs and surf lodges but check rooms as standards vary. For B&Bs check out Headland Rd for a cheap place to stay within walking access of Fistral Beach. Some of the picks include:
£££ **Headland Hotel**, T01637-872211, www.headlandhotel.co.uk. Grand old redbrick hotel overlooking the madness of Fistral Beach. Although at the top end of the scale, residents have access to their tennis courts, golf course, pool and jacuzzi. Often have good deals off peak.
££-£ **Reef Surf Lodge**, Tower Rd, T01637-879058, is a centrally located, clean and modern surf lodge with secure board storage, wetsuit drying room plus fresh bar and café.
££-£ **Home Surf Lodge**, Tower Rd, T01637-851736, is a lively place that openly welcomes groups. It has a late dorm accommodation, board lock up, outdoor shower and a licensed bar. No curfews.
££-£ **Fistral Backpackers**, Headland Rd, T01637-873146, is a short walk to the beach with dorms or doubles plus board storage, drying room and kitchen facilities.
Self Catering **Cornwall Campers**, T01872-571988, www.cornwallcampers.co.uk. Sleeping and transport in one package – a VW camper van! From £395 per week. Also pick up from Newquay Airport.
Headland Village in the grounds of The Headland Hotel (above), T01637 872211, www.headlandvillage.co.uk, beautiful, modern, 5 star 1-3 bed hi-spec cottages with sun deck, cleaning lady and hotel leisure facilities. 2 bed cottage from £665-2170 per week.
Camping The options are pretty limited for groups **Smugglers Haven** (18-30s) at Trevelgue Holiday Park T01637-852000, is one of the only options. Statics and chalets also available. Also try **Sunnyside**, T01637-873338, and **Rosecliston**, T01637-830326.

Eating and drinking

For lunchtime 'caff' food try **Breadline Café** Beachfield Rd. **Red Lion** Beacon Rd, is a popular spot with good value pub grub. The **Fistral Chef Café** over the road is also a good place to grab a meal. For a more expensive slap-up meal, the **Lewenick Lodge** Pentire Headline, has a wide menu from seafood to steaks. Newquay is heaving with bars and clubs. The **Koola Bar** Beach Rd and **The Sugar Lounge** on Bank Street both deliver great sounds in fresh, modern environments. At the other end of the scale **Sailors**, Fore St, is where everyone tends to gravitate to after a few pints to dance the night away to cheesy chart buster.

Directory

Surf Shops There is a massive selection in town including **North Shore**, Fore St, T01637-850 620, which has a good selection of hardware as does **Ocean Magic**, Cliff Rd, T01637-850071, run by legendary shaper Nigel Semmens. **Tunnel Vision**, Alma Pl, T01637-879033, is another well established shop. **Airport** T01637-860600. **Banks** ATMs on Bank St. **Internet** is pricey here try **Tad & Nick's Talk 'N' Surf**, Fore St, and **Cybersurf @ Newquay**, Broad St. **Post office** East St. **Tourist information** Opposite the bus station on Marcus Hill, T01637-854020 www.newquay.co.uk.

Perranporth

This pretty unremarkable resort town offers plenty of cheap accommodation, surf shops, full facilities and access to a huge beach – complete with excellent beach bar, The **Watering Hole** which has decent pub grub and regular live music.

Sleeping

£ **Perranporth Youth Hostel**, Droskyn Point, T0870-7705994. Overlooks the 3-mile bay. There are also lots of cheap B&Bs in town within a short walk of the beach. See www.perraninfo.co.uk for information. There are a number of caravan parks including **Perranporth Caravan Holidays** on Crow Hill, T01872-572385, offering static caravans with sea views across Perran Sands. It's just a short scramble down to the waves.

St Agnes

This pretty ex-mining village is the home of environmentalists SAS and is the heart of Cornwall's most tight-knit surfing community – welcome to the Badlands!

Sleeping

£££ **Driftwood Spars**, T01872-552428, popular 17th-century beamed Inn and hotel by picturesque Trevaunance Cove with traditional bar serving real ales plus separate restaurant – Spindrift.
££ **The Malthouse**, T01872-553318, an excellent, eclectic, surfer-friendly B&B in a central location in Peterville, the lower part of St Agnes. Recommended.
Camping **Beacon Cottage Farm**, T01872-552347, May-Oct camping and electric hook-ups for vans. **Presingoll Farm**, T01872-552333, Easter-Oct on the main road into St Agnes, offers camping and pitches for vans.

Eating and drinking

The **Tap House**, Peterville is popular and crammed at weekends, even in winter. The food is excellent and on Wed off-season does half-price pizzas.
The **Driftwood Spas** (see above) has a pool table, live band, snug bar plus good restaurant - Spindrift.

Directory

Surf shops **Aggie Surf Shop**, Peterville, T01872 552574, is owned by legendary shaper Chops Lascelles' of **Beachbeat Surfboards**, and is one of the best stocked shops in the area with a full range of boards, wetties and accessories. He uses cutting edge shaping technology combined with years of experience to shape boards for some of Cornwall's top surfers. Steve Bunt's **Best Ever Surfboards**, T01872-553532, are also based in the heart of the Badlands and shape boards for local chargers including Drustan Ward, Jamie Kent and Nicola Bunt.

Porthtowan

Accommodation is fairly limited here.
££ **Pentowan Farm B+B**, Towan Cross, T01209-891611, just out of the village and 2 mins' drive to the beach is an excellent choice. This family run B&B also offers wetsuit drying facility.
££ **The Beach Hotel**, Westcliff, Porthtowan offers basic accommodation with en suite rooms and S/C apartments.

Eating and drinking

The **Blue**, overlooking Porthtowan beach, is a great place to enjoy a post-surf beer, offering unrivalled views across the beach and is popular year-round with locals and visitors alike. As well as Wi-Fi access, regular live music at the weekends, they do a good range of food from nachos and pizzas to excellent chicken and sweet potato salads.

Directory

Pure Blue Surf Academy, T01209 890336, www.purebluewater.com, run by British Longboard Champion and British Junior Team Coach, Dominique Kent, who is also a championship level shortboarder and one of the highest qualified female instructors in the UK. Offers lessons and coaching to beginners, intermediate and advanced surfers, also runs exclusive coaching weekends with beachside B&B. Seasonal beachside self-catering accommodation also available, just 5 mins' walk to the surf. **Sick Lame and Lazy**, at the top end of the village stocks a limited range of hardware and is open year round.

Gwithian

Pretty little village backing onto 3-mile beach. **Supertubes** surf shop at Godrevy is fully-stocked and right on the beach, T01736-758510.

Sleeping

Self Catering ££ **Gwithian Holiday Suites**, www.gwithianholidays.com. Well-priced, sleeping up to 5 with full

kitchen facilities, also available as B&B.
Camping **Gwithian Farm**, Church Town Rd, T01736-753127, Mar-Oct. Relaxed site just 15 mins' walk to beach and opposite local pub The Red River Inn.

Eating and drinking
Godrevy Cafe, National Trust car park, has views over the bay from the upper deck – a great spot for a sundowner beer, home-made cake or full meal.
Sandsifter, Godrevy, nestled in the sand dunes is the excellent bar/restaurant/ music venue offering up some of the best nights around plus a tasty brunch for the morning after the night before.

Sennen

This long, sandy crescent is a popular tourist destination and one of Cornwall's most consistent beaches. It has plenty of room to spread out and a pretty chilled atmosphere as well as beach facilities including changing rooms, wet area and café.

Sleeping
££-£ **Whitesands Lodge**, T01736-871776, www.whitesandslodge.co.uk. Popular with dorm accommodation plus single and double rooms – with or without breakfast – camping facilities plus café/restaurant. Also try ££ **Myrtle Cottage**, in the village, T01736-871698.
Camping **Trevedra Farm Caravan and Camping Site**, T01736-871835, offers pitches for tents and vans.

Eating and drinking
The **Beach Restaurant** by the seafront car park is fresh and modern with beautiful bay views.

Directory
Chapel Idne Surf Shop, T01736-871192, Sennen Cove car park. Hardware, clothing, board hire facility.

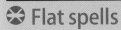

Flat spells

Devon
Cinema **Pendle Stairway Cinema**, High St, Ilfracombe, T01271-863484.

Golf There are a few 9-hole courses in the area: **Ilfracombe & Woolacombe Golf Range**, Woolacombe Rd, T01271-866222, and **Mortehoe & Woolacombe GC** in Mortehoe, T01271-870255. **Saunton GC**, T01271-812436, has 2 top-class 18-hole courses but only for those with handicap certificates. Also **Royal North Devon GC**, on Golf Links Rd, Westward Ho!, T01237-473817.

Sights **Clovelly**, is an outrageously pretty chocolate-box of a village with an outrageously priced car park to match.

Skating **SRP Skate Rock Park**, Pilland Way, Pottington Industrial Estate, Barnstaple, is an indoor park with a street course and mini ramp. You need to be a member (£5) to skate it; a day pass costs the same. Closed Mon. **Bideford Skate Park**, Bank End by the River Torridge, Bideford has rails, banks, fun boxes and a spined mini-ramp.

Cornwall
Cinema **The Regal**, in the centre of Wadebridge, T01208-812791, and **The Plaza**, Lemon St, Truro, T01872-272894, have all the latest releases.

Golf There is a vast number of courses in the area with varying green fees. **Holywell BayGC**, at the fun park, T01637-874354, is a short, cheap links course. There are also a couple of pitch 'n' putt courses overlooking Porth and Tolcarne beaches. **Perranporth GC** links course is snuggled into the dunes at Budnic Hill, T01872- 573701. **Praa Sands GC** Germoe Crossroads, T01736-763445, is a reasonably priced 9-hole course.

ROBERT LUNN

Sights **Eden Project**, signed from the A30, is just north of St Austell, T01726-811911, www.edenproject.com, £14, children £5. This former quarry has been transformed into a magical, giant domed jungle with the aid of a couple of large biomes housing several thousand species of plants and a can-do attitude. In winter the grounds play host to an ice-skating rink, and in summer it hosts a series of bands and musical events.

The tightly packed streets of **St Ives** don't make for the ideal base for a surf trip, but it is an excellent place to visit with surf shops as well as great restaurants and bars. Try the Saltwater Café, on Fish St, T01736-794928, for good seafood at a moderate price. If you're after a bit of culture with a sea view check out **The Tate St Ives**, on Porthmeor Beach, T01736-796226.

The **Minnack Theatre**, T01736-810181, www.minack.com, cut into the cliffs overlooking Porthcurno, is a real experience. It doesn't matter what's on, just wrap up warm and take a picnic.

Skating Practice your lines at the mini-skatepark on the seafront at Crooklets Beach, Bude. **Wooden Waves**, Newquay, T01637-853828, is an indoor park based at Waterworld - helmets required. **Mount Hawke Skate Park**, T01209-890705, is an excellent indoor park - around £2 a session. **Penzance Bowl**, Princess Way Rec, is a big and beautiful concrete bowl.

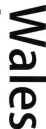

Overview

For centuries the English tried to keep the pesky Welsh over on their side of the border, where they thought they belonged. During the mid- to late-eighth century, huge earth workings – which became known as Offa's Dyke – were constructed over a 150-mile stretch of borderlands, delineating the boundary between these great rivals and providing a defensive wall. While relations are a lot friendlier in the 21st century, this great rivalry seems to have been channeled into the field of sports. This is especially true of the Welsh national obsession, rugby, where a win at the Millennium Stadium will result in a virtual national holiday, and the heroics of players celebrated in song, just as the heroics on the battlefield would have been celebrated in the days of Offa's Dyke.

While Devon and Cornwall have undergone an increasingly large annual influx, there are still parts of the undulating Welsh coastline where pockets of surfers can enjoy isolated waves with a few friends. During the height of summer, the clans gather at Freshwater West - probably the most consistent break on the coastline. "Fresh West is where I started surfing," says Welsh Champion Dan Harris. "Everyone surfs their own areas in Wales but seems to meet up at Fresh West - everyone heads there in the summer. It's pretty consistent, pretty popular. It can get crowded but there's no localism, no hassle." However, during the winter, when huge Atlantic storms heave into the western reaches of the UK, the Welsh coastline lights up. Freshwater West may be a boiling cauldron of whitewater, but along the jagged coastline, gems have come to life and

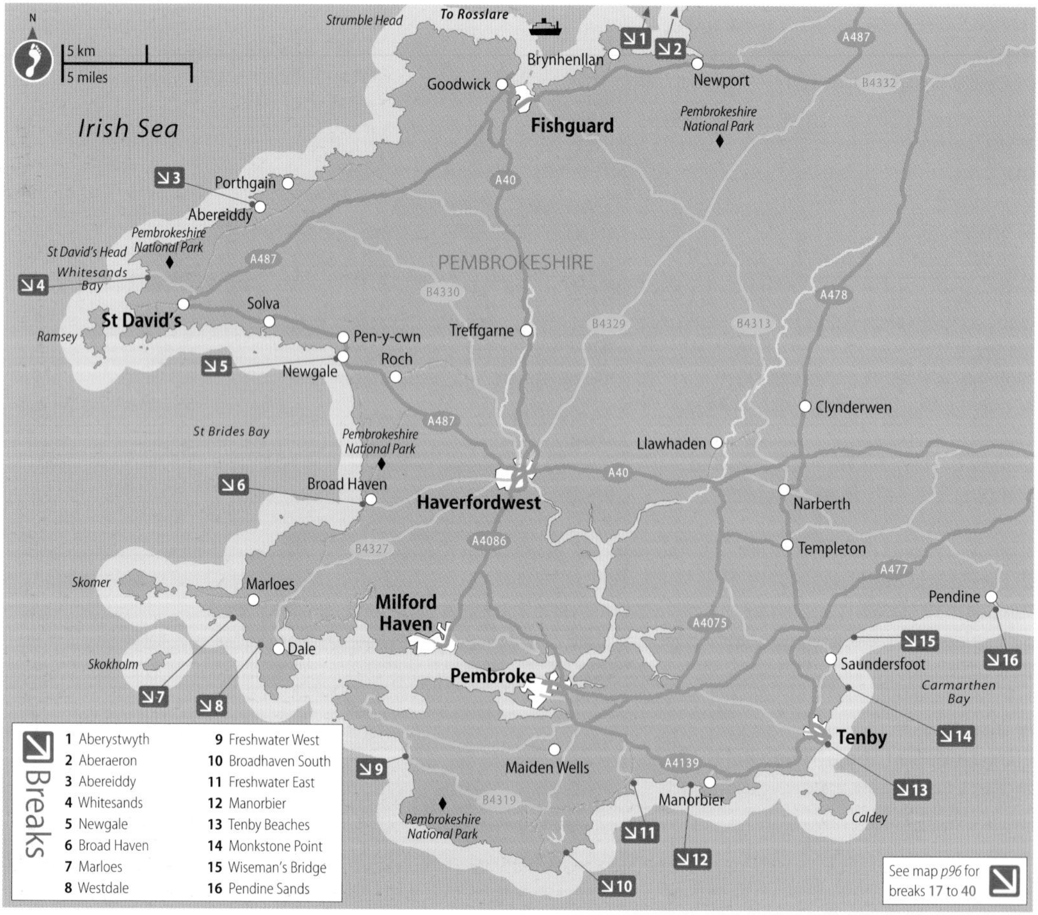

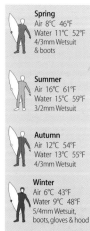

Spring
Air 8°C 46°F
Water 11°C 52°F
4/3mm Wetsuit & boots

Summer
Air 16°C 61°F
Water 15°C 59°F
3/2mm Wetsuit

Autumn
Air 12°C 54°F
Water 13°C 55°F
4/3mm Wetsuit

Winter
Air 6°C 43°F
Water 9°C 48°F
5/4mm Wetsuit, boots, gloves & hood

O'NEILL

THE GILL

9'0" Robert August What I Ride

Shaper: Robert August

9'0" x $22\frac{7}{8}$" x 3"

Built with Surftech's proven TUFLITE construction.

A board that maximizes your fun regardless of conditions. The "What I Ride" utilizes a 60/40 rail configuration which, in combination with a nifty tear drop concave conveniently placed under the nose, greatly enhances your nose riding ability.

Single box with FCs side

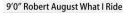

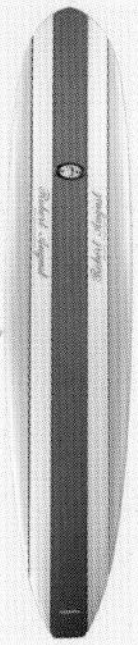

6'2" Brewer Pro Mini

Shaper: Dick Brewer

6'2" x $18\frac{3}{8}$" x $2\frac{1}{8}$"

Built with Surftech's proven TUFLITE construction.

Designed with Hawaiian ripper, Myles Padaca for high performance in waves headhigh and below. Dick & Myles put countless hours into the development of this shape. Semi boxy rails and a flatter deck mixed with subtle concaves for some Brewer magic.

FuturesF4 fins.

Boards by **Surftech**
www.surftech.com info@surftech.com

the clans have scattered to their own, secluded corners of this green land. There are the Gower Reefs, their rocky protrusions offering a challenge to the very best surfers in the land who call these breaks home. Then there are the varied breaks around Porthcawl and Aberavon, from dune-backed beaches to thumping industrial breakwaters. And finally the tight-knit community of Llantwit Major, a breeding ground for some of the country's top waveriders.

"Ahh, but when the big southwesterlies roll through, that's when everyone gets excited. Not only the south coast, but breaks hidden away anywhere along the Welsh coastline can spring into life," says Chris 'Guts' Griffiths, Gower local and former world number five. "It's time to head for your personal favourite. The kinds of places you try to keep quiet and out of the spotlight." Yes, Wales really does seem to have a lot to offer. Luckily for us surfers, the defenses of Offa's Dyke have long since fallen into disrepair, as the breaks of south Wales are such an enticing proposition. It would be a daunting task to have to face the massed ranks of surfers lining the ramparts, boards glistening in the sun, like the shields of a huge army, voices raised to the strains of *Land of My Fathers*. Now that would be taking localism to a whole new level.

Coastline

The Welsh coastline is broken into distinct communities. Around Llantwit Major and Porthcawl a hardened crew surf in brown water, with pollution from the Bristol Channel and the Port Talbot industrial plant up the coast. Here a mixture of reefs and long beaches leads up to the surfing heartland of the Gower Peninsula, which sticks out into the Atlantic Ocean as though thumbing for a ride. This Designated Area of Outstanding Natural Beauty, complete with a series of sandy bays, reefs and points, provides no end of surfing possibilities. Once out of Mumbles the countryside opens up and the water becomes clearer. The wide, open bay at Rhossili has seen surfing for decades and is a spot where many Welsh surfers first learned their trade. To the west, the Pembrokeshire coastline is a rugged and spectacular area with no end of coves, bays and reefs, nestled in pristine countryside – a great place to explore and escape from the crowds.

Local Environment by Surfers Against Sewage

"After heavy rain this region suffers from diffuse pollution around agricultural land and raw sewage being pumped into rivers and the sea. Welsh Water were one of the better water companies, often doing more than the minimum legally required. However, over the last couple of years their pollution record is losing it's shine. Around the River Severn and the larger towns there is industrial pollution." Andy Cummins (www.sas.org.uk)

It would be unusual to experience localism in Wales, but that's not to say that there aren't very tight-knit, competitive line-ups. Crab Island is a very competitive spot, and if you turn up at any of the Gower reefs with a minibus full of friends, don't expect a warm welcome. In general, if you are respectful you should have no problems.

Getting around

Most of the breaks on the Welsh coastline are easily accessible and the road network is excellent. The M4 feeds into south Wales over the Bristol Channel and allows easy access to the surfing regions.

ROGER POWLEY

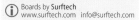

Above: Welsh Champion Dan Harris. **Top left**: Pembroke Peak.

Breaks

REEF BREAK

↘1 Aberystwyth

- **Conditions** Big SW swells, offshore in E to SE winds
- **Hazards/tips** Crowds, backwash at high
- **Sleeping** Aberystwyth ›› *p99*

Harbour Trap is a left and right peak with hollow rights at low tide and long lefts at mid tide. This flat reef works from low to three-quarter tide. **Bath Rocks**, a hollow reef for advanced surfers only, is worth trying at high. It needs to be 6 ft on the south coast to work here and it's always busy when it does. Parking on the promenade. Big student surf club so pretty crowded in water.

LEFT POINT BREAK

↘2 Aberaeron

- **Conditions** Big SW swells, offshore in SE winds
- **Hazards/tips** Crowds, popular with longboarders
- **Sleeping** Aberystwyth ›› *p99*

It was only a matter of time before word got out about the points of west Wales. This is a boulder point that breaks about six times a year producing long, walling left-handers on all tides. These walls are busy when it's on, especially with longboarders. Only really gets to 4-5 ft, worth checking when the south coast is over 6 ft. Head south from Aberystwyth on the coast road for 30 minutes. Out of village but visible from the road.

THE GILL

THE GILL

Above: 2 Aberaeron – classic Welsh point. **Below left:** James Jones – west side.

SLAB REEF BREAK

↘3 Abereiddy

- **Conditions** Big SW swells, offshore in SE to S winds
- **Hazards/tips** Shallow reef
- **Sleeping** St David's ›› *p99*

When Whitesands is too big, check this left-hand reef – it is shallow, wedgy, breaks at mid tide and is really best left to advanced surfers. Found on the south side of bay. Beach car park.

BEACH BREAK

↘4 Whitesands

- **Conditions** Medium NW to SW swells, offshore in SE to E winds
- **Hazards/tips** Crowds, Parking near beach
- **Sleeping** St David's ›› *p99*

Whitesands is a popular and flexible break that works through the tides. There are peaks from sandbanks along the beach and at low tide to the north of the bay is the **Elevator**, a hollow right. There are crowds at the Elevator and surf schools and kayakers on the beach. Picks up less swell than Fresh West.

BEACH BREAK

↘5 Newgale

- **Conditions** Small to medium NW to SW swells, offshore in E winds
- **Hazards/tips** Good for beginners, large uncrowded beach
- **Sleeping** St Brides Bay ›› *p99*

At the northern edge of St Brides Bay, Newgale is part of the Pembrokeshire Coast National Park so enjoys good water quality, and has plenty of room to spread out (almost 2 miles). When small, it is a good spot for beginners. Faces west and so picks up plenty of swell. Beach parking, easy access.

BEACH BREAK

↘6 Broad Haven

- **Conditions** Medium NW to W swells, offshore in SE winds
- **Hazards/tips** Not crowded, flexible beaches. Good for beginners
- **Sleeping** St Brides Bay ›› *p99*

When Newgale gets big, try Broad Haven and Little Haven at the southern end of St Brides Bay. They are good beach breaks and have more protection from the wind. They work on all tides and have plenty of parking.

BEACH BREAK

↘7 Marloes

- **Conditions** Small to medium NW to SW swells, offshore in N winds
- **Hazards/tips** Quiet beach, walk from National Trust car park
- **Sleeping** Marloes » *p100*

A peaky beach break that picks up lots of swell and works up to three-quarters tide. Watch out for scattered rocks on the beach. Walk from car park down track. Car crime can be a problem here.

BEACH BREAK

↘8 Westdale

- **Conditions** Small to medium NW to SW swells, offshore in E wind
- **Hazards/tips** Quiet bay, intermediate and advanced surfers
- **Sleeping** Marloes » *p100*

Westdale is a bay just north of Milford Haven inlet. It has a left at south and right at north. Best from low to three-quarter tide as it is a bit rocky at high tide. Walk from the village car park. There is a surf school based here.

BEACH BREAK

↘9 Freshwater West

- **Conditions** Small to medium NW to SW swells, offshore in E winds
- **Hazards/tips** Rips, rocks, crowds
- **Sleeping** Pembroke » *p100*

Best beach break in Wales with hollow, fast waves like Fistral (see page 79). Picks up the most swell too and is the regular venue for the Welsh Nationals. Works on all states of tide. Although the army used to turn a blind eye to surfers jumping the fence, the firing range beach to the south is out of bounds again. Expect a big fine if you try to sneak in. Beware of rips and rocks in the middle of the bay. The water is clean and Fresh West gets busy when it's on. Beachfront parking.

BEACH BREAK

↘10 Broadhaven South

- **Conditions** Medium to big NW to SW swells, offshore in N winds
- **Hazards/tips** Small take-off zone, crowds
- **Sleeping** Pembroke/Manorbier » *p100*

This southeasterly facing bay needs a solid swell to wrap into the bay. When it does the lines refract off the eastern cliff and meet in the middle producing wedging, hollow lefthanders. This means a tiny take-off zone and pretty heavy peaks best left to advanced surfers. Watch out for rips in a decent swell. National Trust parking overlooks break. Clean water.

BEACH BREAK

↘11 Freshwater East

- **Conditions** Big W swells, offshore in W winds
- **Hazards/tips** Check in westerly storms
- **Sleeping** Pembroke/Manorbier » *p100*

THE GILL

Tasty Welsh wedge.

One of those places that awakens when just the right conditions combine, like those end of the world apocalyptic films where solar and lunar alignments open up a portal to another dimension. A huge westerly swell or storm surf can turn this tranquil, easterly facing bay into a hollow, heavy beach break. Gets crowded when it's on and is best around mid tide. Peaks can throw up excellent lefts and rights with fast barrels. Parking near the beach. Not for beginners when big.

BEACH AND REEF BREAK

↘12 Manorbier

- **Conditions** Medium to big NW to SW swells, offshore in NE winds
- **Hazards/tips** Crowded, easy access, rocks
- **Sleeping** Manorbier/Tenby » *p100*

This bay is home to a fairly average, low tide beach break and a decent high tide right reef. The reef at the western edge of the bay can produce walling right-handers that are always a big draw, but the wave doesn't hold a crowd. Parking is available overlooking the break. Beginners should stick to beach. Swells here are always two thirds the size of Freshwater West.

BEACH BREAK

↘13 Tenby Beaches

- **Conditions** Big W swells, offshore in W winds
- **Hazards/tips** Punchy waves
- **Sleeping** Manorbier/Tenby » *p100*

THE GILL

You don't need a telescope to see the potential of Tenby.

Tenby, with its massive town walls, is the place to head for in huge westerly storms. South beach works on all tides and produces peaks that can be very hollow. Not ideal for beginners. This is a winter break that gets crowded when good. Parking above and at the beach. All amenities in town.

RIGHT POINT BREAK

↘14 Monkstone Point

- **Conditions** Huge W or SW swells, offshore in W winds
- **Hazards/tips** Winter break
- **Sleeping** Manorbier/Tenby » *p100*

This long, walling right-hand point is like a slow Lynmouth (see page 72) so is especially popular with longboarders. Breaking in southwesterly gales from low to mid tide, this sheltered spot is a winter retreat. A long walk out from Saundersfoot harbour car park.

REEF BREAK

↘15 Wiseman's Bridge

- **Conditions** Huge W to SW swells, offshore in NW winds
- **Hazards/tips** Alternative spot in winter storms. Parking at break
- **Sleeping** Manorbier/Tenby » *p100*

Gentle, long, walling right-hand reef that works from mid to high tide. A good alternative to Tenby in huge winter storms.

BEACH BREAK

↘16 Pendine Sands

- **Conditions** Medium to big SW swells, offshore in NE winds
- **Hazards/tips** Good for beginners
- **Sleeping** Manorbier/Tenby » *p100*

This is the nearest break for Carmarthen surfers. Long stretch of sand that produces gentle waves that are good for beginners. The best surf is near the cliff at the west end of the beach in front of the village at mid to high tide. Sheltered in northwesterly winds. Needs decent swell so only check it when Freshwater is 6 ft plus. This flat beach is used for land speed records, so don't expect good banks. Parking on the beach.

POINT BREAK

↘17 Broughton Bay

- **Conditions** Big NW to SW swells, offshore in S winds
- **Hazards/tips** Slow wave, dangerous rips
- **Sleeping** Llangennith » *p100*

Long, walling, left-hand point break that produces fairly slow waves, popular with longboarders. Worth checking when Llangennith is 6 ft. There is a strong rip, so it's not for beginners. Loads of dogfish in the shallows. Walk through caravan site and be courteous to the farmer!

BEACH BREAK

↘18 Llangennith Beach

- **Conditions** Small to medium NW to SW swells, offshore in E winds
- **Hazards/tips** Consistent, popular spot
- **Sleeping** Llangennith » *p100*

One of the hubs of the Welsh surf scene and probably the best known surf spot in the country. The quality doesn't quite live up to its fame as the beach's 3 miles of relatively flat, featureless sand means that sandbank formation is inconsistent. Waves tend to lack punch making it a good place for beginners and relatively safe in small surf. It is, however, a consistent spot that gets very busy, though quieter peaks can usually be found a short walk down the beach. Works on all tides up to about 6 ft when it closes out and channels disappear. Pay parking at Hillend Campsite, which has shop and restaurant. Llangennith is also home to PJ's Surf Shop. When the swell is too big, head south to Rhossili end. This spot is best at mid to high tide and sheltered from strong southerly winds. Parking on top.

BEACH AND REEF BREAK

↘19 Mewslade (Fall Bay and Mewslade Reef)

- **Conditions** Medium W to SW swells, offshore in N winds
- **Hazards/tips** Powerful breaks, not for beginners
- **Sleeping** Llangennith/Port Eynon » *p100*

Fall Bay Wedge is a beach break that works at high tide for spongers, while **Mewslade Reef**, in the middle of the bay, is a sucky, hollow, left reef for experts only. It's a low tide break best in a northerly wind. Mewslade beach is best from low to mid tide and has powerful, semi close-outs. Park at the farmyard car park. Signed from road.

REEF BREAK

↘20 Pete's Reef

- **Conditions** Small to medium W to SW swells, offshore in N winds
- **Hazards/tips** Very crowded, experts only
- **Sleeping** Port Eynon » *p100*

Low tide hollow peak breaking on shallow limestone reef. Gets very crowded when it's on and holds up to 5 ft. Popular with good local surfers. Breaks like a small Porthleven (see page 83). Long walk. Parking difficult.

LEFT REEF BREAK

↘21 Boiler Left

- **Conditions** Medium NW to SW swells, offshore in N winds
- **Hazards/tips** Long walk and parking difficult
- **Sleeping** Port Eynon » *p100*

Low tide, hollow, medium-length left breaking on limestone reef with submerged ship's boiler at the end. Has a big rip and works up to 6-8 ft. Small, sucking take-off zone.

THE GILL

Evening session, Gower.

RIGHT REEF BREAK

↘22 Sumpters

- **Conditions** Medium to big NW to SW swells, offshore in NE wind
- **Hazards/tips** Popular wave with deep channel for paddle out
- **Sleeping** Port Eynon » *p100*

Quality right and another peak nearby. Easier access. Best from low to mid tide producing long, walling rights with the occasional barrel. Not too shallow. Popular wave that holds swells up to 8 ft. Paddle out in deep channel after walking along sewer pipe.

RIGHT POINT BREAK

↘23 Port Eynon Point

- **Conditions** Medium to big NW to SW swells, offshore in N winds
- **Hazards/tips** Access is a walk south from Port Eynon beach car park
- **Sleeping** Port Eynon » *p100*

Powerful, sucky, low tide point break which peels in front of rock ledges. Popular spot that breaks consistently. Quality wave that is best left to the experts.

BEACH BREAK

↘24 Horton Beach

- **Conditions** Medium to big NW to SW swells, offshore in N wind
- **Hazards/tips** Parking at the beach
- **Sleeping** Port Eynon » *p100*

Sheltered beach that needs a good swell to work, but produces dumpy, hollow waves that can close out at high. Works on all tides but is better at low to mid. An alternative to crowded Langland. Good spot for intermediates and a safe beach for beginners. Also popular with kitesurfers and windsurfers.

BEACH BREAK

↘25 Oxwich Bay/Point

- **Conditions** W to SW storm swells, offshore in SW winds
- **Hazards/tips** Safe beach, scenic, Oxwich Bay Hotel for refreshments at a price
- **Sleeping** Oxwich » *p101*

A hollow beach break that's best at high tide. Gets busy when breaking as it can be the only spot in storms. Breaks up to 6 ft, but is usually about 3 ft.

BEACH BREAK

26 Threecliff Bay

Conditions Medium W to SW swell, offshore in NW winds
Hazards/tips Dangerous rips
Sleeping Oxwich » p101

This is a mid to high tide beach break with some good sandbanks, producing lefts and rights. It's the most scenic bay on the Gower and features on many postcards. Park near Penmaen post office, on South Gower Road, and make the long walk to the beach. Usually uncrowded so an alternative to Langland.

THE GILL

REEF BREAK

27 Hunts Bay

Conditions Medium NW to SW swell, offshore in N wind
Hazards/tips Difficult access
Sleeping Oxwich/Mumbles » p101

A right-hand reef where there is difficult access in and out of the water due to rocks. It does produce walling rights, but often with sections. Access from Southgate, a long walk along cliffs. Quiet break.

BEACH BREAK

28 Caswell Bay

Conditions Small to medium NW to SW swells, offshore in N winds
Hazards/tips Popular spot near Mumbles
Sleeping Mumbles » p101

Smallish bay popular with tourists and beginners with a beachfront car park. Works from mid to high tide. Produces short peaky waves that can get crowded.

REEF/BEACH/POINT BREAK

29 Langland Bay (Langland Point/Langland)

Conditions All NW to SW swells, offshore in N winds
Hazards/tips Many spots for surfers of all abilities, gets crowded
Sleeping Mumbles » p101

The **Outside Point** is a reef, but not dangerous. It works at low tide only, best from 2-8 ft, and is not too challenging. A popular spot with longboarders and doesn't get too crowded. The **Inside Point** and **Shit Pipe (Huttons)** is a mid tide reef break with long, walling right-handers. Again a popular longboard wave, nicknamed the 'Malibu of the Gower'. It has a friendly line-up, is sheltered from strong westerly winds but can be rocky and shallow. **Langland Shorebreak** is a virtual close-out, popular with shortboarders on a big swell. It's really a one manoeuvre wave that works at high tide only. Crowded with locals in solid swells and generally ridden in stormy conditions.

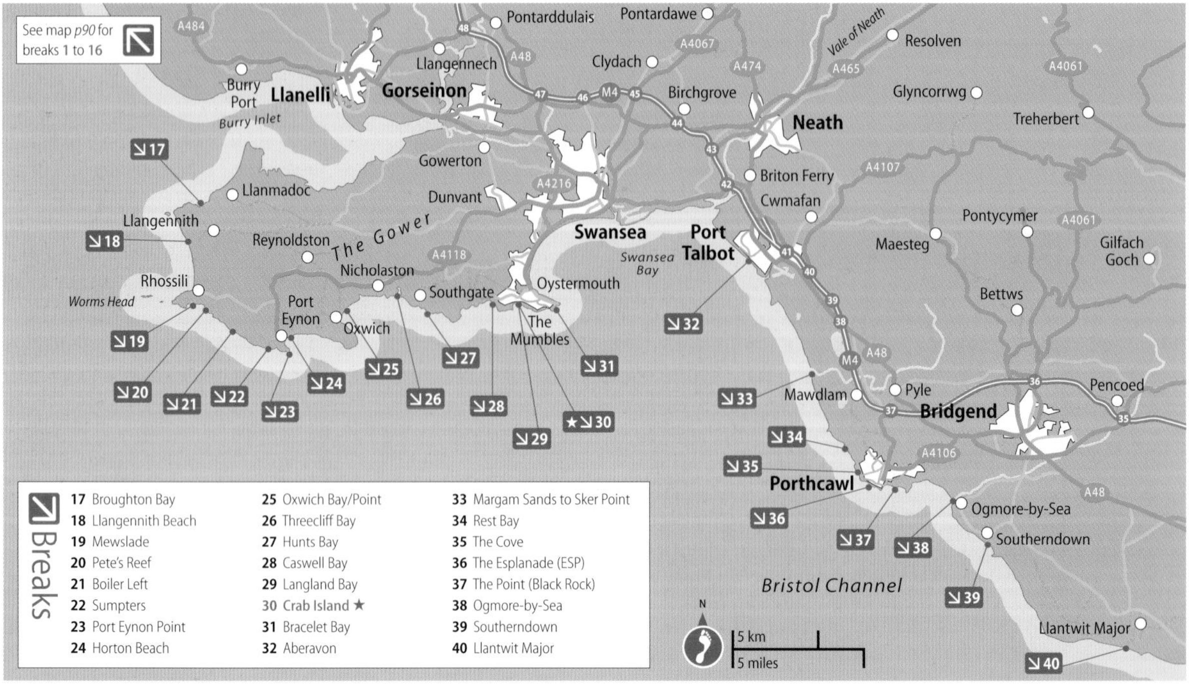

Langland Reef (Kevs) breaks at mid tide, a crowded peak with a mixture of boards and abilities. It's a very busy, short left and long right that is shallow on the peak. **Middle of the Bay (MOTB)** is a left that breaks into strong rip, opposite **The Reef**. This sandbank breaks from low to half tide, producing lefts that can be hollow. Gets very crowded and can be ridden in all winds as it is quite sheltered. **Rotherslade Left** is further out than MOTB, producing walling lefts with sections, over a low tide sandbank. Works best in medium swells when it can be crowded. The **Sandbar** is a low tide, very shallow reef. It has a dangerous, dropping take-off and is best left to advanced surfers only. "This is where Carwyn used to practice for Pipeline," explains Mumbles local The Gill. The peak splits into a left and right, the left is the most hollow. It's a heavy wave where you don't want to get caught inside as it unloads onto the shallow reef. Breaks up to 10 ft.

Gas Chambers is a cocktail of sand, rock and air, for boogie boarders and the brave. At mid tide, **Inside Crab** produces left-hand barrels up to 5 ft. The **Shallow Peak** is a shallow, rocky reef that works up to 5 ft. It produces lefts and rights, sucky all the way.

Below: 29 Langland Bay crowds.
Bottom: 30 Tom Moran, Crab Island.
Opposite page: The Gower.

THE GILL

THE GILL

RIGHT REEF BREAK

↘30 Crab Island

- **Swell** SW
- **Wind** N
- **Tide** When Crab Island appears out of the water towards low tide
- **Size** 2-10 ft
- **Length** 50-100 m
- **Bottom** Rocks
- **Ability level** Intermediate to advanced
- **Best months** Sep-Apr
- **Board** Round to pintail performance thruster
- **Access** Off the rocks
- **Hazards/tips** Rocks on take-off
- **Sleeping** Mumbles » *p101*

Crab Island is Welsh surfing gold. A quality reef with a competitive line-up, offering excellent rights to some of the country's top surfers. This is a long, powerful wave which peels along the trailing edge of a small offshore island – hence the name. The peak is an elevator drop, the nearby rocks always in the back of the mind. It then walls up into a fast section, with barrels opening up in the right conditions. There is a strong rip pushing away from the peak, which can become a test of stamina in a cranking swells.

Sitting not far from the urban centres of Swansea, Port Talbot and Porthcawl, you'd expect the regions surfers to be all over this wave, but a strong pecking order helps keep everything civilised. The long established and respected surf community includes the likes of Guts Griffiths, Frenchie, Matt Stephens, Swinno, Tim Page and The Gill. If you are going to go and surf Crab, it's best to be respectful and try not to snag too many waves.

If you like Crab Island, try ***Thurso East*** *in Scotland (see page 41) or* ***Easkey Right*** *in Ireland (see page 137).*

THE GILL

THE GILL

Above: 12x Welsh Champion Chris Griffiths, Pembrokeshire. **Left**: Crab Island.

RIGHT REEF BREAK

↘31 Bracelet Bay

- **Conditions** Medium to big W to SW swells, offshore in NW winds
- **Hazards/tips** Strong rips
- **Sleeping** Mumbles » *p101*

Nestled under the coastguard station is this low to mid tide right-hand reef. It produces walling rights with sections, breaking up to 8 ft. Has strong rips. Last of the Gower breaks.

BREAKWATER BREAK

↘32 Aberavon

- **Conditions** All NW to SW swells, offshore in E winds
- **Hazards/tips** Dirty water, heavy when big, access off the jetty when big
- **Sleeping** Porthcawl » *p101*

One of the regions classic spots, an A frame with a short right and long left, slightly spoiled by changes to the sea defence in the corner. It's difficult to get back in at high tide when it's big. This sandbar is a real industrial surf spot, breaking next to steelworks and deepwater docks. Very unscenic and crowded.

BEACH BREAK

↘33 Margam Sands to Sker Point

- **Conditions** Small to medium NW to SW swells, offshore in E winds
- **Hazards/tips** Dune backed beach
- **Sleeping** Porthcawl » *p101*

Best at mid to high tide, this long stretch of beach break peaks are hollower at the Sker end. Park at Kenfig Pools, a long walk through the dunes. Quiet spot with better waves towards the Sker end. Local surf schools so safe for supervised beginners.

BEACH BREAK

↘34 Rest Bay

- **Conditions** Small to medium NW to SW swells, offshore in E winds
- **Hazards/tips** Parking in beach car park, strong parallel rips
- **Sleeping** Porthcawl » *p101*

This popular beach produces great peaks, with some excellent waves, which many consider to be some of the best in the area. Works best from low to three-quarter tide on the push. Can have lefts and rights up and down this long beach. The southern peaks are the most popular.

BEACH BREAK

↘35 The Cove

- **Conditions** Small to medium NW to SW swells, offshore in E winds
- **Hazards/tips** Heavy wave with rips
- **Sleeping** Porthcawl » *p101*

This spot is accessible at low tide from Rest Bay. It has heavy peaks, with lefts and rights breaking on a sand bottom. Strong rips.

REEF BREAK

↘36 The Esplanade (ESP)

- **Conditions** Medium NW to SW swells, offshore in NE winds
- **Hazards/tips** Crowds, shallow reef
- **Sleeping** Porthcawl » *p101*

This is a shallow, hollow and fast left reef where the locals dominate. Park on seafront overlooking break. Only works at high tide.

REEF POINT BREAK

↘37 The Point (Black Rock)

- **Conditions** Medium to big NW to SW swells, offshore in N winds
- **Hazards/tips** Drive through caravan park to front
- **Sleeping** Porthcawl » *p101*

This is a high tide right-hand reef point that breaks over knobbly rocks. After a shallow take-off the wave is fast and sucky before becoming a long wall. This is a crowded spot best left to Porthcawl locals and experts.

RIVERMOUTH BREAK

↘38 Ogmore-by-Sea

- **Conditions** Medium NW to SW swells, offshore in E winds
- **Hazards/tips** Can be excellent, watch out for rips
- **Sleeping** Porthcawl » *p101*

A fickle spot that can be a classic, right-hand rivermouth if the banks are right. Best at high tide, the spot can be quite busy, but watch out for rips out from river. Park overlooking break. Locals will be on it when it's good.

BEACH BREAK

↘39 Southerndown

- **Conditions** Small to medium NW to SW swells, offshore in E winds
- **Hazards/tips** Consistent spot
- **Sleeping** Porthcawl » *p101*

A popular break with Bridgend/Cardiff surfers. The beach peaks can produce good, walling waves, suitable for all surfers. A consistent spot that picks up a lot of swell, so gets quite busy. Similar to Llangennith (see page 95).

SELECTION OF REEF BREAKS

↘40 Llantwit Major

- **Conditions** All W swells, offshore in a N wind
- **Hazards/tips** Good quality spot, crowds, pollution
- **Sleeping** Porthcawl » *p101*

Large triangular boulder reef on the Glamorgan coast producing a number of waves at different states of tide. The peak works at low tide in small to medium swells. Perfect right peels off the edge of the reef at low to mid tide and can be classic on its day. At mid to high tide there are hollow peaks on the boulders near the car park. Crowded spot that breaks in swells of 3-8 ft. Best on incoming tides, but beware of rips. Sign-posted to beach. Home of Nathan Phillips, Mark Vaughan and the Bright brothers.

Practicalities

Aberystwyth

Welsh nationalism and language is alive and kicking in this Victorian resort town appropriated by students during term time.

Sleeping

££ **Yr Hafod**, South Marine Terr, just back from the seafront, T01970-617579.
£ **Borth Youth Hostel**, 5 miles north in the village of Borth overlooking the bay, T01970-871827, open all year.
Camping You can camp next to the river at **Aberystwyth Holiday Village**, Penparcau Rd, T01970-624211, Mar-Oct. Also statics. **Ocean View Caravan Park**, T01970-828425, overlooks North Bay and is open Mar-Oct. Heading about 5 miles north, **Borth** also has a couple of camping options: **Swn-y-Mor Holiday Park**, off the B4345, T01970-871233, Apr-Oct. **Brynrodyn Caravan and Leisure Park** in Upper Borth, T01970-871472, Jan-Oct. Both have statics available.

Eating and drinking

As a student town there are plenty of cheap places to grab a bite to eat.
The **Treehouse**, on Baker St, combines an organic shop with a lunchtime café where you can get a tasty bowl of soup and a roll for about £3.50 or something more filling for about £6. Gets busy but worth the wait. **Gannets Bistro**, on St James Sq, is more expensive but a relaxed place serving good home cooking using local fish and meat – the steak is very good. In terms of cafés, the **Dolphin**, on Great Darkgate, is a winner for fish and chips. The **Blue Creek Café**, on Princess St, serves up good veggie and more 'exotic' café food. There is no shortage of pubs here. **Rummers** with its beer garden next to the river on Bridge St, is a popular choice.

Directory

Surf Shops **Stormriders**, Alexandra Rd, T01970-626363, near the train station, is well stocked with hardware and kit. **Internet** Pricey connection at **The Biognosis**, Pier St or head to the library just off Corporation St. **Banks** Great Darkgate St (main street). **Post office** Great Darkgate St. **Tourist information** Terrace Rd, running up towards North Beach, open year round.

St David's

What seems like a tiny village is actually a city (it has a cathedral) and provides easy access to Whitesands Bay.

Sleeping

££ **Glan-Y-Mor**, T01437 721788, have accommodation for surfers.
£ **St David's Youth Hostel**, near the beach, T01473-721831, open Easter-Oct.
Camping There are plenty of campsites in the area including, to the south, **Caerfai Farm**, T01437-720548, with an organic shop, open May-Sep, and the large **Caerfai Bay Caravan and Tent Park**, Caerfai Rd, T01437-720274, open Mar-Nov, with statics to rent. Handier for Whitesands however is **Lleithyr Farm Caravan & Tent Park**, T01437-720245, open Easter-Oct.

Directory

Shapers **Simon Noble Surfboards (SNS)** are based at Trehenlliew Farm, St David's, T07866-737935. **Ma Simes Surf Hut**, can be found on the Hight Street, T01437-720433.

St Brides Bay

At the heart of the **Pemrokeshire Coast National Park**, stretching from Cardigan to Amroth, this pretty bay is a major draw.

THE GILL

Sleeping
£ **Penycwm Youth Hostel**, T0870-7705988, in Penycwm, has excellent facilities and very popular, so best to book ahead.
£ **Broad Haven Youth Hostel**, T0870-7705728, provides an affordable place to stay in the village.

Marloes

Sleeping
££ **Clockhouse B&B**, T01646-636527, has a wetsuit drying area.
££ **Foxdale Guesthouse**, opposite the church on Glebe Lane, T01646-636243, also offers a camping area.
£ **Marloes Sands YHA Hostel**, T0870 7705958, has easy access to the beach.

Pembroke

This market town has plenty of amenities centred around Main St, making it a good base, with easy access to the breaks on the south coast as well as Fresh West.

Sleeping
££ **The Old Rectory**, Cosheston, T01646-684960.
££ **High Noon Guest House**, on Lower Lamphey Rd, T01646-683736.
Camping Year round camping south of Pembroke at **St Petrox Caravaning and Camping**, near St Petrox village.

Eating and drinking
You'll find unexceptional food at moderate prices here. Check out **Henry's**, on Westgate Hill and **Brown's**, on Main St for basic food for around a fiver. For good fish and chips try **Rowlies** on Main St.

Directory
Surf shops **Waves 'N' Wheels**, Commons Rd, T01646-622066; **The Edge**, on Main St South, T01646-686886. In Maiden Wells is **Outer Reef**. **Banks** ATMs on the western end of Main St. **Post office** Main St. **Tourist information** Pembroke Visitors' Centre, Commons Rd, T01646-622388.

Manorbier/Tenby

Manorbier is a pretty village with a well-known surf break. The Norman castle is in a pretty good state of repair and overlooks the sea.

Sleeping
Manorbier Youth Hostel, T070 7705954, open Mar-Oct, also offer camping facilities.

Directory
Surf shops Heading east on the A4139 are **The Edge**, on St George St, T01843-842368, and **Underground**, on Church St, T01834-844234.

Llangennith

Llangennith, at the western edge of the stunning Gower Peninsula, sits just inland from Rhossili Bay, a huge flat beach that opens out in front of a vast area of sand dunes. This area has been at the forefront of the British surf scene since the very early days and is now home to the Welsh Surfing Federation Surf School.

Sleeping
££ **Western House**, just down the road from the King's Head pub, T01792-386620, run by a surfing family.
££ **Bremmel Cottage**, T01792-386308, is also surf friendly.
Camping There are plenty of campsites. Most popular is **Hillend Camping Site**, overlooking the beach and housing the newly opened Eddy's Restaurant. Another

THE GILL

Left: Boyos. **Above**: Gower gold.

option is **Kennexstone Camping and Touring Park**, T01792-386790, open Apr-30 Sep. Heading towards Broughton Bay is **Broughton Farm Caravan Park**, T01792-386213, open Apr-Oct with statics to hire. They also run the **Cross**, a year-round self-catering cottage sleeping up to 8 people from £350 per week, within walking distance of the King's Head. South at Rhossili is the reasonably priced **Pitton Cross Caravan & Camping**, T01792-390593, open Apr-Oct.

Eating and drinking
The **King's Head** is the place for an al fresco pint and some pub grub. **Eddy's** at Hillend Camping Site (see above) is also a good place to grab a cheap bite to eat.

Directory
Surf shops **PJ's Surf Shop**, opposite the King's Head, T01792-386669, has been up and running since 1978 and sells and hires out surf equipment. PJ (Pete Jones) is a dedicated surfer and is a former Welsh, British and European Champion. **Surf schools** **Welsh Surfing Federation**, based at Hillend Campsite, T01792-386426, www.wsfsurfschool.co.uk, has given lessons since 1981.

Port Eynon

Sleeping
On the A4118 from Swansea, Port Eynon has a couple of **camping** options: **Bank Farm Leisure Park**, T01792-390228, overlooks the Bay and is within walking distance of Horton. **Carreglwyd Camping & Caravan**, T01792-390795, is open Apr-Oct. **Port**

Eynon Youth Hostel, T0870 7705998, is right on the beachfront and open Apr-Oct.

Oxwich

Sleeping

Oxwich Bay is a nature reserve as well as a popular surf beach and has a couple of **camping** options: the small **Bay Holme Caravan Site**, T01792-401051, with statics to hire, and **Oxwich Bay Camping Park**, T01792-390777, open Apr-Sep. Further east, overlooking the next beach, is **Three Cliffs Bay Caravan and Camping Park**, T01792-371218, open Mar-Oct, who also run a self-catering cottage.

Mumbles

Mumbles is the general term given to the village of Oystermouth. The name actually came about as a corruption of '*mamelles*' or breasts – the word French sailors used to describe the 2 offshore islands nearby.

Sleeping

££ **Langland Cove Guest House**, Rotherslade Rd, T01792-366003. Within walking distance and overlooking Langland Bay, the B&B is run by legendary shaper and surf photographer The Gill who keeps the breakfasts and stories flowing.

Eating and drinking

There are some good eating options in Mumbles, as recommeded by The Gill. **CJ's** on Mumbles Rd, is a lively bar/restaurant where you can eat for about £5-10. The **Village Inn** further along the road mixes good pub grub with bad karaoke. **Castellamare** pizzeria, overlooking Bracelet Bay, is a great place to spend an evening. The **Antelope**, on Mumbles Rd, is a busy pub with a beer garden and is just one of the places Welsh poet Dylan Thomas is said to have frequented. The **Rock and Fountain**, at the top end of Newton Rd, is a locals' pub with live music. **Bentley's Night Club**, is popular with local surfers, complete with sticky carpet and cut-glass mirror ball.

Flat spells

Climbing Pembrokeshire has some great climbing opportunities. Contact **TYF Adventure**, T01437-721611, www.tyf.com.

Golf There are loads of courses in Wales. A few to get you started include **Bryn-y-Mor**, Aberystwyth, T01970-615104 and the 9-hole **St David's City GC**, Whitesands Bay, Pembroke, T01437-721751. Heading south **South Pembrokeshire GC**, Military Rd overlooking the Pembroke Dock, T01646-621453. In Tenby **Trefloyne GC** in Trefloyne Park off the A4139, T01834-842165 is the best bet. Around the Gower try **Langland Bay GC** off the B4593, T01792-361721, or **Grove GC**, off the A4229 at South Cornelly, near Porthcawl, T01656-788771.

Riding **Pilton Moor Trekking**, Pitton Cross, Rhossili, T01792-390554, for all abilities.

Sights Pembroke castle was originally built in 1093 in wood before being upgraded to stone in 1204. The 25-tonne **Arthur's Stone**, Reynoldston on the Gower, marks a Neolithic burial mound and gives awesome views right across the peninsula.

Skating **New Quay**, just south of Aberaeron, has a free park on Church Rd with mini ramp, fun box etc. Swansea's Cwmdu Industrial Estate on Camarthen Rd is home to **Swansea Skate Park**, T01792-578478. **Jennings Building**, Porthcawl Harbour, T01656-785215, has a park with street course and ¼ pipe etc. Open 1800-2100 weekday, 1000-2100 weekends from £2 a session.

Walking Pembrokeshire's coastline is beautiful, dramatic and much of it has been designated national parkland. Walking just some of the 300-km marked coastal path is a great way to see the true potential of this area and may reveal the odd secret spot.

Directory

Surf shops **Big Drop**, T01792-368861, is on Tivoli Walk. **Guts Surfboards**, T07779 583445, is run by surfer/shaper Chris 'Guts' Griffiths, former British and European champion and world No 5 longboarder. **JP Surfboards**, Woodville Rd, Mumbles, T01792-361621. John Purton has been shaping boards since he was 13 and now shapes for some of the UK's top surfers. **Post office** Mumbles Rd. **Tourist information** Dunn Lane, summer opening only.

Porthcawl

An unspectacular seaside resort town with a couple of camping options and plenty of amusement arcades.

Sleeping

Camping **Happy Valley Caravan Park**, off the main A4106, T01656-782144, is open Apr-Sep and has a bar and café on site.

Directory

Surf shops **Black Rock** and **Porthcawl Marine** are both on New Rd. Just inland at Bridgend's South Cornelly Industrial Estate is **Freelap Custom Surfboards**, T01656-744691, www.oddsurfboards.com, who put out boards under the **ODD** logo. Freelap is run by glasser Albert Harris who has been involved in the surf industry since the 1970s. ODD's Paul Gill has been shaping since 1977 and has made boards for chargers such as Wales's Isaac Kibblewhite and legends such as Mickey 'Da Cat' Dora.

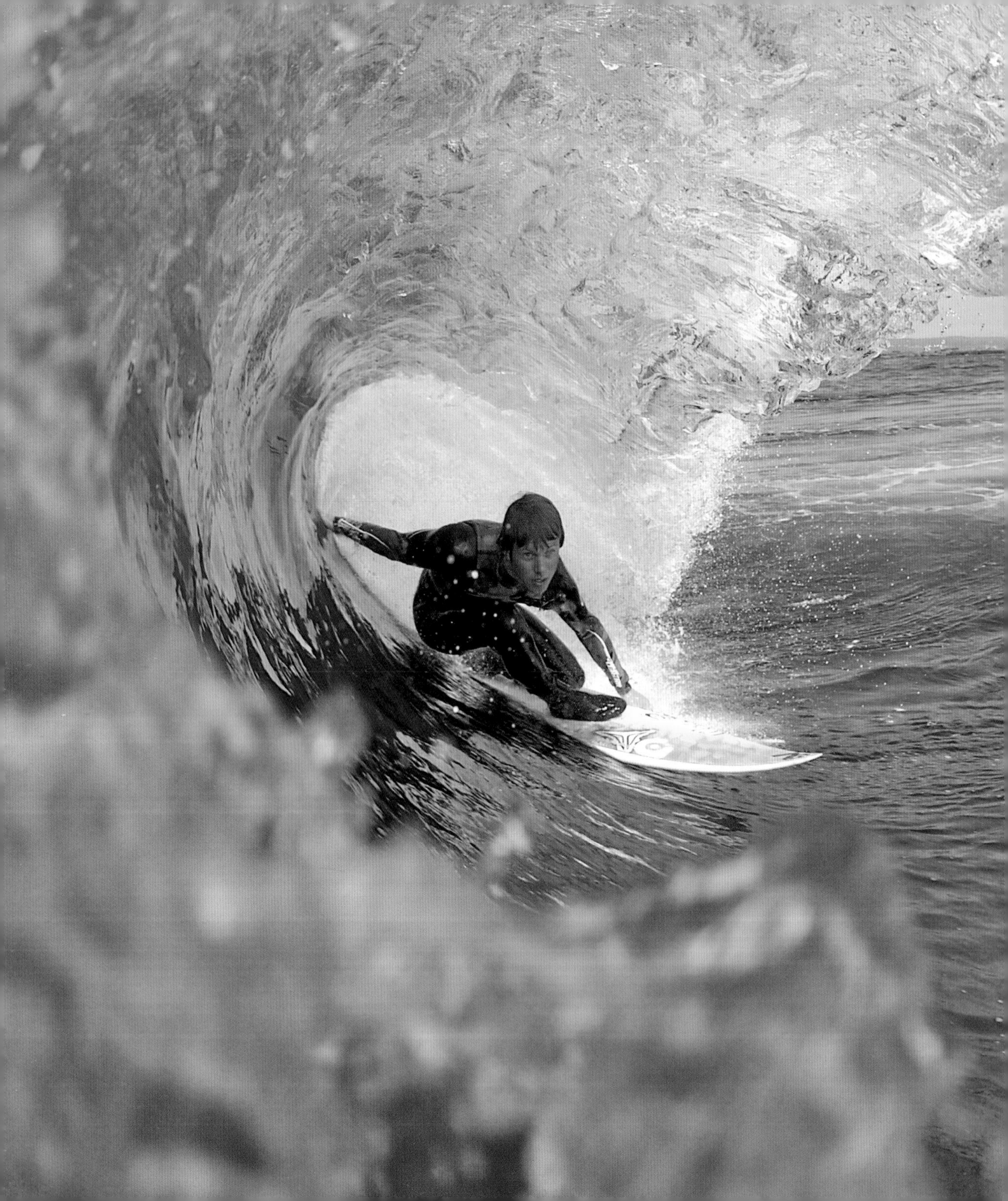

Ireland

Fergal Smith, Bumbaloids.

MICKEY SMITH

Star breaks

1. **Bundoran** Ireland's most famous wave, the Peak, is still under threat, despite the positive influence surfing has on the local economy ▸▸ *p124*.
2. **Pampa Point** Awesome ▸▸ *p124*.
3. **Easkey** Beautiful right-hand reef, with long walls and a mirror-image left looking on ▸▸ *p131*.
4. **Crab Island** Ireland's answer to Pipeline, like playfighting with Mike Tyson – don't overstep the mark ▸▸ *p133*.
5. **Inch Reef** Fickle wave that break for miles – literally! ▸▸ *p143*.

ANDY HILL/TROGGS

Northern Ireland is blessed with some excellent, hollow Hossegor-style beachbreaks.

Surfing in Ireland has undergone a shift of seismic proportions since the end of the 1980s. Just as the flat limestone has tilted and shifted over the millennia to form the almost perfect angling reefs of the west coast, so the resident surfing population has expanded and grown, reclaiming what is theirs while redefining the boundaries of just what is surfable. Back in the mid nineties Aussie charger Joel Fitzgerald showed the world the awesome waves of PMPA Point in the seminal surf film Litmus. Today it is homegrown talent pushing back the boundaries and showing the world just how it is done. Irish surfers such as Fergal Smith adorn the covers of UK surf media, embedded so deeply in a series of saline shells it is as if only a winkle picker could coax them out, while images of local big wave chargers like John McCarthy have featured throughout the US surf magazines, towing into monster waves at Aileen's. The scene has exploded, matured and evolved with Irish surfers flocking the length and breadth of the west, south and north coast in search of waves. But although the economy has boomed, along with the numbers in the line-up, the very sensory experience that has brought surfers to the Emerald Isle remains unchanged. The spectrum of greens refracted as the shadow of a solitary cloud glides across a lowland pasture and drifts up onto fractured limestone of the Burren, the hedgerows painted brilliant red with fuchsias and wild flowers. The aroma of the warm peat fire, the cool iron tinged taste of the black stuff and the background sound of live music wafting over the bar as you recount your best waves of the day. The clover is still the national emblem of Ireland. Its three leaves standing for the holiest of trinities – great surf, great people and great *craic*. Once you've experienced it, it's easy to get hooked.

Surfing Ireland

THE GILL

Northwest Ireland has huge potential for exploration.

✓ Pros	✗ Cons
Picks up loads of swell.	Famous breaks are crowded.
Undulating coastline with loads of potential for surf in all conditions.	Can be inconsistent.
Excellent quality reefs.	Can be cold and wet, especially in winter and spring.
Still plenty of breaks off the beaten track.	Journeys between breaks time-consuming.
Great pubs.	Relatively expensive.
Friendly locals.	
Beautiful Celtic countryside.	
Lots to do on flat days.	

"I think Ireland has waves just as good if not better than anywhere else in Europe. The surf industry and surf awareness has grown in tandem with the big increase in the number of Irish people taking to the water. In terms of surfing standard we are catching up fast with the UK and the rest of the continent. Nicole Morgan and Easkey Britton both Donegal girls have won the last two British Pro (BPSA) titles. At present along with the girls, Fergal Smith, Cain Kilcullan and Mikey Morgan are all surfing as European professionals. 10 years ago that would have been unimaginable. The standard is going up here every year. I think the current and future Irish pros are good enough to give the EPSA a go over the next few years. From there the natural progression would be a follow on to the WQS and beyond. I'd love to see an Irish surfer emerge and do for Ireland what Russ Winter did for British surfing." Irish charger Richie Fitzgerald.

There are many variables and factors that one takes into account when looking at a destination for a surf trip. For different people they carry a different weighting – to one, solitude may rank highly, to another, the social element may be king.
If we were clinical we might sit down and look at Ireland like this: (Low pressures x fetch = swell) ÷ coastal geography = wave quality + (countryside x craic) – drizzle = Ireland.
But surfing in Ireland is not about maths or physics. It's about quality of experience, sights, sounds, tastes and smells. It's experiential not theoretical. Yes this 85,000-sq km island sits directly in the path of swells generated in the North Atlantic storm track, yes these swells break on a quality coastal terrain that ranges from flat limestone reef, to granite boulder points to huge sandy bays. But surfing in Ireland is about more than the sum of all the parts. There is a certain Y factor that also combines with the great scenery, the great people and the great craic. Even the drizzle can't dampen spirits on a trip to the Emerald Isle. Surfing began here back in the 1960s with a surfer called Kevin Cavey, and grew steadily until the surf booms of the 1980s and 1990s. Today, the Irish Surfing Association say there are 5,000 Irish surfers. "There are more people in the water," says Graham Collins, "and that is pushing people to explore more of the coastline. There are so many waves being surfed now that weren't really known a few years ago." Knowledge and access feed growth, and with over 50% of the population living within 10 km of the coast, it's easy to see why these numbers are predicted to carry on rising. The profile of Irish surfing has also risen on the world stage, helped by big wave exploits at breaks like Aileen's near Lahinch and by the next generation of rippers like Cain Kilcullen. Yes, when you do the sums, it all seems to add up. The cool, clear waters of the Irish coastline is a great place to be a surfer and the perfect destination for that autumn surf trip.

Climate

Green. That's one word that describes Ireland. As an island, the climate is very much 'maritime', and at this latitude, it is also 'temperate'. The southwesterly trade winds mean that the west coast receives somewhere between 1,000 to 1,250 mm rain per year, with some form of precipitation on up to 225 days per year in certain locations. However, unlike many countries, the hourly rainfall amounts are generally low. The south and east coasts are the sunniest and the wave-rich west is the wettest. Due to the influence of the Gulf Stream, coastal temperatures rarely tend to drop below freezing in the winter, and generally do not rise above 20 degrees in the summer months. Come here in the summer and you'll be amazed by how warm and mild it can be, with temperatures demanding shorts and T-shirts. In the golden sun the heather takes on a wonderful purple hue and hidden flowers are suddenly revealed. But within 10 minutes the whole scene can be turned on its head. When the wind and rain kick in, Ireland can be transformed into shades of grey – bleak and barren under a blanket of cloud. In the summer the days are long, but surf trips can still be either blessed with glass or cursed with gales. One thing you can guarantee is that on an evening, beside the peat-burning fire, there is always enough music, stories and drink to go round.

Best seasons to go

Summer in Ireland means taking a bit of a gamble. Some years will be blessed with constant swells, others will not. At this time of year Ireland becomes a very popular tourist destination and holidaymakers from all over the world will be sharing the narrow roads, pushing journey times and the price of B&Bs up. The plus side of this time of year is that you stand a good chance of catching decent sunshine (in between showers of course – July particularly can have high levels of rainfall). Air temperatures average around 16°C, with water temperatures lurking just below. To optimize the chance of a wave, head for the more exposed coastlines, such as the northwest.

Autumn is the most glorious time of year to be in Ireland. Low pressure systems leaving the eastern seaboard of North America track through the north Atlantic past Iceland sending long distance, north-westerly ground swell into the famous reefs and points. Continuing to track past Iceland, northerly swell is pushed down into the breaks around Northern Ireland. A lower trajectory will result in westerly swells, lighting up spots such as Inch Reef. While the main breaks remain pretty busy at peak times, it is possible to score good uncrowded, clean waves by exploring off the beaten track. Prices for accommodation drop and the swells increase, coaxing the reefs and points out of hibernation. The air cools to around 12°C and water temperatures begin to creep down signaling the transition from 3/2s to 4/3s.

In winter it can be bleak but there will be a huge amount of swell hitting the coast. This is the time to head for the sheltered coastlines and breaks. Although the days will be short, the line-ups will be quiet and some of the sleeping beauties will awaken. They will also be cold, so pack your 5/4/3, boots and gloves. The warming currents of the Gulf Stream help to keep the winter temperatures reasonably mild and make this a good time to explore less well known parts of the Emerald Isle. Although this is generally a very wet time of year, the line-ups are fairly quiet and there will be plenty of swell around allowing maximum surfing possibilities. Head for a flexible coastline.

Spring can be a fairly unsettled, unpredictable season in terms of swell and as with the majority of Europe big stormy surf happily rubs shoulders with epic glassy days. However this can also be a time of some of the driest weather for the majority of the west coast (well dry in terms of the fact there may only be rain or drizzle for around 13 days each month). The air temperature slowly moves into double figures and the water temperature hovers around a 10°C average meaning 4/3's and boots are a good call.

AL MACKINNON

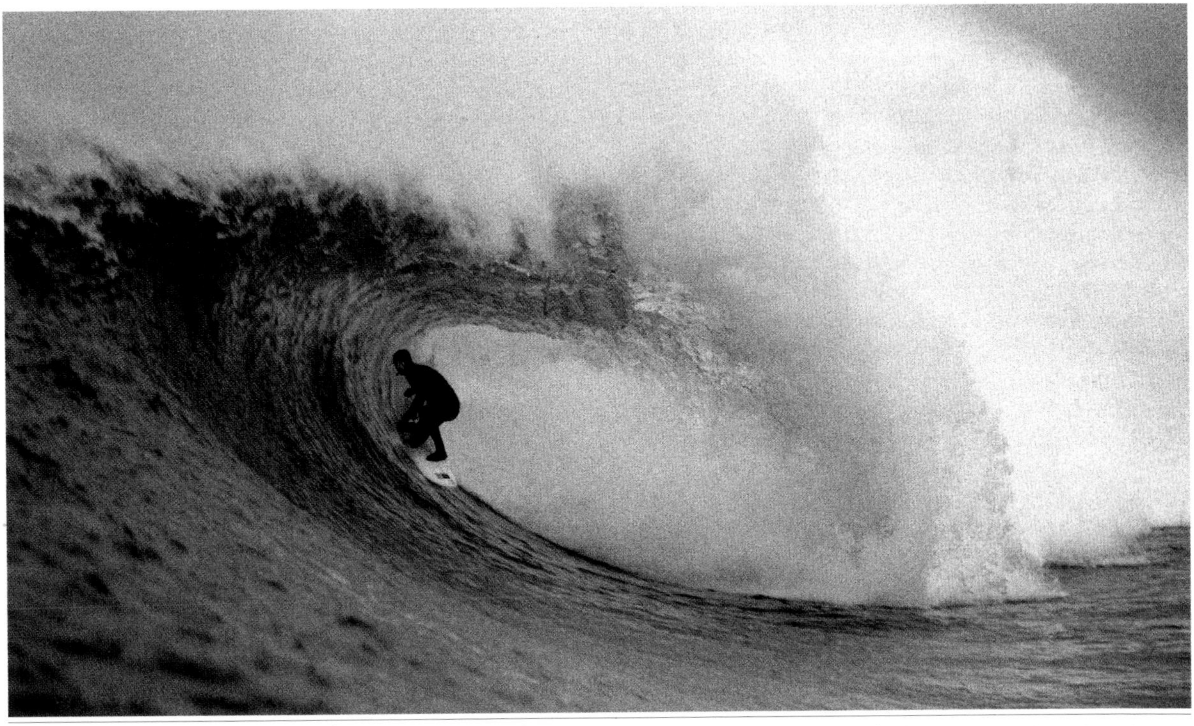

John McCarthy experiencing some west coast pleasure.

MICKEY SMITH

Rusty Long drops into a bomb.

“”

I have been to many places across the world and I have yet to find waves as good as I get at home in Ireland. It might be freezing, windy and cold but there is always the possibility of finding empty amazing waves. It still has that exploration side to surfing and it is quite easy to get to. As long as people come with a friendly attitude and an open mind you will always receive a welcome. Everyone loves the black stuff!!!

Fergal Smith, Irish Champion

Geography and the breaks

Ireland has a diverse, fragmented coastline of islands, inlets and islets, ravaged by the Atlantic onslaught. Northern Ireland packs variety into a small area – west of Portrush a huge dune backed bay stretches out while to the east the coastal fringe is a string of bays and rocky headlands. But even these are varied – Whiterocks is backed by chalk cliffs while further east the unique coastal environment of the Giants Causeway, a puzzle of interlinked rock stacks formed by the rapid cooling of lava to form hexagonal basalt columns, separates the consistent White Park Bay from Porthballintrae. Northwest Ireland, and Donegal specifically, enjoys a series of flat reefs, which act as the perfect foil for the north Atlantic swells that bombard the region and are interspersed by sandy bays and rivermouths. On the west coast the Burren – a huge swathe of flat carboniferous rock – hides unique plants within the cracks in this limestone paving. This bleak, world renown ecosystem is rare, fragile and found in few places in Europe. At Doolin it's possible to see where the limestone pavement runs into the sea to form the reefs and points which have turned the region into an aquatic playground. It's also clear to see that this soft limestone has been slowly dissolved by the sea to form sharp, unforgiving coral-like fingers. The stunning mountains of the southwest, the biggest of which is Carrauntuohil in Kerry, provide a wonderful backdrop to the breaks of this region. Much of the west coast of Ireland is jagged and undulating. There are inlets, huge sandy bays and towering cliffs. To the north of Lahinch, the Cliffs of Moher tower above the Atlantic. These huge sheer faces are a popular tourist destination, but definitely not for those who suffer from vertigo. It is beneath these very cliffs that the big wave spot Aileens waits for those big swells to kick in, providing an excellent vantage point to view the tow surfers at work.

Surfing and environment

Ireland's coastal waters are some of the best quality in the whole of Europe. Main environmental issues include issues such as localized

Ireland: a brief surf history

1960s → Kevin Cavey becomes the first Irishman to surf on the Emerald Isle. **1966** → Ireland are invited to attend the World Surfing Championships – Kevin Cavey is their representative. Roger Steadman and Kevin Cavey establish C&S Surf Board Company, the first Irish surf company. **1967** → Surf Club of Ireland is established in Mount Herbert, Bray, and hosts the first National Championships in Tramore. **1968** → First Irish Intercounty Championships, won by County Down , are held at Rossnowlagh. **1969** → Ireland attends the first European Surfing Championships in Jersey. **1970** → Irish Surfing Association established as the sport's governing body to look after the 400 surfers in the country. **1972** → Ireland host the European Surfing Championships at Lahinch, without any surf **1979** → The Smirnoff International is held in Easkey, Co Sligo, in perfect surf. **1985** → Ireland hosts the Guinness Eurosurf at Bundoran and Rossnowlagh. **1987** → Grant Robinson wins the European Masters title in France. **1996** → *Litmus* – the ultimate film for soul surfers – brings breaks like Pampa Point to world prominence. **2001** → Quiksilver hold the World Masters Championships in Bundoran, attended by a host of former world champions including Tom Curren, Rabbit, Kanga, Simon Andersen, Jeff Hakman and local heroes, Henry Moore and Grant Robinson. **2005** → Ireland finishes 8th in Eurosurf 2005, the European surfing championships held in Portugal. **2006** → 'The Silver Surfari' from Lahinch to Rossnowlagh takes place with nearly 70 local and international pioneers of surfing in Ireland in attendance to celebrate 40 years of surfing Ireland's coastline. **Ireland today** → Surfing in Ireland is going through a boom and is establishing itself as a big-wave spot. The ISA estimates that there are 5,000 surfers in Ireland, 35 surf shops, 27 surf schools, 10 affiliated surf clubs and 5 surfboard shapers nationwide.

Low Pressure Chart for Ireland

In all instances we assume the depressions are deep enough to produce classic swells (say 986 to 992mb). A low leaving the eastern seaboard of the American mainland may deepen as it moves into the **L1** slot, pushing groomed swell lines into the southwest and western coastlines as well as exposed spots in the northwest. The further it tracks towards the **L2** position the less swell can reach the southern coast and Dingle, but the regions around Bundoran and Easkey come alive. Once it reaches **L2**, the angle of swell will turn Northern Ireland on with a classic northwesterly swell.

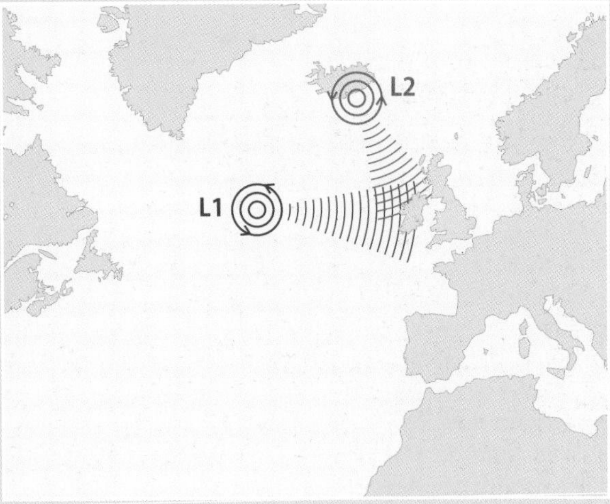

problems with agricultural run-off from farmland. Here excessive fertilizer and animal waste works its way into the water triggering eutrophication and algal blooms, so called red or green tides, where the vast numbers of algae causes fish to suffocate and water to become pretty unpleasant. Proposed development projects can threaten breaks as with a proposed pier extension at Doolin and the proposed marina development in Bundoran. "As most surfers know, The Peak has been under the threat of a marina development," explains Richie Fitzgerald. "The Irish Surfing Association, local surfers and concerned residents, using a number of tactics, have managed to fight off any development so far. As the years go on and the visible popularity and financial benefit of surfing to this area become more obvious, the marina project looks less and less likely. But when dealing with big money and politics you let your guard down to your peril, so the ISA and locals have been keeping the pressure on the local council to drop the idea entirely." Find out more from the Irish Surfing Association, www.isasurf.ie.

The surf community

"For me personally the most radical change over the last half a decade in surfing in Ireland has been the amount of Irish people in the water," says Richie Fitzgerald. "In the 1990s Ireland seemed to be getting crowded from the outside-in, with every second surfer being a foreign national from the USA, South Africa, Australia, New Zealand, France the UK etc. I think we still get the same amount if not many more visiting surfers to our shores, but they are now far out weighed by the number of Irish people taking to the waves. I think it is much healthier for the development and sustainability of surfing in Ireland if it continues to grow from the inside-out."

"Although there are a lot more surfers, the vibe hasn't changed very much," says Cork surfers Graham Collins. "Most of us learnt to surf in an uncrowded environment so the rules weren't really needed but now the rules are slowly getting introduced. It's still pretty laid back. Just don't turn up in two vans full of surfers. That's not going to win you any friends."

Resources

Ireland is home to a comparatively new and small surf community. Watersports' publication, *Fins Magazine* (which features surfing) is currently the country's only homegrown read, www.finsmag.com.

A couple of useful resources on the web include:
www.irishsurfer.com – news, forecasting;
www.isasurf.ie – Irish Surfing Association website with news and event information;
www.irelandsurfari.com – A great website charting the 2006 Silver Surfari, a celebration of 40 years surfing in Ireland and a gathering of those at the vanguard of surfing Eire;
www.worldsurfradio.com – Ireland based, internationally flavoured bi-weekly podcast looking at all aspects of the surf scene;
www.magicseaweed.com – Accurate, detailed surf forecasting.

Essentials

Position

The island of Eire lies off the west coast of Britain in the Atlantic Ocean, separated from its neighbour by the Irish Sea and St George's Channel on its eastern side. The northeastern region is the province of Northern Ireland, a part of the UK and as such has separate government from the rest of Ireland. (see separate box).

Language

English, in a soft, rounded, lilting tone is spoken throughout Ireland – in varying degrees of strength. Irish or 'Gaelic' is spoken in the *Gaeltacht* communities – a collective term for the predominantly west coast regions (such as the Dingle Peninsula) where this Celtic tongue is spoken as a first language. Although English is also widely used, in these areas, Gaelic place names and road signs often feature meaning a good map can be essential to establish that Dubh Linn is in fact Doolin! But the most common Irish phrase you will see written or hear spoken is *Cead mile failte* – a thousand welcomes.

Crime/safety

Ireland is a fairly hassle-free place to be, with the usual problems focused around city centres. If you do need to report anything, head for the Garda – the Irish police force. While Ireland's drink driving laws were once relaxed, they have recently stepped up their action in even the smallest villages. The history of Ireland is interwoven with acts of terrorist violence from members of ideologically opposed groups – Chops Lascelles remembers attending the 1985 European Surfing Championships in Bundoran under armed escort. Following the Good Friday agreement violence has abated but some tensions still remain. In passing through Northern Ireland you may notice the flags, painted street markings and murals delineating loyalist and republican neighbourhoods.

PAUDIE SCANLON

Ollie Flaherty, Lahnich.

Fact file

Capital city: → Dublin
Time zone: → GMT
Currency: → Euro (€)
Coastline: → 3,172 km
Emergency Numbers:
→ General Emergency: 999/112
→ International Operator: 114
Country code: → +353
Electricity: → 220v 3 pin plug
Visa: → None required for citizens of EU countries, or tourists from the US, Canada, Australia and New Zealand. For all up-to-date info check: www.foreignaffairs.gov.ie
Tourist Board: → www.discoverireland.ie, www.tourismireland.com, www.irelandwest.ie, www.discovernorthernireland.com

Health

All visitors should invest in good travel insurance. EU residents need to carry a European Health Insurance Card, www.ehic.org.uk, for free (or reduced cost) healthcare. **NB** This has replaced the E111, and like its predecessor does not cover repatriation costs. For Europe-wide information see the European Commission's website: http://ec.europa.eu/employment_social/healthcard/index_en.htm.

Opening hours

Irish opening times are similar to that of the UK. As a result, business hours are generally Monday to Friday 0900-1730 with shops opening on Saturdays and big supermarkets in big towns suppressing Catholic guilt to open on Sundays. Shops close on St Patrick's Day and over the Easter long weekend (when you may even find some pubs closed, especially in rural areas).

Sleeping

Ireland can seem pricey when compared to some parts of continental Europe. At the top end of the scale, hotel rates are usually highest in the summer months of July and August. More reasonable rates can often be negotiated off peak – during the cold, wet months of November-February. **Bed & Breakfasts (B&Bs)** – usually offering a warm welcome, a bed for the night in a private home and a full Irish breakfast in the morning – can be a good option for a short stay. Rooms range in quality, style – from chintzy to cheap – and price (€40-90 for a room). Around popular holiday resort areas such as Bundoran, **self-catering** is a good and readily available option. It is often the cheapest solution for groups, especially off peak. There is plenty of **hostel** accommodation throughout Ireland from around €18 per night, much of which is run independently. Check out www.hostels-ireland.com for details. **An Oige**, www.anoige.ie, affiliated to Hostelling International, also has a good network of sites across the country. In terms of **camping**, www.camping-ireland.ie, it is extremely difficult to find a site open off-season. Even during the summer, there are not the number of sites you find on the continent. However, it is often worth asking about camping opportunities in the pubs – sometimes you can find a farmer who'll let you pitch for a couple of euros a night. Bear in mind that accommodation gets booked up at peak times such as St Patrick's Day (17 March) July/August, Easter and Christmas. If you can't find accommodation in a village, ask in the local pub.

Eating and drinking

Like many national diets, the cuisine of Ireland has been shaped by the climate and economy. At times both have been hard, so it's no surprise that much of the traditional diet is more about filling, affordable food than fine, flashy fare.

Served with every meal in a multitude of guises, in Ireland the **potato** is king – despite the famine of the 1800s. **Colcannon** (mashed potato and cabbage) is a common occurrence, as a side dish or with grilled cheese on top as a meal on its own. Another staple is bread, particularly **soda bread**, a dense white loaf with a consistency similar to scones – nothing beats a slice of it with a mug of tea after a surf! Warming, hearty **stews** of lamb, beef or pork and veg are an everyday staple. Surrounded by the sea, Ireland is also a place to sample excellent seafood. **Crab's toes** (or crab's claws to you and me), **oysters**, and the **Dublin Bay prawn** (or lobster) as well as some good, old fashioned **fish 'n' chips** – battered, smothered in salt and vinegar and wrapped up in paper. Similar to a full English, the **Irish cooked breakfast** is the real selling point of a B&B and a hearty way to start the day. Cafés will very often serve an all-day Irish breakfast – so get ready for the cholesterol-raising bacon, fried egg, sausages, black pudding, tomatoes and toast all washed down with an industrial-strength mug of tea. And while we're on to washing things down, it is important to note that drinking here is a near-professional pursuit. You can get lager and wine here but you are better off sampling some of Ireland's famous 'black stuff'. Stout is black with a thick, creamy head, the body is rich and filling, with a hint of iron about it – practically a whole meal in itself. It takes time to pour a perfect pint of **Guinness** or **Murphy's** but it is definitely worth the wait. To round off an evening where the beer and conversation flows in equal proportions, enjoy a nip of **Irish whiskey** neat or in an Irish coffee – a coffee revved up with a shot of whiskey and a blob of cream on top.

Getting there

Air Dublin, the capital, Shannon to the west and Belfast in Northern Ireland are the main international gateways to Ireland. Flights from Australia/New Zealand are usually via the UK and it can often be cheaper to book your onward journey with one of the budget airlines. There are plenty of services from North America. Air Canada offers regular flights between Toronto and Dublin (6½ hours), www.aircanada.com. Irish national airline **Aer Lingus**, www.aerlingus.com, operates some of the cheapest routes with regular flights from major cities including LA, SFO, Washington and Orlando to Dublin with flights from Chicago, Boston and NY to Dublin and Shannon with returns starting at about €600. They also offer excellent services across Europe to Dublin, Cork and Shannon. On international flights providing surfboard carriage falls into normal baggage allowance, on all other flights there is a €25 charge is levied. **Ryanair**, www.ryanair.com, also run regular, reasonable services between Dublin or Shannon and an ever expanding number of European destinations including surfing destinations including Biarritz, Faro, Fuerteventura, La Rochelle, Marseille, Porto and Bilbao. They also run between Frankfurt and Kerry or Shannon. Be aware all luggage incurs a fee. **Easyjet**, www.easyjet.com, run flights to Belfast from a more limited selection of airports. To keep prices down, avoid

The Lowdown

"The essence of an Irish surf trip is being prepared for anything from giant, cold, rainy slabs to sunny, superfun beachbreak – and everything in between. That, and not being in a hurry or over-frothing to get surf. I expected a slightly less crowded surf experience, but once I got to Ireland, I realized there are plenty of superkeen surfers at the best known breaks."
Marcus Sander Editor, Surfline

"We depend on the goodwill of landowners and local residents to access many of the spots we surf on a regular basis. Please respect our access and show respect to landowners and local residents. Do not damage fences or leave gates open. If you are unfamiliar with a break check with local surfers regarding access. Please take your litter home." *Irish Surfing Association*

"Visitors tend to think west coast west coast west coast, but our prevailing wind in Northern Ireland is offshore unlike Cornwall, Wales and SW Ireland. We also have a relatively large swell window that does open up to the west with Portballintrae."
Andy Hill, 6x National Champion

"Bring a quiver of boards and a rain jacket because you never know what the surf or the weather is going to do."
Roy Kilfeather, Sligo surfer

Searching for the G Spot.

travelling on a Monday morning or a Friday evening – popular with business commuters – and try to book well in advance.

From UK Aer Lingus, T+353(0)818-365000, run flights between Ireland and the UK at prices which can often rival budget airlines. The cheapest route is usually Gatwick-Dublin. Ryanair offer an awesome range of services from a plethora of UK destinations. Dublin is serviced by almost every conceivable UK airport, while flights to Knock, Kerry, Shannon and Cork run from many UK cities. A twice-daily flight also runs between London Stanstead and Derry in Northern Ireland and provides good access to the north shore. Ryanair flights to Ireland cost from 99p to £150 plus depending on offers and how far in advance you book. Other airlines to consider include easyjet and BMI Baby, www.bmibaby.com, who run flights to Belfast in Northern Ireland (handy for the north) and Flybe, www.flybe.com, who run daily flights between Dublin and Exeter, Norwich and Southampton.

Sea There is a wide range of services between the UK and Ireland, fares varying according to how far in advance you book and the season in which you travel. Irish Ferries, T08705-171717, www.irishferries.com, run between Pembroke and Rosslare in southeast Ireland (3 hours 45 minutes, flexible returns for a car and two adults £220-350). They run two services on the Holyhead-Dublin route, the swift ferry (1 hour 50 minutes, flexible returns £280-400) and the slower (3 hours 15 minutes) *Ulysees* (£240-360). Stena Line, T08705-707070, www.stenaline.com, run a number of services including Holyhead-Dublin, Fishguard-Rosslare, and Stranraer-Belfast services. P&O Irish Sea, T0870-2424777, www.poirishsea.com, run Cairnryan-Larne, Fleetwood-Larne and Liverpool-Dublin services.

From France, Brittany Ferries, www.brittany-ferries.com, run a weekly service between Roscoff in the northwest and Cork. It takes 14 hours and a car and two passengers in Sept costs approx €550 return. Irish Ferries, T0818-300400, www.irishferries.com, run Roscoff-Rosslare and Cherbourg-Rosslare services.

Red Tape: Ireland is a Schengen state (see page 18).

Getting around

Driving (left-hand side) A full driving licence or International Driving Permit is required plus adequate insurance and ownership papers. Since Ireland received a massive EU cash injection, they've been building new roads and resurfacing old roads like there's no tomorrow! Having said that, the roads are extremely windy and smaller roads badly potholed. Journeys anywhere will always take longer than you think. The 308 km from Rosslare to Sligo takes about 4 hours 40 minutes.

Motorways There are snatches of motorway, mainly focused around the Dublin area, but more roads are being upgraded all the time. Check www.nra.ie for a map showing roadworks. Speed limit 112 kph.

Other roads N roads act as motorways and connect the majority of the country. Their standard is improving but some stretches will test even the most robust suspension. Speed limit 96 kph/48 kph in urban areas.

Car hire Car hire can be expensive, from €160 a week for a small car. Fly/drives may offer better deals as will booking ahead if you are coming over from the US. You need to be over 21, and very often companies won't rent to anyone under 23. You also need to have held a licence for more than a year. Budget have bases here, including Dublin airport, T01-8400800, www.budgetcarrental.ie, as do Thrifty, T01-8400800, www.thrifty.ie.

Public transport

The national **rail** company, Iranrod Eireann, T01-836 3333, www.irishrail.ie, or www.iarnrodeireann.ie, has a fairly limited rail network. Main routes fan out from Dublin to Sligo and Ballina in the north, Galway in the west and Tralee, Cork, Waterford and Rosslare Harbour in the south. They don't charge for board carriage, provided you put the board on the train yourself. If you want a few days in the city without your board, you can always send it on ahead of you for a small fee. Price is worked out by weight, contact the freight department on T0185-767676 for details.

Bus Eireann, T01-8366111, www.buseireann.ie, the national bus company, do have a fairly extensive network across Ireland for both long-haul and short-haul trips. However they charge for surfboard carriage a whopping €9 and they can't guarantee that your board will get on – 'luggage' gets priority – making this mode of transport really only viable for long journeys. If you are going to be doing a lot of bus travel, it may be worth investing in an Irish Rover bus pass (check the website for details). Alternatively you can get a combined bus and train pass.

Surfers' tales

Satisfying the Yearn in Easkey: a Cripple's Guide to Surfing Desperation

By Michael Fordham

People who surf are doomed to yearn. When you're away from the coast, you yearn for the sea. When you're at the beach and it's flat, you yearn for a solid, clean swell. When that swell arrives you yearn for a quiet dawn, an empty car park, a light offshore. Truth is that the yearn is what motivates you. It's what keeps you paddling out through the cold, with the aches, despite the pain the slop and the frustration that surfing these islands often entails.

One April morning whilst snowboarding way out on the far side of the Ziller valley above Mayerhofen, I was taken out from behind by a viciously hungover board betty still half full of Jack Daniels and moody cocaine. It wasn't yet nine AM and the piste was icy as hell. I went over at speed and my shoulder popped straight out and stayed that way. Thing is, my annual insurance had just expired, so I couldn't call the emergency services. They probably would have called a heli and it would have cost me thousands. So, idiot that I was, I had to sideslip down the mountain, get a chairlift back up to the top of the far peak, then sideslip down, all the way down the bubble to the village – all of this in big agony. By the time I made it to the predatory orthopaedic surgeon in his lair at the foot of the mountain I was crying like a baby from the pain. Four hundred quid on the Visa card later and I'm on the way home, pissed off as it's possible to be. My tendons, rotator cuffs; everything vaguely meant for paddling around my right shoulder was shot to buggery.

So, a couple of weeks after getting back from Austria I find myself with a photographer on the ferry to Ireland. We'd pre-booked everything and we had a looming deadline. The mission was to take portraits and landscapes shots of the local surfers in the west of Ireland, so I had to go. Typical that the trip coincided with an all time swell generated by a 955mb low that seemed as if it would hover out there forever. I was in a sling, watching all these amazing waves, endless lines, unstoppable sliding, gaffing, gouging, cruising, all the things I needed to satisfy the yearn. I woke up really early one deathly silent morning. It was May and we were at Easkey, and it was cold as it can only be in Mayo in the late spring. Perfect, head high peelers, spaced out and smoking with a dead silent wind, were wrapping and bending into the reef on the right. It was one of those Irish dawns when the day is fresh and new with the tang of peat in the air and the mineral thrall of the breeze opens up your sinuses. All was silent but the surge and the hiss of the waves on the reef. The one or two other wagons parked out on the headland were silent and nothing stirred. Thing is, as well as taking in the beauty of it all, the frustration I had been feeling bubbled to the surface. I really was on the verge of tears. There was only one way out of this situation.

It was tough getting the wetsuit on. If anybody else had been awake they'd have pissed their selves laughing at the spectacle of a one-armed man contorted with pain peeling on the neoprene and then trying to do the zip up. Thing is, when the tension of the wettie finally wrapped my shoulder in its embrace, it felt more snug and secure than it had been since the mountains. Perfect. I picked my way across the rocks and began to get excited by the smell of the brine and the feel of the weed and the boulders beneath my toes. I didn't really know what I was in for or what I was trying to achieve. But when I slipped into the surf between sets it all made sense.

This strange, delicate, lonely bodysurf taught me the greatest of lessons. I realised that surfing has nothing to do with what board you ride or even how you ride it. It mattered nothing that I was floating and kicking and one armed paddling, my right arm limp but strangely comforted by the neutral gravity. Only once or twice did I go over the falls to feel a stab of proper pain. It was the surf of my life, the quietest, most intense, yearn-sating surf with nothing but me and the waves and a wettie. I could feel the weeks of tension, of anger, of bitterness falling from me. Frozen in my mind, each moment was a kind of redemption. By the time the small crew began to paddle out and hour or so later, I was laughing and giggling to myself. I was a holy goof, a half-crippled, laughing fool. But I had learned that you'll always yearn for surf. You just have to get in. No matter what.

Michael Fordham is creative director of The September Project. 'September: Ireland's Dreaming' is available from good book shops or direct from www.september-project.com.

Overview

"The troubles never came into surfing as far as we were concerned. We were surfers and to be honest, for most of my friends I still couldn't tell you if they were catholic or protestant. Now we have surfers coming from all over the world as the surfing here is so good and still relatively uncrowded."

6 x Irish National Champion Andy Hill.

West coasts have always had a magnetic draw to surfers. The earth's complex weather and swell patterns seem to favour this aspect above all others. From California to Chile, Cornwall to the west Algarve, the Mentawais to Margaret River. There are, however, little pockets of classic surfing real estate that are just as blessed as their sunset facing cousins and due to our western fetish, have tended to avoid the mass attention and influx of travellers. Northern Ireland is a classic example of this. It's northerly outlook faces straight into the swells generated by depressions tracking across the higher reaches of the Atlantic, yet this coastline is also blessed with trade winds that blow virtually offshore. Just think Northern Spain or the region around Easkey and you'll get the idea. For decades surfers from the north of England made their regular journeys west, ferries across the Irish Sea plus the overnight dash to the west coast. And yet, had they just turned right a whole coastline of possibilities would have opened up to them. "Visitors tend to think west coast, west coast, west coast," says six times Irish National Champion Andy Hill, "but our prevailing wind is offshore. We also have a relatively large swell window that also opens up to the west with Portballintrae."

But surfing in Northern Ireland is no new discovery. The locals have been enjoying the full potential of the region since the earliest days of Irish surfing. "People have been surfing in the area since 1963, when my father, a customs officer based in Londonderry, first came over with a board," says Andy who also owns Troggs surf shop. "There was an underground interest during the seventies and eighties (maybe 20 locals), but it was with the advent of surf shops like ourselves, opening in the early nineties, that acted as a catalyst for the sport. It has really boomed in the last two years. All the beaches are busy on the weekends and holidays. But it's still very uncrowded during the week." There has been a high standard of surfing

ANDY HILL/TROGGS

Spring
Air 8°C 46°F
Water 9°C 48°F
5/4/3mm Wetsuit & boots

Summer
Air 15°C 59°F
Water 13°C 55°F
3/2mm Wetsuit

Autumn
Air 11°C 52°F
Water 13°C 55°F
4/3mm Wetsuit

Winter
Air 4°C 39°F
Water 8°C 46°F
5/4/3mm Wetsuit, boots, gloves & hood

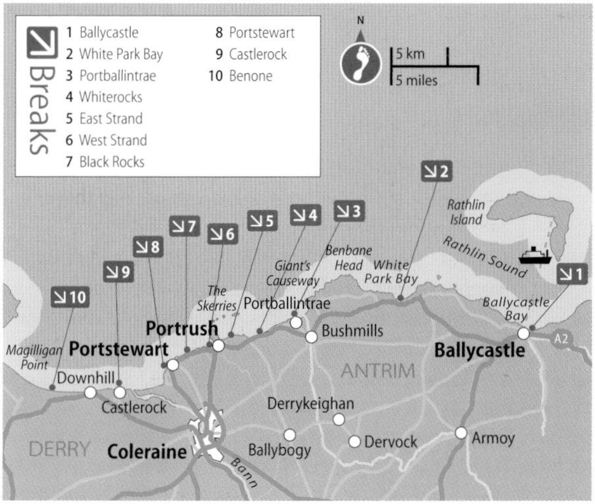

6'0" Rusty Piranha
Shaper: Rusty Presiendorfer
6'0" x 20$^{1}/_{16}$" x 2$^{1}/_{8}$"
Built with Surftech's proven TUFLITE construction.
Wider template, low entry rocker and single-to-double concave make this a greedy fish. The three-wing, pulled-in swallow tail still allows you to surf vertically. Ride 2-4" shorter than standard shortboard. Magic in the knee high, weak to punchy head high surf.
Futures Rusty fins.

6'3" JC SD-3
Shaper: John Carper
6'3" x 18$^{1}/_{8}$" x 2$^{1}/_{4}$"
Surftech's lively, responsive TL2 composite technology.
Single to double bottom contour, slightly fuller rail, lower entry rocker and a slight bump wing at the hips. The 6'3" is designed to get you in early for steeper, deeper barrels with the speed to make it out alive!
Futures JC-1 fins.

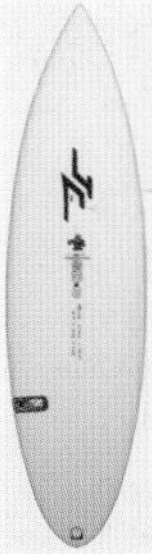

Boards by **Surftech**
www.surftech.com info@surftech.com

coming out of this area as well: Alistair Mennie was 5th on the British circuit in 2004 and is now concentrating on big waves, like Mavericks and Todos Santos. Andy Hill is a 6 times Irish National Champion, local legend Stevie Burns is the current National Longboard Champion and Alan Duke is a 3x Irish National Champ. Isn't it time you checked out the waves of Northern Ireland for yourself, before word gets out.

Coastline

The coastline of Northern Ireland is one of the most interesting and picturesque in Europe, and it boasts one of the UK's most famous landmarks – The Giants Causeway. Lying between the swell magnet beachbreak of Portballintrae and curving sands of White Park Bay, this section of coastline was formed over 60 million years ago when an upwelling of molten, igneous rock came into contact with the cool sea, causing accelerated cooling and rock crystalisation. The results were these spectacular, tightly packed hexagonal stone columns, stacked together as low lying stepping stones or towering high as columnar cliffs. To the west, the coastline of Northern Ireland unfolds into a series of sandy bays with some good rocky reefs interspersed by tumbling headlands. Offshore the horseshoe shape of Rathlin Island cuts out much of the swell bound for Ballycastle Bay, making this an ideal winter bolt-hole when the big storms kick in. West of Portstewart the coastline morphs into a huge section of golden sand backed by rolling dunes. This area, home to rare bird and orchids species, is the ideal place to take your shoes off, feel the sand between your toes and find an empty peak for the day.

Local environment

Although the coastline of Northern Ireland is one of Europe's undiscovered gems, a recent WWF and Wildlife Trust report warned that the region has a less than pristine record of coastal management within the UK. They called on the Government to protect local areas that are deteriorating due to erosion, sand removal and the construction of apartments and marinas. "The Northern Ireland coastline is in danger of being swamped by a tide of development," said Jim Kitchen, Head of WWF Northern Ireland. "New marinas and the apartments that come in their wake, shellfish farming, uncontrolled recreational use, sewage pollution, sand removal – all of these and other threats are putting unprecedented pressures on our fragile coast from Derry to Dundrum."

"There is little in the way of localism here. Some of the breaks are getting busy, especially at peak times, but if people follow the usual surfing etiquette and don't turn up in huge groups, there are no problems," says Andy Hill.

Getting around

The northern coastline of Northern Ireland is well fed by arterial roads such as the A2, which hugs the north shore from Ballycastle west via White Park Bay and Portballintrae through Portrush and across to Downhill. You'll definitely need a car here, but there are many beachside car parks and break access is good. Plenty of scope to explore.

ANDY HILL/TROGGS

Above: 4 David Boyd locking into a cranking Whiterocks.
Left: Andrew Mennie tearing up Portrush.

Quiksilver
roxy
PROTEST
animal
ALDER
ripcurl
BILLABONG
C-SKINS
O'NEILL
troggs.com
* Irelands Premier Surf Retailer
* 1000s of Quality Products
* Shipping Worldwide Daily
* BSA & ISA Accredited Surf School
* Daily Surf Report - 09111 680 090
* Board & Wetsuit Hire
* Live Updated Webcam & Weather Station
ROXY
Irelands Only Official Quiksilver Surf School
Quiksilver
roxy LIFE
British Surfing Association
Governing British Surfing Since 1966
ISA IRISH SURFING ASSOCIATION
Email: surflessons@troggs.com
Tel: +44 7748 257 717
88 Main St., Portrush. BT56 8BN, N.Ireland. Tel: +44 (0) 28 708 25476
72 Ballymoney St., Ballymena. BT43 6AN, N.Ireland. Tel: : +44 (0) 28 256 37651

Breaks

BEACH BREAK

↘1 Ballycastle

Conditions Big to storm size W to NW swells, offshore in SE to SW winds
Hazards/tips Popular winter break
Sleeping Ballycastle ›› *p119*

This is a popular winter break that needs either a big westerly or northwesterly swell to thread its way through Rathlin Sound between the island and the mainland. Check here when Portrush is eight to ten feet. It's a good quality beach break that works through the tides. Surfing has really taken off in Ballycastle over the past five years with a growing surf community.

BEACH BREAK

↘2 White Park Bay

Conditions All N to NW swells, offshore in SW to E winds
Hazards/tips Rocks at northern end
Sleeping Ballycastle ›› *p119*

Head past the Giants Causeway and you'll come to this big, sandy bay with crystal blue waters. It's home to various peaks that break along its length. Port Bradden is a sheltered lefthander found at the southwestern end of the beach that is sheltered in westerly gales. Along the rest of the beach you'll find both lefts and rights, some can be surprisingly long. This is a pretty quiet beach that works best up to six foot from mid tide on the push. Don't surf here alone as the beach is remote and can have strong rips in big swells. Parking by the Youth Hostel off the A2.

BEACH BREAK

↘3 Portballintrae

Conditions Small to medium W to NW swells, offshore in S to E winds
Hazards/tips Heavy and hollow when big
Sleeping Portrush ›› *p119*

This is the north coast's summer swell magnet – if it's flat here it's flat everywhere. A deep water basin helps focus swell onto the beach to produce heavy and hollow waves meaning it can be four foot here when other spots are flat. There are peaks along the beach as well as consistent lefts and rights at the rivermouth. Works best up to six feet on the push, but as the most consistent break, can get very busy in the summer. Drive past the harbour to the car park. This spot is always bigger than it looks.

ANDY HILL/TROGS

3 Swell magnet Portballintrae turning it on.

BEACH BREAK

↘4 Whiterocks

Conditions All N to NW swells, offshore in SE to SW winds
Hazards/tips Strong rips running down the beach
Sleeping Portrush ›› *p119*

This is one of the prettiest breaks along the north coast with a backdrop of white chalky cliffs and sand dunes and views across to the Skerry Islands and Scotland beyond. This 2km beach break runs from Whiterocks west to East Strand, the swell exposure gradually diminishing as you go. There is a consistent right hand sandbank that reels in front of the white rocks at the eastern end of the car park that produces long walls with the occasional quality hollow section on the inside. Best surfed from mid to high on the push, but over 6 ft it can be a mission getting out the back. This is the most popular beach on the north coast and hence gets crowded. Check down the beach for empty peaks. Found two miles outside Portrush on the coastal road, left past the golf course.

BEACH BREAK

↘5 East Strand

Conditions All N to NW swells, offshore in SW to S winds
Hazards/tips Sheltered in big swells when it gets busy
Sleeping Portrush ›› *p119*

East Strand is probably the least consistent break on the north coast due to the protection offered by Portrush Peninsula, but this is also a plus point as it makes it a great spot to head for during big swells and westerly gales. When it's working it really pumps with hollow, powerful lefts and right barrels there for the taking. There is a consistent right found at the end of the promenade or check out the peak by the stream. At four to six foot this beach is a real treat, but can hold bigger swells when rips and access can be a problem. Has a well-earned reputation as a board breaker. Best at mid tide.

Also worth checking is Arcadia Left, a low to mid tide lefthander that breaks by the Salmon fishery. Best during big westerly storms. Access is off the rocks but watch the locals first.

BEACH BREAK

↘6 West Strand

- **Conditions** All N, NW and W swells, offshore in SE to SW winds
- **Hazards/tips** Consistent spot
- **Sleeping** Portrush » *p119*

Another consistent beach break, this time in the heart of Portrush. The lefts and rights here are good quality and although this is a very popular spot, the bay can handle a crowd. Best on the push and suitable for all levels. Beach front parking.

REEF BREAK

↘7 Black Rocks

- **Conditions** All N to NW swells, offshore in SW to S winds
- Hazards/tips Advanced surfers only, rocks
- **Sleeping** Portrush » *p119*

Black Rocks is considered the best reef break on the north coast, but it is fickle, requiring just the right swell direction to produce the goods. But when it does, you'll find a fast, reeling lefthander that begins with a wedgy take-off, then leads into a hollow mid-section before transforming into a fun and walling inside racetrack. The peak has a pretty tight take-off zone so can easily get crowded. Best at four to six feet on a pushing mid tide.

BEACH AND POINT BREAK

↘8 Portstewart

- **Conditions** Small to medium W to NW swells, offshore in SW to SE winds
- **Hazards/tips** National Trust beach front parking
- **Sleeping** Portrush » *p119*

This is a 3 km long stretch of sand that reaches from the edge of town west to the River Bann. Starting at the eastern end, Bailey's is a super long right that can be one of the longest waves on the north shore on its day. The take-off spot can move around making it difficult to line-up but it is a quality wave. Heading down the strand there are many peaks to choose from, spreading out the crowds even on the busiest summer days. At the western end lies The Barmouth, a mechanical lefthander that reels off the groyne where the River Bann meets the sea. These rolling walls may not be as critical as some of the other breaks around but are great fun, with an easy ride in the rip back into the line-up. The whole beach is pretty consistent and works well in swells up to six feet.

BEACH AND POINT BREAK

↘9 Castlerock

- **Conditions** All W to NW swells, offshore in SW to SE winds
- **Hazards/tips** Free parking
- **Sleeping** Portrush » *p119*

This stretch of beach is generally more consistent than nearby Portstewart and is home to a number of banks offering both lefts and rights. The waves here aren't as heavy as many spots, but tend to peel for longer making them popular with beginners and the longboard crowd, but as the swell size picks up so does the quality of the waves. At the eastern end of the beach lies the western groyne at the mouth of the River Bann, The Barmouth offering reeling rights on this side of the river. These excellent rights can reel for up to 200 m on classic days offering perfect walls through to the beach. Free parking at the western end of the beach.

BEACH BREAK

↘10 Benone

- **Conditions** All N swells, offshore in SW to S winds
- **Hazards/tips** Isolated beach
- **Sleeping** Downhill » *p119*

Downhill Strand runs for over 10 km from Downhill in the east to Magillian Point to the west. Benone offers access to a stretch of banks that are less heavy than beaches to the east. At the eastern end lies a consistent right-hander that can break for over a hundred metres, with steep walls sheltered from strong southwesterly to southerly winds by the surrounding cliffs. Heading west the waves get progressively smaller due to the swell shadow cast by Malin Head. You can drive along the beach but beware not to get your car caught in soft sand.

ANDY HILL/TROGGS

Above: 5 East Strand delivers hollow, powerful beach break barrells.

Practicalities

Ballycastle

Ballycastle isn't a consistent swell catcher but the town can make a good base to explore the eastern end of this coastline. It has a growing surf scene and provides easy access onto the Antrim coast road – voted one of the great scenic wonders of the world. If it's flat you could always catch a ferry across to Rathlin Island.

Sleeping

£ **Glenmore House**, 96, Whitepark Rd, T028-2076 3584, www.glenmore.biz. This quiet, family run accommodation has that traditional Brit B&B feel, but is good value and out of town.
£ **Castle Hostel**, 62 Quay Rd, T028-2076 2337, www.castlehostel.com. Only 50 m from the beach, close to the action as far as the town is concerned and with no curfew, a better option for those looking for some nighttime action.

Eating and drinking

There are plenty of pubs in the town. Catch some traditional Irish music with a pint of the black stuff at **The Central Bar** on Ann St.

Portrush

Portrush probably makes the best base for surfers wanting to explore this coastline. It is a popular resort town with plenty of accommodation options and you'll be close to the surfing action. Pop in and check out Troggs Surf Shop in town and they'll be happy to pass on some useful advice.

Sleeping

£ **Portrush Hostel**, 35 Causeway St, T028-7082 4845, www.portrush-hostel.com, is a small, friendly spot with easy beach access, dorms from £10 and doubles from £14. Internet access.
£ **Rick's Causeway Coast Hostel**, 4 Victoria Terr, Portstewart, T028-7083 3789, rick@causewaycoasthostel.fsnet.co.uk. Found just a short drive to the west in Portstewart, this hostel is close to the beach and offers great facilities including small dorm rooms, twins and doubles.
££ **Adelphi Portrush**, 67-71 Main St, T028-7082 5544, www.adelphiportrush.com. The Adelphi offers more luxury accommodation with free broadband and Wi-Fi access. There are some deals available off-season and midweek so it might pay to book ahead. It also has a Bistro serving food sourced from local produce.
££ **Ramada Portrush** 73 Main St, Portrush, T028-7082 6100, www.ramadaportrush.com, is a modern hotel boasting 69 en suite rooms and Wi-Fi access. Deals available.

Eating and drinking

Andy Hill recommends checking out the following spots **The Harbour Bar and Bistro**, on the Harbour, Portrush for fine food and ale as well as **Rogues Wine Bar**, Kerr St. Also worth checking out are **The Ramore Restaurant**, offers a wide menu including oriental, and **Coast Pasta Pizza Bar** which is a bright cool spot to enjoy some Italian cuisine.

Directory

Surf Shops 88 Main St, T028-70 825 476, www.troggssurfshop.co.uk, is Northern Ireland's top surf shop **Troggs** run by 6-times Irish National Champion Andy Hill. They offer all the latest hardware and accessories as well as good surf advice and are open 7 days a week. **Shaper Westbay Surfboards**, http://westbaysurfboards.co.uk, are also based here as well as shaping a range of boards they offer a ding repair service through Troggs. **Internet** The local library is your only option as Portush lacks an internet café. **Pharmacy** Campbell's on Dulce St. **Post office** Dhu-Varren Post Office, 11-13 Portstewart Rd. **Tourist information** Sandhill Drive, Portrush.

Downhill

Sleeping

£ **Downhill Hostel**, 12 Mussenden Rd, T028-07084 9077, www.downhillhostel.com. Recently renovated and looks out over a great surfing beach. Dorms form £10 per night with private rooms from £30. Also board and wetsuit hire.

Flat spells

Golf Northern Ireland has a string of links courses running along the coastline, a couple of well placed suggestions include **Ballycastle GC**, T028-2076 2536, on the A2 west approach to Ballycastle combines links and parkland; weekday green fees from £25. **Bushfoot GC**, at Portballintrae, T028 2073 1317, is a 9-hole course, fees from £15. The queen of the coast, **Royal Portrush GC**, commands royal fees. Natural links Dunluce fees from £170 weekdays – cheaper winter season. Their second flat links Valley course, fees from around £35.

Giant's Causeway This UNESCO World Heritage site lies between Port Ballintrae and White Park Bay on the Causeway Coastal Route and is not to be missed. More than 40,000 hexagonal basalt rock columns of varying heights descend from the cliffs to the ocean

Whiskey **Bushmill's Distillery**, at Bushmills, just south of Portballintrae, T028 2073 3218, www.bushmills.com, has been licensed to distil whiskey since 1608. Tours £5.

Overview

"The main reason Bundoran and the surrounding area has become the lynch-pin of Irish surfing is its high concentration of world class waves within a small area. Beach breaks like Tullan Strand are perfect for beginners and reef breaks like PMPA and the Peak are among Europe's best and are ideal for advanced surfers. So for surfers of all abilities the area is perfect with a huge array of waves within walking distance of each other. The area also receives a lot of surf media attention with European and International magazines regularly featuring the area, its waves and top surfers. This raises the profile of the town and its waves so making it much more popular with Irish and visiting surfers." Richie Fitzgerald

The streets of Bundoran are a buzz with conversation as groups and couples ebb and flow through the door of the Bridge pub. Crossing the road the view of the ocean draws the attention of the initiated away from the giggles and occasional shout towards the steady, rhythmic rumble emanating from the glassy waters of Donegal Bay. A cauldron of white water boils and bounces up the flat reef as the time and tide pushes slowly landward. The sun is setting but the dots in the line-up show no sign of being drawn towards the warmth of the Bridge just yet, not while the Peak is still putting on a show. The waves of revellers may be oblivious to the spectacle unfolding before their blinkered eyes, but the natural wonder of an Atlantic swell line transformed into a classic A frame of symmetrical perfection is not lost on those few, exhausted surfers who linger for an extra minute, an extra glance, before wading into the throng inside. Joining friends and fireside and the mesmerising dark liquid that seems to subtly simmer in the cool confines of its chilled glass.

The bustling resort town of Bundoran is the surfing capital of Ireland, famed for the quality of its waves as well as its scene, but it gives few clues as to the true surfing experience waiting in the rest of the county. Donegal spreads

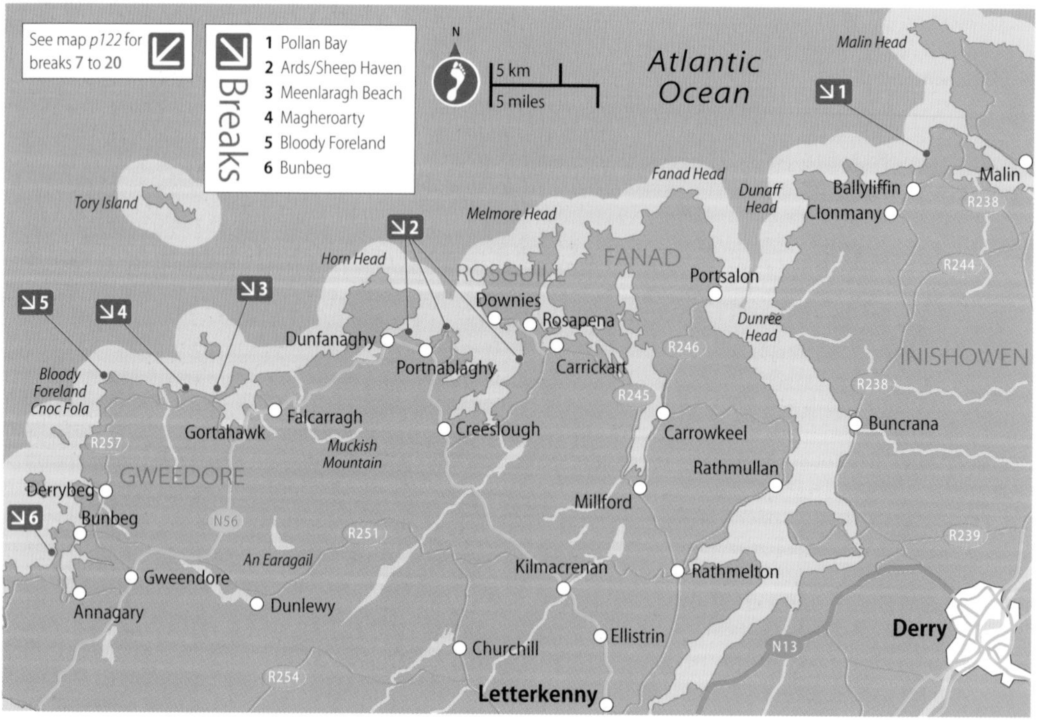

Spring
Air 8°C 46°F
Water 9°C 48°F
5/4/3mm Wetsuit & boots

Summer
Air 14°C 57°F
Water 14°C 57°F
3/2mm Wetsuit

Autumn
Air 10°C 50°F
Water 13°C 55°F
4/3mm Wetsuit

Winter
Air 5°C 41°F
Water 9°C 48°F
5/4/3mm Wetsuit, boots, gloves & hood

BEN SELWAY

15 Fergs charging the shallow, hollow Pampa Point.

6'2" Webber

Shaper: Greg Webber

6'2" x 18½" x 2¼"

Built with Surftech's proven TUFLITE construction.

Single concave fading to flat in nose and tail. Smooth medium rocker with no flats, bumps or breaks of curve. Strong link between planshape and rocker. Perfect board for fast flowing surfing on beach break waves. Broad sweet spot leads to high degree of forgiveness despite great responsiveness.

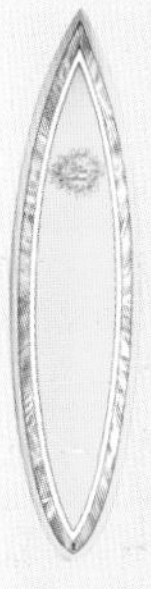

6'8" Brewer Backdoor

Shaper: Dick Brewer

6'8" x 18" x 2¼"

Built with Surftech's proven TUFLITE construction.

Brewer designed this board with Hawaiian Myles Padaca for big gapping barrels. Single to double concave for rail to rail, down the line speed and stability in the tube. When The Peak and Pampa Point are on, this is the board you'll need.

Futures F5 fins.

Boards by **Surftech**
www.surftech.com info@surftech.com

northward, unfolding a mass of surfing potential that few travelling surfers break out to experience. The generous coastline fans out like a giant coral head filled with complex headlands, huge bays and deep inlets, scarred by cool, clear rivermouths. The green blanket laid across the landscape from the heights of the Blue Stack and Derry Veagh Mountains pushes ever on towards the dramatic climax at Bloody Foreland, a headland named for the vivid red hues that the dying sun swathes across the rocky shore at this most northwesterly tip of the Emerald Isle. Here lies a pointbreak that few seek out, where walling rights peel along the angled boulders. Where isolation is the only reward after exiting the water exhausted yet satisfied. Waves relived with a few travelling companions before retiring to find the nearest place that offers a warm fireside and a glass of that mesmerising dark liquid. Some things are a constant no matter where you venture on the Irish coastline.

Coastline

Northwest Ireland has two distinct surfing communities. Around the reefs of Bundoran and the beaches of Tullan Strand and Rossnowlagh are probably the country's largest surfing groups, with a history that goes back to the roots of Irish surfing. The huge inlet of Donegal Bay was perfectly suited to the early surfers, taking on beach breaks with large, cumbersome boards. Today the second and third generations have spread out onto the awesome limestone reefs that lie around that area, and some have taken it to the next level – towing in to the serious reefs that are only brought to life when the most insane swells bombard the region. To the north, heading out of Donegal Bay, the coastline can be summed up in one word – potential. A tour of the beaches alone would keep an explorer busy for weeks. The undulating contours of the coastal fringe delivers up many reefs and headlands that work in any combination of swell and wind, wrapping around past the huge inlets and complex angles around Sheep Haven, Fanad and Inishowen.

Without any major communities living close by, these spots are often quiet. Donegal is the most geologically diverse county in Ireland. Many of the lochs and inlets are glacial by nature and the rock is a complex mix of sedimentary, igneous and metamorphic stone. This county is just crying out to be explored. Head out onto the N56 with a good map and a compass, the beaches are all well marked but in between . . .

Local environment

Donegal is one of the most pristine coastlines in Europe and has the reputation of being virtually unaffected by pollution. One problem can be agricultural run-off where nitrate and phosphate fertilizer and large amounts of animal waste enter the water. As well as being unpleasant, they cause algal blooms, where so called green or red tides occur, robbing the water of oxygen and killing of fish and other ocean life.

As far as localism goes, there are crowd issues in and around Bundoran. Make sure you don't paddle out at breaks that are beyond your ability as this just adds to the crowd factor. Also, avoid turning up at spots with a van full of mates. To the north, many spots here are less well known and traveling surfers need to be respectful and chilled out. "Of course Bundoran like every other surf destination is not immune to the difficulties of a growing surf industry and population local or non local," says Surf World owner Richie Fitzgerald. "You do see and hear some hand bags at dawn arguing in the water, but if you put it in the context of world surfing, Ireland's NW coast still has a mellow vibe in the water. If you do travel here the same rule applies as everywhere else, be respectful of the locals and you will receive respect in return."

Getting around

The N56 will take you north away from Bundoran on a true surf adventure. Coming from Londonderry and Northern Ireland the N13 leads into the northwest of Donegal. Road quality in the county seems to be more neglected than the rest of the country and can be basic. More money seems to be being spent on them since Irelands entry into the EU. Be patient, be friendly and remember that it always takes much longer to reach your destination than you think.

Breaks

PAUDIE SCANLON

Donegal secret.

BEACH BREAK

↘1 Pollan Bay

- **Conditions** Small to medium NW to W swells, offshore in E to SE winds
- **Hazards/tips** Open exposed beach
- **Sleeping** Inishowen ▸▸ p126

Heading north on the R240, take the R238 at Carndonagh to **Pollan Bay**, or continue through Malin to **White Strand Bay**. Both are exposed beaches that pick up westerly and northwesterly swell. The banks here can be very good with powerful, hollow waves on all tides. If the swell has more north, or is big, head to **Tullagh Bay** to the west of Pollan.

BEACH BREAK

↘2 Ards/Sheep Haven

- **Conditions** Medium to big N to NW swells, offshore in SW to SE winds
- **Hazards/tips** Inlet that comes alive in northwesterly swells
- **Sleeping** Rosguill/Dunfanaghy ▸▸ p126

Sheep Haven is a large inlet lying between Rinnafaghia Point and Horn Head. Within the complex contours are a number of beaches, reefs and rivermouths that come alive when north or northwesterly swell angles into its inner reaches. In a straight northwesterly swell, **Rosapenna** is a quality beach break with fast and hollow waves. It is a massive crescent-shaped bay and works in any wind with east in it, the southerly end picking up the most swell. **Ards** has a sandy point that's worth seeking out and, to the north, **Portnablaghy** has a sheltered beach that needs southwesterly winds. **Dunfanaghy** is a very flexible spot that picks up north and northeasterly swell, but is offshore in any westerly wind. Rivermouth banks at the northern end of the beach.

BEACH BREAK

↘3 Meenlaragh Beach

- **Conditions** N to W swells, offshore in E to SE winds
- **Hazards/tips** Watch out for rips
- **Sleeping** Falcarragh ▸▸ p126

At the western end of a 10-km stretch of sand, Meenlaragh is a quality beach that works well in westerly and northwesterly swells. Moving away to the east it curves round from facing due north to face due west, then round the corner to face due north again. This allows it the flexibility to work in a variety of wind and swell combos.

REEF BREAK

↘4 Magheroarty

- **Conditions** All W to NW swells, offshore in SE winds
- **Hazards/tips** Needs a northwesterly or westerly swell
- **Sleeping** Falcarragh ▸▸ p126

Directly out in front of the harbour sits a fairly long, bowly left hand reef that comes alive in a northwesterly or westerly swell. Best surfed mid to high tide when walling waves of up to 8 ft wrap around the reef. Easy paddle out with access from the harbour when big. A good quality spot. Between here and Bloody Foreland are a couple of left reefs worth checking.

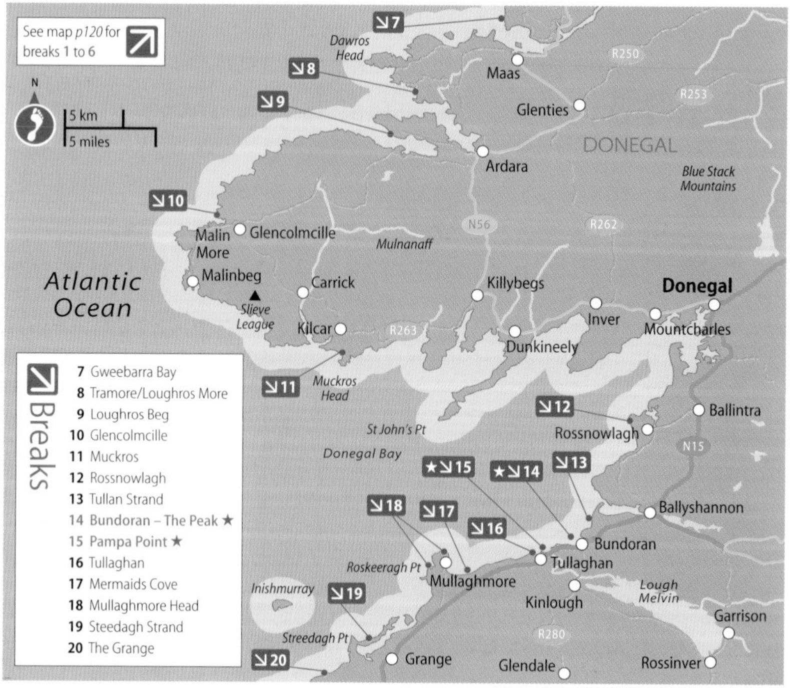

BOULDER REEF BREAK

↘5 Bloody Foreland

- **Conditions** All W to NW swells, offshore in SE winds
- **Hazards/tips** Boulders, rips, powerful waves
- **Sleeping** Falcarragh/Bunbeg ›› *p126*

This exposed headland gets its name from the fact that the rocks turn blood red at sunset. There is a bouldery right-hand point that breaks in north and northwesterly swells. Can be a quality wave in the right conditions and picks up heaps of swell but is exposed to the wind. Needs to be over 3 ft to surf due to rocks, but it can hold a big swell of up to 10 ft.

BEACH BREAK

↘6 Bunbeg

- **Conditions** All NW swells, offshore in SE winds
- **Hazards/tips** Northwest facing beach with offshore islands
- **Sleeping** Bunbeg ›› *p126*

Inishfree Bay is to the southwest of Bunbeg and picks up plenty of swell from a northwesterly direction. Although the bay is littered with offshore islands, the swell still filters through. Works on all tides and has some excellent banks. Very quiet spot.

BEACH BREAK

↘7 Gweebarra Bay

- **Conditions** All NW and W swells, offshore in E and SE swells
- **Hazards/tips** Rips in rivermouth
- **Sleeping** Dungloe/Ardara ›› *p126*

It's a bit of a walk into the bay but it is worth it. A beautiful location with a river at the southern end of the bay. There is a sandbar that forms here and can have excellent lefts and rights on an incoming tide. Watch out for rips as the tide drops. To the north and south there are plenty of banks to explore. The northern end is home to a seasonal surf school who also stock a few essentials including wax and leashes. Check out the bay in front of Narin and Portnoo golf course by Inishkeel.

BEACH BREAK

↘8 Tramore /Loughros More

- **Conditions** Medium to big NW to SW swells, offshore in E to NE winds
- **Hazards/tips** Rips in rivermouth
- **Sleeping** Ardara ›› *p127*

Tramore beach is the northern beach, which has some excellent rights at the top end of the beach in good swells. It is offshore in northeasterly as well as easterly winds. **Loughros** is the next beach to the south, a huge bay with a rivermouth to the south. The sandbanks change with the tides, but there are usually waves near the rivermouth. Part of the Spanish Armada ran aground here.

BEACH BREAK

↘9 Loughros Beg

- **Conditions** Medium to big NW swells, offshore in SE winds
- **Hazards/tips** Quiet bay, rips by rivermouth
- **Sleeping** Ardara ›› *p127*

This is a wonderful beach with sandbanks spread along its length. The rivermouth usually has a decent sandbar, but is best on a pushing tide. A good place to check in southwesterly winds as the south of the beach is overlooked by the heights of Slieve League Peninsula which gives it plenty of shelter.

BEACH BREAK

↘10 Glencolmcille

- **Conditions** Small to medium NW swells, offshore in E winds
- **Hazards/tips** Picks up heaps of swell, very exposed
- **Sleeping** Glencolmcille ›› *p127*

GREG MARTIN/FINDYOURWAVE

13 Tullan Strand.

Follow the road out towards the end of the headland and stop off at the bay. This small beach picks up heaps off swell and although the waves might not be epic, there can be some great little peaks.

BEACH BREAK

↘11 Muckros

- **Conditions** Big NW or medium SW swells, offshore in NE winds
- **Hazards/tips** Works in northerly wind
- **Sleeping** Glencolmcille ›› *p127*

A good beach break that is popular when a northerly wind is blowing out the breaks around Bundoran. Needs a decent northwesterly or a medium westerly or southwesterly swell. Works on all tides.

BEACH BREAK

↘12 Rossnowlagh

- **Conditions** Medium to big W swells, offshore in E winds
- **Hazards/tips** Long surfing heritage
- **Sleeping** Rossnowlagh ›› *p128*

Rossnowlagh was one of Ireland's pioneering surfing beaches with a long tradition that stretches back to the 1960s. The Intercounties Surfing Contest has been held here since 1968. It needs a big northwesterly or a medium westerly swell to get into the beach, but when it does there can be some nice banks on offer. An ideal spot for beginners and intermediates to polish their skills.

BEACH BREAK

↘13 Tullan Strand

- **Conditions** All NW and W swells, offshore in E winds
- **Hazards/tips** Long beach with rips by the cliffs at the south
- **Sleeping** Bundoran » *p128*

Tullan Strand is a huge stretch of sand to the north of Bundoran. Has waves along its length but the most consistent tend to break at the southern cliff side end, where a good quality left usually waits. Tends to take the overspill from Bundoran, so gets crowded, but there are more peaks along the beach to spread out onto. Works on all tides and picks up plenty of swell, so it may be worth checking for waves here when other spots are flat. Inexperienced surfers should watch out for the rip in front of the cliffs. Parking on the cliff top overlooking the bay.

SHARPY

Above: 14 Dylan Pickett deep in the pocket.
Top right: 15 One of the County Donegal's main draw cards. **Bottom right: 15** PMPA.

A FRAME REEF BREAK

↘14 Bundoran – The Peak

- **Swell** W to NW
- **Wind** SE
- **Tide** Low
- **Size** 3-8 ft
- **Length** 50-100 m
- **Bottom** Flat reef
- **Ability level** Intermediate
- **Best months** Sep-Dec
- **Board** Performance thruster
- **Access** In the channel/over the reef
- **Hazards/tips** Shallow reef, gets very crowded
- **Sleeping** Bundoran » *p128*

Lets face it, the Peak is no shrinking violet. It sits out on the end of the headland, in the middle of town, flaunting its wares in front of the surf-hungry masses. And what wares they are. The close take off point peaks into a perfect A frame, before reeling off into a long walling left that spins down the reef, while a shorter hollow right spins away to the west. With more north in the swell the rights become longer and hollower and a huge southwesterly swell will supercharge the left. It is the accessibility and sheer quality of the break that has helped the Peak at Bundoran become one of Ireland's most famous waves. The wave has hosted contests from local to World Masters level and draws travelling surfers from across the country and across the globe. The flat, kelpy reef works best a couple of hours either side of low tide, when a hungry pack will fill the line-up. Many of the country's best surfers will be here, but the high profile of the wave may have just saved its skin. A proposed marina development has been on and off for years now but a group of local surfers, including Bundoran charger and surf shop owner Richie Fitzgerald, fought the plans all the way. "We've been trying to save the Peak by demonstrating that surfing brings a lot into this town, that we're not just a bunch of hippies," says Richie. "There are businesses and holiday accommodation that are supported by visiting surfers. By highlighting the excellent quality of the wave, it has made it more crowded, but we'd rather have a Peak that's more crowded than no wave at all."

LEFT REEF BREAK

↘15 Pampa Point

- **Swell** NW
- **Wind** S
- **Tide** Mid to high
- **Size** 4-12 ft
- **Length** 25-75 m
- **Bottom** Ledge reef
- **Ability level** Expert
- **Best months** Sep-Dec
- **Board** Pintail semi-gun
- **Access** Well timed paddle off the rocks
- **Hazards/tips** Shallow reef, gets very crowded
- **Sleeping** Bundoran » *p128*

When Andrew Kidman's film *Litmus* showed Aussie pro Joel Fitzgerald charging huge gaping lefts at PMPA Point in the mid 1990s, it opened eyes around the world. We'd seen the groomed, polished reefs, feathering barrels and reeling points of Ireland – but this was something else. This was scary. "Pampa is one of my favourite waves in the world," says Irish Hellman John McCarthy of this Jeckyll and Hyde spot. In some swells it can produce

SHARPY

enticing, hollow barrels but it really metamorphosises when the serious swells kick in. "As the wave gets to 8 ft it moves onto the outer ledge. When you look at the 10-footers Joel Fitzgerald surfed in Litmus – that's second ledge. When it gets to that size it takes on a whole different and much more serious persona."

The take off at PMPA is critical, dropping out into a super-steep elevator drop as the lip throws, the wall bowls and begins to speed along the shallow reef. It's all about keeping the speed and locking into the barrel. "It's just so challenging riding backside," says John. "I'm having a good session here if I make 20% of my waves. But whether you make the wave or not, you're going to clock up four or five seconds of tube time on each wave." But there's a proviso here. PMPA is a serious wave for seriously good surfers, who've racked up serious barrel time at seriously heavy reefs. The wave gets its name from a PMPA Insurance sign that used to stand near the break – coincidence or a warning. There's a great opportunity for getting excellent cover, and take the right lines, tuck-in and you'll certainly be claiming it. Get it wrong and it could be a car crash!

RIGHT POINT BREAK

↘16 Tullaghan

Conditions Medium to big NW swells, offshore in southerly winds
Hazards/tips Breaks over boulders
Sleeping Bundoran » *p128*

A big right-hand point break that works in even the biggest swells when it has been described as an Irish take on Sunset Beach. Another *Litmus* star, the waves break over boulders, which is fine in bigger swells but can be a problem when smaller. Tricky exit when big.

BEACH BREAK

↘17 Mermaids Cove

Conditions Medium to big NW swells, offshore in S winds
Hazards/tips Quiet beach
Sleeping Bundoran » *p128*

This beach break is found in front of the caravan park at the eastern end of Mullaghmore beach. A good place to check in a bigger swell. As the swell picks up, move closer to Mullaghmore Head where the beach is more sheltered from swell and wind. Works on all tides.

THE GILL

LEFT REEF BREAK

↘18 Mullaghmore Head

Conditions Big NW to W swells, offshore in SE to SW winds
Hazards/tips Big-wave spot
Sleeping Bundoran » *p128*

Needs a big swell to get going due to the rocks in the line-up. Starts getting ridable in the 8-10 ft range. 100% for advanced surfers only. Has been a tow-in spot. West Mullaghmore has a right reef further round the headland that gets going when the swell is over 4-5 ft.

BEACH BREAK

↘19 Steedagh Strand

Conditions All NW to W swells, offshore in SE winds
Hazards/tips Exposed beach, picks up loads of swell
Sleeping Bundoran » *p128*

This is a great stretch of beach and a fantastic place to escape the crowds. The beach is very consistent. It picks up loads of swell – in bigger swells, check out the peaks near Steedagh Point, which are more sheltered. Offshore in southeasterly and southerly winds. Park and walk along the beach. There are bits of reef and a rivermouth to check.

REEF BREAK

↘20 The Grange

Conditions All NW to W swells, offshore in SE winds
Hazards/tips A series of reefs
Sleeping Bundoran » *p128*

This area has some excellent Easkey-like lefts that break over rocky reefs with boulders. They are best from mid to high tide. Take a right after Grange and explore the headland.

Practicalities

Inishowen

Capping the Inishowen Peninsula and the county of Donegal, Banba's Crown on Malin Head, is the Republic of Ireland's most northerly point and was a strategic lookout point during The Second World War. While fairly quiet during the week it's becoming popular at weekends and well-known for its golfing. Clonmay and Ballyliffin, just south of the Pollan Bay have been undergoing a bit of upmarket development and have several large 'golfing hotels', Malin Head to the east is a quieter proposition, popular with visiting surfers.

Sleeping

€ **Sandrock Holiday Hostel**, Port Ronan pier, Malin Head T074 9370289, is open year round with dorms and doubles – beds from €10. They also offer bike hire.

€ **Malin Head Hostel**, on the R242, T074-9370309, is a relaxed spot, open year round with dorm rooms and doubles. They also offer bike hire, reflexology and aromatherapy treatments and sell organic home grown veggies. Beds from €14. Pubs a couple of kilometres away.

Camping Tullagh Bay Campsite, just behind Tullagh Bay, T074-9378997, open May-Sep is stumbling distance to the Rusty Nail pub where you can grab a pint, a bite and maybe a jam session.

GREG MARTIN/FINDYOURWAVE

Rosguill

This pretty peninsula is a popular summer spot with tourists and locals and is home to a good campsite. Open Apr-Sep.
Casey's Carvan and Camping Park, in Downings, T074-9155301, overlooks the beach and is just 200 m from shops, bar etc. The drawback is that you do have to pay for showers.

Jul-Aug only, there's also the small **Rosguill Park**, campsite on Melmore Rd, Downings T074-9155766.

The **Fisherman's Village Lodge**, is a couple of kilometres north of Downings and has comfortable, quiet B&B accommodation (set in cottages separate for the main house) plus lounge and drying room. Popular with fishing charters (also available from here) T0749 155080, www.rosguill.com.

Dunfanaghy

On the N56, this pretty, unassuming town on the western edge of Sheep Haven has a year-round hostel a few kilometres from the town on the Falcarragh road.

€ **Corcreggan Mill Hostel**, T074-9136409, is a tranquil, retreat kind of place with no TV or radio. The rebuilt millhouse is rustic and relaxed and feels like staying with friends; doubles from €50. For cheaper accommodation, the restored railway car with dorms and doubles is a unique experience with bunks from €16. It also has a cosy lounge with open fire. Campers can pitch up from €8, www.corcreggan.com. For a cashpoint or provisions head to **Ramsey's** in town.

Falcarragh

This town has a significant Irish-speaking community and some beautiful sand dunes to the northwest as well as plenty of bars, café plus amenities like banks, a chemist etc.

Sleeping

€ **Shamrock Lodge**, Main St, T074-9135057, dorm accommodation 15 Jan-15 Dec from €15, private rooms from €20.

Eating and drinking

The hostel is above a popular pub of the same name, which is big at the weekends for traditional music. They also have a pool table and screen the Gaelic matches. A couple of km south at Gortahork, Maggie Dan's is somewhere to nourish your body and soul – they serve basic grub including reasonably priced pizzas and lovely veggie soup, usually with a side order of music, theatre or poetry.

Bunbeg

The villages of Bunbeg and Derrybeg have expanded to meet one another on the R257.

Sleeping

€€ **Bunbeg House B+B**, overlooking the harbour at Bunbeg, www.bunbeghouse.com. Prides itself on it's tranquil setting. A mid-sized hotel, the rooms are a little 'twee' but comfortable and the breakfasts are good Mar-Oct.

€ **Backpackers Ireland Seaside Hostel**, in Derrybeg, T074-9532244, is open Mar-Oct. Groups might try **Bunbeg Holiday Homes**, T074-9531401, modern, comfortable bungalows sleeping 4-8 people at reasonable off-season rates.

Teach Hudi Beag, is the place to head for a pint and some traditional Irish Craic.

Dungloe

Heading south on the N56, Dungloe is the capital of The Rosses and as such has good facilities and amenities, most of which including banks, pharmacy and tourist info are based around Main Street.

Sleeping

€ Atlantic House B&B, Main St, is a frilly but charming traditional B&B with good off-peak rates.

€ Greene's Holiday Hostel, on Carnmore Rd, T074-9521021, is centrally based, open year round, hires out bikes (cheaper for guests) but does have a curfew.
Round the back of the hostel is **Greens's Caravan and Camping Park**, T074- 9521943, open Apr-10 Oct, free hot showers.
Alternatively head south to out of the way Crohy Head and the **Crohy Head An Oige Hostel**, overlooking Boylagh Bay, T074-9521950, basic facilities, open Jun-Sep. South at Dooey Point overlooking Gweebarra Bay **Roaninish Hostel**, T07495 44329, www.gweebay.com, has simple, well placed accommodation.

Eating and drinking

Grab a bite to eat in the average **Doherty's** café on Main St.

Ardara

Not for the yarn-a-phobic, this place is a magnet for tweed-tourists who flock to this weaving hub. As a result there are a couple of good accommodation options as well as banks, a pharmacy and post office around Main St.

Sleeping

€€ Green Gate B&B, T074-9541546. Run by a writer, this is a lovely, eclectic yet traditional cottage, just out of town. The set up is relaxed and breakfast is served anytime – perfect. Just what a B&B experience should be.

€ Drumbaron Hostel, on the main square, T074-9541200.

Camping Head up to **Tramore Beach Caravan & Camping Park**, T074-9551491, just behind the beach with easy break access. Open Easter-Sep.

Eating and drinking

Head to **Nancy's** on Front St for good seafood – whether just a sandwich or a full fish supper. Great ambience and often live music.**Charlies Café** on Main St does basic grub at basic prices.

Flat spells

Bowling **Bundoran Glow Bowl**, Main St, T071-9842111, can while away many a flat hour.

Bloody Foreland Drive out to Cnoc Fola and watch the sunset turn the rocks here blood red. Legend has it that Balor of the evil eye, the Celtic God of Darkness, was slain on these hills, with his blood colouring the landscape, giving Bloody Foreland its name.

Cinema **Bundoran Cineplex**, has 5 screens showing the latest films, T071-9829999, for information.

Golf Green fees can be fairly pricey around these parts as they attract the dedicated golf tourist. Courses include: **Ballyliffin GC**, Inishowen Peninsula, T074-9376119, from €75, cheaper in winter. **Rosapenna GC**, Rosguill, T074-9155301, Old Tom Morris Links Course fees from €50. **Dunfanaghy** par 68 links course, T074-9136335. Fees from around €30. **Bundoran GC**, T071-9841302, is an 18-hole, par-70 links course, green fees from €45. www.bundorangolfclub.com. For those who like their golf to be crazy, look no further than **Crazy Golf and Pitch 'n' Putt** at **Tyrconnell Holiday Homes**, Bundoran, T071-984227.

Island hopping **Tory Island** 11 km north of the mainland, Tory Island is the place to rub shoulders with royalty. They have their own king - currently Patsy-Dan - who more than likely will greet you off the ferry. **Donegal Coastal Cruises**, T074-9531320, www.toryislandferry.com, run between Bunbeg and Tory Island throughout the year, returns around €20. **Arranmore Island**, off the west coast of Donegal is part of the Gaeltacht and Ireland's second largest inhabited island (around 500 residents). It's all about the scenery. The ferry from Burtonport on the mainland runs year round and takes about 25 mins, T07495 20532, www.arranmoreferry.com, returns from €26, car and driver or €9 adult.

Mountain walks Head to **Muckish Mountain**, and climb the 670-m monster for some great views of the area - when it's not covered in cloud that is ... **Errigal**, at 751 m is the highest of the impressive Derryveagh Mountains. It should take around 1-1½ hours to hike to the top. On the south side of the mountain, on the R251, is a handy carpark and the start of the trail.

Glencolmcille

There are a couple of good hostels near this beautiful craft-loving parish which combines several settlements.

Sleeping

€ Dooey Hostel, T074-9730130, www.dooeyhostel.com, is an independent, friendly, inviting, cliff-top spot with dorms doubles plus an area for campers who want to pitch up and utilize the facilities. Beds from €10.

€ Malinbeg Hostel, south at Malinbeg, T074-9730006, is not as convenient but is a very comfortable, new-build place with bunks from €14 and doubles/twins from €16 per person, Jan-Nov. Popular with those wanting to climb the nearby Slieve League Mountains.
Further south still at Kilcar,
€ Derrylahan Hostel, on the Kilcar-Carrick

Rd, on the southern shore of the peninsular, T074-9938097, is very handy for Muckros Head. It's a warm modern place with dorms from €14, private rooms from €18 and camping from €6.

Rossnowlagh

Rossnowlagh is home to one of Ireland's oldest surf communities and one of Ireland's largest surf clubs. With a great swathe of sand known as the Heavenly Cove, this is a popular spot with holidaymakers but quiet off season.

Sleeping

Accommodation here is fairly pricey, and most surfers stay in Bundoran.

€€€ Sandhouse Hotel, http://sandhouse-hotel.ie (they also have a handy webcam), is vast and has a fantastic location on the edge of the beach as well as an on-site spa. The rooms are a good size and pleasantly furnished but the real reason for staying here is location. Check for off-season deals.

€€-€ Ard-na-mara, http://ardnamara-ire.com, on the wonderfully named Coolmore cliffs overlooking the bay is comfortable family run B&B where you receive a warm welcome and a fantastic Irish breakfast. Request a room with a seaview and you will be made. Short stroll down into town and onto the beach and a couple of door from Smugglers Creek.

Eating and drinking

Smugglers Creek Inn, an old beamed, award winning bar/restaurant overlooking the beach on Cliff Rd, T071-9852366, is a great place to eat some good seafood and enjoy a pint. B&B also. Savour a drink or two at the **Surfers Bar**, at the Sandhouse hotel overlooking the beach.

Bundoran

Bundoran is not your typical Irish village. It doesn't have the multi-coloured terraced houses, or an old world charm. But what this 1970s-style resort town does have is far more appealing. Bundoran is home to some of Ireland's most famous waves as well as a serious surfing community with an infrastructure to match.

GREG MARTIN/FINDYOURWAVE

13 Tullan.

Sleeping

The surf boom in this part of the world has resulted in the opening of a couple of new, dedicated surf hostels in the town.

€ Turf'n'Surf Lodge, Bayview Terrace, T071 9841091, www.turfnsurf.ie, is a good budget B&B set up with surfers in mind – en-suite dorms from €20 and doubles from €50 including seaviews, internet and breakfast.

Bundoran Surf Lodge, Main St, T071 9841968, www.bundoransurfco.com, is a good set up – comfortable private and dorm rooms with en-suite bathrooms, lounge area with free Wifi and internet access, kitchen plus board storage and drying room – dorms from €20, private €25 per person.

Homefield Hostel, Bayview Av, T071-9841288, www.homefieldbackpackers.com, has warm, relaxed dorm €20 and double accommodation €25 per person, breakfast included with use of self catering kitchen plus lounge with open fire. As part of an equestrian centre, also offer horse riding.

Self-catering **Tyrconnell Holiday Homes**, T071-9842277, www.tyrconnell-group.com, is one of the best bets for groups. This low-rise holiday village, just 10 mins walk from the seafront, and just by the pitch 'n' putt has a good range of warm, comfortable houses and apartments with pretty reasonable off-season rates.

Heading north out of town on the Tullan Strand Rd, **Surfers Cove Holiday Village**, T071-9842286, www.surferscove.com, offers a similar deal.

Eating and drinking

Being a tourist draw, there are plenty of excellent places to eat in Bundoran.

The **Ould Bridge Bar** on Main St however is the complete deal – food with a view. Nourish your body with reasonably priced steak, seafood, burgers or a vegetarian bite and feast your eyes on the Peak.

Richie Fitzgerald also suggests dropping by the **Astoria Wharf**, on Atlantic Way, for good value food with a bit of atmosphere and "for possibly the best pint of Guinness in Ireland (and yes they have won the award 5 times). No night would be complete without a visit to **Brennans Bar**, Main St, Bundoran – it's a Guinness drinker's Nirvana!"

Directory

Surf Shops **Fitzgerald's Surf World**, Main St, T071-9841223, surfworld@eircom.net, www.surfworldireland.com, is Bundoran's original surf shop and an Aladdin's cave of hardware and goodies which has been serving the local and international visiting surf community since 1990. When not pioneering big-wave spots along the coastline, it is run by the hard-charging and knowledgeable, Richie Fitzgerald. Richie has pretty much become Bundoran's cultural surf ambassador, helping to balance media interest of the region with the preservation of the local surf scene. **Bundoran Surf Co.**, Main St, www.bundoransurfco.com, has a good range of hardware for all standards plus accessories. Shaper Jim Barnes's **Legend Surfboards**, is based in Bundoran, T087-9711718, www.legendsurfboards.com, and also offer ding repair. **Bank** Main St. **Pharmacy** Main St. **Police** Garda Station on Church Rd, T071-9841203. **Tourist information** Bundoran Bridge, www.donegaldirect.com.

Overview

"The essence of an Irish surf trip is being prepared for anything from giant, cold, rainy slabs to sunny, superfun beachbreak – and everything in between. That, and not being in a hurry or overfrothing to get surf."
Marcus Sanders, editor, Surfline

The 1970s was a decade when globe trotting surf explorers combed the ocean's tropical fringes for their own personal nirvanas. But in scouring the maps for new destinations, a cooler section of dynamic coastline came into view. Even with whole tracts of the Central American jungle still untouched and infinite Indonesian Islands waiting to be 'discovered', the glint of the Emerald Isle exerted a kind of pull that these pioneers found hard to resist. While Biarritz had been a chance to experience the warm summers and glamour of the French beach lifestyle, Ireland offered a purity of surfing experience and a warmth of culture that was addictive. The lush green landscape, the swell receptive, harsh grey limestone pavement contorting the cool clear waters into textbook, empty reefs and peeling points. The craic, the warm welcome, the evenings by an open fire and live music washed down with a pint of the black stuff. These weren't yet comfortable clichés, or hackneyed phrases, they were new, exciting experiences. This was the real deal. For surfers from the USA or Australia, the contrast with tropical explorations couldn't be more different.

Word of mouth created a gentle simmer of interest but as contests, images and snatches of footage were thrown into the pot over the ensuing decades and words committed to paper, by the 1990s the breaks of west coast of Ireland had become a regular features on surfing's menu. Easkey, Spanish Point and Lahinch saw a new wave of surfers from Britain, Australia and beyond heading for line-ups to join a small core of locals who initially welcomed the influx of these visitors. As the new millennium dawned, a domestic boom occurred accompanied an Irish economic upturn. The Irish surfing population has undergone a huge growth spurt, and endured a few growing pains in the process. But while the headline acts maybe busy, occupied by the demands of their many adoring fans, there is still a huge scope for exploration of the 'unknown talent' out there. It may sound like a cliché but if you get off the beaten track, it's easy to find the elements that attracted the original searchers here to the west coast in the 1970s and 1980s. Bring that true spirit of exploration and friendship and you'll be roundly rewarded, for this is the real deal.

Coastline

Starting at the home of the ISA, Easkey, and heading west, this coastline has a geology and geography perfectly suited for surfing. The same rock that forms the unique mountain top limestone pavements also lays down some wonderful flat limestone reefs and point breaks. These are interspersed with sheltered sandy beaches that have allowed these golden grains to accumulate, either in sheltered bays or around rivermouths and inlets. The undulating nature of the coastline allows for almost any swell to be surfed as the wind is usually offshore somewhere. Stand on the vertigo inducing Cliffs of Moher, worth a trip for their sheer scale alone, and in a big, clean swell you can watch the thundering big wave 'Aileens' detonate within this stunning arena, while local and international chargers tow into some truly life threatening bombs.

Local environment

Ireland has a wonderfully rich and diverse marine environment. Its biodiversity is helped by the close proximity of the continental shelf where nutrient up-wellings occur. However with many of the country's large urban populations and factories situated in close proximity to the coastline or on estuaries, some pollution and sewage found its way into the coastal waters over the years. Tougher new legislation helped massively, but contaminated sediment is still present in some larger rivermouths where years of discharge may have occurred. Agricultural run-off is also an issue. Chemicals such as fertilizer and pesticide runoff can be washed from the land into river and on into the sea.

There are many factors that have contributed to the boom in Irish surfing over the past 10 years or so. The vast improvements in wetsuit technology, the increasing availability of surf products, the excellent surfing environment and the coverage Ireland has received in media at home and across the globe have all played their part, as has the fact that 50% of the Irish population lives within 10 km of the coastline. Probably the main factor is that surfing is so addictive that what is being experienced in Ireland is reflecting a global trend. The increase in numbers in line-ups has the inevitable effect of causing increased tension and more competition for waves. When your local break goes

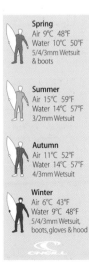

Spring
Air 9°C 48°F
Water 10°C 50°F
5/4/3mm Wetsuit & boots

Summer
Air 15°C 59°F
Water 14°C 57°F
3/2mm Wetsuit

Autumn
Air 11°C 52°F
Water 14°C 57°F
4/3mm Wetsuit

Winter
Air 6°C 43°F
Water 9°C 48°F
5/4/3mm Wetsuit, boots, gloves & hood

MICKY SMITH

Mole demonstrating West Coast Ireland's big wave pedigree.

6'1" Byrne Tom Carroll

Shaper: Phil Byrne

6'1" x 18¼" x 2⅛"

Built with Surftech's proven TUFLITE construction.

Designed with two-time world champ Tom Carroll, this highly responsive round pin works well in just about any surf from 2 ft-6 ft.

FCS TC Redlines fins.

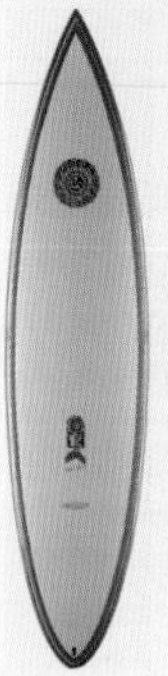

6'7" Wayne Lynch Free Flight

Shaper: Wayne Lynch

6'7" x 18¾" x 2⅜"

Built with Surftech's proven TUFLITE construction.

Solid semi-gun perfect built for powerful waves and round barrels. Single to double concave with extra nose and tail rocker to handle the elevator drops when Crab Island is pumping.

FCS G7 fins.

Boards by **Surftech**
www.surftech.com info@surftech.com

from four guys in the line-up to forty, it is bound to cause frustration in some quarters. The bottom line, as with anywhere is don't turn up with a van full of mates, bring a chilled outlook and there should be no problems. Don't try to take more than your share of waves, even if you are the best surfer in the line-up. Enjoy the surfing and the company and you won't go far wrong.

Getting around

The roads in western Ireland are not built for speed. Sometimes they feel more like they are designed to test the build quality of your car. When trying to work out how long it takes to get between breaks always factor in extra time. Be warned that the *garda* are always on the look out for drink driving and will often set up checkpoints heading out of towns or even in the smallest villages.

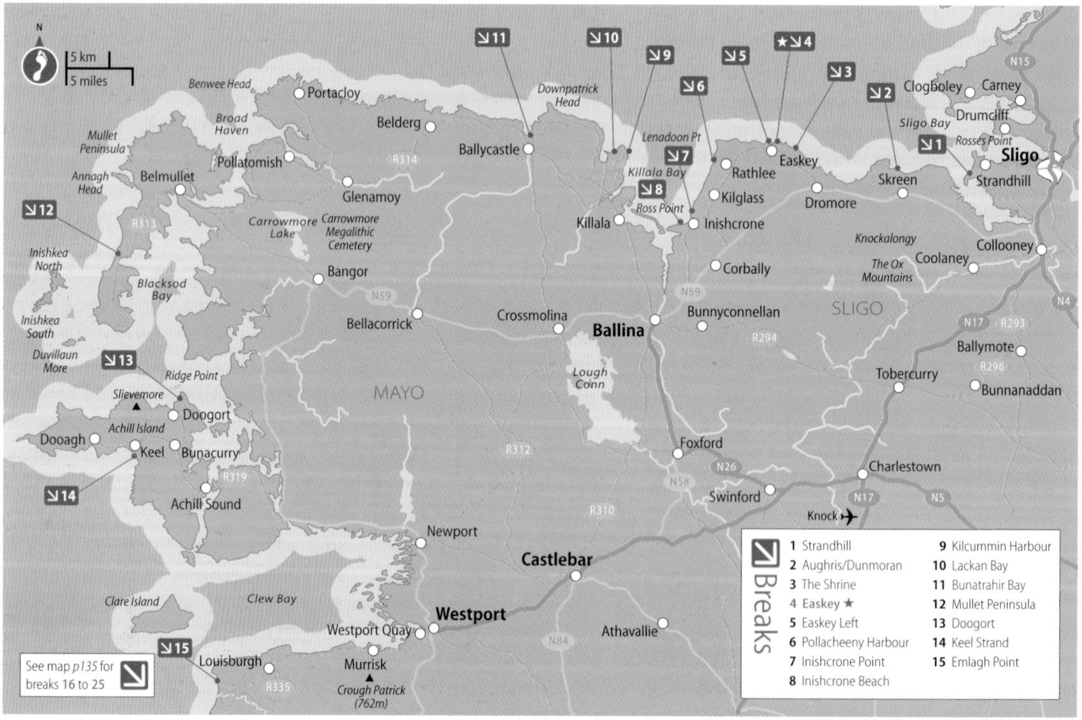

Breaks

BEACH BREAK

↘1 Strandhill

Conditions All NW swells, offshore in E to SE winds
Hazards/tips Popular beach
Sleeping Strandhill ▸▸ *p137*

The beach is a long arc of sand with numerous peaks, generally working best at mid tide in an easterly. The most popular peaks are by the car park. Waves can push up to the promenade at high. There is a decent right that can break off the bouldery point to the north that needs a northeasterly wind. The rivermouth to the southwest can also have excellent waves breaking on a sandbar. Strandhill is a real surfers village. Its proximity to the 2 km beach as well as the large urban population of Sligo has made it one of Ireland's most popular surf spots. Weekends see the line-up bustling, especially in small clean swells. Check www.strandhillsurfcam.com.

BEACH BREAK

↘2 Aughris/Dunmoran

Conditions Medium to big NW swells, offshore in S winds
Hazards/tips Quiet spot
Sleeping Strandhill/Easkey ▸▸ *p137*

This beach break is pretty mellow and less intense than the reefs to the west. A good spot for beginners and intermediate surfers. Works on all tides. The west of the beach is sheltered in larger swells and westerly winds, making it popular spot with surfers from nearby Sligo.

LEFT REEF BREAK

↘3 The Shrine

Conditions Medium NW swells, offshore in S to SW winds
Hazards/tips Shallow and heavy
Sleeping Easkey ▸▸ *p137*

Follow the road to the shrine of St Farnan where you will find a ledgy, hollow left-hand reef. It needs a decent swell to get going but produces quality waves around mid tide.

RIGHT REEF BREAK

↘4 Easkey

Swell NW
Winds S
Tides Low
Size 3-10 ft
Length 50-100 m
Bottom Flat reef with boulders
Ability level Intermediate plus
Best months Sep-Nov
Board Performance thruster
Access Paddle round in channel or off the point
Hazards/tips Rock reef, crowds
Sleeping Easkey ▸▸ *p137*

Of all the surf destinations and all the waves in Ireland, Easkey is probably the Queen. She has been a legend since the 1970s, when surf explorer/journalists Kevin Naughton and Craig Peterson famously rocked up here and showed the world that Easkey was holding. The pages of Surfer Magazine helped inspire many travelling surfers to follow in their footsteps, and some – including the legendary Mickey Dora, stayed on for a time to add an international flavour to this small, traditional village.

The reason Easkey is so popular, and why people keep coming back, is pretty simple. It's easy to find, consistent, not an overly heavy wave and great quality. Swells hit the flat reef and throw up long, walling right-handers that wrap along the reef before closing out on the inside. There's quite an easy paddle out to the west of the break in the huge channel and it can handle swells up to 8-10 ft. That's not to say it's easy at 8-10 ft! At this kind of size it's really the realm of the expert. Easkey Right is a low tide break but when it's on, it's rarely quiet. Expect crowds, especially with a good chart, anytime during the holidays, bank holiday weekends and through the summer. Don't come in large groups and bring a relaxed attitude into the line-up, and remember this is a region where there is massive surf potential. There is a surf centre in the village.

ⓘ *If you like **Easkey Right**, try **Thurso East** in Scotland (see page 40) or **Crab Island** in Wales (see page 97).*

SHARPY

4 Sam Lamiroy enjoying the walling Easkey Right.

THE GILL

THE GILL

Top: 7 Inishcrone – likened by some to the legendary J Bay. **Above: 9** Oli Adams, Kilcummin.
Right: 16 Local charger John McCarthy, Crab Island.

LEFT REEF BREAK

↘5 Easkey Left

- **Conditions** All NW swells, offshore in S winds
- **Hazards/tips** Crowds
- **Sleeping** Easkey ▸▸ *p137*

Just to the western side of the bay lies Easkey Left – on its day another world-class reef. It starts to work in smaller swells and produces excellent wrapping walls by the mouth of the small river. The left also has an easy paddle out, this time in the channel from the harbour wall that overlooks the break. Easkey left is more flexible in that it works through all the tides. Again, very busy and very popular. To find both of the breaks, take the turn down to the castle tower from the village. There are toilets and camping here too.

RIGHT REEF BREAK

↘6 Pollacheeny Harbour

- **Conditions** Medium to big W to NW swells, offshore in SE winds
- **Hazards/tips** Quality wave, heavy when big
- **Sleeping** Easkey/Inishcrone ▸▸ *p137*

Follow the bumpy track down to the bouldery natural lagoon. There are two waves that break here, the outside and inner point. They are both quality hollow waves breaking over a bouldery reef. Works best in a southeasterly wind and at low tide.

RIGHT POINT BREAK

↘7 Inishcrone Point

- **Conditions** Medium to big NW swells, offshore in SE winds
- **Hazards/tips** Excellent, fast breaking reef
- **Sleeping** Inishcrone ▸▸ *p137*

Standing on the harbour at Inishcrone you should see a fast, quality right-hand point break wrapping along the headland just to the northeast. In a good swell and with southeasterly winds, fast hollow waves reel down the point over the shallow reef. A very nice wave that has been largely overlooked, but those in the know enjoy a speedy wave that challenges the surfer. Best at low tide. Park near the harbour. Best left to advanced surfers.

BEACH BREAK

↘8 Inishcrone Beach

- **Conditions** Medium NW swells, offshore in S winds
- **Hazards/tips** Good all-round beach
- **Sleeping** Inishcrone ▸▸ *p137*

A good sized beach with plenty of peaks along the bay. Not too powerful or heavy so worth checking when big swells close out most of the reefs. A fun spot for beginners and intermediates at other times. Works through the tides.

LEFT-HAND POINT BREAK

↘9 Kilcummin Harbour

- **Conditions** All W to NW swells, offshore in SW to S winds
- **Hazards/tips** Can work in W wind
- **Sleeping** Ballycastle ▸▸ *p137*

Follow the road round to the harbour and from here there's a good view north to a quality left peeling down the point towards you. Kilcummin is famous for its excellent walls and barrel sections but it does get busy in a westerly wind as it can be one of the few waves still working.

BEACH BREAK

↘10 Lackan Bay

- **Conditions** Medium NW swells, offshore in S winds
- **Hazards/tips** Big beach
- **Sleeping** Ballycastle ▸▸ *p137*

Worth checking in a westerly wind – the headland provides a degree of shelter. It is a long beach with banks that change with the tides. A great location, suitable for surfers of all abilities and not one of the regions better known spots. Check the headland to the west for a left-hand reef break.

REEF BREAK

↘11 Bunatrahir Bay

- **Conditions** Medium NW swells, offshore in S wind
- **Hazards/tips** Quiet break
- **Sleeping** Ballycastle ›› *p137*

A point break located by a harbour, Bunatrahir has a nice little left-hand reef to the north of the breakwater. The wave needs a medium swell from a northerly direction to really fire. Park responsibly near the harbour.

BEACHES AND REEF BREAK

↘12 Mullet Peninsula

- **Conditions** All NW to SW swells, offshore in E winds
- **Hazards/tips** A huge variety of breaks
- **Sleeping** Belmullet ›› *p137*

The Mullet Peninsula has amazing potential. The beaches on the western side are exposed to the full force of the Atlantic so are ideal for exploring in the summer. It has a long sandy beach, with plenty of peaks to choose from, and virtually no surfers. The southern tip is more sheltered and worth checking when the swell really kicks in.

BEACH BREAK

↘13 Doogort

- **Conditions** Medium to big W swells, offshore in SE winds
- **Hazards/tips** Access over the fields from the village
- **Sleeping** Achill Island ›› *p138*

It's a long drive round from Belmullet to Achill Island and this flexible spot. There are a couple of beaches here that work in big swells and winds from easterly through to southwesterly. Ridge Point picks up the most swell whereas the western beach is more sheltered. Works on all tides.

BEACH BREAK

↘14 Keel Strand

- **Conditions** Medium to big W to SW swells, offshore in NE winds
- **Hazards/tips** Likes a southwesterly swell
- **Sleeping** Achill Island ›› *p138*

Keel is a small village at the northern end of this 3 km long, open, sandy bay. You can access the long, curving beach from either end or in the middle via Dookinelly. A little exposed to the wind but it remains flexible due to the fact that it works in an easterly, northeasterly or northerly wind. Has some good banks, especially around the stream that drains out of Keel Lake. Faces southwesterly but also worth checking in massive northwesterly swells.

BEACH BREAK

↘15 Emlagh Point

- **Conditions** All NW to SW swells, offshore in SE winds
- **Hazards/tips** Long open beach
- **Sleeping** Achill Island ›› *p138*

This is an amazing beach about as far away from the crowds as you can get. Between Emlagh Point and Tonakeera Point lie nearly 10 km of beaches broken by the occasional reef and rocky point. There are plenty of high quality sandbanks to check out in an easterly or southeasterly wind.

RIGHT REEF BREAK

↘16 Crab Island

- **Swell** NW to SW
- **Wind** Light E to SE
- **Tide** Low to mid
- **Size** 3-12 ft plus
- **Length** 50-75 m
- **Bottom** Jagged reef
- **Ability level** Advanced
- **Best months** Sep-Nov
- **Board** Pintail thruster to semi-gun
- **Access** Long paddle in the channel from the harbour
- **Hazards/tips** Long paddle offshore, heavy wave, shallow reef
- **Sleeping** Doolin ›› *p138*

"It's the kind of paddle I wouldn't consider in Australia or South Africa," says big wave charger and Lahinch local John McCarthy, of the 20 minutes of deep blue channel that needs to be navigated to reach the back of Crab Island. "Fortunately there's no such

AL MACKINNON

thing as a shark attack in Ireland," he adds. Even so, this can be an un-nerving spot and a place where the lack of crowds adds to the eeriness. The reef is a serrated, unforgiving limestone slab waiting just below the surface, in stark contrast to the cold, deep-water channel. Half hidden at the back of the offshore island, the wave can be misleading from the distance of the shore. Get the measure of it before heading out as once in the line-up it can be sobering to see the size of the barrels detonating into the whitewater cauldron. "Do not overestimate your ability," warns Tom Buckley of nearby Lahinch Surf Shop. "It is a serious wave and has broken many boards and leashes, dislocated a few shoulders and put out a few backs. If you lose your board then the swim home can be very, very difficult due to the currents in the channel between the island and the mainland."

The swell jacks up out of deep water and unloads onto the shallow ledge making the take-off critically steep as the wave suddenly stands up into a vertical peak. The glassy wall then opens up for the brave before the lip throws into a cavernous barrel wrapping and bowling with a thundering bass rumbling through the water as the pitching lip zippers along the impact zone. "Crab can be quite short," says John McCarthy, "but has a lot of intensity. At fully low tide it's only a couple of feet deep so the take-off can be very challenging, but you can get some perfect tubes. If you get a big west or southwest swell with no wind, you can surf it at 12 ft and maybe bigger. There are always some random peaks that catch you out, but if you get to know the wave you can avoid most of the swimming."

*If you like **Crab Island**, try **Coxos** in Portugal (see page 298) or **El Basurero** on Isla Graciosa (see page 267).*

RIGHT POINT BREAK

↘17 Doolin Point

Conditions All NW to SW swells, offshore in E winds

Hazards/tips Long walling wave, entry and exit can be tricky in big swells

Sleeping Doolin ▸▸ *p138*

It's a short walk from the car park to the wrapping righthand walls of Doolin Point. These big, open faces peel over an intimidating, jagged limestone reef that must be tip toed over to reach the waters edge. From its outside line-up, long, walling waves provide bowling rides of up to 8 ft. The wave is best surfed at low to mid tide, before the waves start to push onto the limestone ledges, making exit difficult. The reef is sharp and dangerous. Best left to experienced surfers. There is also a good left just to the southwest of the point towards the cliffs.

MICKEY SMITH

Lahinch local Tom taking on one of the area's primo spots.

BEACH BREAK

↘18 Lahinch

- **Conditions** Medium to big NW to SW swells, offshore in E winds
- **Hazards/tips** Excellent beach for beginners to advanced surfers
- **Sleeping** Lahinch »p139

Very popular beach and centre of local surf community. Works through the tides and can have good to excellent banks. Good for beginners and advanced. Busy peaks by town, spread out north and south. Avoid high tide by sea defenses as beach disappears.

PAUDIE SCANLON

LEFT REEF BREAK

↘19 The Lefts

- **Conditions** Medium to big NW to SW swells, offshore in E winds
- **Hazards/tips** Good quality waves, experienced surfers
- **Sleeping** Lahinch »p139

Heading south from Lahinch, there are a number of left reefs that pick up more swell as you go. The first is **The Left**, which sits at

THE GILL

PAUDIE SCANLON

Top Right: 19 This series of Lefts are a goofy footers dream. **Above: 19** Neil Bru Acheson, Cornish Left kicking in. **Top: 17** Doolin Point.

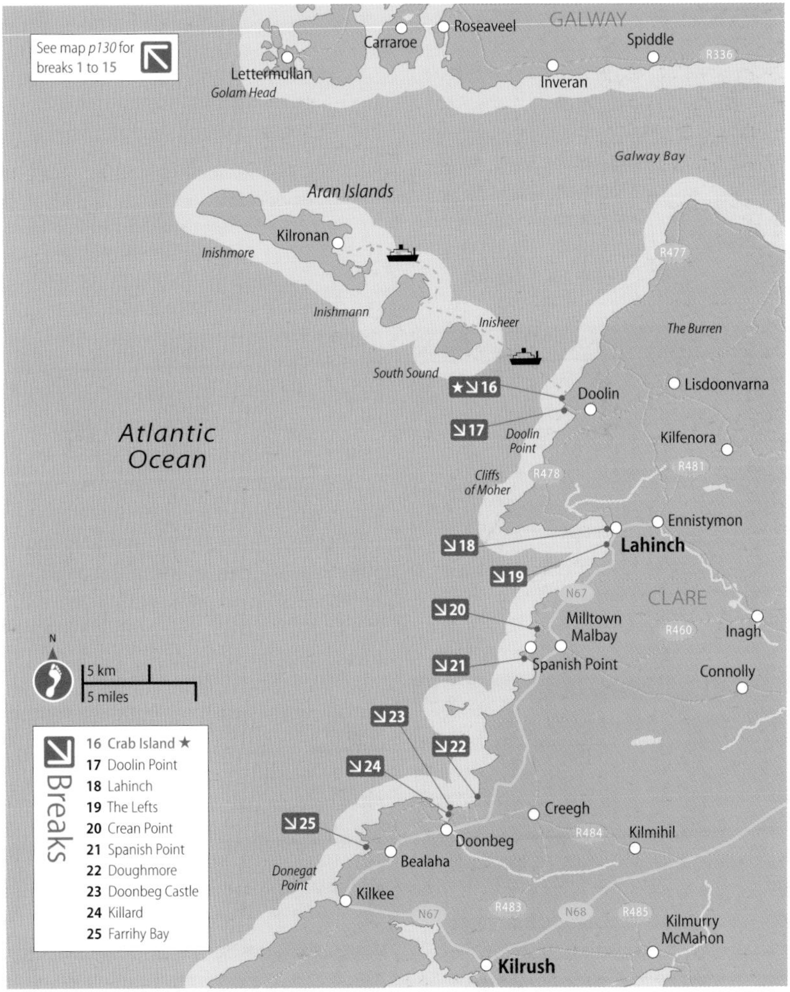

PAUDIE SCANLON

Above: 22 Eoin McCarthy-Deering – Dougmore, Co. Clare.

the end of the beach and is the most popular. In good swells it produces long walls up to 300 m and is best from low to mid tide. Just to the south is **Cornish Left**, a faster, hollower wave that works through the tides. **Cregg** has a left and right that works through the tides, and a low tide right. Next is **Aussie Left**, a quality wave that needs a big swell to fire.

RIGHT POINT BREAK

↘20 Crean Point

- **Conditions** Big NW to SW swells, offshore in E winds
- **Hazards/tips** Advanced surfers only
- **Sleeping** Lahinch/Kilkee ▸▸ *p139*

A huge right-hand peak that comes alive in massive swells. One to watch and admire, unless you have your tow-in set up with you.

REEF BREAK

↘21 Spanish Point

- **Conditions** All NW to SW swells, offshore in E winds
- **Hazards/tips** Series of excellent reefs
- **Sleeping** Lahinch/Kilkee ▸▸ *p139*

One of Ireland's first star breaks, it seems to have slipped a bit from the limelight in the last decade. Not that the crowds have passed it by – it's more popular than ever with Irish surfers. There are three right-hand reefs to choose from. The **outer point** picks up a massive amount of swell and is pretty much unsurfed, except by the very competent. It can look perfect but upon closer inspection its size can be awesome. The **middle point** is a high quality right-hand reef and the most popular and consistent of the three. It works on a medium swell and has great walls with hollow sections. Best at mid tide. Easy paddle out. The **inside point** needs a large swell to get going. It's a fast, walling wave that benefits from being the most sheltered. The houses around Spanish Point are frequently swamped by surfers, so make sure you park respectfully and don't rock up with the stereo pumping. This will quickly lose what little goodwill is left. Farmers have been known to remove cars that have parked irresponsibly with their tractors.

BEACH BREAK

↘22 Doughmore

- **Conditions** Small to medium NW to SW swells, offshore in SE winds
- **Hazards/tips** Difficult access
- **Sleeping** Kilkee ▸▸ *p139*

Wonderful, dune-backed beach that picks up heaps of swell. Excellent fast, hollow banks but when the swell hits head-high tends to close out. All tides. Access is a bit tricky as you have to cross farmland to reach the sea. Always check with the farmer first and make sure you don't block any of the access roads.

REEF BREAK

↘23 Doonbeg Castle

- **Conditions** Big NW to SW swells, offshore in SW winds
- **Hazards/tips** Great spot when other breaks closing out
- **Sleeping** Kilkee ▸▸ *p139*

This is a pretty good left-hand reef that produces walling lefts in massive swells. The corner by the castle is sheltered and provides a decent spot to surf when other breaks are closing out. Take the turn by the church, just south of the village. Works on all tides except low.

BEACH BREAK

↘24 Killard

- **Conditions** Big NW to SW swells, offshore in SW winds
- **Hazards/tips** Sheltered spot
- **Sleeping** Kilkee ▸▸ *p139*

Another sheltered spot to check in big swells, this time offshore in southwesterly or westerly winds. Easy parking. Works through all tides and can produce walling lefts and rights, depending on the sandbanks.

BEACH BREAK

↘25 Farrihy Bay

- **Conditions** Small to medium NW to SW swells, offshore in E winds
- **Hazards/tips** Consistent spot
- **Sleeping** Kilkee ▸▸ *p139*

Just north of Kilkee, this bay picks up heaps of swell and can have some great beach-break waves in small swells. Tends to close out in bigger swells. Take the turning for Corbally and follow it to the bay.

Practicalities

Strandhill

This is a popular beach resort for surfers and families from the Sligo area with a great stretch of beach and a thriving surfing community watched over by the 1078-ft summit of Knocknarea.

Sleeping

€ Dunes Tavern, Top Road is just behind the golf course and a short walk to the beach, T0719168131. Run by a couple of local surfers they offer simple, clean B&B accommodation from €35 per person and budget bunks from €20, The downstairs bar gets pretty lively and has regular DJs and live bands. Recommended.

€ Strandhill Lodge and Hostel, Shore Rd, T071-9168313, is on the seafront has internet access plus doubles and bunk rooms.

Camping **Strandhill Caravan and Camping Park**, on the airport road, T071-9168111, with outdoor surfers showers and indoor pay showers, Easter-Sep.

Directory

Surf Shop **Perfect Day**, on the seafront, T071-9128488, is well stocked an operate a surf school from here.

Easkey

This is a pretty, traditional, Irish village centred around the main street. It has been heavily influenced by the influx of surfers – Mickey Dora once lived here and the Irish Surfing Association, www.isasurf.ie, has set up home in the Easkey Surf and Information Centre, Main St, who, handily peddle blocks of wax. Stop for a pint in **McGowans** – popular with locals.

Sleeping

Easkey Surfing and Information Centre Main street, T096-49020, has an up-to-date list of surfer-friendly rooms and apartments. Also www.westsligo.com, for information.

Self Catering **Riverbank**, T096 49525, www.easkeybreak.com, a well furnished, stylish 3 bed, modern house on the banks of the River Easkey also offers views over the break and is ideal for couples from €450 per week.

Camping **Atlantic 'N' Riverside Caravan and Camping Park**, in the village, next to the river, T096-49001, is a 5-min walk from the breaks, open Apr-Sep, Register at the Post office.

Inishcrone (Enniscrone)

Popular Irish holiday resort with that really only opens from Easter. If you do turn up off season ask in the pubs as very often they'll be able to help you find B&B accommodation. During Easter weekend you may find the pubs closed, but seek and you may find that one of them may have a crafty lock-in. Stop off at **Walsh's**, on Main St for live music, good food and internet access.

Sleeping

€€ Gowan Brae B&B, on Pier Rd, T096-36396, is a large, reasonably priced Georgian house with views towards Killala Bay.

Camping **Atlantic Caravan Park**, on the seafront, T096-36132, has excellent access to the beach, static caravans to hire as well as room for vans.

Directory

Surf Shops **Kilcullen's Surf Shop**, at the northern end of the bay by the famous Seaweed Baths stocks all the essentials.

Ballycastle

Not to be confused with Ballycastle, Co. Antrim, this small and pretty village, on the northern shores of County Mayo is centred around its sloping Main Street. Most visitors here are drawn to the Céide Fields megalithic excavation site and visitor's centre, 5 miles west.

Sleeping

€€€ Stella Maris, T096 43322, www.stellamaris.com. This former 19th Century coastguard headquarters has been transformed into a hotel that is elegant and comfortable. The home cooking is great but the real pull is the location and views afforded by the huge conservatory overlooking Bunatrahir Bay. Pricey but a spot to secret yourself away with someone special.

€ Céide House, Main St, T096-43105. Lively pub with good value rooms open year round.

Mullet Peninsula

An awesome stretch of pristine coastline with huge sand beaches and many undiscovered reefs. The main settlement is the small market town of **Belmullet**, with

THE GILL

21 Spanish Point.

PAUDIE SCANLON

Kevin Doyle, Lahinch.

banks, supermarkets, post office plus a few places to eat and drink. The **Square Meal Restaurant**, on the Square, for hearty post-surf food.

Sleeping

€ **Drom Caoin**, is 1-2 km out of town with views towards Blacksod Bay, T097 81195. It offers comfortable B&B with rooms sleeping up to 3, Wi-Fi access plus a store and drying room. On site s/c apartments also available. € **Kilcommon Lodge Hostel**, just off the peninsula in Pollatomish, 20 mins to the east of Belmullet, T097-84621, is a welcoming place in a beautiful valley and offers some of the cheapest local accommodation, with excellent dorm and private accommodation from around €12.

Achill Island

This windswept peninsula juts into the Atlantic, forming a typically striking Celtic landscape which has been a constant draw to creatives. When the sun is out it is stunningly pretty, when the sky is grey and the wind blows, it is harsh, bleak and devastatingly beautiful.

Sleeping

€ **Valley House Hostel & Bar**, T098-47204, www.valley-house.com, is a good, affordable choice, also with the option of camping, on the road to Dugort from Bunacurry. It may be a little basic but the roaring fire on a cold day soon makes you forget.
Camping Keel Sandybanks Caravan & Camping Park, at the northern end of Keel Strand, T098-43211, www.achillcamping.com, overlooks the bay and has mobile homes available May-Sep. **Seal Caves Caravan and Camping Park**, T098-43262, open May-Sep, is well placed by the beaches at Dugort.

THE GILL

SHARPY

Above: The Cliffs of Moher, Aileens. **Bottom**: Swinno sets his rail on a secret west coast reef.

Eating and drinking

For a good evening meal check out **Calvey's Restaurant**, Keel, with views over the nearby sands. They pride themselves on using local produce from lobster and crab to locally grazed lamb and steaks.

Directory

Banks ATM in Achill Sound, plus various mobile banks. **Tourist information** Cashel on the Achill Sound-Keel road, www.achilltourism.com.

Doolin

This tiny village that stretches out along the valley, has become a centre of Irish music. The pubs have regular live bands that play to audiences including locals, surfers and US tourists. Boats run from the quay to the Aran Islands. There are no banks or ATMs in Doolin – Cliff of Moher visitors centre, Lahinch or Ennistymon are the closest ATMs.

Sleeping

€€ **Atlantic View House**, Pier Rd, T065-7074189, is a large, comfortable B&B with great views of the sea.
€€-€ **Doolin Activity Lodge**, T065-7074888, www.doolinlodge.com, offers fantastic B&B in clean, warm, modern ensuite rooms (single, twin, family) as well as offering apartments which can be rented on a B&B or self-catering basis with full kitchen facilities. The lodge has a 'wet entrance' plus purpose-built dry room and lock up storage facilities, excellent, well priced option. Packed lunch available on request. Popular with climbers and divers.
€ **Aille River Hostel**, by the river at top end of the village, T065-7074260, is a converted farmhouse and very popular with fairly basic but free facilities including laundry and internet. The atmosphere makes up for it through. Camping available on site.
€ **Doolin Hostel**, Fisher St, T065-7074421, www.doolinhostel.com. Popular with walkers and just a short stagger from the pubs with dorms and double rooms. **Fisher Street House** hostel is run by the same people, same contact, similar facilities.
Camping Nagles Doolin Camping and Caravan Park, T065-7074458, open May-end Sep, is a great place for campervans. It is within walking distance of the breaks, has fully equipped kitchens, a phone and a shop.

Eating and drinking
McDermott's is where the locals go for good beer, pub grub and live music. **Doolin Café** serves excellent dishes including seafood specials, good if a bit pricey, as does the **Lazy Lobster**, who deliver fantastic seafood dishes (as well as vegetarian and carnivore dinners) for around €20.

Lahinch

Lahinch is a popular tourist centre with a long sandy beach backed by sea defences. It is also one of Ireland's main surfing centres with a surf club of over 50 members.

Sleeping
€ **Lahinch Hostel**, Chuch St, T065-7081040, is clean and comfortable with dorm and private rooms plus board storage facilities.
€ **St Mildred's B&B**, Church St, T065-7081489, is a little basic but the rooms are comfortable with views of the beach at very reasonable prices.
Camping **Lahinch Camping and Caravan Park**, on the southern edge of town a short walk from the sea, T065-7081424, May-Sep.

Eating and drinking
O'Looney's, overlooks the sea and delivers good pub grub, an excellent atmosphere and a nightclub after sundown. **Mrs O'Brien's**, for pub grub, bands, DJs and pricey internet access. For a chilled-out pub with music head to **Flanagans**.

Directory
Surf shops **Lahinch Surf Shop**, Old Promenade, T065-7081543, was Ireland's first dedicated surf shop opening in 1989. They have a great range of hardware and accessories as well as managing a daily surf report, T0818-365180, www.lahinchsurfshop.com. **Surf school** Irish champion, the lovely John McCarthy runs **Lahinch Surf School**, T0879609667, www.lahinchsurfschool.com. **Banks** No banks, but there is an ATM at the northern end of Main St. Also on Main St are the **Post office**, a **petrol station** and a **pharmacy**. **Tourist information** Main St, T065-7082082, can book accommodation.

Flat spells

Ancient monument **Carrowmore Megalithic Cemetery**, just to the southwest of Sligo, is a fantastic collection of over 60 megalithic tombs, half of which are open to the public

Céide Fields Ballycastle - an extensive 5,000-year-old settlement first uncovered in the 1930s, although it's now been covered over again, the visitor centre is worth a stop by T096-43325.

Aran Islands Apr-Oct, catch the ferry that runs from Doolin harbour to the spiritual home of the knitted jumper – the Aran Islands – 3 isles covered in stunning flora and littered with ancient and Neolithic forts and tombs. The largest, measuring around 9 miles by 2 is Inishmore and one of the best ways to explore its treasures is by bike – which you can hire from the pier on arrival at the island. The journey from Doolin takes around 20 minutes, T065 7074455, www.doolinferries.com. For more info on the Aran Islands check out www.aranislands.ie.

Caves At Doolin, peer into the sea caves to the north of the harbour. One is called Hell and is a drop into a maize of sea caves, called the Green Holes of Doolin, that only the most experienced cavers should enter.

Cliffs of Moher Just south of Doolin. Spectacular, sheer cliffs with a drop of 214 m into the sea and one of those rare places where you can actually see it raining upwards!

Golf **Strandhill GC**, T071-9168188, www.strandhillgc.com, links course with fees from €40. **Enniscrone GC**, T096-36297, 2 courses including one par 72 championship links course. Weekday fees from €55. There is also a pitch and putt course in the village for those who prefer to fool around than play a round.

Spa To unwind, check out **Killcullen Seaweed Baths**, T096-36238, www.kilcullenseaweedbaths.com, if it's been flat too long and you're missing the sea, try out a therapeutic seaweed bath. Massage also available.

Mountain High **Knocknaea Mountain**, to the southwest of Sligo town stands a 1,078-ft mountain, capped off by a huge cairn or burial mound which, legend has it, is the tomb of the warrior Queen Maeve – this is an important archeological site which has been damaged by visitors climbing on the cairn. It takes around 40 minutes to climb the 'mountain of the moon' and the views over the bay are awesome.

Kilkee

Summer sees the population swell 10-fold with local holiday makers, while off-season is a mellower proposition. The holiday crowd means there are good local amenities plus plenty of places to drink and eat – try **The Pantry** for home baked lunches and evening meals. O'Curry St has a **Bank of Ireland** and ATM.

Sleeping
€€-€ **Bayview B&B**, T065-9056058, is well placed with sea views, quaint rooms, has a pub next door and is open year round.
Camping **Green Acres Caravan and Camping Park**, at Doonaha, T065-9057011, open Apr-Sep, sits on the coast and offers beach access and static caravans.

Southwest Ireland

Overview

Cresting the road – the climb to 1,300 ft complete – the summit of the Conor Pass lays out a stunning panoramic vista. A huge, rolling expanse that smoothly transitions from the peak of Mount Brandon – at 3,200 ft Ireland's second loftiest – down to sea level at Bá Bhreandáin, without a single sharp angle in sight. From this vantage point the Atlantic bends across the horizon, white clouds drift across a vast sky shadowed by a darker twin that rakes the land below. This is the perfect place for a surf check, worth the drive even on the flattest days. Brandon Bay is laid out below, the region's most consistent spot, and swell lines marching into the bay make a heart quickening sight, like a sudden shot of adrenalin. Nice view and all that – but time to go!

The Dingle Peninsula in southwest Ireland is one of the country's premiere tourist draws. The picture perfect scenery has provided the backdrop for many a big budget Hollywood production, from 'Ryan's Daughter' to Tom Cruise's 'Far and Away'. The town of Dingle is no less perfect, with brightly painted cottages and warm, welcoming traditional pubs slowly piping black magic into angled glasses. For a surfer the attraction is much more clear. The Atlantic ocean ravages the rugged and complex coastline, eeking out bays and eroding cliffs into beaches now linked by narrow country lanes, fringed by a mass of red fuchsias that proliferate at the roadside. These winding tracks weave down to coves fringed with golden sand, and lapped by waters that would rival any Caribbean location for sheer translucent perfection. Bays like Coumeenole, tranquil and soothing one day, the next, raging with gaping barrels that spit contempt at any but the most serious challenge to their all-conquering power.

The guilt of an enhanced 'carbon footprint' must be off-set later – driving is a sheer necessity to track down those elusive waves that are out there. Somewhere. Just another check of the map and another bend in the road. "I think the thing I've noticed is that as the economy has picked up, more younger surfers seem to have cars, so there's more surfers about on the roads," says local charger Paul McCarthy. "Although the line-ups haven't got that much busier on a day to day basis in the past five or six years, there's certainly more people at spots like Brandon Bay on a Bank Holiday or a weekend." Here four wheels are as necessary a companion on your search as a surfboard.

Spring
Air 8°C 46°F
Water 10°C 50°F
5/4/3mm Wetsuit & boots

Summer
Air 15°C 59°F
Water 14°C 57°F
3/2mm Wetsuit

Autumn
Air 11°C 52°F
Water 14°C 57°F
4/3mm Wetsuit

Winter
Air 5°C 41°F
Water 9°C 48°F
5/4/3mm Wetsuit, boots, gloves & hood

PAUDIE SCANLON

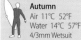

Sam Pollard tucks into an Irish Gem.

Coastline

The southwest corner of Ireland is blanketed in a lush green baize, laid across the windswept countryside like a patchwork quilt. Its highpoints are the towering hills and the summit of Mount Brandon, which rolls down to the jagged coastline scoured by the raging Atlantic. Summers here are warm and mild and the blue waters around Dingle have an almost tropical clarity. While not the most consistent region in the country, the many hidden coves and open beaches can provide rich surfing when the northwesterly swells roll in. Brandon Bay to the north is the most consistent spot. Hidden in the fjord-like Dingle Bay, Inch Reef is the area's most famous break, like a sleeping giant waiting for a westerly swell to hit. And to the south, the amazing Ballinskelligs Bay has a whole raft of boulder reefs waiting for the southwesterly swell lines to roll in. In this region, if you're willing to get out and explore, you will truly be rewarded.

Local community

"Even though surfing has seen a massive increase in participants across Ireland in the last six years, the amount of local surfers on the Dingle peninsula has not increased all that much" says Ben Farr from Finn McCool's Surf Co, Dingle. "Some guys have moved away, there are some new faces and some have moved on and started picking up kites. However the amount of surfers from across Ireland who visit Dingle in the summer has massively increased. You'll see plenty of cars with boards on top searching for waves and the line-ups at Inch and Brandon on a sunny weekend can be fairly crowded – especially on a Bank Holiday. Also with the addition of three or four new surf schools and the fact that many of these 'weekend warriors' are beginners, you'll find that most of the deeper breaks are still fairly empty and

THE GILL

10 Waiting on the other side of Glenbeigh Woods.

certainly many are put off by the climb down the cliff at Inch reef to risk it with their shiny new boards. In the wintertime you can still find loads of peaks amazingly devoid of surfers – particularly on a rainy, November, Tuesday morning."

Getting around

The roads in Ireland are not built for speed but to get you there, eventually. Some go by the longest, most convoluted way you could imagine. Even the relatively easy task of reaching the next bay around the headland can become a lengthy trek inland before turning back to the coast. But once you accept that most trips will take longer than you think, you can sit back and enjoy the scenery. Checking swell and wind directions and chatting with the locals can save hours in the car.

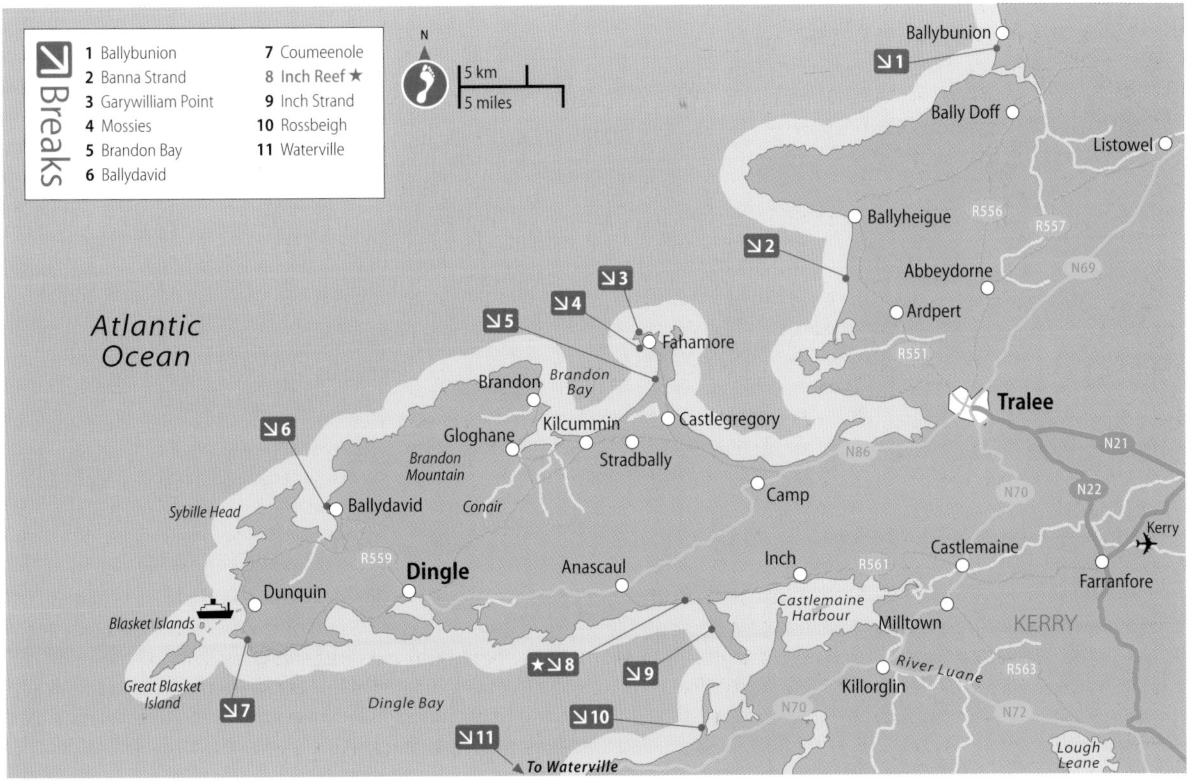

Breaks

BEACH AND REEF BREAK

↘1 Ballybunion

- **Conditions** All NW to SW swells, offshore in E winds
- **Hazards/tips** Three popular breaks
- **Sleeping** Ballybunion » p144

A flexible stretch of beach with easy access to some fairly good banks. Lefts and rights break on the main beach through the tides. Towards the southern end of the beach is a low tide left that breaks over rocks and boulders. This spot produces good walls and the odd barrel section, but gets too fat as the tide pushes. At the northern end of the beach is a right that starts breaking in front of the cliff and peels through to the inside with nice walls to attack. The right works on all tides except low.

BEACH BREAK

↘2 Banna Strand

- **Conditions** All W and medium to big SW to NW swells, offshore in E winds
- **Hazards/tips** Beautiful beach
- **Sleeping** Ballyheigue » p144

This massive, open beach is exposed to a medium westerly and northwesterly swell. The beach offers some great peaks with the northern end being the most sheltered and the southern end picking up the most swell. There are a couple of rivermouths worth checking out for sandbanks. Follow the R551 from Tralee or Ballybunnion.

REEF BREAK

↘3 Garywilliam Point

- **Conditions** Small to medium NW to W swells, offshore in SE winds
- **Hazards/tips** Exposed reef for experienced surfers
- **Sleeping** Dingle » p144

Out on the end of the point breaks this exposed right-hand reef. It picks up plenty of swell but is easily affected by winds, so likes still days or southeasterlies. The wave hits and throws out sending fast, hollow barrels racing along the shallow reef. Best at low tide. Experienced surfers only.

REEF BREAK

↘4 Mossies

- **Conditions** Medium W to NW swells, offshore in SE winds
- **Hazards/tips** Offshore reef with mellow waves
- **Sleeping** Dingle » p144

A mellow reef break that has both lefts and rights peeling along a reef just inside Brandon Bay. It's a bit of a paddle out to the wave, which is best at low to mid tide. Follow the road out towards Fahamore.

BEACH BREAK

↘5 Brandon Bay

- **Conditions** All NW to W swells, offshore in SE to S swells
- **Hazards/tips** Huge bay exposed to northwesterly swell
- **Sleeping** Dingle » p144

This is the most likely spot to have waves on the Dingle Peninsula as it faces due northwest. Take a drive up from Dingle and park on the pass at Conair to check the bay.

THE GILL

3 Garywilliam Point.

Just south of Mossies is **Dumps**, a section of hollow peaks that works at all tides. It picks up plenty of swell producing short, barrelling lefts and rights. Further round the bay at Stradbally is **Peaks**, a section of good banks that work from mid to high tide. At **Kilcummin** is a popular area that is offshore in southerly winds, but the waves here aren't as powerful nor the banks as good.

RIGHT POINT BREAK

↘6 Ballydavid

- **Conditions** Big NW swells, offshore in S winds
- **Hazards/tips** Heavy wave
- **Sleeping** Ballydavid » p145

Sitting on the edge of the village of Ballydavid is a reeling wave that only rouses itself in the biggest swells. This heavy, right point has a difficult take-off, solid, hollow waves and long hold-downs. Check it from the harbour and if it's on, you'll probably need your gun. Works on all tides. On the other side of the bay is **Black Strand**, a left that breaks at high tide. This part of the beach picks up more swell.

BEACH BREAK

↘7 Coumeenole

- **Conditions** Small and medium SW to large NW swells, offshore in NE winds
- **Hazards/tips** Hollow powerful break, not for beginners
- **Sleeping** Dingle » p144

This looks like a very picturesque bay where holidaymakers paddle and picnic. In reality it's a solid beachbreak that really packs a punch. There are some great banks here including a hollow, heavy right that works from low up to three-quarter tide. A board breaker. There's a steep road down the cliffs to the beach, demanding careful parking – check your handbrake!

RIGHT REEF BREAK

↘8 Inch Reef

- **Swell** W or big NW
- **Wind** NE
- **Tide** All but high
- **Size** 3-8 ft
- **Length** Up to 800 m (according to legend)
- **Bottom** Flat, rock reef
- **Ability level** Intermediate
- **Best months** Nov-Apr
- **Board** Longboard or thruster with volume
- **Access** Over the rocks from the cliff
- **Hazards/tips** Rips, tricky entry and exit
- **Sleeping** Dingle ▸▸ *p144*

A great name for a reef that can break for nearly half a mile in perfect conditions. Inch needs a big northwesterly swell or a solid westerly swell to get into the narrows of Dingle Bay. The R561 that runs above the break and provides a great vantage point to check the break. Has become increasingly busy as the local and semi-local surfing communities have increased over the last few years. If it breaks on a weekend, expect all surfers from the greater area to converge here. "You can still get it pretty quiet during the week, early morning or in the winter," says local surfer Paul McCarthy. There can be punishing rips pushing away from the peak. Spectacular location with views running down the peninsula.

*If you like **Inch Reef**, try **Immessouane** in Morocco (see page 378) or **Ribeira d'Ilhas** in Portugal (see page 299).*

> There has definitely been an increase in numbers of surfboards you see on roof racks, but it's still possible to score pretty uncrowded waves. You just need to read the conditions right.
>
> *Paul McCarthy*

THE GILL

Top: 8 Inch Reef – Ireland's longest wave. **Bottom:** 7 Coumeenole

BEACH BREAK

↘9 Inch Strand

- **Conditions** Big W swells, offshore in E winds
- **Hazards/tips** Mellow beach
- **Sleeping** Dingle ▸▸ *p144*

The beach is quite mellow and has a feel of Llangennith or Saunton as the waves lack real punch. A good spot for beginners or longboarders. A stunning location looking down Dingle Bay with spectacular scenery on both sides. Parking available at the beach.

BEACH BREAK AND BOULDER POINT

↘10 Rossbeigh

- **Conditions** Medium to big W swells, offshore in SE winds
- **Hazards/tips** Mellow beach
- **Sleeping** Glenbeigh ▸▸ *p145*

On the south side of the bay there is another stretch of beach and a boulder point accessed at Glenbeigh Wood. Picks up more swell than Inch, and is offshore in winds from the southeast.

BEACH BREAK

↘11 Waterville

- **Conditions** All SW and big W to NW swells, offshore in NE winds
- **Hazards/tips** SW facing sheltered bay
- **Sleeping** Waterville

A tight knit surfing community surf this bay, waiting for just the right lows to push in medium or big southwesterly or big westerly swells. To the west of Waterville is a stretch of average beach break. To the left of the village are a number of boulder reefs that work at various stages of tide including a low tide left and a low to mid there is a right. At mid to high in the right conditions you'll also see a couple of lefts.

THE GILL

Practicalities

Ballybunion

Ballybunion is a golfer's paradise with world-class course and plenty of pubs, accommodation and facilities. Travelling from County Clare to Kerry, save yourself the loooong (nearly 3 hrs) 140 km drive around the Shannon Estuary, by hopping on the Killimer-Tarbert ferry. Operated year round by Shannon Ferries, T065-9053124, www.shannonferries.com, the crossing takes 20 mins with regular services daily (from Killimer until 2100 in summer and 1900 winter, 30 mins later from Tarbert). Return for a camper and passengers around €27. In Tarbert **Ferry House Hostel** on the square, is a comfortable, handy and open year round with dorms and twins from €14, T068-36555 www.ferryhousehostel.com. Heading along the R551 to the resort town of Ballybunion, the **Parklands Holiday Park** on Listowel Rd, T068-27275, Easter-Sep, has mobile homes to rent.

Ballyheigue

Heading south along the R551, Ballyheigue has all the basic amenities including a supermarket, post office, pubs and takeaways.

Sleeping

Self Catering **Banna Beach Holiday & Leisure Complex**, just south at Banna Strand, T066-7134103, www.bannabeachhotel.net, is a family focused park with kids activities and entertainment laid on. That aside, it also has quality, modern detached bungalows sleeping up to 6 within easy reach of the beach for around €350-760 per week, making it a good option for groups also. **Camping** **Sir Roger's Caravan & Camping Park**, just back from Banna Beach, T066-7134730, www.sirrogerscaravanpark.com, is a great spot, open Mar-Nov. Board hire also available.

Dingle

On the southern shore of the beautiful Dingle Peninsula, a finger of land that beckons to the passing Atlantic lows, the town of Dingle is compact, cosmopolitan, and home to good craic. Well, what would you expect from a small town that is home to more than 50 pubs? Centred around Main and Goat St, traditional painted shop-fronts and bars blend with businesses – and there are plenty of amenities from a supermarket, banks plus a good surf shop. The harbour here is the adopted home of Fungie the dolphin and a whole micro-industry has sprung up around him. Although English is widely spoken, Dingle lies within the *Gaeltacht* or Irish-speaking community so is as authentic an experience as you could imagine.

Sleeping

€€ An Capall Dubh, Green St, T066-9151105, www.ancapalldubh.com, is an excellent option, especially for couples. The 6 B&B rooms are bright, cute and clean with en suite bathrooms. They also have reasonably priced self-catering apartments or town houses available to rent.
€ Ballintaggart House Hostel, on the Dingle-Tralee Rd, T066-9151454, www.dingleaccommodation.com, is an excellent option – around 20 min walk into town. Originally a hunting lodge in the 1700s, it has been well converted into a hostel with spacious dorms, €13 a bed, and double rooms from €40. May-Sep they also operate a campsite for tents and vans.
€ Grapevine Hostel, centrally located on Dykegate, T066-9151434, is small, friendly and centrally located with dorms available from €16 and private rooms from €21 p/p.
€ Rainbow Hostel, about a mile from the town centre, T066 9151044, www.rainbowhosteldingle.com, is light and airy with dorms and private rooms. They have internet access plus board storage as well as camping available on site.

Eating and drinking

Adams, on Main St, is a pub/restaurant and as traditional as they come. This mid-priced, dark, cosy bar serves, among other more basic fare, excellent locally caught crab salad. **An Café Liteartha**, Dykegate St, is a great little café-cum-bookshop that serves good, affordable soups, sandwiches and snacks. For an evening meal, try mid-priced **Global Village**, on Main St, open Mar-Nov, which fuses foods from across the world to create something lovely and relaxed. **Dick Mack's**, is a great spot with a Hollywood Boulevard-style pavement outside with all their famous visitors recorded in stone – including queen of Country, Dolly Parton! A locals favourite, its interior has remained unchanged from the days when it doubled as a hardware store. The **Conair Bar**, Spa St, has a good vibe and live music at the weekends. But if these aren't your cup of tea (or beer) fear not there's another 50 or so pubs to choose from.

Directory

Surfshop **Finn McCool's – The Surf Company**, Lower Green St, T066-9150833, www.finnmccools.ie, have a good range of hardware including Rip Curl and C-Skins wetties, boards plus surfing's necessities – ding repair, fins, wax etc. **Internet** **Dingle Internet Café**, Main St, Mon-Sat also International phone calls. **Banks** Main St.

THE GILL

Reef watch Southwest Ireland.

Bike hire **Foxy John's** on Main St from €9 a day. **Pharmacy** Holy Ground. **Post office** Main St. **Tourist information** The Quay, www.dingle-peninsula.ie, year round.

Ballydavid

On the north shore of the Dingle Peninsula at Ballydavid, **Tigh An Phoist Hostel**, on Bothar Bui, T066-9155109, www.tighanphoist.com, is open Apr-Oct and offers good access to Ballydavid Point. Dorm beds from around €15, private rooms around €20 per person. Self catering apartments also available sleeping 5-6. Near Ballydavid, at Gallarus, **Teach An Aragail Campsite**, T066-9155143, is Europe's most westerly site. This friendly spot is open Apr-Sep and is within walking distance to the local pubs.

Glenbeigh

Heading south on the N70, Glenbeigh sits on the Iveragh Peninsula, home of the stunning road circuit known as the Ring of Kerry. Camp in the village within sight of Rossbeigh beach at **Glenross Caravan and Camping Park**, T066-9768451, www.killarneycamping.com. Open May-Sep, they also have mobile homes available from €220 for 6 people. Just above the beach at Rossbeigh itself, the self catering **Rossbeigh View Beach House**, T087-6735943, www.rossbeighbeachhouse.com, is a new-build, comfortable, semi, sleeping up to 7 from around €370 per week and available to rent Apr-Jan.

Flat spells

Blasket Islands The Blaskets, T066-9156422, www.blasketisland.com, a group of islands off the coastline, were inhabited until 1953 and are now home to colonies of puffins, gannets and guillemots among others. Tra Ban (white strand) is a beautiful and popular beach in the summer. In the autumn, Atlantic seals make their annual trip to Great Blasket. Blasket Island Ferries run regular services from Dunquin harbour. For services from Dingle, T066-9151344, www.dinglebaycharters.com.

Cinema **Kerry Omniplex Cinema**, Ivy Terr, www.omniplex.ie, Tralee, just next to the tourist information office has 8 screens showing the latest movies. **Phoenix**, in Dingle on Dykegate, T066-91512222, www.phoenixdingle.net.

Dogs Head to the **Kingdom Greyhound Stadium**, in Oakview, at the north of the town, T066-7124033, for an evening at the dogs. Races Tue, Fri, Sat entry €10.

Fishing Sea angling is available out of Dingle marina from about €20 p/p, T066-9151344, www.dinglebaycharters.com. Shore angling is also popular with some excellent spots near Coumeenole and Ballydavid.

Fungie the dolphin There are boat trips out of the harbour to see Fungie the dolphin, (although you can also see him from the nearby beach). The dolphin first appeared in 1984 and has become the region's major attraction. If Fungie stimulates your interests in all things aquatic, you can visit **Oceanworld** on Dingle Harbour, which has a shark tank and an ocean tunnel tank.

Golf **Aqua Dome**, Dingle Rd, Tralee, T066-7128899, is home to Aqua Golf, an 18-hole mini-golf course (and about €150 cheaper than the Tralee golf course!). **Dingle Golf Links** near the Three Sisters, out towards Ballyferriter, T066-9156255, is Europe's most westerly course. For the less serious golfer, there's a pitch and putt course just outside Dingle on the road to Ventry (R559). **Castlegregory Golf Links**, on the northern edge of the Dingle Peninsula, has a lovely 9-hole course fees from €20, T066-7139444, www.castlegregorygolflinks.com.

Mountain **Mt Brandon** is Ireland's second largest peak, situated on the north coast of the Dingle Peninsula. At 950 ft, it is a serious trek, but the views it reveals are worth the walk.

Walking One of the best ways to explore some of this region's awesome scenery is using foot power.

Rosslare

If you're coming or going, a night here is fine (emphasis on fine, not to be confused with good) otherwise there are plenty more interesting places to explore on the south coast.

Sleeping

€ **An Oige Rosslare Harbour Hostel**, Goulding St, T053-33399, is fine for a night and clean with dorm rooms for around €15. Summer only For a more sumptuous affair try the old fashioned, pretty.

€ **St Martins B&B**, on St Martins Rd, T053-33133.

France

Fanning the fires of La Nord.

THIERRY ORGANOFF

Star breaks

1. **La Sauzaie** Quality A-frame reef that is the heart of the Vendée surf community ▶▶ *p171*.

2. **Lacanau** Heaving summer-holiday destination and traditional centre of surfing in the Gironde, its sandbanks have been the stage for surf competitions since the early days of French surfing ▶▶ *p178*.

3. **La Gravière** A thumping sandbank with heavy, hollow barrels on the golden beaches of Hossegor ▶▶ *p183*.

4. **Les Cavaliers** Another outstanding sandbank that offers year-round barrels. One of the original 'old skool' surf spots from the 1970s ▶▶ *p191*.

5. **Lafitenia** Classic right-hand point in the heart of the Côte Basque ▶▶ *p194*.

LAURENT MASUREL

Shoulder high, evening glass. This is why you came.

France is Europe's 'Grande Dame' of surfing. Her lineage can be followed back to some of the first waves ridden on this continent – and what great waves they are. Her torso is ruled by a 225-km stretch of classic beach breaks, capped off by reeling reefs and firing points at either end. And then there's that climate which helped make the southwest region, and Hossegor in particular, the destination of choice for generations of Eurogroms embarking on their first big surfing adventure. Not forgetting the pull of the food, the bars, the culture, the flesh. In the summers of the neon eighties and back-to-black nineties all roads led to Hossegor. A melting pot of nationalities rocked up to the makeshift camp that was Estagnots car park, while a rainbow nation of tents and languages spread through the pine shaded campsite, living it up on barrels, baguettes, cheese and cheap wine.

But as new spots hit the headlines and low-cost airlines touch down at an even more extensive array of airports, is southwest France still Europe's destination de rigueur? The collection of bumper stickers in the beachfront car parks is no longer limited to the European codes. With expanded numbers comes a whole new generation from across the global surf tribe. Read the signs and you'll find they now go from AUS-ZA. As for the class of yesterday, they may have graduated onto world travel and more comfortable accommodation, but there is still something drawing them back. Golden sands, thunderous barrels, nightlife, earlies on the offshore peak and a couple of hours watching the 'CT charge Gravière – France just has that 'something' that is truly hard to beat; an extra, irresistible ingredient – a certain je ne sais quoi.

Surfing France

There is something very special about the late summer and autumn seasons in southwest France. The hit of endless miles of golden sand, the fix of clear blue waters and the score of epic beach break barrels cut with the cafés and bars pulsing with activity, the beachside pads, the parties. There is an overall comfort in the feeling of being in one of the surfing world's classic venues that seems to entice surfers not only from the four corners of Europe, but from the four corners of the globe. Like nowhere else in Europe, this region has an addictive draw that we all find hard to resist. In an era when line-ups are busier than ever, the northern and central reaches of France offer the perfect antidote to the amped mass of Hossegor or buzzing waters of Biarritz. Yet, few decide on a crowd detox in Brittany or to rehabilitate their surfing spirits on the Central coastline, where an altogether more diverse surfing experience awaits. Here the classic point breaks harnessing the raw power from the North Atlantic, and the ledging reefs that explode into hollow perfection on the angled rocky platforms are very much an all-French preserve. This really is a soul surfer's retreat. You're certainly not going to bump into people you know from back home here.

But maybe that's part of what makes the southwest such a draw: the tradition and promise of the familiar, the industry endorsement, the lure of the famous names, the camp grounds filled with familiar faces of surfing's nomads who return on their annual pilgrimage. It's certainly the most consistent stretch of coastline in France and when the sun is out, it's hard to beat. Whichever region you feel pulled to, and whatever the reason, you can be sure that it's a great place to be a surfer. Vive la France!

Pros

- The best beaches in the world.
- Rugged and varied breaks in the northwest.
- Consistent swell outside the summer months.
- Plenty of *aire de camping* locations.
- Great seafood, chocolate and wine.
- See the world tour come to town in September.
- Still quiet breaks in Gironde and Les Landes.
- Good climate.

Cons

- The straight, southwest coast is easily blown out by westerly winds.
- Busy breaks in the summer around the southwest.
- Quite expensive.
- Wet in the winter.
- Competitive line-ups..

> Oh, I love France. I love Hossegor and the French lifestyle. Baguettes, cafe au lait and beautiful girls. This together with those powerful beachbreaks make Hossegor and Les Landes one of my favourite places to be.
>
> *Lars Jacobsen, Editor Surfers Magazine*

Climate

The French coastline is dominated by a temperate maritime climate. The general rule of thumb is that the summers tend to be warm to hot thanks to the continental high pressure over Europe, while the winters

DAMIEN POULLENOT

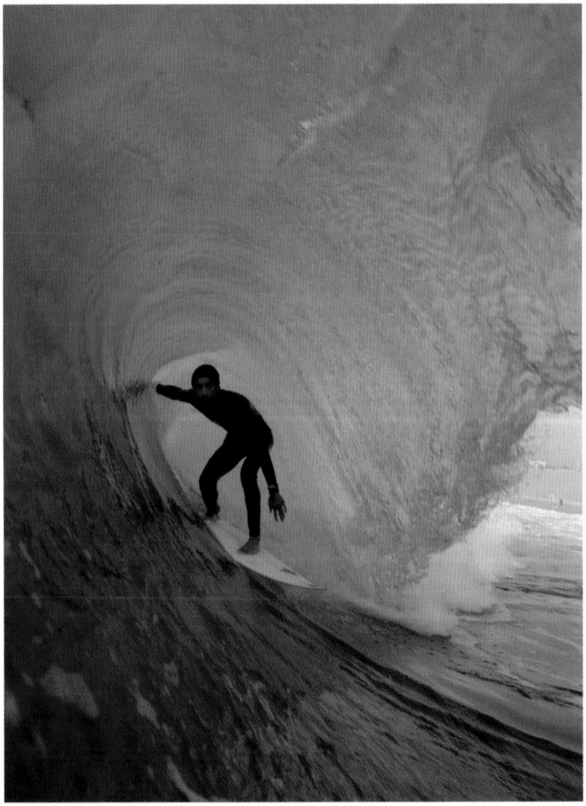

Above: Arnaud Darrigade – La Piste.
Opposite page: Avalanche – screaming into the Basque region's big wave arena.

LAURENT MASUREL

are cold, damp and unpredictable, thanks to lows coming in off the Atlantic. December in Hossegor could mean T-shirts or snow.

Best seasons to go

The **summer** surf season in France is a lottery. The weather over July and August is usually hot and sunny in the southwest, and there's a good chance of this extending north into Brittany. The surf is at best a gamble, with the exposed southwest your best bet. Some years there can be consistent swell, offshore winds, and hot sunny days broken only by the occasional thunderstorm rolling in off the Pyrénées while others are blighted by persistent onshore slop or long flat spells. Still, with air temperatures averaging around 22°C and the water warm enough for boardies, it's hardly surprising that holidaying surfers flock here, not only from inland France, but also from Britain, Germany, Spain; in fact anywhere in Europe. These two months see prices rise (from ferries to accommodation) and the roads pack out but this is also the honey-time when resorts like Hossegor come to life. "The best fun season is summer," says *Trip Surf* Editor Bertrand Portrat, "with a lot of travellers from all over the world, a lot of parties, girls (and boys), open-air concerts and festivals." The bars and clubs will be heaving, the cafés packed and the beautiful French women will still want nothing to do with you.

For surf quality, **autumn** and **spring** are the best times to visit. Spring is the quieter option as the seas have yet to warm up. In the south, the autumn weather can stay hot and sunny into November. With quick, early season sessions in boardies just about do-able and averages hovering around a very respectable 17°C, it gives good reason for the presence of the residual hangover crowd from the summer. The northern reaches around Brittany however begin to feel the chill with the seasonal average around 13°C and making surfing (in 4/3's) a more solitary experience. Mid-September sees most prices return to normal but unfortunately also signals the closure of many of the larger campsites. The swells beginning to hit the coastlines can be clean and glassy. They can also pump, as anyone seeing the images from the Quiksilver Pro France events can testify. When a deep depression tracks across the northern reaches of the Atlantic, a steady stream of swell can hit the southwest for days at a time. In spring the depressions can be just as severe but can track more to the south, colliding with the coastline in a mass of onshore winds and storm surf.

KRISTEN PELOU

The geology of Brittany ensures that as conditions alter, it has a full complement of reefs, points and peaks waiting to be explored.

KRISTEN PELOU

Erwan Simon – surfing for the soul in Brittany.

Winter is the time when the quiet little secret spots of Brittany and Vendée come to life, the jagged coastline providing some real gems that break when the surf pumps. In these northern and central regions, 5/3's with boots and hoods are a necessity with the air dropping to around 7°C, the wind chill increasing and the water around a mean 10°C. In the southwest, travelling surfers are now few and far between. The resorts are quiet, and the wind and rain can lash the coastline for days on end – those heady sun-scorched days now just a distant memory. But there are still occasions when the heavy winter swells clean up into perfect, powerful and punishing barrels sculpted in cold green water. Lows are much more consistent but their trajectory is always more of a lottery at this time of year. "Winter is a really good season for massive swells but it's so cold and there's no more light at five o'clock," says Bertrand. "All the French surfers who have money and time go away (to tropical, warm islands)!"

Boards

A classic board for a French trip would be a flexible beach break board. It should be fuller and wider for the summer – a good wave catcher – but can be more performance orientated for the autumn and spring when the swells kick in. A squash tail or swallow tail will give the board more drive in smaller waves. This would work well on the beaches of Les Landes and Brittany/Vendée as well as the reefs when they are up to head high. When the serious swells hit and the points and reefs of the north or the big banks around Hossegor fire, a longer board with a pin or rounded pin tail will come into its own.

Geography and the breaks

When seen from the air, the coastline of Les Landes and Gironde is a stunning natural phenomenon. A huge sand dune stretches from the River Gironde south to Hossegor, forming a coastal spine separating the emerald-green ocean on one side from the deep green pine forests on the other. The elements of wind and sea conspire to create this barrier, the defining symbol of an area that truly is the backbone of French surfing. The banks and channels here are constantly changing and the local surfers seek out the areas that are consistently the best, or the rogue 'superbanks' that spring up from time to time, offering the select few perfect waves that will be added to the region's surfing folklore. The downside to this awesome 225-km straight sandbank series is that it leaves few places to run to in huge conditions. Heading into the Basque

France: a brief surf history

1956 → While filming in Biarritz with actress wife Deborah Kerr, scriptwriter Peter Viertel surfs the waves of Biarritz, lending his board to interested locals - George Hennebutte, Joel de Rosney, Rott and Barland. **1958** → Barland Surfboards (Barland & Rott) set up shop as France's first surfboard shapers. **1959** → Deborah Kerr becomes patron of Waikiki, France's first surf club. **1964** → The French Surfriding Foundation establishes itself in Biarritz. **1966** → Guéthary hits the world stage after featuring in *US Surfer* magazine. **1968** → *Evolution*, staring Nat Young and Wayne Lynch, highlights the surf potential of Europe, featuring among other spots the beach break at La Barre, Anglet. **1971** → France hosts the European Surfing Championships. **1979** → The Lacanau Pro is established as an annual event and becomes an international affair with everyone from Rabbit, to Carroll, to Curren to Slater winning the event. **1984** → Quiksilver set up offices in southwest France and other international brands quickly follow suit. **1985** → France wins the European Surfing Championships and goes on to win more than ten times. **1986** → France's first magazine *Surf Session* sets up shop in Biarritz. **1987** → Biarritz hosts its first pro contest, the Surf Masters. **1989** → François Payot founds the EPSA in Capbreton, France, in order to support and promote European surfing. France today remains the nerve centre for European surfing. **1990** → Tom Curren founds environmental pressure group Surfrider Foundation Europe in France in order to protect Europe's seas and coastline. Today SFE has more than 15 chapters operating across Europe. **1994** → Eric Chauche sets up *Trip Surf* magazine in Biarritz, edited today by Bertrand Portrat. In recent years, France has seen several of its riders take to the world stage. In 2003, French surfer Marie Pierre Abgrall became Europe's first female surfer to join the competitive WCT while in 2004 Eric Rebière became the first Frenchman to join the elite 44 on the world tour. **Today** → Southwest France host the prestigious Quiksilver Pro France WCT event in Hossegor - the European headquarters for many of surfing's International organizations. Mickey Picon sampled life on the 'CT in 2006, while Jeremy Flores (originally from Reunion but an adopted French man) became the youngest ever WCT qualifier.

Low Pressure Chart for France

In all instances we assume the depressions are deep enough to produce classic swells (say 986 to 992mb). **L1** tracking through the Atlantic will push swell into the whole of the French coastline, from Brittany south to the Basque region. Its easterly trajectory may see it veer to the north above Ireland pushing a northwesterly swell into Landes, Hossegor and Biarritz until the swell window is closed by the Emerald Isle's land mass. If **L1** tracks into Biscay it may bring stormy weather to the southwest coastline but push swell into the more sheltered parts of southern Brittany.

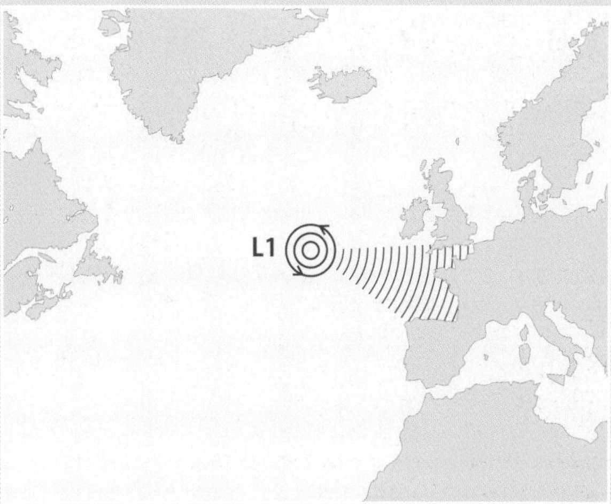

country, VVF in Anglet marks the end of the unbroken beachies and the start of the consistent bays, rocky points, headlands and reefs which handle the larger swells bombarding the coast and mark the region out as a premier surf destination.

In the north, the jagged coastline of Brittany will be familiar to anyone who knows the sandy bays and rolling headlands of Devon and Cornwall, and has the benefit of reefs and points as well as beach breaks. Loire Atlantique, Vendée and Charantes have always been dominated by the power and force of the ocean. The maritime geography here is a complex mix of rivers, islands and rocky coastlines with stretches of long sandy bays. This patchwork makes it ideal for surfers, for though it picks up less swell than the southwest, any that does arrive is usually rideable at any number of spots.

Surfing and environment

The jagged coastline of Brittany has always had a pretty fearsome reputation. In 1999 the oil tanker Erika sank off the coast off the Gulf of Morbihan, spilling thousands of tonnes of oil onto the shore. Luckily it was not quite on the scale of the Prestige oil disaster in Spain in 2002, but it shows the potential for environmental disasters in European waters.

Water quality around the mouths of major rivers such as the Loire and the Gironde, and around heavily urbanized areas, can be poor. It is best to avoid surfing those breaks near rivermouths after heavy rains: talk to the locals who will offer advice. Most beaches are clean and free from most pollution. There are occasional factories dotted along the coastline, but the importance of the tourist industry and the preservation of the beaches have kept much industrial development in check. The environmental organization, the Surfrider Foundation www.surfrider-europe.org, has its European headquarters based in southwest France where it campaigns hard for improved water quality. As well as educating the masses, they publish the annual name and shame, 'Black Flags' highlighting the most polluted beaches on the coastline.

The Surf Community

Southwest France in the summer holidays: a small swell after a flat spell and bang – chaos. Chambre d'Amour, Cavaliers, Lancanau, Hossegor and Côte des Basque will be full to the brim. Line-ups jammed with locals and travellers scrambling over waves. Here drop-ins and the odd vibe may be common, but outright localism is still pretty rare. Breaks in the Basque region have a very low tolerance for anyone not following surfing etiquette. Fred Papageorgiou has been surfing in Biarritz for 20 years and says that Grande Plage is a very competitive beach: "It is very busy here in the summer and can be very intense. There are many local surfers who all want to get their waves." True localism would be very unusual in France. As long as travelling surfers show respect, they will generally be treated with respect. And a few words of French go a long way.

Resources

France supports two excellent surf magazines *Trip Surf* (www.trip-surf.com) and *Surf Session* (www.surfsession.com), plus free magazines *Surftime* and *Beachbrother*. A pick of the online resources include: www.surf-report.com, excellent site with surf forecasting, webcams plus news and stories; www.viewsurf-attitude.com, network of webcams including snapshots of majority of coastline; www.surfing france.com, national surfing association including news, clubs and schools; www.surfrider-europe.org, for up to date environmental reports and activities.

Essentials

Fact file

Capital: → Paris
Time zone: → GMT+1
Currency: → Euro (€)
Coastline: → 3,427 km
Emergency Numbers:
→ General Emergency: 112
→ Police: 17
→ Ambulance: 15
Country code: → +33
Electricity: 220v, continental dual pin adaptor
Visa: None required for citizens of EU countries, or tourists from the US, Canada, Australia and New Zealand. For all up to date info check with the French embassy
Tourist Board: www.tourisme.fr, www.franceguide.com, www.francetourism.com, www.brittanytourism.com, www.vendee-tourisme.com, www.charante-maritime.org, www.tourisme-aquitaine.fr, www.tourisme-gironde.fr, www.tourismelandes.com, www.bearn-basquecountry.com

Position

The largest country in western Europe, France is bordered by three major bodies of water and seven countries. Moving anti-clockwise from its northern tip, France rubs shoulders with: La Manche (the Channel), Atlantic Ocean (the business end), Spain (along the mountainous Pyrenees), tiny Andorra, the Med plus Italy, Switzerland, Germany, Luxembourg and Belgium.

Language

French is the official language, and spoken by about 122 million people worldwide. English is understood in major cities and many coastal resorts, but it is important to flex your linguistic muscles, even if it is just for the amusement of the locals. They will either correct your appalling pronunciation, roll their eyes and pretend not to understand or, even more humiliating, reply in perfect English. In Brittany, the Celtic language of Breton is just about surviving while the Basque influence is very high profile in the southwest.

Crime/safety

France is as relatively crime-free as most European countries. The biggest problem for surfers is probably car break-ins – especially foreign cars. Use common sense and avoid leaving anything visible in your car or 'hidden' in the boot. To report anything, head for the Police Nationale or Gendarmerie Nationale (same but different). Recreational drugs are illegal – the police do have amazing powers of search and are happy to use them.

Health

All visitors should invest in good travel insurance. EU residents need to carry a European Health Insurance Card, www.ehic.org.uk, for free (or reduced cost) healthcare (this has replaced the E111 and so does not cover repatriation costs). Be aware you have to pay upfront for care/medicine and ambulance call out, recouping costs at a later date. For Europe-wide information see the European Commission's website: http://ec.europa.eu.htm. For minor ailments head to the local *pharmacie* – there will always be a local 24-hour chemist open on rotation.

Opening hours

As lunch is generally the most important meal of the day, opening hours tend to be Monday-Saturday 0800-1200 and 1400-1700. Most businesses (especially in smaller villages) tend to close on Sunday.

Sleeping

From *première classe* to *aire de campings*, France welcomes visitors with open arms, well nearly. With *l'herbergement* (accommodation) already pricier than its continental cousins, a *tax de séjour* is often levied on top of these rates, and often only included when it comes to pay the bill. July-August is the peak period when booking in advance is key and prices take a steep hike north– some rates almost double. Bastille Day, 14 July, can be an especially crazy time to get a room for the night. **Hotels** are graded 1 to 4 star with an 'L' thrown in for good measure at quality establishments. At the lower end of the scale, rooms will generally have use of a communal bathroom. **Formule 1**, www.hotelformule1.com, are worth checking out – they offer a chain of clean, basic, budget, hotels with rooms sleeping up to three people for around €30, although they are usually out of town. Youth Hostelling hasn't really caught on here however there are a smattering of auberges de jeunesse dotted around although many are fairly basic, and require an HI card. A bed for the night should cost around €15-20. Check out www.fuaj.org and rival gang **LFAJ** www.auberges-de-jeunesse.com, for details.

Camping is king with thousands of sites in fantastic locations all over the country. It is not always a particularly cheap option (especially if you head to one of the popular super-sites on the coast) and many sites do shut over the winter period. See the excellent www.campingfrance.com and www.les-campings.com, for listings. In

DAMIEN POULLENOT

Cap Frehel – this tempting peak lies just west of St Malo.

many popular areas, you can also find aire de campings, basic (usually car park style), regulated free-camping-style areas for vans and motorhomes – ideal for an overnight stop – where a minimal fee of around €5 is sometimes charged. There are also usually facilities including water and electric hook-up available at a minimal charge. For details of the sites, check out www.airecampingcar.com. Although actual free camping is not technically allowed, it is widely and discreetly practiced in, for example, beach car parks off-season and usually tolerated. Be aware certain car parks (including the one at Cavaliers) have become late night cruising spots and flashing lights may attract new 'friends'.

Eating and drinking

Food here is not just a necessity but an art form. A morning stop by the *boulangerie* (bread shop) results in food gold – *pain au chocolat*, rich, buttery croissants or even a humble baguette. And when washed down with *un grand café au lait* or *chocolate chaud* after an early session is the breakfast of champions. Lunch can be a simple affair involving a *pain* (fatter than a baguette) and a wedge of your favourite *fromage* (cheese) – a creamy Camembert, a salty Roquefort or even a sublime Brie de Meaux. If you want a serious sandwich, you can't do better than an *'Américan'* – a baguette stuffed with hamburgers, salad and french fries or opt for the ubiquitous *croque-monsieur* – cheese and ham toastie, French-style.

For something more civilized, head to a café or restaurant for lunch (1200-1430) or dinner (1900-2200) and sample a *menu* or *formule* – a two- or three-course meal, often good value. No French trip is complete without dabbling in some of the excellent seafood these shores have to offer, whether it's shucking *huîtres* (oysters) in Arcachon, sucking on grilled gambas (giant prawns) in the Basque country or enjoying the staple *moules et frites* (mussels and chips) countrywide for around €10. Oh, and don't miss out on having a *crêpe* – a thin pancake with a range of fillings from sugar or Nutella to booze, or even something savoury. And of course, no meal is complete without a glass of something special to wash it down. Home to some of the world's most celebrated vineyards, France has something for everyone: from real Champagne to full-bodied vins rouge from Bordeaux or a light Sancerre from the Loire Valley. A cognac from just north of the Gironde will cap off any good evening. *Le bière blonde* (lager) also flows freely in France and draught or *pression* is the cheapest way to enjoy it.

Getting there

Air The main international airports – Paris Orly (T0149-751515) and

Surfers' tales

The Vendée, another way of surfing by Thierry Organoff

At first glance this is one of the regions that doesn't seem made for surfing, yet the Vendée, for those who know it well is packed with great spots. This region is shaped both geographically and culturally around the ocean. The Vendée Globe Challenge, one of the most prestigious sailing races, starts at the Sables d'Olonne. With a varied coastline, the region boasts a mix of sandy and rocky beaches making it perfect for a variety of surfing conditions. Despite the fact that Patrice Chatillon started surfing at "Les Roches" as early as the summer of 1959 on a homemade plywood surfboard, even though he had never set foot in Biarritz, surfing developed later here than elsewhere.

Head for La Sauzaie if you're searching for virtually perfect waves at the risk of running into crowds. La Mine or Bud Bud are also great spots and often much quieter. Then there's the mythical right of La Tranche Sur Mer, a small coastal town and a great out-of-season spot without the crowds. There are plenty of beach breaks and reef breaks to be discovered for those who have the time and patience to search a little.

The swell hits the Vendée with less ferocity than Hossegor due to the continental shelf which runs the length of the coastline, this however doesn't prevent some excellent quality waves reaching the shore with both large and small surf. This region can also be highly recommended for its seafood restaurants and for those who enjoy fishing. As with many coastal areas it's best to avoid the summer rush between mid July and the end of August.

ALEX LAUREL

Hoss – The Boss.

Paris Charles de Gaulle (T0148-622280) – receive direct flights from the US, Australia and New Zealand with carriers including **Air France**, www.airfrance.com, and **British Airways**, www.british-airways.com. Flights vary widely in price according to season and availability. Domestic connecting flights are not particularly cost effective and with the UK's vast network of budget airlines, transit via London can often be an easy option.

From Europe There is a large network of regional airports serviced mainly by budget airlines. Some of the best connections to coastal France are from the UK including: Brest in Brittany with **Flybe**, www.flybe.com, and **Ryanair**, www.ryanair.com; La Rochelle in Charente Maritime with **Flybe**, **Ryanair** and **easyJet**, www.easyjet.com; Bordeaux in Aquitaine with **BMI**, www.flybmi.com, **easyJet** and **Ryanair**. For quick access to the southwest there are **Ryanair** flights to Biarritz from Stanstead, Dublin, Shannon and Frankfurt. Fares (excluding board carriage and luggage in the hold) range from a few euros up to about €200 return. For details of all airports in France check www.aeroport.fr.

Rail From the UK you can take the **Eurotunnel** train from Folkestone to Calais (about 35 minutes). Singles from around £50 per vehicle. Book in advance for deals, T08705-353535, www.eurotunnel.com. **Eurostar**, from London St Pancras, can deposit you in Lille or Paris in around 3 hours. Returns to Paris start at around £60 but can be a lot more so book ahead and look out for offers, T08705-186186, www.eurostar.com. No item longer than 2 m can be taken on the train. Boards under this size incur a £20 Registered Baggage Charge (T08705-750750). **Rail Europe**, www.raileurope.com, has a handy interactive route map and booking facility for journeys across Europe.

Road France is a well connected country. From Northern Spain, the coastal N1 becomes the N10 as it trickles over the border at Irun/Hendaye. The E5 toll road crosses here too. From Belgium, Luxembourg/Germany and Switzerland, the main E17, E50 and E60 run to Paris respectively. From Italy the E80 crosses into France by Monte Carlo, following the Mediterranean coast round past Marseille to Perpignan, from where it's just 450-km of navigation past the Pyrénées to Biarritz.

Sea The main ports providing links with the **UK** and **Ireland** are on the northern coast, with Dover to Calais the shortest and cheapest route – the 90-minute crossing costs from around £140 for a van and two people with **P&O**, www.poferries.com, similar with **Sea France**, www.seafrance.com, T0871 6632546. **Norfolkline**, T0870 8701020, www.norfolkline-ferries.co.uk, Dover-Dunkerque route – around 1 hour 45 minutes is similarly priced. **Note** Savings made in crossing times add up to more hours of driving time. The popular Portsmouth-Cherbourg crossing with **Brittany Ferries**, T08709-076103, www.brittany-ferries.com, takes around 4¾ hours with returns slightly more than the Dover-Calais route. Their Plymouth-Roscoff crossing is an excellent entry point for exploring Brittany, depositing you just 100 km from Quimper and costing around £300 for a van and 2 people. The showcase route however is Brittany Ferries overnight Portsmouth-St Malo crossing (meaning you don't waste any holiday time). It takes 8-11 hours (St Malo suffers massive tides) and costs more – around the £350 mark. However, in comparison to the other ports, it also shaves around 160 km off the journey south. From **Ireland**, **Irish Ferries**, www.irishferries.com, run Rosslare-Cherbourg Mar-Jan and Rosslare-Roscoff April-September, crossing around 19 hours from €250 for a van and 2 passengers. Other routes into France do exist – check carries for details.

Getting around

Driving (right-hand side) A full driving license or International Driving Permit is required plus adequate insurance and ownership papers. The roads are of a generally good standard making travel in this large country fairly straightforward, if a little monotonous. But the French make road travel a more high-octane experience; they hate getting stuck behind slow moving or foreign vehicles – especially vans so will speed up, close in and can't wait to overtake.

Toll Roads or *péages*, **Speed limit 130 kph** Making up a great deal of the motorway system, they are efficient and speedy if a little costly. Savings in journey time and distance often outweigh the charges. For example Calais-Biarritz in a camper via péage is around 1070 km taking 12 (ish) hrs at a charge of about €100. Sans péage is only a few km more but will take approximately 16+hours – that's half a day's surfing time wasted. See www.autoroutes.fr, for pricing and route details.

Motorway *autoroute* **Speed limit 110 kph** The extensive and efficient motorway system, spreads out like spiders' legs from Paris, and are peppered with excellent motorway services, complete with cafés serving real food and pretty, wooded picnic areas.

Other roads **Speed limit 110 kph dual carriageway, 90 kph single carriage, 50 kph urban areas** (unless otherwise indicated). Routes nationales **N** or **RN** roads are of a good standard, often with stretches of dual carriageway, but can get extremely busy with motorists avoiding the *péages*. Local roads are of a generally good standard and can be a great way to explore the countryside and get off the beaten track.

Car hire There are plenty of car-rental companies operating in France including all the big multinationals such as **Hertz**, www.hertz.com, and **Europcar**, www.europcar.com, who have offices in all the main towns, ports and airports. Rental starts at about €450 for two weeks but you usually need to be over 25. Hire cars are especially attractive propositions to thieves so try to remove obvious signs.

Public transport The train network of France offers a quick and easy way to travel. The fastest services are on the TGV – for example a direct journey Paris-Biarritz should take around 5 hrs and cost around €80, www.tgv.com. The regional TER are also pretty efficient, www.ter-sncf.com. The slowest are autotrains, which generally stop in every one-horse town. The excellent www.sncf.com, website is a one stop shop with route details for all networks nationwide. To send your board on ahead (provided it's shorter than 3 m) Sernam, T+33 (0)825 845845, offer a luggage service which takes 2 days to send luggage between 2 branches costing around €40 for a board. They only have around 60 offices nationwide so are not always near a train station (for example the nearest to Biarritz is in Bayonne).

The Lowdown

"In France we have four seas: North Sea, Manche, Atlantic Ocean and Mediterranean Sea. We have all kinds of waves: beach, reef, point and outside breaks, from little and fun to huge waves like Belharra or hollow ones like Hossegor. We have good food, good wine, welcome and open-mind people, a fiesta culture, beautiful & varied landscapes, and a very present nature." *Bertrand Portrat, Editor* Trip Surf

"In France people often say 'not possible', like when you're asking for no onions on your pizza they say, "It's not possibl". Of course it's possible. But you can't let it bother you, you just need to shrug it off." *Dan Malloy, US pro surfer*

"France – fun waves, nude beaches, great ambience." *Ian Cairns, surf legend*

"Northwest France – it's very far from everywhere, flat during the summer, stormy and you need to know somebody who can tell you where is the best spot of the day. You gonna drive a lot to find the good waves. But it's beautiful, wild, preserved, stony, with awesome waves, true people and always an offshore place." *Bertrand Portrat, Editor* Trip Surf

"The big advantage of Basque coast is that you can surf it from 2 ft to 20 on rocks, reef break, point break, sand bar – you have everything out there. You can surf all kinds of waves difficult ones to really cool ones. You can also surf with different winds as the coast turns. When it is south wind you go south (and even to Spain) when it is north you can surf Lafitenia or Les Cavaliers protected by the hills or the piers." *Damien Poullenot, surf photographer*

"For the northwest, make sure to have tidal charts and be ready to drive a lot... The best area is the western tip (Finistere) with spots like La Palue or La Torche and around. The north shore has many spots still to be discovered with southerly winds. It can be very rainy ..." *Kristen Pelou, photograher*

Surfers' tales

Hoss et gore by Sharpy

Hossegor… Just the word conjures up the sweet waft of pine forests, the sting of drying salt on your back, the tang of a good Bordeaux red, the gravely sand stuck between your toes, the aroma of good espresso, the sight of pert bronzed flesh, the taste of moule-frites and… Waves, perfect beachbreak waves of every flavour around an unassuming little town that runs the full gamut through the seasons from crowded, summer-holiday hell to brooding, ghost-town in the winter.

The Hoss' is many things to many people: the undoubted surf capital of Europe, the surf-trip cherry-taker for many, a world-class, world championship tour destination, the hub of the European surf industry, a late night party town and -for the forgotten few thousand that actually live there year round- home.

All quite impressive for a backwater town that outside of surfing circles is minorly famous for having a nice golf course, a good seafood restaurant, a casino and a small marina.

Surfing's love affair began with the region in the seventies but it wasn't until the eighties when the world really sat up to take notice – images of Maurice Cole, Carwyn Williams, Rabbit, Curren et al pulling into macking La Graviere shacks shook off the notion that France was a small wave longboarding gig, the focus shifted North from the softer waves of Biarritz to 'the shorebreaks'. The feral travelling surfers, the surf industry and the world tour soon arrived and the region instantly became a firm favourite with anyone that likes good surf – especially the pros – sweet waves, enthusiastic spectators, sublime lifestyle and a culture intriguing as it was maddening hooked everyone.

Which brings us neatly to 1991. The first time yours truly set foot on the golden sands of the Landes. It was a trip of firsts- my first overseas surf trip, my first barrel (pulled in, the lip came over, I freaked out and shut my eyes, opened them a few seconds later riding out on the open face again), first experience of nude sunbathing (and yes it did burn), my first sighting of an international pro surfing (mind-blowing) and my first nuclear grade, sand-whomping, oh-god-I'm-gonna-die wipeout. After that month of heaven Hossegor became Nirvana to my teenage mind, every year was based around scraping together enough cash to spend the summer down there, by whatever means possible…

In sixteen years of 'doing the season' I've done it all. Got the twenty-four coach down from London and walked everywhere (which sucks major ass when you're carrying camping gear and boards). Driven down in a small car with four other guys and lived out of the motor for six weeks sleeping on the beach (in the car when wet) and lived on nothing but baguettes, ham, cheese and cheap red. Been civilised and actually rented an apartment (with twice the recommended amount of people for the gaff). Lived in vans in the forest for months at a time (the ideal solution). Flown down, rented cars and stayed in hotels (on other peoples dime) and for three years called the place 'home'. There are many options but the aim is the same- to get stuck into some of those thumping beachies…

The beauty of Hossegor and its surrounds lies in the variety. There's a wave to suit every ability and every mood. From the fluffy softness of La Sud smack out front of the 'Party Plaza' otherwise known as 'La Centrale', north to the tow-in friendly peak of La Nord, the Backdoor style, A-Frame death-bowls of La Graviere shorebreak, the quiet but classy peaks of Cul Nul and north through the longer more rippable banks of Estagnots, Bourdaines, Penon and Casernes. Not forgetting the epic barrels just south of the river that start at La Piste and stretch south in increasingly secret locations all the way to the river Adour at Bayonne.

Everyone who has ever got amongst it in Hossegor will have a story. It is a town of stories: Tales of 200-metre long sand bars only accessible by trekking miles up the beach or through forests – of getting arrested by military police in those same forests for trespassing. Wide-eyed yarns of sharing a peak with the world champ/next big thing/old school legend and getting hooted into a bomb. Dark accounts of the darkness and violence of the ocean, of dead bodies washed ashore, police searches and bundles of cocaine washed up from a deal gone wrong. Legends of parties in the forest that go on all night for weeks. Anecdotes of seedy goings on in bars and clubs with people or pros who shall not be named and 'they never did that did they? In the toilet? Eeeew…' moments. Fish tales of waves caught, barrels surfed and moves pulled. Narratives of life changing waves, of life changing moments all brought into keen focus by the sheer quality of the waves.

For this writer it was that stretch of Atlantic chewing away at the old continent of Europe that put me where I am today…

1994. Just finished university. Plan was to head down to Hossegor for September for a month of post degree surfing, celebrating and de-stressing. Prior to departure I'd dropped £35 on a second-hand, piece of crap, recycled Russian destroyer bit of pig iron that was supposedly an SLR camera and a few dodgy

SHARPY

Even Andy Irons can make mistakes here.

lenses. Aim being to take a few line ups and shots to wind up the crew at home that couldn't make it down.

On the third day we'd been feasting since dawn on a clean 2 ft swell at empty VVF in Capbreton (not so empty now but this was over ten years ago) and at 10.30 I made the call to get a wave in as a box of ten Pain Au Chocolates had my name all over them in Leclerc's supermarche. The wave in was a peach, a clean little micro barrel, just big enough to squeeze into. Spoilt by that I paddled out for one more 'last wave' same deal, took off, pulled in, but got caught, flipped in the lip and pile driven head first into the sandbar which felt like concrete. I wandered up the beach in a daze, concussed and confused and for some reason insanely thirsty. Turns out I'd snapped my collarbone and got concussion from head-butting the bottom. The people in Bayonne hospital were awfully nice and fixed me up a treat and the long and the short of it is I spent the next three and a half weeks sat on the beach watching some of the best Graviere and Estagnots I've ever seen. Taking photos, a lot of photos. As I had nothing else to do and every time I moved any part of my body it was agony. So I had a three-week induction in what it means to be a surf photographer. To be stood on the beach all day watching insane waves and not being able to surf them. Considering the equipment the shots were okay, but that wasn't the point, I was hooked. That wipeout was the best thing that ever happened to me. I wouldn't be sat here now – in a rented cottage in Bundoran waiting for an impending swell with a crew of American, English and Irish pros – if that hadn't happened. I'd be doing some real world job and probably be happy with a wife, mortgage, 2.4 kids and two weeks abroad a year. I wouldn't have been round the world a couple of times shooting surf photos, I wouldn't of lived in Hossegor for three years editing a surf magazine, I wouldn't know all the weird, wonderful and talented people that orbit in the surfing universe and I wouldn't be looking forward as keenly as ever to getting back down to Hossegor. It's a hell of a place…

Roger Sharp is one of Europe's leading surf photographers.

O'NEILL
PHOTO McBRIDE

oneilleurope.com
CORY LOPEZ

Overview

It would be a cruel trick, but if you showed a water shot taken at one of Brittany's cliff-edged beach breaks to a Cornish surfer and asked them to identify which Cornish beach it was, they'd probably have a good bash. "Maybe it's near Aggie" or "I'm sure that's that a spot in north Cornwall." The truth is that the coastlines of Cornwall and Brittany are amazingly similar. In fact, in many ways Brittany has the edge. Those southerly neighbours have less crowded beachies, a number of decent reefs, as well as a good few high-calibre point breaks. They even have a number of quality, proper secret spots hidden away to be surfed by just a few locals – something you definitely won't find in Kernow. The two regions do share many common features. The roots of Brittany (which literally translates as Little Britain) lie in Celtic Britain, whose inhabitants were driven out, emigrating to this French

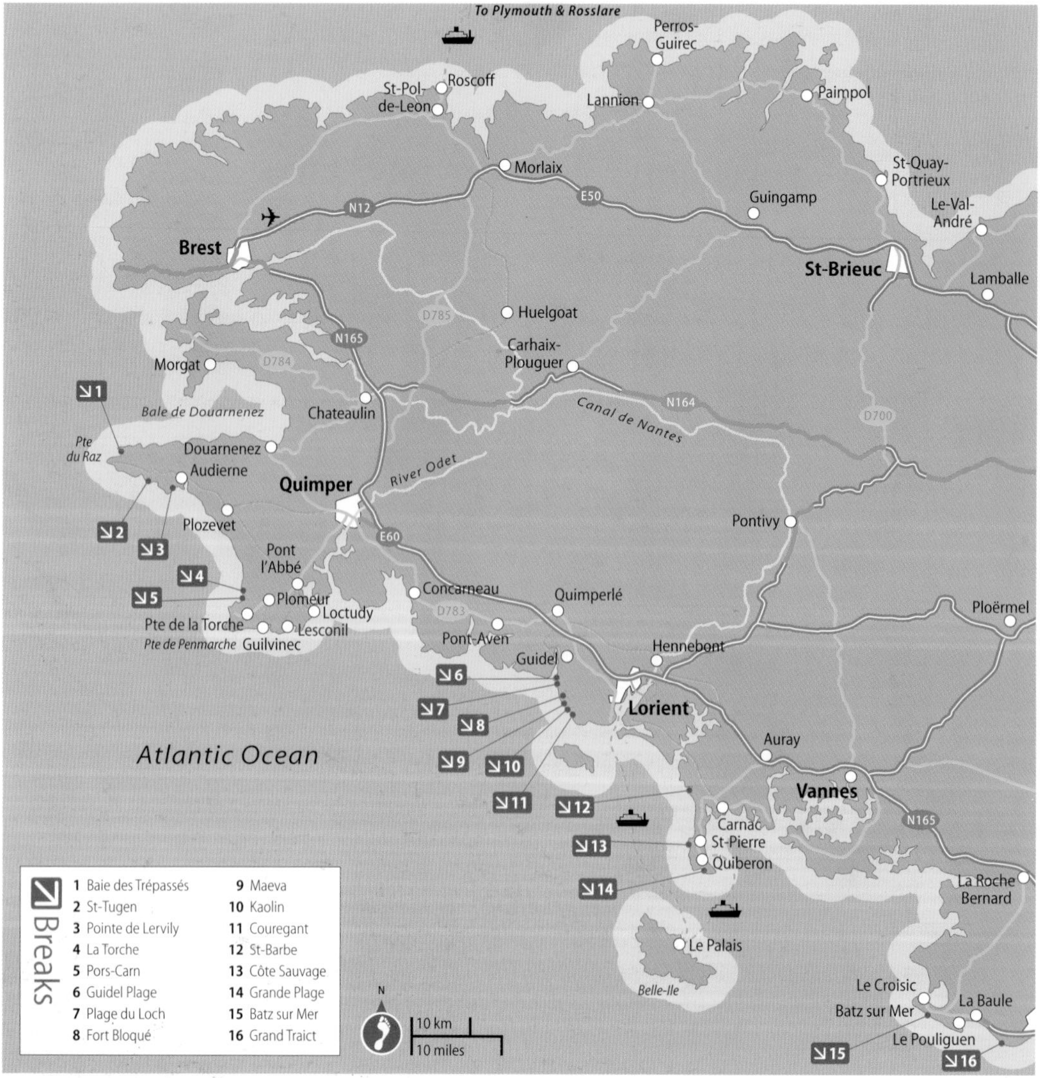

Spring
Air 10°C 50°F
Water 11°C 52°F
4/3mm Wetsuit & boots

Summer
Air 17°C 63°F
Water 16°C 61°F
3/2mm Wetsuit

Autumn
Air 13°C 55°F
Water 15°C 59°F
4/3mm Wetsuit

Winter
Air 6°C 43°F
Water 11°C 52°F
5/4/3mm Wetsuit, boots, gloves & hood

KRISTEN PELOU

Above: Brittany doing a good impression of Cornwall. **Below right**: Winter swells highlight the true potential of the region.

haven in the fifth century. The southwest region of Brittany is known as Cornouaille (Cornwall), they share the legend of King Arthur, and each have their own languages – Cornish and Breton – kept alive by a dedicated few. These are elemental landscapes: storm-lashed jagged coastlines and beautiful secluded coves.

In the 1970s Brittany Ferries started a Roscoff to Plymouth route, re-establishing historical trading links that existed between the two regions from the 1800s when 'Johnnies' from Roscoff braved the Channel crossing to sell their strings of onions in Britain, cycling from town to town. What began as an economic link now offers British surfers easy access to some of Europe's best and least crowded waves. From the exposed points north of Brest, to the beaches of the Côte Sauvage, there is a vast area waiting to be explored.

Coastline

Like many of Europe's Celtic regions, the northwest of France takes the full brunt of the storms that roll in off the Atlantic and the jagged coastline is a testament to this. It is the undulating nature of the geography that makes this area so flexible. "It's a region that catches most swell directions," says surf photographer Kristen Pelou. "We've got points, bays, beaches, reefs; there's always an offshore wave somewhere." Sandy coves, powerful beaches and crumbling cliffs culminate in the Pointe du Raz, a French version of Land's End. In fact the region in which it lies, Finistère, literally translates as the 'end of the world'. Heading south this ragged coastline has been littered with wrecks for centuries, highlighting the fact that these are some of the most dangerous waters on the French coastline. Fishing villages are nestled in rivermouths and rocky coves, away from the storms and treacherous currents and, on the west-facing Côte Sauvage, all swimming has been banned due to the number of drownings. Further south, the major surfing area of La Baule demonstrates how powerful the ocean can be. The rocky ex-island has been snared by a long peninsula of sand and colonized by beach homes and holiday cottages.

Local environment

In 1978 the Amoco Cádiz ran aground just off Brittany causing what was, at the time, the largest oil spill in history. One and a half million barrels of oil were lost into the sea along the 100 miles of coast. Tankers patrolling the Channel, the busiest in the world, are occasionally known to illegally clean out tanks before hitting port. The Channel aside, the waters of Brittany are still mostly pristine. Around more densely populated areas however there is some pollution from sewage and run-off while, due to farming and agriculture river-water flowing from major estuaries can be poor.

There are breaks in this region that do draw a crowd – especially at the weekend but little out-and-out localism. Some breaks are isolated, with dangerous rips so it pays to keep the locals onside and learn a few tips from them.

Getting around

Heading west of Quimper, it takes longer to reach places than you would think, especially in the summer when tourists hit the area. The N165 provides a good fast link between the cities, but there is excellent coastal access via minor roads.

6'0" Stretch Ratboy

Shaper: Stretch

6'0" x 18¾" x 2¼"

Built with Surftech's proven TUFLITE construction.

Surfing Magazines 2005 Shaper of the Year, William "Stretch" Reidell designed with Aerialist Jason "Ratboy" Collins. Steep drops, fast walls, wobbly sections and open face bliss, designed to be extremely forgiving yet as fast and loose as possible.

Futures F4 fins.

6'10" Rawson Hyper Skate

Shaper: Pat Rawson

6'10" x 18¾" x 2½"

Built with Surftech's proven TUFLITE construction.

Designed for all around surf in the 6' to 8' + range. Fast and drivey through turns and cutbacks with enough stability to hold in the steep sections.

Futures FTP1 fins.

Boards by **Surftech**
www.surftech.com info@surftech.com

DAMIEN POULLENOT

Breaks

BEACH BREAK

↘1 Baie des Trépassés

- **Conditions** All NW to W swells, offshore in E to SE winds
- **Hazards/tips** Beautiful location
- **Sleeping** Audierne ›› *p167*

This northwesterly facing Brittany beach certainly has a dramatic 'end of the world' feel. It picks up loads of swell and is sheltered from south and even southwesterly winds by the Pointe du Raz. Magnificent cliffs overlook some quality peaks. This area is popular with walkers and holidaymakers in the summer. Breaks up to 8 ft producing some great right-handers.

BEACH BREAK

↘2 St-Tugen

- **Conditions** All W to SW swells, offshore in NE winds
- **Hazards/tips** Quality waves with parking at the beach
- **Sleeping** Audierne ›› *p167*

This good-quality, 300-m-long white sand beach break can have excellent hollow and powerful waves, especially when a southwest swell kicks in. Works through the tides, though better at low as high can close out. Head east along the D784, then follow signs to the beach.

RIGHT POINT BREAK

↘3 Pointe de Lervily

- **Conditions** Medium to big SW swells, offshore in N to NE winds
- **Hazards/tips** Rocky point for experienced surfers
- **Sleeping** Audierne ›› *p167*

A walling right-hand rocky point that works in medium to big southwesterly swells.

KRISTEN PELOU

Above: 5 Porscarn. **Far right: 6** Guidel Plage.

Breaks best on high tides when the shallow waves are home to a small, but committed local crew. Be respectful. Currents and rocks make this one for the more experienced.

BEACH BREAK

↘4 La Torche

- **Conditions** All NW to SW swells, offshore E to SE winds
- **Hazards/tips** Consistent, most famous break in region
- **Sleeping** Pointe de la Torche ›› *p168*

This rocky point flanked by beach breaks is the home of Breton surfing. It has good exposure to northwesterly swells, making it one of the area's most consistent breaks. A good peak breaks near the point. The right peels towards the point, the left away. There is a rip that runs out along the point which the locals call l'ascenseur or 'the lift' as it picks you up and deposits you at the peak. Does the same to unsuspecting swimmers. The waves here work on all tides and gets crowded when it's on, especially holidays and weekends. There is a long stretch of beach heading north so try Tronoën if Le Torche is packed out.

BEACH BREAK

↘5 Pors-Carn

- **Conditions** Medium to big NW to W swells, offshore in a SE wind
- **Hazards/tips** Just south of La Torche, always less crowded
- **Sleeping** Pointe de la Torche ›› *p168*

Less swell gets in at Plage Pors-Carn to the south of the point, but a powerful right-hander breaks here at low tide. The wave is punchy and can be hollow. Worth checking in a big southwesterly storm as the headland offers some protection. If the wind is northerly, head east along the D53 and south on the D102 to Lesconil where there is a reef near the harbour.

BEACH AND RIVERMOUTH BREAK

↘6 Guidel Plage

- **Conditions** Medium to big W to SW swells, offshore in NE winds
- **Hazards/tips** Very dependent on sandbanks
- **Sleeping** Lorient ›› *p168*

Sandbanks build up just to the south of the Laïta rivermouth and in clean swells there can be either a series of rights or one long classic reeling wave. Low tide to mid tide usually best. There are also other good sandbars just to the south, providing plenty of options. Easy parking overlooking the break on the coastal road.

BEACH BREAK

↘7 Plage du Loch

- **Conditions** Medium to big W to SW swells, offshore in E to NE winds
- **Hazards/tips** Popular break
- **Sleeping** Lorient ▸▸ *p168*

Loch is considered the best beach break in the area and can produce excellent, hollow waves well into the overhead range. Good banks build up here, especially at low tide. This is a popular spot that can get crowded on weekends and is particularly busy in the summer. Needs a southwesterly swell or a big northwesterly swell to work. Just south of Guidel on the D152. Parking by the break.

BEACH BREAK

↘8 Fort Bloqué

- **Conditions** Medium to big SW to NW swells, offshore in E winds
- **Hazards/tips** Good beginner break
- **Sleeping** Lorient ▸▸ *p168*

Just by Camping L'Atlantys you'll find this pretty sluggish beachie. Not as high quality as the surrounding spots, though good for beginners. Needs a good southwesterly swell.

KRISTEN PELOU

Brittany has a series of islands perfectly primed as swell receptors including Belle-Île lying off the southern tip of the Quiberon peninsula.

DEMI TAYLOR

REEF BREAK

↘9 Maeva

- **Conditions** Medium to big SW to W swells, offshore in E winds
- **Hazards/tips** Average reef by beach
- **Sleeping** Lorient ▸▸ *p168*

Check from the beach and you should see this reef break peak with walling lefts and rights that work up to 6 ft. Works best at high tide when it can be busy with local surfers.

RIGHT REEF BREAK

↘10 Kaolin

- **Conditions** Medium to big SW to W swells, offshore in E to NE winds
- **Hazards/tips** Heavy, hollow break
- **Sleeping** Lorient ▸▸ *p168*

Kaolin is a short, powerful, hollow reef break especially popular with the area's bodyboarders. Swell comes out of deep water lunging onto this flat slab reef producing heavy right-hand barrels. Needs a big westerly or a southwesterly swell to work. Best from low to three-quarter tide and offshore in an easterly. A serious wave respected by the locals. Mostly breaks in the winter in cold northeasterly winds.

REEF BREAK

↘11 Couregant

- **Conditions** Medium to big W to SW swells, offshore in E winds
- **Hazards/tips** A long paddle, experienced surfers only
- **Sleeping** Lorient ▸▸ *p168*

Continuing along the D152, this heavy peak breaks over a rocky reef, a long way off the point at Couregant. It is worth the paddle though as it is a long, quality wave. Works best at low in a big westerly or southwesterly swell.

BEACH BREAK

↘12 St-Barbe

- **Conditions** All W to SW swells, offshore in E winds
- **Hazards/tips** Popular beach, crowds
- **Sleeping** Quiberon ▸▸ *p168*

This is a long beach leading to the sandy peninsula connecting the mainland with the rocky Côte Sauvage. It is pretty consistent as it is well exposed to westerly and southwesterly swells. It has lefts and rights that can be long and walling, and very popular with longboarders. Heading south along the peninsula, there are several other beach breaks worth checking out – **Tata, Les Crevettes, Les Palisades** and **L'Isthme**.

BEACH BREAK

↘13 Côte Sauvage

- **Conditions** Medium to big NW, all W and SW swells, offshore in E winds
- **Hazards/tips** There can be dangerous currents here
- **Sleeping** Quiberon ›› *p168*

This rocky peninsular points due south, with a series of excellent sandy bays on the western side that have a definite Cornish feel to them. Those familiar with the coastline around St Agnes will have a definite feeling of déjà vu. This 'Wild Coast' is considered treacherous and swimming is banned due to the dangerous waters. The quality beach breaks are a succession of cliff-backed sandy coves and headlands which join up at low tide. There is parking at Port Blanc and access along a path to Port Blanc, Port Maria, Port Rhu and Port Bara. **Port Blanc** has peaks breaking over sand and rock (as the tide pushes, a big rock appears in the line-up, interfering with the right at mid-tide), works well in westerly swells in northeasterly winds and is popular with locals. **Port Maria** produces some good lefts and rights, but to the south **Port Rhu** is the most powerful break, with quality peaks breaking over sand and rock. **Port Bara** has a good left, sand-covered reef.

DAMIEN POULLENOT

KRISTEN PELOU

Top: 10 Cool, green Morbihan perfection. **Above:** 13 Port Blanc.

BEACH BREAK

↘14 Grande Plage

- **Conditions** Big SW or W swells, offshore in N to NE winds
- **Hazards/tips** Very popular tourist beach in the summer
- **Sleeping** Quiberon ›› *p168*

This sandy beach nestles inside the breakwater at Quiberon on the southern tip of the peninsula and needs a very big swell to work. The pretty Breton town fronts a beach that can have some fun waves at low to mid tide. Closes-out at high tide. Good in northwesterly through to northeasterly winds.

REEF BREAK

↘15 Batz sur Mer

- **Conditions** Big W and SW swells, offshore in NE winds
- **Hazards/tips** Rocky
- **Sleeping** La Baule ›› *p168*

West of St-Nazaire, **La Govelle** is a right and left walling, sand-covered, flat rock reef. Best at mid tide when there can be some good waves in decent swells. Works up to 8 ft. Gets crowded when good. In a large swell you can head to the versatile and popular crescent-shaped beach, offering some shelter at **La Baule**.

REEF BREAK

↘16 Grand Traict

- **Conditions** Big W to SW swells, offshore in NE winds
- **Hazards/tips** Rocks
- **Sleeping** La Baule ›› *p168*

This spot near St-Marc needs a big swell to produce mediocre, walling right-hand waves. Best mid to low tide. A break that comes to life during the winter season as it is quite protected from the wind.

Practicalities

Calais

The port town of Calais is fine for a night's stopover on your way in or out.

Sleeping

€ Auberge de jeunesse, just back from the campsite on Av Marechal Lattre Tassigny, T0321-345940, B&B from €17.
Camping Camping Municipal, west of the ferry terminal on Av Raymond Poincare, T0321-978979, open year round.

Cherbourg

Cherbourg is a busy but unglamorous port of entry into France.

Sleeping

€ Moderna, R de la Marine, T0233-430530, www.moderna-hotel.com, is handy for the ferry port and has Wi-Fi access.
€ Auberge de jeunesse, R de l'Abbaye, T0233-781515, is a big hostel offering B&B with no curfew, convenient for those with late arrivals or early departures.

St-Malo

A preferable port of entry is pretty St-Malo with an impressive *citadelle*. It's worth arriving early to spend an evening or afternoon walking around the 17th-century ramparts. There are plenty of good places to eat within the walls – most have a similar set menu involving some sort of *moules et frites* combo.

Sleeping

€ Le Croiseur, within the walls on Pl de la Poissonnerie, T0299-408040, www.hotel-le-croiseur.com, has a contemporary feel and is well placed.
Camping La Cité d'Alet, T0299-816091, Mar-Sep, overlooks the bay and is housed in a Second World War fort with bullet-riddled emplacements. **La Fontaine**, rue de la Fontaine aux Pèlerins off the D155 to Le Mont St Michel, T0299-816262, open year round with chalets available.

Roscoff

This Finistère port town is a mellow entry point (the town is small and countryside immense) and good jump-off for exploring Brittany.

Sleeping

Camping Aux 4 Saisons, overlooking the sea at Pointe de Perharidy, T0298-687086, Apr-Oct with chalets available. There's also a free motorhome service and parking point on the sea front at Sainte Barbe.

Audierne

In the heart of Finistère, this pretty fishing town nestles in the banks of the Goyen estuary and is home to a good Sat market. On the other side of the river is the popular beach Gwendrez.

Sleeping

€ Hotel Baie de Trepasses, on the beach of the same name, T0298-706134, Feb-Nov, is dramatically placed.
€ L'Horizon, RJJ Rouseau, T0298-700991, is close to the Audierne beach front.
Camping Le Loquéran, near the bridge on Bois de Loquéran, T0298-749506, is reasonably priced, open May-Sep. Also offers gîtes, dorms from €12.50, doubles around €30. **La Corniche Campingn**, south at Plozevet, T0298-913293, is open Apr-Sep with Wi-Fi and cabins. Vans also **free-camp** in the car park behind the dunes at **Baie de Trépassés**.

KRISTEN PELOU

Roscoff is famed for its artichokes, Johnnies and links with Celtic cousin Cornwall.

Flat spells

Belle-Île This spectacularly beautiful and rugged island is just 20 km long and very popular in the summer. Regular ferries run between Port Maria in Quiberon and Le Palais on the Belle-Île (also accessible from Lorient). Returns about €25 with **SMNN**, T0820-056000, www.smnn-navigation.fr. Hire a bike for the day at the port for around €15 and explore. There are a couple of campsites on the island as well as a hostel near the port, T0297-318133. Tourist office open year round at Quai Bonnelle, www.belle-ile.com.

Carnac Tucked away behind the Quiberon peninsula is the village of Carnac home to a fantastic array of Neolithic monuments. Predating the Pyramids and Stonehenge, rows upon rows of *menhirs* (standing stones) stretch northwards and eastwards from Carnac in lines and grids or 'alignments'. It is a spectacular site and believed to be Europe's oldest settlement. Pick up a free map of the sites from the Carnac tourist office, pack a picnic and head off. Carnac-Plage tourist office is open year round on Aves des Druides, www.ot-carnac.fr.

Quimper Head inland along the D785 to the oldest city and heart of Brittany. Sitting on the banks of the Oder, it's all about the ambience.

Pointe de la Torche

This spot is popular with surfers and windsurfers and has plenty of surf shops and a good campsite.

Sleeping

Camping Pointe de la Torche, southwest of Pont l'Abbé on the Plomeur-Pointe de la Torche road, T0298-586282, www.campingdelatorche.fr, is about 2 km from the sea, open Apr-Oct, with cabins.

Directory

Juanito Surfboards, on the Meju Roz Route de Tronöen, T0298-826167, sponsor local ripper, Simon Joncourt and do repairs as well as custom shapes. **Twenty Nine** surf shop is next door to the *crêperie* at Pointe de la Torche and have been catering to the areas surf scene for more than 10 years.

Lorient

The port town of Lorient is a huge natural harbour in the Morbihan region, flattened during the Second World War and rebuilt without much inspiration. Still, if you do want to stay.

Sleeping

Camping There are several campsites just to the west by the surfing beaches including **Plage du Forte Bloque**, next to the beach of the same name, T0297-059546, www.campingplageguidel.com, Apr-Sep. It isn't flashy but has statics for rent. Heading north on the coast road towards Guidel Plage, **Pen er Malo**, T0297-059986, is slightly cheaper, open year round, also with statics. Also try the **Parc de Loch Malo**.

Directory

Actionline, surf shop at Guidel, stocks hardware as well as all the basics.

Quiberon

The pretty Presqu'île de Quiberon peninsula, with a port at its southern tip and excellent beaches, is a massive tourist draw in the summer.

Sleeping

€ Hôtel Restaurant au Bon Accueil, Quai de Houat in Port Maria, T0297-502862, is reasonably priced and well located, closed Jan.

Camping Plenty of options on the Presqu'île de Quiberon. At St-Barbe, just inland, try **Kersily**, T0297-523965, open Apr-Oct, statics available. South on the peninsula at Sables Blancs is the massive **Camping Muncipal**, T0297-523715, Apr-Sep. At Kerhostin is **L'Ocean**, T0297-309129, Apr-Oct, cabins to rent. Continuing south along the D768 to St-Pierre Quiberon is the pricier **Park er Lann**, T0297-502493, Apr-mid Oct. There are a couple of aire de campings including just north of the breaks plus a freecamp area by the railway lines on the isthmus.

Eating and drinking

Head to **Crêperie la Pourlette**, rue Jean Bart, for a traditional crêpe or two.

Directory

Surf Shops Ocean Gate, on the road leading to Port Blanc stocks all the hardware and accessory essentials. **Tourist information** R de Verdun, www.quiberon.com.

La Baule

Just north of the Loire, this popular, upmarket holiday resort was once an island until, in 1779, a huge storm raged through depositing a sandy peninsula in its wake. The crescent-shaped bay is a bustling tourist beach in the summer and a popular surfing, sailing and windsuring spot.

Sleeping

€ Marini, on Av Clemenceau, T0240-602329, close to the railway station, has clean, comfortable rooms and a swimming pool.

Camping There are plenty of campsites around La Baule and Batz sur Mer. Between Le Pouliguen and Batz, on the coast, there is the summer-only **Camping Govelle**, R de la Côte Sauvage, T0240 239163. **Camping Ajoncs d'Or**, on Chermin du Rocher, T0240-603329, open Apr-Oct, is just back from the bay at La Baule, with statics available.

Directory

Surf Shops Airslide, Esp Francois Andre, is a surf/skate/wake shop but stocks all essentials as does **Holywind**, Blvd des Oceanides, in nearby Pornichet. **Tourist information** Pl de la Victoire.

DEMI TAYLOR

ALEX LAUREL

Top: Buckwheat crêpe and a glass of cider to wash it down.
Above: 4 Flying the flag.

France Northwest France Practicalities

St-Nazaire

River Loire

Nantes

Pornic

Ile de Noirmoutier

Noirmoutier

Cholet

Barbatre

Beauvoir

Fromentine

Perrier

Challans

St-Jean-de-Monts

Port-Joinville

Ile d'Yeu

☒ 1

St-Gilles-
Croix-de-Vie

La Roche

★☒ 2

Brétignolles
sur Mer

☒ 3

☒ 4

☒ 5

VENDÉE

Les Sables-d'Olonne

☒ 6

Fontenay-
le-Conte

☒ 7

Longeville

Luçon

☒ 8

La Tranche

☒ 9

☒ 10

Niort

Atlantic Ocean

Ile de Ré

La Rochelle

☒ 11

☒ 12

St-Denis

CHARENTE
MARITIME

St-Pierre d'Oléron

Rochefort

Ile d'Oléron

Le Chateau

☒ 13

☒ 14

St-Trojan

Marennes

Pen. de Maumusson

Saintes

☒ 15

Phare de la Coubre

N
10 km
10 miles

St-Palais-sur-Mer

Royan

Cozes

Verdon

Pons

River Gironde

Breaks

1	St-Gilles-Croix-de-Vie	**9**	La Terrière
2	La Sauzaie ★	**10**	Le Pointe du Grouin/ Le Phare
3	Les Dunes	**11**	Pointe de Chassiron
4	Sauveterre	**12**	Les Huttes
5	L'Aubraie	**13**	Vert Bois
6	Tanchette	**14**	St-Trojan
7	Les Conches	**15**	Côte Sauvage
8	Bud Bud		

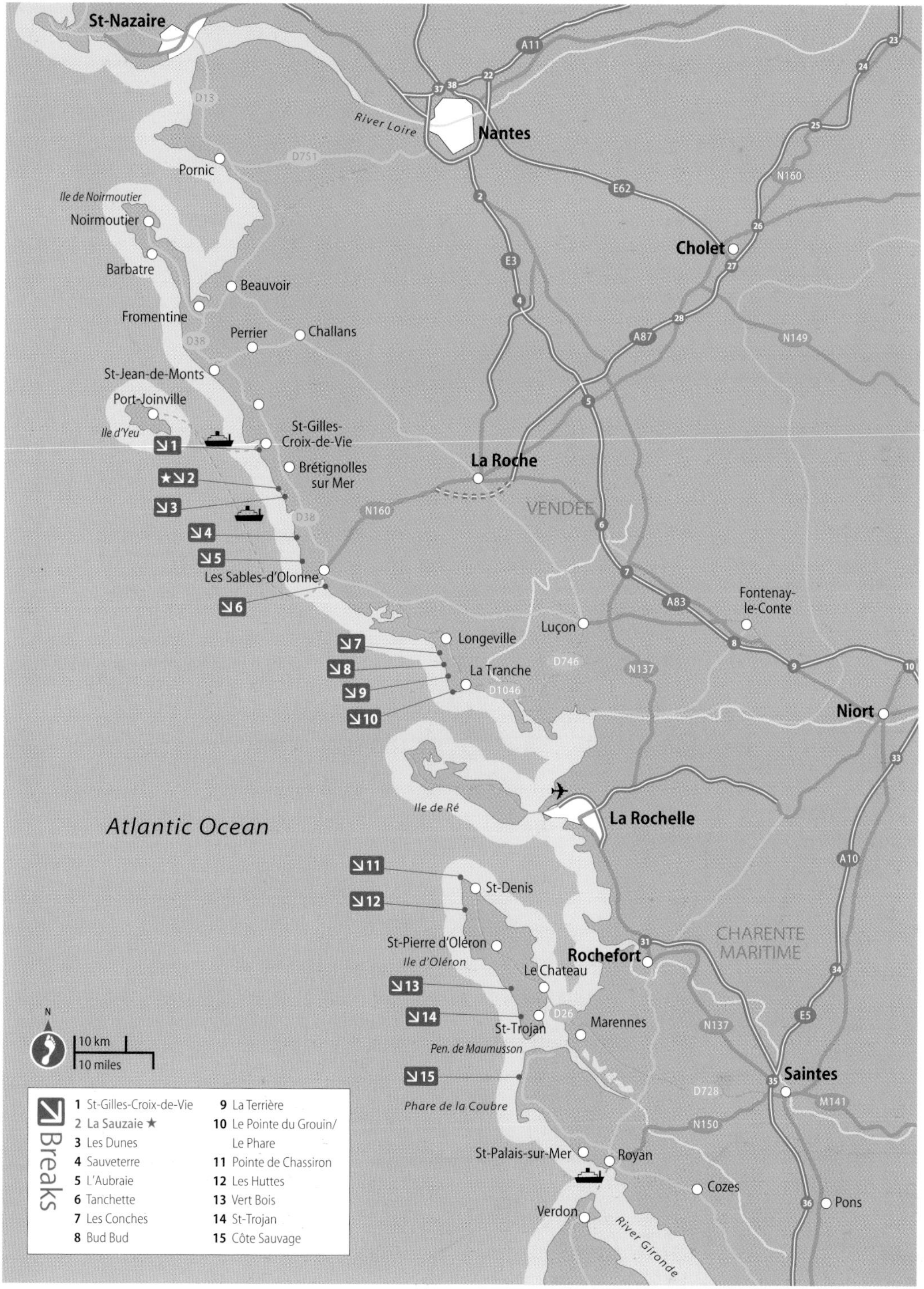

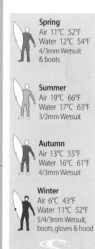

Spring
Air 11°C 52°F
Water 12°C 54°F
4/3mm Wetsuit
& boots

Summer
Air 19°C 66°F
Water 17°C 63°F
3/2mm Wetsuit

Autumn
Air 13°C 55°F
Water 16°C 61°F
4/3mm Wetsuit

Winter
Air 6°C 43°F
Water 11°C 52°F
5/4/3mm Wetsuit,
boots, gloves & hood

O'NEILL

Overview

The southbound A-83 toll-road is a hypnotically smooth and quiet stretch of tarmac. This arterial route pumps traffic efficiently and quickly in a southerly direction towards the beaches of Les Landes and the Côte Basque. It is as if the local surf community clubbed together to divert the flow of holidaymakers away from their own beaches and reefs and towards those further south. If you do decide to make the turn for La Roche, be warned that this stretch of road seems to go on forever: dual carriageway follows roundabout follows dual carriageway until you think your eyeballs will bleed, until, eventually, the town of Sables-d'Olonne comes into view.

LAURENT MASUREL

Above: Vendee has a reputation for turbulant waters and difficult navigation – neither of which seem to pose a problem to the locals who dominate this reef. **Above right: 2** La Sauzaie: "a good hollow right, short but intense barrels", says Bertrand Portat.

The shore that lies between the great rivers of the Loire and the Gironde angles away inexorably towards the southeast, each subtle twist and turn, each island and bay offering unique surfing possibilities. This stretch of coastline is all about balance – although it may not be as exposed as the southern provinces, it does have an ever-changing geography that allows everything from fun summer peelers through to macking winter storms to be utilized by the local waveriding fraternity. While Vendée and Charente may not be the raw, empty swell magnet that Brittany is, it does have some sweet points and reefs, and although it may not offer the thundering beachbreaks of Landes to the south, it doesn't have the same thronging crowds. Central France is, perhaps, the perfect halfway house.

Coastline

This spectacular coastline is a patchwork of features and a geographer's delight. Dense, pine-fringed beaches demonstrate the classic features of succession – the naked beach, the dunes colonized by marram grasses, the pine tree forests that are quick to follow. Tidal rivermouths have rich mud flats and cities like La Rochelle, Rochefort and Royan have sprung up in their calm waters. Sitting offshore are a series of islands with their own raison d'être. While Île de Ré has a unique microclimate and receives the most sunshine in western France, Île d'Oléron is second only to Corsica in size.

This physical complexity makes the region a diverse surfing destination. There is a healthy mix of reefs, beach breaks and even some rivermouth sandbars. To the south, the River Gironde marks the start of one of the world's longest beaches – bliss or monotony, depending on your standpoint. But one thing's certain, you won't find coastline as diverse as Vendée and Charente until you cross the border into Northern Spain.

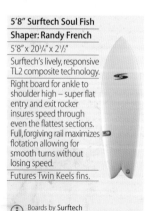

5'8" Surftech Soul Fish

Shaper: Randy French

5'8" x 20¾" x 2½"

Surftech's lively, responsive TL2 composite technology.

Right board for ankle to shoulder high – super flat entry and exit rocker insures speed through even the flattest sections. Full, forgiving rail maximizes flotation allowing for smooth turns without losing speed.

Futures Twin Keels fins.

Boards by **Surftech**
www.surftech.com info@surftech.com

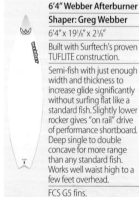

6'4" Webber Afterburner

Shaper: Greg Webber

6'4" x 19⅛" x 2⅜"

Built with Surftech's proven TUFLITE construction.

Semi-fish with just enough width and thickness to increase glide significantly without surfing flat like a standard fish. Slightly lower rocker gives "on rail" drive of performance shortboard. Deep single to double concave for more range than any standard fish. Works well waist high to a few feet overhead.

FCS G5 fins.

Local environment

It always pays to try a bit of French in the line-up. Outside the French summer holidays the vibe at most of the breaks here is pretty relaxed. La Sauzaie is probably the only exception, where the crowds will be on it whenever it breaks. Just bring a relaxed attitude and you'll be fine.

Getting around

The road links in Vendée and Charente are very good, with the coastal areas all served by main D roads. Getting around outside the busy summer season should be no problem. Watch out for bridge tolls between islands – in the summer they can be as high as €16.

Breaks

BEACH BREAK

↘1 St-Gilles-Croix-de-Vie

- **Conditions** All W to SW swells, offshore in NE winds
- **Hazards/tips** Popular with longboarders and beginners
- **Sleeping** St-Gilles-Croix-de-Vie ▸▸ *p174*

Crumbly, mellow beach break with lefts and rights, protected from big swells. A real longboarders' wave, making it an ideal location for the Vendée Longboard Pro Am. An urban spot with a breakwater at the northern end. At high tide there is backwash from the concrete defences, so best at low to mid.

THIERRY ORGANOFF

REEF BREAK

↘2 La Sauzaie

- **Swell** NW or SW
- **Wind** NE
- **Tide** Quarter to high tide
- **Size** 3-8 ft
- **Length** 50-100 m
- **Bottom** Rocky reef and sand
- **Ability level**: Intermediate to advanced
- **Best months**: Sep-Jun
- **Board** Performance Thruster
- **Access** Via the channel
- **Hazards/tips** Busy, breaking over reef
- **Sleeping** St-Gilles-Croix-de-Vie/Les Sables-d'Olonne ▸▸ *p174*

This is a short, but high quality A-frame reef and one of the region's premier spots. When southwesterly or westerly swells hit the reef, powerful and hollow lefts and rights produce nice barrel sections. The wave breaks in front of rocks. This reef hosts the annual WQS Pays de La Loire Surf Pro contest. As you would expect at such a good break, it does get busy year round, with a committed group of local surfers competing over a small take-off zone. Best surfed from mid to high tide. There are other reefs in the area worth checking out.

Head south from St-Gilles on the D38 and turn right at La Sauzaie.

If you like La Sauzaie, try Porthleven in Britain (see page 83) or The Bubble in Fuerteventura (see page 268).

BEACH BREAK

↘3 Les Dunes

- **Conditions** All NW to SW swells, offshore in E to NE winds
- **Hazards/tips** Popular longboarders' wave
- **Sleeping** Les Sables-d'Olonne ▸▸ *p174*

This beach break has lefts and rights and is a touristy spot with lifeguards in the summer. A fairly weak wave, popular with longboarders, its swamped when small, better at 4-5 ft.

REEF AND BEACH BREAK

↘4 Sauveterre

- **Conditions** All NW to SW swells, offshore in E to NE winds
- **Hazards/tips** Lovely location, busy in the summer, beach car park
- **Sleeping** Les Sables-d'Olonne ▸▸ *p174*

There are a couple of options to chose from, **Pic du Large** and **Pic du Phoque** – both are right-hand, sand-covered reefs with nice long walls that work well in big northwesterly swells. Follow the small coast road north from Sables-d'Olonne into the pine forests and in a good swell you'll see the surfers' cars parked by the footpath through the pine forest to the sea.

BEACH BREAK

↘5 L'Aubraie

- **Conditions** All NW to SW swells, offshore in E to NE winds
- **Hazards/tips** Beach break with rocks
- **Sleeping** Les Sables-d'Olonne ▸▸ *p174*

At low tide there are good rights on the beach. There are a couple of sand-covered rocky breaks – **Pic de L'Abraie** is the best and has a fast hollow left, considered one of the best waves in the region, which works best at mid tide. Watch out for the rocks. These spots sit about 2 km north of Chaume in a beautiful forest location.

LAURENT MASUREL

DEMI TAYLOR

Top: Tucking into a Vendée barrel. **Above**: 7 Les Conches.

BEACH BREAK

↘6 Tanchette

- **Conditions** All SW to W or big NW swells, offshore in NE winds
- **Hazards/tips** Good potential
- **Sleeping** Les Sables-d'Olonne » *p174*

There is a pretty average beach break at Sables-d'Olonne but there are pretty good, long right-handers breaking off the rocks. The right can handle a big swell but be careful with the rips and currents.

BEACH BREAK

↘7 Les Conches

- **Conditions** All Big NW and all W to SW swells, offshore in E to NE winds
- **Hazards/tips** Very pretty location
- **Sleeping** La Tranche » *p174*

This a quarter way down a large, slowly arcing sandy beach backed by dunes with views south to Île de Ré. It offers a combination of peaks, lefts and rights and quality varies with the swells, from mellow and cruisey to punchy and powerful. Works on all tides. This access point serves as a good indicator as to whether the rest of the Longville beaches are working. This area is less busy than the spots to the south. Popular with holidaymakers in the summer, the beach resembles Les Landes but with green, cloudy waters.

BEACH BREAK

↘8 Bud Bud

- **Conditions** All NW to SW swells, offshore in E to NE winds
- **Hazards/tips** Can get busy, can be powerful when big
- **Sleeping** La Tranche » *p174*

Quite a well-known break, this is a good quality beachbreak that offers pretty consistent and occasionally hollow peaks. Picks up more swell than the other sections of beach and the banks offer both lefts and rights here. It works all through the tides but can get crowded. Park back from the beach on the road in the pines and walk through the dunes on the walkway. Signposted.

BEACH BREAK

↘9 La Terrière

- **Conditions** All NW to SW swells, offshore in E to NE winds
- **Hazards/tips** Popular tourist beach in the summer
- **Sleeping** La Tranche » *p174*

There is easy access to this part of the beach which increases crowds. There is, however, plenty of room to spread out if there is a crowd. Works on all tides and has a pretty chilled vibe. No high-top van access in the car park.

RIGHT POINT BREAK

↘10 Le Pointe du Grouin/Le Phare

- **Conditions** Massive NW or W swells, offshore in NE winds
- **Hazards/tips** Check here in the biggest swells
- **Sleeping** La Tranche » *p174*

When a huge swell is running, this is a great place to check as it wraps around the point and peels along the flat, rocky reef point. Follow the signs for Le Phare (the lighthouse) to the car park with special campervan-free camping area. Needs to be surfed at high, when mellow walling waves can peel for over 200 m. Surf down the point and walk back up. Bring a longboard or fish for winter fun. There is also a weak right-hander to the south towards the jetty called Embarcadère. Popular wind and kite surfing spot.

REEF BREAK

↘11 Pointe de Chassiron

- **Conditions** Medium to big W to NW swells, offshore in S to SE winds
- **Hazards/tips** Low tide, shallow reef, strong rips
- **Sleeping** Île d'Oléron »» p175

The Île d'Oléron points in a northwesterly direction into the turbulent waters that surround this stretch of coastline. At low tide, as the sea recedes off northern tip of the island, a long, flat, sharp, striated reef is revealed along which quality lefts and rights peel. It's a long walk out over the rocks to the break, so booties are essential at any time of year. This is a heavy reef break with very real dangers posed by rips and currents, so this is a spot best left to experienced surfers. Respect the locals who are happy to offer advice to travellers. Head for the lighthouse from which there are view out over the peak. In a massive swell check out the left points at St-Denis and Les Boulassiers.

BEACH BREAK

↘12 Les Huttes

- **Conditions** Medium to big NW to SW swells, offshore in E winds
- **Hazards/tips** Rips
- **Sleeping** Île d'Oléron »» p175

In a big southwesterly or good northwesterly swell, this stretch of beach really comes into its own with powerful and hollow waves

YANNICK LE TOQUIN

11 Pointe de Chassiron.

breaking through the tides. Park up and walk over the dunes. The best beach break on the island when it's on, but watch out for powerful rips.

BEACH BREAK

↘13 Vert Bois

- **Conditions** Medium NW to SW swells, offshore in NE winds
- **Hazards/tips** Very popular break
- **Sleeping** Île d'Oléron »» p175

The main surf checkpoint, this stretch of beach is also the most popular spot on the island. This area can have some excellent waves on all tides, but needs a decent clean swell. The beach stretches south so check it out if the main peaks are crowded.

BEACH BREAK

↘14 St-Trojan

- **Conditions** Medium NW to SW swells, offshore in E winds
- **Hazards/tips** Quiet spot
- **Sleeping** Île d'Oléron »» p175

Take the D126 and walk down the Grande Plage, which is dune-backed and has massive potential. Can be busy by the main access points in the summer but is such a big stretch of beach that there are always empty peaks to be had. A beautiful and quiet spot that has a real Les Landes feel to it. Watch out for rips and currents, especially near the southern Maumusson end.

BEACH BREAK

↘15 Côte Sauvage

- **Conditions** All NW to SW swells, offshore in an E wind
- **Hazards/tips** Rips, can be polluted
- **Sleeping** Royan »» p175

Access points through the forest lead to the dune-backed beaches of the 'Savage' coast. The southern end near the lighthouse, Phare de la Coubre, is the busiest – check to the north where it is much quieter. The banks can be excellent with hollow, powerful waves in clean swells. Watch out for powerful rip currents.

Practicalities

St-Gilles-Croix-de-Vie

This popular French resort town is the venue for the Vendée Longboard Pro Am and, despite having a fairly functional feel, makes a good base for exploring the reefs to the south.

Sleeping

Camping **Bahamas Beach**, on R des Sables, T0251-546916, 2 km from the town and about 800 m from the beach, Apr-Sep, is very family-focused. Just to the south, at Givrand, is **Domaine des Beaulieu**, T0251-555946, about 1 km from the sea, open year round with cabins to rent.

Eating

Casa Pizza, by the church on R Achard, serves pizzas and good grills.

Directory

Surf Shops South of St-Gilles in Bretignolles sur Mer, check out **Atlantic Lezard**, on R de Plage, www.atlanticlezard.com, as well as **Sunset Surf Shop**, R Marais Girad. **Tourist information** Blvd de L'Egalité.

Les Sables-d'Olonne

This popular holiday spot is the starting point for the Vendée Globe Challenge, www.vendeeglobe.org – the single-handed, non-stop round the world yacht race which launches every 4 years.

Sleeping

€€ Hôtel les Voyageurs, R de la Baudere at Pl de la Gare, T0251-951149, spacious rooms with baths plus a bar and restaurant below. **€€ Auberge Vendee**, R des Ramparts, just back from the beach, T0251-320398. **Camping** **Dune des Sables**, just by the sea at La Paracou, T0251-323121, open Apr-Sep, cabins. **Camping Roses**, R des Roses, 500 m from Rembai beach, T0251-951042, open Apr-Oct.

DEMI TAYLOR

Above: The dune-backed Côte Sauvage. **Right**: 8 Bud Bud is well known for producing hollow Landes-style barrrels.

Directory

Surf Shops **Bahia Surf Shop**, R de Ramparts, is well stocked with hardware and accessories. **Tourist information** Promenade Joffre, in a glass-fronted building near the seafront.

La Tranche

This is a pretty town, sheltered in the natural harbour behind Pointe du Grouin du Cou. It has good amenities and is quiet off season. Just to the north sits Longeville, a long stretch of pine-fringed beach with a number of campsites.

Sleeping

Camping In Longeville sur Mer, try the pine-shaded **Clos des Pins**, 250 m inland from Les Conches, T0251-903169, Apr-Oct, and the family orientated **Les Dunes**, also on Ave Dr Joussemet, T0251-333293 – both a short walk to the beach. Just north at Plage Rocher check out the cheaper **Camping Municipal du Rocher**, T0251-903157, Apr-Sep. The local beach isn't as good but Les Conches is only a 5-min drive away.
South at **Le Phare** there are a couple of good choices:
€ Face aux Flots, R de la Phare, T0251-304711, year round, is very reasonable, a short stumble to the beach and has a pizzeria downstairs. Over the road is a well placed **stationment de camping car** with direct beach access – plus you can always grab a decent breakfast or pick up a takeaway at the hotel. **Camping La Vieux Moulin**, R Vieux Moulin, T0251-274847, Mar-Oct, is a large municipal site shaded by vast pines.

Directory

Surf shops **Le Palmier**, on R Pertuis Breich in Tranche sur Mer. **Nova Fun**, on the main R Victor Hugo (by the banks etc) open Mar-Nov plus weekends and holidays.

Île d'Oléron

This 30-km long island is joined to the mainland by a 3-km bridge. Fringed by 20 km of beautiful beaches, it gets very busy in the summer. Le Château on the southeast of the island is a popular base with easy access to the breaks on the western coast. Check out the Sun market for local produce.

Sleeping

€ Le Castel, R Alsace-Lorraine, T0546-752469, has comfortable and clean rooms.

Camping The island is literally a series of campsites. A few choices include: **Phare Ouest**, St-Denis, about ½ km south of the lighthouse at the northern tip of the island, T0546-479000, Apr-Sep. Nearby **Cap Soleil**, off the D734, T0546-478303, is open Apr-Oct. In the middle of the island, at picturesque St-Pierre, traditional family site **Trois Masses**, T0546-472396, Easter-Sep, offers good access to all the breaks.

Directory

Surf shops The excellent **Island Surf Shop**, on R Bouline, in St-Pierre is well stocked with hardware, accessories and essentials. They have also opened up a girls' shop next door. **Post office** On Blvd Victor Hugo. **Tourist information** Pl de la République.

Royan

At the mouth of the River Gironde this is a good base to explore the beaches of the Côte Sauvage. It is also a good place to bisect the river: take the ferry across to Verdon for the start of Gironde and beach break country.

Sleeping

€ Hermitage, Front de Mer, T0546-385733, is slightly utilitarian but affords views of the marina and glimpses of Plage Grande Conche, has excellent deals available off season and is handy for an overnight stop.

Camping Plenty available in and around Royan. **Clairfontaine**, a well-equipped site 300 m from the beach in Pontaillac, T0546-390811, May-Sep. **Camping Chenes**, 2 km to the north at Medis, T0546-067138, open Mar-Oct. **Camping La Triloteie**, on Av Alienor d'Aquataine, just out of town on the road to Bordeaux, T0546-052691, is open year round. Northwest of Royan at La Palmyre and with direct access to the Cote Sauvage is **Le Parc de la Cote Sauvage**, T0546-224018, Apr-Sep.

Directory

Surf shops There are several shops on R Gambetta. There is also the well stocked **Neway**, on Esp du Bac. In La Palmyre try **Palmyr Wind**, Ave du Limousin, which has a good range of boards and surf staples.

KRISTEN PELOU

Flat spells

Golf Get a round in at **Fontenelles GC**, 6 km east of St Gilles Croix de Vie, T0251-541394. The 18-hole **Golf de Royan**, to the west of Royan in St-Palais-sur- Mer, on Maine Gaudin, T0546-231624.

Sights About 1½ hrs' drive east from La Rochelle is **Hennessy**, T0545-357268, www.hennessy-cognac.com, the spiritual home of cognac with distillery tours daily Mar-Dec. Ask at the tourist office on R 14 Juillet for more details.

Île de Ré From the city of La Rochelle with an attractive old port and lively cafés and bars, it's only a short, hop over the toll bridge to explore the beautiful, beach-fringed Île de Ré – free to those on foot and on bikes. With environmental foresight, the city of La Rochelle has come up with a genius concept – the famous yellow bikes – free to hire for the first two hours and just €1 for each hour thereafter. Place de Verdun (plus Quai Valin May- Sep), T546 340222 to reserve your bike, and then just pretend you're in San Francisco!

Île d'Yeu From St Gilles Croix de Vie or Sables d'Olonne take the ferry across to Port-Joinville on Île d'Yeu which – with forest, dune-backed beaches and rocky outcrops – is like a France sampler. **Compagnie Vendeenne**, T0825 139085, www.compagnievendeenne.com, do a day return from St Gilles for around €20 and from Sables d'Olonne for around €28. Hire a bike for the day from Port-Joinville for around €10.

Overview

The sun is dropping down towards the horizon and the evening light is beginning to take on a pinky hue. Shaper Phil Grace is sipping on a beer looking out over the jostling Hossegor crowds. "Jeff first surfed here back in '71. He was on his way to Biarritz and just turned right. There was only one guy out surfing." Jeff Hackman smiles as the memory reappears. "And he was naked," laughs Jeff. The swell is pumping, fanned by a light offshore breeze. It's glorious September, and the town is buzzing with life. The tourist season is coming to an end accompanied by fanfare and an explosion of energy as the Quiksilver Pro France brings the world tour to town. Salt crusted, we're sitting at an outside table, nursing préssions, feeling surfed out and contented, listening to one of Phil's classic stories. This is prime Landes season. There are 225 km of classic beach break spreading from Pointe de Grave south to Anglet – empty barrels reeling, peaks where a soul could surf alone for weeks. So why be here? Why are so many drawn to Hossegor from across the continent? Is it the unconscious pull of the tribe, is it the atmosphere, to see just what's going on or is it for the parties? Summer in Hossegor has become a surfing pilgrimage. Despite the crowds, it's still a place where grommets come for fun, adventure and great waves – it gives birth to stories you can tell for decades to come. Even if you don't see a naked guy pulling into a barrel...

Coastline

Gironde and Les Landes consists of 140 miles of straight beach heading north to south, broken only by the Bassin d'Arcachon. The west-facing strip is backed by a huge spine of sand dunes behind which stretches a dense, aromatic pine forest. An extreme example of this can be found to the south of Arcachon, where the huge Dune de Playa dominates the landscape.This massive sand dune – the largest in Europe at 120 m high – affords bird's eye views of the coastline. As the dune slowly encroaches landward, it swallows up massive pine trees in its advancement.

All the sand moving around this coastline means one thing – sandbanks and lots of them. Currents and storms can create and destroy perfect sandbars with amazing regularity. However, as one bank is swept away, another will come to life.

One big drawback to this open coastline is that when a big swell hits, there are few sheltered spots. Capbreton will always be crowded in big swells and the breaks around Soulac-sur-Mer are also popular. If all else fails, head south into the Basque region where the bays will have plenty to offer.

Spring
Air 12°C 54°F
Water 12°C 54°F
4/3mm Wetsuit & boots

Summer
Air 21°C 70°F
Water 20°C 68°F
Shortie

Autumn
Air 17°C 63°F
Water 16°C 61°F
3/2mm Wetsuit

Winter
Air 7°C 45°F
Water 11°C 52°F
5/4/3mm Wetsuit, boots, gloves & hood

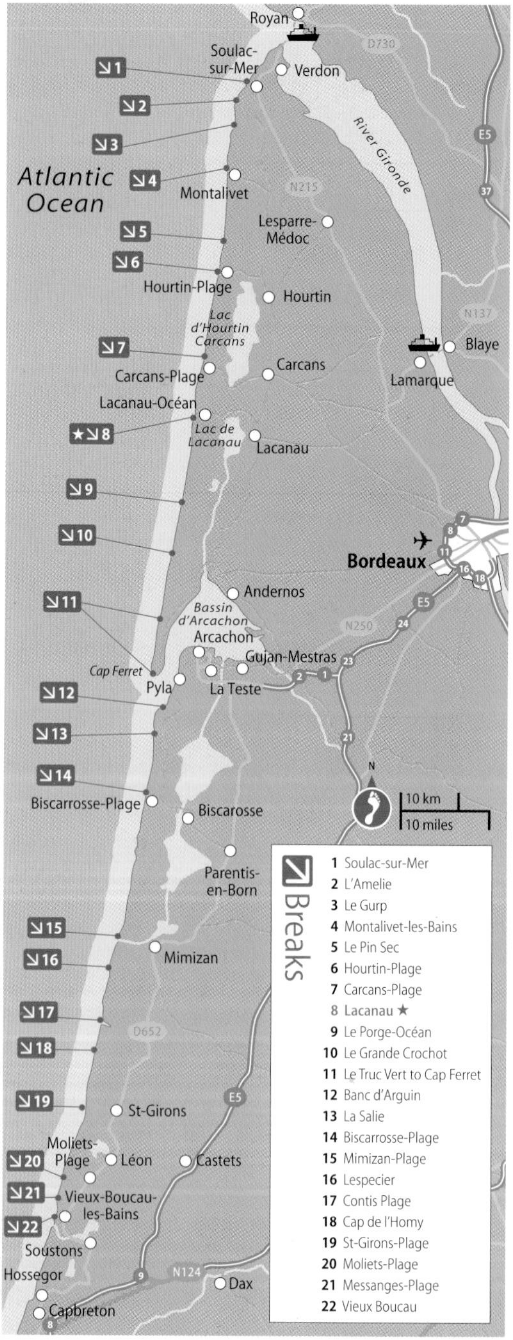

DAMIEN POULLENOT

LAURENT MASUREL

Above: 31 Patrick Bevan, VVF. **Top:** Fred Basse – power-assisted surfing at one of Les Landes' regular tow-in spots.

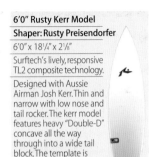

6'0" Rusty Kerr Model

Shaper: Rusty Preisendorfer

6'0" x 18 1/4" x 2 1/8"

Surftech's lively, responsive TL2 composite technology.

Designed with Aussie Airman Josh Kerr. Thin and narrow with low nose and tail rocker. The kerr model features heavy "Double-D" concave all the way through into a wide tail block. The template is suited for the fast, rampy waves of Hossegor.

Futures Rusty fins.

6'3" Stretch F-4

Shaper: Stretch

6'3" x 18 11/16" x 2 1/8"

Surftech's lively, responsive TL2 composite technology.

Lightning fast! Half-moon template elongates the rail-line for positive drive and release off the tail. Deck channels give added strength while moderating a progressive flex pattern into the four fins. When the Beach Breaks are reeling, it will make every section!

Futures Quad fins.

Boards by **Surftech**
www.surftech.com info@surftech.com

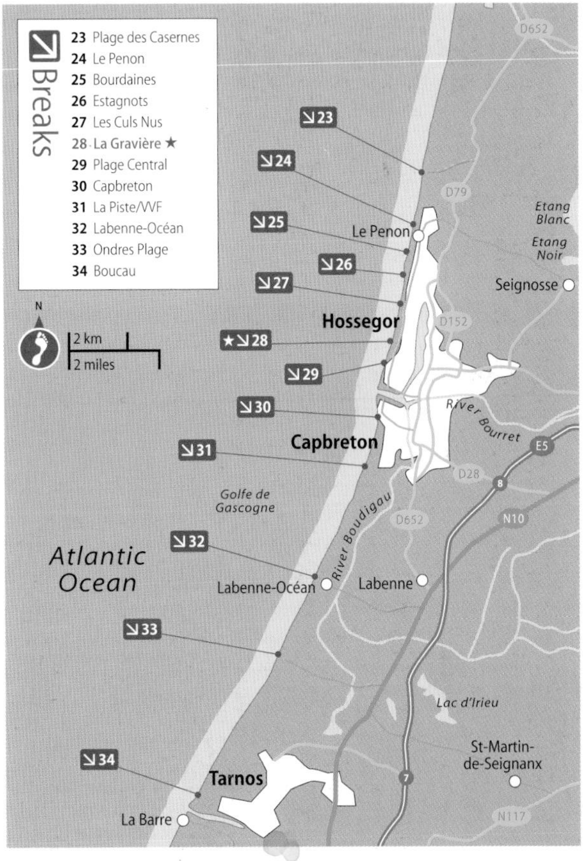

Local Environment

Water quality is generally good, although caution should be exercised around rivermouths after heavy rains and thunderstorms that can fire through the region with regularity in late summer/early autumn. The beaches of Les Landes were also hit by some of the oil from the Prestige disaster. Surfrider Foundation Europe is active in this area highlighting beach litter and other forms of pollution. "The sand dunes in Les Landes act like a bacteriological filter. The low urbanisation affords this area a general good quality of water." Surfrider Foundation.

The European headquarters for the majority of surf brands are based in and around Hossegor and has seen both the electorate and elected embracing the surf scene like no other community in Europe. You'll find some of the busiest breaks in Europe here. There will also be many top riders in the water, especially when the world tour is in town in September/October. The breaks will be very competitive around Hossegor but as you head north the spots get quieter and more chilled. Many spots in Les Landes and Gironde can be empty, even in early Autumn. If you're prepared to walk, you can have your pick of empty peaks – get out and explore.

Getting around

For a fast north to south journey the N10 inland is the best bet. There is a whole series of D roads that follow the coastline and allow easy access to every resort along this huge beach. There is always ample parking by the beach, and a short walk should yield a decent bank to surf.

Breaks

Gironde

BEACH BREAK

1 Soulac-sur-Mer

Conditions Medium to big NW to SW swells, offshore in E winds
Hazards/tips Good spot to check in big swells
Sleeping Soulac-sur-Mer » p185

Sitting 9 km south of Pointe de Grave, Soulac marks the start of an epic stretch of sand running south to Biarritz, broken only by the Bassin d'Arcachon. Offshore sandbanks deposited by the River Gironde affects the amount of swell getting into the beach here, making this a good area to check in big swells. Works on all tides but best from low to three-quarters. Not the prettiest spot.

BEACH BREAK

2 L'Amelie

Conditions Medium NW to SW swells, offshore in E winds
Hazards/tips Rips when big
Sleeping Soulac-sur-Mer » p185

L'Amelie has some good peaks and works best in medium swells. As with most spots along this stretch of coastline, it works through all tides. However when a big swell hits it can have strong rips and be difficult to paddle out. In small swells these beaches are suitable for supervised beginners. Follow the D101 south to this quiet beach.

BEACH BREAK

3 Le Gurp

Conditions Medium NW to SW swells, offshore in E winds
Hazards/tips Quiet beach, especially outside summer
Sleeping Soulac-sur-Mer » p185

Classic beach breaks along this stretch produce some great banks in clean swells. Can take a bigger swell but banks tend to move around quickly and change with tides.

BEACH BREAK

4 Montalivet-les-Bains

Conditions Small to medium NW to SW swells, offshore in E winds
Hazards/tips Good beach break
Sleeping Montalivet-les-Bains » p185

This extension of a huge stretch of beach picks up a bit more swell, and again can have some good banks. Popular in the summer but very quiet off-season.

BEACH BREAK

5 Le Pin Sec

Conditions Small to medium NW to SW swells, offshore in E winds
Hazards/tips Good beach break
Sleeping Montalivet-les-Bains/Hourtin Plage » p185

Another quiet spot and super French beachie with various quality peaks that bleed into one another. Like much of this coast, it doesn't handle a big swell. Plenty of scope for exploration around here.

BEACH BREAK

6 Hourtin-Plage

Conditions Small to medium NW to SW swells, offshore in E winds
Hazards/tips Good beach break
Sleeping Hourtin Plage » p185

A popular summertime beach with many tourists and day trippers from Bordeaux. Plenty of room up and down the beach - pack a lunch and head off. Easy access with parking near the beach.

BEACH BREAK

7 Carcans-Plage

Conditions Small to medium NW to SW swells, offshore in E winds
Hazards/tips Good beach break
Sleeping Carcans-Plage » p185

Sitting among the pines and dunes you'll find this small village with amenities and parking near to the beachfront. Not as busy or commercial as Lacanau, but still a very popular spot in the summer. The peaks near the village fill up first but a short walk should provide quieter peaks. Just back from the coast sits the largest Freshwater lake in France.

BEACH BREAK

8 Lacanau

Swell Small to medium NW to SW swells
Wind E
Tide All tides
Size 2-8 ft
Length 20-75 m
Bottom Sand
Ability: All levels
Best months: Sep-Nov, Apr-May
Board Performance Thruster or fish
Access From the beach via channels
Hazards/tips Heavy when good, very busy
Sleeping Lacanau-Océan » p185

The popular resort town of Lacanau-Océan has been on the surfing map since the early, hazy days of French wave riding, and for good reason. Sandbanks build up, assisted by the occasional groyne, to produce miles of consistent, powerful, sometimes hollow beachbreak. The Lacanau Pro has been an annual feature since 1979 and has been won by just about every big name on the circuit from Rabbit, through to Carroll, Curren, Occy and Pottz. Lacanau is slowly expanding and spilling into the generous pine forests that fill

YANNICK LE TOQUIN

THIERRY ORGANOFF

Above: 3 Le Gurp churns out classic lefts. Above left: 8 Geoff Hennou tearing it up in Lacanau.

the gap between ocean and lake. In the summer months, the beach and town throngs with the bronzed and the beautiful, the pros and the poseurs, but in the autumn months, the crowds die back and the swells kick in to reveal the true beauty of the area.

*If you like **Lacanau**, try **Praa Sands** in England (see page 83) or **Praia de Fontella** in Spain (see page 247).*

BEACH BREAK

↘9 Le Porge-Océan

- **Conditions** Small to medium NW to SW swells, offshore in E winds
- **Hazards/tips** Good beach break
- **Sleeping** Lacanau-Océan ➤➤ *p185*

Another good section of beach backed by pine trees which is quiet except during the peak summer season when the area becomes a holiday hotspot. Works on all tides but the high tide close-out shore break in bigger swells can be challenging.

BEACH BREAK

↘10 Le Grande Crochot

- **Conditions** Small to medium NW to SW swells, offshore in E winds
- **Hazards/tips** Good beach break
- **Sleeping** Lacanau-Océan/Cap Ferret ➤➤ *p185*

The D106 leads the Bordeaux surfers straight to this popular beach. Another stretch of golden sand that can have excellent banks through the tides. Surfers are here year round, becoming very popular in the summer.

BEACH BREAK

↘11 Le Truc Vert to Cap Ferret

- **Conditions** All NW to SW swells, offshore in E winds
- **Hazards/tips** Good beach break
- **Sleeping** Cap Ferret ➤➤ *p186*

The huge stretch of beach from Le Truc Vert to Cap Ferret, with roads down through the pines to a series of spots, is a great place to lose the crowds. Cap Ferret is worth checking in a bigger NW swell on an incoming tide as the cape cuts out some of its force. There are nasty rips on an outgoing tide as water empties from the Basin d'Arcachon – the massive lagoon here.

BEACH BREAK

↘12 Banc d'Arguin

- **Conditions** Small to medium NW to SW swells, offshore in E winds
- **Hazards/tips** Huge shifting offshore sandbank
- **Sleeping** Dune de Pyla ➤➤ *p186*

A lot of sand is shifted around this area by winds and currents. Winds have created the towering sand dune Dune de Pyla, the biggest in Europe, that overlooks the southern edge of the Basin d'Arcachon. The swift currents have helped sculpt the Banc d'Arguin, a huge sandbank sitting in the mouth of the inlet. Worth exploring for a unique surf session but watch out for rips in big tides. Best left to the experienced. Boats leave from Dune de Pyla for the sandbank see www.bateliersvarcachon.com or T05-5772 2828 for information.

BEACH BREAK

↘13 La Salie

- **Conditions** Medium NW to SW swells, offshore in E winds
- **Hazards/tips** Quiet spot
- **Sleeping** Dune de Pyla ➤➤ *p186*

Heading south on the D218, there is a turning that leads through the pines to the beach. Protected by the Pointe d'Arcachon and the sandbanks in the river, this area doesn't pick up as much swell as Biscarrosse to the south and the banks shift around due to the currents. Nice quiet location.

YANNICK LE TOQUIN

DAMIEN POULLENOT

Above: 11 The stretch of sands leading to Cap Ferret can be a great place to find empty peaks.
Top: 6 Hourtin turns it on with banks that Landes has become legendary for.

Les Landes

BEACH BREAK

↘14 Biscarrosse-Plage

- **Conditions** Small to medium NW to Wswells, offshore in E winds
- **Hazards/tips** Excellent beach break
- **Sleeping** Biscarrosse-Plage ›› p186

The overall increase in popularity of Landes has had an impact on all these breaks. Once the retreat of those escaping the crowds to the south, these spots have become much more popular, especially at weekends and during the vacations. Quality wise, Biscarrosse is an excellent beach with plenty of peaks. From the top of the dunes you can see banks all the way north and south, with the ones by the main beach access getting busy. There are also nice hollow peaks by the northern access point. Busy at weekends but with a more chilled vibe in the water than further south.

BEACH BREAK

↘15 Mimizan-Plage

- **Conditions** Small to medium NW to W swells, offshore in E winds
- **Hazards/tips** Rips when big
- **Sleeping** Mimizan ›› p187

Mimizan is another classic Landes ocean-side village with a river mouth on its southern flank and endless sand to the north. Beachfront parking overlooks the most popular banks by the surf club. Although busy at lunchtimes, weekends and during holidays, there is still a good atmosphere in the water. There are two groynes with banks. There is a very smelly factory by the river on the road in, so water quality at the rivermouth may not be the best. Between Biscarrosse and Mimizan is a restricted military zone.

BEACH BREAK

↘16 Lespecier

- **Conditions** Small to medium NW to W swells, offshore in E winds
- **Hazards/tips** Beautiful, quiet location
- **Sleeping** Mimizan ›› p187

This is a secluded spot reached by quite roads through the Forêt de Mimizan, either from Mimizan to the north or via Bias inland. Good quality beach break with numerous banks to the north and south. Dune backed and pine fringed.

BEACH BREAK

↘17 Contis Plage

- **Conditions** Small to medium NW to W swells, offshore in E winds
- **Hazards/tips** Summer resort, quiet of season
- **Sleeping** Mimizan ›› p187

This tiny resort has a rivermouth and stone groyne to help sculpt the sand into banks. Some excellent waves also form in front of the old bunker. Check the surf from the car park on top of the dunes just to the north of the village. A summer resort, quiet outside the holidays. Great lighthouse marooned in the middle of the woods. The car park is a popular autumn free-camp spot over looking the surf.

BEACH BREAK

↘18 Cap de l'Homy

- **Conditions** Small to medium NW to W swells, offshore in E winds
- **Hazards/tips** Emptier banks away from main access
- **Sleeping** Mimizan/Moliets-Plage ›› p187

There is a campsite overlooking the sea with some great banks stretching to the north and south. The bank in front of the access fills up first but a short walk should yield empty waves. Chilled-out location.

BEACH BREAK

↘19 St-Girons-Plage

- **Conditions** Small to medium NW to W swells, offshore in E winds
- **Hazards/tips** Beautiful, quiet location
- **Sleeping** Moliets-Plage ▸▸ *p187*

Accessed via the D42, this is another small resort village, quiet out of season when the windswept sand gives it a slightly run-down feel – a contrast to the bustling summer trade. Produces some great waves in the right conditions, without the crowds further south.

BEACH BREAK

↘20 Moliets-Plage

- **Conditions** Small to medium NW to W swells, offshore in E winds
- **Hazards/tips** Pleasant resort with good waves
- **Sleeping** Moliets-Plage ▸▸ *p187*

The D117 hits the coast at one of the most pleasant resorts on this stretch of Les Landes' endless sandy coastline. The banks here shift around but there are generally some great peaks to be had.

BEACH BREAK

↘21 Messanges-Plage

- **Conditions** Small to medium NW to W swells, offshore in E winds
- **Hazards/tips** Excellent spot, quiet off season
- **Sleeping** Moliets-Plage/Vieux Boucau ▸▸ *p187*

Excellent series of banks, plenty of peaks to choose from in a good swell. Low tide sees some hollow, grinding barrels jacking up onto the sandbars. In a bigger swell it can be a hell of a paddle without a decent channel. Works through all tides, and although busy in the summer, off season it is quiet.

BEACH BREAK

↘22 Vieux Boucau

- **Conditions** Small to medium NW to W swells, offshore in E winds
- **Hazards/tips** Popular spot with strong surf community
- **Sleeping** Vieux Boucau ▸▸ *p181*

Vieux Boucau became a refuge for those seeking a bit of peace away from the busy summer Hossegor waves. There are great banks here and a much more mellow scene than just to the south. The breaks by the surf club and main access are the busiest, but there are plenty of waves up and down the beach. The surf club in the dunes (founded in 1973) has a wooden clubhouse that is shaped like a breaking wave, in tune with the natural surroundings.

BEACH BREAK

↘23 Plage des Casernes

- **Conditions** Small to medium NW to W swells, offshore in E winds
- **Hazards/tips** Beautiful, quiet location
- **Sleeping** Seignosse/Hossegor/Capbreton ▸▸ *p187*

The place to go to find quiet banks during the high season. This long stretch of beach has miles of sandbars and endless possibilities. From the car park, follow the tracks through the pines. Always used to be a popular surfers freecamp area.

Hossegor

BEACH BREAK

↘24 Le Penon

- **Conditions** Small to medium NW to W swells, offshore in E winds
- **Hazards/tips** Quality beach break
- **Sleeping** Seignosse/Hossegor/Capbreton ▸▸ *p187*

Most northerly of the world-renowned Seignosse/Hossegor breaks, Le Penon can offer some pretty awesome waves and, when the whole of Hossegor is going off, can be one of the least busy spots. Park in front of the apartments and check the surf from the dunes. Banks cluster around the pier and also further to the north where it is a bit quieter. Works on all tides.

YANNICK LE TOQUIN

13 Glenn Le Touquin finding the quiet banks of La Salie very accommodating.

DEMI TAYLOR

DEMI TAYLOR

Above: 21 Messanges, a typically French sight to feast on. **Right: 27** Culs Nus bearing its soul.

BEACH BREAK

↘25 Bourdaines

- **Conditions** Small to medium NW to W swells, offshore in E winds
- **Hazards/tips** Less busy than breaks around Gravière
- **Sleeping** Seignosse/Hossegor/ Capbreton ›› *p187*

This stretch of beach starts to the south of the jetty and continues towards Estagnots. A good option in the summer, when it is less busy than the breaks to the south. Can have some excellent banks, through the tides.

BEACH BREAK

↘26 Estagnots

- **Conditions** All NW to W swells, offshore in E winds
- **Hazards/tips** Heavy shore break at high tide
- **Sleeping** Seignosse/Hossegor/ Capbreton ›› *p187*

This stretch of beach has an excellent reputation for producing quality consistent banks that churn out left-hand waves. At low there can be long walling waves, breaking closer in at high when it can also have a punishing shore break, especially in bigger swells. Was the traditional home of the Rip Curl Pro.

BEACH BREAK

↘27 Les Culs Nus

- **Conditions**All NW to SW swells, offshore in E winds
- **Hazards/tips** Parking on coast road, popular nudist beach
- **Sleeping** Seignosse/Hossegor/ Capbreton ›› *p187*

Sandwiched between Estagnots and La Gravière, this spot always attracts a crowd. It is home to some quality sandbanks, which work through the tides. It can also hold a large swell. Punishingly heavy shore break at high tide and rips when the tide drops out. The official nudist beach for Hossegor – the name (bare arses) says it all.

BEACH BREAK

↘29 Plage Central

- **Conditions** Medium to big NW to W swells, offshore in E winds
- **Hazards/tips** Crowds when small, heavy when big .
- **Sleeping** Seignosse/Hossegor/ Capbreton ›› *p187*

In the big autumn and winter swells, **La Nord** comes to life. There is an outside bank that breaks at huge sizes and has become a popular tow surf spot for locals and visiting pros. Near the shore there's an epic bank that has become an alternate site for the Quik Pro when Gravière gets too big. Heavy, hollow and punishing. To the south there's a huge river of a rip that's best avoided, but nearer the river mouth is **La Sud** one of the few spots in big swells that will provide comfortable waves for mortals. Therefore busy when working.

BEACH BREAK

↘30 Capbreton

- **Conditions** Medium to big NW to W swells, offshore in E to SE winds
- **Hazards/tips** Sheltered in big swells
- **Sleeping** Seignosse/Hossegor/ Capbreton ›› *p187*

A series of groynes breaks up the beach just south of the river. The area nearest the river is known affectionately as **Kiddies Corner** as it is very sheltered and surfable in the biggest swells. Sandbanks build up by the groynes and can produce good rights peeling off the south side of them. Parking is on the seafront, but difficult when the surf is good.

Beach break

↘28 La Gravière

- **Swell** NW to W
- **Wind** E
- **Tide** All tides
- **Size** 2-12 ft
- **Length** 25-75 m
- **Bottom** Sandbar
- **Ability** All levels
- **Best months** Sep-Nov
- **Board** Performance Thruster
- **Access** Off the beach
- **Hazards/tips** Crowds, rips, heavy hollow waves
- **Sleeping** Seignosse/Hossegor/Capbreton ▸▸ *p187*

Andy Irons dropping down the vertical face of a 10-ft peak, no time to bottom turn, spray angling off the rail as it bites into the clean green face – suddenly he's gone, under the huge throwing lip. A plume of spray spits contempt into the channel, clearing to reveal Irons, arms raised. The crowd goes wild. Another ten point ride. Already renowned throughout the surfing world as one of the best beach breaks on the planet, the exploits at the annual Quiksilver Pro have only further enhanced the reputation of La Gravière. Held in peak season, the sight of the world's top 44 pulling into epic Pipe-like barrels has become almost expected – the sight of scaffolders and technicians working on the beach has become a signal for the swells to kick in.

Along this huge stretch of shifting peaks and moving banks, Gravière is one of the few constants. Just a five minute walk to the north of Place de Landais, the sandbar forms close in to the shore. Heavy swells and shifting currents help to sculpt a consistent bank, making it one of the most reliable spots in the region. On 3 ft summer days it looks fun as the crowd hustles over the peelers, enjoying the brief boardshorts window of opportunity. When the solid, clean, autumnal swells kick in, that's when the real Gravière comes to life. The peak throws out heavy, hollow lefts and rights, the scuttling groms replaced by the serious chargers. This wave is made to look deceptively easy by the top class surfers who take it on. During the contest season it becomes a gladiatorial pit with broken boards and heavy hold-downs just feet from dry land. Best left to the experienced as the super competitive line-up is not difficult to get out to, but once there the rips, high tide shore dump and powerful waves can make you wish you stayed on dry land.

If you like *La Gravière, try low tide* ***Croyde*** *in England (see page 72) or* ***Supertubos*** *in Portugal (see page 296).*

LAURENT MASUREL

28 La Graviere – it's all about the barrels.

> La Gravière, Hossegor– my number one wave, mainly because it's home and only a short drive from Anglet, where I live and surf. But also because I've surfed there some of the most perfect waves of my life. Just intense and powerful barrels. Absolute beach-break perfection.
>
> *Franck Lacaze, former editor* Trip Surf

BEACH BREAK

↘31 La Piste/VVF

- **Conditions** Small to medium NW to W swells, offshore in E winds
- **Hazards/tips** Hollow banks in front of the WW2 bunkers
- **Sleeping** Seignosse/Hossegor/ Capbreton ›› *p187*

An excellent, high quality stretch of beach break, heading south from the huge old bunkers. There are many banks that work through the tides. Popular spot with some very hollow rights in clean swells and light offshores. Gets busy in the summer. Easy parking at VVF which includes a camping site for vans. Watch the rips.

BEACH BREAK

↘32 Labenne-Océan

- **Conditions** Small to medium NW to W swells, offshore in E to SE winds
- **Hazards/tips** Much less crowded than Hossegor
- **Sleeping** Seignosse/Hossegor/ Capbreton ›› *p187*

A great place to escape the crazy summer days in Hossegor. Take the D126 off the N10 and a whole range of quiet peaks are available. Works best in a small to medium swell on a low to three-quarter tide. As usual, the banks around the main access points fill up first. Pack a picnic and take a hike – you'll be surprised at how quiet it can be.

BEACH BREAK

↘33 Ondres Plage

- **Conditions** Small to medium NW to W swells, offshore in E to SE winds
- **Hazards/tips** Good option for quiet waves
- **Sleeping** Seignosse/Hossegor/ Capbreton ›› *p187*

Amazing to find such quiet waves in the heart of the surfing southwest. If the main peaks are busy, a short walk north or south will yield something quieter. Banks change with tides, but lower tides seem to be better.

LAURENT MASUREL

DAMIEN POULLENOT

Top: 29 La Nord is a pretty serious proposition at the best of times. **Above: 31** Bunkers – this wave breaks in front of the decaying ruins of huge bunkers left over from the Second World War.

LEFT-HAND JETTY BREAK

↘34 Boucau

- **Conditions** All NW to W swells, offshore in E to SE winds
- **Hazards/tips** Not for beginners
- **Sleeping** Seignosse/Hossegor/ Capbreton ›› *p187*

Not to be confused with Vieux Boucau, this left-hand wall peels along the sandbar built up along the northern side of the concrete jetty at the mouth of the River L'Adour. The jetty also offers some protection from southerly winds. The waves here can be pretty awesome in the right conditions, though those arriving in groups may find a frosty welcome. Parking available in front of the break.

Practicalities

Gironde

Getting there

To circumnavigate the Gironde can be a serious commitment of over 200 km, involving a trip to Bordeaux before virtually doubling back to Soulac. If you're hankering after some beachbreak action, the river- crossing alternative is a lot less painful. A year-round ferry service at the mouth of the Gironde connects Royan (T0546-383515) with Verdon (T0556-733773) on the south bank in just 20 mins. They operate regularly in the summer, every couple of hours in winter, around €3 passengers, from €37 for a van.

If the summer queues send you over the edge, drive two-thirds of the way down the river and take the Blaye-Lamarque ferry (20 mins, about €3 passengers, from €20 vans, T0557-420449) shaving almost 100 km off your journey.

Soulac-sur-Mer

Sitting on the northern tip of Médoc, this fairly uninspiring resort town all but closes in winter months. As with the majority of towns and villages on this stretch, the beach is the focal point, with most amenities on the handily named R de la Plage. This includes a couple of surf shops, **Cangoo** and **Aloha Beach**, as well as the post office, tourist information office, daily food market and a plethora of cafés, bars and restaurants.

Sleeping

There are a couple of sleeping options on R de la Plage including the unexceptional **€ Hôtel La Dame de Coeur**, T0556-098080.

Camping There are plenty of seasonal camping options. **Palace**, Blvd Marsan de Montbrun at northern end of town, T0556-098022, May-Sep. Heading south on the D101 to L'Amélie sur Mer, the smaller **Les Sables d'Argent**, T0556-098287, nestles in pine forest on the beachfront, Apr-Sep, with the option of cabins and statics. The slightly cheaper and larger **Amélie Plage**, T0556-098727, right on the seafront, Mar-Dec.

Montalivet-les-Bains

This truly seasonal resort all but closes outside Apr-Oct. In summer the main Av de l'Océan is home to a massive daily market selling goodies from across the region but the area is better known for the nearby **Euronat**, Europe's largest naturist park. A walk north up the beach will yield a skate park, just behind the beachfront car park.

Sleeping

€ L'Océan, beachfront, T0556-093005, you pay more for a seaview. They also have apartments for 4 at €400-500 per week, and one of the only restaurants open out of season.

Camping **Soleil D'Or**, is the closest site to the beach, about 100 m away, T0556-093137, www.campingle soleildor.com, open Apr-Oct.

The pine-shaded **Camping Municipal**, south of the town on Av de l'Europe, T0556-093345, open May-Sep is also close to the beach.

Eating

There are plenty of seasonal cafés and restaurants on the main drag including the excellent **La Guinguette** pizzeria where you can eat in or take away.

Globe Trotter, Av de l'Océan, is open year round (Oct-Apr, Thu-Sun only) and do a mean chicken fajita.

Directory

Spyder Surf Shop, Av de l'Océan, is open year round and has been delivering surf essentials to the community since '89. **Surf & Co**, who also hire out bikes and skateboards, are open summer only. **Tourist information** on the main Av de l'Océan.

Hourtin-Plage

Heading south on the coast road you pass plenty of right turns offering endless beach possibilities. At the top of Forêt d'Hourtin sits the summer resort of Hourtin-Plage with its own surf shop, **Surf & Co**, on R Jean Lafitte.

Sleeping

Camping In a pine forest just back from the beach is the massive **Côte d'Argent**, T0556-091025, mid-May-mid-Sep, fairly pricey with statics available and many of the amenities don't really kick in until Jul-Aug peak period. At Hourtin, 9 km inland, cheaper camping options include **Les Ourmes**, on Av du Lac by the massive Lac d'Hourtin (which does attract an exsanguinating number of mozzies), T0556-091276, Apr-Sep, statics available.

Carcans-Ocean

Backed by the largest freshwater lake in France, Carcans-Plage is another seasonal seaside resort which offers a little relief for those trying to escape the Lacanau hordes. There are even a couple of surf shops here **Rods** who shapes and stocks a good range of hardware and the well stocked **He'Enalu**. **Camping Municipal**, just back from the beachfront, T0556-034144, open Mar-Sep is a mellow pine-shaded site. Inland at Carcans, **Le Lierre**, on Route de Philibert, T0556- 034009, is open year round. Grab a pizza to restore you post-surf at **Le Galipo** on Av de Plage.

Lacanau-Océan

Follow the D6 from Bordeaux or the coast road south from Carcans-Plage to the summer resort of Lacanau-Océan. Slowly expanding between awesome dunes and pine forest, this is a popular, busy summer resort for families and surfers and has played host to the annual Lacanau Pro since 1979.

Sleeping

€ Villa le Zenith, Av Adjudant Guittard, T0684-608808, www.lacanau-zenith.com, just a short walk from the beach with beds from €17 and kitchen and laundry facilities acts as the local hostel Apr-Sep. There are plenty of good self catering options depending on season and size of group - contact the tourist board for more information.
Camping Airotel de l'Océan, R du Repos, T0556-032445, Apr-Sep, statics available. **Grands Pins**, T0556-032077, www.lesgrandspins.com, open Apr-Sep, is excellent, set in pine forest with private access across the dunes to Plage Nord - about a 15-min walk into town along the beach. It also has a good, reasonably priced on-site restaurant serving anything from pizzas to coquilles St-Jacques.
Free-campers, regularly pitch in the dunes between the campsite and the town with little bother.

Directory

Surf shops there are plenty here including Lacanau's first, **Surf City**, on the main Blvd de Plage, which opened in 1978 and sells everything from boards to boardies. There is also **Pacific Island**, on Allées Pierre Ortau. **Tourist information** Pl de l'Europe, www.lacanau.com, with year round Wifi summer internet access.

Cap Ferret

This chic little finger of land at the mouth of the Bassin d'Arcachon marks a pause in the stretch of sand dunes and beach breaks. To the north, on the Route de Forestière, is camping **Truc Vert**, T0556-608955, www.trucvert.com, May-Sep, set back from the beach in the pine trees. In the main town **Camaro** and **Tutti Frutti** surf shops on Blvd de la Plage, can service your basic needs.

Dune de Pyla

From Cap Ferret, the road goes round the triangular Bassin d'Arcachon before heading south towards the natural wonder, Dune de Pyla, which – at over 100 m – is Europe's highest sand dune. It's also slowly progressing eastward as the western side succumbs to marine erosion.

Sleeping

Camping There are a couple of seasonal campsites here, all on the D218 Route Biscarosse. **La Fôret**, T0556 227328, nestled between the forest and the imposing sand dune, open Apr-Nov, has statics and lovely wooden chalets. Continuing along the road, **Panorama**, T0556 221044, is on the edge of the dune, open May-Sep, also has statics. **Petit Nice**, a terraced site with easy beach access, T0556 227403, is open Apr-Sep.

Les Landes

Biscarrosse-Plage

Heading south, Biscarosse is the first town in Les Landes – a region of flat, sandy pine forest. With good atmosphere and amenities, it's an excellent base. Off season, the 'plage' half of the town pretty much closes. There are few locals and most visitors focus on the fabled beach breaks of Hossegor to the south.

Sleeping

Camping Aire de camping: year round, vans can park up at the Le Vivier Aire de Camping, R de Tit, Biscarosse-Plage (next to Campeole de Vivier) . It is free to camp except Jul-Aug – pay and display. Inland **Porte de Navarrosse Aire de Camping**, has a multi-service point and electric hook-up Jul-Aug. In terms of 'proper' sites, **Camping Maguide**, Chemin de Maguide, T0558-098190, is open year round and has statics. Another good, but seasonal, option is **Campeole Plage Sud**, R Becasses, T0558-782124, open May-Sep, chalets available and a short walk to the beach.

Eating and drinking

In season seafood restaurants and cafés line Av des Plages. For everything else – pizza, pasta, takeaway – there's **La Florentin**, open year round. It's wrong but…there is a **McDonald's** in Biscarosse-Bourg on Av Laouadie the town also has plenty of places to eat off-season.

Directory

Surf shops There are a couple including seasonal **Blue Hawaii**, Bvd d'Arcachon, off the main square open Apr-Sep, **Tamaris Surf Shop**, on rue des Tamaris and **So What Surfboards**, open July-Aug plus weekends and holidays. **Banks** Several ATMs in the semi-pedestrianised centre. **Internet** The seafront surf club may check the charts for you. **Tourist information** Pl de la Fontaine, www.biscarrosse.com.

LAURENT MASUREL

Days end.

LAURENT MASUREL

Marie-Pierre Abgrall.

DAMIEN POULLENOT

28 Gravière in perspective.

Mimizan

Mimizan is another seaside town of 2 halves, Bourg and Plage. There are several good camping options here including the swanky **Club Marina**, just back from the front at Plage Sud, T0558-091266, open May-mid Sep, cabins available. **Camping de la Plage**, Blvd de l'Atlantique, T0558- 090032, www.mimizan-camping.com, Apr-Sep, is slightly cheaper and also offers cabins.

Directory

Surf Shop **Karukera**, on the Ave Maurice Martin sells hardware as well as clothes as does seasonal **Silver Coast**, at Plage Sud. **Pharmacy** Av Maurice Martin.

Moliets-Plage

Heading south along the D652 you pass a handy Aire Natural (free-camping spot) on the way into this mellow seaside resort. **Camping Saint Martin**, Av de l'Océan, T0558-485230, www.camping-saint-martin.fr, is a good choice as has a pool, is open Apr-Oct and close to the beach. **Les Cigales**, T0558-485118, Apr-Sep is another option. **L'Open** is a popular seasonal surf bar. Off-season the town follows form and shuts down. **Café de l'Océan**, on the beachfront, is one of the only decent cafés that stays open off season – except for Tue. In terms of surf shops, best bet is to head south to Messanges and the excellent **Desert Point**, centro commercial.

Vieux Boucau

The pretty resort town of Vieux Boucau is a popular yet relaxed spot with an excellent beachfront campsite. The town centre has plenty of amenities, even off season, including **Locacycles** renting bikes on Grand' Rue and the **Wishbone surf shop** on Av des Pêcheurs – open half days and weekends from Nov depending on the weather. There is also a nice **skate park** in the town near the sports centre, opposite the *pelote* stadium, complete with rails, midi-ramps, quarter ramps, spined ramps and a fun box.

Sleeping

Camping **Camping Les Sableres**, Blvd de Marensin, open Apr-15 Oct, is just a short walk from the beach with statics from €185 per week for 4. There is also a handy *aire de camping* at Port d'Albret.

Hossegor

Seignosse-Hossegor-Capbreton

This chic, affluent, sprawling, modern collection of low-rise resort towns – with 2 golf courses, 1 lake, hundreds of bars and cafés plus a similar number of surf shops as well as the European headquarters for many of the world's international surf brands – has become synonymous with surfing in

Flat spells

Aventure Parc Get in training for your next session at this wooded, army assault course style, fun park in the trees at Biscarosse on the Route de la Plage, T0558-825340, entry from €20.

Bike hire Head into Arcachon and hire bikes at **Locabeach 33**, on the main Blvd de Plage, and explore the cycle routes around the basin. In Lacanau **Locacycles**, Av de l'Europe, have 'touring' bikes plus VTT (*vélo tout terrain*) or mountain bikes – check out the nearby lake by cover up well to avoid the mossies. In **Locavelo**, Av Paul Lahary, Hossegor, and Av M. Leclerc, Capbreton, hire out touring bikes and serious off-roaders.

Bordeaux The home of vin rouge, what better place to learn how to appreciate the plonk you've been necking? The **Maison du Vin**,1 Cours de 30 Julliet run a 2-hr course for about €20 for a. If this has whetted your appetite, they can also recommend a selection of nearby châteaux where you can sample more wine.

Dune Surfing Liberate a bodyboard, climb the huge dune at Pyla , and take the drop!

Golf Get a round in at **Golf d'Ardilouse International Golf** on the main road in from Lacanau town, T0556-039298. The par-68 course at **Golf de Biscarosse** on the Route des Lacs, T0558-098493 is cheaper during the week. Around Hossegor, check out the par-72 **Golf de Seignosse**, T0558-416830, or the par-71 **Golf Club d'Hossegor**, T0558-435699.

Go-Karting Drive inland to Chemin d'en Hill, Biscarosse-Bourg, for a go at some serious driving, at **Karting Biscarrosse**, T0558-788850. Near Hossegor, burn round the 855-m outdoor track at **Karting Gaillou**, on Blvd des Cigales, Capbreton, T0558-418009.

Oysters are to Arcachon what wine is to Bordeaux so head to the port of Gujan Mestras, home of Banc d'Arguin oysters, for a sampling session. A dozen freshly shucked oysters will set you back around €3.

Skating Near Pyla, there's a mini-ramp at La Teste on the N250. In Biscarosse-Bourg, there's a full-on skate park – complete with midi-ramp, rails and fun box – at the roundabout on Av Daudet, you can't miss it. **Hall 04**, Zone Artisanale, Soorts-Hossegor, T0558 419025, is home to an excellent pay-to-play wooden skate park with bowls, banks, rails, fun boxes etc. **Capbreton skatepark**, with a midi-ramp, fun box, rails and banks, overlooks the Port de Plaisance.

France. While Hossegor is the focal point, Seignosse and Capbreton take up the flanks to the north and south respectively.

Sleeping

There are hundreds of self catering apartments available to rent (often the best/cheapest bet for groups/extended stays) but they are best booked through the tourist office or an agent such as **Seignosse Immobilier**, T0558-433226.

Camping **Aire de Campings**: Just south of Seignosse Golf Club is an Aire du Stationnement, as well as one in Hossegor just off the Route des Lacs. The most popular one is by VVF which has been updated to include electricity and water hook-ups. Most cost around €6 in the summer months but are free off season.

Seignosse **Camping Oceliances**, Av Tucs between the golf club and Estagnots, T0558-433030, www.oceliances.com, open Apr-Sep, is close enough to the action and popular with surfers. Just back from Plage Cascernes at Le Penon, and within a short stroll of the nudist area, is the all-singing **Campeole Les Oyats**, T0558-433794, open mid May-mid Sep, with cabins - popular with families. There are several other seasonal sites but none close to the beach.

Hossegor € (except July-Aug **€€**) **Les Fougeres**, Ave de Gaujac – on the Casino road – is a 10 min walk to the beach and recommended, T0558 437800, www.hotel-lesfougeres.com. Open Mar-Nov, the hotel has a great vibe and is used to surfers staying, the rooms are en-suite, with balconies, some come with a fridge and a couple of hobs for cooking plus there is a pool on-site. **Camping du Lac**, Route des Lacs, T0558-435314, open Apr-Nov also has bungalows available and is the only site in Hossegor itself.

Capbreton Crossing the river into Capbreton, summer-opening **Labarthe**, R des Campeurs, T0558-720234, has chalets. **Municipal Bel Air**, Av du Bourret, T0558-721204 is open year round and well placed. There are several other sites in Capbreton but these are not too far from the action.

YANNICK LE TOQUIN

8 Rico et Sarah styling, Lacanau.

Eating and drinking

There are all the usual seaside eateries and watering holes here as well as a few firm favourites, mainly clustered close to the seafront at Hossegor.

Leading down from the main square **La Napoli**, rue des Landais, is highly recommended serving up vast pizzas, huge salads and good pasta (as well as seafood and steaks) at good prices – pizzas from around €9. It is thronging in the summer and during WCT week when a good number of the top 44 will certainly make an appearance or two. **Pinnochio**, just up the road is slightly cheaper but has less of a buzz about it.

Further up the road **Hossegor Sandwiches** is admittedly just a tiny café, but they don't serve up any old sarnies – the American (burger, fires and salad, encased in a baguette) can keep you going for a week at least.

For a spot of reasonably priced Vietnamese and Japanese with a good vibe, head to **Boul.eat caphe** on Ave Le Penon, opposite Estagnots or if you've been doing a spot of browsing at the Billabong factory shop inland at Soorts, stop off at the excellent **Nori Sushi** on Ave des Sabotiers – tasty, healthy, good portions and fair prices.

Cream Cafe Plage des Bourdaines is where the parties happen – planned or otherwise. They also serve great food until 2100.

Le Rock Food, Pl des Landais (main square), is a self-styled Hard Rock Café for the surf frat – surf memorabilia line the walls and you can watch the sun go down on your last session with a beer for comfort.

Opposite, **Dick's Sand Bar** has become a bit of an institution – the bronzed and beautiful flock here to party hard every night and with photo's lining the walls from the season's sessions it has that Aussiegor Gold Coast feel … they also have internet access through the day plus Wi-Fi.

BEN SELWAY

31 The vast flank of the bunker acts to marshall the sand into sweet banks.

Directory

Surf shops If you can't find one here, you're obviously not looking! Heading away from the beach and into Hossegor town, cross over the canal by the casino and surf shops stretch out as far as the eye can see on Av Paul Lahary and Av Touring Club de France, taking in all the big names as well as a couple of independents. North at Seignosse, there are a couple on the beachfront Ave de la Grande Plage including **Zao Boutik** and **L'Agreou** which both stock a good range of brands and hardware. **Internet** **Dick's Sand Bar**, Places de Landais or **Powder Monkey**, Av Touring Club in Hossegor town with Wifi also plus computer repairs. **Pharmacy** **Beau Pharmacie de la Plage**, place des Basques (by Place des Landais). **Post office** Av de Paris, Hossegor. **Tourist information** Av du Lac, Seignosse, www.tourisme-seignosse.com; Av de Paris, Hossegor, www.hossegor.fr; Av G Pompidou, Capbreton, www.capbreton-tourisme.com.

Overview

Young groms on scooters buzz like gnats around the car park at Chambre d'Amour, boards or sponges under arm, overstressed two stroke motor filling the air with blue grey fumes and a high pitched scream. Raised voices and excitement spark like electricity around the groups that line the beachfront promenade, just waiting for the tide to drop back from the angular, block strewn sea wall. The line-up will soon be filled with frenetic energy and overenthusiastic drop-ins. This is the young face of Anglet hanging outside the glass fronted surf boutiques. To the south, another group of surfers sit way, way out back. They float high out of the water on their guns. The equipment and style is very much old skool, but Guéthary is that kind of place. This isn't a

This is where everything started in France for surfing – when you are surfing "la Côte des Basques" and Biarritz you can imagine the pioneers surfing here.

Damien Poullenot, surf photographer

place for aerials or shortboard mayhem. This is a classic wave that demands a class-act. It's about size, it's about speed and it's about carving. Individually they scan the horizon as shifting peaks and walls of water angle in

Breaks

1 La Barre	7 Plage de la Côte des Basques	12 Cenitz
2 Les Cavaliers ★		13 Lafitenia ★
3 Anglet Beaches	8 Ilbarritz	14 Peyo's Left
4 Sables d'Or & Le Club	9 Bidart	15 Erromardie
5 VVF	10 Guéthary	16 Sainte Barbe
6 Grande Plage	11 Les Alcyons & Avalanche	17 Socoa
		18 Hendaye

N
2 km
2 miles

Atlantic Ocean

Bayonne
La Barre
Chiberta
Chambre d'Amour
Anglet
Biarritz
Bidart
Arcangues
Arbonne
Guéthary
Ahetze
St-Jean-de-Luz
Ciboure
Cabo Higuer
Corniche Basque
Hendaye Urrugne
SPAIN
Biriatou
River Nivelle
Ibarron
Ascain
St Pee-s-Nivelle

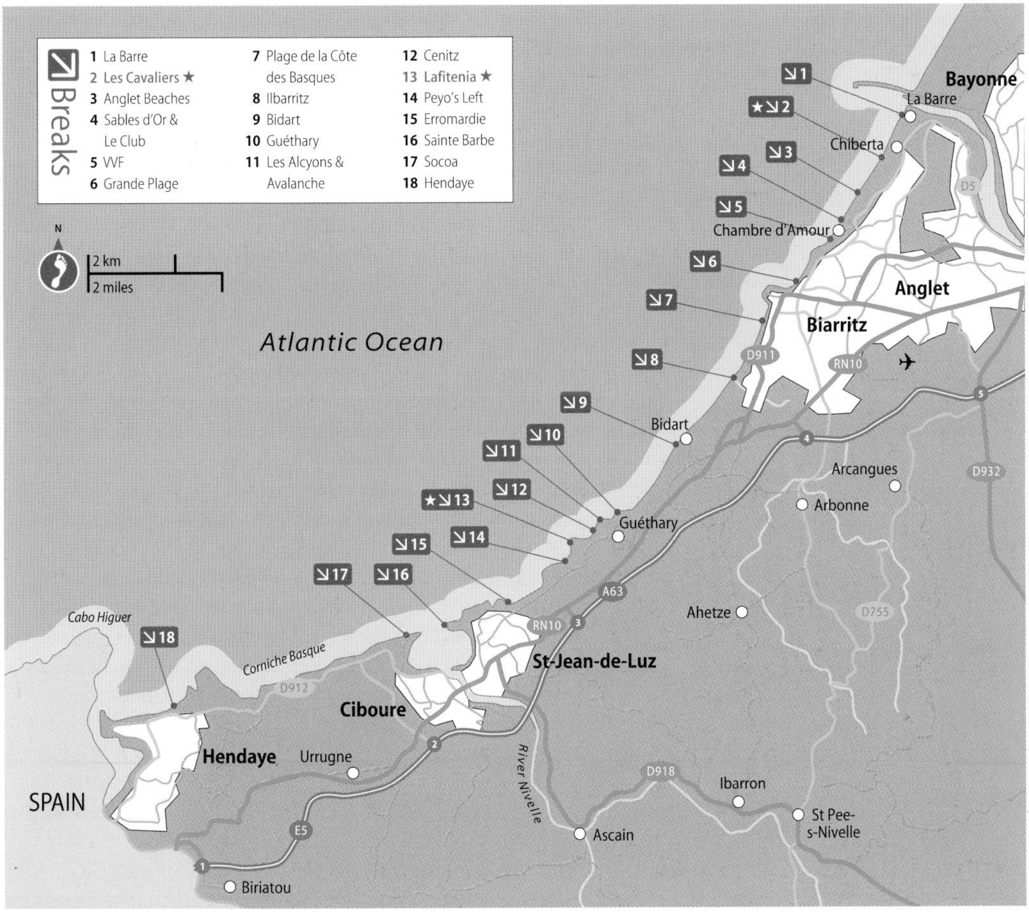

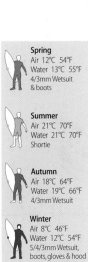

Spring
Air 12°C 54°F
Water 13°C 55°F
4/3mm Wetsuit
& boots

Summer
Air 21°C 70°F
Water 21°C 70°F
Shortie

Autumn
Air 18°C 64°F
Water 19°C 66°F
4/3mm Wetsuit

Winter
Air 8°C 46°F
Water 12°C 54°F
5/4/3mm Wetsuit,
boots, gloves & hood

6′1″ T.Patterson A-Team model
Shaper: Timmy Patterson
6′1″ x 18⅜″ x 2⅛″
Surftech's lively, responsive TL2 composite technology.
This board features a single to slight double concave and a nice hard edge coming off the tail to give you the speed and drive you need to go big. Designed for mid-sized punchy beachbreaks.
FCS GYU fins.

Boards by **Surftech**
www.surftech.com info@surftech.com

6′6″ Lynch Round Pin
Shaper: Wayne Lynch
6′6″ x 19½″ x 2 9/16″
Built with Surftech's proven TUFLITE construction.
A little extra overall volume and softer plan shape curves, creates great paddling qualities plus the ability to run across flat sections and maintian speed. Works well when Lafitenia starts to get overhead.
FCS fins.

DAMIEN POULLENOT

Classic Anglet beachbreak session.

towards the reef, trying to catch them off guard. They paddle as one, heading into position. The north/south divide – the old and the new. This is the Yin and Yang of Basque surfing.

A surfing hypermarché, all waveriding needs are catered for by the region's geography. It doles out 'fun' shories for aerialists and near death sand-gratings for the unsuspecting, stacks the shelves with thundering beach break barrels and reeling points and keeps the massive outside reefs for XXL tow-ins locked away in a cabinet for specialists only. For the traveling surfer it offers a hyper-reality of opportunity and reward – both in and out of the water. The surfing can be insane, intense, matched only by the rich culture and heritage of these Basque lands. Sit outside the cafes and drink in a little of the atmosphere, kick back on Dora's bench and feast on the panorama, the story. With an undulating coastline of bays, beaches and reefs, through to green rolling hillside pastures leading up to the jagged, snow capped peaks of the Pyrénées, this is a complete land. This is a truly 'special offer'.

LAURENT MASUREL

4 Walking the board, by golden sands.

Coastline

The Côte Basque is wave-rich and varied with excellent beaches and fine reefs. The rivermouth at La Barre was the site of one of the original great European waves, until a stone groyne was built through its heart. To the south stretches nearly 5 km of golden sand reaching all the way to VVF in Anglet, compartmentalized into separate beaches by a series rocky groynes. Below the chic resort of Biarritz, the rocky coastline comes alive when a good swell hits. The beaches of Bidart can be a great place to lose the crowds. The reefs of Guéthary stretch far out to sea and can work in 20-ft swells – the two rock fingers with deep water channel permits access on the biggest days. To the south of St-Jean-de-Luz there are offshore reefs that only wake during monster swells. It was here at Belharra, that a group of French surfers shocked the wave-riding world and the judges of the Billabong XXL surf contest, forcing them to look afresh at the reality of Europe's big wave potential.

Local Environment

There are few places on the Côte Basque with out and out localism. "Compared to what I've seen in Hawaii, the French are pretty friendly and cool," says Peyo Lizarazu. "Especially if guys are really respectful and say 'Hi' when they paddle out. Obviously don't expect to take all the waves, even if you are a better surfer."

Town breaks like Grande Plage and Plage Côte Basques can get extremely busy but the atmosphere is generally good. Certain breaks are dominated by local surfers such as Lafitenia (once a localized spot but now just plain crowded), or less well known breaks that the locals would like to keep that way. If you surf respectfully, you should have no problems.

Getting around

Very painless, even in the summer. The main coastal N10 is excellent and stays just inland from the sea down to St-Jean-de-Luz, before carrying on to the Spanish border. The only real bottlenecks are probably getting through Biarritz at rush hour and around St-Jean-de-Luz on a Sunday evening when everyone is heading home.

Breaks

LEFT GROYNE BREAK

↘1 La Barre

- **Conditions** Big NW to W swells, offshore in E to SE winds
- **Hazards/tips** Pollution
- **Sleeping** La Barre/Anglet ▸▸ *p195*

La Barre is famous as one of European surfing's first great casualties. It starred in several 1970s surf films, ridden by the likes of Nat Young and Wayne Lynch, and was one of the first European waves to feature in *Surfer* magazine. Today two block breakwaters have somewhat ruined the wave. There is still a good left-hander that breaks in big swells from low to three-quarter tides next to the mouth of the river Adour. The water quality is pretty poor.

BEACH BREAK

↘2 Les Cavaliers

- **Swell** NW
- **Wind** E
- **Tide** All tides, better low to three-quarters.
- **Size** 3-10 ft
- **Length** 50 m plus
- **Bottom** Sandbar
- **Ability level** Intermediate +
- **Best months** Sep-Dec
- **Board** Performance Thruster
- **Access** Channel from the beach
- **Hazards/tips** Rips, heavy wave, crowds
- **Sleeping** La Barre/Anglet ▸▸ *p195*

Cavaliers is a legendary spot. It is contest venue, alpha A-frame and a location that draws traveling vans to congregate in the car park in corrals of many nationalities. As the morning winds waft through the car park at first light, the short walk onto the promenade promises so much and often delivers more. Sunny autumn days are prime time for this classic beach break, with all day A-frames breaking through the tides and helping to ease the lunchtime crowds. This stretch of coastline lost La Barre as its reigning monarch, but gained this new king of the Anglet beach breaks.

At times this peak can be a heaving cauldron of surfers and bodyboarders, at other times there may be just a few out. But on any day it can be one of the best waves in the country forming hollow, fast lefts and rights. The bank works through all tides, but is best from low to three-quarter tide. This break was a regular site for WCT and is still a WQS contest venue due to the quality of the wave and its consistency. In small swells it provides fun walls, but breaks right up to thundering conditions when huge, hollow, cavernous waves can pound the beach. Definitely a spot for your 'To Do' list.

ⓘ ***If you like** Cavaliers, try **Supertubos** in Portugal (see page 296) or **Fistral** in England (see page 79).*

LAURENT MASUREL

DEMI TAYLOR

Above: 2 Les Cavaliers. **Top: 1** La Barre – one of the first waves in France to enjoy international acclaim.

BEACH BREAK

↘3 Anglet Beaches

- **Conditions** Small to medium NW to W swells, offshore in E winds
- **Hazards/tips** Rips, crowds
- **Sleeping** Anglet ▸▸ *p195*

This is a long stretch of sand that runs south from Cavaliers, broken by huge rock groynes into individual beaches, each with pretty similar characteristics. Sandbanks build up alongside the breakwaters forming good lefts and rights on low to three quarter tides. In big swells the paddle out is a mission and in the summer the breaks become very busy. Plage des Dunes and Plage de l'Océan are the best bets for less busy summer waves. Good beach facilities including showers.

BEACH BREAK

↘4 Sables d'Or and Le Club

- **Conditions** Small to medium NW to W swells, offshore in E winds
- **Hazards/tips** Crowds
- **Sleeping** Anglet ›› p195

Two good quality beachies again separated by block groynes in front of the bars and surf shops of Sables d'Or. These breaks are busy year round due to the beachfront parking and easy access. **Le Club** (in front of the surf clubhouse) is popular with young local surfers but disappears at high when the tide reaches the concrete sea defences. Try heading north to Marinella, Corsaires or Madrague or south to VVF.

BEACH BREAK

↘5 VVF

- **Conditions** Medium to big NW to W swells, offshore in E winds
- **Hazards/tips** Crowds
- **Sleeping** Anglet ›› p195

VVF is the most southerly of the Anglet beaches and sits in the lee of the cliffs and watched over by a 1970s-style hotel. Works well at high tide in big swells, 6-10 ft, when all the other beaches are maxed out. There is a large car park right in front of the break which means it's always crowded, especially in the summer.

BEACH BREAK

↘6 Grande Plage

- **Conditions** Medium NW to W swells, offshore in E to SE winds.
- **Hazards/tips** Crowds.
- **Sleeping** Biarritz ›› p196

A glitzy surf location in downtown central Biarritz, the promenade and golden sands are overlooked by the casino and grandiose Hôtel du Palais. In a medium, clean swell, the beach can produce excellent hollow waves. Outcrops of rocks and swirling currents help to sculpt some consistent banks which are fought over by the large local crew. Works on all tides with the southern casino end, being the busiest. This is home to one of the oldest surf clubs in France and the annual Reef Trophy contest.

DAMIEN POULLENOT

LAURENT MASUREL

Above: 3 La Madrague – sundowner session. **Top: 3** Tim Boal, Marinella – here the banks are groomed into neat drills by a series of man-made rocky groynes separating each of the bays.

BEACH BREAK

↘7 Plage de la Côte des Basques

- **Conditions** Small to medium NW to W swells, offshore in E to SE winds
- **Hazards/tips** Popular with longboarders
- **Sleeping** Biarritz ›› *p196*

The northern end of this beach has been a long time, longboard haven. The waves here are less powerful and heavy than on the rest of the beaches in the area, hence perfect for those taking their first steps along a Mal. As a result the vibe in the water is friendly, even though it does get crowded in the summer. Best from low to mid tide – at high the beach disappears. Parking on the Boulevard du Prince de Galles. Moving south away from the promenade, the beach picks up more swell and clusters of rocks appear, but crowds thin.

BEACH BREAK

↘8 Ilbarritz

- **Conditions** Small to medium NW to W swells, offshore in E to SE winds
- **Hazards/tips** Rocky
- **Sleeping** Biarritz ›› *p196*

A series of beaches heading south from Plage Marbella with sandbars and rocky reefs. Great place to explore and get away from the heaving crowds in the summer. There are no hidden classic waves here but there are a few OK rides if you check them through the tides; visible from the clifftop at Ave Notre Dame.

BEACH BREAK

↘9 Bidart

- **Conditions** Small to medium NW to W swells, offshore in SE winds.
- **Hazards/tips** Quieter beach, closes out easily.
- **Sleeping** Bidart ›› *p197*

The beaches around Bidart traditionally pick up less swell, but this is a good thing as they tend to close out easily. Can be excellent on their day, or frustratingly fickle. Definitely worth checking in a small or medium clean swell. Also home to a fantastic beach front restaurant.

LAURENT MASUREL

11 Riding out the avalanche.

REEF BREAK

↘10 Guéthary

- **Conditions** Medium and big NW to W swells. Offshore in SE winds.
- **Hazards/tips** For experienced surfers only
- **Sleeping** Guéthary ›› *p197*

The picturesque Basque village of Guéthary is home to the legendary big-wave spot Parlementia. The steep hills overlook the huge peak and provide an excellent vantage point to take in the action – there is even a bench dedicated to one time resident Mickey Dora. The reef sits 400 m offshore where swell comes out of deep water to form huge, shifting peaks. This is Europe's very own Sunset, where peaks roam around a take-off area the size of a football pitch, rogue sets swinging in wide to catch the pack off guard. This is not really a wave for shortboarders. Old skool boards and old skool style rules here. The experienced locals jostle around, paddling their big boards into the elevator drops. The wave then fattens out into a long right-hander, that can sometimes connect through to the inside section where it walls up again. It is a pretty straightforward paddle out in the channel, but be warned, the wave looks easier and smaller than it is. The lefts can sometimes be good too.

> “”
>
> Guéthary, on a good, big day when the surf is a solid 10-12 ft, with offshore winds and swell breaking on both sides of the bay, lefts and rights, the set-up is so classic.
>
> *Nick Lavery*

LEFT REEF BREAK

↘11 Les Alcyons and Avalanche

- **Conditions** Medium to big NW swells, offshore in SE winds
- **Hazards/tips** Big wave, heavy, crowded.
- **Sleeping** Guéthary ›› *p197*

On the left-hand side of the harbour is a serious, heavy, hollow reef break. It has a jacking take-off followed by a barrelling left that reels along the shallow reef toward the channel. Can break up to 12 ft when it is an awesome sight. Best left to the experts – looks hard and is. On the outside edge of the bay sits a true big-wave spot, Avalanche, a left reef that works in the biggest swells. It's a long paddle and a heavy wave for big-wave chargers only. Used to be surfed by a few hardy locals, but with the upturn in big wave surfing, is becoming more popular. Big rips and long hold downs.

THE GILL

13 Lafitenia.

REEF AND BEACH BREAK

↘12 Cenitz

- **Conditions** Small to medium NW to W swells, offshore in E to SE winds
- **Hazards/tips** Popular with locals
- **Sleeping** Guéthary ▸▸ *p197*

On the southern fringes of Guethary, Cenitz is a popular break with the locals. It has a left point at the south of the bay that works best at mid tide. It is a walling wave that peels into a deep channel opposite a right-hander that breaks from low to mid tide. To the north of this is another right that breaks way out the back. It is a long paddle from the rocky beach and there are rips to negotiate. This is a break where locals come to get away from the excesses of Lafitenia and Anglet. If you surf respectfully and share the waves you will be OK; if you come to hassle and drop in you will not be tolerated.

RIGHT-HAND POINT BREAK

↘13 Lafitenia

- **Swell** NW to W
- **Wind** S to SE
- **Tide** Low to three-quarter
- **Size** 3-10 ft
- **Length** 50-200 m plus
- **Bottom** Reef and sand
- **Ability** Intermediate to advanced
- **Best months** Oct-May
- **Board** Slightly longer Thruster
- **Access** Paddle off the beach
- **Hazards/tips** Heavy when big, crowded in the summer
- **Sleeping** Guéthary/Lafitenia ▸▸ *p197*

After the endless drifting and shifting sand of Les Landes, this classic right hand point comes as a refreshing and reinvigorating change. The do or die barrels of Hossegor are left behind for the long winding walls of Lafitenia, wrapped in the horse shoe shaped bay and hemmed in by steep wooded banks. This spot was for years a haven away from the chaos and the locals tried to keep the crowds down. But it's hard to keep a wave of such quality secret and today it has become renowned across the globe. It was the venue for the Quiksilver World Masters contest from 1999 to 2000. When a good swell hits the Basque coast, the car park above the bay throngs, surfers line the view point, necks craning to check out the set waves before rushing to their open boots to pull on their wetsuits.

The crowds add to the challenge this wave poses. In big swells it has a shifting, heavy take-off out over the rocky reef on the point. The pack often jostles, pushing too deep and allowing the wily to sit inside and pick off some of the best set waves. From the steep drop the wave walls into a fast middle section, perfect for big carves, leading to the inside which, on a low tide, can get pretty fast and hollow. It is a classic point set-up with a dry hair paddle out from the beach. It is one of Patrick Beven's favourite waves: "It's such a special place and you can work your line and do big manoeuvres." Ex-world champion Barton Lynch loves the wave: "It's a real surfers' wave. Great walls, just great fun."

__If you like Lafitenia__, try __Devil's Rock__ in Morocco (see page 388) or __Skaill Bay__ in Orkney (see page 52).

BIG LEFT REEF BREAK

↘14 Peyo's Left

- **Conditions** Big to huge NW to W swells, offshore in E winds
- **Hazards/tips** Experts only
- **Sleeping** Guéthary/Lafitenia ▸▸ *p197*

Out on the southern fringes of Lafitenia bay sits an enormous left-hander that breaks out on the outside reef, providing an intense drop and a huge, walling ride into the outer edges of the bay. Only occasionally surfed until the recent big wave upsurge. Named after French big wave rider Peyo Lizarazu. Also a tow-in spot.

BEACH BREAK

↘15 Erromardie

- **Conditions** Small to medium NW to W swells, offshore in SE winds
- **Hazards/tips** Quiet beach
- **Sleeping** St-Jean-de-Luz ▸▸ *p197*

Just to the north of St-Jean-de-Luz sits this beach break, overlooked by campsites. It is a fairly average break, which can have decent rights at the north end of the beach.

RIGHT BREAKWATER BREAK

↘16 Sainte Barbe

Conditions Big NW swells, offshore in SE winds.
Hazards/tips Peaks at end of breakwater
Sleeping St-Jean-de-Luz » p197

When big swells pound the coast, a crazy right- hander peels from outside the jetty at Sainte Barbe, past the end and wraps its way through into the sheltered bay. Slightly insane take-off. In these conditions, it can get crowded.

SAND-COVERED REEF BREAK

↘17 Socoa

Conditions Big N and NW swells, offshore in S winds
Hazards/tips Crowds
Sleeping St-Jean-de-Luz » p197

Big northerly or northwesterly swells thread their way through the harbour entrance and find a few banks to break on inside the bay. If everywhere is maxed out, check it out, but don't expect too much.

BEACH BREAK

↘18 Hendaye

Conditions Medium to big NW swells, offshore in S winds
Hazards/tips Long, flat safe beach
Sleeping St-Jean-de-Luz » p197

"I learnt to surf at Hendaye," says top Basque surfer Peyo Lizarazu. "It is basically the flattest beach on all the coast, with the weakest waves." This is a good beach for beginners and a good place to check out in big swells. There can be OK waves here with a few peaks.

Practicalities

La Barre

The once-famous sandbank at La Barre was ruined long ago by a huge breakwater. However on the south bank of L'Adour, La Barre has an Aire de Camping (around €5 a night) that is basically just part of the **ice hockey** car park. Useful overnight spot with good access to Cavaliers, plus there's a **McDonald's** handy for breakfast.

Anglet

The beaches north of Biarritz are part of Anglet home to some excellent breaks and places to stay. Much of the action is centred around Chambre d'Amour where there are surf shops, bars and restaurants overlooking the sea. Inland there are several huge hypermarches including a Leclerc at the Centre Commercial, Blvd de Bab towards Bayonne.

Sleeping

€€ Hôtel Residence Mer & Golf, Blvd de la Mer, just back from Plage de VVF, T0559-527000. Apartments for 2-6 people, all with balconies overlooking either the sea or the golf course. Reasonable outside the summer holidays.
€ Arguia, Av des Cretes, T0559-638382, open 15 Apr to 15 Oct, is reasonably priced and a 10-min walk to the beach. Rooms are light, airy and excellent value. Group rooms and breakfast also available.
€ Villa Clara, Blvd des Plage, T0559-520152, is an excellent choice – chilled hotel with views over the dunes to the sea. Used to surfers – the floors are tiled floors. Open year round, they also have studios to rent, with basic kitchen facilities sleeping 2 or 4 with one apartment sleeping up to 6 (just).
Camping Although usually fairly relaxed about a bit of subtle freecamping you are not allowed to park up overnight by the beach Jul-Aug. You will get moved on. **Camping Fontaine Laborde**, Allée Fontaine Laborde, just north of Chambre d'Amour, T0559-034816, is open Easter–Sep and has a party spirit. **Camping de Parme**, out by the airport on R de l'Aviation, T0559-230300, open Mar-Nov, is relatively pricey and with fairly basic facilities has little going for it.

Eating and drinking

There is a good selection of bars/cafés/restaurants around Sables d'Or and the beachfront.
Mama Nature, is a lively spot that serves large portions of great food at reasonable prices – most pasta dishes are around €10 – a popular spot with local surfers. **Chilli's**, on the same strip does good Mexican food. **Croq des Sables** does the showcase post-surf takeaway feast. The Americana is awesome – a baguette filled with burgers, fries and salad. Excellent value lunch.

Directory

Surf shops There are several centred around Chambre d'Amour including **Rusty, Billabong, Rainbow** and **Waimea Surf Shop**. All stock hardware, accessories and clothing. **JP Stark**, Allée Louis de Foix, T0559-639478, www.starksurf.com, are well established – Jean-Pierre has been shaping boards for more than 25 years – and also do good board repairs. **Internet** From around €4.50 per hr, access available as a bowling alley side order at **Cyber Bowling**, Anglet just off the N10. **Banks** are ATMs on Av de l'Adour, Le Barre and Chambre d'Amour. **Post office** in Anglet centre on R du 8 Mai, about 10 mins' drive from the beaches. **Tourist information** Av de Chambre d'Amour, www.anglet-tourisme.com.

ALEX LAUREL

3 Cavaliers, Anglet.

Flat spells

Adventure Park In the Foret de Chiberta, Ave de l'Adour, **Evolution 2** is an awesome treetop adventure park complete with traverses, rope ladders and zip lines. Prove you're not chicken from €25, Apr-Nov, T0559 420306.

Aquarium **Musée de la Mer**, on the seafront on Esplanade du Rocher de la Vierge, is open year round and comes complete with de riguer sharks and seals €7.50.

Golf Get a round in at the 18-hole, par-70 **Golf de Chiberta**, Anglet, Blvd des Plages, T0559-525110. There's also a 'mini golf' course nearby at Pl de Docteurs Gentilhe in Chambre d'Amour.

Party Do not miss **Casetas**, a 5-day festival that takes place in the summer and again in the winter. All the local bars set up under one huge marquee and a massive party takes place into the early hours.

Skating In Biarritz, head to R 8 Mai by the Lycée College for some mini-ramp and fun box action at this small skate park.

Snowboarding Running the length of the France/Spain border, the Pyrenees, although lacking the consistency of the Alps, has some great snowboarding on offer – but you've got to be on it to make the most of it as fresh powder doesn't hang around. The mellow resort of **La Mongie**, accessed via the A64 from Bayonne, is home to one of the largest snowfields in the Pyrenees and great for a spot of affordable freeriding. A pass should be arpund €30 and a board for the day around €18. Check the tourist board for accommodation and snow reports, T0562-955071, www.bagneresdebigorre-lamongie.com.

Biarritz

The faded grandeur of this beautiful old resort – a previous playground of the glitterati – has been given a new shine and reinvented as a chic surf city, after all this is where Deborah Kerr's husband, the screen writer Peter Viertel, surfed the first French waves in the 50's sparking off a Gallic surf fever. The impressive Hôtel du Palais – formerly the summer residence of Napolean III and Empress Eugenia – overlooks the truly Grande Plage.

Sleeping

In Jul-Aug, prices sky rocket but there are still a couple of bargains to be found.

€ Hôtel Argi Eder, R Peyroloubilh, T0559-242253, www.hotel-argieder.fr, is near the top of Côte de Basque. They have rooms for up to 4 people plus Wi-Fi access and probably some of the most reasonably priced peak rate rooms.

€ Hôtel Palym, R du Port Vieux, T0559-242583, is a warren of a hotel above a pizzeria and recommended as a budget option. There are an amazing number of rooms of varying size and layout, all eclectically decorated. Some rooms are en suite. Parking available by the harbour, free off season.

Camping **Biarritz Camping**, off Av de Milady on the R d'Harcet (near Ilbiarritz), T0559-230012, open May-Sep. **Aire de Camping Cars**, just off the Av de Milady opposite the turning for Plage de Marbella, is free for motorhomes off season and even has limited electric hook-up points and water and toilet emptying facitlities.

Eating and drinking

La Pizzeria, opposite the Casino on Av Edouard V11, is the showcase place to eat in Biarritz. That's why there is always a queue, but it's worth the wait. Fantastic pizzas, amazing tarts and very reasonable – about €38 for 2 plus a *pichet* or jug of wine. **Taco'Mex**, R Lavernis, is a great little Tex-Mex restaurant with a small menu of excellent food including help yourself fajitas. Head down to the Port des Pecheurs – the fishing port – where there are a couple of great seafood restaurants including **Chez Albert**, an excellent eatery with prices to match. If you're hankering after some tapas, get down to **Bar Jean**, rue des Halles, which has a real buzz about it so gets packed out quickly. **Le Surfing**, overlooking Cote Basques is the ubiquitous surf bar with old boards and memorabilia adorning ceilings and walls. For a complete change, dust down your boardies and head to the beautiful café at the **Hôtel du Palais** to soak up the ambience and grab a coffee. **Ventilo Caffe**, rue Mazagran, is a great spot to enjoy a couple of cocktails and DJ sets plus there are a couple of other bars on the same strip to move on to.

Directory

Surf shops There are more than 10 here – most of which are a little boutiquey given

LAURENT MASUREL

5 VVF – the most southerly of the Anglet beachbreaks.

LAURENT MASUREL

15 Erromardie.

DAMIEN POULLENET

10 Parlementia watched over by Dora's bench.

the locale – including **Rip Curl**, on Av Reine Victoria, **Billabong**, Place Bellevue and the **Roxy** store, R Mazagran. **Wilbur**, R Gambetta, carries retro boards and small US import labels. **Internet** **Newquay Bar**, place Clemenceau, the tourist office also have internet access. **Chemist** **Pharmacie de L'Ocean**, R Gamebetta. **Post office** R de la Poste. **Tourist information** Square d'Ixelles, behind the Hôtel de Ville and police station, www.biarritz.fr, **Aéroport** **International de Biarritz-Anglet- Bayonne** is a 10-min drive into town, T0559-438383.

Bidart

This pretty, traditional Basque village and wonderful beach, have quick access to Biarritz and is a good stopover.

€ Motel Mil, R Chiripa, T0559-547171, is open year round with clean, comfortable, well priced rooms plus chalet-style apartments.

There are plenty of campsites around Bidart. **Camping Berrua**, 1 km from the beach, R d'Arbonne, T0559-549666, is open Apr-Oct. **Camping Pavillion Royal**, Av Prince de Galles, T0559-230054, is a well kept family site next to the sea open mid May-Sep.

For wonderful seafood, on the beach, head to **La Tantina** Plage du Centre, T0559-265356. Plats of grilled fish are around €12-15 – the *gambas* are amazing – it is very popular so it's worth booking ahead.

Guéthary

A village at the heart of the Côte Basque and at the heart of surf community, Guéthary is about tradition. The streets are lined with beautiful houses painted in classic Basque colours of deep red and white, the steep seafront overlooking one of the world's most famous breaks has been capped off with a bench dedicated to the memory of the one-time resident and surf deviant/deity Mickey Dora. The terraces on the town square catch the sun's rays making this an awesome spot to chill and enjoy a biere. In the evening head down to **le trinquet**, the pelota venue and if you've brought your skate, there's a mini **concrete bowl** nearby on Cemin de Tranchet.

Sleeping

€ Le Madrid, T0559-265212, is right on the square, with an old skool feel to the beamed rooms, at reasonable rates with breakfast included. Restaurant and bar with terrace. The only downside is the proximity to the railway line.

Eating and drinking

Bar Basque, on the square, is a great place for a drink or a bite to eat. Sit outside on the terrace and watch the world go by – it also has Wifi access. The eclectic **Hetero Clito** is not to be missed, the opening hours and service is random but the food is good and the atmosphere is electric. Menu around €25 – try to nab one of the outside tables for sunset. **Les Alcyons** Chemin du Port is a real treat open May-Sep specializing in grilled meat, fish and awesome sea views – around €30 (their lunch special is a lot cheaper). On the beachfront at nearby Cenitz the terrace at the wooden **Ostatua** affords incredible views and is a great place to enjoy 'a la plancha' grilled meat or fish. Open Apr-Sep it is popular so booking can be a good idea T0559-265916. Lunch from €10, dinner is more pricey.

Directory

Surf shop **2nd Sky**, Chemin du Port. **Tourist information** Excellent centre next to the railway station, www.guethary-france.com.

Lafitenia

Home of the amazing right-hand point break, but little in the way of accommodation. However, **Camping Playa**, T0559-265585, www.camping-playa.com, open Apr-Oct/Nov (depending on demand), must have one of the most amazing views in the surfing world as this terraced site overlooks the break. Feel your tent shake when the surf's big.

St-Jean-de-Luz

St Jean de Luz is a pretty, grand fishing town, so has quite a 'towny' vibe about it but can be a handy stopover. Basque privateers (pirates) sailed from this port, attacking British merchant ships, and many of the fine houses were paid for this way.

€ Hôtel Bolivar, R Sopite, T0559-260200, is close to the beach, a little spartan but is clean and comfortable.

In terms of camping **International d'Erromardie**, just north of the town and on the beach T0559-263426, open Apr-Sep, is the best bet.

Spain

Kepa Acero cutting a swathe through green Spain.

LAURENT MASUREL

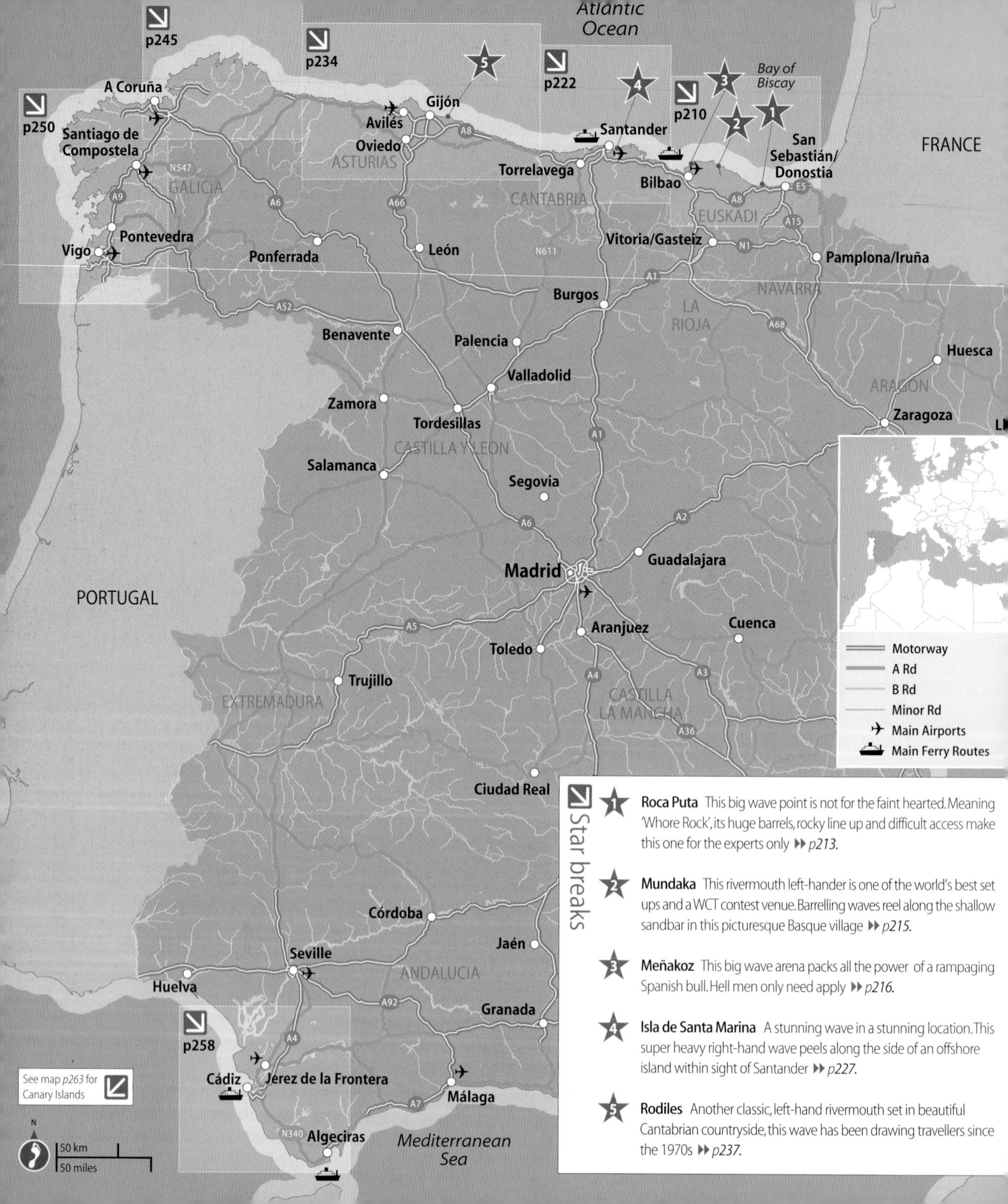

Star breaks

1 Roca Puta This big wave point is not for the faint hearted. Meaning 'Whore Rock', its huge barrels, rocky line up and difficult access make this one for the experts only ▸▸ *p213*.

2 Mundaka This rivermouth left-hander is one of the world's best set ups and a WCT contest venue. Barrelling waves reel along the shallow sandbar in this picturesque Basque village ▸▸ *p215*.

3 Meñakoz This big wave arena packs all the power of a rampaging Spanish bull. Hell men only need apply ▸▸ *p216*.

4 Isla de Santa Marina A stunning wave in a stunning location. This super heavy right-hand wave peels along the side of an offshore island within sight of Santander ▸▸ *p227*.

5 Rodiles Another classic, left-hand rivermouth set in beautiful Cantabrian countryside, this wave has been drawing travellers since the 1970s ▸▸ *p237*.

JAKUE ANDIKOTXEA

Galician gold.

For many tourists a trip to Spain is all about the Costa del Sol. For the initiated, however, it's all about the Costa del Surf – the rain-soaked, weather-ravaged Costa Verde or 'Green Coast'. It seems fitting that, as wave riders, we cannot resist the subconscious pull of the north shore. Here, Spain is bombarded by the turbulent Bay of Biscay, with its ever-changing weather patterns so loved by us, so loathed by sun worshippers. The coastline mirrors the climate – lush and verdant, undulating and never constant – always offering somewhere to enjoy the consistent swells that break here.

France and Spain are such different neighbours, and as soon as you cross the border the impact is immediate. Conservative France likes to keep itself to itself, looking chic and well coiffured, whilst noisy neighbour Spain stays up all night, machine-gun voices raised in impassioned debate, fuelled by a high-octane combination of tapas, espresso and Rioja. They eat late, they sleep late, and they even came to the surf party late: but they've more than made up for it, making friends quickly and bringing a unique brand of exuberance and determination. They have produced some of the continent's best waveriders, brought up on a high-carb diet of reeling rivermouths, rocky reefs and terrifying big wave spots. There is a passion attached to everything they do here – from driving down the line at Mundaka to running with the bulls at Pamplona. Spain is an epic experience. Don't worry about the calories – just tuck in.

Surfing Spain

For many years, the idea of travelling to Spain to surf really meant surfing in the Basque region – or more specifically, a trip to Mundaka. The majority of the northern coastline remained off the beaten track, literally. Even those wandering explorers road tripping down through northern Europe to the warmth of Morocco usually 'cut the corner' off their journey by taking their vans on the inland stretch from Mundaka down to Ericeira. Today however, the vast potential of this consistent, flexible, undulating coastline with its waves of every conceivable persuasion and awesome scenery punctuated by classic Spanish towns, is most definitely on the itinerary. You just can't keep a secret that's this big. Aided by new destinations from low cost airlines and the crowd pressures of so many other regions, surfers have pushed out to explore new areas, places outside the usual comfort zones and with names that aren't part of the common surf vernacular. This change of focus has only been enhanced by the sheer quality of surfing coming out of Northern Spain, where riders like the Acero brothers and Michel Velasco rank as some of the most talented in Europe and where a committed crew of big wave hellmen charge monstrous points along the Green Coast. And there's Mundaka, still pulling them in despite her short vacation. Add to the mix Spain's propensity for fiestas plus love of late nights and general partying and it's easy to see why so many travelling surfers are making a pilgrimage to the pristine beaches, classic rivermouths and reeling point breaks of Northern Spain. With so much on offer, so much of this big country to explore, perhaps the best way is the Spanish way, sample a little taste at each spot before moving on to the next.

Climate

Northern Spain exhibits a classic temperate maritime climate, characterised by relatively mild winters, warm summers and a high level of rainfall throughout the year. You'll hear this said time and time again but they don't call this region 'Green Spain' for nothing – it can have an annual rainfall higher than northern Scotland. Moist winds roll in off the Bay of Biscay, hitting the mountains that fringe the ocean. This causes the air mass to rise to a higher altitude where it cools. The colder air holds less moisture and releases the excess as rainfall. The benefits of this are that the rainfall has helped to carve a varied and jagged coastline punctuated by many rivermouth breaks. The mountains are being slowly eroded and some of the debris carried by the water ends up deposited as rivermouth sandbanks at breaks like Mundaka or Rodiles. It also keeps away those surfers who need a guaranteed helping of sun with their waves. But if it's pure wave quality you are after, the odd cloudy or drizzly day is a price well worth paying.

Andalucía on the other hand, is the exact opposite. Hot summers of small surf and mild winters make this a popular stop on the classic trail to Morocco.

Best seasons to go

If swell was the only criteria for a trip, the question would not when is the best season to go, but where is the best spot. In the summer this area is one of Europe's most consistent swell catchers and if there is going to be surf anywhere in Europe, stretches of northern Spain will be getting it. As a general rule, the breaks that face northwest pick up the most swell. Spots around Sopelana in the Basque region, Liencres and Suances in Cantabria, and Asturias west of Gijón are some of the most consistent summer breaks while the coastline north of Ferrol in Galicia picks up every ocean ripple. Combined with ocean temperatures of between 18 and 20°C and air temperatures in the 20s, you can see why this region is a real surfing hotspot. The stunning scenery, beautiful beaches and towering mountains provide a stark contrast to the over-developed costas of the Mediterranean and prove a big draw to holidaying Spaniards. Consequently, prices hike-up, road networks become congested and become breaks around resort towns become very busy. Noja, Reinante, Zarautz and Laredo are typical. But this is not to say that there isn't the odd uncrowded beach to enjoy. If you don't mind the odd rainy day, this is great time to be here: long, warm days filled with surfing and nights filled with fiestas and tapas. Most travelling surfers head for Spain for the autumn swell season. In late September and early October daytime temperatures can still be in the high teens or low 20s and the water is a mild 17-18°C. Swells start to kick in as spiralling lows track across the North Atlantic. While well-known breaks like Mundaka, Rodiles and Pantín prove to be the biggest draws, there are countless other reeling spots going unridden. This is the time of year that the ASP WCT and WQS world tours choose to role into Mundaka, Tapia and Pantín for their professional surfing contests.

The winter and spring seasons are predominantly left to the locals and just a handful of hardy travellers. But while the coastline can be battered by storms for days on end, the undulating geography means that there are always spots working in even the most severe weather. This is also the time when the big wave spots such as Punta Galea and Santa Marina really kick into action. In between the storms, cool, crystal clear swells can break under crisp, sunny, winter skies while the snow-topped Picos de Europa look on impassively. Water temperatures drop to around 13°C – time to break out the 4/3's but if you want empty line-ups, this is the time to go. For Andalucía, the transition from Autumn to Winter is the most popular time with the swells picking up and fine weather still dominant. The water remains warm at around 15-18°C.

JAKUE ANDIKOTXEA

El Quemao, Islas Canarias.

Boards

A good two board selection for Spain would have a performance Thruster as its mainstay. Something flexible for small days through to overhead. A good rounded squash tail or swallow-tailed thruster, about 18½" wide will give plenty of range. For the big days, or for when the points fire, a good semi-gun will definitely be a help, something like a nice 6'8" to 7'0" pin tail.

Geography and the breaks

In general, northern Spain is a rugged mountainous region with a thin strip of land acting as a buffer between the towering peaks and the raging Bay of Biscay. In these green and fertile areas, wide rivermouths and large beaches can be found, often with excellent breaks peeling along the white sandy bay in front of pristine sand dunes. In some areas the mountains fall directly into the sea. Here the only options are low tide coves that shelter under towering cliffs or rivermouths where thousands of years of erosion have opened up some breathtaking surfing possibilities. Many of Europe's best point breaks peel along this coastline – some hidden deep in the eucalyptus forest, some within plain view of the coastal highway. Many are rocky, sleeping giants needing a big swell to bring them to life. In Andalucía the wide open coastline has huge stretches of sandy beach interspersed with rocky points, while overhead vultures and storks soar on warm thermals.

Surfing and environment

There are parts of the coastline where the industrial landscape rivals any region in Europe. Smoke stacks belch noxious fumes that are wafted by offshore winds into the line-up and burning chimneys illuminate the night sky. Franco's hatred of the northern territories that had dared to hold out against his rule, meant that little thought went into the environmental impact of the steel works, petrochemical plants and power stations that sprung up as the struggling Spanish economy tried desperately to modernise. Playa de la Arena, Playa de la Concha and the breaks north of Gijón are typical of this kind of development which led, not just to a visual blight on the landscape, but to a legacy of air and water pollution. Port towns and urbanised zones such as, Bilbao, Getxo, Santander, Gijón, Aviles and A Coruña still

Pros

- Long and rugged coastline which picks up loads of swell from the Atlantic low pressure systems.
- Has a massive variety of breaks.
- Beautiful and deserted surf spots.
- Bustling urban breaks.
- High standard of wave riding around surfing hotspots.

Cons

- Some localism at busiest breaks.
- Oil residue from the *Prestige* disaster.
- When Portugal is basking in the sun, the Basques can be shivering in the rain.
- Some breaks polluted by industrial waste.

Low Pressure Chart for Spain

In all instances we assume the depressions are deep enough to produce classic swells (say 986 to 992mb). For many travelling surfers the ideal northern Spain chart always translated into the ideal chart for Mundaka. A deep enough low tracking between **L2** and **L3** will push groundswell into the legendary rivermouth break. But this is a flexible coastline and just about any clean or storm swell will have somewhere reeling. A depression travelling from **L1** will hit western Galicia and tracking through **L2** to **L3** the whole of the coastline should come alive.

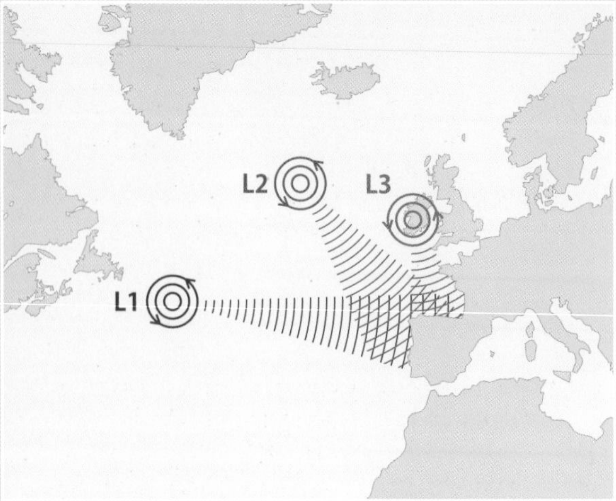

suffer from both industrial pollution and sewage. However, huge swathes of countryside look as though they've completely missed the industrial revolution and vast coastal stretches have been given over to national parkland where the water quality is good. Northern Spain missed the '70s holiday boom and is desperate to protect its natural habitat. As with anywhere, avoid rivermouths following heavy rains.

The events of 19 November 2002 left a lasting impression on the coastline when the oil tanker *The Prestige* broke in two and sank, a hundred miles off the Galician coastline, causing one of Europe's worst environmental disasters. It became a huge environmental and political issue in Spain. The clean up operation is complete but fears remain for the oil still trapped within the decaying hull of the tanker. Some scientists warn that more oil may be released as the two halves of the ship break down further, creating an environmental time-bomb. The threat over rivermouth dredging and coastal developments continue to shadow the breaks here – Rodiles and Gijón respectively.

The surf communities

The Spanish are passionate about life and about their surfing. With an ever-increasing number of surfers, some breaks are suffering greater tensions in the water but few suffer out-and-out localism. Usually surfers riding respectfully will have no problems. Tensions grow at breaks that are very busy, have a small take-off zone, rarely break, are dangerous or all of the above. A good example of this is the rivermouth at Rodiles. A low tide break popular with travelling surfers since the '70s, Rodiles has a small take off zone and large local surfing population. Some people surf there and have the session of their lives. Others come away with tales of intimidation, drop-ins and acts of aggression. At certain spots, a breach of etiquette may have serious consequences due to the dangerous nature of the break. Places like Roca Puta, Santa Marina and Menakoz are for experienced surfers only and fools are not suffered lightly. Picking up a few words of Spanish as well as a few words of Basque can help defuse potential conflicts.

Resources

Spain supports several good surf magazines including *3Sesenta,* www.3sesenta.com and *Surfer Rule,* www.gruposr.com. A pick of the online surf resources include: http://frussurf.com (tide tables and forecasting), www.partedeolas.com (forecasting site with swell charts), www.alaplaya,com (surfing in Euskadi), www.euskalsurf.com (Euskadi Surf Fed with beach and forecasting info as well as news), www.surfasturias.com (Asturias Surf Fed with beach and forecasting info as well as news), www.federacioncantabradesurf.com (Cantabria Surf Fed with links to regional tide tables and forecasting, news etc) www.fgsurf.com (Galicia Surf Fed with links to handy webcams plus forecasting, tide tables, news etc).

Spain: a brief surf history

1963 → Having got his hands on a Barland surfboard from the French Basque region, Jesús Fiochi becomes the first Spanish surfer at Sardinero, Santander. **1964** → The surf scene begins to spread through Cantabria. **1965** → Basque surfer Raul Dourdil and friends begin surfing at Bakio. **1969** → José Merido begins making Spanish surfboards under the MB mark. **1969** → Surfing spreads to Galicia with the discovery of breaks like Ferrol and Doniños. **1970s** → Surfing goes national travelling south to Cádiz and across the water to the Canaries. **1973** → Following on from Santa Marina and Geronimo surfboards, the first Pukas boards are shaped. **1987** → The first Spanish surf magazine, *Tres60*, is launched. **1988** → Spain holds its first International surf contest the Pukas Pro. **1989** → The first international surf contest, organized by the EPSA is held at Mundaka, helping to project the wave onto the world stage. **1990** → *Surfer Rule* magazine launches. **2001** → Spain's successes in competitive surfing culminate in Euskadi's Eneko Acero being crowned European surfing champion. **Today** → Spain hosts one of the WCT's most prestigious events, the Mundaka Pro, as well as several WQS events including rounds held at Tapia and Pantín.

Essentials

Position
With the lion's share of the Iberian Peninsula (which it co-habits with Portugal), Spain stretches out westward from continental Europe and south towards Africa. It is bound by the Atlantic along the North, northwest and southwest coastlines, the Mediterranean to the south and east, and is the second largest country in Western Europe after France.

Language
For the majority, the main language is Spanish (Castellano or Español) spoken at breakneck speed. A grasp of basic Spanish is a necessity – even in the tourist hubs of Bilbao and San Sebastián – as English is not widely understood . In the Basque country, the regional language 'Euskara' is making a comeback and appears on all road signs. Here it's *hondartza* not playa, *pintxos* not tapas and *eskerrik asko* not gracias. In Galicia you may come across a smattering of 'Galego' (*praia* not playa) and in Asturias 'Babel' raises its head on road signs, (with a helping hand from some locals who change the j's to x's).

Crime/safety
This is a relatively safe destination but car/van break-ins have been a particular problem for visitors, especially in and around urbanized areas. Just be aware and don't leave anything valuable on display.

If you need to report anything lost/stolen the **Polícia Nacional** deal with most urban crimes while the **Guarda Civil** handle roads, borders and law and order away from towns. **Polícia Local/Municipal** deal with traffic issues and some crime in large towns and cities. The Basques have their own force, **Ertzaintza**, who deal with local issues.

Health
In towns at least one pharmacy will be 'on-call' and open round the clock. Manned by highly trained staff, they can be a good first port of call and many prescription drugs (like antibiotics) can be bought over the counter after a consultation with the pharmacist. Recreational drugs are illegal (including cannabis brought over the border from Morocco). See page 19 for general EU health care rules.

Opening hours
Lunchtime governs the country. General opening hours are 1000-1400 and 1700-2000 Monday to Saturday with banks opening at 0830 and large supermarkets staying open throughout the day.

Sleeping
There are plenty of accommodation – *alojamientos* – options here but you can never judge a place from the outside – always request to see the room first. **Hotels** are the priciest, listed as H or HR and often

JAKUE ANDIKOTXEA

Ibon Amatriain at the temple.

charge a 7% tax on top of the asking price. The quality of lower end **hostales** (listed Hs or HsR) is often similar to **pensiones** (P) which are usually cheaper, family run places or rooms above bars. Offering good rates for double and twin rooms, pensiones are the accommodation of choice. Off the beaten track **casa rurales/agroturismos** – cottages rented out or run as hotels – can prove a popular and affordable option but may not be near many amenities. **albergues** (youth hostels) are few and far between and when compared with pensiones are not usually the best, or most affordable choice. There are plenty of **campings** (campsites) across Spain, many of which have great facilities including pretty comfortable wooden chalets (camping-light). A number are summer opening only, so check ahead; don't just rock up. www.campinguia.com and www.vayacamping.net are handy resources. Responsible free-camping away from tourist spots (and 1 km away from official campsites) is generally tolerated although in many areas isn't safe and the local police may move you on.

Eating

Breakfast is not particularly exciting with many favouring coffee and a pastry (cigarette optional). The sugar rush option is *chocolate con churros* – hot chocolate thick enough to stand your *churro* (sugar-covered fried dough sticks) in. Here lunch, 1330-1530, is the most important meal of the day. The best and cheapest way to eat is to grab a three-course *menú del día* from a local café, workers bar or *venta*. Wine or water plus bread is usually included in the €6-10 cover price. What's on offer differs region to region. Dinner is eaten late – usually 2200 onwards (later at weekends). If you've been surfing and need to refuel head to a café for a cheap *plato combinado* – usually fairly average chicken/steak/egg with chips. Better yet, embrace the tapas culture. Tapas (*pintxos* in Euskadi) are available all day but usually eaten from about 1930 onwards and are little nibbles (hot or cold) ranging from tortilla (potato omelette) to glamorous regional delights with seafood, ham or sausage. They should only cost about €2-4 each. Either help yourself from the selection on offer and keep a note of what you've had for when you come to pay, or ask the bartender to serve you. *Raciones* are slightly larger portions. The Spanish favour a 'food crawl' – soaking up the ambience, having a bite to eat and a small drink at each stop.

Each region has its own delicious speciality whether it's the *pintxos* in Euskadi, the *fabada* (bean and pork stew) in Asturias or the *pulpo* (octopus) in Galicia.

ALEX LAUREL

Sanchis challenges Newton's laws in Spanish waters.

Fact file

Currency: → Euro (€)
Capital city: → Madrid**Time zone**: → GMT+1
Length of coastline: → 4,965 km
Emergency Numbers:
→ General Emergency: 112
→ Police: 092
→ Local Police: 092
→ International Operator: 1008
Country Code: → +34
Electricity: → 220v continental dual pin
Visa: → None required for citizens of EU countries, or tourists from the US, Canada, Australia and New Zealand. For all up to date info check: www.ukvisas.gov.uk
Tourist Board: → www.spain.info plus www.euskadi.net, www.turismodecantabria.com, www.infoasturias.com, www.turgalicia.es, www.andalucia.org, www.turismodecanarias.com

Getting there

Road The main route into northern Spain is from southwest France via the E5/E70 motorway heading towards San Sebastián. You can avoid the tolls and take the slower but more scenic N-10, which becomes the N-634.

Sea P&O operate a year round ferry service between Portsmouth and Bilbao which they run more like a cruise so charge accordingly. Cabins are mandatory and a September return for van and two people can be around €1200. Prices vary hugely according to season and availability but booking in advance can be cheaper. Check www.poferries.com for occasional off peak specials. **Brittany Ferries**, www.brittanyferries.com, offers a twice-weekly service, mid March-mid November, between Plymouth and Santander. It's a little shorter taking around 20 hours and, with the option of reclining seats or cabins, can often be the cheapest choice. A September return for van, cabin and two people is around €800.

Air Madrid is the main international airport although for most longhauls it is often easier, quicker and cheaper to connect via another European destination – the UK offers some of the best low cost routes direct to the north and south coasts. For details of all airports in Spain www.aena.es. For the Canary Islands see page 263.

From Europe The key entry points for Northern Spain include Bilbao in Euskadi, Santander (Carmago) in Cantabria, Asturias, plus A Coruña, Santiago de Compostela and Vigo in Galicia. Budget airline **easyJet**, www.easyjet.com, offers some of the cheapest flights to Bilbao, which can be anywhere between €30 and €180 depending on time of year and availability plus board carriage. Other operators include **Ryanair**, www.ryaniar.com, and **Air France**, www.airfrance.com, who can sometimes offer good off-season deals. Avoid banditos **Iberia** who have ridiculously excessive board carriage charges. Another great budget alternative is to fly into Biarritz with **Ryanair**. The French airport is about 30 minutes from the Spanish border and flights are available from around €10 plus taxes up to about €180 plus board carriage. For Andalucia, **easyJet** has budget flights between London and Málaga (more expensive in peak periods), **Ryanair** operates between Stanstead and Jerez, near Cádiz.

Rail Using Paris as the European connection point, the best and cheapest way to get to Northern Spain by train is via TGV www.tgv.com to Hendaye. From there use Spanish networks **RENFE FEVE** to reach your destination. Rail Europe www.raileurope also has a route map and booking facility for journeys right across Europe.

Getting around

Driving (right-hand side) A full driving licence (photo type or IDP) is required plus liability insurance (bring it with you). You also need to carry two warning triangles. On the spot fines are levied for speeding/traffic offences (get a receipt). Blood/alcohol limits are lower than the UK. Since its transition into democracy and entry into the EU, new and improved road links are opening regularly, and the motorway network is expanding rapidly right across the country. The coastal routes are generally very good and now that the motorways have taken the strain of the goods vehicles, are a great, scenic alternative. There are only a few **toll roads**, most of which are reasonable except in Euskadi which are nothing short of rude. See www.aseta.es for details of tolls nationwide.

Motorway *autovía/autopista* – **Speed limit 120 kph**. Stretches across the majority of Northern Spain and is signed in blue. Running southwards, the motorway connects both Cádiz and Huelva to the north via Madrid. Toll roads are indicated by a red circle and are reasonable (except in Euskadi).

Other Roads **Speed limit 100 kph/50 kph urban areas** (unless otherwise indicated). Urban speed limits are vigorously enforced and heavy fines are not uncommon. *Rutas Nacionales* N roads are main roads that take over where the motorway finishes and are of a good or fair standard. Secondary/provincial roads signed B, C or province initials (ie. AS Asturias) vary but provide access to many hard to reach spots.

Car hire: Seems pretty pricey when compared to other living costs – from about €400 for two weeks. All the big boys operate in Spain including **Hertz**, www.hertz.com, **Europcar**, www.europcar.com, and **Avis**, www.avis.com, but fly/drives may offer better deals. You usually need to be over 21 and pay by credit card. If you've booked ahead prepare yourself for other charges they'll try to slip in such as extra insurance.

Public transport

If you need to go public, the bus routes are quicker with greater access but you'll have little joy getting on with a board under your arm.

Rail **RENFE**, www.renfe.es, is good for major routes with handy connections from Madrid and cross-country. In the North, **FEVE**, www.feve.es, takes the scenic route offering greater coastal coverage. **EUSKOTREN**, www.euskotren.es, services the Basque region while Bilbao relies on its efficient metro service, www.metrobilbao.net.

The Lowdown

"The police are inflexible. The papers of the vehicle and your insurance must be in order, if not your vehicle will be immobilised, and you will receive a hefty fine. Do not try and bribe the police."
Willy Uribe, Spanish surf photographer

"The high and beautiful mountains makes the best gift to the surfers when in the middle of the winter, the magic off shore south wind creates a fan effect and you can enjoy the dry air over 20° C, sunny with a perfect swell increasing and not many people in the water. Everybody that has experienced a south wind in our winter, knows the feeling. . . And the best thing is that is the normal situation from September to February."
Dani Garcia, Spanish surfer

"Asturias is a complex mix of industrialised urban areas cut by great swathes of countryside and is probably the least explored area of northern Spain. Most travellers don't look beyond Rodiles but if they do they'll find plenty of beaches, reefs and points just begging to be surfed." *Dan Harris, Welsh surfer*

"To explore the full surf potential of the Canary Islands would take several lifetimes." *Willy Uribe*

Surfers' tales

Big-wave surfing in Spain by Tony Butt

I can't remember why I started surfing in the early seventies; nor can I remember why big waves started to take my interest around the mid-eighties. Maybe it was because I always wanted to do something different. Or maybe it was because I was fed up with the line-up becoming more and more crowded and competitive. I was never really a very competitive person and have always hated crowded situations. I'd heard that, in big waves, there was this camaraderie in the water where surfers looked out for each other and, at some spots there was no snaking or dropping in because you could ride four on a wave.

I first arrived in the Basque Country around 1990. I'd heard rumour of a big-wave spot called Meñakoz. Not much was known about this spot and I had never seen any photos of it, but, apparently, it could hold waves of over twenty foot and was only surfed by a handful of locals. This sounded perfect. I went on to be obsessed with Meñakoz for the next 15 years. For the first few years, on the big days I'd go out there on my own, wishing someone else would join me.

On that first trip, we drove back through the Basque Country during a huge swell, Mundaka closing out from end to end. We took the coast road up through Gipuzcoa and on towards France. We saw perfect lefthanders breaking at the bottom of inaccessible cliffs, a right-hand pointbreak at one side of a large bay, and several huge peaks breaking just a few metres from the road. But we didn't see one other surfer.

A few years later, New Years Day 1998 to be precise, from the cliff top at La Galea I saw the biggest waves I've ever seen. The 177-metre-long Pride of Bilbao was climbing up the face, slamming down the back of the wave and then disappearing in the trough as if it were a small fishing boat. As far as I know, nobody surfed any big waves that day and there was nothing in the magazines. Most people weren't particularly interested; those of us who were just didn't know where to go.

Nowadays, all those spots along the coast road between Mundaka and the French border have names and many of them are surfed. And if a swell like the one of New Years Day 1998 arrived again, people would be on it from the word go: there would be a mad frenzy of mobile phones, web pages, jet skis, cameras, helicopters, brand-name logos, fame and money, a good week before. Big-wave surfing in Spain has suddenly become popular.

For someone like me, this could be quite depressing. Big-wave line-ups might start to get just as crowded as the small-wave line-ups I got sick of in the 1980s. Strangely, this hasn't happened, so far. On the 25th February 2006, I surfed one of those spots between Mundaka and the French border, fifteen-to-twenty foot with four others. Nobody watching, no cameras. Meanwhile, about 10 km down the road, over a thousand people lined the road and cliff top while Ibon Amatriain and Mikel Agote rode some rather bigger waves, before being on prime-time national television, in all the newspapers and on the cover of several European surf magazines.

JAKUE ANDIKOTXEA

Tony Butt, Meñakoz.

Why? Well, clearly because the waves they rode were of 'record' size. But Ibon and Mikel were towsurfing, not surfing. Towsurfing has brought the biggest change on the North Coast of Spain in the last couple of years. On one hand, this is very worrying. People might start to towsurf in waves too small to justify it, or people might start to towsurf around people who are already surfing. This, of course, has already happened and, although the Spanish hate any rules and regulations, they really need to quickly follow the precedent of places like South Africa and Australia, and not towsurf under any circumstances if someone is out there surfing. It is also worrying because of the contaminating nature of jet skis and the fact that surfers ought to be getting more, not less, environmentally friendly.

On the other hand, if towsurfing is getting all the hype, then normal, traditional big-wave surfing might just be left alone. At Meñakoz, for example, towsurfing is not allowed. Over the last few years, even though the line-up has become a little more crowded on the smaller days, you'll still find the same crew of five

JUAN FERNANDEZ

Northern Spain resident and big-wave charger Tony Butt has been striking out in Asturias to discover new challenges.

or six out there on the big days. Whether this will continue remains to be seen.

Another thing that has suddenly sprung up is the big-wave contest. I'm not sure what the motivation behind a big-wave contest is supposed to be. The worst aspect is that it makes people more aggressive and competitive in the water when there are big waves (perhaps because they are "practising" for the contest, even without realising it). At least some contest organisers have decided to respect local surfers and keep some spots contest-free. In summary, things in Spain have changed a lot over the last few years as far as big-wave surfing is concerned. The simple fact that I'm writing this article is testament to that. The fact that we've only recently realised that the North Coast of Spain contains big waves easily rivalling those in California or Hawaii gives us a unique opportunity to start off on the right foot. Hopefully, our big-wave spots are difficult and dangerous enough to be able to protect themselves – otherwise we really need to make sure they don't become a primordial soup of boards, surfers, leashes, jet skis, noise, fumes, money and greed.

Tony Butt lives in the Basque Country and holds a PhD in Physical Oceanography and Big Wave Surfing. His excellent book 'Surf Science' has become essential reading for surfers and is available through most surf shops and from www.swell-forcast.com.

Overview

Euskadi is probably the most famous and popular surfing region in the whole of Spain. This province is a complex mix of bustling, frenetic urban energy and huge lush swathes of Celtic countryside. A place where the pounding swells generated in the tumultuous Bay of Biscay have shaped the coastline into a land with a big country, Nor Cal feel; where huge surf thunders along forest-shrouded Jurassic points into the realm of XXL contention. Not that the local big wave chargers crave the spotlight; many actively avoid it, fearing the 'Mundaka-ization' of their precious breaks. Euskadi – the Basque Country (El País Vasco) – is home to a proud and patriotic people. Suppressed by Franco, Basque culture is now booming. The beret is on show in every harbourside bar and city café as the headwear of choice and is used to crown new surf contest champions. *Euskara*, one of the continent's oldest languages, was once outlawed, but has been revived by a whole new generation.

In cities like San Sebastián, (or Donostia in *Euskara*), the bustling historic heart of Parte Vieja is lined with *pintxos* (tapas) bars. Excited conversations spill over into the warm evenings as football, surfing, politics and life are debated with equal fervour long into the early hours of the morning – punctuated only by the consumption of another tasty morsel, washed down with a *txikiteo*. In Bilbao, the capital of Bizkaia, the sparkling titanium curves of Frank Gehry's Guggenhheim are a testament to the region's ability to adapt, transforming the city into a popular tourist destination and cultural hotspot. While the Basque region may be relatively expensive when compared to other parts of Spain, the sheer quality of experience it offers has made it great value for money; a destination that tops virtually every travelling surfer's list, whether from the new world or the old.

JAKUE ANDIKOTXEA

The geography of the region lends itself well as a foil for peeling points.

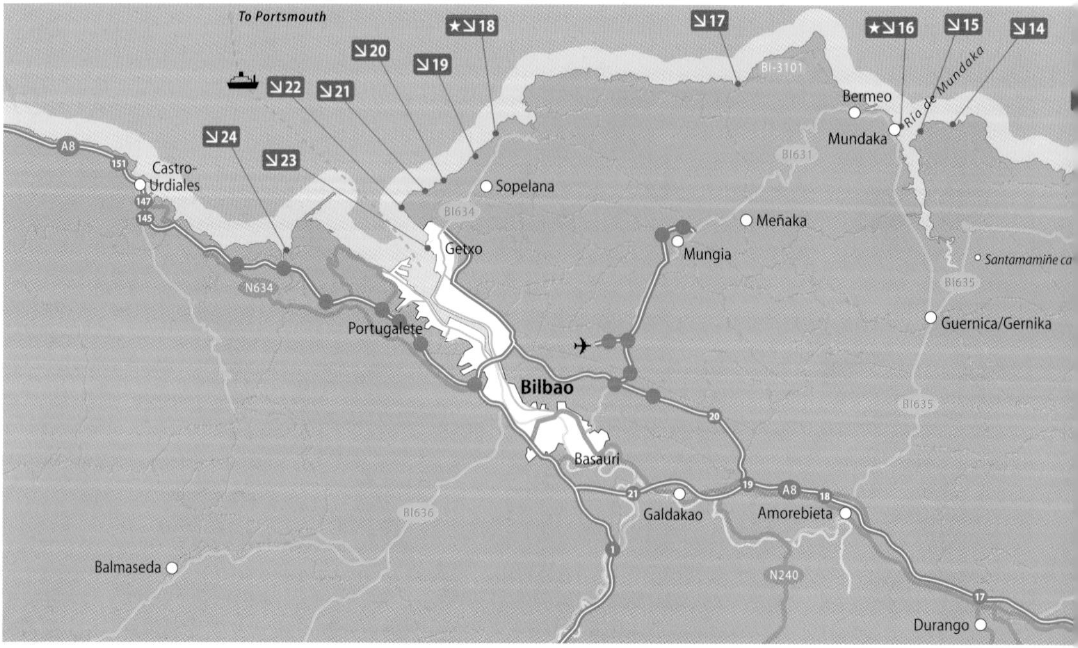

Coastline

Tucked into the corner where Spain meets France, the mountainous interior of Euskadi can be blamed for the area's high precipitation levels. It can also be thanked as it is this freshwater run-off that has carved a number of quality rivermouths into the landscape, converting otherwise average beaches into quality spots. But Euskadi has something for everyone: from the world-class rivermouth to quality beachbreaks, challenging reefs and points and classic big wave spots which are gaining in reputation. From Mundaka to Getxo the coastline is lined with high cliffs where access points can often lead to reefs and rewards.

Local environment

Although there are some pristine breaks in Euskadi, these are mostly away from the urban centres. Around Bilbao, there are also a number of spots blighted by pollution. Playa de la Arena to the west is backed by petrochemical plants and those precious offshore days can see the line-up filled with pretty noxious fumes. Rivermouths can also suffer from run-off from agriculture and storm drains after rains.

The standard of surfing in the Basque region is as high as anywhere in Europe. It enjoys a thriving surf scene and industry and is also home to internationally respected board manufacturers, Pukas. The economic benefits of surfing were fully appreciated following the dredging of the Ría Mundaka, resulting in not only the cancellation of the 2005 Mundaka Pro but also many planned trips to the region. The wave has now returned and the contest, surfers and their welcome euros have followed. Euskadi is also the busiest region in Spain with a high number of both local and visiting surfers. "In the past few years there has been a

change at Mundaka," says top Basque surfer Eneko Acero. "It's not like 30 or 40 people in the water – it's like 100 people. I think some of the local guys get a bit tired of it because it's so crowded. You can't get so many waves, a lot of people are dropping in. It's getting more localized now than it was years ago." The region has a competitive surf scene – not even the top 44 were spared drop-ins while free-surfing epic Mundaka – but actual acts of aggression are not common.

Getting around

The minor road networks are of good quality and provide good access to the Basque coastline. The motorways are a fast way to cross the region, if a bit pricey. The bus and rail networks are also a convenient way to get around and provide access to all the major cities.

6'3" Stretch F-4

Shaper: Stretch

6'3" x 18¹¹/₁₆" x 2⅛"

Surftech's lively, responsive TL2 composite technology.
Lightning fast! Half-moon template elongates the rail-line positive drive and release off tail. Deck channels give added strength while moderating a progressive flex pattern that runs the four fins. Want to get deeper in the barrel at Mundaka than anyone else?

Futures Quad fins.

ⓘ Boards by **Surftech**
www.surftech.com info@surftech.com

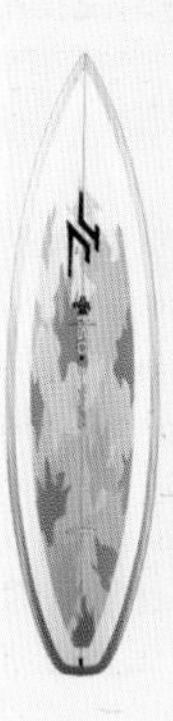

6'0" JC SD-3

Shaper: John Carper

6'0" x 18¼" x 2⅛"

Built with Surftech's proven TUFLITE construction.

Single to double bottom contour, slightly fuller rail, lower entry rocker and a slight bump wing at the hips. Catch waves easy and generate speed instantly. Extremely fast board with forgiving rails. Made for the epic beach breaks that Euskadi has to offer!

Futures JC1 fins.

Breaks

1 Hondarribia	8 Roca Puta ★	14 Playa de Laga	21 Playa de Aizkorri
2 Playa de la Zurriola	9 Zumaia	15 Playa Laida	22 Punta Galea
3 Ondarreta	10 Playa de Deba	16 Mundaka ★	23 Getxo
4 Orio	(Santiago)	17 Playa de Bakio	24 Playa de la Arena
5 Zarautz	11 Punta Pitxarri	18 Meñakoz ★	
6 Karramarro	12 Playa de Karraspio	19 Playa de Sopelana	
7 Playa de Gaztetape	13 Playa de Ogella/Ogeia	20 Sopelana – La Salvaje

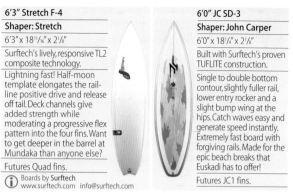

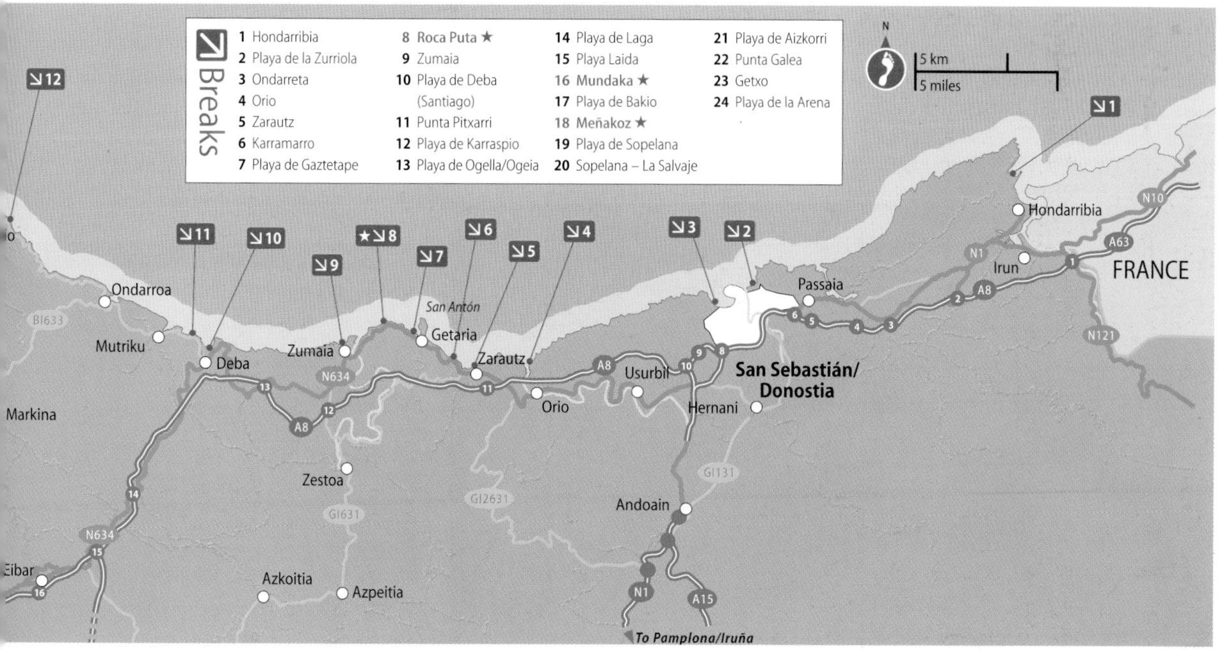

Breaks

BEACH BREAK

↘1 Hondarribia

- **Conditions** Big N swell, offshore in S to SW wind
- **Hazards/tips** Moderately polluted.
- **Sleeping** San Sebastián » *p218*

This sheltered town beach is a place that's worth checking in massive storms when everywhere else is maxed out as it needs big north or northwesterly swells to work. On the push it can produce good waves.

BEACH BREAK

↘2 Playa de la Zurriola

- **Conditions** Small to medium NW to N swells, offshore in S winds
- **Hazards/tips** Crowds, urban break
- **Sleeping** San Sebastián » *p218*

A large, crescent-shaped, sandy beach in San Sebastián working through the tide. Zurriola produces good quality peaks along the beach plus a right breaking at the eastern end near the sea wall. Can have excellent waves in small and medium swells but tends to close out in bigger conditions. The east end plays hosts to a WQS contest. Has a strong local crew so there can be some localism on crowded days and water quality is sometimes poor. A pleasant urban beach with showers and drinking water.

BEACH BREAK

↘3 Ondarreta

- **Conditions** Big N or NW swells offshore in S to SW winds
- **Hazards/tips** Parking is a problem in San Sebastián
- **Sleeping** San Sebastián » *p218*

The second town beach in San Sebastián. Sheltered by a headland and the small island – Isla de Santa Clara. There are two stretches of sand. To the east, **La Concha** is not renowned for its waves. **Ondarreta** works on the push and also has a high-tide point break.

BEACH BREAK

↘4 Orio

- **Conditions** Big N or NW swells, offshore in SW to S winds
- **Hazards/tips** Antilla is visible from the motorway viaduct, has a massive car park, a beachfront campsite, cafés and showers
- **Sleeping** Playa de Orio » *p219*

O'NEILL

A pleasant sandy beach break that works through the tides, situated slightly north of the town of Orio at the rivermouth. Although quite a small beach, in large swells it can have a peak towards the west and a right towards the east. The huge breakwater at Orio cuts out a lot of swell but gives shelter in large westerly storms. Not too crowded or polluted.

BEACH BREAK

↘5 Zarautz

- **Conditions** Small to medium N to NW swells, offshore in S winds
- **Hazards/tips** Crowds, has beachfront skatepark
- **Sleeping** Zarautz » *p219*

Zarautz is a pretty town with a popular beach that is busy throughout the year. It works through the tides and has a variety of shifting peaks all along its shore. Also has a popular peak near the skatepark. Home to a WQS contest in September. A local hotspot, Zarautz has a high standard of surfing and can be crowded. Summer parking can be difficult but off season you should be able to find a spot on the road parallel to the beach. The seafront is lined with modern art and has showers.

LEFT REEF BREAK

↘6 Karramarro

- **Conditions** Big NW to N swells, offshore in S winds
- **Hazards/tips** Gets crowded, experienced surfers only
- **Sleeping** Zarautz » *p219*

This low-tide, rocky reef works in big northwesterly swells. Waves of up to 10 ft draw surfers from Zarautz and beyond. For experienced surfers only. Check from the N-634 just north of Zarautz.

BEACH BREAK

↘7 Playa de Gaztetape

- **Conditions** Small to medium NW swells, offshore in S winds
- **Hazards/tips** Not too crowded or polluted, parking available overlooking the break
- **Sleeping** Zarautz » *p219*

Just west of the San Antón headland at Getaria, this is a small, quiet, crescent-shaped bay that all but disappears at high tide when the waves break onto the rocky sea defences. At low through mid tide, in small to medium northwesterly swells, it produces peaks along the picturesque sandy beach. Doesn't hold a crowd. It is offshore in southerly winds, but the surrounding hills provide good protection from westerlies and easterlies.

WILLY URIBE

Above: 8 Ibon Amatriain, Roca Puta. **Below left:** 5 Michel Velasco, Zarautz.

RIGHT POINT BREAK

↘8 Roca Puta

- **Swell** Medium to big N to NW swells
- **Wind** S
- **Tide** Low to mid
- **Size** 4-12 ft
- **Length** 200 m plus
- **Bottom** Boulders
- **Ability Level** Advanced
- **Best months** Oct-Apr
- **Board** Gun or semi-gun
- **Access** Off the rocks on the inside
- **Hazards/tips** Rocks, crowds, heavy wave
- **Sleeping** Zarautz » *p219*

When Roca Puta comes to life, it can see huge, heavy right-hand waves – from head high to well over 12 ft – reeling off the rocky point just east of Zumaia. In Spain it has established a reputation as one of the region's classic big-wave spots, and has a hard-core crew of chargers who rule the line-up here. It is however still relatively unknown to the outside world. Setting the scene, the name translates to 'Whore Rock', and the sets detonate out on the end of the point from where the wave speeds along rocky coastal defences. The jagged substrate means the swell needs to be over head-high to start working and avoid the large boulders that litter the line-up. Once a big swell kicks in, the point is transformed. This low-tide spot should really only be tackled by experienced surfers. Clean water but rocky line-up. A great spectacle when it's working, the lay-by on the coast road provides a good vantage point.

*If you like **Roca Puta**, try **Isla de Santa Marina** (see page 227) or **Safi** in Morocco (see page 376).*

BEACH BREAK

↘9 Zumaia

- **Conditions** Small to medium NW swells, offshore in S winds
- **Hazards/tips** Parking can be a problem at peak times
- **Sleeping** Zarautz » *p219*

On the western side of the town **Playa de Itzurun** is a sandy beach with fingers of reef that reach out into the Bay of Biscay. These fingers act like groynes and aid the build-up of sand. It is a consistent spot that picks up lots of swell and works best up to high tide when it can be prone to backwash from the cliffs. Contest venue on the Euskadi circuit. It is also a beautiful spot: to the west, a red sandstone cliff of vertical slabs stretches out to the headland and to the east lies a contrasting blue slate cliff with the sandy beach nestled in-between.

RIGHT REEF AND BEACH BREAK

↘10 Playa de Deba (Santiago)

- **Conditions** Big N and NW swells, offshore in S winds
- **Hazards/tips** Heavy wave for experienced surfers
- **Sleeping** Deba/Mutriku » *p219*

This low-tide reef is a fairly consistent big-wave spot that breaks best at 6-8 ft (but up to 15 ft in big northwesterly swells). Considered by local surfers as a dangerous spot suitable for experienced big-wave surfers only. The reef sits at the east end of a sandy beach that works through all tides producing lefts and rights. At the western end of the beach is a sheltering rocky groyne. There are toilets and plenty of parking at the beach.

DEMI TAYLOR

WILLY URIBE

Top: **14** Playa de Laga. **Above: 10** Deba.

LEFT POINT BREAK

↘11 Punta Pitxarri

- **Conditions** Medium NW swells, offshore in S winds
- **Hazards/tips** Shallow when small
- **Sleeping** Deba/Mutriku » *p219*

A short but fun left-hand rocky point that works best at low tide on the push. Pitxarri needs a bigger swell from a more northerly direction as well as southerly offshore winds to form peeling walls that spin off the point along the rocky reef. Park off GI-638 when you see the large clifftop villa and scramble down the disused track.

BEACH BREAK

↘12 Playa de Karraspio

- **Conditions** Medium NW swell, offshore in S winds
- **Hazards/tips** Popular weekend and evening break, just off the coast road east of Lekeitio
- **Sleeping** Lekeitio » *p219*

A very pretty beach break with an island at the western end and a rocky point at the east. A left breaks near the island, along a rivermouth sandbar. There can also be peaks on the beach in a medium swell. Can break on all tides depending on swell size as the river flow affects sandbar deposition.

SAND/REEF BREAK

↘13 Playa de Ogella/Ogeia

- **Conditions** Medium and large NW swells, offshore in S winds
- **Hazards/tips** Very difficult to find, off small back roads
- **Sleeping** Lekeitio » *p219*

Situated west of Lekeitio in beautiful countryside, this low-tide peak produces fast, hollow rights and fast walling lefts. Quality break. Fairly localized.

BEACH BREAK

↘14 Playa de Laga

- **Conditions** Small to medium NW to N swells, offshore in S winds
- **Hazards/tips** Crowds when good and weekends/lunchtime.
- **Sleeping** Mundaka » *p219*

Sitting under a spectacular cliff, this picturesque beach produces some excellent banks with hollow lefts, rights and peaks. Geographically close to Mundaka, Laga tends to get overlooked by travelling surfers who flock here to surf the left-hand legend, and also because it's a drive down the estuary and back out to the east to reach it. This high-quality beach break works on all tides, so when it is on expect there to be a strong local crew, especially at lunch and after work. It works best at low to mid tide. Car parking area, toilets and bar.

BEACH BREAK

↘15 Playa Laida

- **Conditions** Small to medium NW swells, offshore in S winds
- **Hazards/tips** Can produce nice waves, but it's not what people come to Mundaka for
- **Sleeping** Mundaka » *p219*

Laida is an extension of the beach at the Ria de Mundaka. It is a break that can produce some fun waves through the tides and, at any other location, would probably be surfed a lot more. Access from Mundaka village means paddling across the river or driving inland to Gernika and then following the river road back out to the coast – a bit of a trek. In the summer you can hop on a foot passenger ferry.

LAURENT MASUREL

16 Locked into Mundaka.

Left rivermouth

↘16 Mundaka

Swell Medium to big N to NW
Wind S
Tide Low to three quarters
Size 2 to 12ft plus
Length 200 m plus
Bottom Shallow rivermouth sandbar
Ability Level Advanced
Best Months Oct-Apr
Board Semi-gun or pintail thruster
Access Entry via harbour, exit on rocks south of harbour
Hazards/tips Very crowded, powerful, rips. Check someone isn't deep in the barrel before dropping in
Sleeping Mundaka » *p219*

The rivermouth sandbank that rests in the mouth of the Ria de Mundaka must surely rank as one of nature's architectural masterpieces. The forces of ice and rain, and the power of erosion from flowing water have weathered the inland peaks high above this green coastline. Minute particles of rock have been carried by the flowing waters of the river, through boiling rapids and deep green pools until, eventually, their turbulent journey ends where fresh water mingles with the saline fringes of the Bay of Biscay. Here, the loss of kinetic energy causes the particles to be deposited in such a way that they have built up into a long, shallow sandbank, groomed and sculpted by tide and current. It is a geometrical curve so perfect it produces long, peeling, barreling, lefts – one after the other – never sectioning, never closing out. All it needs to fire is another of nature's natural wonders – the lined corduroy of a perfect groundswell. The confusion and disorder of an open ocean storm transformed into metronomic pulses of energy, each evenly spaced – 12-second intervals, eight foot faces. Mathematics, geology, physics, combined as one.

Deposited by the river's current, the jostling pack of neoprene-clad silhouettes mingle and angle around the peak; inside sits a second group – the outsiders. Order, disorder. Pecking orders enforced. Psychology and sociology together.

This tiny Basque village looked very much the same when, on the 26 April, 1937, a squadron of German planes angled out over the sea and poured up the rivermouth, bound for the town of Gernika just to the north. In the most notorious act of the Spanish Civil War they bombed the civilian population as they crammed into the square on market day. Over 1600 people died as fire

JAKUE ANDIKOTXEA

16 Mundaka.

bombs rained down. The raid so affected Picasso that he produced his most famous painting, and named it after the scene of the attack. "I looked across to see planes banking into the Ria and following the river south to Gernika. The sky seemed filled with them." Leaning on the iron railings watching another perfect set reel along the sandbar, Jerónimo Alonso recalls that fateful day as if it were yesterday.

ⓘ ***If you like** Mundaka, try **Rodiles** (see page 237) or **Gills Bay** in Scotland (see page 38).*

“”

The best time to go to Mundaka is late autumn, as it's still warmish and you can get long spells of offshore winds. Its a very unpredictable wave, which is part of what makes it so fun, but the crowds have always been a problem – even in the early '80s it wasn't uncommon to get over a hundred guys out on the weekend. As far as boards are concerned, generally you want enough length to get you into the take-off, but if your board is too long, you increase the chances of snapping it, and it won't trim so well in the barrel. The estuary is very treacherous, so be careful. Mundaka can be a punishing wave. Locals have their injuries to prove it. Backs, shoulders and especially knee injuries are the norm. So treat it with respect. Try not to hassle the locals on the peak. Try to pick off waves a bit further down the line. The Basques drink at a steady pace for a long night, and do not appreciate loud, drunken foreigners. Try to speak a bit of Basque and they may open up some more.

Nick Lavery grew up surfing Mundaka and beat many of the world's best, including the likes of Wayne Lynch and Maurice Cole, in the annual Mundaka Surf Classic.

BEACH BREAK

↘17 Playa de Bakio

- **Conditions** Small to medium W to N swells, offshore in S winds
- **Hazards/tips** Crowds
- **Sleeping** Mundaka » p219

This is a consistent, high-class beach break that works through the tides. A testament to its quality is the fact that it is a regular alternative staging post for the annual Mundaka Pro contest. As a town beach it is usually crowded. In big swells there can be a large, hollow right-hander at the western end of the beach. The town end of the beach is open and sandy with peaks running along its length. From the stream east, the beach has rocky outcrops, but the sand builds up into some quality banks. Good beach for surfers of all abilities. Park in bays on main road from east. Has showers.

RIGHT REEF BREAK

↘18 Meñakoz

- **Swell** N to NW
- **Wind** Southeasterly
- **Tide** Mid to high
- **Size** 6 to 18 ft
- **Length** up to 200 m
- **Bottom** Rock
- **Ability Level** Advanced
- **Best Months** Sep-Apr
- **Board** Semi-gun or pintail thruster
- **Access** From the bay
- **Hazards/tips** Heavy wave, dangerous rocks
- **Sleeping** Sopelana » p220

WILLY URIBE

WILLY URIBE

Top: 17 Bakio. **Above: 18** Asier Ibanez, Meñakoz.

Along with Mundaka, Meñakoz is the region's most famous spot. It is a big wave with a big reputation and one of the first big-wave spots in Europe to come to the attention of the wider world. It is also a definite 'experts only' proposition. "Meñakoz is an extreme example of 'You just can't paddle out there first time and have it wired'," says oceanographer Tony Butt, a British surfer who has spent many years taking on the Basque regions biggest waves. Working from mid to high tide, the powerful right-handers break up to 18ft while some of the main hazards include rips, rocks, difficult access, wide sets, long hold-downs and very powerful waves. "I have been trapped at the bottom of the cliff with a broken foot, seen a friend break seven ribs in his back and another almost lose his leg. I have seen countless boards lost, broken or smashed to pieces, and, (in winter 2003) I became a member of the 'two-wave hold-down club', explains Butt. "Despite all of this, the opportunity to take off on a 20-ft wave and make it, still far outweighs all the inconveniences of this place. Surfing here has given me, without doubt, the most intense experiences of my life." The line-up here is not so much localized, as only really accepting of surfers who truly have the competence to take on these giant waves.

BEACH BREAKS

↘19 Playa de Sopelana

- **Conditions** Small to medium NW swells, offshore in SE winds
- **Hazards/tips** Car and van crime has been a problem here
- **Sleeping** Sopelana » *p220*

Playa de Atxibiribil and **Playa de Arrietara** are two beaches in Sopelana that break through the tides. They offer a variety of peaks and reefs that break either left or right along and near rocky fingers. This area has a large and very committed surf population and boasts some of Europe's top surfers. Surf shops nearby on road to the beach (Calle Loiola Ander Deuna).

BEACH AND REEF BREAK

↘20 Sopelana – La Salvaje

- **Conditions** All W to N swells, offshore in S to SE winds
- **Hazards/tips** A very popular spot, which may have some localism and car crime
- **Sleeping** Sopelana » *p220*

Heading west from Playa de Sopelana lies Salvaje, a quality beach break boasting some excellent waves at all states of tide. **La Triangular** is a rocky finger of reef producing, as the name suggests, both lefts and rights which can be fast and long with hollow sections. This break attracts the area's best surfers so standards are high. Parking on the cliff top.

BEACH AND POINT BREAK

↘21 Playa de Aizkorri

- **Conditions** All W to N swells, offshore in SE
- **Hazards/tips** Due to its proximity to Getxo the water quality is not good
- **Sleeping** Getxo » *p220*

The next bay west boasts nice, quality peaks and an excellent left-hand point at the west of the bay that pumps in large swells. Good alternative to Sopelana as tends to be less crowded. Access from car park at eastern end of the beach.

JAKUE ANDIKOTXEA

RIGHT POINT BREAK

↘22 Punta Galea

- **Conditions** Biggest NW swells, offshore in SE winds
- **Hazards/tips** Dangerous spot where access is a problem
- **Sleeping** Getxo » *p220*

A huge right-hand point breaks here in the biggest swells. Close to the cliffs and rocks, this is a spectacular spot that even experienced surfers think twice about before tackling. Recent staging post for big-wave contest. Works on mid to high tide, offshore in south and easterly winds.

BEACH AND POINT BREAKS

↘23 Getxo

- **Conditions** Big N to NW swells, offshore in SE winds.
- **Hazards/tips** Busy and very polluted.
- **Sleeping** Getxo » *p220*

The two beaches inside Punta Galea are **Arrigunaga** and **Ereaga**. Both are rocky and sand-covered rock. Can work through the tides on massive swells when Arrigunaga can have good quality right-hand waves whereas Ereaga boasts both lefts and rights. Both are popular breaks due to their proximity to urban hubs of Getxo and Bilbao. Parking overlooks these polluted spots.

JAKUE ANDIKOTXEA

Above: 24 West side, La Arena. **Top: 20** Sopelana.

BEACH BREAK

↘24 Playa de la Arena

- **Conditions** Small to medium NW swells, offshore in SE winds
- **Hazards/tips** Polluted, smelly, yet busy
- **Sleeping** Bilbao » *p220*

This beach is just to the west of Bilbao and can have some good-quality waves with various peaks along the beach at different states of tide. However, the drive-in will give you a clue as to why this may be a spot to avoid. Huge petrochemical plants belching noxious fumes are not the prettiest of backdrops, and in an offshore wind, the smell is pretty hideous. Parking and camping available near the beach. Suitable for all surfers with a sturdy disposition.

Practicalities

San Sebastián/Donostia

Just 30 mins from the border along the N1, San Sebastián is an excellent introduction to Euskadi. Cocooned by three beaches, this is a young, buzzing city of tightly packed bars and cafés, where tapas is a gastronomic art form. The Parte Vieja or 'Old Town' has it all: cheap *pensiones*, great tapas bars, and it's only a short walk over the bridge to Zurriola.

Sleeping

Places get booked up quickly, especially during the Gran Semana festival in mid-Aug and International Film festival in Sep, so best to book ahead. All places listed here are in the Parte Viejo.

€€-€ Pension Edorta, C Puerto, www.pensionedorta.com, with lovely, old, beamed rooms and internet access.

There is a glut of very affordable places to stay including:

€ Pensión Loinaz, C San Lorenzo, wwwpensionloinaz.com. Shared bathrooms, laundry room and internet.

€ Pensión Amaiur, C 31 de Agusto, www.pensionamaiur.com. Handy choice with kitchen and internet facilities.

€ Pensión San Lorenzo, C San Lorenzo, www.infobide.com/pensionsanlorenzo. The rooms have private bathrooms, Wi-Fi and fridges, making it a popular option.

€ B&B Isabella, C Ondaribe www.roomsisabella.com. Near Ondarreta beach has double or singe rooms plus apartments sleeping 2 or 6

Camping Camping Igueldo, Paseo Padre Orkolaga, behind Monte Igueldo, 5 km out of town, www.campingigeldo.com. Year round. Only campsite with bungalows.

Eating

San Sebastián has more than its fair share of Michelin-starred restaurants but tapas, or *pintxos*, as they are known in Euskadi, is *the* thing to do here. The Parte Vieja is buzzing with great bars, serving their own take on *pintxos*. Although available all day, from about 1930 onwards, the bars begin to pack out as locals go from spot to spot having a bite and *txikiteo* (small drink) at each stop. Almost anywhere you go is going to be good but C Fermin Calbeton and C 31 de Agosto are good starting places where a couple of plates of *pintxos* and *zuritos* (small beers) for 2 will set you back about €6. **Bar Egosari** for the classics and **Goiz Argi** for the prawn brochettes, C Fermin Calbeton, and **La Cepa**, C 31 de Agosto, for 'jabugo' ham, are all recommended.

JAKUE ANDIKOTXEA

22 Punta Galea big wave contest.

Transport

Driving and trying to find somewhere to park in San Sebastián can be an experience and there is no access through the old town by car. Sometimes it's best to bite the bullet and opt for the underground parking (cars only) which can limit the chances of getting broken into – around €1.50/hr or €14 for 24 hrs, good for overnights. There are a couple near the Almeda del Boulevard. The Paseo Nuevo on the headland just west of the river is a bit of a walk into town but you can usually find a spot and it's free off season. It's also a good place to park vans (but don't leave anything tempting in sight).

Directory

Surf shops There are plenty in San Sebastián, the pick of the bunch being the Pukas stores – one in the Parte Vieja on C Nagusia and another on the seafront at Av Zurriola, which is also lined with a variety of surf shops. **Hawaii**, C Bartolome near Playa Concha is another well stocked option. If you need a new board, Pukas (www.pukassurf.com) have their factory, **Olatu**, to the east in Oyarzun.
Hospitals Hospital Nuestra Señora de **Aranzazu**, on Av Doctor Begiristain near the Plaza de Toros, T943-007000. **Internet** Most of the *pensiones* offer internet access or try **Ciber Networld**, C Aldamar in Parte Viejo. **Police** The main police station is on Larramendi, T943- 450000. Dialling 091 will get you the help of the local police. **Tourist information** Reina Regente in Parte Vieje, www.donistia.org, on, open year round

Playa de Orio

Beach west of San Sebastián, just off the N-634, with showers, toilets, bars and cafés and large **campsite**, www.campingeuskadi.com/orio, open Mar-Nov.

Zarautz

Zarautz marks the start of the truly coastal route. The popular seafront is littered with candy-striped change tents and sculptures, With its combination of long sandy beach and pretty old town, it is a popular and fairly chic seaside resort and regular staging post for WQS events. The beach is also home to a good concrete midi-ramp with banks, ledges and rails.

Sleeping

The old town is set back from the beachfront and has plenty of places to eat, drink and sleep.

€€-€ Txiki Polit, Musika Plaza, T943-835357, www.txikipolit.com, is a nice option with rooms sleeping up to 5, and a cider restaurant below.

Camping Gran Camping Zarautz T943-831238, www.grancamping zarautz.com, east of Zarautz in Talaimendi, is large, open year round but gets packed out in the summer.

Eating

For cheap eats head to the old quarter which has a good range of options including **Bar/Restaurante Klery**, C Azara, where a chicken and chips *plato combinado* will set you back €8 or try the *menu del dia*. Zarautz also has a good line in *pintxos*, best sampled with a glass of *txakoli*, a tart, sparkling local wine.

Directory

Surf Shops Pukas, is on Nafarroa, the main road through town, and sells all the essentials. **Internet** **Mega Ciber**, on C Orape, next to *Txiki Polit*. **Tourist information**, C Nafarroa, www.turismozarautz.com, year round.

Run for your life

Since the sixties Pamplona's Fiesta de San Fermín has proved to be an irresistible attraction for surfers, when the streets are filled with an intoxicating mix of adrenaline, alcohol and thundering hooves, as the world famous 'running of the bulls' takes over. Starting on 7 July, six bulls are released daily at 0800 to run a course through the city to the Plaza de Toro, charging headlong through a tight warren of streets. They are accompanied by a mass of runners (dressed in white with natty red neckerchiefs) trying to stay ahead of the game and out of horns' reach. With each bull weighing more than a family car, serious injury can and does regularly happen.

Fiesta time sees prices rocket and rooms get booked up months in advance, although there may be the odd room going spare – ask at the tourist office. A popular, free and relatively hassle-free option is sleeping out in one of the parks and a left luggage store is set up for the duration of the festival on the Plaza San Francisco, next to the tourist office. **Camping Ezkaba**, T948-330315, www.campingezcaba.com, is 5 km from town and open all year. Check out the excellent www.sanfermin.com for details on every aspect of this event.

Deba

Nestled in a valley with a mountainous backdrop, pretty but functional Deba is a typical Basque working village. **Camping Itxaspe** on the N-634, 8 km from the beach, T943-199377, www.campingitxaspe.com, open year round, with apartments and bungalows sleeping 2-6. Apartments for 4 from €95.

Mutriku

The most westerly village on the coast of Gupuzkoa, this place is a camper's paradise with 4 sites to choose from: **Aritzeta**, T943-603356, east of the town, and **Santa Elena**, T943-603982, to the west, are open all year and on the Deba–Gernika route; **Galdona**, is on the same road, T943-603509, open Jul-Sep; and there's also **Saturraran**, T943-603847, open Jun-Sep.

Lekeitio

A traditional Basque village complete with a bustling fishing port. Lined with bars and cafés, this is a hotspot for holidaying locals. Accommodation is fairly pricey.

Sleeping

€€Hotel Zubieta, Portal de Atea, www.hotelzubieta.com. Open Feb-Oct. In this grand looking former coach house the rooms are pretty and intimate and the bar has a great vibe.

€ Pinupe, on Pascal Abaroa, T946-842984. One of the cheapest with a downstairs bar.

Camping **Camping Leagi**, T946-842352, www.campingleagi.com, has year-round camping on the Lekeitio-Mendexa route.

Mundaka

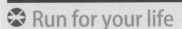

With a year-round influx of surfers and annual WCT contest, the legendary left has had a definite impact on this traditional Basque fishing village. But that's not to say it has the feel of a surf town; it doesn't. The winding, narrow cobbled streets lead to the pretty fishing harbour while the bars that cluster around it greet the surf tourists blowing through with an disinterested ambivalence. But that's all part of the charm. The unique geography that formed the awesome wave has also led to the creation of the Urdaibai Biosphere Reserve, a natural sanctuary to local flora and fauna as well as a steady stream of migrating birds, while Bilbao is just over an hour away by train or bus.

Sleeping

Accommodation in Mundaka is a little pricier than other Basque towns.

€€ Hotel Mundaka, C Florentino Larrinaga, T946-876700, www.hotelmundaka.com. The favourite with WCT surfers, has decent rooms and Wi-Fi access as well as an internet corner.

€€-€ El Puerto, on the seafront, has rooms with views over the harbour. They also have a couple of self-catering apartments available in the village – a more basic flat sleeping 4 and as well as a flat sleeping 6 costing €60-100 and €90-180 respectively

€ Albergue Islakale on Banutegúi, T946-876071, www.islakale.com. Hostel-style bunk accommodation.

Camping Portuondo, on road into Mundaka, T964-877701, www.camping portuondo.com. Year-round, has pitches and cabins and comes complete with an Aussie-style communal seating area. It's fairly pricey and the only choice for miles around – but the showers make up for it.

Eating

Hotel El Puerto, has a lovely little café overlooking the harbour – when it's warm you can sit out and watch the world go by. They do great *bocadillos de jamón*. On the main square, **Batzoika** does a good value 3-course *menú del día* for about €6 and is always busy. **El Casino**, C Kepa Deuna, also does a decent set menu for around €10.

Directory

Surf Shops Mundaka Surf Shop, C Txorrokopuntako, www.mundakasurf shop.com, is owned by ex-pat Aussie, Craig Sage, and has been serving surfers since 1983. There's always a good selection of second-hand and new boards perfect for tackling the legendary left. Their own brand is MSC, shaped by Bruce. **Internet Hotel Mundaka** has access at about €4/hr. **Chemist** On main road Goiko. **Tourist information** C Kepa Deuna near the harbour front, www.mundaka.org, closed Mon. Also in the same block are the **post office** and **police**.

Sopelana

Marking the end of the rural Basque country, this busy, grey, town services a thriving surf community, who try to keep the number of visiting surfers in check by removing and altering the *hondartza* (beach) signs. Parking is easy in front of hondartza Atxabiribil and parking overlooking La Salvaje, but car crime is prevalent. Bilbao is within easy reach, as Sopelana is a stop on the city's metro system

Sleeping

Sopelana is not exactly overrun with places to stay.

€€ 'Hotel' Goizalde, on the beach road, Av Atxabiribil, T946-763937, www.hotelgoizalde.com. Expensive for what it is and not especially nice.

Camping Camping Sopelana, T946-762120, www.campingsopelana.com, signed from the main road and open year round, is probably the best option with cabins for 1-6 people.

Eating and drinking

El Sitio is a great café to sit and watch the surf at Atxabiribil. On the road to Arrietara is **La Triangu**, a busy bar popular with local surfers, complete with boards on the walls, sport on the screens and table football. Just down the road is **Dingo**, a self-styled Aussie surf bar and restaurant – handy for Wi-Fi access.

Directory

There are a couple of surf shops on C Arrietara. On Loila Ander Deuna, the main road through town, there's a whole row of surf shops including **Waves & Wind**, **Eukaliptus**, and **Uhaina**.

Getxo

Separated by the Ría Nervion, and joined by the awesome hanging bridge, Puente Vizcaya (around E1.50 per car), Getxo and Portugalette are two very different animals. While Getxo, all relaxed elegance, is home to an international jazz, blues and folk festival, Portugalette has always been more hardworking, giving over her side of the river to industry, and more of a stopover than somewhere to stay. Parking isn't a problem on the Arrigunaga and Ereaga beachfronts.

Sleeping

There's no campsite in Getxo and the *pensiones* are usually cheaper at the weekends. During the week they are packed with business travellers from Bilbao.

€ Areeta, C Mayor, near the bridge in the popular Las Arenas district, T944-638136, is one of the best cheap options.

€ Pensión Basagoiti, on the avenue of the same name, in the Algorta district, is fairly average, T608-577446.

Directory

There are a couple of surf shops in Getxo, including **Swell/Koral Dream**, on Avenedia Basagoiti, just back from Ereaga. The **Tourist information**, on the seafront at Ereaga, is open year round.

Bilbao

Set back from the sea front and spread across the two banks, or 'bi albo', of the

DEMI TAYLOR

Flat spells

Art **The Parque de Los Pueblos de Europa** Guernika, near Mundaka is a free park dedicated to peace and filled with sculptures of Henry Moore and E Chilida. Also in Guernika, on Allende Salazar see a tile replica of the Picasso's 'Gernika', in which he immortalized the 1937 raid on the village. In Bilbao, set on the banks of the river, the **Guggenheim**, T944-359080, www.guggenheim-bilbao.es, Tue-Sun, €10, created by architect Frank Gehry, has to be seen to be believed. The curved lines of the building constructed in granite, glass and titanium create wave-like contours and can sometimes be more impressive than the art inside. Buses or trains to **Bilbao** from Mundaka leave roughly every half hour – pick up time tables from the tourist office. The train station is at the back edge of town (www.euskotren.es). The bus stop is on Goiko Kalea, the main road through Mundaka. **Cueva de Santamamiñe** is north of Guernika on the BI-635. Although closed, the caves house the 12,000 year old art of prehistoric man as well as some awesome rock formations close by. The nearby forest at Oma has been converted by visionary painter Agustín Ibarrola, into the 'Bosque Pintado de Oma' – a living work of art. Both are free and worth the short trip out.

Drinking From Jan-Apr an afternoon spent at a *sagardotegiak* (cider house) is not a wasted one. The Basque cider, which is flat and tart, is brewed in massive barrels and as part of the traditional menu (from about €25) you can use it liberally to wash down your slab of meat, cheese, quince jelly and walnuts. Pour your cider from a good height for a professional finish. Petritegi Bidea, in Astigarraga, 10 mins from San Sebastián, www.petritegi.com, is one of the few places you can sample the menu year round. See www.sagardotegiak .com (natural cider association of Guipozcoa) for details of cider presses. Alternatively try *txakoli*, a tart, dry, sparkling white wine. Head to Getaria near Zarautz to sample this local speciality.

Football At the Estadio de Anotea in San Sebastián watch **Real Sociedad**, www.realsociedad.com, take on Spain's finest. Tickets available from the stadium. In Bilbao, head to the Campo de San Mames to see **Athletic Bilbao**, www.athletic-club.net. Tickets available from the stadium from around €30.

Nervion, the capital of Bizkaia has shown the world it is more than just a working port. From agriculture, to heavy industry, to sophisticated metropolis, Bilbao has changed with the times to secure its fortune. One of its greatest successes to date, the opening of the Guggenheim Museum Bilbao has transformed it into both a tourist hotspot and thriving cultural capital. Bilbao has double and even triple parking down to a fine art, although there are a few underground car parks, including a handy one in the pedestrianized Casco Viejo, near the Plaza Nueva.

Sleeping

A lot of the accommodation gets pretty booked up so if you want to be sure of somewhere to lay your head, call ahead. The Casco Viejo, over the river from the train station, has the best selection of cheap sleeping options as well as a dense population of bars and cafés.

€€ Iturrienea Ostatua, C Santa Maria, is a lovely, reasonably priced pension with exposed beams and quirky touches surrounded by cobbled streets that lead to some of the city's best pintxos.

€ Pensión Ladero, on Lotería, T944-150932, is probably one of the cheapest with rooms and shared bathrooms from about €23.

€ Gurea on Bidebarrieta, T944-163299, is another very cheap and basic option.

Eating

Hit the pintxos path – in the old town start out at the Plaza Nueva, **Victor Montes** if you can squeeze in, then head and on to C Santa María, which has its fair share of bars including the relaxed **Irintzi**and popular **Gatz**. Cutting across it, C Jardines is home to **Berton**, which is packed with hooves on the ceiling and people at the weekend. The **Siete Calles** (7 streets) is the oldest part of town with fantastic ambience and pintxos to match.

Transport

An easy way to get round the city, apart from on foot, is using the metro – a day pass will set you back about €3.

Directory

Surf Shops **Wakalouka**, C Diputazio, www.wakalouka.es, as with many shops here is more of a boutique but also sells a good range of boards and hardware **Internet** **Laser Internet**, C Sendeja, on the east bank of the river, charges by the min. **Hospital** **Hospital de Basurto**, on Av Montevideo, T944-006000. **Police** Policía Municipal on Luis Brinas; emergency T092. **Post office** There are 2; one in the centre on Alameda Urquijo and the other in the Casco Viejo on Epalza. **Tourist information** Several including one just off the river in the Casco Viejo on Arenal, open year round, www.bilbao.net.

Overview

The modern, clinical black tarmac of the E-70 cuts a clean swathe through the lush green of the Cantabrian countryside, a 20th-century artery feeding tourists along the northern fringes of one of Spain's most picturesque regions. A province where the Spanish come to holiday, its stunning coastline is watched over by the towering limestone of the Picos de Europa – crawling with walkers and naturalists in the summer, snowcapped in the winter and a suitably dramatic year-round backdrop to some of the continent's most spectacular surf breaks. For those racing along the auto-route, attention focused on the white line, this panorama is all but lost in a peripheral blur.

For centuries pilgrims have walked the coastal fringe of northern Spain, trudging west through the regions of Euskadi, Cantabria, Asturias and Galicia to the holy city of Santiago de Compostela. You still see them today, slowly making their steady progress along the old coastal road, now mainly left to the local cars and lorries which speed by on the school run or delivering groceries. Yet the pilgrims have time to notice every curve in the shore, the beauty in the strange, cylindrical waves rolling down the rocky point, the dark silhouettes bobbing in the line-up. For those who really want to explore this diverse and challenging coastline, the motorway must be sacrificed for the winding ocean-side crawl. Time spent stuck behind a lazy tractor may be rewarded with the glimpse of a reef that would have been missed had they not been forced to slow down. The surfing pilgrimage is all about sacrifice. Sacrificing the time to make the journey. Sacrificing the known for the unknown. And to the pilgrim, the sacrifice may ultimately bring reward. On the coastal routes first used centuries ago by those making the long trek to Santiago lie some truly enlightening experiences – for those who keep their eyes open for the signs.

Coastline

Cantabrian breaks east of Laredo sit in pristine countryside but, protected by the headland between Noja and Santander, pick up less swell than those to the west. Breaks around Galizano and Suances are some of Europe's best and their northwesterly orientation means they are swell magnets. The natural harbour of prosperous Santander severs the coast. It is Spain's principal port and a first entry point for many entering the country via the ferry link from the UK. While not as lively as San Sebastián, the many tapas bars and seafood restaurants serve as a gentle introduction to the Spanish experience. Just

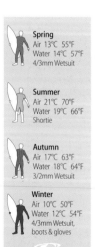

Spring
Air 13°C 55°F
Water 14°C 57°F
4/3mm Wetsuit

Summer
Air 21°C 70°F
Water 19°C 66°F
Shortie

Autumn
Air 17°C 63°F
Water 18°C 64°F
3/2mm Wetsuit

Winter
Air 10°C 50°F
Water 12°C 54°F
4/3mm Wetsuit, boots & gloves

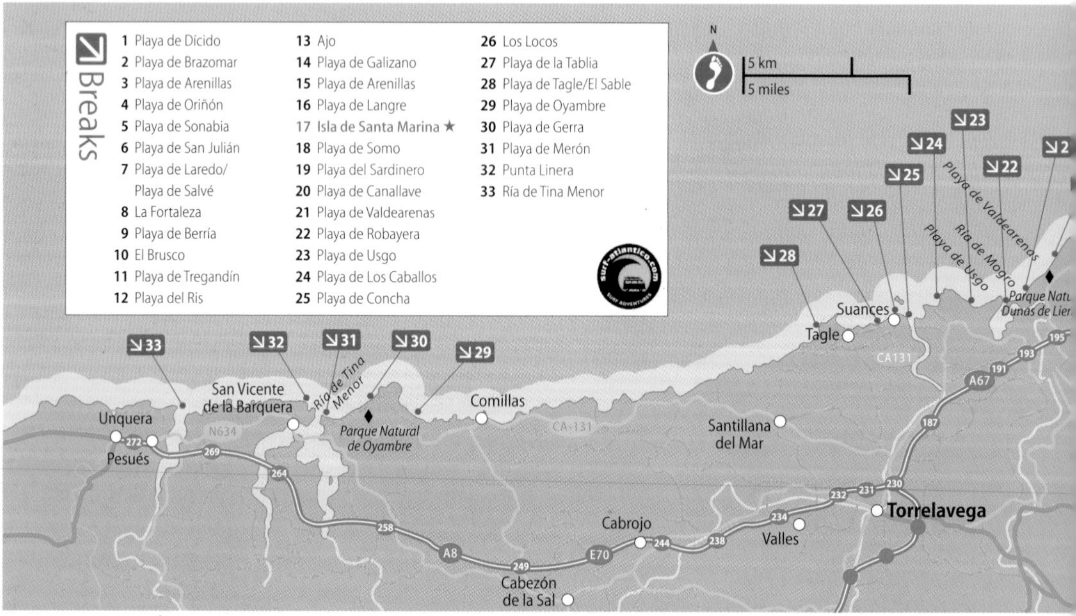

5'10" Xanadu Rocky

Shaper: Xanadu

5'10" x 19¾" x 2$^{1}/_{16}$"

Built with Surftech's proven TUFLITE construction.

Flatter entry rocker with rounder outline,"wider nose, wider tail" makes up for shorter length. Should be 4" -6" shorter than shortboard. Flatter deck makes the rails fuller for better performance in smaller waves. Can be tri-fin, twin fin, or with small trailer fin.

FCS YU fins.

6'2" Rawson Hyper-Skate

Shaper: Pat Rawson

6'2" x 18¼" x 2¼"

Built with Surftech's proven TUFLITE construction.

The 6'2" Hyper-Skate is a high performance single concave design with added double concave over the bottom half of the plan shape. A touch of vee behind the fins make this design ideal for all conditions worldwide.

Futures FTP1 fins.

15 km west of the city, Liencres plays host to the Parque Natural Dunas de Liencres – the region's longest stretch of sand and the scene of some high-quality, consistent beach breaks. Further west, the surf spots around Oyambre also sit in beautiful national parkland and have a relaxed atmosphere. The flexible jagged coastline, with coves and inlets, means there will always be waves to surf somewhere – if you don't mind a bit of a drive.

Local environment

Some rivermouth breaks can suffer from industrial pollution, for example at La Concha. Out of season, the resort of Laredo has a lot of beach litter and can suffer from pollution discharged into the sea. The breaks around the busy port of Santander can also be affected by common urban and industrial pollution. Many of the breaks around Cantabria sit in countryside and, during the week, can be surprisingly quiet and laid-back. "Normally, most of the people here are friendly in the water, so with a good attitude you won't have any problems and you will really enjoy it," says local pro, Michel Velasco. Despite the recent boom in surf schools, there has only been a real increase in summer surfers. Several surfing hotspots do draw big crowds – Los Locos and Los Caballos get busy during peak times – and there can be some tension in the line-up. Car crime has also been a problem at Los Caballos. El Brusco is always busy when it's working and has developed a reputation as a localized spot. The popular resort Noja can get crazy busy during the summer.

More common in the countryside areas is the strategic removal of beach signs, which means that a bit of exploring is sometimes needed to actually find the break.

Getting around

The road system through Cantabria is very good. The coastal roads, such as the N-634 in the east, the CA-141 from Noja, the CA-231 from Santander, and the CA-131 from Suances all provide good access to the breaks. The A-8 motorway dissects the county and provides a fast, toll-free route that stays close to the coastline. Much of the road system is of a good standard with an ongoing motorway improvement programme. A run straight across the region should take around 1½ hours.

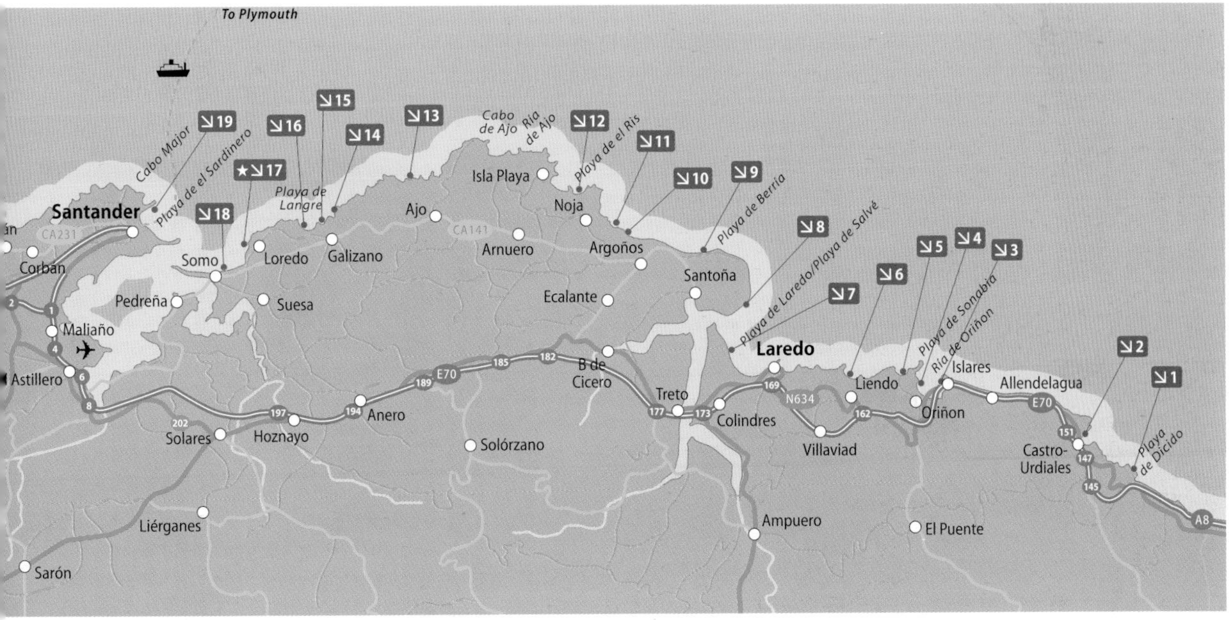

Breaks

BEACH BREAK

↘1 Playa de Dícido

- **Conditions** Medium to big N to NW swells, offshore in S to SW wind
- **Hazards/tips** Suitable for all surfers
- **Sleeping** Castro Urdiales » *p231*

This small, sheltered, crescent-shaped sandy bay is visible from the N-634 coast road. Works in big northwesterly swells with hollow peaks that are best at low tide. It's usually uncrowded and offshore in a southerly wind. Small village with a climbing wall outside the local sports centre.

BEACH BREAK

↘2 Playa de Brazomar

- **Conditions** Big N to NW swells, offshore in SE winds
- **Hazards/tips** Parking available near the beach
- **Sleeping** Castro Urdiales » *p231*

This is one of the town beaches at the popular summer vacation spot of Castro Urdiales. The bay is quite sheltered from swell and so only usually comes to life out of the tourist season. When it works there are peaks on this sandy beach, best at low tide.

BEACH BREAK

↘3 Playa de Arenillas

- **Conditions** Medium NW swells, offshore in S winds
- **Hazards/tips** Rips can be present in big swells on a dropping tide
- **Sleeping** Islares/Oriñón » *p231*

At the Ría de Oriñón the mountains plunge dramatically into the sea, framing this picturesque rivermouth. Right-handers peel towards the river over sand, from the eastern bank and work best in medium swells at low to mid tide. Can have some very good waves but maxes out in big northwesterly swells. Waves break in front of rocks. Parking is available by the popular restaurant Lantarón Hosteria.

JAKUE ANDIKOTXEA

4 Playa de Oriñon.

BEACH BREAK

↘4 Playa de Oriñón

- **Conditions** Medium NW swell, offshore in S wind
- **Hazards/tips** Rips near the river
- **Sleeping** Islares/Oriñón » *p231*

On the opposite bank to Arenillas is a wide beach where good quality waves can be found. Decent lefts peel into the rivermouth, from low through mid tide. In bigger swells, good quality peaks can be found on the western side of the beach. A popular holiday spot that is very quiet out of season. Can be checked from the motorway and the N-634.

BEACH BREAK

↘5 Playa de Sonabia

- **Conditions** Medium NW swells, offshore in S winds
- **Hazards/tips** Quiet, picturesque spot
- **Sleeping** Islares/Oriñón » *p231*

A quiet, cliff-lined beach that works best at low tide producing peaky waves. Follow the road round from Oriñón.

BEACH BREAK

↘6 Playa de San Julián

- **Conditions** Medium to big NW swells, offshore in SW winds
- **Hazards/tips** Beautiful and quiet location, perfect to escape the crowds
- **Sleeping** Laredo » *p231*

Small, crescent-shaped sandy beach nestled under impressive cliffs. Best at low, in a big northwesterly swell it can have either a peak or hollow, wedgy right-handers. Offshore in a southwesterly or westerly wind, but the surrounding hills provide a lot of shelter. Can be hard to find as local surfers have removed the signs. If you pass the shrine to San Julián, you're on the right track. Cliff-top parking.

BEACH BREAK

↘7 Playa de Laredo/ Playa de Salvé

- **Conditions** Big N to NW swells, offshore in W winds
- **Hazards/tips** Suitable for all surfers. A good place to head for in stormy, westerly conditions
- **Sleeping** Laredo » *p231*

The resort town of Laredo has a huge stretch of northeasterly facing sands. In big conditions swell wraps into the beach, which offers the flexibility of being offshore in south, southwesterly and westerly winds. Wave quality varies with conditions, but this is a popular beach with local surfers working through all the tides. Dirty beach out of season. In the winter drizzle it's a bleak, urban break but it comes to life in the summer as a popular holiday spot – though it is usually flat then. Banks vary and huge sections of the beach can close out. The middle of the beach is worth checking. A road runs along the length of the massive crescent-shaped beach, one block back from the seafront, providing easy access and good parking off season.

POINT BREAK

↘8 La Fortaleza

- **Conditions** Big, clean NW swells, offshore in W to S winds
- **Hazards/tips** Known as Spain's Chicama
- **Sleeping** Laredo/Santoña » *p231*

This is one of Spain's classic surf spots, but a rare and sought-after beast. When conditions combine, long, long, left-hand waves wrap around the point – but only in the biggest swells. The reeling walls attract a large local crew who wait for such a day, so if you're lucky enough to score here, take your turn and be prepared for a long paddle. Works best from low to mid tide with light west to southerly winds.

WILLY URIBE

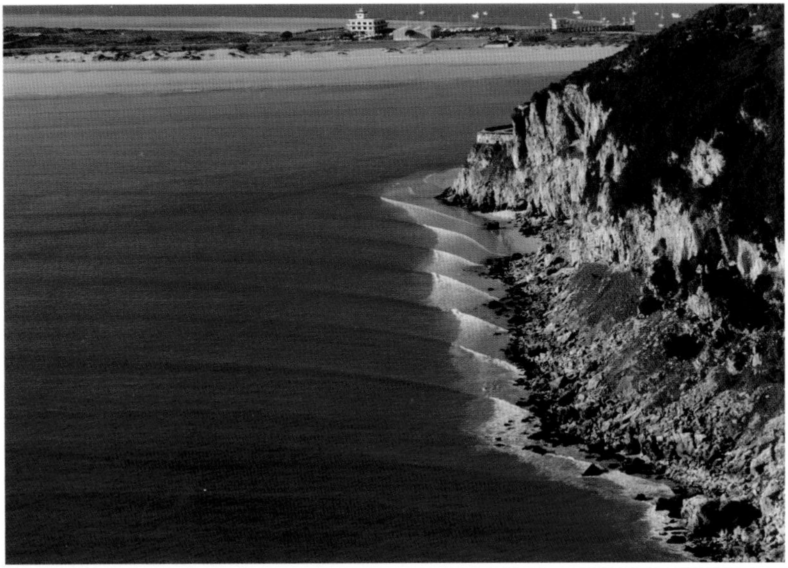

8 The rare sight of firing Fortaleza.

BEACH BREAK

↘9 Playa de Berría

- **Conditions** Small to medium NW swells, offshore in S to SW winds
- **Hazards/tips** Eastern end of the bay picks up the most swell, cliffs offer protection from easterly wind
- **Sleeping** Santoña » *p231*

A long sandy beach that works through all states of tides. Can have some excellent hollow waves and consequently is popular with local surfers. This break hoovers up any swell in the Laredo/Santoña area. A pretty beach that isn't spoilt by the fact that it's overlooked by an imposing prison and a cemetery.

BEACH BREAK

↘10 El Brusco

- **Conditions** Medium to big NW swells, offshore in S winds
- **Hazards/tips** Localism, heavy waves, crowds. Access along the beach road until you can drive no more
- **Sleeping** Santoña/Noja » *p231*

Situated at the far eastern end of Tregandín beach (where the rocks stop), this beach break has a reputation as a bit of a Spanish 'Supertubes', producing waves of excellent quality – fast hollow barrels and reeling walls. "It has two main peaks that give powerful rights and lefts," says Michel Velasco. "It's not a long wave, so you have to make good use of the beginning (section) to get a hollow tube and after this start doing turns, airs, etc." Works best at high tide and in a southerly wind, when board-snapping lefts will be visible from the car park. It has a reputation as a bit of a localized spot, so bear this in mind. Picks up less swell than Ris to the west.

BEACH BREAK

↘11 Playa de Tregandín

- **Conditions** Big NW swell, offshore in southerly winds
- **Hazards/tips** Rocks!
- **Sleeping** Santoña/Noja » *p231*

Needs a big northwesterly swell to produce left-hand walls along a low tide sandbar, offshore in southerly or southeasterly winds. This beach has scattered jagged rocks that look like tank traps on a Normandy landing beach. Excellent skatepark on the beach road with concrete bowl, midi, rails and even concrete cars to skate, plus a climbing wall.

BEACH BREAK

↘12 Playa del Ris

- **Conditions** Small to big N to NW swells, offshore in SW to SE winds
- **Hazards/tips** Crowds and some localism
- **Sleeping** Noja » *p231*

North of the resort of Noja is this popular and consistent crescent-shaped beach break. Picks up loads of swell and can produce some excellent hollow waves. Works through the tides, but best at high. Gets crowded when good and in the summer. Very sheltered from the wind and picks up most swell in the Noja area. Campsites at the western end.

DEMI TAYLOR

BEACH BREAK

↘13 Ajo

- **Conditions** Small to medium NW swells, offshore in S winds
- **Hazards/tips** Left breaks off the western end of the beach when big
- **Sleeping** Ajo » *p232*

Playa de Cuberris and **Playa de Antuerta** both consistently produce good waves in small and medium northwesterly swells and work best from low to mid tide. This is a good sized beach which picks up lots of swell. Suitable for all surfers. Beach parking.

Left: 12 Playa del Ris.
Below: 10 El Brusco.

JAKUE ANDIKOTXEA

BEACH AND RIVERMOUTH BREAK

↘14 Playa de Galizano

- **Conditions** Small to medium NW swells, offshore in SE winds
- **Hazards/tips** Locals have removed sign to beach. Also known as La Canal
- **Sleeping** Loredo » *p232*

A low-tide, rivermouth beach break with powerful, hollow rights at the east and lefts at the western side. Can produce excellent waves in a medium swell and works up to 6 ft, where stand-up barrels are common. This small bay disappears at high tide.

BEACH BREAK

↘15 Playa de Arenillas

- **Conditions** Small to medium NW swells, offshore in S to SW winds
- **Hazards/tips** Take the CA-441, hang a left at the 1 km marker
- **Sleeping** Loredo » *p232*

This small, sandy bay is surrounded by cliffs and can produce some excellent, long walling or barreling waves. At the west end a left peels off a sandbar formed on a rocky outcrop and on the eastern end right-handers can be found. Works best from low to mid tide and is offshore in a southerly or southwesterly wind. Can hold up to a 6-ft swell. Popular fishing spot. Both here and Galizano becoming busier.

BEACH BREAK

↘16 Playa de Langre

- **Conditions** Small to medium swells, offshore in south/southwesterly winds.
- **Hazards/tips** Picturesque and quiet stretch of coastline.
- **Sleeping** Loredo » *p232*

Another cliff-lined bay immediately west of Arenillas, works best from low to mid tide. The cliffs here offer some protection from the wind. Good peaks. Larger yet more sheltered bay with a good left that can be found at the western end.

SAND/REEF BREAK

↘17 Isla de Santa Marina

- **Swell** N to NW
- **Wind** SE
- **Tide** Mid-high
- **Size** 6-12 ft plus
- **Length** 50-200 m plus
- **Bottom** Sand and rock
- **Ability Level** Advanced/ big wave surfers
- **Best Months** Nov-Apr
- **Board** Semi-gun
- **Access** Long paddle out from beach
- **Hazards/tips** Just about all the difficulties you could imagine. Take-off peppered with huge rocks at low.
- **Sleeping** Loredo ›› p232

Isla de Santa Marina is an offshore wildlife sanctuary that also doubles as the region's premier big-wave spot. A powerful right-hander reels down the western side of the rocky island – from take off, a long, macking wall hollows out into a gaping, inside section. Dominated by local big-wave chargers, access is via a long paddle from the rocks between the eastern end of Playa de Loredo and the small car park overlooking the island. The surf is always way bigger than it looks and without someone in the line-up to give it some scale you may find the 3 ft surf you were expecting is nearer three times that. Surfers at this break have long hold-downs, broken boards and rocks to contend with, but the payback is some awesome, huge barrelling waves. "You can surf it really big, it holds any size", says Santa Marina regular Michel Velasco. "I feel really good surfing (here) – the bigger the better. It's a huge rush of adrenaline." Catch it on the right day and it has a feel of a mini-Mavericks. Access from Loredo, out past the campsite, and then turn left onto the headland. In the right conditions, a wedgy left-hander breaks on the eastern side of the island.

If you like Isla de Santa Marina, try Meñakoz (see page 216) or Tullaghan in Ireland (see page 125).

JAKUE ANDIKOTXEA

BEACH BREAK

↘18 Playa de Somo

- **Conditions** Small to medium N to NW swells, offshore in S winds
- **Hazards/tips** Crowds from nearby Santander
- **Sleeping** Loredo/Santander ›› p232

Somo is a high quality beach break that can produce some quality sandbanks. Usually works through all tides and this consistency, combined with the fact that the beach looks over to Santander, ensures that when it's on, it always draws a crowd. This big sandy beach is suitable for surfers of all abilities. A pretty, dune-backed shoreline that joins up with Loredo to create a massive beach. Maxes out in surf over 6 ft.

JAKUE ANDIKOTXEA

Top: 17 Santa Marina beginning to turn up the heat.
Above: 18 Consistent Somo.

BEACH BREAK

↘19 Playa del Sardinero

- **Conditions** Big N to NW swells, offshore in W winds
- **Hazards/tips** Crowded urban beach with usual amenities, suitable for all
- **Sleeping** Santander ›› p232

As the main town beach for Santander, there are usually some surfers in the water, even when small and onshore, and with a decent swell it will be heaving. Needs a really big north or northwesterly swell to get any quality waves, with a westerly or north-westerly/southwesterly wind. Surfing is banned in the summer but there is usually no swell here in any case.

DEMI TAYLOR

WILLY URIBE

Above: 23 Playa de Usgo. Right: 19 Surfing at urban Santander.

BEACH BREAK

↘20 Playa de Canallave

- **Conditions** Small to medium NW swells, offshore in S to SE winds
- **Hazards/tips** Crowds in summer, localism
- **Sleeping** Liencres ›› *p233*

After the town beaches of Santander, this is a refreshing change: drive down through the beautiful national park of lush evergreen trees and park up among the sand dunes. **Parque Natural Dunas de Liencres** is a great backdrop to the longest stretch of beach in Cantabria – home to some world-class beach breaks. Canallave is one of the area's most consistent and high-quality spots working through the tides, except for high. **La Lastra** produces fast, hollow right-handers. This is quite a large stretch with plenty of banks to spread out, but like many breaks in this area, **Canallave** has a number of highly competitive local surfers and there may be localism issues when crowded. The banks nearest the car parks fill up first. On the plus side, there is loads of parking and good facilities.

BEACH BREAK

↘21 Playa de Valdearenas

- **Conditions** Small to medium NW swells, offshore in S to SE winds
- **Hazards/tips** Crowded spot in the summer, some localism, quieter out of season
- **Sleeping** Liencres ›› *p233*

A high-quality, sandy beach that spreads out to the west of Canallave. It picks up loads of swell and produces sucky, fast and powerful waves in northwesterly swells. Works through all tides. Again, a big beach where the peaks nearest to the car park fill up first. Doesn't handle a big swell.

RIVERMOUTH BREAK

↘22 Playa de Robayera

- **Conditions** Medium NW swells, offshore in S to SE winds
- **Hazards/tips** Can be crowded spot, rips in big swells and dropping tides, not suitable for inexperienced surfers
- **Sleeping** Liencres ›› *p233*

This sandy rivermouth break has excellent, fast and hollow lefts. These peel from the rocky stack at the western (rivermouth) end of the beach, with peaks further to the east. This is quite a consistent spot where a quality sandbank is formed in the Ría de Mogrois. Best at low to mid tides on the push. Watch out for rips.

BEACH BREAK

↘23 Playa de Usgo

- **Conditions** Small to medium NW swells, offshore in S to SW winds
- **Hazards/tips** Usually uncrowded
- **Sleeping** Liencres ›› *p233*

A crescent-shaped beach that works best on a small to medium swell but tends to close out over 6 ft. At low to mid tide, wedgy rights break off the banks with some powerful, hollow waves on offer.

REEF AND BEACH BREAK

↘24 Playa de Los Caballos

- **Conditions** Small to medium NW swells, offshore in S to SE winds
- **Hazards/tips** Crowds, localism, car crime
- **Sleeping** Liencres ›› *p233*

This crescent-shaped, cliff-lined bay is an excellent spot, with high-quality waves on offer from low to mid tide. A left peels off a sand-covered rocky finger of reef while beach-break peaks can be found in the bay. Above 6 ft there tends to be too much water moving around to work properly. Can be crowded and locals can be aggressive. Car crime has been a problem so park carefully. Take the road to Playa de Cuchia and bear right.

DEMI TAYLOR

DEMI TAYLOR

Above: 25 East of the rivermouth breaks a long, walling right. **Left: 24** Los Caballos.

BEACH BREAK AND RIVERMOUTH

↘25 Playa de Concha

- **Conditions** Big NW swells, offshore in S swells
- **Hazards/tips** Very poor water quality due to river pollution
- **Sleeping** Suances » *p233*

Concha needs a big swell to get going, but when it does, quality lefts and rights peel at low tide while the beach works through the tides and can have good rights. A good place to check is from the road out to Los Locos. From Los Caballos to Concha is a frustrating 30-minute round trip just to reach the other side of the narrow river. The road heads inland, crosses the bridge, before heading back out to the coast; you will notice the factories.

BEACH BREAK

↘26 Los Locos

- **Conditions** All NW swells, offshore in S winds
- **Hazards/tips** Consistent beach, gets busy, localism
- **Sleeping** Suances » *p233*

One of the most popular and consistent breaks in the area, busy whenever a northwesterly groundswell hits this excellent beach break. Fast hollow barrels and long walls form in small and medium swells. Gets crowded in the summer, at weekends and during lunch, though it is still possible to score it pretty uncrowded early in the day and out of summer season. Works through the tidal range and areas of the bay are offshore in south, southeasterly, easterly and northeasterly winds, making this a very flexible beach. Has a reputation for localism when busy. Follow the signs from Suances. Plenty of parking available on top of the cliffs.

BEACH BREAK

↘27 Playa de la Tablia

- **Conditions** Small to medium NW swells, offshore in S to SE winds
- **Hazards/tips** Crowds in summer, car crime
- **Sleeping** Suances » *p233*

Next bay along from Los Locos, La Tablia is another cliff-lined beachie that has peaks in the middle of the bay and lefts at the western end. Works from low tide on the push, but the beach disappears at high. Again, another high quality break that can get busy, especially at weekends. As with all the breaks in this area, it is advisable to be careful about where you park your car and what you leave visible inside. Follow the coast road west and look for 'La Tablia' building. Park on the cliff top.

BEACH BREAK

↘28 Playa de Tagle/El Sable

- **Conditions** Medium NW swells, offshore in S to SE winds
- **Hazards/tips** Picturesque, quiet beach
- **Sleeping** Suances » *p233*

Follow the signs down to this smallish bay overlooked from the headland by a wind-ravaged ruin. Tagle is a sandy beach with good lefts and rights in medium swells. Waves can be fast and powerful with barrels at low tide, but the beach disappears at high. This picturesque location can be a quiet spot off-season. The car park has a little touch of Malibu with some great and subtle 'Da Cat Vive' graffiti as well as a café and shower.

BEACH BREAK

↘29 Playa de Oyambre

- **Conditions** Medium to big NW swells, offshore in S to SW winds
- **Hazards/tips** Sheltered in big westerly storms
- **Sleeping** Oyambre » *p233*

O'NEILL

JUAN FERNANDEZ

Above: The beaches of Northern Spain can really pack a punch as rising star Raphael Ayme discovers.
Right: 26 Pablo Solar enjoying the quality of Liencres.

This long, flat sandy beach is set in the beautiful countryside of the Parque Natural de Oyambre. It is quite sheltered from northwesterly swells and works on all tides, but is best from low to mid. Needs a big north or northwesterly swell, and winds from the south, southwest or west, to produce lefts and rights. Average waves along most of the beach, but the banks can throw up high-quality peaks. The western end is very sheltered and is the place to hit in big westerly storms.

BEACH BREAK

↘30 Playa de Gerra

- **Conditions** Small to medium NW swells, offshore in S to SE swells
- **Hazards/tips** Excellent banks, big beach, in national park
- **Sleeping** Oyambre ›› *p233*

Overlooked by green pasture, this stretch of beach can produce Hossegor-style waves. The break has some excellent banks and throws up consistent hollow waves. Off season it is a good place to escape the crowds. This pretty location has peaks along its 1-km length and works through all states of tide. Look for the signs to the surf school where there is a car park; in front are some really nice peaks. To the west there is beachfront parking. This beach is also part of the Parque Natural de Oyambre.

BEACH BREAK

↘31 Playa de Merón

- **Conditions** Medium NW swells, offshore in S to SW winds
- **Hazards/tips** Town beach in San Vicente
- **Sleeping** Oyambre/San Vicente de la Barquera ›› *p233*

The beach from Gerra runs west until it joins up with this sandy rivermouth spot, a popular place for local and travelling surfers alike. Banks can produce excellent, fast and hollow waves at all states of tides. It has a rocky jetty with a lighthouse. These sucky waves are slightly sheltered from a westerly wind.

POINT BREAK

↘32 Punta Linera

- **Conditions** Medium N to NW swell, offshore in S winds
- **Hazards/tips** Beautiful, rugged, typically Celtic spot
- **Sleeping** San Vicente de la Barquera ›› *p233*

Fairly exposed, consistent, flat rock point that produces fast and sometimes hollow lefts. Worth checking as the waves can be excellent and the crowds quite small. Is offshore in south and southeasterly winds. Works from low on the push with long rides possible. Drive out of town following signs to the *punta*. Small car park overlooks the break.

BEACH BREAK

↘33 Ría de Tina Menor

- **Conditions** Small clean NW swells, offshore in S winds
- **Hazards/tips** Very quiet, crystal clean water, difficult access
- **Sleeping** San Vicente de la Barquera ›› *p233*

This low-tide, rivermouth right-hander breaks over a sandbar and occupies a spectacular setting: the ría winds through a plunging gorge to the sea where hanging cliffs overlook this very sheltered break. This spot needs a small, clean swell and is offshore in a south or southwesterly wind. Access – now there's the trick!

Practicalities

Castro Urdiales

Heading west, this is the first coastal town in Cantabria, complete with Gothic church, working harbour, castle-cum-lighthouse and a beach – Brazomar.

Sleeping

There are quite a few *pensión* options around the port.
€ Losio, on Los Huertos to the west of the harbour, is one of the cheapest, T942-860299.
Camping Castro, Easter-Sep, is about 1 km from the beach.

Eating and drinking

The fish is excellent. Good cheap eats can be found on Bilbao, La Mar and Ardigales.
Bajamar, C La Mar, good *menú del día* €8.

Directory

Surf shops Banzai Surf, C Ardigales, back from the harbour. **Tourist information** Av de la Constitución, near harbour, www.turismo.cantabria.org, year round.

Islares and Oriñón

Sleeping

€€-€ Hostería Lantarón, on the beach, T942-862212. Has spa centre offering thallasotherapy, decent accommodation and popular lunchtime spot.
Camping Just off the N-634, Playa de Arenillas is serviced by campsite **Playa Arenillas**, T942-863152, www.cantabria.com, 1 Apr-30 Sep, also offers bungalows. Across the river, **Oriñón** overlooks the beach, T942-878630. Not the prettiest of campsites, open May-Sep.

Laredo

This lively summer resort town is home to Salvé – a 5-km stretch of golden sands and decent waves. In winter, the town pretty much shuts down – condoms and crap replace towels and tourists on the beach.

DEMI TAYLOR

13 Swell magnet Ajo.

Sleeping

€€-€ Hotel Cortijo, Av Gonzalez Gallego, is no great shakes but only 30 m from La Salvaje beach.
€ Cantabria, T942-605073, and **€ Salomón**, T942-605081, both on Menéndez Pelayo, are fairly average and open year round.
Camping There are several summer opening campsites: **Playa del Regatón**, on the Laredo-Regatón road, Apr-Sep plus Easter, T942-606995, is just back from the beach and also has apartments available; **Laredo**, on the Irún-A Coruña road, T942-605035, www.campinglaredo.com, Jun-Sep plus Easter week and weekend opening Easter onwards.

Directory

Surf shops Atlantic and **New Wind**, C Marquís Comilla, the main town road, and **Chacahua**, where you can pick up all your surf essentials, on Menéndez Pelay. **Tourist information** Alameda de Miramar, year round.

Santoña

The basic, functional camping compound **Playa de Berría**, T942-662248, may be hemmed in by a prison to its rear and a cemetery to the east, but it does have an awesome view and fantastic access to the beach. Open Jun-15 Sep plus Easter.

Noja

Another popular, sprawling seaside resort with no real core, which turns into a ghost town off season. On the beachfront at Tregandin however is a great concrete skatepark with bowl, midi ramp and even concrete cars to abuse.

Sleeping

€€ Hotel Juncos, Playa Ris, www.hotellos juncos.com, is clean and some rooms have little balconies overlooking the beach.
€€ Las Olas, overlooks Trengandin. The rooms are fine if a little sterile.
€ Residencia Ris, Av de Ris, T942-630131, is one of the cheapest *pensiones*.
Camping The camping is centred around Playa Ris, to the west of the town, including:

 Playa de Ris,T942-630415, Apr-Sep; **Suaces**, T942-630324, 15 Apr-30 Sep; and the massive **Playa Joyel**, T942-630081, www.playajoyel.com, Apr-Sep, with bungalows and mobile homes. **Los Molinos**, is further west on La Ría, T942-630426, www.campinglosmolinos.com, open Apr-Sep, and offers bungalows.

Eating and drinking

The main square has a couple of good breakfast options – **El Horno** bakery, or **Plaza Cafetería** for an eat-in option

Ajo

Travelling west along the CA-141, the little village of Ajo has a couple of campsites. **Arenas**, 100 m from the beach, T942-670663, is open year round. For food, Michel Velasco recommends the paella at **Restaurante Labu**, on Av Benedicto Ruiz.

Loredo

Across a small stretch of water from Santander, hidden among the trees, Loredo has plenty of camping options as well as basic amenities to satisfy the steady influx of visitors and holidaymakers. Year round try **El Arbolado**, 500 m from the beachfront on the Loredo-Ribamontan al Mar road, T942-504414. The larger **Rocamar** has good access to Isla de Santa Marina and a half pipe opposite, T942-504455.

Somo

Just down the road from Loredo, Somo also services the area and is a good base, just outside of the city.

Sleeping

€ Hong Kong, on Las Quebrantas, T942-510013, is one of the cheapest *pensiones*.
€ Hostal Meve, in the centre, T9420-510279, is fairly quaint and used to surfers. Also has self-catering apartments.
Camping **Somo Parque**, just inland towards Suesa, T942-510309, www.somoparque.com, open year round, with bungalows. **Latas**, is just 200 m from the beach, T942-510249, 15 Jun-15 Sep only.

Eating and drinking

Michel Velasco recommends **Mar Salada**, run by surfers and a great place for some post-surf fare and ambience.

Directory

Surf shops **Xpeedin'**, Isla de Mouro, is well stocked and has been around since the 1970s. **Tourist information** Av de Trasmiera, summer only.

Santander

This port town doesn't have the same buzz or beach culture as, say, San Sebastián. It's a more sedate experience and, if you've just stepped off the ferry, is a gentle introduction to Spain with plenty of places to stay, eat and drink. Off season there's plenty of beachside parking. Summer is a different matter and using the underground parking may prove a good option for cars.

Sleeping

Santander can be pricey, especially around the upmarket Sardinero area in the summer. For cheap accommodation, head for the area around the bus station and ferry port.
€ La Corza, C Hernán Cortés, T942-212950, is a good option, handy for eating and drinking also well placed for underground parking and the ferry. Some rooms come with enclosed balconies overlooking the plaza.
€ Gran Antila, C Isabel II, T942-213100, large, basic and cheap.
€ Los Caracoles, on Marina – just off Hernán Cortés, T942-212697. Not glamorous but another cheap option well located for eating and drinking.
Camping If you've just driven your van off the ferry and want to camp over, **Cabo Mayor**, to the north of Sardinero, T942-391542, is handy, but is only open Apr-15 Oct. The smaller **Virgen del Mar**, is just out of town on the CA-231 San Román–Corbán road, T942-342425, www.campingvirgenmar.com. Mar-Dec,

Flat spells

Sightseeing **Ramales de La Victoria**, southeast of Laredo on the N-629, has an entire series of caves. Covalanas has the most impressive Palaeolithic paintings and free entry. The spa town of **Puente Viesgo**, south of Santander on the N-632 (T942-598425, 45 minutes, €2), is home to a series of caves, deep in the heart of Castillo Mount, again featuring the paintings of Palaeolithic man. Open to the public through guided tours. **Altamira**, by Santillana del Mar, south of Suances, houses 14,000-year-old paintings of bison, boar and deer. The caves are closed to the public to preserve the paintings in its place they've opened **Neocueva** (T942-818815, closed Monday, €2.40) a replica cave and museum which is only so interesting. **Potes**, south of Oyambre, on the N-621, has plenty of activities for flat days, including kayak, rafting, paragliding. Check out **Europicos**, T942 730 724, www.europicos.com, for details. Dani García recommends the nearby **Picos de Europa** for walking and climbing. **Santillana del Mar**, just southeast of Suances, is a beautiful medieval town. Avoid in peak summer when it gets swamped.

Skiing/snowboarding Michel Velasco recommends the ski resort of **Alto Campoo**, which is only an hour and a half from the coast. From Santander, drive south to then follow the CA-183 eastbound to the resort. Check there's snow before you go (T942-779222, www.altocampoo.com.

chalets are available sleeping up to 8 people.

Eating and drinking

For some of the freshest and cheapest – but not necessarily most upmarket – dishes around, get down to the Barrio Pesquero (fishing port). For tapas head for the Plaza Canadio and check out the roads leading off it, including Daoiz y Verlade, home to the heaving **Casa Ajero**. Hernán Cortés also has a great selection of tapas bars and bodegas including **Bodega Bringas**, and the popular old **Bodega Mazón**. For some of the best *chocolate y churros* in Spain don't miss **Chocolatería Aliva**, on Daoiz y Verlade, open 0700-1200 and 1700-2130, where fur coats rub shoulders with overalls.

Directory

Internet **Heladería Lugano**, C Hernán Cortés, is a café/ice-cream shop/cyber bar. In the shopping district try **Insistel**, on Méndez Nuñez. **Surf shops** Santander has a thriving surf community and as such has plenty of specialist stores – **Surf 33**, off Cadiz, is near the bus station and has a good range of hardware, as does **Sports Aventura**, on C Reina Victoria, and **Black Ball**, on C Panama, both back from Sardineiro. If you're in the market for a new board, **Full & Cas Surfboards** www.fullcas.com, are based just south of Santander, in the Camargo, and shape boards for some of Spain's top surfers including Pablo Gutierrez. **Tourist information**, in the Mercado del Este, open year round, extremely efficient with info on the whole region.

Liencres

Though just 15 km from Santander, Liencres is a world away, with Cantabria's longest stretch of sand dunes, the Parque Natural Dunas de Liencre.

Sleeping

Camping **Playa de Arnia**, is right on the beach at Arnia, T942-579450, but is small and only open mid-Jun to mid-Sep. West of the national park, Playa Mogro offers an alternative, **La Picota**, Apr-Sep, T942 576 432, handy for Robatera, Usgo and Caballos.

JAKUE ANDIKOTXEA

12 Iker Fuentes tearing it up at Ris.

Suances

Crossing the Río Saja is a mammoth task – about half an hour's drive to cross a 50-m gap, which is a traffic nightmare in the summer. Once there, Suances sprawls out from the marina to the headland with plenty of places to eat, drink and sleep throughout the year. There is a year-round surf community here. The beaches have good facilities and fairly easy parking. Due to the proximity to Santander, it can be fairly pricey.

Sleeping

€€ Hotel El Castillo, T942-810383. Get past the fabulous mock castle façade and the rooms are clean and pretty but more importantly is right next to Los Locos. Also has clean apartments available overlooking Locos sleeping 4-6. **€ Posada Marina**, Plaxa de la Cuba, T942-811474, is an understated gem. It may be over 1 km from the beach but more than makes up for with its views over La Concha. **€ Posada del Mar**, on Cuba de Arriba, T942-811233, is not the prettiest of places but has very reasonable off-season rates with doubles from around €28. **Camping** **Camping Suances** is on the road into town and open Jun-Sep plus Easter and Christmas week, T942-810280.

Eating and drinking

If you're after a simple, filling bite head to **Pier Pizzeria & Pasta**, on the Paseo de la Marina. On the headland, the café at hotel **El Caserío** overlooks both Los Locos and La Concha and offers good tapas and breakfast.

Oyambre

Parque Natural de Oyambre encompasses pasture, cliffs, estuaries, dunes and beach, making this beautiful stretch of coastline popular with holidaymakers in the summer.

Sleeping

Camping **La Playa**, on the beach, T942-722616, is the largest and open year round. Statics also available. **Rodero** is 300 m from the beach, open year round with cabins and mobile homes, T942-722040. **Playa de Oyambre**, open Apr-Sep with bungalows, T942-711461, www.oyambre.com.

San Vincente de la Barquera

San Vincente has banks and supermarkets. There are plenty of places to stay, including the campsite **El Rosal**, T942-710165. Eat on the harbourfront at **Dulcinea**, a popular spot for tapas, while **Urquiza** does a substantial *menú del día* for about €10.

Asturias

Overview

The 2500-m summits of the Picos de Europa look down upon the dramatic coastline squeezing eastern Asturias towards the sea. The mountains that surround this region allowed the Asturians to hold out against the all-conquering Moors, the only area not to fall under the north Africans' rule. This set a trend for the centuries that followed and the region developed a strong will and proud people. In 1934 the army was sent in to put down a strike by the local miners and during the Civil War the region fought against Franco and his Nationalist troops.

The Asturian countryside still has vast swathes of ancient woodland and some pristine coastline. Fossils and dinosaur footprints can be found in the sands; wolves and bears still roam the Parque Nacional de los Picos de Europa and the region has managed to preserve much of its natural heritage. And although the area around Gijón and Avilés is home to some heavy industry, this is the exception to the rule.

When it comes to socializing the *sidrería* is the heart of the local community. Raised voices, cigarette smoke and card games are the order of the day, and glasses are kept full with a constant stream of still cider poured from above the bartender's head. As a result, the cuisine in the region also differs, with bean and sausage stews, excellent meats as well as the staple seafoods on offer.

Coastline

The coastline has a distinctly Celtic feel with small villages, clean sandy beaches and rugged, rocky points. Between the towns there may be nothing but smallholdings, rolling green fields and sheltered, hidden bays, only reached on foot. If you want to escape the crowds, this is one of the few places in Europe where you can truly have a beach to yourself.

The drive into Rodiles takes you through some beautiful scenery and coastal villages like Luarca and Cudillero, with its pretty harbour front, make great places to overnight. To the west, Tapia, with its small rivermouth break, is home to one of Spain's oldest surfing communities and is a regular European contest site. As for the rest of the coastline, it is a surf explorer's dream, with break after break just waiting to be discovered. While surfers are used to seeing their pound of flesh while stripping off in the car park, Asturias takes it to a whole new level with many of the area's surf spots doubling

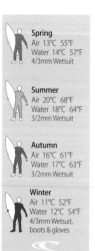

Spring
Air 13°C 55°F
Water 14°C 57°F
4/3mm Wetsuit

Summer
Air 20°C 68°F
Water 18°C 64°F
3/2mm Wetsuit

Autumn
Air 16°C 61°F
Water 17°C 63°F
3/2mm Wetsuit

Winter
Air 11°C 52°F
Water 12°C 54°F
4/3mm Wetsuit, boots & gloves

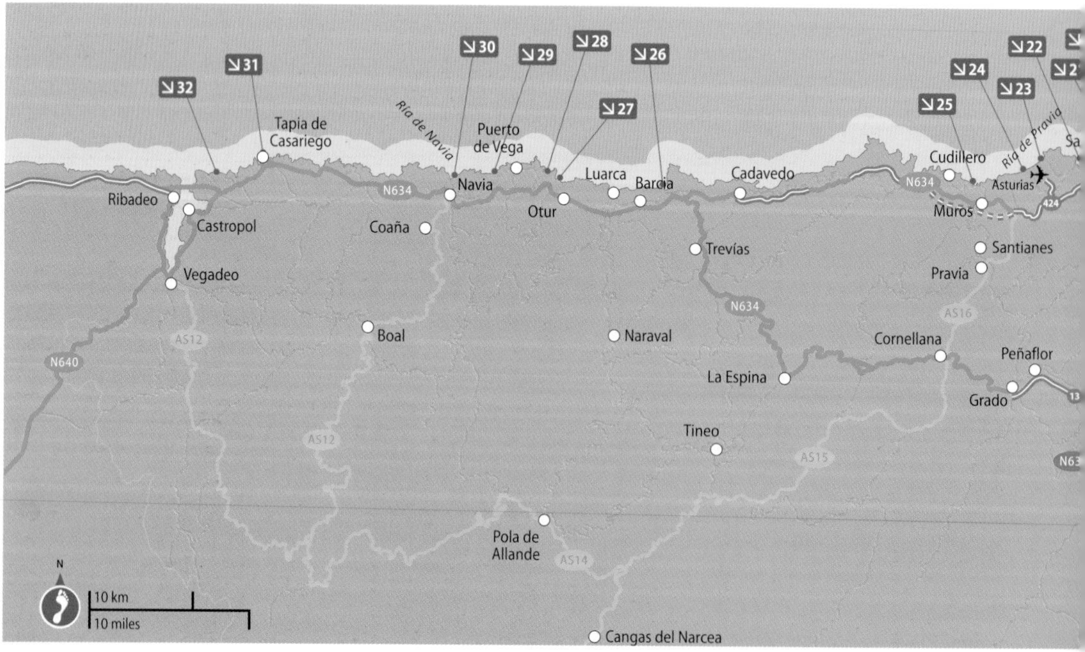

as nudie beaches, making it a draw for naturists as well as the naturalist. Toimbra and the huge expanse of Vega are popular in the east as is Otur in the west, even in the city they're not shy with Peñarrubia one of Gijón's favourite spots to bear all.

Local Environment

Rodiles, the regions most famous and high quality wave, has been under the threat of dredging. Local surfers fear a fate similar to that which befell Mundaka in 2005. "Mundaka, which is the site of a WCT professional event every year, lost its wave for nearly two years due to a dredging project that caused the sandbar to disappear. The local economy was devastated, and local business owners made instantly aware of the positive impact that visiting surfers have had on their pocketbooks for decades," says Will Henry of Save the Waves. "The surfers in Rodiles have been touting Mundaka's example as what could happen to their local businesses if the dredging project goes through. A wave as perfect as this, which is enjoyed by thousands of people every year, should never be sacrificed in order to make a few people rich."A harbour expansion at Gijón is also under discussion. If it goes ahead as planned, it is predicted that the construction of a huge new sea wall will effectively block swell from reaching many of the area's quality breaks including Peñarrubia and El Mongol.

Asturias is generally very laid-back and has few places where localism is a problem. That said, Salinas and some spots around Avilés can get crowded and may have tension in the water. Rodiles has always been a flash point and has been subject to acts of aggression and localism.

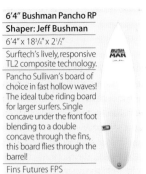

6'4" Bushman Pancho RP
Shaper: Jeff Bushman
6'4" x 18¾" x 2½"
Surftech's lively, responsive TL2 composite technology.
Pancho Sullivan's board of choice in fast hollow waves! The ideal tube riding board for larger surfers. Single concave under the front foot blending to a double concave through the fins, this board flies through the barrel!
Fins Futures FPS

6'2" G&S Mini Magic Fish
Shaper: Steve Seabold
6'2" x 20¼" x 2½"
Built with Surftech's proven TUFLITE construction.
A MAGIC board that skates down the line at surprising speeds, and yet still turns on a dime. Relaxed rocker and the wide fish tail give this board extra lift and speed. Works well in all types of surf 1' - 6'.
Futures FT1 center fins with FTT side fins

Getting around

The A-8 motorway follows the coast through eastern Asturias until Avilés. The N-634 and then the N-632 provide good access to the coastal breaks. The N-634 between Avilés and Cudillero can be a real bottleneck during rush hour with big queues of traffic. The rest of the coastline through to Ribadeo is pretty plain sailing on the N-634.

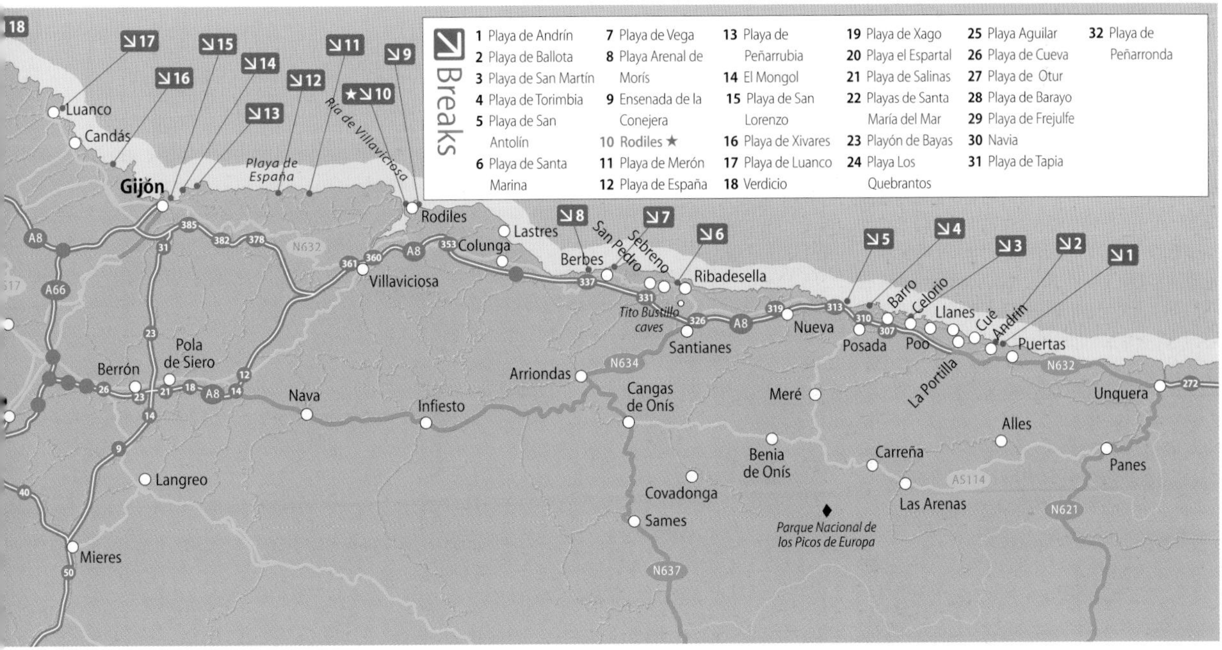

Breaks

BEACH BREAK

↘1 Playa de Andrín

- **Conditions** Medium N to NW swell, offshore in S to Se winds
- **Hazards/tips** Quiet, sheltered bay with wedging waves
- **Sleeping** Andrín/Llanes » *p242*

This quiet, sandy, cliff-lined cove is a beautiful location to escape the crowds. Check the surf from the top of the cliffs, which give a great view over the small cove. The small offshore Isla de Ballota blocks out a lot of the swell, which wraps around the rocky isle and enters the bay at two angles, converging in a wedgy peak in the middle of the bay. Worth checking in small to medium swells. The banks produce both lefts and rights through all tides. Follow the signs from the N-634.

BEACH BREAK

↘2 Playa de Ballota

- **Conditions** Medium N swell, offshore in S to SW winds
- **Hazards/tips** Quiet spot
- **Sleeping** Andrín/Llanes » *p242*

This picturesque bay is the next cove round from Andrín. It faces in a more northeasterly direction, needing more swell to get going. Its advantage is that it is sheltered from all but dead onshore winds. Both bays are very pretty and, overlooked by a popular tourist viewing point, are a great introduction to Asturias.

WILLY URIBE

BEACH BREAK

↘3 Playa de San Martín

- **Conditions** Small N swells, offshore in S to SE winds
- **Hazards/tips** Worth checking village of Poo out for the novelty value and postcards
- **Sleeping** Llanes » *p242*

Although the nearby Playa de Poo sounds tempting, you are more likely to find waves at low tide in this pretty, sandy cove. Needs small swells.

BEACH BREAK

↘4 Playa de Torimbia

- **Conditions** Small to medium N to NW swells, offshore in S to SE winds
- **Hazards/tips** Quiet spot
- **Sleeping** Llanes » *p242*

Sandy bay that works well in small and medium swells, is an attractive location for a day's surfing and is usually uncrowded. Has a powerful peak in the middle of the bay and a right at the eastern end. Parking overlooking the bay.

BEACH BREAK

↘5 Playa de San Antolín

- **Conditions** Medium NW swells, offshore in S to SE winds
- **Hazards/tips** Visible from road, rips when big, rivermouth
- **Sleeping** Llanes » *p242*

A large beach with numerous peaks that work through the tides. Can have fast and hollow lefts and rights. Check out the sandbar formed by the ría that enters the sea on the beach near the car park as this can have quality waves. Access from the AS-263 under the railway line.

BEACH BREAK

↘6 Playa de Santa Marina

- **Conditions** Medium NW swell, offshore in southerly winds.
- **Hazards/tips** Rivermouth can be polluted after rains
- **Sleeping** Ribadesella » *p242*

Sandy beach close to Ribadesella with good waves at all tides apart from high. Picks up a reasonable amount of swell.

JUAN FERNANDEZ

Spain Asturias Breaks

BEACH BREAK

↘7 Playa de Vega

- **Conditions** Small to medium NW swells, offshore in S winds
- **Hazards/tips** Water quality can be poor
- **Sleeping** Ribadesella » *p242*

This long beach picks up lots of swell and produces a number of good-quality peaks through all tides. Doesn't get overly crowded.

BEACH BREAK

↘8 Playa Arenal de Morís

- **Conditions** Small to medium N to NW swells, offshore in S to SE winds
- **Hazards/tips** Quiet spot
- **Sleeping** Ribadesella » *p242*

Long beach that is worth checking on all swells. Consistent beach, which can have good banks at low tide. Has parking.

Far left: 10 The region's MVP lining out.
Left: Spots like this one around Ribadesella hide in plain view just off the motorway.
Below: 10 Tucking into a piece of Rodiles.

JUAN FERNANDEZ

POINT BREAK

↘9 Ensenada de la Conejera

- **Conditions** Big N to NW swells, offshore in S to SW winds
- **Hazards/tips** Access is difficult. Found to the east of Punta Rodiles
- **Sleeping** Rodiles » *p242*

Excellent and long lefts break along this sand and rock point that is secreted away east of the Punta Rodiles. A quality spot that breaks up to 8 ft in big northwesterly swells. Best at low to mid tide but needs a big swell to get going. Difficult to find.

RIVERMOUTH BREAK

↘10 Rodiles

- **Swell** N to NW
- **Wind** S to SW
- **Tide** low to mid
- **Size** 2-10 ft
- **Length** 200 m plus
- **Bottom** Sandbar
- **Ability Level** Intermediate-Advanced
- **Best Months** Sep-Apr
- **Board** Performance Thruster
- **Access** Beach
- **Hazards/tips** Crowds, rips, localism, car crime, avoid after heavy rains
- **Sleeping** Rodiles » *p242*

The rivermouth left at Rodiles is one of the most famous waves in the whole of Spain – a kind of little sister to that other great Spanish rivermouth, Mundaka. Unlike its relative, however, the river here is hemmed in by rocky groynes. Looking out through the eucalyptus trees that line the dune-backed beach, it is possible to be transfixed by the perfect hollow lefts that reel away from the rivermouth at low to mid tide. But it's not all perfection: when it's on it experiences a similar level of crowding to Mundaka, and this has led to incidents of localism. Vehicles are frequently broken into.

The beach also has some excellent waves with sandbars producing lefts and rights through the tides. As with many Spanish breaks, get there early morning to beat the crowds. There is parking in the car park near the river or in the tree-shaded picnic area where there are also showers and toilets. An outstanding break in beautiful countryside, but watch out for the rips in big swells.

Just as its sister wave in the Basque region was damaged by thoughtless dredging, so this wave too has a dark cloud hanging over its future. "This classic rivermouth break is still under threat by a proposal to dredge a larger channel next to the break", says Will Henry from the 'Save the Waves' campaign. "The proposal is supported by real-estate developers who own waterfront land inside the port, and want to build high-priced homes. The port is currently accessible through the rivermouth via a narrow channel between two seawalls, but the developers want the channel deepened to allow for larger yachts and more consistent and safe access. 'Save the Waves' hopes that through an increase in awareness of the level of income surfers bring to the region and the impact this loss will have, pressure can be brought to bear on the local government. Stay tuned at www.savethewaves.org.

***If you like** Rodiles, try **Mundaka** (see page 215) and **Torrisdale** in Scotland (see page 44).*

BEACH BREAK

↘11 Playa de Merón

- **Conditions** Small to medium NW swells, offshore in S winds
- **Hazards/tips** Picks up more swell than Rodiles
- **Sleeping** Rodiles/Playa de España » *p242*

High-quality right-handers break on this sandy beach at low tide. A good alternative worth checking if Rodiles is packed. Good water quality and more chilled.

BEACH BREAK

↘12 Playa de España

- **Conditions** Medium NW swells, offshore in S to SE winds
- **Hazards/tips** Popular beach for day trippers from Gijón
- **Sleeping** Playa de España » *p243*

Its close proximity to the bustling city of Gijón and the quality of waves that break here make this a popular spot. This beachbreak is a consistent swell catcher that works through the tides and can produce fast and hollow waves up to 6 ft. Sits in a picturesque setting.

JUAN FERNANDEZ

WILLY URIBE

LEFT REEF BREAK

↘13 Playa de Peñarrubia

- **Conditions** Medium to big NW swells, offshore in S to SE winds
- **Hazards/tips** Can be very polluted
- **Sleeping** Gijón » *p243*

This rocky left-hander can be a quality break and handles swell up to 6-8 ft when reeling walls are a popular draw. Works best at mid tide, but the water quality can be poor. Found between Cabo San Lorenzo and Punta Cervigon.

POINT BREAK

↘14 El Mongol

- **Conditions** Big NW swells, offshore in S to SE winds
- **Hazards/tips** Crowds, localism, experienced surfers only
- **Sleeping** Gijón » *p243*

This urban point break needs a big swell to get going and when it does, steep heavy rights reel along the rocky bottom. Be ready for waves up to 10 ft. A popular spot that produces long, quality waves, El Mongol can be found along the Paseo Marítimo. With a name like this, it's obviously not a small, fun plaything. Crowds, pollution and localism all add to the experience.

BEACH BREAK

↘15 Playa de San Lorenzo

- **Conditions** Medium to big NW swells, offshore in SE winds
- **Hazards/tips** Crowds
- **Sleeping** Gijón » *p243*

Gijón is a big town with a big surfing community so this city beach always attracts surfers into the line-up, and gets especially busy if good. Works best at low to mid tide with lefts and rights breaking along the seafront. Beach all but disappears at high. Limited parking and showers on seafront.

BEACH BREAK

↘16 Playa de Xivares

- **Conditions** Medium to big NW swell, offshore in S to SW winds
- **Hazards/tips** Pollution, smells bad
- **Sleeping** Gijón ›› *p243*

This popular and pleasant looking beach is very close to the industrial plants that ring Gijón. The wave quality can be good with fast and hollow waves when the banks allow, and is consistent through the tides. Works best up to head high. Needless to say the air is pretty foul, and on offshore days the smell of sulphur and other chemicals fills the air. A stream runs into the sea here from the direction of the industrial plants so water quality is extremely questionable. Has cafés and a first-aid point.

BEACH BREAK

↘17 Playa de Luanco

- **Conditions** Big and storm swells, offshore in W to SW winds
- **Hazards/tips** Very sheltered spot
- **Sleeping** Gijón/Luanco ›› *p243*

This beach north of Gijón faces northeasterly so needs a big swell to get going. It also has a huge breakwater that cuts out the swell even more. This means that it is the ideal spot to head for in big westerly or northwesterly storms. A low-tide town break, with fast, hollow rides when everywhere else is maxed out. The town beach has seafront parking. Not the prettiest of towns.

BEACH BREAK WITH ROCKS

↘18 Verdicio

- **Conditions** Medium NW swells, offshore in a SE winds
- **Hazards/tips** Uncrowded spots
- **Sleeping** Avilés ›› *p243*

Around the headland these two northwesterly facing beaches, **Playa de Tenrero** and **Playa de Aguilera**, both pick up a lot of swell, making them consistent spots worth checking. They work in medium northwesterly swells and are separated by a rocky finger, causing sandbanks to form which can produce some great waves. Usually uncrowded, with parking at the eastern end of the beaches.

JUAN FERNANDEZ

Above left: 16 The Celtic stylings of Playa de Xivares. **Below left: 14** El Mongol, Gijón.
Above : Locked inside the industrial workings of a barrel at San Juan de Nieva near Avilés.

BEACH BREAK

↘19 Playa de Xago

- **Conditions** Small to medium NW swells, offshore in SE to E winds
- **Hazards/tips** Busy in summer
- **Sleeping** Avilés ›› *p243*

Due to its exposed location, this beach picks up even the smallest swells. It's a very popular spot, and gets busy in the summer when there's always a good chance of a wave. It is also a popular weekend destination out of season. The atmosphere, though, is usually pretty good as it's a real family location with BBQ areas and cafés and bars. It is offshore in any easterly wind. The drive into Xago is very unpromising as you pass a big industrial zone but you are soon in a beautiful ecological sanctuary. The beach has many facilities nestled under its eucalyptus trees, including cafés and a modern wooden shower and toilet block. The eastern end of the beach is overlooked by a beautiful, towering, rust-coloured cliff face and the sand dunes act as a buffer between the sea and the forest.

BEACH BREAK

↘20 Playa el Espartal

- **Conditions** Medium NW swells, offshore in SE winds
- **Hazards/tips** Not the cleanest stretch of water, worse after the rains, localism when busy
- **Sleeping** Avilés ›› *p243*

This stretch of sand runs from the rivermouth south to Playa de Salinas, and is a sandy, urban beach. It needs a medium-sized, northwesterly swell to work, but when it's on the quality waves draw a large local crew. The sandbanks sometimes produce hollow peaks, as well as lefts and rights; in all tides. Offshore in southeasterly winds, it can take light easterlies and northeasterlies. This is part of the town beach at Salinas, which is a pretty unremarkable place.

BEACH BREAK

↘21 Playa de Salinas

- **Conditions** Medium NW swells, offshore in SE winds
- **Hazards/tips** Pollution, crowds, localism, urban break
- **Sleeping** Avilés » p243

Works in the same conditions as Espartal and is as popular, also suffers from localism when busy. Not the prettiest location with tower blocks and sea defences overlooking the sea. There is a midi-ramp near the beach.

BEACH BREAK

↘22 Playas de Santa María del Mar

- **Conditions** Medium NW swells, offshore in S winds
- **Hazards/tips** Relatively quiet breaks
- **Sleeping** Avilés » p243

Playa de Santa María del Mar, **Playa Bahinas** and **Playa Munielles** are three beaches heading from east to west, each requiring a bit less swell to get going. Quality sandbanks change with the swells but are fairly consistent and work through all tides.

BEACH BREAK

↘23 Playón de Bayas

- **Conditions** Small to medium NW swells, offshore in E winds
- **Hazards/tips** Long stretch of sand which joins up with Los Quebrantos
- **Sleeping** Avilés » p243

This beach faces northwest and picks up plenty of swell. It works through the tides and has banks that produce both lefts and rights. Isla de la Diva sits at its eastern end.

BEACH BREAK

↘24 Playa Los Quebrantos

- **Conditions** Medium NW swells, offshore in S to SE winds
- **Hazards/tips** Crowds when good
- **Sleeping** Avilés/Cudillero » p243

This beach works up to 6 ft when excellent lefts can be had. In smaller swells the usual peaks and beach break fare is on offer. Big breakwater at Ría de Pravia.

BEACH BREAK

↘25 Playa Aguilar

- **Conditions** Medium N to NW swells, offshore in S to SE winds
- **Hazards/tips** Quiet spot, rocky
- **Sleeping** Cudillero » p243

Two small sandy bays, separated by rocks, that work on all states of tide. A lovely location to escape the crowds, catch a few peaky waves in a pretty spot and then enjoy a drink afterwards. Lefts and rights break in front of a large, anvil-shaped rock. Worth checking in clean, medium swells. The road to this secluded bay winds down through dense trees with easy parking and a beachfront café.

BEACH AND RIVERMOUTH BREAK

↘26 Playa de Cueva

- **Conditions** Small to medium NW swells, offshore in S to SE winds
- **Hazards/tips** Isolated spot
- **Sleeping** Luarca » p244

This pebble and sand beach has good lefts at the western end of the beach and rights at the

Below: 19 Playa de Xago. **Right: 30** Navia

WILLY URIBE

JUAN FERNANDEZ

eastern rivermouth end at low to mid tide. Needs a small to medium northwesterly swell to get going but will work in easterly winds. This beautiful, isolated spot, overlooked by pastureland and cliffs, has great potential.

BEACH BREAK

↘27 Playa de Otur

- **Conditions** Small to medium N to NW swells, offshore in S winds
- **Hazards/tips** Consistent spot
- **Sleeping** Luarca » p244

Take the winding road from Luarca to Playa de Otur off the N-634 to this picturesque bay with a quiet, dark-sand beach. It has shifting banks that work on all tides. Can be excellent when conditions combine. It is sheltered from winds but best in a southerly. Good lefts at the western end and rights at the eastern end, with many peaks in between. Has parking on the beach plus a bar (open in the summer).

BEACH BREAK

↘28 Playa de Barayo

- **Conditions** Medium swells, offshore in southerly winds.
- **Hazards/tips** National park, no parking at beach, quiet break.
- **Sleeping** Luarca/Navia » p244

Barayo is place to escape the rat race. The beautiful valley leads down to the beach through an area of ecological special interest, accessible only on foot. You can, however, check it from the car park before your 30-minute walk. This is a consistent beach break that works on all states of tides and can produce quality banks, especially at the rivermouth. There are two car parks, one on the eastern side of the beach and one on the west (access via Vigo). No dogs or camping allowed in the park.

WILLY URIBE

Above: Navia; city surfing Salinas.

BEACH BREAK

↘29 Playa de Frejulfe

- **Conditions** Small to medium NW swells, offshore in S to SW winds
- **Hazards/tips** Known as Frexulfe in Asturian, litter-strewn car park on the headland
- **Sleeping** Navia » p244

Beach break to the west of Puerto Vega which can turn on in small, clean northwesterly swells. Doesn't get too crowded. The beach works on all tides except for high. Has a small stream at the eastern end where there are some wedgy rights. A finger of reef towards the western end allows sand to build up, producing some nice high tide waves.

BEACH BREAKS

↘30 Navia

- **Conditions** All N to NW swells, offshore in S winds
- **Hazards/tips** Navia can be checked from the headland, then take the small road round to Moro
- **Sleeping** Navia » p244

Playa del Moro is a low tide rocky break that produces hollow rights in most swells. Works up to 8 ft. Moro picks up more swell than sheltered Navia to the east. Playa de Navia is a good quality rivermouth beach break with lefts and rights that is best at low tide. The water can be polluted.

WILLY URIBE

31 This popular competition site also has a great natural amphitheatre for watching the action.

BEACH AND REEF BREAK

↘31 Playa de Tapia

- **Conditions** Medium to big N to NW swells, offshore in SE winds
- **Hazards/tips** Crowds
- **Sleeping** Tapia de Casariego » p244

Tapia is one of Spain's better known breaks, but this doesn't seem to be due to its quality – more down to the fact that it's a regular contest venue on the WQS tour. While not world class, good quality waves do form in the sheltered rivermouth, producing a peak in the middle of the beach. Best at low tide. There is also a left-hand reef that can hold waves up to 8 ft. A big local surfing population ensures that it's usually crowded. Good facilities and car parking overlook the break.

BEACH BREAK

↘32 Playa de Peñarronda

- **Conditions** Medium NW swells, offshore in S winds
- **Hazards/tips** Picks up more swell than Tapia, but is more exposed
- **Sleeping** Tapia de Casariego » p244

This is a big bay with an island at the western end. Good waves can be had in southwesterly winds at all tides – except high – and it doesn't get too crowded. Rights and lefts break up to about 6 ft. Also worth checking is **Puente de Los Santos** in a big northwesterly swell. Low tide rights can be found in southerly or southwesterly winds.

Practicalities

Andrín

Andrín is the first port of call on the 145-km stretch of Asturian coastline. It has a good off-season free-camp potential. Otherwise try **Camping Río Purón**, to the east of the beach, T985-417199, open Mar-Oct, also cabins.

Llanes

This pretty, working fishing harbour has a walled medieval centre interspersed with cafés and shops. It houses the tourist office as well as the 15th-century Basílica de Santa María. The town also has good facilities.

Sleeping

€€-€ Pension La Guia, on Plaza Parres Sobrino, T985-402577, www.pensionlaguia.com, is in an ideal central location and open year round, with plain but attractive (and fairly small) rooms.

Camping There are plenty of places to camp in and around the town. **Las Bárcenas**, T985-402887, Jun-Sep, has cabins. **Entreplayas**, between Llanes's 2 beaches, T985-400888, late Dec-Sep. Heading west towards Poo (snigger) is **Las Conchas**, T985-402290, with cabins, is open year round. Further west, at Celorio, is **Camping María Elena**, T985-400028, late Dec-Sep. Taking the LLN-11 from Celorio to Barro is **Playa de Troenzo**, T985-401672, on the beach and open year round.

Eating

For breakfasts, coffee or snacks, head to **Café Xana** on the harbourfront. **Sidréría Alloru**, C Gutiérrez de la Gandara has good food, a great vibe and is heaving at the weekends. A popular local spot is **Casa Canene** , C Manuel Cue, just off the harbour, with a good, filling *menú de la noche* for about €12 including wine.

Ribadesella

Ribadesella is divided by the Río Sella which gives the town its name and in August attracts hordes of canoe fans from across the globe for the Canoe Festival or International Descent of the River Sella. Eat, drink and sleep in the old part of the town and get a good fish supper on the harbour front. There is also a surf shop here, **Waikiki**, on Trav La Iglesia.

Sleeping

Camping **Ribadesella**, west of the river, in Sebreno and 1 km to the beach, T985-858293, www.camping-ribadesella.com, open Jul-Sep plus Christmas week, with wooden chalets. **Los Sauces**, between San Pedro and the beach Jun-Sep, T985-861312, with cabins. West along the N-632 **Playa de Vega** is just back from the beach, T985-860406, camping Jul-Sep, lovely wooden chalets sleeping 4 are available year round from €70 per night.

Rodiles

Signed from the A-8 motorway and the N-632 coast road, Rodiles lies on the eastern bank of the Ría de Villaviciosa, nestled amongst eucalyptus trees. Popular in the summer, it has great peak-season facilities including toilets, showers, parking, cafés and bars. Just inland, the large town of Villaviciosa has good facilities including banks, restaurants, shops plus some cheaper accommodation.

JUAN FERNANDEZ

JUAN FERNANDEZ

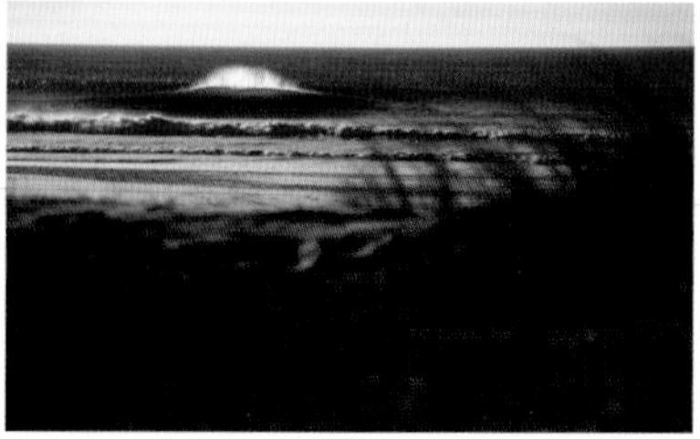

Above: The coastline around Asturias is primed to convert swell.
Right: Solitary peaks can be found along this stretch of coastline.

Spain Asturias Practicalities

Sleeping

La Casona del Terienzu, 2 km from the beach, opposite bar-restaurant Casa Covian, T985-996003, offers apartments for up to 5 people from €80–115, and is a good option for groups. **Rodiride**, www.rodiride.com, run a free-surf camp Apr-Dec from €425/week including board and lodgings. In nearby **Villaviciosa € Pensión Sol**, C Sol, T985-891130, and **€ Pensión El Charcon**, C Piedrafita, T985-974950, are a couple of cheap options. Good food and cider (for which the town is famous) can be had around the town hall.

Camping Free-camping along the tree-lined beach is officially prohibited but there are plenty of designated campsites: **La Ensenada** is just back from the beach and open year round, T985-890157; **Fin de Siglo**, T985-876535, is larger and has cabins but is only open Jun-Sep; **Nery**, on the road out to Selorio, T985-996115, is much smaller and open May-Sep.

Directory

Surf shops **Rodi Ride**, shape and fix boards and have a shop on the Rodiles-Villaviciosa road. **Internet** **Hotel la Ría**, C Marques de Villaviciosa. **Tourist information** Parque Vallina, summer only.

Playa de España

Heading west along the AS-256, turn towards Marines along the VV-2 or VV-3 for camping **Playa España**, T985-894273, Mar-30 Sep.

Gijón

This is the largest town in Asturias and has a friendly rivalry with the official capital, Oviedo. Gijón is relaxed and stylish with a thriving surf community and enough beautiful people clogging up the summer sands to give it a feel of Biarritz.

Sleeping

In terms of cheap places to stay, head for Gijón's old town between the port and the west end of the beach. San Bernando has a few places to stay including **€ González**, T985-355863.

Camping **Camping Gijón**, on the Punta del Cervignon to the east of Playa de San Lorenzo, T985-365755, is open Jun-30 Sep with good access to both San Lorenzo and Peñarrubia. Heading out of Gijón on the N-632, **Camping Deva-Gijón**, T985-133848, www.campingdeva-gijon.com, has good facilities and open year round, with great wooden cabins from €60 for 4,

Eating and drinking

The old town is the place to head for good food, drink and ambience. **La Turuta**, on Av María out on the headland, has a fantastically relaxed ambience while the Plaza Mayor offers a wide selection of alternatives.

Directory

Surf shops With a good surf scene, there are plenty of shops to pick up essentials in Gijón. **Tablas Surf Shop** , right on the seafront along Paseo del Muro de San Lorenzo, www.tablassurfshop.com, has been serving the area since 1979, and is one of the best. **Tourist information** Head to the port for year-round information on the whole region, www.gijon.info.

Luanco

Sleeping

Luanco is not the prettiest town but there are a couple of handy **campsites for a stop over**. Just south in Antromero is **El Penoso**, year round, T985-880164. To the north, at Playa de Bañugues, is the large site of **El Molino**, next to the beach, T985-880785, May-30 Sep and Christmas week, also offers cabins.

Avilés

If you can get past the factory fog and industrial smoke haze Avilés has a beautiful, historic centre, home to one of the best carnivals in northern Spain. The pollution

WILLY URIBE

The art of pouring.

levels here can be fairly high although there are plenty or surf shops as a substitute including **Deportes Valentín** and **Vertical Surf Shop** on Av Los Telares. Across the river to the east, the industrial zone gives way to a sanctuary at Playa Xago with a large eucalyptus-shaded car park, facilities block and busy beach bar **Mari Mar**.

Sleeping

Camping West of Avilés there are a couple of campsites open year round – **Las Lunas** in Naveces, T985-519771, and the larger **Las Gaviotas** in Santa María del Mar, T985-519491.

Cudillero

This pretty cobblestoned village 20 km west from Avilés hangs above the fishing port, where freshly caught skate are stretched out to dry as *curadillo*. Although small, Cudillero has banks and food stores and the Fri market is a great place to pick up fresh produce.

Sleeping

Accommodation is fairly pricey here.

€€ Casona de Pio, is tucked away on Rio Frio. The pretty farmhouse-style rooms have exposed brick walls, shuttered windows and, most importantly Jacuzzi baths. The restaurant downstairs does an excellent, rich seafood stew.

One of the cheapest year-round options is **€ Casa Miguel**, west at Concha de Artedo, T985-596350.

Camping Just to the east in El Pito there are a couple of campsites: **L'Amuravela**, T985-590995, www.lamuravela.com, is open year round and offers wooden cabins; **Cudillero**, on the road from El Pito to Playa de Aguilar, T985-590663, www.camping cudillero.com, has cabins, open Jun-Sep and Christmas week; to the west **Yolimar** is just inland at Artedo, T985-590472, Jan-Sep; **Los Pradones** is just back from Playa de Artedo, T985-591108, cabins, Jun-Sep.

Eating

You can pick up breakfast from **Bar Julio** on the main plaza, and in the evening **Sidrería El Patrón** goes off. For good food with ambience head to the harbour.

Luarca

The pretty town of Luarca winds out along the Río Negro. With an important fishing past and present the focal point of the town is the harbour, lined with cafés, bars and the fish market.

Sleeping

€ Moderna, C Crucero, T985-640057, is one of the cheapest *pensiones*.

Camping There are a couple of sites near the town including the excellent **Playa de Tauran**, to the west in San Martín, T985-641272, www.campingtauran.com, open Apr-Sep; you can rent their cabins year round (if booked in advance). **Los Cantiles** on the N-634 in Luarca is open year round, T985-640938. West at Otur along the N-634, **Camping Playa de Otur**, is about 500 m from the beach, T985-640117, www.inicia.es, open Easter-Oct, (may be open to year round bookings if agreed in advance); it's a pretty site with free Wi-Fi access and bungalows to rent.

Navia

Navia combines a large commercial port with a pretty old town. Navia itself is not a particularly inspiring destination although the town is a good place to stock up, especially at the **Consum** supermarket where their lunch menu will set you back about €6. To the east in Puerto de Vega is the summer campsite **El Ancla**, 25 Jun-10 Sep, T985-648205. A series of historic hill forts wind inland along the river, some of which are more than 2000 years old.

Tapia de Casariego

Tapia is a pull for travelling surfers who have drooled over the contest photos in the European surf mags, and rightly so as it is a relaxed town with several good beaches. It also has a thriving surf scene – with shops **Uluru** and **Picante Surf** – as well as plenty of locals to fill the waves. As with most places, eat, drink and be merry around the harbour. www.goanna.es

Sleeping

€ Puente de los Santos, on the main road, T985-628155, www.hotelpuentedelos santos.com, ain't pretty but the rooms are fine, it has internet access and is one of the cheapest places in town. **Casa Germana**, on the main road Av Primo de Rivera, T985-628181, www.casagermana.com, has self-contained apartments for up to 4 for €60-110, and is open year round.

Camping **Playa de Tapia**, T985-472721, Jun-15 Sep. To the west, **Camping Playa Peñarronda**, T985-623022, www.campingplayapenarronda.com, is 50m from the beach, open Easter-Sep, and has internet access as well as statics.

Flat spells

Golf There are plenty of courses including (from east to west): **La Cuesta Golf Club**, between Cue and Andrín, T985-417084, www.golflacuesta.com, 18 holes; **La Rasa de Berbes Golf Club**, Berbes, T985-857881, 9 holes; **Villaviciosa Golf Club**>, just off the N-634 near Rodiles, T985-358289, 9 holes, driving range and putting green. There are a couple of clubs in and around Gijon including the 18-hole **La Lloreda Municipal Golf Course**, on the N-632 between Gijón and Villaviciosa, T985-333191, www.golflalloreda.com. To the south, 18-hole **Real Club de Golf Castiello**, in Castiello de Bernueces, T985-366313, www.castiello.com, comes complete with a driving range and putting green.

Sights Loved by canoeists and anthropologists alike, Ribadesella is famed for its Jurassic remnants and prehistoric art hidden in the **Tito Bustillo** caves, T985-861120, open mid Mar-mid Sep Wed-Sun, entry €3.50), limited to 375 visitors per day.

Los Picos de Europa (the peaks of Europe) consist of three main limestone massifs, shaped and eroded over 300 million years by glaciation. The peaks cover 64,660 ha over three provinces – Cantabria, Asturias and León – are barely 20 km from the sea in parts and are a walker's/caver's/potholer's/nature lover's paradise. Head south from Ribadesella on the N-634 to **Cangas de Onís**, the Asturian base of the national park's visitor centre (T985-848005, open year round).

Snowboarding Under two hours from the coast you can hit the snow. From Oviedo head south along the A-66 then the N-630 to Pajares to the **Estación Invernal y de Montaña Valgrande-Pajares**, www.valgrande-pajares.com. Check ahead for the snow report (T985-957097).

Overview

"Galicia, a land of magic and antiquity. Finisterre, Costa da Morte (the Coast of the Death) are names loaded with mythical symbolism and epic histories in which the sea has tirelessly waged war against its tortured coastline. The unique geography of this coast and its situation with respect to the powerful Atlantic storms singles Galicia out as a land with one of the greatest wave potentials in Europe, and a place in which virgin waves still exist."

Fernando Muñoz of Spanish surf magazine, Surfer Rule

Dominating the northwest corner of the Iberian Peninsular and open to any passing swell Galicia, with her rugged, undulating coastal morphology full of rivermouths, bays, inlets headlands and spectacular points, simply delivers. But that isn't to say that the breaks here are handed to you on a plate, whether secreted away behind a curtain of dense forest on the northern fringe or waiting on the fractured western coastline at the very edge of a peninsular, they demand to be sought out. When you see what they can offer in return, you'll realize that their demands are well worth listening to.

Looking at Galicia it is obvious that this is a land controlled by the elements. Houses in many coastal villages have stones strategically placed on their roofs to prevent tiles being blown away in winter gales. Exposed to the full force of the ocean, and accompanying weather fronts that sweep in from the Atlantic, coastal communities have for generations harvested the rich pickings from the sea. Today major ports like A Coruña and Vigo supply Europe with high quality seafood, which can be enjoyed in the local bars and restaurants.

Galicia has a Celtic heritage that extends beyond the huge annual rainfall to a history that even includes bagpipe music.

Coastline

Northern Galicia between Ortigueira and Viveiro is a lush green landscape of eucalyptus trees and sheltered coves, a real gem. The coastline from Cedeira to Ferrol, however, has more of a Celtic feel to it. The countryside is more open with smallholdings and large beaches. The geography of the open west coast with its fjord-like inlets means it has massive surf potential, one that few travelling surfers venture far enough west to sample.

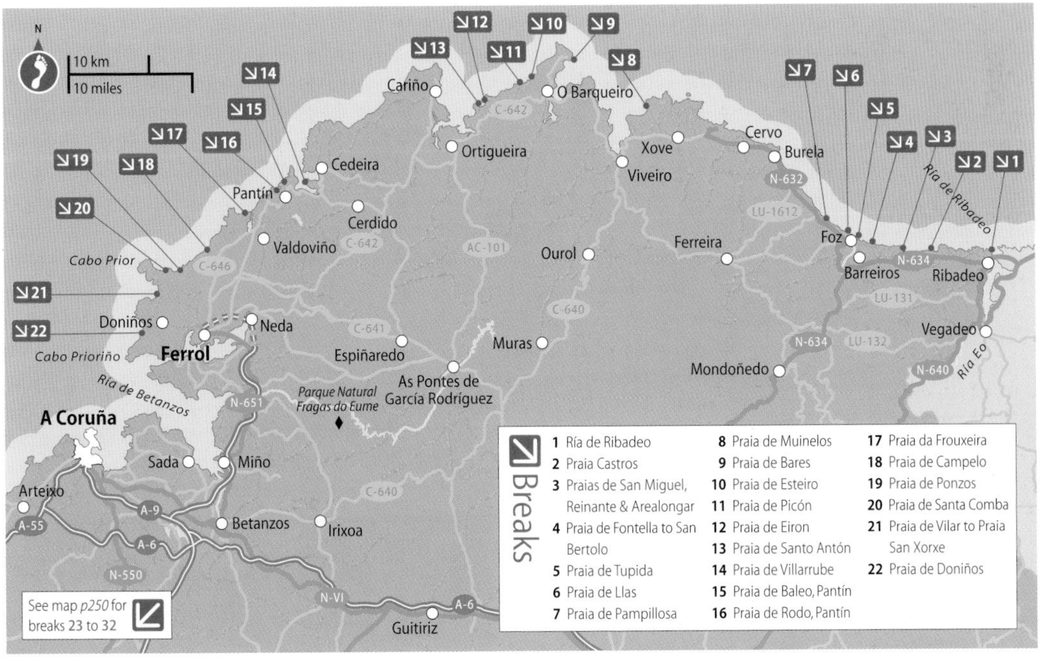

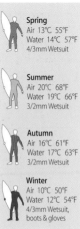

Spring
Air 13°C 55°F
Water 14°C 57°F
4/3mm Wetsuit

Summer
Air 20°C 68°F
Water 19°C 66°F
3/2mm Wetsuit

Autumn
Air 16°C 61°F
Water 17°C 63°F
3/2mm Wetsuit

Winter
Air 10°C 50°F
Water 12°C 54°F
4/3mm Wetsuit, boots & gloves

Local environment

Galicia is home to some of Europe's most unspoilt natural environments, where jagged coastlines seem to be almost untouched by human hands. This made the impact of the Prestige oil spill of 2002 an even greater disaster. More than 60,000 tons are thought to have gone into the water and, while the clean up has helped to remove a portion of the oil, the black stuff is pervasive and notoriously difficult to break down. There is also oil remaining aboard the unstable hull. Don't be surprised to find isolated pockets still turning up. As Galicia lies alongside busy shipping lanes there is also the problem of illegal discharges from passing ships flushing tanks.

Although many of the excellent breaks here have small dedicated crews, few suffer the population pressures that have led to localism at other spots in Europe. Many surfers are friendly and will be inquisitive towards respectful travelling surfers, especially out of season. There are a couple of spots where a few locals have developed a reputation for localism. Clustered close to Ferrol and the city of A Coruna with its large surf community, Pantín and Doniños are known places where pressures in the water can lead to drop-ins and other acts of localism.

Getting around

There really is only one way to truly experience Galicia and that is by exploring the smaller roads that lead off the main arteries. The network of minor roads that hug the coastline are of good quality while from Ferrol, an expanding motorway system runs south to Portugal cutting through Santiago de Compostela, Pontevedra and Vigo.

6'6" JC SD-3

Shaper: John Carper

6'6" x $18\frac{1}{4}$" x $2\frac{1}{4}$"

Surftech's lively, responsive TL2 composite technology.

The 6'6" SD-3 is Shane Dorian's go to board when the waves turn on. Single to double concave, slightly fuller rail, lower entry rocker and a slight bump wing at the hips. Ideal step up board for hollow waves is the 6'-10' range.

Futures JC-1 fins.

7'2" Surftech MAC Fish

Shaper: Randy French

7'2" x 22" x $2\frac{7}{8}$"

Surftech's lively, responsive TL2 composite technology.

Recommended for ankle to shoulder high surf - the super flat entry and exit rocker insures speed through even the flattest sections. The full, forgiving rail maximizes flotation allowing for smooth turns without losing speed.

FCS G5 fins.

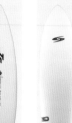

Boards by **Surftech**
www.surftech.com info@surftech.com

DEMI TAYLOR

JAKUE ANDIKOTXEA

Top: 4 Praia de Fontela. **Above:** Machacona – one of east coast Galicia's top spots.

Breaks

RIVERMOUTH BREAK

↘1 Ría de Ribadeo

Conditions Big NW to N swell, offshore in S to SW winds

Hazards/tips Urban break, water quality varies

Sleeping Ribadeo » *p254*

This rivermouth break is slightly sheltered so needs a big northwesterly swell to get going. Shifty sandbanks form at the rivermouth, with mostly left-handers breaking at low tide. There is some protection offered from westerly winds. Parking by the break in this fairly unremarkable town.

BEACH BREAK

↘2 Praia Castros

Conditions Small to medium N to NW swells, S to SW winds

Hazards/tips Gets busy in the summer

Sleeping Ribadeo to Foz » *p254*

Castros is the first in a series of beaches along this stretch, following the coast road. It is a small, cliff-lined cove with a sandy beach that throws up some nice peaks. There are a few scattered rocks. Park overlooking the break.

BEACH BREAKS

↘3 Praias de San Miguel, Reinante and Arealongar

Conditions Small to medium N to NW swells, offshore in S to SW winds

Hazards/tips Busy in summer

Sleeping Ribadeo to Foz » *p254*

The Estrada da Costa is a well signposted road that hugs the shore and links a series of pretty, sandy bays, separated by rocky headlands. These beach breaks work best on low to mid tide, but there are some waves at high. Watch out for the scattered rocks on some of the beaches, especially as the tide pushes. There's plenty of parking overlooking each break, but gets busy with holidaymakers in the summer. Some beaches have showers. Praia Reinante even has a brothel next to the campsite – don't mistake it for a 'club' in the traditional sense of the word.

Below: 3 Arealonga – one of many rocky coves on the Estrada Costa. **Bottom: 4** Another beach in this series, Olinas do Mar has consistantly good banks.

JAKUE ANDIKOTXEA

JAKUE ANDIKOTXEA

BEACH BREAKS

↘4 Praia de Fontella to San Bertolo

Conditions Medium N to NW swells, offshore in S to SW winds

Hazards/tips Massively popular in the summer

Sleeping Ribadeo to Foz » *p254*

Continuing west on the Estrada da Costa is another series of fine, white-sand beach

JAKUE ANDIKOTXEA

Above: This chunky left point breaks between Foz and Ribadeo on the Marina Orientale. **Right**: The Pantin we know and love. **Bottom right**: **16** The eastern edge of Rodo, macking, on steroids.

breaks. Again, they generally work best on low to mid before some of the bays disappear as the tide pushes into the low-lying, rocky headlands that overlook the coves. The beaches at the eastern end of this stretch pick up most swell. There are campsites, cafés and car parks galore.

BEACH AND RIVERMOUTH BREAK

5 Praia de Tupida

- **Conditions** Big N and NW swells, offshore in SW and S winds
- **Hazards/tips** Parking on the seafront, rips when big
- **Sleeping** Foz » *p254*

On the eastern side of the *ría* looking over at Foz is this large expanse of sandy beach with a rocky outcrop. Currents conspire to create a rivermouth sandbar that produces fast, quality lefts on low. To the east peaks form on the main beach. Follow signs for the Moby Dick restaurant.

BEACH BREAK

6 Praia de Llas

- **Conditions** Medium N to NW swells, offshore in SW winds
- **Hazards/tips** Crowds
- **Sleeping** Foz » *p254*

On the west side of Foz is this large, white, sandy beach with a few rocks. The beach works best on the push from low to three-quarter tide and can produce some nice rights. Good beachfront facilities including parking and toilets overlooking the beach. Foz has an active surfing community and this is a popular break.

BEACH BREAK WITH RIVERMOUTH

7 Praia de Pampillosa

- **Conditions** Medium to big N to NW swells, offshore in S to SW winds
- **Hazards/tips** Break visible from the N-642
- **Sleeping** Foz » *p254*

Pampillosa is a long beach with a rivermouth at the western end and a pretty, scrub-backed stretch of sand with peaks at all tides. This is a quality break where reeling lefts can be found in big swells.

BEACH BREAK

8 Praia de Muinelos

- **Conditions** Small to medium swells, offshore in a southeasterly/easterly wind.
- **Hazards/tips** Beautiful location, faces west, picks up plenty of swell
- **Sleeping** Viveiro » *p254*

Low tide sees high-quality lefts breaking along a sandy beach with some rocks. **Praia de Esteiro**, the next beach, is also worth checking and works in similar conditions. These are the first breaks in Galicia that face northwesterly and are both set in fantastic locations, with evergreen forest, parking and beautiful clear water.

BEACH BREAK

9 Praia de Bares

- **Conditions** Huge N and NW swells, offshore in a W to NW winds
- **Hazards/tips** Beautiful location, stunning scenery, parking at the beach
- **Sleeping** Viveiro » *p254*

Easterly facing beach break with a small harbour at its northern end. This is a good place to head for if Galicia is being pounded by one of its huge westerly storms as the swell will have to wrap 180° into the sandy beach. This beach disappears at high and works best from low to mid on a rising tide.

BEACH BREAK

10 Praia de Esteiro

- **Conditions** Medium NW swells, offshore in E and SE winds
- **Hazards/tips** Quiet spot
- **Sleeping** Viveiro » *p254*

Follow the track down to this beautiful beach and in a clean swell there should be an A-frame peak with short rights and long lefts breaking in the middle of the sandy bay. Best on the push from low to three-quarter tide, but high-tide wedges are fun. This picturesque bay is hemmed in by cliffs at each side and backed by dunes. Great location with parking on the beach. Not to be confused with the other Praia de Esteiro, north of Xove.

BEACH BREAK

↘11 Praia de Picón

- **Conditions** Small to medium NW swells, offshore in SE to S winds
- **Hazards/tips** Rocks, quiet beach
- **Sleeping** Viveiro/Cedeira » *p254*

Turn left in the tiny village of Picón to the cliff top where access can be gained down to this beach break. The rocky beach is not a classic but has occasional peaks that work on all tides providing short, fun rides. When the swell gets over 6 ft it will close out. Parking is on the cliff top.

BEACH BREAK

↘12 Praia de Eiron

- **Conditions** Small to medium NW swells, offshore in S to SE winds
- **Hazards/tips** Rocks
- **Sleeping** Viveiro/Cedeira » *p254*

Rocky beach which works on low tide. Lefts peel off a rocky outcrop and rights break on the beach. Part of the same bay as Santo Antón, but is more sheltered so can handle bigger swells. Has showers and a toilet.

BEACH BREAK

↘13 Praia de Santo Antón

- **Conditions** Small to medium NW swells, offshore in S to SE winds
- **Hazards/tips** Less rocky than Eiron
- **Sleeping** Viveiro/Cedeira » *p254*

A flexible and popular beach that is sheltered from all winds except northwesterly. Works on all tides and is quite popular. Town break with parking and toilets at the western end of the bay.

BEACH BREAK

↘14 Praia de Villarrube

- **Conditions** Big and huge NW swells, offshore in a SW to S winds
- **Hazards/tips** Can be checked from the C-646 to Pantín. Spectacular location
- **Sleeping** Cedeira » *p254*

Pretty and unique break that nestles inside the estuary south of Cedeira. The enclosed geography, narrow entrance and sheltering hills make this the place to head for in huge northwesterly storms. The beautiful sandy beach sits on the western side of Ría de Cedeira, but when swells angle between the headlands long peeling rights reel off the northern end of the beach. The surrounding eucalyptus-covered hills offer good protection from the wind. Works best at low tide. There is also a left at the southern end of the beach.

BEACH BREAK

↘15 Praia de Baleo, Pantín

- **Conditions** Small to medium W to N swells, offshore in SE winds
- **Hazards/tips** Rips, localism, crowds
- **Sleeping** Cedeira » *p254*

Pantín is the most famous surf destination in Galicia due to the WQS events held here. It is

JAKUE ANDIKOTXEA

JAKUE ANDIKOTXEA

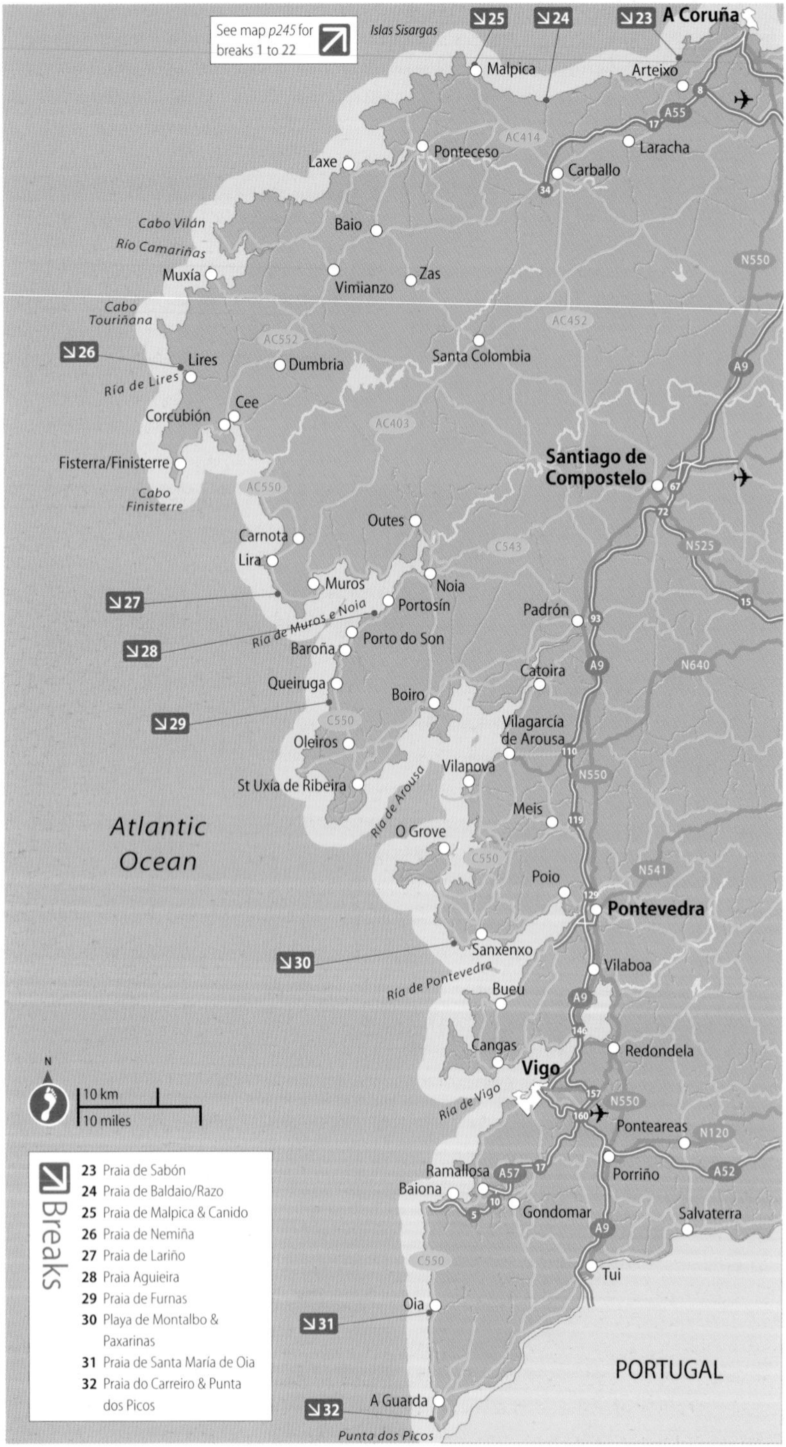

actually two beaches, with Baleo being the north bay separated by a short drive. It is a popular, medium sized sandy bay that can produce excellent rights and lefts. Working on all tides and in all westerly and northwesterly swells up to 6 ft makes this a consistent spot. It picks up more swell than Rodo and is less crowded. A big peak can break in the middle of the bay with long lefts and rights. In bigger swells watch the rips at the north and south of the bay. Parking overlooking the bay with picnic area.

BEACH BREAK

16 Praia de Rodo, Pantín

- **Conditions** Small to medium W to N swells, offshore in an E to SE winds
- **Hazards/tips** Localism, crowds
- **Sleeping** Cedeira » *p254*

Rodo is the larger of the two bays and is also more popular than nearby Baleo. There are various peaks along the bay that can get crowded during the summer and at weekends. Works on all tides serving up hollow pits and long, walling rides. Depending on who you talk to, Pantín is either a localized spot, or a break with a few grumpy guys who try to intimidate non-locals. The consensus seems to be that if you are chilled and don't go in big groups, you will be OK. This beach is where the WQS event is actually held.

BEACH BREAK

17 Praia da Frouxeira

- **Conditions** All W to N swells, offshore in S to SE winds
- **Hazards/tips** Whole beach can be checked from C-646
- **Sleeping** Cedeira » *p254*

This massive, dune-backed beach just south of Pantín stretches out for 3 km to the west and can have quality peaks all the way along. At the eastern end is a rivermouth that opens into a lagoon. This is a quality beach that picks up loads of swell and has some excellent banks with fast lefts and rights. At the town end of the shore a right breaks towards the rocky island in big swells. This end is usually the busiest, but off season the rest of the beach can be very quiet. This bay works on all tides and all swells. Massive potential.

BEACH BREAK

↘18 Praia de Campelo

- **Conditions** All NW swells, offshore in S to SE winds
- **Hazards/tips** Consistent spot. Rips when big
- **Sleeping** Cedeira/Ferrol » *p254*

An excellent beach break that picks up heaps of swell and has some sick banks waiting to produce long, hollow rights and lefts. Rights reel off the eastern end of the beach and lefts further down to the western end. A quality set-up. The cliff-lined beach virtually disappears at high tide but it continues to break in big swells. Works best at low to mid tide. Car park overlooks bay. Access is off the C-646 down a small signposted road.

BEACH BREAK

↘19 Praia de Ponzos

- **Conditions** Small to medium N to NW swells, offshore in a S wind
- **Hazards/tips** A beautiful, quiet location
- **Sleeping** Cedeira/Ferrol » *p254*

Big, sandy bay with plenty of room to spread out, backed by dunes. Sheltering rocky headland at the south. Picks up lots of NW swell and works on all tides. Peaks break all along the bay and there is a low tide left that breaks off the headland at the south. Parking by the beach at the southern end.

BEACH BREAK

↘20 Praia de Santa Comba

- **Conditions** Medium to big NW swells, offshore in S winds
- **Hazards/tips** Very quiet out of season
- **Sleeping** Cedeira/Ferrol » *p254*

JAKUE ANDIKOTXEA

JAKUE ANDIKOTXEA

Above: 22 Surfing around Ferrol and A Coruña can be highly competitive. **Top: 22** Praia de Doninos – home to some of the region's best waves.

Another beautiful, dune-backed bay separated from Ponzos by a rocky headland. This long, sandy bay works on all tides, but is not as good at high. It is more sheltered from swell than Ponzos and has a rocky finger towards the southern end. There is parking at the northern end overlooking the bay with a right-hander in front of the car park. Excellent potential in a stunning location.

BEACH BREAKS

↘21 Praia de Vilar to San Xorxe

- **Conditions** All NW swells, works in E to S winds
- **Hazards/tips** A big bay with big potential
- **Sleeping** Cedeira/Ferrol » *p254*

A series of small coves leading to the massive beach at San Xorxe. **Vilar** faces west and picks up the least amount of swell. Moving south, **Fragata** and **Esmelle** are the next two

JUAN FERNANDEZ

The fractured coastline around Pontevedra can yield great returns.

coves which pick up more swell and have rocky fingers separating them. All work best on low tide with lefts and rights breaking off the rocks. **Xorxe** is a long, crescent-shaped sandy beach that picks up a lot of swell despite being in the shadow of Cabo Prior. It works on all tides and the shape of the beach gives it loads of potential in different swell and wind directions. The car park overlooks this dune-backed beach.

BEACH BREAK

↘22 Praia de Doniños

- **Conditions** All W to NW swells, offshore in E to SE winds
- **Hazards/tips** Rips, crowds, some localism
- **Sleeping** Ferrol » p255

This beach is very popular with surfers from the Ferrol area and gets crowded in the summer and at weekends. It's a 2-km long beach that picks up lots of swell. It has excellent peaks that work on all tides. High quality beach break with some of the region's best waves. Beach has bars, cafés, parking and a bus link to Ferrol (hence its popularity). Has a reputation as a localized spot and beware of rips. Worth checking off season.

BEACH BREAK

↘23 Praia de Sabón

- **Conditions** Small to medium N to NW swells, offshore in S to SE winds
- **Hazards/tips** A busy break that can be packed on small summer days
- **Sleeping** A Coruña » p255

This beach is just south of the city of A Coruña and picks up any swell going, making it a popular summer spot. Works on all tides.

BEACH BREAK

↘24 Praia de Baldaio/Razo

- **Conditions** Small to medium N to NW swells, offshore in a S to SW winds
- **Hazards/tips** A great stretch of coastline to explore
- **Sleeping** Malpica » p256

A huge stretch of beaches with fantastic dunes, great banks and beautiful scenery. Picks up loads of swell. Can have excellent rights and lefts in even the smallest swells.

BEACH BREAK

↘25 Praia de Malpica and Canido

- **Conditions** Medium NW to N swells, offshore in S to SW swells
- **Hazards/tips** Parking by the beach
- **Sleeping** Malpica » p256

A busy summer beach that is quiet out of season. Works on medium north or northwesterly swells. A great stretch of beach that joins up with Canido. Access via the AC-414.

BEACH BREAK

↘26 Praia de Nemiña

- **Conditions** Medium to big W to NW swells, offshore in an E wind
- **Hazards/tips** Consistent, quiet, rips when big
- **Sleeping** Muxía » p256

A beautiful stretch of dune-backed beach that picks up plenty of swell and reaches down to the Ría de Lires. Along the beach are numerous excellent peaks while the rivermouth throws out a classic left at low to mid tide. A great, consistent spot that is usually fairly uncrowded.

BEACH BREAK

↘27 Praia de Lariño

- **Conditions** Medium S to W or big NW swells, offshore in a NE wind
- **Hazards/tips** Visible from the main coast road, quiet spot
- **Sleeping** Muros » p256

West-facing stretch of beach just off the C-550 that is usually very quiet. Set in beautiful countryside. Needs a swell from the west or south or a big swell from the northwest. From here north there are many spots worth checking just off the C-550. Try **Suresco, Lira, Xaxebe** and **Carnota**.

JAKUE ANDIKOTXEA

WILLY URIBE

Left: 25 Praia de Maplica. Above: 26 Nemia, a quiet little spot to enjoy the glide.

BEACH BREAK

↘28 Praia Aguieira

- **Conditions** Huge NW and W swells, offshore in S winds
- **Hazards/tips** It's only worth checking here in the biggest of swells
- **Sleeping** Porto do Son » p256

Heading south from Noia you will find the beautiful Praia Aguieira. Set in pine forest, this excellent dune-backed beach has quality waves that come to life when the big swells roll in. Awesome location.

BEACH BREAK

↘29 Praia de Furnas

- **Conditions** All NW and W swells, offshore in S to E winds
- **Hazards/tips** Stunning, unmarked stretch of coastline, crystal-clear water
- **Sleeping** Porto do Son » p256

Furnas picks up loads of swell and is one of many high-quality breaks on this stretch of coastline. Works best at low tide. When it's on it has fast, hollow rides on a beautiful, uncrowded beach. Other breaks worth checking include **Baroña** and **Queiruga** to the north and **Portinos**, **Ladeira** and **Ferreiras** to the south.

BEACH BREAK

↘30 Praia de Montalbo and Paxarinas

- **Conditions** Medium to big NW to W swells, offshore in E to NE winds
- **Hazards/tips** Crowds, rips when big
- **Sleeping** Sanxenxo » p256

Close to the town of Sanxenxo sit the beaches of Montalbo (Montalvo) and Paxarinas. **Paxarinas** has an excellent, hollow left-hander that gets going in big swells and draws surfers from across the region. **Punta Montalbo** is a rocky point that throws up a hollow right-hander at low to mid tide. The beach is also home to some excellent waves. This is a spot that can get very busy. There is parking at the beach, signposted from the main road.

REEF BREAK

↘31 Praia de Santa María de Oia

- **Conditions** All N to W swells, offshore in S to SE winds
- **Hazards/tips** Rocky reef, powerful waves
- **Sleeping** A Guarda » p256

This is a stunning stretch of coastline with a rich maritime history, where beautiful bays are separated by rocky points. The beach break at Oia has a reef that works in northwesterly swells producing beautiful, crystal-clear lefts up to 8 ft on all but low tides. Popular with a small but committed local crew.

BEACH AND POINT BREAK

↘32 Praia do Carreiro and Punta dos Picos

- **Conditions** All W and NW swells, offshore in E winds
- **Hazards/tips** These are the last breaks in Spain before crossing into Portugal
- **Sleeping** A Guarda » p256

The beach at Praia do Carreiro is always worth checking, as is Punta dos Picos. This works in a northeasterly wind and, in big swells, can produce walling rights. Head south from A Guarda and follow signs.

Practicalities

Ribadeo

Crossing over the Ría Eo into Galicia, Ribadeo (see how they got the name there) is the first place you hit and it even has a surf shop. Holaola, www.holaola.com, is on Av Carlo Sotelo.

Sleeping

In peak season, accommodation can be fairly pricey.

€€ Mi Norte, wwwminortehabitaciones.com, just off the N-634 highway, is quite a fun place to stay and a bit different with amusingly themed rooms (try the James Bond).

€ El Pinar, on Villaframil, T982-131157, is fine, one of the cheapest pensions.

Camping Ribadeo, summer campsite to the west of the town, Jun-Sep, T982-131167, also offers cabins.

JAKUE ANDIKOTXEA

Galicia, one of the few places in Europe where waves peel unwatched and unridden.

Ribadeo to Foz

The Ribadeo to Foz stretch is notoriously packed with trucks hurtling towards A Coruña. The beach signs off the N-634 don't give you much notice so hit the Estrada de Costa (coast road) as soon as possible. It feels pretty seedy round here but don't let this colour your opinion of the region.

Sleeping

East of Foz, camping **Nosa Casa Reinante**, on Playa Reinante, T982-134005, is open year round and has the option of cabins.

A Gaivota, is between Playa de Barreiros and the N-634, T982-124451. Open Jun-Sep. It has full facilities as well as cabins.

Benquerencia, www.camping benquerencia.com, between Benquerencia and Barreiros, T982-124450, is open year round and is the largest site in the area.

Foz

This is a fairly unremarkable fishing town with a large port servicing a cluster of good seafood cafés and restaurants. It also has a couple of surf shops servicing the local scene.

Sleeping

There is not a wide choice of cheap accommodation here.

€ Hotel Leyton, on the main Av Generalisimo, T982-140800, looks like a knocking shop but is a cheap bet off season.

Camping Rapadoira-Llas, just back from Praia Llas, T982-140713, is the smaller of the 2 campsites, open Jun-Sep. To the west is **San Rafael**, by Praia de Peizas, T982-132218, May-Sep.

Eating

Asador, on the N-634 before Foz, is a popular and reasonable place to grab a chicken and chips.

Viveiro

The drive from Xove to Viveiro is an aromatic experience and more what Galicia is about – the road is thickly lined with lush eucalyptus trees. Viveiro, itself is a busy working port, nestled in this heady green valley at the neck of the river. A visit to the old town and the replica Lourdes grotto may even cure your surfing ails – locals leave offerings in return for good health and if not a trip to the local surf shop might: check out **T Hachece** opposite the bridge on the east side of town, and **Koala**, Av Ferrol.

Sleeping

€ As Areas II, on the west side on Av Santiago, T982-50523, has parking, large but fairly basic rooms and good off-season rates.

Camping Viviero, at Praia de Covas on the west of the town, T982-560004, Jun-Sep.

Eating

Eat good cheap fish along the waterfront – check out the **Galicia Café**, on Av García Navia Castrillón. On the main road by **O Barqueiro**, the clean, friendly café **O'Boliche** does a great *menú del día* for about €6.50 and is popular with the locals.

Cedeira

Cedeira on the C-646 is a good base for exploring Pantín and the surrounding breaks as it has all the basic amenities including banks and supermarkets.

Sleeping

€ Chelsea, T981-482340, is not the prettiest, but it is friendly, functional and one of the cheapest places to stay here.

Camping Heading west, **A Lagoa**, is just back from Praia Frouxeira, T981-487122, open Jun-15 Sep. **Valdoviño**, off the C-642, T981-487076, has plenty of facilities including cabins, and is open year round.

DEMI TAYLOR

10 Praia Esterio

Further along, **Fontesín**, T981-485028, is simpler and cheaper, Jun-Sep.

Eating

Pizza Lanus, on the riverfront of the old town, does a good pizza as well as a selection of pasta and salads. **Café Plaza**, Praza Sagrado, is a great place to grab a coffee and a *napolitana* for breakfast. Heading west towards the village of Pantín, **Casa Ramos**, overlooking the WQS break, Praia Rodo, is an interesting place to get a beer or a coffee and have a game of pool after a surf.

Ferrol

The drive from Cedeira crosses moorland, rugged countryside and bypasses jagged cliffs interspersed with large expanses of beach. Ferrol itself – the birthplace of Fascist dictator, Franco – is fairly unremarkable but has a large port, a large surf community and several surf shops.

Sleeping

€ Da Magdalena, on Magdalena, T981-355615, open throughout the year and one of the cheapest options around.
Camping As Cabazas on the Cobas-Ferrol road, T981-365706, Jun-Sep, also has cabins.

A Coruña

A Coruña is a relaxed, beautiful city surrounded by water. A warren of seafood restaurants and tapas bars is headed up by a square paying tribute to the city's saviour, María Pita, who stopped the city from being ravaged by Drake and the plundering English in the 1500s. To the north, the Torre de Hércules looks out towards Britain and having been erected by the Romans in the 2nd century AD, is said to be the oldest working lighthouse in the world (although most of the structure actually dates from the 1700s). You can climb to the top and look out over the world. There is plenty parking dotted along the main arteries including underground car parks at Plaza de María Pita and Av de la Marina.

Sleeping

A couple of cheap options can be found on Praza de Galicia near the church of St Lucía, including **€ Palacio**, T981-122338, www.hostalpalacio.com. The rooms are large and comfortable but fairly basic (doubles from around €25).
€ Carbonara, Rua Nueva, T981-225251, is closer to the action and clean and massive.
Camping Camp out of town at Valcobo south at in Arteixo on Lugar de Valcobar, T981-601040, Apr-Sep.

Eating and drinking

Sandwiched between R Nueva and Plaza María Pita is the tapas zone and the best place to head for ambience. A Coruña is all about the seafood, especially *pulpo* (octopus) and C Franja off the square is the place to sample it. If fish doesn't float your boat, head to **El Serrano**, on Galera, which,

Flat spells

Sights **Lugo** An hour south from the coast, the Roman town of Lugo still retains its walled centre – erected in the 3rd century AD – as well as the remains of Roman baths. A UNESCO World Heritage Site, the entire wall circuit is intact and is one of the best examples of late Roman fortifications in western Europe. Grab a bite to eat on the Rua Nova which stretches down towards the cathedral. **Pontevedra**, off the A9 in the south, is a very pretty city, complete with old quarter, gothic architecture and a beautiful 16th-century church, Basílica de Santa María a Maior. **Vigo** in southwest Galicia is about the fish and as one of the world's largest fishing ports it's no surprise that you can pick up some good quality, reasonably priced seafood – head for the market on R de Pescadería or check out the cafés nearby. There's also an abundance of surf shops here – good for a bit of light browsing. In **A Guarda**, Galicia's southernmost coastal town, trek up the **Monte Santa Trega** for awesome views across the river to Portugal and out to sea. Nearby are also the remains of a Celtic village. Head south of Ferrol to the pretty river town **Pontedeume** and explore the **Parque Natural Fragas do Eume** – a vast woodland of ancients oaks, hazel and chestnut trees in a canyon carved out by the River Eume.

Museums Head to the **Domus** on Santa Teresa for the museum of mankind and catch a movie at the **Imax** cinema, T981-189840.

Football Watch erstwhile La Liga contenders **Deportiva La Coruña** at Estadio de Raizor, in A Coruña, just back from Praia de Raizor.

Golf There are plenty of courses in the region. Get a few rounds in at **Club de Golf Campomar**, in Ferrol, C Nicaragua, T619-659832. Get some practice at **Golpe Pitch & Putt** in Carballo, southwest of A Coruña, T981-739699, www.carballo.org, or have a full round at the **Campo Municipal de Golf Torre de Hércules**, Av da Torre, A Coruña, T981-209680. In the south try **Golf a Toxa** on Isla da Toxa near O Grove, T986-730818, www.latojagolf.com.

DEMI TAYLOR

15 Praia Baleo – Pantin's less crowded option

as the name and the ceiling suggests, is a *jamonería* serving a good selection of tapas and raciones. In the early evening the Plaza is a popular spot to have a beer and watch the world go by.

Directory

Surf Shops There are plenty of surf shops here including **Surf & Rock** www.surfandrock.com just back from Praia de Raizor on C Alfredo Vicente. One road back, on Fernando Macías, is the vast **Raz**with a good range of, well, everything www.raz.es (with handy webcams of the surrounding coast west).
Internet Estrella Park C Estrella. **Tourist information**: Plza Maria Pita and Plza Orense www.turismocoruna.com.

Malpica

The fishing town of Malpica is on the Costa da Morte, or 'coast of death', at the end of the AC-414 from Carballo. Offshore, Islas Sisargas is a haven for birds.

Sleeping

€€ Hotel Fonte do Fraile, on the seafront overlooking Playa de Canido, www.fontedofraile.com, is a nice spot and well priced off season from €50. The modern/rustic rooms are a good size and there is a jacuzzi area to chill out in.
€ Hostal JB, C Playa, T981-721906, is one of the cheapest hotel options with rooms overlooking the beach from around €28.
Camping **Sisargas**, T981-721702, large, seasonal campsite open Jun-15 Sep, also offers cabins.

Muxía

South of the Río Camariñas, Muxía is home to a couple of campsites: **Lago Mar**, T981-750628, also cabins, open Jun-Sep; and **El Paraiso**, T981-750790, open year round; are between Merexo and Muxía on C Playa de Lago. **Playa Barreira Leis**, in Leis, T981-730304, is reasonable, open year round and has cabins. For a change of scene, head to the 'end of the world', **Cabo Finisterre**, a dramatic place to walk around and experience the power of the Atlantic.

Muros

Set on the Ría de Muros e Noia, this pretty fishing town has plenty of eating and accommodation options.

Sleeping

€ Hostal Playa Atlantica, on San Francisco de Louro, T981-826451, offers some of the best room rates.
Camping **San Francisco**, C Playa, T981-826148, 20 Jun-20 Sep. **A Vouga**, T981-826284, open year round on the road down from Finisterre. **Ancoradoiro**, on the road from Corcubión, T981-878897, by the (nudist) beach of the same name and the smallest of the 3 sites, open Jun-Sep.

Porto do Son

Heading south on the C-550 this is a pretty place to stay and one of the most lively around the Ría de Muros e Noia.

Sleeping

Accommodation here is not particularly cheap.
€€ Hotel León II, C Praia Ornanda, T981-766188, is one of the most cost effective, though the rooms are a bit stark.
Camping There are a couple of places to the north including: **Punta Batuda**, near Praia de Ornanda-Gaviotas, T981-766542, www.puntabatuda.com, large site with great facilities and cabins to rent; and **Cabiero**, T981-767355, which is smaller, has fewer facilities, but is cheaper. Both are year round.

Sanxenxo

Overdeveloped and slightly disappointing, this resort town is a popular spot, indicated by the high number of campsites crammed into such a small area. It does however have good facilities. The waterfront is packed with bars and cafés and there are hundreds of places to stay so shop around for a deal and take your pick.

Sleeping

Camping Highlights include the all-singing, all-dancing **Boavista**, handily placed by Praia Montalvo, T986-720478, open Apr-Sep, with cabins. Also near the beach is the lower grade **Montalvo Playa**, Jun-Sep, T986-724087. **Monte Cabo** is just north of Portonovo by the Punta Faxilda, T986-744141, and is year-round; as is **Baltar**, www.campingbaltar.com, T986-691888, 100 m from the beach of the same name with statics available.

Directory

Inland at Pontevedra there are several surf shops where you can pick up essentials, including **Puerto Escondido**, on Cruz Gallastegui, and **Mission**, on Sagastra. In Poio in the commercial centre is **Sinsemilla**.

A Guarda

Sitting at the bottom of the C-550, this is the last Atlantic town in Spain.

Sleeping

Camping Camp out year round in **Salcidos**, at Santa Tecla, T986-613011, which is crammed full of amenities including cabins to rent. Heading north, Oia also has a couple of campsites: **O Muinoz**, on the C-550, T986-361600, with cabins and more facilities than you can shake a tent pole at, Mar-Sep; and **Camping Mougas**, to the north near Baiona, www.campingmougas.com, T986-385011, Apr-Sep, which has the choice of camping and wooden chalets.

Overview

It's a massive jump in distance, geography and culture from the lush, green Celtic fringe of Northern Spain to the parched, brown hues of Moorish Andalucía. Long, sun-warmed beaches of golden Saharan sand are backed by tinder-dry pines that gaze across the narrows of the straits of Gibraltar toward the northern shores of Morocco. This geological bottleneck creates a natural wind machine, funneling the dry siroccos from the Sahara and the leventes from the west, drawing windsurfers and kitesurfers from across the globe. But the province isn't without its surfing draws. The huge expanses of beach are linked by some surprisingly good points and the occasional rivermouth gem – just be ready to be on it when the wind dies.

This region has a turbulent past. It was the first to fall to the Moors in AD 711 and the last to be reclaimed by Spain. Moorish architecture and culture dominate, with walled cities and palaces set around tiled courtyards with fountains and shady palms. Then there's the Alhambra in Granada, one of the country's biggest tourist attractions. The western Costa de la Luz is watched over by the port town of Cádiz to the north and the walled town of Tarifa to the south. Cádiz has an amazing old centre, a thriving surf community and some excellent city beaches. Tarifa meanwhile has become a traditional overnight stop for those making the trip south to the surf potential of Morocco. Locals will tell you that the endless winds make Tarifa the suicide capital of Spain, (and if you have spent any time here waiting for the winds to die so you can make the crossing to Morocco, you can see why) but it has also meant that the picturesque Moorish town is Europe's windsurfing Mecca. It overlooks the busy shipping lanes of the Straits of Gibraltar and offers glimpses of the heights of the north African continent, only 14 km away through the haze.

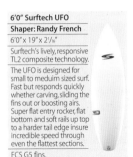

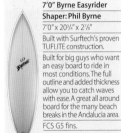

DEMI TAYLOR

6 Playa del Palmar

Coastline

The coastline of Andalucía is a mixture of long, dune-backed, sandy beaches and rocky points. The region around Cádiz is dominated by massive tracts of beach break. This area picks up less swell than the south due to the blocking effect of Cabo San Vincente in Portugal. The rocky points around Cabo de Trafalgar and Cabo Garcia can have some excellent point breaks in good swells and the southern stretch of beach towards Tarifa. Although not Europe's most consistent coastline, it enjoys mild winters which can have great waves set against the backdrop of Africa's Northern Rif mountains.

Localism environment

Around the port town of Cadiz the water quality can be low as the sewer system is dated, and can be especially poor after the rains with stormwater run-off making its way into the line-up. The same can be said of rivermouth breaks such as Barbate. As far as localism goes many of the breaks are pretty relaxed and there are many uncrowded spots to be discovered. Spots in Cádiz and at Roche can get very busy and the coastline has developed a bit of a reputation for car crime. Park with care and don't leave valuables in the car.

Getting around

The city beaches in Cádiz are accessible on foot, but if you really want to get out and explore the region you will need wheels. The N-340 south runs parallel to the coast with smaller roads accessing the beaches. Some spots are accessed via rough pistes.

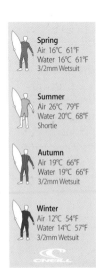

Spring
Air 16°C 61°F
Water 16°C 61°F
3/2mm Wetsuit

Summer
Air 26°C 79°F
Water 20°C 68°F
Shortie

Autumn
Air 19°C 66°F
Water 19°C 66°F
3/2mm Wetsuit

Winter
Air 12°C 54°F
Water 14°C 57°F
3/2mm Wetsuit

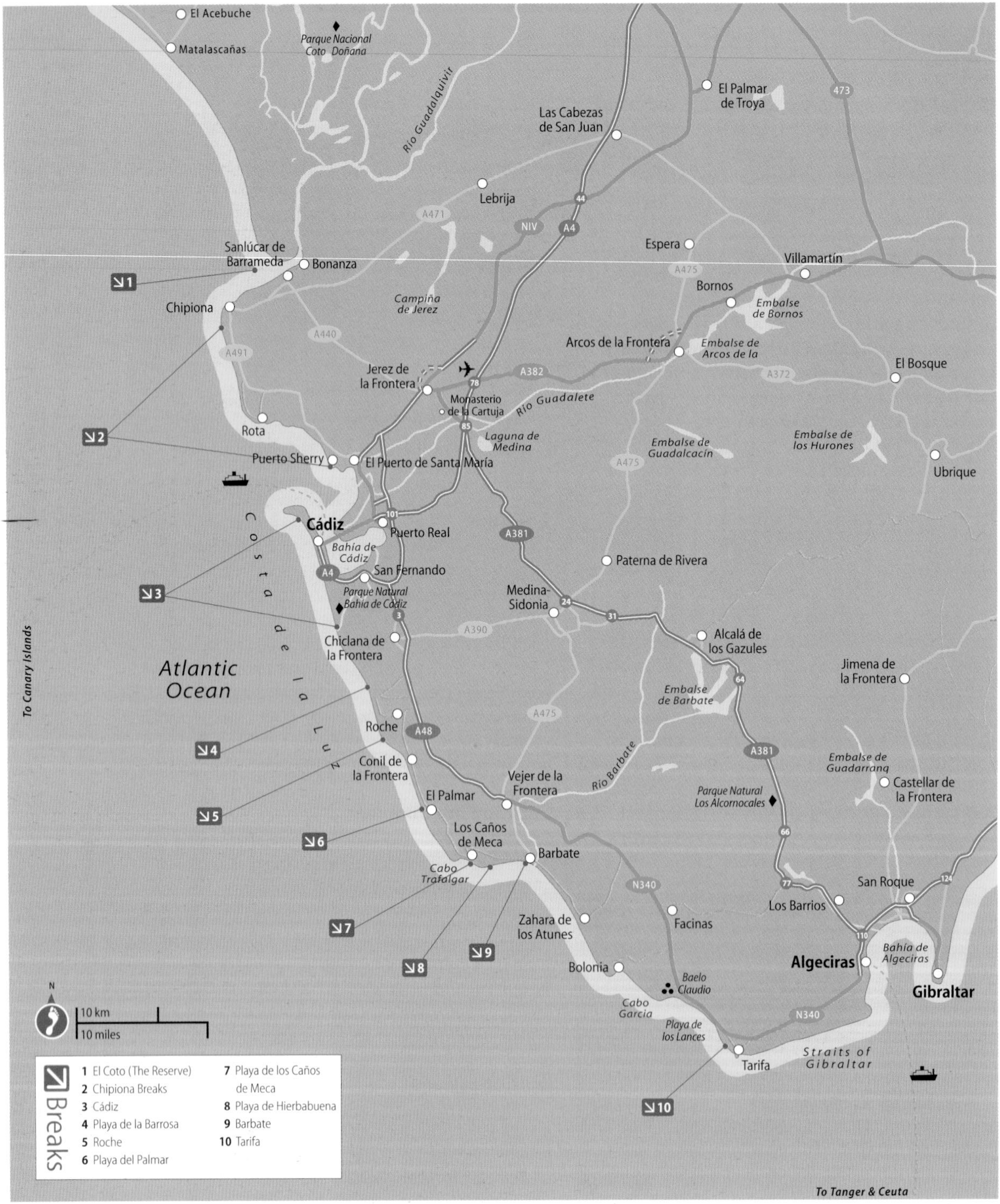

El Acebuche
Matalascañas
Parque Nacional Coto Doñana
Río Guadalquivir
El Palmar de Troya
Las Cabezas de San Juan
Lebrija
Sanlúcar de Barrameda
Bonanza
Chipiona
Campiña de Jerez
Espera
Villamartín
Bornos
Embalse de Bornos
Arcos de la Frontera
Embalse de Arcos de la
El Bosque
Jerez de la Frontera
Monasterio de la Cartuja
Río Guadalete
Laguna de Medina
Rota
Puerto Sherry
El Puerto de Santa María
Embalse de Guadalcacín
Embalse de los Hurones
Ubrique
Cádiz
Puerto Real
Bahía de Cádiz
San Fernando
Costa de la Luz
Parque Natural Bahía de Cádiz
Paterna de Rivera
Medina-Sidonia
Chiclana de la Frontera
Alcalá de los Gazules
Atlantic Ocean
To Canary Islands
Jimena de la Frontera
Embalse de Barbate
Roche
Conil de la Frontera
Vejer de la Frontera
Río Barbate
Embalse de Guadarranq
Castellar de la Frontera
Parque Natural Los Alcornocales
El Palmar
Los Caños de Meca
Barbate
Cabo Trafalgar
San Roque
Los Barrios
Zahara de los Atunes
Facinas
Bolonia
Baelo Claudio
Algeciras
Bahía de Algeciras
Gibraltar
Cabo Garcia
Playa de los Lances
Tarifa
Straits of Gibraltar
To Tanger & Ceuta
A471
A4
NIV
44
473
A475
A440
A491
A382
A372
78
85
101
A381
24
31
3
A390
64
A48
A475
A381
66
77
N340
124
110
N340
N
10 km
10 miles
1
2
3
4
5
6
7
8
9
10
Breaks
1 El Coto (The Reserve)
2 Chipiona Breaks
3 Cádiz
4 Playa de la Barrosa
5 Roche
6 Playa del Palmar
7 Playa de los Caños de Meca
8 Playa de Hierbabuena
9 Barbate
10 Tarifa

Breaks

ROCKY RIVERMOUTH BREAK

↘1 El Coto (The Reserve)

- **Conditions** All W and SW swells, offshore in NE winds
- **Hazards/tips** Busy wave in national park
- **Sleeping** Chipiona » *p261*

When a clean westerly or southwesterly swell comes out of the Atlantic this mid to high tide wave can turn on producing walling right-handers. The wave breaks at the northern mouth of the Río Guadalquivir on the edge of the Parque Nacional Coto Doñana. This is a quality wave that can get busy but is still pretty chilled.

JAKUE ANDIKOTXEA

You can even find the odd wave lurking east of Tarfia.

BEACH BREAKS

↘2 Chipiona Breaks

- **Conditions** All SW to W swells, offshore in NE to E winds
- **Hazards/tips** Quality breaks south of Chipiona
- **Sleeping** Chipiona » *p261*

Playa de Regla is a white-sand urban beach best at mid to high tide. On the same stretch of beach to the south is **Playa de Tres Piedras**, a dune-backed beach break with some rocks to the eastern edge. It has lefts and rights and works best at mid to high tide. Both need winds from the northeast or east and southwesterly or westerly swells. To the south breaks a quality right-hander, **Cien Metros**, a fast and powerful wave that breaks between mid and high tide. **Playa de la Ballena** is another mid to high tide break. All found north of Cádiz on a long stretch of coast between Chipiona and Rota.

DEMI TAYLOR

2 Chipiona.

BEACH BREAKS

↘3 Cádiz

- **Conditions** All W to SW swells, offshore in E winds
- **Hazards/tips** This huge stretch of beaches becomes less busy as you head south
- **Sleeping** Cádiz/El Puerto de Santa María » *p261*

Cádiz sits on the northern end of a peninsula, which provides a huge expanse of sandy beaches that stretch south all the way to the river at Sancti Petri. The town beach, **La Playita**, has two boulder groynes along which the sand builds up. It works best at low to mid tide. **Las Caracolos** stretches to the south of the city and works best on a mid to high tide. At the end of Playa de la Victoria is **La Cabañita**, a hollow, right-hand high tide wave. **Torregorda** and **Campo Soto** are both picturesque dune-backed beaches with golden sand.

BEACH BREAK

↘4 Playa de la Barrosa

- **Conditions** All W to SW swells, offshore in NE winds
- **Hazards/tips** Picks up less swell
- **Sleeping** Chiclana de la Frontera » *p262*

A continuation of the sandy beaches heading south, La Barrosa has peaks that work best at low to mid tide. This is a fairly quiet spot with some shelter that needs a bigger swell to get going.

BEACH BREAK

↘5 Roche

- **Conditions** All W to SW swells, offshore in E winds
- **Hazards/tips** Crowds, localism when busy
- **Sleeping** Conil de la Frontera » p262

Roche is a popular beach break that is one of the region's most consistent waves. It has powerful, high-quality lefts and rights that are best from low to mid tide. Gets busy and can have a degree of localism. Take the turning off the N-340 for Roche.

BEACH BREAK

↘6 Playa del Palmar

- **Conditions** All W and SW swells, offshore in NE and E winds
- **Hazards/tips** Gets busy at peak times
- **Sleeping** Conil de la Frontera » p262

Palmar is a popular spot that can produce high-quality lefts and rights, with powerful and hollow waves breaking consistently on the sandbanks. Works on all tides with a high tide shore break, but is best from low to mid tide.

REEF BREAK

↘7 Playa de los Caños de Meca

- **Conditions** All W to SW swells, offshore in a N to NE winds
- **Hazards/tips** Gets busy when it's working
- **Sleeping** Barbate » p262

This is a long, sandy beach but the break itself is a flat slab reef that works best from low to mid tides. This left-hander can be fast with decent cover-up sections. Popular spot with a small take-off zone.

RIGHT-HAND POINT BREAK

↘8 Playa de Hierbabuena

- **Conditions** Big W to SW swells, offshore in N to NE winds
- **Hazards/tips** Crowds, car crime
- **Sleeping** Barbate » p262

This rocky point is hidden away among scrub and pine trees west of Barbate. It can produce excellent long right-hand walls on all tides, but needs a decent swell to get going. Breaks up to 6 ft. At the end of a long sandy track – you'll need to go by foot unless you have a 4WD. This area has a reputation for car crime. Don't leave any valuables in sight.

RIVERMOUTH BREAK

↘9 Barbate

- **Conditions** Medium to big W to SW swells, offshore in NE winds
- **Hazards/tips** Busy break, may have localism when crowded
- **Sleeping** Barbate » p262

Barbate is the region's most famous break and many travelling surfers visit here, drawn by photos of this mini Mundaka-like set-up. The rivermouth currents sculpt a sandbar ready for when a good size swell hits, sending long, reeling lefts spinning through to the inside. Classic spot but not very consistent, so the locals will be on it when it breaks. Like many rivermouths, a low tide spot.

BEACH BREAK

↘10 Tarifa

- **Conditions** All W to SW swells, offshore in NE or E winds
- **Hazards/tips** Windy, packed with windsurfers, can be damp in winter
- **Sleeping** Tarifa » p262

From Tarifa north is a huge stretch of sandy beach with the occasional rocky finger point. This coastline is peppered with campsites and draws windsurfers from all over the world for good reason. However, there can be waves when the wind drops and a decent swell kicks in. At the northern end of the beach is a right-hand point accessed in front of the Jardín de Las Dunas campsite. This stretch is offshore in a light northeasterly wind. Great views across to Morocco and if you feel the need to learn to kitesurf, this is the ideal place. For many surfers, however, the constant wind can be a test of sanity.

DEMI TAYLOR

7 Caños de Meca, just east of Cabo Trafalgar.

Practicalities

Chipiona

Heading south from Sevilla on the A4/E5 toll road, take the A-471 west and you'll soon hit the Costa de la Luz or 'coast of light'. Less built-up than the high-rise Costa del Sol to the east, Andalucía's west coast is an easy stopping point before heading south to Morocco. Chipiona, south of the Río Guadalquivir, is the first coastal port of call and with four long white sandy beaches is a popular summer resort.

Sleeping

The large **Camping El Pinar de Chipiona**, T956-372321, is open year round on the road south to Rota.

El Puerto de Santa María

Given its proximity to Cádiz, this pretty town is a popular spot with urban holidaymakers and weekenders. It's also a popular spot for anyone interested in sampling the local **sherry** – drunk very cold and very dry – in one of the many bodegas that line the river and road into town.

Sleeping

Camping Las Dunas, on the Paseo Marítimo La Puntilla, T956-872210, is fairly large, just back from the beach and open year round.

Eating

Around the harbour are plenty of good seafood eateries, try the relaxed **Romerijo**, on the Ribera del Marisco.

Directory

Surf Shops On the main road into the town check out the retail park which houses a **Decathlon** sports store who do a cheap range of own-brand wetsuits, boots and gloves as well as a few boards. Surf/skate store **Kalima**, on Av del Descubrimiento, can sort out your basic needs, as can **Nomadas Surf Shop**, in the Centro Comercial.

Cádiz

Set at the end of a long peninsula, Cádiz is an important port town and, having been settled by the Phoenicians in 1100 BC, is also one of the oldest towns in Spain. Head to the Plaza de San Juan, just back from the port, where the streets are a warren of watering holes and beds for the night.

Sleeping

€ Pensión Las Cuatro Naciones, on Plocia, T956-256255, is one of the best sleeping options where rooms range from about €17.

DEMI TAYLOR

An indicator of how regular a feature the wind really is here.

Camping **El Pinar** is the nearest campsite, 11 km away in Puerto Real on the N-IV from Madrid, T956-830897.

Eating

Look out for *freidurías* – fried fish shops

Flat spells

Bodegas Laid-back entertainment can be found at one of the many bodegas in the birthplace of sherry where a tour and generous product sampling can set you back about €8. One of the best known is **Pedro Domecq**, T956-357016, www.domecq.es. Head to the tourist office on Larga, the main road, for help organizing a tour.

Golf Get 9 holes in at the reasonably priced**Vista Hermosa Golf** nestled in the Bahía Cádiz, T956-541968.

Horses **Sanlúcar de Barrameda** is home to some intense beach horse racing in August – hit the tourist office on Calzada del Ejército for more info. While you're there, enjoy a glass of *manzanilla* sherry which has helped make a name for the place. **Jerez**, north of Cadiz, is all about horses and sherry – in almost equal quantities. The **Horse Fair** in May is a grand affair and sees horses put through a series of events and shows.

Morocco If you're not heading south for the winter, from Tarifa take a day trip to Morocco or overnight there. You can book a return to Tanger for about €40 from any one of the kiosks along the main road or at the harbour front.

Nature reserve North of the Río Guadalquivir in the Huelva region lies the **Parque Nacional Coto Doñana**, the largest nature reserve in Spain. Home to flamingos, birds of prey and lynx among others, entrance is controlled. The best way to see (a bit of) the park is by boat tour on the Real Fernando from the Bajo de Guía quay in Sanlúcar de Barrameda. Tickets for the 4-hr tour are about €14 and need to be pre-booked on T956 363 813, or at the park exhibition centre on the Bajo de Guía.

Skiing Head east and hit the slopes on the Sierra Nevadas where night skiing is on offer, www.sierranevadaski.com.

where you can eat in or, better still, take your meal away with you wrapped in a paper cone.

Directory

Post office Plaza de Topete. **Surf Shops** Sitting at the top of a long stretch of breaks, Cádiz is home to a healthy surf community and has plenty of surf shops including **Hot Water**, along the waterfront on Paseo Marítimo, **Oasis Surf Shop**, in Chiclana, and **Tavarua** on Tolosa la Tour. **Tourist information** On Ramón de Carranza, just off the plaza San Juan de Dois, www.andalucia.com.

Chiclana de la Frontera

Sleeping

Heading south on the N-340 from Cádiz to Tarifa, there is **Camping La Barrosa**, on the road from Barrosa, T956-494605, open May-Sep, bungalows to rent.

Directory

Etnica Surf Shop, on the beach at Barrosa, www.etnicasurf.com.

Conil de la Frontera

This pleasant, whitewashed fishing village, has a laid-back attitude and is fast becoming a favourite with holidaying locals. As such there are plenty of reasonable places to eat, drink and be merry along the beachfront. There are also a couple of internet posts.

Sleeping

The centrally located **€ Hostal La Villa**, Plaza de España, T956-441053, is reasonably priced and convenient.
Camping Plenty of campsites here including year-round **Cala del Aceite**, T956-442950, www.caladelaceite.com, with cabins, **La Rosaleda**, on road to Pradillo, T956-443327, open year round, as is **Roche**, on Pago del Zorro, T956-442216, www.campingroche.com, with cabins, **El Faro**, on Puerto Pesquero near the beachfront, all year, T956-444096, www.campingelfaro.com. **Los Eucaliptos**, on El Padrilo, Apr-Sep, has cabins, T956-441272. To the south **Camping El Palmar**, is well placed on the coast off the Conil-Caños de Meca road at Playa El Palmar, T956-232161, 1 Apr-31 Sep. Off season, the police seem to tolerate responsible free-camping near the beach but move vans on in the run up to the summer.

Eating

Keep an eye out for *chiringuitos* dotted all along the seafront – fairly seasonal beach bars where you can pick up a cheap and tasty lunchtime or evening snack of fried fish. There is also a good supermarket, as well as local fish and vegetable markets.

Directory

The beachside **El Palmar Surf** (www.elpalmarsurf.com), offers a surf camp, shop as well as a surfboard factory.

Barbate

On the run down to Tarifa, the classic rivermouth of Barbate is a popular stop off.

Sleeping

Camping Faro de Trafalgar, on the Vejer-Caños de Meca route, T956-437017, 3 Apr-15 Sep. Just down the road is **Caños de Meca**, T956-437120, with cabins, Apr-15 Oct. **Bahía de la Plata**, south at the fishing village of Zahara de los Atunes, T956-439040, www.campingbahiadelaplata.com, is open year round.

Directory

As well as campsites, the village has a couple of surf shops including **Coco's**, on Av del Generalísimo.

Tarifa

Separated from Africa by a 14-km stretch of water, the Moors' influence on this old walled town is obvious. The constant hammering of the levante winds from the east and the poniente winds from the west has brought Tarifa international acclaim within the world of windsurfing. Spring sees the Playa los Lances overrun with some of the world's best windsurfers for the **Redbull Skyride**, which includes a race across the Straits of Gibraltar. Tarifa's a great place to stop off if you want to try kitesurfing or stock up on surf essentials before heading off to Morocco.

Sleeping

Camping The N-340 on the Atlantic side of Tarifa is littered with year-round campsites on both sides of the road but probably due to the fact they are popular with windsurfers they seem pricey.
Jardín de las Dunas is just off the main road at Playa de Valdevaqueros, near a popular free-camping site, T956-689101, www.campingjdunas.com.
Paloma, T956-684203, www.campingpaloma.com, has cabins. **Río Jara**, T956-680570, on N-340, is just down the road from **Camping Tarifa**, T956-684778, www.camping-tarifa.com.
Torre de la Peña I, T956-684903, www.campingtp.com, has cabins. **Torre de la Peña II**, T956-684174, runs onto the beachfront and is popular with windsurfers.

Directory

Surf Shops Plenty of windsurf/surf shops, including a **Quiksilver Boardrider**, **Art of Surfing**, **Xtrem**, **Surf Division** and **Fly Cat**, on Batalla del Saludo. **Internet** Check the charts online at **Top Clean Tarifa**, Av de Andalucia 24, T956-680303. They also have a coffee shop and you can get your laundry done as well! Send your last cards from Europe at the **Post office** C Coronel Moscardo. **Tourist information** Paseo de la Alameda.

Canary Islands

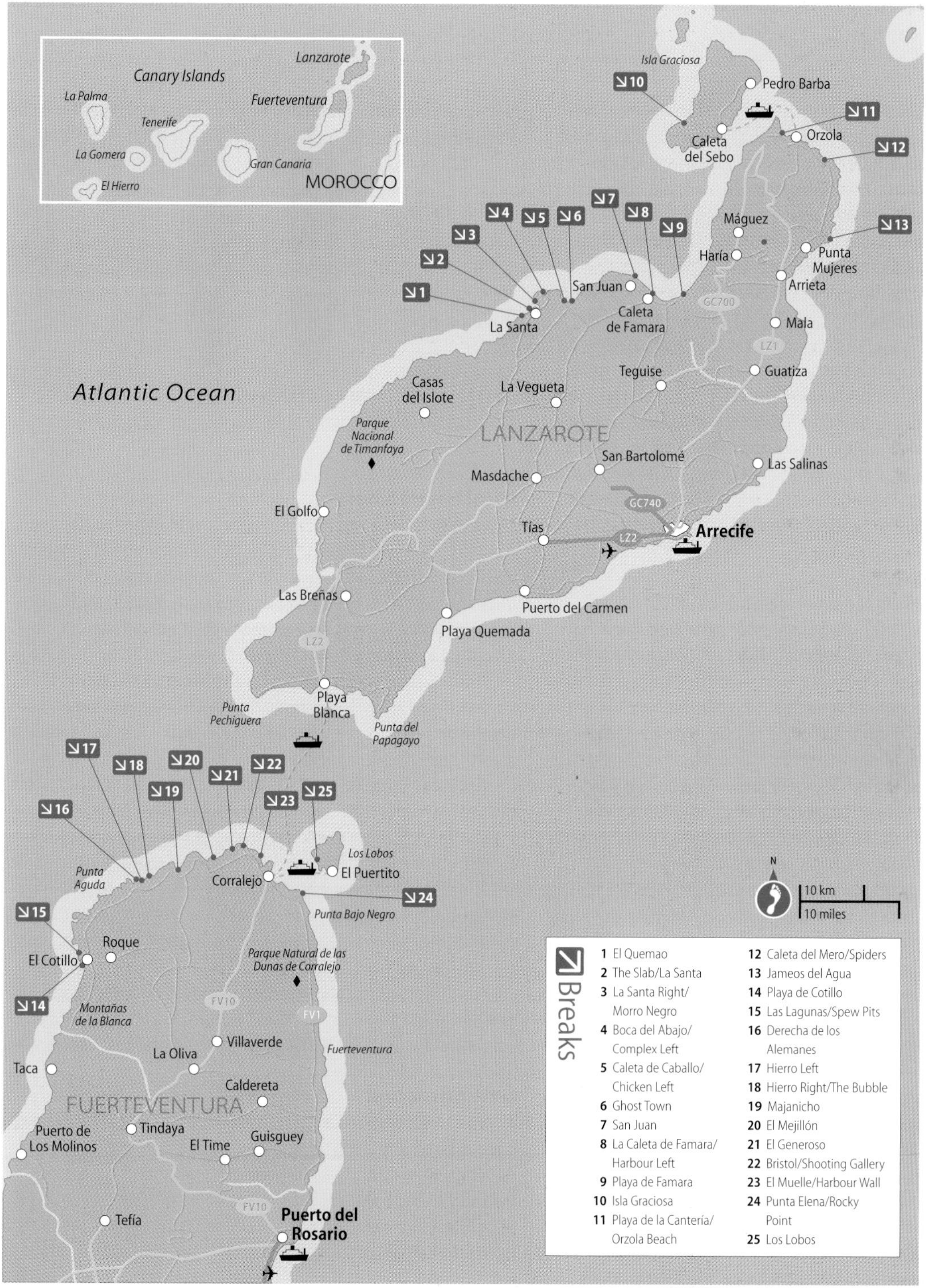

Breaks

1 El Quemao
2 The Slab/La Santa
3 La Santa Right/Morro Negro
4 Boca del Abajo/Complex Left
5 Caleta de Caballo/Chicken Left
6 Ghost Town
7 San Juan
8 La Caleta de Famara/Harbour Left
9 Playa de Famara
10 Isla Graciosa
11 Playa de la Cantería/Orzola Beach
12 Caleta del Mero/Spiders
13 Jameos del Agua
14 Playa de Cotillo
15 Las Lagunas/Spew Pits
16 Derecha de los Alemanes
17 Hierro Left
18 Hierro Right/The Bubble
19 Majanicho
20 El Mejillón
21 El Generoso
22 Bristol/Shooting Gallery
23 El Muelle/Harbour Wall
24 Punta Elena/Rocky Point
25 Los Lobos

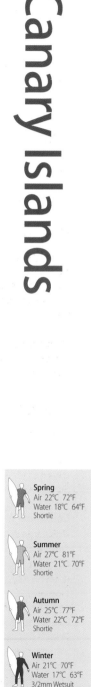

Spring
Air 22°C 72°F
Water 18°C 64°F
Shortie

Summer
Air 27°C 81°F
Water 21°C 70°F
Shortie

Autumn
Air 25°C 77°F
Water 22°C 72°F
Shortie

Winter
Air 21°C 70°F
Water 17°C 63°F
3/2mm Wetsuit

Overview

It's an old cliché, but the Canary Islands really are Europe's very own Hawaii. Just as the 'Aloha State' floats way off the west coast of California in the tropical blue of the Pacific, our very own islands are anchored off the desert coast of Africa, more than 1000 km away from their European roots. Each offers a winter getaway for northern hemisphere surfers eager to shake off the cold and gorge on classic waves. Both are famed for their challenging volcanic reefs, where *cojones* and rhino hides are a plus. Both possess a 'North Shore' whose fire is ignited through the winter months, converting every passing swell into huge, powerful, shallow waves and life-threatening barrels and where an uneasy spirit of local domination rules the line-up.

November through February sees some of the most consistent surf in the Canary Islands, with a constant stream of low-pressure systems pushing regular, chunky swell down from the North Atlantic. This is when the northeasterly trade winds – which in the summer can turn the islands into frustrating dust bowls – also ease off. The water, although tempered by the cooling Canaries Current travelling south towards the equator, remains at a manageable 18-21°C. Winter on these 'Lucky Islands' is nigh on perfect.

A less savoury aspect of surfing here is the 'localismo' that has taken hold at some spots. "The *surfista* visitor should used their common sense and their imagination," says surf photographer Willy Uribe. "There are uncrowded waves out there for those prepared to look, and with a bit of time management it is even possible to ride the most famous breaks when the numbers of local *surferos* are low." Visiting surfers tend to head straight for the north coast of Lanzarote or to the south coast of Tenerife, where the waves are already busy. Bear in mind that there are many other surfing possibilities on the islands. Central and southern coasts of Fuerteventura, the north coast of Tenerife, the greater Chinijo archipelago and other islands that are not quite so famous hold some interesting secrets.

Coastline

The Canary Islands are a group of volcanic islands sitting 100 km off the African coast. They are the tips of volcanoes, some of which are still active, protruding above the Atlantic waves. Fuerteventura is the closest to Africa and sand from the Sahara has built up on the eastern seaboard to provide idyllic tourist beaches. The lava rock reefs that fringe the island make for excellent surfing but are definitely not for beginners. Lanzarote is the least mountainous of the islands. It doesn't catch as much rainfall as the others and is therefore less green. It has 300 volcanoes and the northeast corner of the island is home to some comparatively fresh and savagely jagged lava reefs. The north shore is often compared to Hawaii as swells hit the islands with full force, unhindered by a continental shelf to slow them down. As we said, not a place for beginners.

Local environment

As a popular holiday resort, the Canaries have long been subject to coastal development issues including the creation of artificial beaches and the construction of sea walls to dampen the effects of the ocean: the south west coast of Tenerife has particularly suffered. Alongside this, the sewage systems have to try and cope with an influx of millions of tourists every year.

When discussing surfing in the Canaries the vexed subject of localism always raises its ugly head. There have been some very unpleasant incidents over the years and everyone knows someone with a story to tell, and while some of it may be in the realm of the urban myth, some of it definitely isn't. On Lanzarote, the locals now only allow certain visitors to surf the two main breaks at La Santa. "Don´t try to surf in La Santa left or El Quemao if you don't wanna have problems," says José Gonzáles, editor of *Radical Surf* magazine based in the Canaries. The locals maintain that if you surf respectfully, you will have no problems, but this is not always strictly true. Avoiding key breaks at peak times will minimize the risks and many surfers who visit report no problems, but maybe you'll just want to take your surf buck elsewhere.

An influx of surf tourists is frustrating for locals who work long hours, wait for the good swells to kick in and then find the breaks crowded with unfamiliar faces. But this situation is not unique to the Canaries.

Getting around

To get to the breaks on Lanzarote and Fuerte you will definitely need a hire car, preferably a 4WD if you intend surfing the more out-of-the-way spots. The main roads are pretty good, but the dirt tracks, including Fuerteventura's infamous North Track, can be very poor. Make sure you fill up with gas and take all the provisions you need for a full day on the road.

Breaks

Lanzarote

LEFT-HAND REEF BREAK

↘1 El Quemao

- **Conditions** Big W swells, offshore in SE winds
- **Hazards/tips** Crowds, localism, heavy wave, shallow, experts only
- **Sleeping** La Santa » *p271*

One of the heaviest waves in Europe, this predominantly left-hand lava reef challenges the best with elevator drops, heaving thick lips and shallow razor-sharp bottom waiting for the slightest error in trajectory. Comes to life in big conditions, with westerly swells being from the optimum direction. Heavy, hollow fast lefts reel along the sharp, urchin-infested reef, but there are also occasional very fast, very hollow rights. Open ocean swells give this a real Hawaiian feel with sets breaking up to and over 10 ft. Most definitely a wave for experts only.
This is also one of the most localized waves in Europe and there have been violent incidents here. The waves break out in front of the village of La Santa with the harbour providing a good vantage point. Considered to be the Pipeline of the Canaries, this is the wave that showcased the surf in Lanzarote to a worldwide audience.

A-FRAME REEF BREAK

↘2 The Slab/La Santa

- **Conditions** All N to W swells, offshore in E winds
- **Hazards/tips** Heavy, shallow, powerful, heavy localism
- **Sleeping** La Santa » *p271*

A heavy, thick A-frame ledge offering serious barrels for the seriously skilled barrel rider. "Perfect, powerful and hollow," says Michel Velasco. "One of the best waves of the Canary Islands – good for barrelling when it's big (around 2 m) and good for sick turns when it's small." Not surfable at low tide but good from mid to high. If you choose to surf here, best to paddle out alone as it is considered by the area's surfers to be a 'locals only' wave, probably the most localized on the island. Best to park away from the break as cars have been vandalized. Can be checked from the road.

RIGHT-HAND POINT BREAK

↘3 La Santa Right/Morro Negro

- **Conditions** All N to W swells, offshore in SE winds
- **Hazards/tips** Heavy wave when big, tricky entry
- **Sleeping** La Santa » *p271*

A true quality right-hand point reef that works through all tides and is offshore in southeasterly winds. More of a long, walling wave than a hollow one, but in bigger swells it can really fire with the three sections joining up to form one huge wave. One of the island's best-known waves. Jump off the lava rocks to get into the line-up or take the safer option of the long paddle round. Not as localized as El Quemao so surf with respect and you should have no problems. A serious wave in big swells – surfers have drowned here in the past.

ALEX LAUREL

1 Eric Rebiere – calm in the eye of a storm.

WILLY URIBE

An aerial perspective of La Santa.

LEFT REEF BREAK

↘4 Boca del Abajo/Complex Left

- **Conditions** Big W to medium NW and N swells, offshore in S winds
- **Hazards/tips** Heavy wave
- **Sleeping** La Santa » *p271*

Found on the back of La Isleta by La Santa's sports complex, this is another awesome, high-quality left reef that wraps over a lava reef into a sheltered bay. It can hold a big swell, when it does a great barrelling impression of Padang Padang. Used to be pretty quiet but is now more localized and busy. Pictures of Tom Curren charging here were seen in surf mags worldwide.

REEF BREAK

↘5 Caleta de Caballo/Chicken Left

- **Conditions** Medium NW to N swells, offshore in SW wind
- **Hazards/tips** Crowded when good, sharp lava reef
- **Sleeping** La Santa/Caleta de Famara » *p271*

This is a pleasant spot close to La Santa that offers both lefts and rights, nestled in the western end of the bay. The left point breaks over a rocky reef and works up to 6 ft. It does get crowded, especially at peak times, as it is a less intense, less 'performance' wave. The right can be fast and hollow. Likes north swells.

RIGHT REEF BREAK

↘6 Ghost Town

- **Conditions** Medium to big NW to N swells, offshore in S winds
- **Hazards/tips** Heavy reef
- **Sleeping** La Santa/Caleta de Famara » *p271*

Fun barrels at head high but when the serious swells kick in it can do a thundering imitation of Backdoor or Off The Wall. Can break between 4 and 10 ft over a rocky reef. Can get pretty crowded when working.

LEFT REEF BREAK

↘7 San Juan

- **Conditions** All W to N swells, offshore in S winds
- **Hazards/tips** Shallow, heavy, crowded
- **Sleeping** La Santa/Caleta de Famara » *p271*

This is a consistent, quality left reef with long, hollow waves breaking over a huge, urchin-encrusted slab reef. Consequently this makes it a wave for the experts only. The inside section gets shallower as the tide drops, going dry at low, but the outside is still surfable. Not a good place to get caught inside in a decent sized swell. This can be a localized break and has parking in front. Swell magnet. Venue of the La Santa Sport 4-star WQS surf contest.

LEFT-HAND POINT BREAK

↘8 La Caleta de Famara/ Harbour Left

- **Conditions** Big W swells, offshore in S winds
- **Hazards/tips** Shallow, heavy, crowds
- **Sleeping** Caleta de Famara » *p271*

Harbour Left doesn't break that often but when it does it reels off long, hollow good quality lefts. Works best in a big westerly swell where it wraps along the reef and is best surfed at high tide. As the tide drops, areas of the wave section and dry out. A crowded wave when it's good.

BEACH BREAK

↘9 Playa de Famara

- **Conditions** All W to N swells, offshore in S to SE winds
- **Hazards/tips** Safe at southern end
- **Sleeping** Caleta de Famara » *p271*

A rarity here, not just a beach break but a spot that's suitable for beginners. The south end of

WILLY URIBE

2 La Santa Claus.

WILLY URIBE

9 Famara, Lanzarote.

the beach is a safe area of crystal-clear waves that are popular with the island's surf schools. Works on all tides. Further north the beach picks up much more swell and can have good peaks. Probably the only place you are guaranteed to have no localism issues.

LEFT AND RIGHT REEF BREAKS

↘10 Isla Graciosa

- **Conditions** All W to N swells, offshore in S to SE winds
- **Hazards/tips** Localism, 20-min ferry journey to island from Orzola.
- **Sleeping** Isla Graciosa » *p272*

Once a deserted idyll, this island off the northwest coast of Lanzarote is home to some excellent surf and has great potential. The main breaks – **El Corral**, a long perfect left, **El Basurero**, a thumping right-hander, and **Yellow Mountain**, with its pipe-like barrels – are now popular spots. Localism can be a problem here.

BEACH BREAK

↘11 Playa de la Cantería/ Orzola Beach

- **Conditions** Medium N swells, offshore in SW winds
- **Hazards/tips** Quiet beach
- **Sleeping** Caleta de Famara » *p271*

A beautiful beach in a stunning location on the north of the island with views over to Graciosa. Can have some fun waves from mid to high tide when there are lefts at the western end, rights at the eastern end, and peaks in the middle section of the beach, all of which are usually pretty quiet.

A-FRAME REEF BREAK

↘12 Caleta del Mero/Spiders

- **Conditions** Big NW to W swells, offshore in W to SW winds
- **Hazards/tips** Sharp reef, tricky entry/exit
- **Sleeping** Puerto del Carmen » *p272*

LAURENT MASUREL

7 San Juan.

This is an A-frame peak with a sucky take-off that throws into grinding lefts and fast hollow rights. Works best at mid tide. The rock in this area is very sharp fingers of lava (like a spider's legs), which is hard to walk on and makes entry and exit a bit tricky. Boots and helmets recommended.

LEFT REEF BREAK

↘13 Jameos del Agua

- **Conditions** Big N swells, offshore in W to SW winds
- **Hazards/tips** Rocky reef with urchins
- **Sleeping** Puerto del Carmen » *p272*

In the heart of the Malpaís de la Corona – literally the 'bad lands' – the waves here break over urchin-infested fingers of solidified lava. There is a big outside left that picks up loads of north swell, an inside left point that works at mid to high tide, and a short, fast right. Crowded at times.

Fuerteventura

BEACH BREAK

↘14 Playa de Cotillo

- **Conditions** All W to NW and big N swells, offshore in E winds
- **Hazards/tips** Heavy waves when big, crowds
- **Sleeping** El Cotillo » *p272*

When northeasterly winds blow out the north shore many people head for the beach break at Cotillo on the western side of the island. Good quality waves break on this sandy beach to the south of the village. Coming out of deep water, waves can be powerful and hollow producing clear water barrels. The beach picks up plenty of swell and can still work in everything from a southeasterly to a northeasterly wind. As with many spots, can get crowded.

REEF BREAK

↘15 Las Lagunas/Spew Pits

- **Conditions** All NW and W swells, offshore in E winds
- **Hazards/tips** Very shallow lava reef, advanced surfers only, crowds.
- **Sleeping** El Cotillo » *p272*

The name really gives a hint to what to expect here – sucking, spitting, hollow barrels lurking just north of Cotillo. There's a difficult take-off over an unforgiving lava reef. Competition can be tight with a consistent presence of local surfers and bodyboarders. It does, however, produce some sick waves with hollow lefts or rights on offer, depending on the swell direction.

RIGHT-HAND REEF BREAK

↘16 Derecha de los Alemanes

- **Conditions** All N to NW swells, offshore in S winds
- **Hazards/tips** Crowds, sharp reef
- **Sleeping** El Cotillo/Corralejo » p272

This right-hand reef produces hollow waves which can reel over the lined-up lava reef. It picks up plenty of swell from north and northwesterly directions and is flexible enough to work through the tides. Follow the track along the north shore past the Bubble. As this spot takes longer to reach and is further out of the way, it is usually less crowded than other breaks. Gets its name from the fact that it is popular with German surf camps.

LEFT-HAND REEF BREAK

↘17 Hierro Left

- **Conditions** Small to medium N to NW swells, offshore in S winds
- **Hazards/tips** Crowds
- **Sleeping** El Cotillo/Corralejo » p272

Sometimes just known as Hierro, this spot is a walling left-hander that works well in small and medium swells. A fun wave that's not as intense as many on the north shore, so can get crowded. Along with Los Alemanes, Hierro is a gentle introduction to the reefs of the Canaries.

REEF BREAK

↘18 Hierro Right/The Bubble

- **Conditions** All NW to N swells, offshore in S winds
- **Hazards/tips** Sharp reef, board breaker, crowds
- **Sleeping** El Cotillo/Corralejo » p272

At its best, this wave is a picture-perfect A-frame with a fast hollow right and less intense left. Waves come out of deep water and hit the triangular reef with a lot of power. The small take-off zone doesn't help the crowding problems, which are worse at mid to high tide – the safest time to surf as there is more water covering the reef. Follow the road west from Majanicho. The Bubble is one of the best-known waves on the island, attracting many visiting surfers and locals.

REEF BREAKS

↘19 Majanicho

- **Conditions** All NW to N swells, offshore in S winds
- **Hazards/tips** Sharp reef, crowds
- **Sleeping** Corralejo » p272

The ubiquitous shallow, jagged reef here produces nice walling waves at high and gets hollower and less forgiving as the tide drops out. Check outside for a left reef point that breaks in big swells. To find the break head towards the little fishing village of Majanicho, which lies at the end of the pitted North Track. Continue out of town on the eastern side and you should see the reef breaking.

Left: Some nice little spots can be found around Cotillo.

LAURENT MASUREL

LAURENT MASUREL

REEF BREAKS

↘20 El Mejillón

- **Conditions** Medium to big NW to swells, offshore in S winds
- **Hazards/tips** Heavy hold-downs
- **Sleeping** Corralejo » *p272*

This spot picks up a lot of swell and when the lines stack up, the shifty lefts and rights really come alive. Not really a place for the inexperienced as the hold-downs can be long, the waves are heavy and there's a lot of water moving around.

LEFT REEF BREAK

↘21 El Generoso

- **Conditions** All NW and big W swells, offshore in S winds
- **Hazards/tips** Rocky reef
- **Sleeping** Corralejo » *p272*

A great, long, walling left that really comes alive when the swells hit. There is also a short right off the peak at high tide in swells with more north in them, but be sure to pull out before the inside as it heads towards the rocks. A less intense wave with a less intense vibe.

LEFT REEF BREAK

↘22 Bristol/Shooting Gallery

- **Conditions** All NW and big W swells, offshore in SW winds
- **Hazards/tips** Crowds
- **Sleeping** Corralejo » *p272*

A long, left-hand reef break that really attracts the crowds when it's on. At low it is intense with barrel sections, at high it is more forgiving with long walls. Popular with local surfers.

LEFT REEF BREAK

↘23 El Muelle/Harbour Wall

- **Conditions** All NW swells, offshore in S winds
- **Hazards/tips** Crowds
- **Sleeping** Corralejo » *p272*

This fast, hollow, shallow left-hander breaks by the harbour wall in Corralejo and due to its easy access is always very popular. It will break in a huge range of swells, up to 10 ft. Hollower at low, more walling at high, there will always be a crowd here.

REEF BREAK

↘24 Punta Elena/Rocky Point

- **Conditions** Medium to big NW swells, offshore in S to SW winds
- **Hazards/tips** Crowds
- **Sleeping** Corralejo » *p272*

This spot has fast and hollow rights that tend always to draw a crowd. Gets crowded when big swells hit the north shore as it needs a decent swell to get going. Also throws up lefts too. Head southwest from Corralejo to Punta Elena.

JORDAN WEEKS

JORDAN WEEKS

Top: 17 Hierro Left.
Right: 23 Harbour Wall.

Right: Room with a view.
Left: 25 Getting inside Los Lobos.
Below: 25 Los lobos – lip-smackingly good.
Bottom: 25 Island walls.

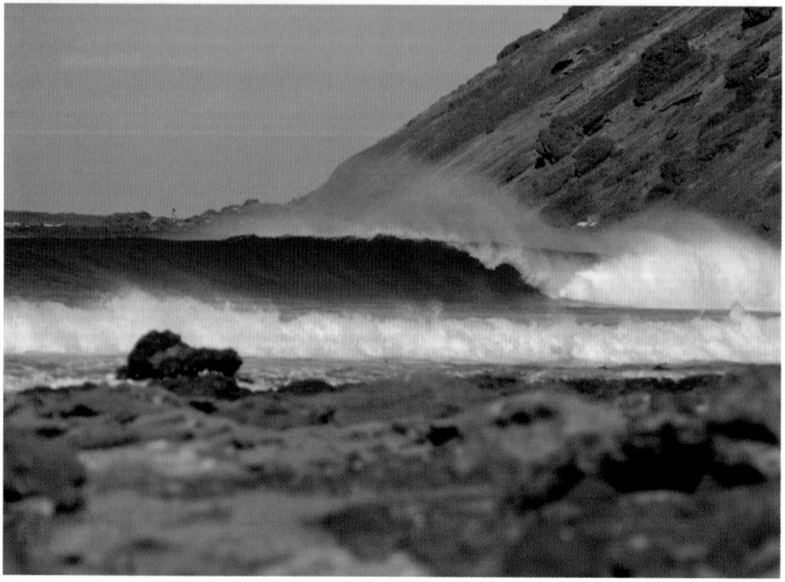

RIGHT POINT BREAK

25 Los Lobos

- **Conditions** Medium to big NW swells, offshore in SE winds
- **Hazards/tips** Classic breaks on offshore island
- **Sleeping** Los Lobos » *p273*

One of the truly classic waves of the Canary Islands, this awesome, long, right-hand point break can produce waves up to 300 m long in ideal conditions. Northerly or northwesterly swells peel down the western side of this offshore island, producing long walling waves with hollow sections. In big swells the waves become much more powerful and hollow. Access into and out of the water needs to be well timed as the rocks are unforgiving. Getting to the island means a ferry trip from Corralejo which leaves daily at 1000 to make the 2-km crossing and returns at 1600.

> After the take-off barrel section, you can get some nice re-entries off the lip, quite challenging on your back-hand...and if you walk to the top of the volcano and look down onto the wave, through the light, almost Caribbean blue, you can see how perfectly the wave peels.
>
> *Welsh surfer Nick Lavery on Los Lobos*

Practicalities

The volcanic Islas Canarias archipelago erupted from the Atlantic and lies more than 1000 km from the Iberian peninsula and just 100 km from the coast of Africa. While the islands are very much part of Spain, Africa still influences their make-up, the Sirocco winds depositing tons of Saharan sand on the islands. Lanzarote and Fuerteventura are the least mountainous of the seven main islands and so receive very little rainfall. This leaves them dependent on desalinated seawater for drinking.

JORDAN WEEKS

Getting there

Air The Islands international airports are Arrecife (Lanzarote), T928-846000, and Puerto del Rosario (Fuerteventura), T928-860600. There are no direct flights from the US or Australasia; connections are via Madrid or the UK. There are regular flights between the Islands and Madrid with **Spanair**, www.spanair.com, **Iberia**, www.iberia.es (who charge heavily and randomly for board carriage – be warned) and **Air Europa**, www.air-europa.com. **Air Europa** also run services to Lanzarote from Barcelona, Bilbao, Santiago de Compostela and Asturias.

From UK: The best deals can often be found with package holiday companies such as **Thomsons**, www.thomsonfly.com, T0870-190 0737, or **First Choice**, www.firstchoice.co.uk, T0870-850 3999. **Jet2**, www.jet2.com, operates flights between Lanzarote and Leeds. While **BA** also runs regular services between London and the islands.

Sea Trasmediterranea, www.trasmediterranea.es, run a weekly ferry service between Cadiz, southwest Spain, and the Canary Islands. The journey to Las Palmas (then onwards to Fuerteventura or Lanzarote) takes around 36 hours and has a hefty price tag to reflect this. **Fred Olsen**, www.fredolsen.es, T902-100107, and the slightly cheaper **Naviera Armas**, T902-456500, www.naviera-armas.com, run regular, reasonably priced inter-island ferry connections between the big seven. Journeys between Playa Blanca, Lanzarote, and Corralejo, Fuerteventura, take about 20 mins and cost around €30 return.

Lanzarote

Named after the Genoese sailor, Lancelotto Malocello, who landed here in the 1300s, Lanzarote is the most easterly of the main islands and, despite its arid landscape, is home to a UNESCO biosphere reserve.

La Santa

Sleeping

€€-€ Club La Santa, www.clublasanta.com, is a complex of apartments just outside La Santa and there can be some good off season (best surf season) deals for groups sharing.

Eating

Riminis Italian Restaurant, on the main street, offers reasonably priced pizzas.

Directory

La Santa, on the north shore, is a small village with 2 surf shops on the high street: **Sefon Surf Shop** and **Sense Surf Shop**. Sefon offers hardware and clothing, ding repair and has a shaper in house.

Caleta de Famara

Famara is a small fishing village flanked by a cliff of the same name and a 3-km stretch of beach.

Sleeping

€ Playa Famara Bungalows, T928-591617, is a groovy looking selection of 1970s style bungalows ranging in price and size for 2-6 people.

€ Famara Surf Shop, info@famarasurf.com, can organize basic but clean accommodation for up to 3 people within walking distance of the nearby breaks.

Eating and drinking

Casa García Restaurant, close to the beach opposite Famara Surf Shop, is a relaxed spot offering tapas and Spanish/Italian food.

Above: 13 Jonathan Gonzales, Jameos del Agua.

Restaurant Casa Ramón, is a more formal and expensive option a few doors down on Av El Marinero but it does have excellent seafood.

Directory

Surf shops **Famara Surf Shops**, on the main Av El Marinero, is a small and friendly shop selling clothing and hardware as well as dealing with board rental, while **Lennys** stocks all the usual kit and offers internet access.

Isla Graciosa

Separated from Lanzarote by the straits of El Río, Graciosa is a quiet island with limited facilities. The **Lineas Marítimas Romero** ferry (T928-842070) runs a service 3 times a day (winter) 5 times a day (summer) between Orzola, on the northern coast of Lanzarote, to Caleta del Sebo – the focus of island life. It takes about 20 mins and costs about €18.

Sleeping

There are a couple of *pensiones* in Caleta de Sebo including **€ Pensión Girasol**, right on the seafront, T928-842118.

Camping El Salao, T928-842000, is pretty basic.

Puerto del Carmen

About 30 mins' drive from the north shore breaks, this is the main tourist development on the island, with wall-to-wall cooked English breakfasts, so it has the most to offer in terms of nightlife and tourist accommodation.

Sleeping

Most of the accommodation in town is monopolized by the tour operators.
€€-€ Pensión Magec, C Hierro, T928-515120, is clean and comfortable.

Eating and drinking

The action really gets going around 2300. Check out Av de las Playas for most of the bars, clubs and the casino. **Hawaii Bar** is on the main road at the north end of town, it plays funky tunes, has friendly staff and DJs at the weekend. **San Miguel Bar** is situated in the old town and is a smart bar serving food with good music and a big screen to boot.

Directory

Surf shops **El Niño** and **Blue Planet** are on the main drag. **Tourist information** Av de las Playas. **Bike hire** **Renner Bikes** in Centro Comercial Marítimo. **Internet** **Cyber Jable** on C Bernegal. **Post office** C Guardilama.

Fuerteventura

Named after the 'fuerte' (strong) 'viento' (wind), Fuerteventura can certainly live up to its name, especially in the summer months when the island becomes overrun by windsurfers. The beaches of this arid island are littered with circular stone shelters, which offer some protection from the relentless onslaught. For info, visit www.fuerteventuraturismo.com.

El Cotillo

This is a sleepy little village on the northwest coast. There are a couple of sleeping options here including the chilled out **€ La Gaviota**, T928-538567, an apartment with a pirate ship out front. Check out the **Onit Surf Shop**, on C 3 Abril 1979. As well as offering all the usual surf shop facilities, they hire bikes, run a book swap, have clothes washing facilities as well as internet access for around €0.10/min.

Corralejo

Corralejo was a little fishing village but is now a resort town full of bars, facilities and Brits abroad. South of the town the sand dunes of the protected Parque Natural de las Dunas stretch out like a mini Sahara towards Puerto del Rosario.

Sleeping

If you're not on a package holiday it can be hard trying to find affordable accommodation in the town.
€€-€ Hotel Corralejo, on the seafront at C la Marina, T928-535246, with beach views.
€ Hostal Manhattan, on C Gravina, T928-866643.

€ Hostal Sol Y Mar, just behind C Milagrosa, is the cheapest place to stay on the island and has room for boards as well as a communal kitchen and lounge. Popular with kiteboarders.

Radical Surf magazine, T928-535877, reservas@radicalsurfmag.com, have a couple of basic apartments to let: **Apartamento Guarda Mar** sleeps up to 4 (1 room) while **Apartments San Rafael** can squeeze in up to 6 bodies.

Eating and drinking

The main Av General Franco is littered with large pubs, bars, clubs and eateries, including **Corky's Surf Bar**, which screens surf flicks and has a reasonably priced grill house **Parilla Poco Loco**. Just off the main drag, on C Iglesia, **Blue Rock** has live bands playing regularly.

Directory

Surf shops Pretty thick on the ground on Av General Franco, with **No Work Team International**, **Deportes Chacón**, **Matador** and **Sixties Surf Shop**. There's also **Home Grown**, on R Jose Segura Torres, and **Puro Nectar**, on R Juan de Tustria. **Internet** **Orange Projekt**, on C General Franco. **Banks** C General Franco. **Pharmacy** On the main C General Franco and Primero de Mayo. **Post office** C Lepanto. **Tourist information** Plaza Grande de Corralejo.

Los Lobos

This tiny island, which takes about 2½ hrs to walk around, lies in the El Río Strait between Lanzarote and Fuerteventura and is named after the 'Sea Wolves' or monk seals that used to frequent these shores. A couple of daily ferry services run to the island from Corralejo port including the **Isla de Lobos** and the glass-bottomed **El Majorero** (around €10 return). There are few facilities on the island but there is a good *chiringuito* serving reasonably priced fresh fish. If you want to camp, you'll need to get a permit from the Oficina del Medio Ambiente in Puerto del Rosario (see below).

Puerto del Rosario

Sleeping

Close to the airport, this port town is Fuerteventura's capital. There's not a lot going for it but it does have a couple of affordable sleeping options close to the waterfront – handy if you've just flown in and haven't booked ahead – including **€ Hostal Tamasite**, on C Leon y Castillo, T928-850280, with internet access.

Eating

You could grab a pizza at the nearby **Pizzeria El Patio**.

Directory

Airport El Matorral, T928-860600. **Pharmacy** Primero de Mayo. **Police** C Fernandez Castaneyra. **Post office** Primero de Mayo. **Tourist information** C Canalejas.

Flat spells

Lanzarote

Art Artist César Manrique took some of the island's most awesome, natural phenomena and 'enhanced' them, to reflect 'man's harmonious actions on nature'. They are pricey but worth exploring, including Jameos del Agua, T928-848020, a gallery of caves shaped by lava tubes more than 3000 years ago, and the nearby Cueva de los Verdes, T928-848484, a lava tunnel complex now also used as a concert venue. **Mirador del Río** (€4), perched on a cliff edge with great views over to Isla Graciosa, is a domed, encrusted 1970's viewing platform which has been given the Manrique touch and is definitely worth experiencing.

Fishing There are plenty of deep sea fishing charters on the island including **Ana Segundo**, based in Puerto del Carmen on C Teide, T928-514322.

Go-karting Head to **Gran Karting Club Lanzarote**, just to the west of the airport, T619-759946, www.grankarting.com, where you can hit 80 kph.

Golf Get a round in at the 18-hole **Golf Costa Teguise**, T928-590512, www.lanzarote-golf.com. Green fees are pricey, from €41.

Sights Visit the island's volcanic heart in the centre of the 50 sq km lava-encrusted Parque Nacional Timanfaya.

Fuerteventura

Biking The barren landscape makes this ideal terrain for a bit of off-roading. Get some pedal power at **Vulcano Bikes**, on C Acorazado España in Corralejo.

Diving There are a couple of dive centres dotted along the island including **Dive Centre Corralejo**, on C Nuestra Señora del Pino, T928-535906, www.divecentercorralejo.com.

Golf Get a round in at the **Fuerteventura GC**, at Caleta de Fuste, just south of the airport, T928-163922.

Sights Lucha Canaria Catch men in leotards (or at least short shorts) wrestling 'Canaries style' in one of the *terreros* (wrestling rings) dotted across the island. **Mirador Morro Velosa** Just off the FV30, this vantage point serves up weird and wonderful views across this lunar landscape.

Portugal

JOSH SWARD

Coxos, Ericeira – an internal examination of one of the country's premiere reefs.

Star breaks

1. **Supertubos** Heavy, fast, heavy, hollow and heavy. In a big swell it does as good an impression of Pipeline as you'll see in Europe, but don't think the sand bottom is any less painful than a reef ▸▸ *p296*.

2. **Coxos** Awesome and heavy wave with long barrels and equally long hold-downs. This right-hand reef break sees waves come out of deep water onto a shallow point ▸▸ *p298*.

3. **Ribeira d'Ilhas/Pontinha** Very popular beach/point set-up that can have long, walling right-handers and an easy paddle out. Venue for world tour event ▸▸ *p299*.

4. **Pedra Branca** Sitting near the heart of Ericeira, this is a goofy footer's dream. Hollow and shallow, a true barrel fest ▸▸ *p300*.

5. **Carcavelos** Supertubos look-a-like at the heart of the Lisbon surfing scene ▸▸ *p302*.

GREG MARTIN/FINDYOURWAVE

The Algarve's elusive charms.

What's not to love about Portugal? The climate is hard to beat, the locals are friendly, the port flows freely and the surf pumps. The combination of great geology and a constant influx of Atlantic swell means there's few places that aren't worth exploring along the 1,793 km of amazing coastline. Lisbon also has the ace up its sleeve of being the only European capital with surf right on its doorstep. The competitive and polluted breaks around Estoril may not be what you travelled half way round Europe for, but the capital does deliver easy access to spectacular waves just a short commute up or down the coast. It also boasts the buzzing bars of the Bairro Alto, where you can sample late night *fado*, and the cutting edge boutiques where you browse the latest designs from this cultural capital's hip young things. Although central Portugal can be a hot, arid environment, with scorched landscapes dominated by rusty earth tones and brown-greens, the coastal fringes are awash with a riot of spring flowers. And, with its sea faring tradition, it is only natural that these fringes are also animated by the bustling communities of whitewashed villages that cluster around small working harbours and the golden, sandy beaches fringed by crystal-blue waters.

But perhaps, one of the best things about Portugual is that local surfers will still take travellers at face value. While you probably won't be welcomed with open arms, if you are friendly and respectful you will find that Portuguese surfers are among the most hospitable and stoked in the whole of Europe.

Surfing Portugal

"Portugal is home to probably one of the best point-break waves in Europe. I've had some challenging surfs at Coxos and the biggest barrel I've ever surfed in Europe. There are some really good waves around too and the Portuguese lifestyle is really cool. Cruisey and mellow people, great food and wine, and cheap too."

Franck Lacaze, former editor Trip Surf magazine.

Through the late '60s and early '70s Europe had been swept up by the new wave of radicalization, liberation and free love. Hendrix had played the Isle of Wight festival, John Lennon had staged his love-in peace protest from the comfort of this honeymoon bed, Jane Birkin had been seduced by Serge Gainsbourg, 20 years her senior, and together had topped the charts for more than half a year smouldering, "Je t'aime, oui, Je t'aime ...". France was hip and chic, with scantily clad bronzed bodies on the beaches and a laid-back, long-haired surf community. Americans, Australians and Brits were making the pilgrimage to the beaches of Hossegor and the Basque region.

For Portugal, however, the revolution was late in coming. Life was hard under the repressive military regime and many young people were abandoning the country. It was a time of economic stagnation, political prisons and secret police. Few could afford an imported surfboard and few travellers rolled through. On the 25 April 1974 the 'Carnation Revolution' brought the people onto the streets signalling the beginning of the end for the military dictatorship and ushering in a brave, new era of democracy for the country. Hungry for the freedoms surfing affords, by the late '70s a few small surfboard manufacturers had popped up near the capital and in 1982 Semente opened its doors. Portugal had a lot of catching up to do and it was soon apparent to surf travellers that there were some amazing waves to be had here. Portugal caught on quickly and, following the surf boom of the '90s, it has become one of Europe's most popular destinations. It's hip and chic and filled with the bodies beautiful, but there still exists a few places where, when you turn up at the beach, it's as quiet in the line-up as it was in the '60s.

Climate

Portugal enjoys an almost Mediterranean-style climate (although admittedly somewhat tempered by the unpredictable Atlantic). On the coast, the winters are generally mild and the summers long and warm, with the majority of rainfall happening during the winter months. The north of the country is wetter and cooler, becoming dryer and hotter as you travel south. On the west coast, the ocean currents conspire to keep the ocean temperatures at a refreshing level year round, while the south facing Algarve coast enjoys slightly warmer waters.

Pros

- Massive variety of breaks on offer in every region.
- Excellent quality reef breaks.
- Main breaks very busy but still plenty of scope to explore quiet spots.
- Warm, sunny winter climate and mild water temperatures.
- Good surf close to Lisbon.
- Great food and buzzing nightlife in main towns and cities.

Cons

- Some localism around certain areas.
- Pollution in urban areas.
- Main breaks can be very busy.
- Getting more expensive as a destination.

JOAO MAYA

Sundowner session on mainland Europe's most westerly shores.

Seasons

During the **summer** months Portugal can be a wonderful place to be, with warm sun, cool seas and the occasional swell coming from Atlantic low pressure systems pushing northwesterly swells onto the more exposed breaks. With temperatures around 22°C and the water averaging a balmy 18°C, the beaches around Peniche, Guincho and Costa da Caparica bustle with holidaymakers and surfers alike and the heaving cafés and bars of Cascais and Ericeira are lively into the early hours of the morning. This is also the season when the sands of the Algarve positively sag with the sheer weight of tourists visiting but with the water on the south coast between 19-21°C and the air temperature pushing up through the mid 20s, it's little surprise.

Autumn is the best time to head for Portugal. In line with the rest of Europe, low pressures tracking across the north Atlantic will push swell south and onto the breaks and beaches with a northwesterly or westerly aspect. The days are long, the temperatures are more than comfortable, and powerful swells regularly peel along the world-class reefs and beaches that abound along the huge coastline. Even in northern Portugal, where the temperatures are least favourable, 3/2s still cut it with water temps around 16°C and it's not really until November that things feel decidedly chilly with the air temperature dropping to around 13°C. In the south, the water is at least a couple of degrees warmer, but the real difference is with the air temperatures which average around 19°C. It is during this season that streams of vans and campers descend upon the car parks and campsites of the central coastline from all across northern Europe and Spain. Line-ups become a collage of nationalities and locals seek out those secret breaks to escape the crowds.

In the north, late **winter** and **spring** bring chilly winds and rain as far south as Lisbon and sees the air cool to around 12°C. Many breaks pick up southwesterly swells coming from low pressures out in the Atlantic to the south, especially those breaks along the southwest coastline of the Algarve and the Lisbon coast. This is a good time to check out the Estoril coast when the big swells wrap into the Lisbon coastline and the urban breaks like Carcavelos come alive. During these chilly months, with the water around 13-14°C, a 4/3 wetsuit is essential to keep out the cold and a warm *café com leite* or white coffee is always welcome after a classic session. However, heading south, the Algarve is the sunniest corner of Europe and hence one of the continent's most popular holiday destinations. The fact that it still picks up loads of swell makes the southwest corner of Portugal an ideal winter escape.

Boards

Portugal has a wide variety of breaks so flexibility is the name of the game. A staple would be a beach break Thruster that works in everything from knee high to overhead. A back-up would be a longer pin tail for when the points or hollow beaches fire.

Geography and the breaks

"The uniqueness of surfing in Portugal is directly related to its geography," explains João da Câmara Valente, Editor of *Surf Portugal* magazine. "Although it is a somewhat small coast, it displays an

JOSH SWARD

Cave – slab surfing Ericeira style.

Above: Portugal's coastline is an instruction in diversity – point, rivermouths and reefs interspersed with cranking, cliff-backed beachies.
Right: City surfing at Lisbon's draw card Carcavelos.

enormous variety of breaks within very short areas. Point breaks, reef breaks, beach breaks, rivermouths, whatever – Portugal has it all. Sometimes I think to myself how lucky we are that the whole Portuguese coast is not made of just an enormous beach break monotony. Also, for its number of surfers, it's amazing how many spots remain uncrowded – once one decides to step away from the 'sheep-factor'. Surfing in the south can also be an inspiring experience for its wildness, being the most preserved stretch of coast in Europe."

The geography of Portugal is a lot more complex than a cursory glance at a map would lead you to believe. North of Porto is a subtle patchwork of beach, reef, point and cove, making the Costa Verde a flexible destination year round. From Porto to Peniche empty beahbreaks take over, broken only by the huge point of Figueira da Foz – mostly high-tide close-outs with the occasional rocky groyne that aids in the sculpture of banks. The coastline south of Peniche is one of Europe's premiere regions with a network of rocky reefs, interspersed with long sandy bays, cliffs, points, rivermouths as well as the more urban breaks of Lisbon. With a west and south facing coastlines, the Algarve has become a winter haven and is one of the most flexible destinations in large swells.

Surfing and environment

Although Portugal does have some, pristine coastal regions, with areas of crystal-clear waters around the southwest and the Algarve alive with dolphins and myriad seabirds, Portugal as a whole does not have a great track record in terms of sewage treatment. Around major urban areas the picture is particularly murky. The River Douro that flows out at Porto is severely contaminated and one by-product of the resulting raised water temperatures is the effect this has had on the species of fish found in the area. Due to high pollution levels, many local surfers strongly advise against surfing the city beaches in Porto, which can be particularly uninviting. Lisbon as a capital city saw major growth without the appropriate updating of the sewage facilities and the Costa Estoril can be grim. To counteract this in 2004 €270 million was pledged for the continued upgrade and installation of sewage treatment facilities and the reduction in pollution of the River Tejo

Low Pressure Chart for Portugal

In all instances we assume the depressions are deep enough to produce classic swells (say 986 to 992mb). Portuguese surfers scan the charts for two scenarios. Most Portuguese breaks will pick up long distance swells from **L1** including the sheltered spots on the Algarve and the southwesterly facing breaks of Lisbon. In line with the rest of Europe, **L2** will push swell onto the reefs and beaches with a northwesterly or westerly aspect as this low tracks in an easterly direction.

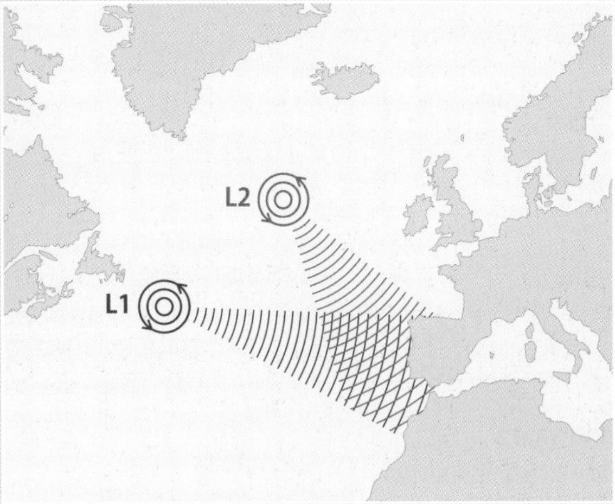

until 2008. Meanwhile, Sines in the south is home to a vast and thriving petro-chemical industry.

The surf community

Many people come away with an impression that Portuguese line-ups are somewhat unfriendly. However, although the line-up can seem a bit 'hassley', it's just the local way. Competing over waves is just as big a tradition as riding the waves. If you're respectful and friendly, and have a chat with local surfers out of the water, you'll find they have a tendency to respond in kind. "Break the locals' ice with a smile and a little talk," recommends João. "Even if they don't react immediately, they eventually will and you should be in for some great new friends and, who knows, easy access to some secluded spots." Remember that surfers have been coming to Portugal since the 1970s. Locals have been dropped in on and visiting vans have left litter and waste. It is understandable that you may have to prove you are here to share waves and not take waves.

Surf directory

Surf Portugal, founded in 1987, is one of the most established surf magazines in Europe. There is also *Onfire Surf Magazine*, www.onfiresurfmag.com.

JOAO MAYA

Some of the best online resources include:
www.beachcam.pt – which, as the name suggests includes webcams as well as charts, reports and beach information including useful updates such as tide times etc;
www.surftotal.com – combines news, surf forecasting and beach webcams
www.surflower.com – a women's surf site with news and articles
www.surfingportugal.com – Portuguese Surfing Federation site with news and competition information

Portugal: a brief surf history

1950s → Portuguese surfers PedroLima and Antonio Jonet begin surfing in Costa de Caparica while to the north of the Rio Tejo, Paulo Inocentes begins surfing Carcavelos. **1976** → US based *Surfer Magazine* runs images of awesome waves in Portugal bringing the surf potential of the country to the attention of the world stage. **1977** → Portugal hosts its first international surfing contest in the waves of Peniche. **1979** → Nick Urrichio and Antonio Perira Caldas create Portugal's first surfboards under the 'Lipsticks' label in Costa de Caparica. **1980** → Aleeda in Costa de Caparica becomes Portugal's first surf shop. 1982 – Nick Urrichio and Miguel Katzenstein set up Semente Surfboards who today sponsor, among others, Tiago Pires. **1987** → *Surf Portugal* magazine is established, reflecting the national growth of the sport. **1988** → The Costa brothers and Fernando Horta set up Polen Surfboards who today sponsor, among others, top surfer Justin Mujica. **1994** → The Surf Experience sets up camp in the Algarve. **1996** → Portugal hosts and wins the Junior European Championships. **1997** → Following on from the previous year's success, Portugal wins the Senior European Championships. Tiago Pires takes an impressive second place in the 2000 Rip Curl Sunset Pro, but just misses a WCT berth. **Today** → Pires is still one of Europe's top surfers and on the verge of the WCT.

Essentials

Position

The westernmost country in continental Europe, Portugal shares its borders with Spain on its northern and eastern flanks, with its south and west coasts washed by the Atlantic ocean.

Language

Portuguese is the native tongue but though about half the population have a working knowledge of English efforts to speak the language are greatly appreciated. Just don't go mixing it with Spanish.

Crime/safety

A relatively safe destination, as with many urban areas in Europe, pickpockets and petty criminals are the main problems in Portugal's city centres. If you do run into any unpleasant situations head for the **Policia de Seguranca Publica** (PSP) in the cities or the **Guarda Nacional Republicana** (GNR) in smaller towns. Generally their English is not forthcoming or limited and they do demand respect. While possession of small amounts of drugs for personal use has been decriminalized, don't spark up in public unless you want to spend your holiday money on a hefty fine.

Health

See page 19 for EU healthcard details. Chemists or *farmacias* can advise on minor matters and sell many prescription drugs, including antibiotics, over the counter. Large towns will have at least one pharmacy open 24 hours.

Opening hours

As with Spain, lunch is king, reflected in the opening hours which are generally 0900-1300 and 1500-1900 Monday to Friday, shutting up shop for the weekend at 1300 Saturday. Monday also sees most museums and monuments closed.

Sleeping

Portugal has a good range of accommodation – *o alojamento* – to suit any budget and operates on similar principles to neighbouring Spain. *Pousadas* are high-end, government-run establishments, usually a former castle or palace, and not really suited to most surfers' needs or budgets, www.pousadas.pt. Still at the premium end of the scale, **hotels** – graded 1-4 stars – can break the bank in the height of the summer but are worth checking out off season when rates can drop considerably. Perhaps the best choice is a *pensão* or *residencial* offering affordable **B&B** style accommodation – a double will usually be between €20-45. As a rule, you'll be shown the most expensive room first – normally with an en suite bathroom – but cheaper options with a shared bathroom may be available. Slightly cheaper are *hospedarias* (boarding houses). There are a limited number of *pousadas de juventude* (**youth hostels**) dotted around Portugal, for which you need a Hostelling International (HI) card but with certain curfews and when compared with the cost of a double in a *pensão* are not usually the cheapest or best choice, www.pousadasjuventude.pt. There are plenty of cheap *parque de campismo* (**campsites**) across Portugal. Although some close off-season, you can usually find a conveniently placed municipal or state-run site open year round. See the excellent www.roteiro-campista.pt for a list of sites plus the privately run and slightly pricier Orbitur, www.orbitur.com. Responsible **free-camping** away from tourist spots (and 1 km away from official campsites) is legal except in the Algarve.

Eating and drinking

If coffee and a roll is your idea of a great breakfast then you'll be in heaven in Portugal. If you're after more of a sugar rush, head to a *pastelaria* (cake shop) for a *pasteis de nata* or a custard tart. Lunch (massive portions, high on carbs and protein, low on vegetables) is served between 1230 and 1430, with the *pratos do dia* (dish of the day) usually the cheapest option around €5. *Ementa turistica* are a similar idea to the 'menu del dia' of Spain – an affordable, set 2-3 course meal and drink. Snack bars have a selection of *pratos combinados* – filling and basic 'with chips' dishes. Dinner is an earlier affair than in Spain with restaurants serving between 1900 and 2200. If you are going to eat out then the **fish**, which will usually be excellent and fantastic value. Portions can often be huge and it is common to ask for *uma dose* meaning one portion between two. Be advised, the little plates of nibbles lying innocuously on your table are not complimentary and will be charged for if you choose to snack on them. *Sardinhas assadas* (grilled sardines) is one of the most popular and cost-effective dishes and there's no avoiding the *bacalhau* (salt cod). *Churrasqueira/ churrascaria* (grill houses) are the showcase and most towns have them. Post surf, order half or quarter of a *frango assado* (roast chicken) served with rice and/or chips and usually a scoop of pickled veggies washed with a beer or a coke for about €5 and you won't be disappointed.

Where drinking is concerned, there are two main brands of beer, Superbock and Sagres, which are cheap and pretty strong. The wine is generally of a good quality and very reasonable. As well as the usual red and white, it is home to *vinhos verdes* (green wine) – referring to the age of the grapes – which is light, refreshing and with a gentle sparkle very drinkable. On the other end of the scale is the heavy, yet very drinkable fortified wine **port** which hails from the Douro valley, inland from the city of Porto, which gives the drink its name.

Getting there

Road There are plenty of routes leading from Northern Spain into Portugal depending on how far along the coast you get. From Galicia, crossing near Valenca do Minho, the A3/E1 will lead you to Porto on toll roads. Alternatively, avoiding tolls, take the coastal N13 leading to the IC1 and Porto.

Air Portugal has three main airports: Porto to the north, Faro on the Algarve and Lisbon; see www.ana.pt for details. Lisbon is the entry point for long-haul flights from New York with either **Continental**, www.continental.com, or **TAP**, www.flytap.com, taking around 7 hours. There are no direct flights from Australia, New Zealand or west coast USA so journeys will need to be broken via another European destination, with the UK offering some of the cheapest options into Faro. As with most European destinations, peak summer, Easter and Christmas see flights book up and prices rocket. Service providers from a wide array of UK destinations include: **easyJet**, www.easyjet.com, **Fly Be**, www.flybe.com, **Jet2** www.jet2.com, **BMI Baby** www.bmibaby.com and **Monarch**, www.flymonarch.com, who offer returns to Faro for £40-140, depending on availability and timing.
Note Budget airlines do charge board carriage – usually around £15 each way per board bag. For flights to Lisbon from the UK try **TAP** plus **Monarch** and **easyJet** To Porto, look at **TAP** and **Ryanair** www.ryanair.com.

From Ireland, **Ryanair**, www.ryanair.com, fly between Dublin and Faro as do **Aer Lingus**, www.aerligus.com, who also run flights from Cork as well as between Dublin and Lisbon. From France, **Air Portugal (TAP)** and **Air France** run daily flights between Paris and Lisbon or Porto. From Spain, **Portugalia**, www.pga.pt, **Spanair**, www.spanair.com, **TAP**, www.tap-airportugal.com, and **Lufthansa**, www.lufthansa.com, operate services between Madrid and Lisbon.

Train Train travel can be a fairly pricey way to get to Portugal (£225-300 for a London-Lisbon return taking around 24 hours on a clear run). The easiest route, using Paris as your main connection, is to take the **TGV Atlantique** to Irun/Hendaye, then catch the **SudExpress** to Lisbon or Porto. Check Rail Europe, www.raileurope.com, for journeys right across Europe.

Getting around

Driving (right-hand side) A full driving licence or International Driving Permit is required plus adequate insurance and ownership papers. Thanks to generous EU funding, Portugal's road network is rapidly improving. The country is linked north to south and east to west by a comprehensive motorway system – much of which is toll road (see www.brisa.pt for details and charges). There are however, also plenty of dirt tracks to explore along the coast as well as substantial stretches of road on popular, main routes that are potholed and in serious need of maintenance and modernisation. The roads may be improving but the driving isn't – Portugal has the highest rate of road accidents in Europe, which is no surprise when you've experienced overtaking à la Portuguese.

Fact file

Capital: → Lisbon
Time zone: → GMT
Currency: → Euro (€)
Coastline: → 830 km
Emergency Numbers:
→ Fire/Police/Ambulance: 115/112
Country code:→ +351
Electricity: → 220v continental dual pin
Visa: → None required by EU citizens, or tourists visiting from North America and Australia
Tourist Board → www.visitportugal.com

Motorways *auto estrada* **Speed limit 120 kph**. The A3/A1 runs from the Spanish border near Valenca do Minho to Lisbon where the A2 takes over for the run down to the Algarve. Offshoots run east towards the main border with Spain. The toll roads, or *portagem*, prefixed with an A, are fast and well built, but the €3-9 charges soon add up.
Other roads **Speed limit 90 kph/50 kph urban areas** (unless otherwise indicated). Due to the high accident rate, speed limits are vigorously enforced and fines are readily doled out. **Estrada Nacional N** roads are improving but can often be slow, clogged with vehicles avoiding tolls and in need of resurfacing, while on the smaller, provincial roads quality varies wildly between dirt *piste* and very good.

Car hire There are plenty of car rental companies operating here including all the big multinationals who have offices in all the main towns and airports. Rentals are slightly cheaper than the majority of western Europe – deals can be found from around €300 for two weeks but usually you do need to be over 21. Hire cars are especially attractive propositions to thieves so be extra vigilant.

Public transport

The public transport system in Portugal is fairly efficient, especially in the southern half of the country. The state-run **railway Caminhos de Ferro Portugueses** (CP) is the cheapest, if not always the quickest, option for long distance travel and will usually try to accommodate your board, www.cp.pt. Lisbon is serviced by the handy **metro**, www.metrolisboa.pt, from 0600-0100 daily. The **bus** services are fairly consistent, largely managed by **Rede Expressos**, www.rede-expressos.pt, and fairly affordable – around €18 from Lisbon to Porto or Faro. Board carriage as always on buses or coaches can be difficult, so if you do have to go public, try to stick to trains.

Northwest Portugal

Overview

The huge headland at Figueira da Foz, with its endless rights and town beachfront surf contest, offers only a temporary concession to the gargantuan that is the twenty first century surf culture machine. One tiny, logo-covered foothold along the vast expanse of the 'Silver Coast'. But soon the bustle of a crowded line-up fades into the background, into the memory and it's back to the arrow straight beaches, the groins and the sandbanks, fed only by the occasional piste road and witnessed only by the truly adventurous surf explorer.

Coastline

The area to the north of Porto has been christened the **Costa Verde**, due to the green, rain soaked landscape. The coastal area is one long strip of beach, broken with rocky outcrops, inlets and subtle reefs and points. There are areas of the dunes that have been cultivated and fertilized with seaweed to produce excellent crops. Occasional rivermouths and resort villages pepper this stretch, but many beaches are virtually empty outside the holiday month of August. **Porto** is an industrial city and the water around the rivermouth and urban beaches is very polluted. Heading south the sandy beaches continue on what is known as the **Costa de Prata**, the silver coast, until the giant point of **Figueira da Foz** suddenly ruptures the coastline. These unspoilt stretches of beach break are again backed by dunes and pines, with spots like **Costa Nova** perfect for those wanting to escape the crowds.

Local environment

With endless miles of open coastline there are only occasional pollution hotspots, the worst of which is Porto. The beaches around the city are notorious for the chemical and sewage pollution. The rivermouth sandbank only breaks under the worst conditions, after heavy rains with all its associated storm-water runoff. There is very little in the way of localism but there has been problems with car crime in the past, so make sure no valuables are left in the car or on show in the van.

Getting around

From the northern border with Spain, the A3-E1 toll road runs south and inland to Porto, where the A1-E80 takes over – a good way to cover a large distance in little time. There are plenty of other more scenic coastal hugging routes.

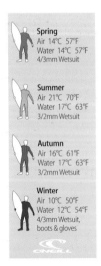

Spring
Air 14°C 57°F
Water 14°C 57°F
4/3mm Wetsuit

Summer
Air 21°C 70°F
Water 17°C 63°F
3/2mm Wetsuit

Autumn
Air 16°C 61°F
Water 17°C 63°F
3/2mm Wetsuit

Winter
Air 10°C 50°F
Water 12°C 54°F
4/3mm Wetsuit, boots & gloves

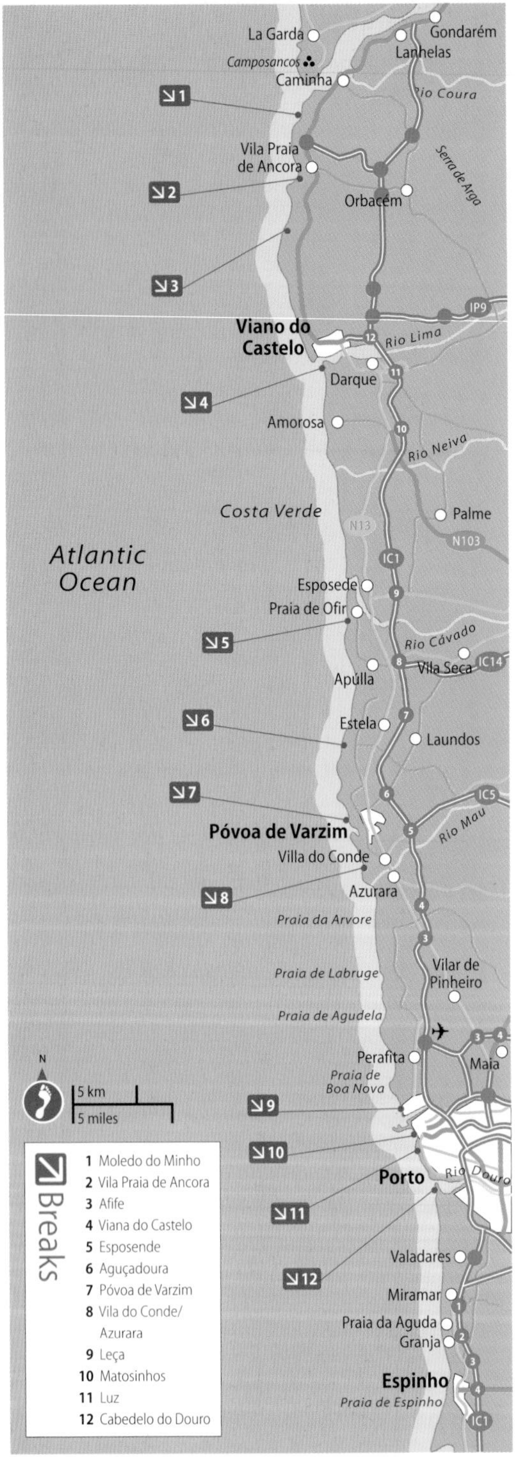

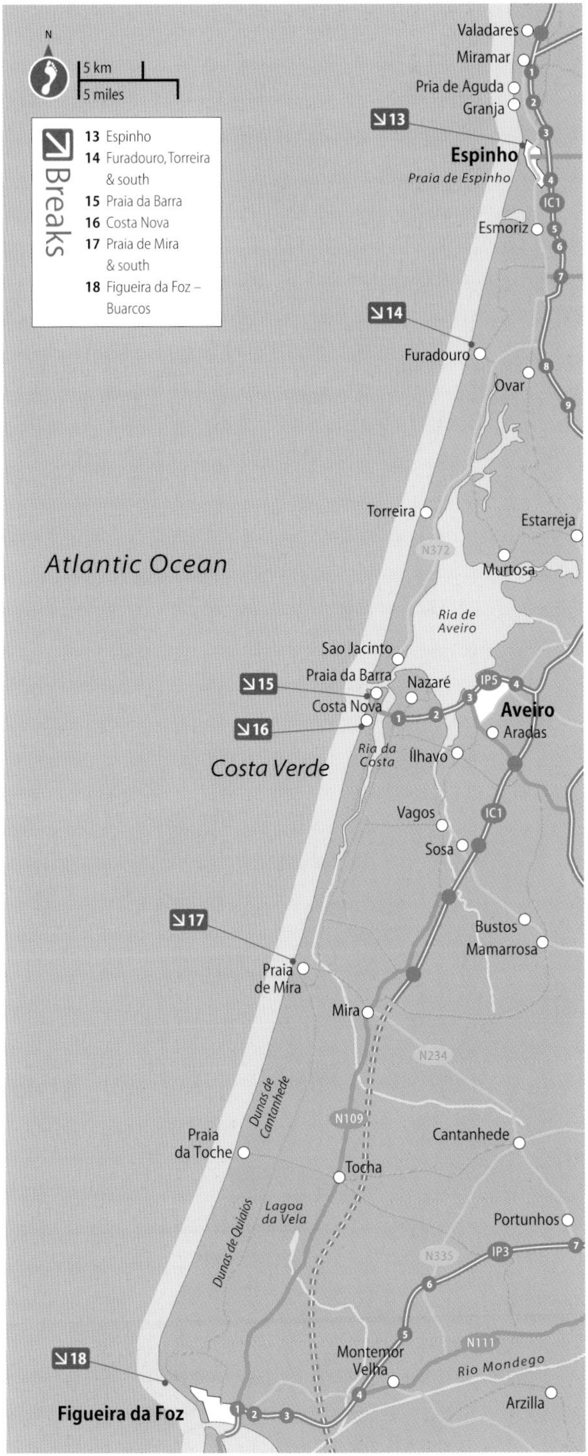
N
5 km
5 miles
Breaks
13 Espinho
14 Furadouro, Torreira & south
15 Praia da Barra
16 Costa Nova
17 Praia de Mira & south
18 Figueira da Foz – Buarcos
Valadares
Miramar
Pria de Aguda
Granja
13
Espinho
Praia de Espinho
IC1
Esmoriz
14
Furadouro
Ovar
Torreira
Estarreja
N372
Murtosa
Atlantic Ocean
Ria de Aveiro
Sao Jacinto
Praia da Barra
Nazaré
IP5
15
Costa Nova
Aveiro
16
Aradas
Costa Verde
Ria da Costa
Ílhavo
Vagos
Sosa
Bustos
Mamarrosa
17
Praia de Mira
Mira
N234
Dunas de Cantanhede
N109
Praia da Toche
Cantanhede
Tocha
Lagoa da Vela
Dunas de Quiaios
Portunhos
IP3
N335
N111
Montemor Velha
Rio Mondego
18
Figueira da Foz
Arzilla

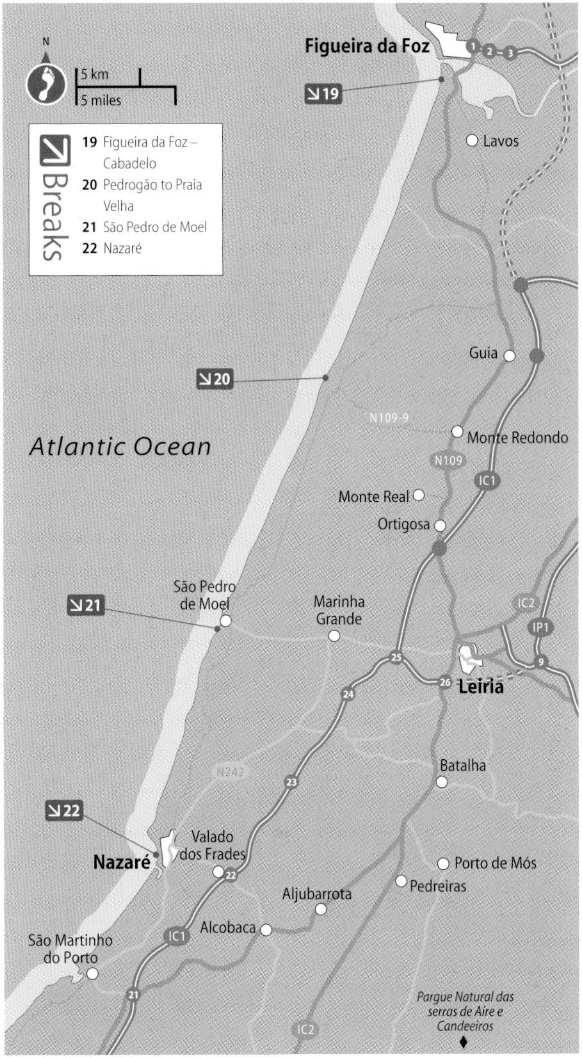
N
5 km
5 miles
Breaks
19 Figueira da Foz – Cabadelo
20 Pedrogão to Praia Velha
21 São Pedro de Moel
22 Nazaré
Figueira da Foz
19
Lavos
Guia
20
N109-9
Monte Redondo
N109
IC1
Atlantic Ocean
Monte Real
Ortigosa
São Pedro de Moel
21
Marinha Grande
IC2
IP1
Leiria
N242
Batalha
22
Valado dos Frades
Nazaré
Porto de Mós
Pedreiras
Aljubarrota
Alcobaca
São Martinho do Porto
Pargue Natural das serras de Aire e Candeeiros

Breaks

BEACH BREAK

↘1 Moledo do Minho

- **Conditions** All NW to SW swells, offshore in E winds
- **Hazards/tips** Rips near the river
- **Sleeping** Viana do Castelo »» *p290*

A fairly consistent, busy beach that gets crowded in the summer. Shifting sandbars work through the tides with left-handers to the south. There is reputed to be a wave in the rivermouth though it is very inconsistent.

BEACH BREAK

↘2 Vila Praia de Ancora

- **Conditions** Small to medium NW to SW swells, offshore in E winds
- **Hazards/tips** Consistent beach suitable for all surfers
- **Sleeping** Viana do Castelo »» *p290*

A short trip south on the N13 brings you to Ancora. This is a long, consistent beach break with various peaks working through the tides.

Below: Northern Portugal affords plenty of opportunities to escape the crowds.

JOAO MAYA

BEACH BREAK

↘3 Afife

- **Conditions** All NW to SW swells, offshore in easterly winds
- **Hazards/tips** Susceptible to the wind
- **Sleeping** Viana do Castelo »» *p290*

This beach produces some fine sandbars and is the place to come when there is any swell. Praia do Bico has a good local reputation for always having a wave and also producing high quality, hollow waves. In easterly winds and clean swells at low to mid tides, the beach will turn on and can even hold a big swell. Easily blown out with light onshores. A popular spot with locals.

BEACH BREAK

↘4 Viana do Castelo

- **Conditions** All NW to SW swells, offshore in E winds
- **Hazards/tips** Nice town with excellent waves
- **Sleeping** Viana do Castelo »» *p290*

Rivermouth divides beach breaks that can both hold quality waves. The crescent shaped beach to the south, Cabadelo, has a breakwater that can produce quality rights in big northwesterly swells. The beach stretches south and can be worth exploring at low to mid tide for good peaks.

BEACH BREAK

↘5 Esposende

- **Conditions** All NW to SW swells, offshore in SE to E winds
- **Hazards/tips** Quiet beaches with good banks, pretty uncrowded
- **Sleeping** Esposende »» *p290*

If the swell is small and the wind southerly, this is the place to check. To the south of Esposende stretch miles of quiet beaches, broken by rock breakwaters. Check Praia de Ofir where the sandbanks can be very good with both lefts and rights on offer.

BEACH BREAK

↘6 Aguçadoura

- **Conditions** All NW to SW swells, offshore in E winds
- **Hazards/tips** Quiet beaches with good banks
- **Sleeping** Vila do Conde »» *p290*

Take the turning off the N13 and a coastal road opens up a whole stretch of excellent quality, fairly cosistent beach-break waves. Works through the tides and usually uncrowded.

LEFT REEF AND BEACH BREAK

↘7 Póvoa de Varzim

- **Conditions** Medium NW to SW swells, offshore in E winds
- **Hazards/tips** Crowded, rocky
- **Sleeping** Vila do Conde »» *p290*

A left-hander breaks off the rock in the middle of the beach but needs a decent size

JOSH SWARD

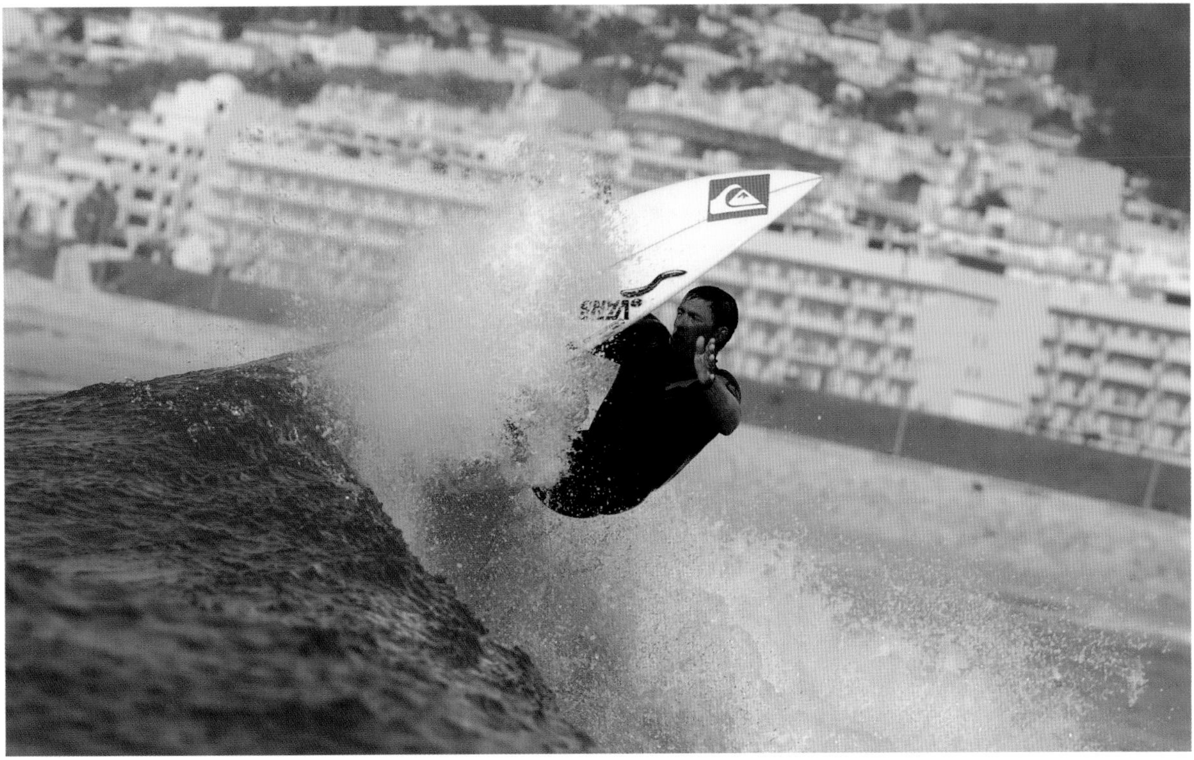

swell to get going. Has a small take-off zone and can easily get crowded. Popular with bodyboarders. A short wave that works best on a mid to high tide, but rocky and not a classic. Watch out for rocks. There are other waves worth checking on the beach.

BEACH BREAK

↘8 Vila do Conde /Azurara

- **Conditions** Medium NW to SW swells, offshore in E to NE winds
- **Hazards/tips** Rocks and rips
- **Sleeping** Vila do Conde ›› *p290*

Praia Azul at Vila do Conde is a west-facing beach break that produces excellent lefts and rights on all tides. Shouldn't get too crowded but is popular with bodyboarders. Azurara, just to the south, is the place to head for a bit of shelter if the wind is from the north. There can also be excellent banks with some nice right-handers.

BEACH BREAK

↘9 Leça

- **Conditions** Medium NW to SW swells, offshore in E winds
- **Hazards/tips** Dangerously polluted
- **Sleeping** Porto ›› *p290*

An urban beach located near the harbour in a quite industrial setting, Leça is a polluted and crowded wave. Works through the tides once a swell of over 3 ft has kicked in. Very poor water quality.

BEACH BREAK

↘10 Matosinhos

- **Conditions** Medium to big NW to SW swells, offshore in NE winds
- **Hazards/tips** Urban waves with poor water quality
- **Sleeping** Porto ›› *p290*

DEMI TAYLOR

Top: Figueira da Foz is northern Portugal's best known surf destination. **Above: 6** Just one of a stretch of fine beachies.

When the swell is over 6 ft, Matosinhos Bay is the place where the local surfers head. As local Francisco Garcia says: "Here you can choose the size of waves you want to ride since the waves are bigger as you walk south on the beach. On the north side of the beach there is a right point break, in the centre of the beach there is a right and left beach break, and at the southern end where the waves are biggest, you can surf a right beach break and left point."

RIGHT POINT BREAK

↘11 Luz

- **Conditions** Big NW swells, offshore in E winds
- **Hazards/tips** Pollution, rocks
- **Sleeping** Porto » p290

In downtown Porto, this high tide, right-hand, urban point break can handle big swells. As with other breaks in this area, the poor water quality is a massive drawback – often outweighing the quality of the wave.

RIVERMOUTH BREAK

↘12 Cabedelo do Douro

- **Conditions** Medium to big NW to SW swells, offshore in E winds
- **Hazards/tips** Rips and pollution, experts only
- **Sleeping** Porto » p290

One of Portugal's most legendary waves. A sandbar at the southern edge of the mouth of the Douro can produce epic, barreling right-handers peeling away from the rivermouth with shorter lefts. The water is coffee brown in colour and very polluted. The wave only comes to life when conditions conspire every couple of years, but when it does it is one of the country's best. It needs heavy rains followed by a big swell but when it does it will give northern Spain's Mundaka a run for its money. There are fears for the wave with a new rivermouth breakwater being built.

BEACH BREAK AND JETTY

↘13 Espinho

- **Conditions** Medium to big NW to SW swells, offshore in E winds
- **Hazards/tips** Localism and car crime can be a problem
- **Sleeping** Espinho » p291

An average beach break that works on all tides but is easily blown out. A hollow right-hander breaks off the southern jetty, which is reputed to hold big swells. If you get it early on a mid or low tide it can be a good wave. Easterly winds are offshore and the jetty offers a little protection from the northwesterlies. The crew here are quite tight but there aren't real localism problems. Not an affluent area so keep valuables hidden. Get up early to beat the crowd.

DEMI TAYLOR

BEACH BREAK AND JETTIES

↘14 Furadouro, Torreira and south

- **Conditions** Small to medium NW to SW swells, offshore in E winds
- **Hazards/tips** Water quality is poor
- **Sleeping** Furadouro » p292

"Maceda next to Furadouro always, and I mean always, has a wave waiting for you," says Francisco Garcia. The other breaks are average beaches broken occasionally with jetties and sand-covered rocky breaks. Good waves may be found alongside the jetties but the area easily maxes out and is affected by wind.

BEACH BREAK

↘15 Praia da Barra

- **Conditions** All NW to SW swells, offshore in E winds
- **Hazards/tips** Start of a huge stretch of beach
- **Sleeping** Costa Nova » p292

Banks form near the breakwater, which provides some shelter from the northwesterly swells that this region Hoovers up. High tide can close out but mid to low can see good quality waves.

BEACH BREAK AND JETTIES

↘16 Costa Nova

- **Conditions** Small NW to SW swells, offshore in E winds
- **Hazards/tips** Rips when bigger
- **Sleeping** Costa Nova » p292

The longshore drift on this coastline is kept in check by a series of jetties that allow sandbanks to build up on either side. These banks change according to swell direction but can produce some excellent waves. Better in smaller swells and susceptible to winds from directions other than the east. A pretty resort that is fairly uncrowded during the week but can get busy at weekends and during the summer. The open beaches are more prone to rips. Better low to mid tides.

BEACH BREAK AND JETTIES

↘17 Praia de Mira and south

- **Conditions** Small NW to SW swells, offshore in E winds
- **Hazards/tips** Rips in bigger swells
- **Sleeping** Praia da Mira ›› *p292*

The breaks at Praia de Mira are again a series of jetties, which break better low to mid tide. To the south is an open expanse of beach fronted by sand dunes. It is an exposed stretch best in small summer swells with either no wind or light easterly winds.

RIGHT-HAND POINT BREAK

↘18 Figueira da Foz – Buarcos

- **Conditions** Medium to big NW to W swells, offshore in E to NE winds
- **Hazards/tips** Rips when big
- **Sleeping** Figueira da Foz ›› *p292*

This long, sand-covered rocky point can produce excellent, long walls on medium to large swells. Works on mid to low tides when rides of 100-200 m may be possible. When large swells wrap round the headland the peeling rights can be an impressive sight. Rips can push down the headland making a long paddle just that bit harder. May be crowded in the summer, but not too bad out of season.

BREAKWATER WITH BEACH BREAK

↘19 Figueira da Foz – Cabadelo

- **Conditions** Medium NW to SW swells, offshore in E winds
- **Hazards/tips** Crowds and pollution
- **Sleeping** Figueira da Foz ›› *p292*

DEMI TAYLOR

Opposite: 18 This point can peel for up to 200 m.
Above: 22 Nazaré.

A huge breakwater runs out to sea at the southern mouth of the Rio Mondego. It provides shelter from big northerly swells and northerly winds, allowing some quality sandbars to be deposited in its shadow. Can produce some excellent waves and is a very popular spot, home to both regular surfing competitions and a thriving local surf scene. Works on all states of tide, but due to its proximity to the rivermouth water quality can be poor.

BEACH BREAK

↘20 Pedrogão to Praia Velha

- **Conditions** Small NW to SW swells, offshore in light E winds
- **Hazards/tips** Rips on the open beaches can be a problem
- **Sleeping** Figueira da Foz ›› *p292*

A long stretch of sandy beach, with occasionally jetties and the odd rock outcrop. The area picks up loads of swell but, like the beaches to the north, it is easily maxed or blown out. Works best low to mid tide in small swells and an easterly or no wind. A huge area with surfers mostly around the occasional village beach.

BEACH BREAK

↘21 São Pedro de Moel

- **Conditions** Small to medium NW to SW swells, offshore in E winds
- **Hazards/tips** Rips in bigger swells
- **Sleeping** São Pedro de Moel ›› *p292*

Rocky outcrops help hold sandbanks and produce pretty consistent waves on the cliff enclosed town beaches. A good place to check in small to medium swells. Best in easterly winds and works at all states of tide. There are beaches to the north and south that are best on low to mid tide.

BEACH BREAK

↘22 Nazaré

- **Conditions** All NW to SW swells, offshore in E winds
- **Hazards/tips** Bad rips when big, powerful waves
- **Sleeping** Nazaré ›› *p292*

An underwater trench channels swell into the region around the headland, into the beach north of the town, producing big and powerful waves. However, in big swells there is a lot of water moving around on the beaches and bad rips. The town beaches are a more sheltered option and work in northeasterly winds.

Practicalities

Viana do Castelo

Sleeping

€ Margarida da Praca, Largo 5 de Outubro, T258-809630, is a good choice year round with breakfast included and newly refurbished rooms with Wifi overlooking the river.
€ Residencial Jardim, Largo 5 de Outubro, T258-828915, is slightly cheaper with clean, en suite rooms.
€ Residencial Magalhães, R Manuel Espregueira, T258-823293, is good value and centrally located.
€ Pensão Guerreiro, R Grande, T258-822099, is another good cheap option with clean and good size rooms and café attached.
€ Youth Hostel Viana Castelo, R Limia, by the river T258 800 260 is open year round with beds from around €11.
Camping **Orbitur Viana do Castelo**, on the south 'Cabedelo' side of the river, T258-322167, has direct beach access, a pool plus cabins, year-round.

Eating and drinking

Dolce Vita, R do Poço, is a good value restaurant with a selection of basic and filling pasta and pizzas. The café at **Pensão Guerreiro** serves seafood and regional specialities. For coffee and pastries try **Pastelaria Brasileira** on R Sacadura Cabral. The **Foz Caffé** at Cabedelo is a fun place to grab a post surf beer.

Directory

Surf Shops There are several including **Omni Surf Shop**, R do Poço and **Viana Locals Surf Shop** in Complexo Turistico Minho Hotel which have the basics plus hardware. **Internet** Get online at the youth hostel. **Banks** Praça da República. **Tourist information** R Hospital Velho, www.rtam.pt.

Esposende

This relaxed resort sitting at the mouth of the Rio Cávado has plenty to offer. The dune-backed beaches kick in a few kilometres north while the beautiful white sands of Praia Ofir stretch out from the pine forests to the south.

Sleeping

€ Residencial Acrópole, close to the tourist office on Praça D Sebastião, T253-961941. Just south of the river is the year-round **Campismo Fão**, T253-981777. Continuing south to Estela **Rio Alto Orbitur Campismo**, T252-615699, has direct beach access and bungalows available year round.

Vila do Conde

Close to Porto, this bustling, popular fishing town has managed to maintain its historic, seafaring heart and is a more relaxed stopover than nearby Póvoa de Varzim. Stop by the **Big Wave**, surf shop on Av Julio Graca for essentials.

Sleeping

€ Pensão Princesa do Ave, R Dr António José Sousa Pereira, T252-642065, good value and 500 m to the beach.
€ Le Villageois, Praca da Republica, T252-631119, has a couple of rooms above an excellent restaurant serving seafood.
Camping There are a couple of year-round campsites to the south of the town. **Campismo Ârvore**, near Praia Arvore on R Cabreiro, T252-633225. Further south still and slightly cheaper is **Campismo Vila Cha**, R do Sol, T229-283163, with apartments sleeping 4 from €45-68 a night.

Porto

Portugal's second largest city, Porto, lies at the heart of the Douro region and sprawls across the bank of the Douro River, towards its sister town Vila Nova da Gaia. Porto is an industrial, hardworking place – it gave the county its name, to the world it brought port, and it hasn't stopped grafting since. Although the Ribeira district, complete with cobbled streets, has been presented with a world heritage title from UNESCO, the city itself is not the most glamorous of destinations and you do need to watch your pockets.

Flat spells

Golf Between Esposende and Povoa de Varzim enjoy a round at **Estela**, T052-601814 – head north along the N13 and take the turning to Rio Alto. Further south get 9 holes in at the beachside **Miramar** golf course, just south of Porto on Av Sacadura Cabral, T227-622067. Or if you're feeling flush, head south out of town on the N109 and get a round in at **Oporto GC**, T027-342008 , one of the oldest courses in the country.

Port You can't leave Porto or Portugal for that matter before you've done the tour, drunk the stuff and got the T-shirt. Head over the river to Vila Nova da Gaia and try **Caves Ramos Pinto**, on Av Ramos Pinto, T223-707000, www.ramospinto.pt, or British producers **Taylor's**, R do Choupelo, T223-742800, who have been producing port for more than 300 years, for a cellar tour and an all important tasting.

DEMI TAYLOR

The dune backed coastline.

Sleeping

There is plenty of accommodation in the city, some of which at the cheapest end can be fairly grotty so ask to see the room before you agree to staying.

€ **Pensão Astorio**, R Arnaldo Gama, T222-008175, near the old town walls, combines simplicity with a hint of faded grandeur for a friendly stay. Can be a bit chilly in the winter.

€ **Pensão Porto Rico**, on the main R do Almada, T223-394 690, have extremely good room rates for up to 4 people.

€ **Pensão Duas Nações**, Praça Guilherme Fernandes, T222-081616, centrally based near the north bus station, is clean, modern and popular with budget travelers perhaps as it has internet access and heating in the winter!

Camping Orbitur Angeiras, north of the city near Matosinhos, T229-270571, is a site popular with locals escaping the city for the weekend. Access to Praia de Angeiras, cabins, open year-round.

Eating and drinking

In a city this size there is something for everyone. For cheap chicken 'n' chips or other grilled delights, check out **Pedro dos Frango** on Bonjardim, just up from the tourist office near Praça Dom João.

At the other end of the scale on Cais do Riberira, **Taverna dos Bebos** – literally tavern of the drunks – dates from the 19th century and serves up generous portions of traditional fare and fish suppers, some of which can be pricey. Way out east on R Bonfim is a vegetarian's delight, **Suribachi**, dishing up cheap, macrobiotic fare.

Directory

Surf shops As you'd expect there are plenty dotted around the area. To the north, check out **Surf Local Surf Shop**, Av Dr Fernando Aroso, in Leça or the **Waimea Surf Shop**, R 1 Dezembro, at Matosinhos or **Matosinhos Surf Centre**, R Roberto Ivans. South, in Vila Nova de Gaia, head for **Malibu Surf Shop**, on R Padua Correia. **Banks** Av dos Aliados. **Post office** Av dos Aliados. **Tourist information** There are a couple of helpful offices, the main one on R Clube Fenianos, another in the Ribeira district on R Infante D. Henrique, www.portoturismo.pt.

Espinho

On paper, Espinho has little going for it. It's a pretty rundown, 1970s-style resort that has become a suburb of Porto. The roads arranged in a grid system are numbered – not named. The water is polluted and these harsh conditions have bred tough surfers, especially the breakwater right-hander. "It can be very crowded, it's true", says local surfer Francisco Garcia. "But here in the north we don't have any localism. When I go to Espinho I leave my board on the top of my car and go eat far from the car, where I can't see my board. I've never had a problem." It's also home to one of the largest **markets** in the region good for stocking up on provisions – Mon, Rua 22, 23 and 24.

Sleeping

The reasonably priced € **Hotel Mar Azul**, T227-340824, is on the romantically named Av 8.

Camping Espinho, is a year round municipal site T227-343718.

Directory

Surf shops There are a couple here, including the mianly body boarding **Invert Surf Shop**, Rue 32, by the municipal swimming pool. **Tourist information** Rua 6.

Furadouro

Heading 5 km west from the pretty market town of Ovar lies Praia de Furadouro, home to the beachside **Campismo Furadouro**, T256-596010, a shady spot nestled just north of the town among the pine trees. In Ovar itself is the **Animal Surf Shop** on R Gonçalo Velho stocking boards, essentials and clothing.

Costa Nova

Just to the south of Aveiro on the coast, Costa Nova is a small and pretty resort that is busy during the weekends with day trippers from the city. With a huge beach stretching from Praia da Barra to the north all the way down to Figueira da Foz, Costa Nova makes a good base for a couple of nights.
There is a large and well equipped **Campismo Costa Nova**, T234-369822, which is open year round.
Just north is **Praia da Barra** also open year round with great beach access and mobile homes available to rent, T234-369425.
In Costa Nova is the surf shop, **Loja da Tribo do Sol**.
Praia da Mira is home to an excellent, beach side **Orbitur**, T231-471234, site open Jan-Nov with cabins available to rent.

Figueira da Foz

Sitting at the mouth of the Rio Mondego, this lively fishing port is a popular Portuguese resort and regular staging ground for national, European and WQS events.

Sleeping
There are plenty of rooms available in private houses if you are willing to hunt around. There is also a good selection of accommodation around R Bernado Lopes including:
€ Pensão Central, T233-422308, with large rooms.
Alternatively try the more basic
€ Residencial Bela Figueira, R Miguel Bombarda, T233-422728, with good beach access.
€ Paintshop Hostel, R. da Clemencia 9, T233-425489, is a fantastic, modern, clean hostel with dorm beds from €16 and doubles from €35 with internet access, bar, games room and no curfew. Or if you rock up in your van, you can negotiate use of kitchen and bathroom facilities for a reduced rate. Recommended.
Camping There are several good campsites in the area including the inland **Camping Municipal**, T233-402810, and **Foz do Mondego**, set across the river near Praia Cabedelo, T233-402740, open 15 Jan-15 Nov. Further south at Praia Cova Gala is the year-round **Orbitur** site, T233-431492, which also offers good rates on cabins off season. Heading north to Praia de Quiaios is another, year-round **Orbitur** site, about 8 km from Figueira da Foz, T233-919995, set in pine trees.

Eating and drinking
If you feel a long way from home and are in need of a curry, head to the reasonably priced **Pensão Bela Figueira**. To sample the delights of the sea venture out to the fantastic **Dory Negro** at Largo Caras Diretas in Buarcos.

Directory
Surf Shop Ze Surf Shop, Centro Comercial Atlantico. **Banks** Overlooking the river on Av Foz do Mondego. **Post office** The most convenient is on R Miguel Bombarda, running parallel to the beach. **Tourist information** Av 25 de Abril just back from the seafront, http://figueiraturismo.com.

JOAO MAYA

São Pedro de Moel and Nazaré

São Pedro Moel is home to fantastic year round **Orbitur** set just north of the village in pine forest, T244-599168, handy for a stop over.
Nazaré has a couple of handy year sites **Vale Paraiso** north of town on the N242 also has apartments and cabins to rent, T262-561 800, and **Orbitur Valado**, set back 2 km from the town in the pine trees, with very groovy Star-trek like pods available to rent, T262 561111. There are also a couple of surf shops here – **H20** and **Yeti** which both have a good range of goods.

Peniche, Ericeira & Lisbon

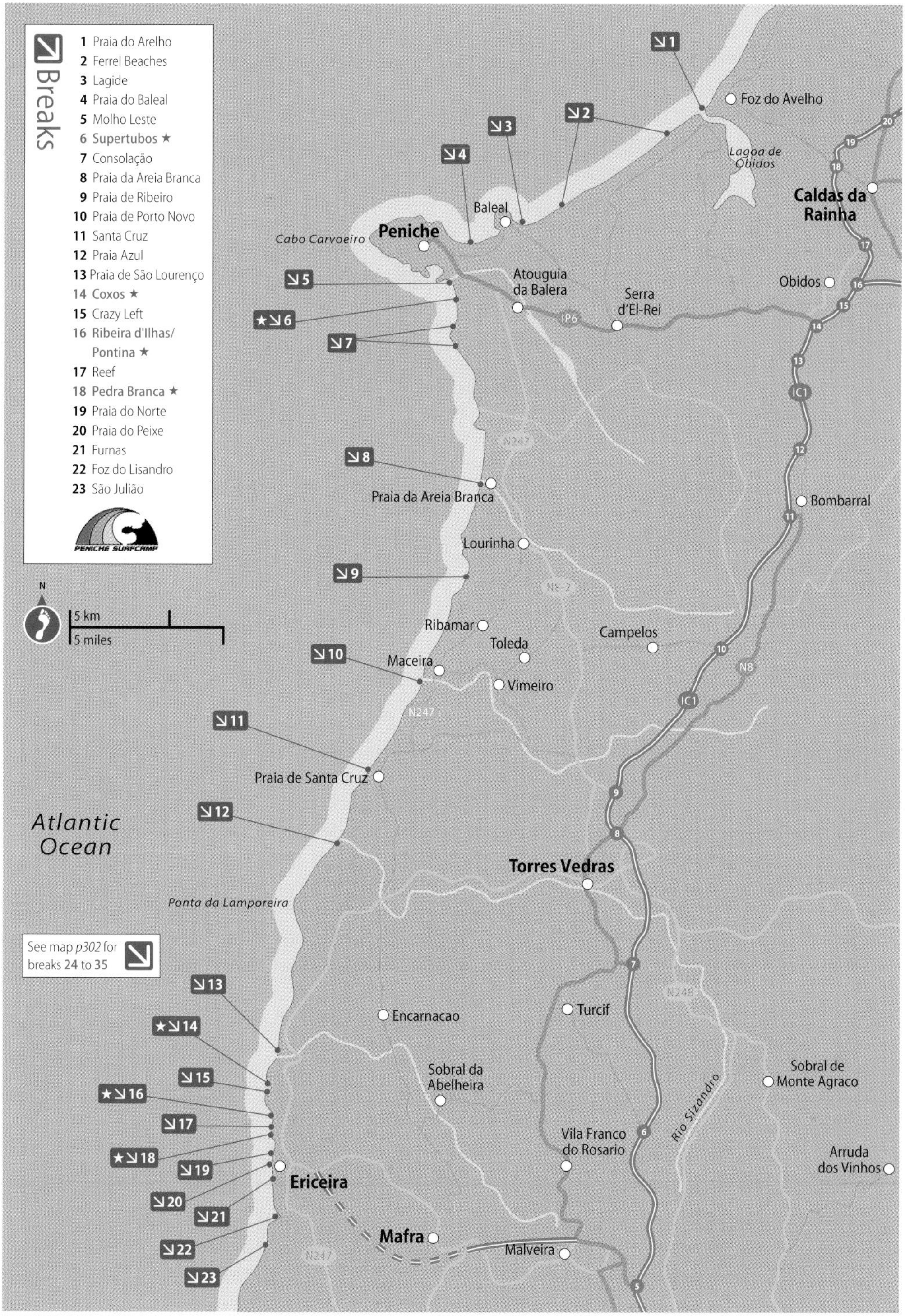

Spring
Air 16°C 61°F
Water 14°C 57°F
4/3mm Wetsuit

Summer
Air 22°C 72°F
Water 18°C 64°F
Shortie

Autumn
Air 18°C 64°F
Water 17°C 63°F
3/2mm Wetsuit

Winter
Air 11°C 52°F
Water 14°C 57°F
4/3mm Wetsuit, boots & gloves

Overview

This stretch of coastline is the true surfing heartland of Portugal. Hop in a car at Cascais and drive north to Peniche and the winding, two-hour journey will take you past some of Europe's finest breaks and through a coastal fringe rich in surfing heritage. There are razor-sharp reefs, precision points and shifting sandbanks liberally scattered along the way, each working in slightly different conditions, each requiring a subtle combination of factors to fire. The coastline changes constantly, like the moods of the ocean itself, and when the ocean changes its mood, the coastline always offers somewhere to capture the moment.

Presiding over this shore are Portugal's three main surf towns. Peniche is all raw power, beach breaks, Supertubos and fish factories. Come in prime season and, if you don't mind getting wet in less than perfect conditions, you could surf every day. Ericeira is smart and precise; white-washed walls and shallow, finely tuned reef breaks. You don't come here for onshore Coxos. It's all or nothing. Get things wrong and the jagged rocks will punish you for stepping out of line. Get things right and you'll be rewarded beyond the dreams you scribbled on text books as a grom. Watching over is Lisbon, with her bustling trams, bouncing down cobbled streets, Fado music drifting from backstreet bars and the draw of the brooding breaks of the Costa do Estoril. Moody, polluted, localized, crowded urban breaks. Reefs, points and beaches that wait for the big swells to yawn, open-jawed, into action. If the urban chaos is too much, there's the bridge south and the escape. The waiting sandy expanse of the Costa de Caparica, winding away into the heat haze, empty sandbanks shimmering like mirages in the distance. Lost on an empty beach, hopping over hot sand, aiming for the cooling water's edge. One of Europe's major capital cities, just a stone's throw away, is just a faded impression on the boundaries of your vision.

Coastline

Flexibility. Consistency. These are the words that best sum up Peniche. The town was built on a rocky island on the end of a sand peninsula and at the western end of a huge crescent-shaped bay. Geographically designed as an impregnable fortress town, the planners unwittingly conspired to lay out a smorgasbord of beach breaks for future generations to enjoy. This geographical set-up means that there are beaches facing almost every direction. The result is a place that once you've arrived, you'll find very hard to leave behind. Ericeira is so very different. The jagged coastline faces due west and is a series of high quality reefs with occasional sandy beaches. It lacks the flexibility of its neighbour, but the sheer class of the waves on offer more than compensates. The flat, razor-sharp rock is unforgiving and many spots are carpeted in urchins for good measure. Lisbon is built on the hills around the natural harbour in the Rio Tejo, protected from the fierce Atlantic storms. The breaks dotted along the Linha de Estoril look out in a southerly direction, a series of polluted jetties, sand covered reefs and points. The population explosion on this coastline combined with a lack of sewage infrastructure has left its legacy. Follow the road out past the popular suburb of Cascais and Guincho will unfold before your eyes. The westerly aspect here makes for Libon's most consistent break, the wide sandy bay bearing the brunt of the Atlantic's power.

Local environment

The west coast breaks may suffer a few localized pollution issues near harbours and village storm-water run-offs but are generally clean. The Lisbon breaks are the most polluted in the region in terms of sewage as poor infrastructure struggles to cope with the large population. Nearer the city other industrial pollutants make their way into the line-up. As far as localism issues goes, Nick Uricchio of Semente says, "Portuguese people in general are warm folks. The invasion of foreign surfers has taken its toll a bit on certain locations, so there is a bit of bitterness these days. Do not travel in mobs and don't hog waves even if you are a better surfer." Nick also advises visitors to make sure they don't leave valuables on display in their vans or cars.

Getting around

The N247 allows access to the breaks around Ericeira and then heads north past the Semente factory and nearby Coxos. Follow the coast road north (or the faster A8 or N8 roads that runs inland) and soon the bustling fishing port of Peniche comes into view. Access to the breaks around Peniche is straightforward, with the local council even providing convenient signposts to Supertubos from the main road, the breaks around Ferrel take a little exploring down piste. In terms of the city, the A5 is a quick an easy route out of Lisbon to the west coast – a reasonably priced toll road that runs just shy of Guincho. The busy N6 follows the coast out to Cascais giving acces to the urban breaks as do the cheap and regular trains on the Linha de Cascais.

6'3" Rusty Pro-ject

Shaper: Rusty Preisendorfer

6'3" x 18 3/4" x 2 3/16"

Built with Surftech's proven TUFLITE construction.

Moderate rocker with triple concave finished with a slight release vee through the tail. The 6'3" Pro-ject is a design that shines brightest in waist-to-overhead waves.

Futures FEA fins.

Boards by **Surftech** www.surftech.com info@surftech.com

6'6" Bushman Pancho Model

Shaper: Jeff Bushman

6'6" x 19 3/8" x 2 1/2"

Built with Surftech's proven TUFLITE construction.

Jeff Bushman designed this board with Pancho Sullivan for hollow, powerful waves on the North Shore and beyond which makes it perfect for Coxos. Single to double concave for down the line speed and power gouges in the pocket.

FCS fins.

Breaks

BEACH BREAK

↘1 Praia do Arelho

Conditions Small to medium NW to W swells, offshore in E to SE winds
Hazards/tips Quiet spot with good waves
Sleeping Baleal/Peniche » *p304*

With a northwesterly swell and crowds at Peniche it's worth checking this spot next to Lagoa de Obidos. Very consistent and usually pretty uncrowded. Can have excellent and powerful beach break waves through the tides.

BEACH BREAK

↘2 Ferrel Beaches

Conditions Small to medium NW to W swells, offshore in SE winds
Hazards/tips Tricky access
Sleeping Baleal/Peniche » *p304*

Turn left at the 58 surf shop and follow the *piste* roads to a long series of beach breaks with some excellent quality waves. Left turns lead down to a series of beaches popular with local surfers. Pick up a lot of swell. Formerly an area metaphorically and physically off the beaten track, this series of breaks is becoming more popular with surfers visiting the region. **Praia da Almagreira** has nice, sucky, sandbars. Park above the breaks. Show respect to locals, don't turn up in large groups. Access can get tricky after heavy rains.

LEFT-HAND REEF BREAK

↘3 Lagide

Conditions Small to medium NW to W swells, offshore in E to SE winds
Hazards/tips Urchin-infested reef
Sleeping Baleal/Peniche » *p304*

Lagide is a lovely, long, walling left-hand reef that breaks in front of the car park at

CARLA TOME

4 Baleal – Meio da Baia.

Above: 6 Standing in the waist-deep impact zone watching another thunderous set approach.

6 Supertubes.

Baleal. The wave peels over a flat reef, but it's no death or glory charge – even when the swell picks up, but watch out for the urchins. There's an easy rip out to the peak just to the west of the break, the take off is straightforward and the wave is easy to surf. All these things add up to big crowds! It's the first thing that fills the windscreens of those pulling into the car park. The tiny take-off point means surfers take off on the wrong side of the peak to steal a march on the masses, so drop-ins happen all the time. Catch it quiet and you're stylin'. On the other side of the channel the beach can have some fun little waves in small to medium swells but it easily closes out when the swell picks up.

BEACH BREAK

↘4 Praia do Baleal

- **Conditions** All N to W swells, offshore in W/S/E winds
- **Hazards/tips** Rips when big
- **Sleeping** Baleal/Peniche ›› p304

A fantastically flexible, crescent-shaped bay that picks up loads of swell. Due to the curvature, parts of the bay will be offshore in winds from the west through south to east. A fast, hollow right breaks near Baleal. Further round a nice left works in all swells and the rest of the bay consists of many shifting banks that can be found on all tides. The western edge of the bay can be a good place to head in large W swells. Loads of room to spread out.

BEACH BREAK

↘5 Molho Leste

- **Conditions** Small to medium W to SW swells, offshore in E to NE winds
- **Hazards/tips** Small take-off point, localized spot
- **Sleeping** Baleal/Peniche ›› p304

A right-hand sandbar at the mouth of the stream alongside the harbour wall south of Peniche. This can be a great wave in smaller swells but tends to close out in bigger swells. There is a large local crew here who have the tiny take-off zone wired and always seem to be in the best place for the best set waves. Parking by the break. Can offer some protection in Northerly winds.

BEACH BREAK

↘6 Supertubos

- **Swell** Southwesterly to Northwesterly
- **Wind** Easterly
- **Tide** All tides, but better around mid tide
- **Size** 2-10 ft
- **Length** Up to 50 m
- **Bottom** Very shallow sandbar
- **Ability Level** Intermediate to Advanced
- **Best Months** Sep-May
- **Board** Semi-gun or performance Thruster
- **Access** Channel off the beach
- **Hazards/tips** Very shallow, very hollow and powerful, board breaking, crowds
- **Sleeping** Baleal/Peniche ›› p304

Why here? The long, curving crescent shaped beach arcs away for at least two miles to the south, and yet the sandbanks always form just here – 200 m to the left of the car park. There must be something in the underwater topography, in the currents, that conspires. At low the sandbars are visible just below the surface, huge and wide, the stage on which the swells perform. Each day slightly different, but the theme remains the same, the adjectives to describe them. Pitching, hollow, shallow, steep. That's why the crowds come.

The town of Peniche doesn't quite have the whitewashed charm of many Portuguese towns. It has all the elements – the town walls, the cobbled streets, the 16th century castle and the harbour. But it isn't polished, hasn't been changed to draw the tourists and that makes it much more attractive. It's still a grafting town, a working town. With fish factories and the occasional ammonia stench of offal. Surfers pitched up here in the 1970s, just after the revolution, and they've been coming back ever since. The campsite on the edge of town a short hop from the break, the break just a short walk from the car park. The car park filled with a united nations of surfers. Autumn brings the migration of Saffas, Aussies, Yanks, Scandos, Brits, Germans. Passing through, heading south. The locals are friendly in the car park. Make small talk. In the line-up it's a different matter. You want their waves and they know them better. Not agro, tactics.

Just because this is a beach break, don't make the mistake of underestimating it. When it's truly on, it breaks like a reef – on classic days like the most famous reef in the world. Six to eight foot barrels spiraling left and right. The locals taking the lions' share, having a sixth sense about just which ones will close out and which ones will stay open. Some days there's the peak, some days just the left will work, others a second right will also open across the channel – but it will always be busy. The take off drops away beneath your feet – it's just pull in, grab the rail and aim for the exit. Be patient, wait for the right one, emerge from behind the curtain and wave to the crowd.

If you like ***Supertubos****, try* ***Carcavelos*** *(see page 302) and* ***La Gravière*** *(see page 183) and* ***Les Cavaliers*** *(see page 191), both in France.*

LEFT- AND RIGHT-HAND POINT BREAKS

↘7 Consolação

- **Conditions** Medium to big NW to SW swells, offshore in E winds
- **Hazards/tips** Rocky breaks with urchins
- **Sleeping** Baleal/Peniche ›› *p304*

The peninsula at Consolação is visible from Supertubes, jutting out to the south. The rocky headland has a left point on the north side and a right on the southern side. The left can be a classic wave with long, peeling walls that work at all states of tide, but seems to be the least consistent of the two. It is usually uncrowded and has easy access from the beach. The right point breaks in big swells and although the set-up looks promising, the waves look better than they actually are. There is a big drop on take-off after which the wave flattens out and it can be hard work making it through to the inside. Sheltered on northwesterly winds. Access from the rocks, but watch out for urchins.

To the south of Consolação is another right-hand point that comes alive in the biggest swells. Access is tricky and the point breaks over rocks. For experienced surfers only.

BEACH BREAK

↘8 Praia da Areia Branca

- **Conditions** Small to medium NW to SW swells, offshore in E winds
- **Hazards/tips** Large, quiet beach with rips in big swells
- **Sleeping** Praia de Areia Branca ›› *p305*

Follow the N247 south to this excellent and underrated beach break. It is a great place to escape the crowds of Peniche and usually has some decent banks (near the rivermouth). Check the whole beach from the cliff top. Mellow vibe off-season.

BEACH BREAK

↘9 Praia de Ribeiro

- **Conditions** Small to medium NW to SW swells, offshore in E winds
- **Hazards/tips** Sheltered beach with few surfers
- **Sleeping** Praia de Areia Branca/Santa Cruz ›› *p305*

A sheltered sandy beach with a peak in the middle that has lefts and rights. Doesn't break at high tide.

BEACH AND RIVERMOUTH BREAKS

↘10 Praia de Porto Novo

- **Conditions** Small to medium NW to SW swells, offshore in E winds
- **Hazards/tips** Take a packed lunch and water!
- **Sleeping** Praia de Areia Branca/Santa Cruz ›› *p305*

Porto Novo has a rivermouth break at the northern end and a massive stretch of beach heading south, which has various peaks working at different states of tide. A great place to get away from the crowds and explore.

CARLA TOME

7 Consolação right.

BEACH BREAK

↘11 Santa Cruz

- **Conditions** Small to medium NW to SW swells, offshore in E winds
- **Hazards/tips** Heavy waves, rips, easily blown out
- **Sleeping** Santa Cruz ›› *p305*

No Steamer Lane here, but a thumping beach that on its day can rival any in Europe. The beaches to the north of the town are home to some powerful, high quality breaks – dare one say like Hossegor. There are a series of sandbanks and sand-covered reefs. There is even the sand-covered shipwreck of a boat that sank just after the Second World War and produces an excellent sandbank. Sitting between two surf Meccas, Santa Cruz has managed to avoid attention and is a great place to escape the crowds. Go on an offshore wind though.

JOSH SWARD

ALEX LAUREL

Above: 14 Portugal's top player Tiago Pires at home. **Top: 11** Just one of the excellent sand covered reefs found.

BEACH BREAK

↘12 Praia Azul

- **Conditions** Small to medium NW to SW swells, offshore in E winds
- **Hazards/tips** Heavy when big, rocks
- **Sleeping** Santa Cruz ›› *p305*

One of the most consistent breaks in the area and can have some excellent peaks. Always worth checking in small, clean swells. There is also a bonus reef at the north end of the bay.

SAND-COVERED REEF BREAK

↘13 Praia de São Lourenço

- **Conditions** Medium to big NW to SW swells, offshore in E winds
- **Hazards/tips** Big-wave spot, heavy, rocks, rips
- **Sleeping** Ericeira ›› *p305*

This big right-hand reef only gets going when big swells kick in. It has heavy, walling waves that peel through to the beach but the peak can shift around a lot and getting caught inside is not a pleasant experience. Doesn't usually get that crowded. For experienced surfers only.

RIGHT-HAND REEF POINT BREAK

↘14 Coxos

- **Swell** Northwesterly to southwesterly
- **Wind** Easterly/southeasterly
- **Tide** Low to mid tide
- **Size** 3-12 ft
- **Length** 50-100 m plus
- **Bottom** Sharp rock reef
- **Ability Level** Advanced
- **Best Months** Sept-Dec
- **Board** Semi-gun or pintail thruster
- **Access** Off the point (with good timing) or from the inside
- **Hazards/tips** Heavy waves, sharp rocks, rips, crowds
- **Sleeping** Ericeira ›› *p305*

The naked rock tapers down the headland and lies in wait below the surface of the translucent

JS CALLAHAN/TROPICALPIX

16 Ribeira doing a canny impression of Bells Beach.

DEMI TAYLOR

14 Putting Coxos into razor-sharp perspective.

blue waters. Dry, jagged, splintered, angry rock, the colours blend from fiery orange, to dark brown, to white as the water fizzes up this barren headland. Timing the jump off, that's the trick. Now that you know what waits below the surface, it's always there, in the back of your mind. The outside line-up centres on a ledge, where the waves lunge out of deep water and spill into a thick-lipped right hand barrel before wrapping around the outer edge of the point, one of the black wetsuited locals locked deep inside. Could be Tiago Pires, could be Miguel Fortes or João Pedro exiting, cutting back and setting up for the next section – a long winding wall. Then the wave feels the shallow, jagged bottom again throwing into a thin-lipped tube for a race through the inside. It wasn't by chance that the Semente factory set up shop just a two-minute hop from this, one of Europe's premier waves. Depending on swell direction this can be long and walling or a fast, heavy, hollow wave with barrel sections.

If you like Coxos, try Inishcrone in Ireland (see page 132) and Lafitenia in France (see page 194).

REEF BREAK

15 Crazy Left

- **Conditions** Medium S to SW swells, offshore in E winds
- **Hazards/tips** Shallow, heavy, rocky
- **Sleeping** Ericeira ›› p305

Rarely surfed left-hand reef found in the same bay as Coxos. It is fast, shallow and hollow and needs a swell from a southerly direction to work. Best left to the experts. It's not called Crazy for nothing.

SAND-COVERED REEF BREAK

16 Ribeira d'Ilhas/Pontina

- **Swell** Westerly/northwesterly
- **Wind** Easterly
- **Tide** All
- **Size** 2-12 ft
- **Length** Up to 200 m
- **Bottom** Sand covered reef
- **Ability Level** All
- **Best Months** Sep-May
- **Board** Thruster and longboard
- **Access** Off the left-hand side of beach – use rip
- **Hazards/tips** Crowds
- **Sleeping** Ericeira ›› p305

Looking down on a classic day at Ribeira from the cliff top lay by and you'd be forgiven for thinking you'd been transported to Victoria and were now looking down on Bells Beach. The cliff lined sandy bay, the reeling right – peaking on the outside, backing off, speeding up, wrapping round and going, going going. It may look like a stand-in for the Antipodean stalwart, but Ribeira is most certainly its own quality act. Its beauty is in its flexibility. This long walling point starts working at 2 ft and then just keeps going, pumping out the endless walls way into the 10-ft plus region. Rides of well over 200 m are common, and the ease of access, via a rip to the south of the wave, only helps enhance its popularity. Add the beach front parking, the fact it works through the tides, shows all its wares to the coastal road and is longboard friendly means you've got to get up pretty early to beat the crowds. There is a second, outside reef called Pontina on the northern edge of the bay that works in medium swells. Access at low tide is on foot along the reef below the cliffs, or by paddling north from the bay. It's a short fun right of average quality.

RIGHT-HAND REEF BREAK

17 Reef

- **Conditions** Small to medium NW to W swells, offshore in E winds
- **Hazards/tips** Shallow reef with urchins
- **Sleeping** Ericeira ›› p305

Just to the south of Ribeira, this shallow right-hand reef sees waves coming out of deep water and peeling along a sharp, rock ledge producing hollow waves that finally empty onto virtually dry land. Popular with bodyboarders and experienced surfers only. Just north of Pedra Branca, access via the same dirt road opposite the campsite.

LEFT REEF BREAK

↘18 Pedra Branca

- **Swell** Westerly/northwesterly
- **Wind** Easterly
- **Tide** Mid/high
- **Size** 3 to 6 ft
- **Length** 50 to 75 m
- **Bottom** Shallow rock reef
- **Ability Level** Expert
- **Best Months** Sep-May
- **Board** Short pintail Thruster
- **Access** Paddle off the rocks
- **Hazards/tips** Very shallow, crowded, urchins
- **Sleeping** Ericeira ›› *p305*

Pedra Branca, or White Rock, gets overshadowed by the nearby breaks of Coxos and Ribeira. See it on a small summers day and it might look like a fun, playful, shallow wall, but when the Autumn swells kick in it's transformed into a shallow, jacking, death or glory left-hand barrel. The swell comes out of deep water lunging onto a shallow ledge to produce hollow, fast waves. The reef slab can hold a swell up to 8 ft plus but starts to get too shallow at mid tide, especially in smaller swells. Out on the end of the headland, it is susceptible to unfavourable winds. Take the short dirt *piste* road opposite the campsite down to the headland and there it is. Popular with bodyboarders.

BEACH BREAK

↘19 Praia do Norte

- **Conditions** All NW and SW swells, offshore in E winds
- **Hazards/tips** Popular wave, easy access from village
- **Sleeping** Ericeira ›› *p305*

Praia do Norte has a long right-hander that peels in front of the car park on the northern edge of the village. This can be a good quality, walling wave and is one of the area's most consistent spots. Best from quarter to high tide. To the north is a short, hollow left that's worth checking at mid tide. Not considered one of the area's prestige waves and as such can often be overlooked.

BEACH BREAK

↘20 Praia do Peixe

- **Conditions** Massive NW swells, offshore in E winds
- **Hazards/tips** Crowds, polution
- **Sleeping** Ericeira ›› *p305*

This break only works when massive swells are closing out the coastline. There is a left peeling actually inside the harbour in front of the small pier, but the water quality isn't great and there is bound to be a crowd.

BEACH BREAK

↘21 Furnas

- **Conditions** Big NW to SW swells, offshore in E winds
- **Hazards/tips** Check in big swells
- **Sleeping** Ericeira ›› *p305*

A right-hand wave breaking off the breakwater and assorted beach-break waves to the south of Ericiera. Can be the only place working in big northwesterly swells, but not a high quality spot.

BEACH BREAK

↘22 Foz do Lisandro

- **Conditions** Small to medium NW to SW swells, offshore in E winds
- **Hazards/tips** Fickle rivermouth
- **Sleeping** Ericeira ›› *p305*

Just south of Ericeira, this rivermouth is worth checking because when it's working it is a high quality beach without the crowds found to the north. Best from low up to three-quarter tide.

Left: 22 Luca Guichard, Foz do Lisandro.
Below: 15 Reef.

JOSH SWARD

ALEX LAUREL

BEACH BREAK

↘23 São Julião

- **Conditions** Small NW to SW swells, offshore in E winds
- **Hazards/tips** Very consistent spot
- **Sleeping** Ericeira ▸▸ *p305*

This is a very consistent spot that works through the tides. A good place to check in smaller conditions as it Hoovers up the swell, but doesn't handle bigger swells. Can be excellent when the banks are right with hollow lefts and rights on offer.

BEACH AND REEF BREAK

↘24 Sintra Area Beaches

- **Conditions** Small to medium NW to SW swells, offshore in E winds
- **Hazards/tips** Rocks, rips and access can be a problem on some of these beaches
- **Sleeping** Praia Grande ▸▸ *p306*

Stretching north of Praia Grande are a series of breaks that can be surprisingly fun and devoid of crowds. They lie in a string of beaches, coves and rivermouths – some under cliffs accessed by steep paths. Many are beach breaks, but some offer sand covered reefs and all are offshore in easterlies and usually work best low to mid tide. Explore **Magoito, São Julião, Adraga** and **Praia das Maças**. You will find many of them uncrowded, but they don't handle big swells preferring instead small, clean surf making them ideal summer getaways.

BEACH BREAK

↘25 Praia Grande/Praia Pequena

- **Conditions** All NW to SW swells, offshore in E winds
- **Hazards/tips** Crowds, powerful board-breaking waves
- **Sleeping** Praia Grande ▸▸ *p306*

As the name suggests, **Praia Grande** is a large, sandy beach and has some great banks at low tide that can produce fast, hollow waves. Popular beach with surfers and bodyboarders. Can have a heavy shore break. The beach picks up lots of swell making it the preferred destination for the area's surfers. **Praia Pequena** is a smaller bay at the north end of the beach. Again the sandbanks here work through the tides, but a right-hander breaks off the northern point at low tide. This can be a quality wave so is worth checking in a decent swell. Park on top of the cliff. Very busy in the summer, both in and out of the water, so be careful where you park as it is easy to get blocked in.

JOSH SWARD

16 Eric Rebiere locked into White Rock.

BEACH BREAK

↘26 Praia do Guincho

- **Conditions** All NW to SW swells, offshore in E winds
- **Hazards/tips** Exposed beach, powerful waves, dangerous rips
- **Sleeping** Guincho/Cascais ▸▸ *p306*

Guincho is the favoured haunt for Lisbon surfers when the swell doesn't reach the city beaches. It picks up loads of swell and the waves can really pack a punch. It works through the tidal range with low often being better, however it's famed for the strong rips and swimmers have drowned here. Pick a good line up point on the beach and keep an eye on it. Not recommended for beginners. This beach is a windsurfer's Mecca as roaring winds often scour the beach on summer afternoons – get in early for the morning glass. At the southern end of the beach is **Little Guincho**, a smaller bay that can also have good banks.

RIGHT REEF BREAK

↘27 Monte Estoril

- **Conditions** Medium to big SW to W swells, offshore in NE winds
- **Hazards/tips** Rocks at low tide, pollution
- **Sleeping** Cascais/Lisbon ▸▸ *p306*

Walking east from Cascais you will come to a jetty, which occasionally has rights breaking off the far side. Access is from the end of the concrete pier but watch out for rocks as the tide drops out. Water quality is poor as there is a sewage pipe in front of the break. These Lisbon breaks all work on either good southwesterly swells or massive, wrapping northwesterly storm surf.

SANDY REEF BREAK

↘28 São João

- **Conditions** Medium to big SW to W swells, offshore in NE winds
- **Hazards/tips** Urchins, crowds, pollution
- **Sleeping** Cascais/Lisbon » p306

The breaks at São João need a decent size swell and northeasterly winds to work although the water quality of each of these breaks is dubious. **Bolina** is the first spot in São João, a shallow, hollow wave over a rocky/sandy reef. It's a crowded spot, popular with bodyboarders, best at mid tide. **Poca** is next, a good left and fast right with a steep take-off; very popular so respect the locals. Rocky reef that works through the tides but better at mid, bar and restaurant on the beach. A short walk to the east, **Azarujinja** is a powerful right and left that breaks over a sand-covered reef. A quality wave that breaks best at mid to low and therefore busy. Can suffer from localism.

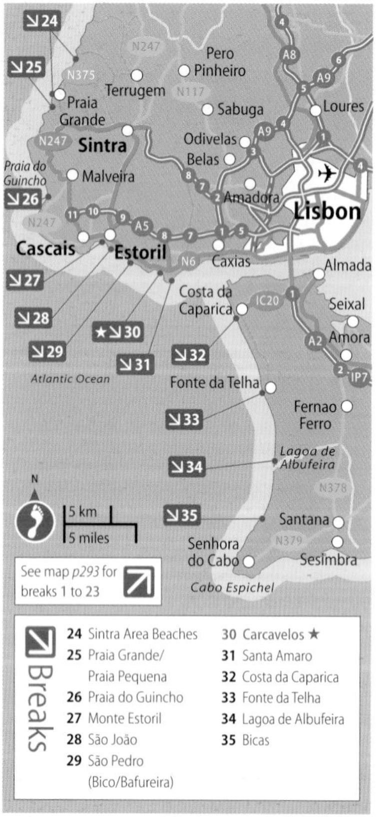

RIGHT-HAND SANDY REEF BREAK

↘29 São Pedro (Bico/Bafureira)

- **Conditions** Medium to big SW to W swells, offshore in NE winds
- **Hazards/tips** Crowded and poor water quality
- **Sleeping** Cascais/Lisbon » p306

Bico is a fat right-hander that produces fun waves in big swells. It gets very crowded even though the waves lack power and the water quality is fairly bad. Next to Bico, **Bafureira** is the less crowded right-hander, with shorter but better waves – probably an all-round better bet.

RIGHT-HAND SANDY REEF BREAK

↘30 Carcavelos

- **Swell** Southwesterly or northwesterly
- **Wind** Northeasterly
- **Tide** All tides
- **Size** 3-10 ft
- **Length** 50 m plus
- **Bottom** Sandbank
- **Ability Level** All
- **Best Months** Oct-May
- **Board** Performance Thruster
- **Access** Off the beach
- **Hazards/tips** Powerful, crowded, polluted
- **Sleeping** Cascais/Lisbon » p306

The long, sandy beach stretches away towards the fort at the eastern end of the bay. It is quite fitting that here, beneath the battlements, sits the areas most localized break, known as the **Zone**. The sandbank here produces mostly lefts, which can be high quality, very hollow and very crowded. Carcavelos was one of the first waves in Portugal to reach the attention of the world and now attracts surfers and bodyboarders from all over the capital. Not really a summertime wave, it comes to life during the autumn and winter swells when it can be quite consistent. In serious swells the wave can be a board breaker so is obviously a spot for experienced surfers only. The sandbars shift around and swell direction can also affect the types of waves formed. When the banks are properly aligned the beach produces long, hollow powerful lefts and sometimes rights. You have to be on it at first light to beat the locals.

Nearby **Parede** is a high quality right-hand point break that comes to life in huge swells. Raved about when conditions combine to produce classic conditions here.

This stretch of coastline used to be home to the elite of Lisbon until a boom in development in the 1980s saw the area expand rapidly. The extra sewage waste from the new housing was simply dumped in the sea. The area has suffered from pollution issues ever since, but now local surfers are speaking out. As Surf Portugal editor João Valente explains: "In the winter it can be very bad, especially with a southern swell. Sometimes you can see the waves are brown – polluted with sewage."

*If you like Carcavelos try **Supertubos** (see page 296), **Hossegor** in France (see page 181) and low tide **Croyde** in England (see page 72).*

RIGHT-HAND POINT BREAK

↘31 Santa Amaro

- **Conditions** Big SW to W swells, offshore in N winds
- **Hazards/tips** Very heavy, polluted, debris, localism
- **Sleeping** Cascais/Lisbon » p306

An inconsistent spot that works only on the biggest swells producing hollow, powerful waves. Best at mid to high tides, when long, punchy rights are ridden by Lisbon's best surfers. When it's on, everywhere else will be maxed out. Has a heavy reputation as one of the best waves in Lisbon but the bottom here is rocky with metal debris and the water is very polluted. Rideable in 10-ft plus range.

BEACH BREAK

↘32 Costa da Caparica

Conditions Big NW and medium to small W to SW swells, offshore in E winds

Hazards/tips Crowds and pollution at the northern end

Sleeping Costa da Caparica » *p307*

Crossing the spectacular bridge heading south opens up access to a huge, sweeping stretch of golden sand. This is a very popular destination for Lisbon's surf community with miles of endless beach breaks, getting less crowded as you head south. This northern end of the bay has groynes to trap the sand, which helps produce reliable sandbars. Each section may have a regular crew of bodyboarders or surfers, but the further south you go, the more the crowds thin out and the water quality improves. Easterly winds are offshore and the beach picks up southerly, westerly or large northerly swells. Works through all states of tide.

Five minutes from Caparica is **Cova do Vapor**, a left that breaks along a rocky groyne. It's the best wave in the area, producing fast and hollow lefts at low tide. Dominated by a large pack of bodyboarders, it gets very crowded and non-locals may find they get dropped in on. A lot. The beach is suitable for surfers of all abilities. Some of the groynes (*vapor*) for experts only.

BEACH BREAK

↘33 Fonte da Telha

Conditions Small to medium NW to SW swells, offshore in E winds

Hazards/tips Shifting peaks

Sleeping Costa da Caparica » *p307*

Driving south about 10 km you come to Fonte da Tehla. Towards the middle of the bay the peaks tend to shift around more without the groynes. Still crowded but less polluted. Low tide tends to be a better option but some high tide peaks do form. A much better bet in smaller swells but can work in medium and bigger swells as well. Much less crowded than the Costa Estoril.

DEMI TAYLOR

THIERRY ORGANOFF

Top: 26 This large, exposed beach picks up loads of swell. **Above: 30** Carcavelos.

BEACH BREAK

↘34 Lagoa de Albufeira

Conditions Small to medium NW to SW swells, offshore in E winds

Hazards/tips Rips in big swells

Sleeping Costa da Caparica » *p307*

Hollow, fast waves near the mouth of the lagoon. Works on all tides but can get busy at the weekend or in the summer. In the winter it is usually quiet. Produces nice rights when the lagoon opens into the sea.

LEFT REEF BREAK

↘35 Bicas

Conditions Big NW to W swells, offshore in E winds

Hazards/tips Watch out for rocks

Sleeping Costa da Caparica » *p307*

Rocky left reef that works best on low to mid tide. Bicas can handle a big northwest and westerly swell, needing 3-6 ft waves to really get going. Only breaks a few times a year but can produce high quality waves. The nearby beach has waves with a left and hollow right.

Baleal

Lying just east of Peniche, this small village has spilled off the island peninsula it occupies and onto the mainland. The car park overlooking Lagide is a busy focal point during the day and gives good access to both the popular eastern end of Praia do Baleal and the reef at Lagide – depending on wind direction and tides.

Sleeping

Baleal Surf Camp, R Amigos do Baleal, T262-769277, www.balealsurfcamp.com, is based on the mainland near the car park. They have several accommodation options including the year-round Surf House – just 200 m from the beach this is a great choice sleeping up to 20 people in dorms and doubles with kitchen, lounge and free internet access. Jul-Sep they also offer private, pricier accommodation – good for couples. Guiding is available year-round for competent surfers (not Jul-Aug) taking in the breaks between Foz do Arelho and Santa Cruz. Lessons also available. 7 nights accommodation from €95-175 with reductions for longer stays.
Peniche Surf Camp, Ave do Mar T962-336295, www.penichesurfcamp.com, is short walk from Lagide and offer lessons, guiding as well as simply dorm-style accommodation in apartments for visiting surfers with Wi-Fi access. 1 week from €89-189.
There are also private rooms available to rent, the best being in the old village, over the causeway.

JOSH SWARD

14 Coxos line up.

€ Pequena Baleia, T262-769370, or **€€-€ Casa das Marés**, T262-769200, www.casadasmares1.com, 3 separate establishments in a large white building overlooking the sea with pretty, light and airy rooms.

Eating and drinking

Danau Bar, is a popular if unspectacular bar that has live music and good views of the surf at sunset. There are also a couple of restaurants close to the causeway. **Bruno's Bar** on the beachfront at Baleal is run by the guys who own the surf camp and is a great place for a sun-downer beer or a well priced simple bite to eat with surf inspired names, fittingly the Occhilupo is a plate of sausage, chips and egg!

Directory

58 Surf Shop sits just inland on the main road east and has a good range of hardware and accessories.

Peniche

Peniche is one of the centres of the Portuguese surf scene, but lacks a touristy feel. Once an island, it became a pretty, fortified fishing town that is now home to a couple of fish factories so in the right conditions you can smell Peniche for miles! It has a faded beauty, a definite charm and a proud working-class feel to it. The main road into town now crosses a peninsula of sand that helps to make it such an excellent surfing destination. They hold a vast open-air **market** on the last Thu of each month near Forteleza.

Sleeping

There are plenty of budget sleeping options in town.
€ Katekero, Av do Mar, T262-787107, has good, clean rooms and is in a great location for restaurants, with parking available at the marina or just over the bridge.
In the same area are **€ Residencial Maciel**, R José Estevão, T262-784685, and **€ Residencial Rima Vier**, R Castilho, T262-789459, which has good value double rooms.
Camping Parque Municipal de Campismo, T262-789529, is a decent and very cheap campsite on the EN114. Open year round, it has free hot showers and is a popular option with surfers in vans as it is only 2 mins from Supertubos.
Camping Peniche Praia, T262-783460, on the far side of town, is further from the breaks and so less popular with surfers.

Eating and drinking

There are some great seafood restaurants on R do Mar including **Restaurante Populaire**. Check out the fish kebab or pick any fresh fish or seafood and watch it cooked in the open kitchen. Any of the numerous fish restaurants on this road are pretty good, but if seafood isn't your thing there's a fairly good Italian restaurant on the roundabout at L do Muncipal. The best place for a post-surf binge is **Inter Churrasco**, Av 25 de Abril, near the skate park, eat in or take out excellent grilled chicken or ribs, cooked over charcoal, with chips, rice and Coca Cola (from a glass bottle) – all from around €5.

Directory

Surf Shop **Rip Curl Surf Shop**, on R Alexandre Herculano just up from the *turismo*, has hardware and accessories. **Peniche Surf Shop**, R. Dr Francisco Sera is also well stocked and carries Pukas boards. Shaper **Fatum Surfboards**, T967-124494, www.fatumsurfboards.de, on the EN 247 to Lourinha, (closed Mon) have been shaping since 1998 and in Peniche since 2000.
Banks off the square near the *turismo*.
Hospital R General Humerto Delgado.
Internet Cyber Café on R António Cervantes, www.cm-peniche.pt. **Tourist information** year round R Alexandre Herculano.

Praia da Areia Branca

A good size beach sits in front of this modern village, which is an amazing cocktail of architectural styles and very quiet out of season.
€ **Casal dos Patos**, Alameda Ver O Mar, T261-413768, www.casaldospatos.online.pt, is a lovely, comfortable little B&B with sea views Mar-Oct. They also have apartments available to rent at very reasonable prices.
€ **Youth Hostel Aeira Branca**, T261-422127, with internet access overlooks the beach and has doubles, dorms and an apartment available.
Camping Campismo Municipal da Praia da Areia Branca, T261-412199, is an excellent site near the beachfront at the bottom end of town.

Santa Cruz

Heading south on the coastal N247, the cliff top town of Santa Cruz overlooks a tempting stretch of beaches. Popular with Portuguese holidaymakers in the summer, it is very quiet out of season when cheap rooms can be found by asking in the local bars. **Campismo Praia de Santa Cruz**, T261-930150, on the edge of town, is busy in the summer and quiet off-peak. It's well shaded, full of caravans, but fairly expensive. R José Pedro Lopez has amenities including a bank, mini-mercado and a number of cafés. **SPO Surfboards**, T261-937558, www.spo surf.com, based near Santa Cruz in Silveira, are a co-operative of European based shapers.

Flat spells

Boca do Inferno 2 km west of Cascais the 'Mouth of Hell' blowhole can be a spectacular swirling cauldron during stormy weather.

Casino Estoril is the home of players and playboys so it's only fitting that it hosts Europe's biggest Casino. In terms of dress code, think Daniel Craig a la but Bond and you won't go far wrong.

Cinema Often in Portugal films are shown in English with Portuguese sub-titles, check before buying your tickets 'Versao original com legendas?' In Peniche, head to the small cinema on R Dr João de Matos Bilhau, by the Centro Commerical. In Ericeria, on the main square try **Cinema de Ericeira**. At the Cascais Shopping Centre, there's a multiplex showing all the latest releases, mostly in English.

Fortaleza Peniche If you want to know more about the history of the country check out the 16th-century fortress, converted into a notorious political prison by General Salazar and in use until 1974.

Go Karting On the 1250-m **Kiro** track at Bombarral, just off the main Obidos to Torres Vedras road, generating speeds of up to 75 kph is one way to enjoy the ride on a flat day.

Jesus at Costa da Caparica. If you're looking for supreme vision, hand over your €2 to climb up inside this huge monument (think Rio) and take in the views.

Motor racing Estoril is famous for its motor racing circuit which hosts both Moto GP and Formula 1 grand prix. To see if a race coincides with your visit, T21-460 9500, www.circuito-estoril.pt.

Towns Don't miss **Obidos** – a walled hilltop village, so pretty it was once given as a wedding present. It used to overlook the sea before the bay silted up and is now 20 mins inland and just east of Peniche. Lying west of Lisbon, **Sintra**, with it's crazy Moorish architecture is like an urban planner's, acid-inspired fantasy and is a lovely way to soak up some free-form ambience and while away a flat day. And don't forget **Lisbon**. Although much of its historic side was destroyed by a double whammy of natural disasters in the 18th century, the city has a great buzz to it with plenty going on in the evenings and is just 30 mins from Cascais by train and around €3 return.

Ericeira

Since the 1980s, Ericeira has become the epicentre of Portuguese surfing. This picturesque, traditional fishing village with cobbled streets and classic blue and white school colours has expanded to become a popular holiday town, with new developments and holiday apartments set back from the old centre but has lost none of its charm in the making.

Sleeping

€ **Residencia Vinnu's**, R Prudencio Franco da Trindade, north of the central square, T261-863830, has light and pretty rooms sleeping 2 or 3 in a good central location. Some rooms have kitchenette facilities also.
€ **Hospedaria Bernado**, T261-862378, is close to the square and has nice, clean rooms and friendly owner.
The tourist office can also supply a comprehensive list of apartamentos for rent.

There are a couple of **surf camps** here. **Rapture Camp**, T191-724 5704, www.rapturecamps.com, overlooking Lizandro, south of the town offers surf guiding (plus free lessons) with comfortable dorm-style accommodation complete with beach views, a garden for chilling and secure board and wetsuit lock up, from €250 per week They also have deals based accommodation, breakfast daily plus dinner 5 nights a week.
Ribeira Surf Camp,

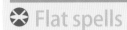

 www.ribeirasurfcamp.com, camp based next to the beach car park at Ribeira d'Ilhas is a series of heated wooden cabins – shared or private plus onsite bar and restaurant. They offer accommodation only options from €190-285 plus 'with lessons' and guiding packages.
Camping Parque Municipal de Campismo de Mil Regos, T261-862513, on the N247 coast road at the northern edge of town, is a large, popular and cheap campsite with bungalows available sleeping 4 or 6 from €40-100. Out of season it is mainly inhabited by surfers and empty caravans and is just a short walk across the road to the breaks around Pedra Branca.

Eating and drinking
Seafood in Ericeira is excellent and there are many fish restaurants here, although they are pricier than Peniche. **Mar a Vista** on Largo das Ribas has good fish, particularly its grilled sardines or monkfish. Don't miss **Tik Tak**, R 5 Outubro, for excellent steak or fish at very reasonable prices – from around €8. Josh Sward of Rapture Surf Camp recommends **Prim Restaurant**, R 5 de Outubro, for the best food in town – Brasilian and Portuguese, also offering seafood. There is the obligatory **Casa dos Frangos**, on R de Santo Antonio, doing takeaway grilled chicken and chips. During the week there are some great cafés and bars to sit outside on the main square. At the weekends, the town comes to life with an influx of visitors from nearby Lisbon. **Bar Big Waves** Praça dos Navigantes is a great spot, as is **La Luna**, while the one and only **Disco-Bar Ouriço**, overlooking the fisherman's beach heaves with local and visiting surfers as well as hot young things.

DEMI TAYLOR

Peniche Prison-eye view of Supertubes.

Directory
Surf Shop **Ericeira Surf Shop**, R Prudencio Franco da Trindade, has a wide selection of hardware and clothing as does the **Billabong** shop on R Dr Eduardo Bumay. **Semente Surfboards**, is on the N247 at Ribamar, about 2 km north of Ericeira, T261-863552, www.semente.pt. Created by Nick Uricchio and Miguel Katzenstein in 1982 and sponsoring among other Tiago Pires, they are the country's top board manufacturer. **Shapers Board Culture**, T261-862000, www.board-culture.pt, whose team includes Edgar Nozes also have a base in Ericeira in Urbanizacao S Sebastiao.
Banks and ATMs on the main square. **Police**: R de Outubro. **Post office** R Prudencio Franco da Trindade.
Taxis available from the main square back to the campsite. **Tourist information** P da Republica, www.ericeira.net, large, modern and very helpful office on the main square.

Praia Grande

West of Sintra and on the edge of the N247 this summer resort is a halfway house between the hubs of Ericeira and Lisbon and is fine for an over night stop.
Praia Grande Campismo, on the EN135 Sintra–Praia das Maças road, T21-929058, is a good size campsite open year round.

Guincho

This windswept beach is heaving in the summer and also popular with windsurfers.

Sleeping
Except for the expensive **€ Fortaleza do Guincho**, which has truly seen better days, accommodation near the beach is limited. Better options are in nearby Cascais.
Camping Just behind the beach and set in tree-topped dunes, **Orbitur Campismo Guincho**, T21-4870450, is a large site with some shady pitches and good facilities including cabins to rent. An excellent option if you want a cheap place near Lisbon. Has bus access to the train station in Cascais, for regular 30-min train service to Lisbon.

Cascais

With a name that sounds like a sneeze, Cascais ('kesh-kysh') has traditionally been an upmarket suburb of Lisbon due to its excellent transport links to the centre, great bars, restaurants and beachfront culture. It makes a great base for a surf trip to the Lisbon area as there is a regular **train** service into central Lisbon (costing less than €2) with stops at all the best breaks along the Costa Estoril. Station is on the EN6/Av Marginal.

Sleeping
Cascais traditionally attracts the jet-set crowd and has a number or boutique, design hotels, but there are good value options around if you explore.
€ Cascais Beach Hostel, R da Vista Alegre, T309-906421, isn't on the beach but has clean, comfortable modern hostel accommodation including dorm beds from €18, doubles from €49 and suites from €69 with a pol, BBQ area and Wifi access.
€ Residencial Avenida, R da Palmeira, T21-4864417, is probably the best value and has some good double rooms in a central location.
Nearer the beaches in the older part of town is **€ Residence Parsi**, R Afonso Sanchez, T21-484 5744. A good but noisy location.

Eating and drinking
Grilled fish, especially sardines, *sardinhas assado*, is a local speciality. Check out **Esplanada Santa Marta**, for their grilled fish served on a terrace overlooking the tiny beach of the same name. **Jardim dos Frangos**, Av Com da Grande Guerra, is the obligatory grilled chicken establishment, a

popular spot with tables outside. **Dom Monolo's**, Av Marginal, offer a good value menu with grilled fish and meat. Recommended are the catch of the day and the grilled chicken all served with chips and salad.

Directory

Tourist information R Visconde da Luz.

Lisbon

Lisbon is a bustling city best seen on foot. A good idea if you are in a van is to leave it in Cascais and get the cheap and regular metro train into the centre. The station (Cais do Sodré) is near the river and just a short walk east to Baixa. This is the heart of the city and is dissected by the pedestrianised R Augusta, which runs from the river up to Rossio near the main railway station. Walking through the archway on Praça do Comércio, you enter the bustling city centre where men in macs appear to offer knock-off watches before melting away. There are cafés and restaurants along the length of what is the heart of the city, rebuilt following the cataclysmic double hitter earthquake and tidal wave of 1755. There are some good cheap accommodation options in this area and it makes a great base from which to push out and explore.

Sleeping

There are a couple of new breed 'design hostels' with good, clean, facilities including: **€ Lisbon Poets Hostel**, R do Duque, just east of the Barrio Alto T21-3461058, dorm beds €18-20, doubles from €44, breakie €3. **€ Lisbon Lounge Hostel**, relocated to R de S. Nicolau T21-3462061. It features contemporary, comfortable rooms with floor to ceiling windows, Wifi access, and breakfast included. Dorms €18/20, doubles €50/54.

€ New Aljubarrota, R da Assunção, T21-346 0112, is well located just off R Augusta, has a selection of great rooms with or without showers, and does rooms sleeping up to 4 as well. Breakfast included.

€ Pensão Norte, R dos Douradores, T21-887 8941, has a wide selection of clean rooms with either a shower or bath. It is a good, well-located (near Rossio), 'no-frills' option and relatively quiet for such a central location.

Camping Lisboa, Estrada Circunvalacao, T21-7628200, is about 5 km out of town, fairly pricey from around €33 for a van and 2 people per night but is open year round and has bungalows also.

Eating and drinking

The city is home to all types of food and a short stroll through the Barrio Alto should yield a good selection. Below are a couple of well priced options: **Rei do Frangos**, on Trav De Santo Antão, really is king of the chickens. For vegetarians, head to **Terra Restaurante Natural**, R da Palmeira, for a wonderful organic feast of Mediterranean and traditional dishes. Sit outside and drink in the atmosphere over lunch at **Académica** on Largo do Carmo in Bairro Alto. Enjoy a coffee and pastry for breakfast or a lunch of grilled sardines. **Pasteis de Belem**, R de Belem, is like the holy temple of the pasties de nata (the humble custard tart). The interior is like an apothecary and the flavour is like medicine for the body, mind and spirit.

Lisbon has an amazing assortment of bars and clubs and with new ones opening practically every week, there's something for everyone. There are Jazz clubs, Fado bars and even a club part-owned by John Malkovich. It's best to get out and explore.

Directory

Internet **Acores Café Bar**, R. Vitor Cordon, by the Praca do Comercio in the Baixa district is reasonably priced. **Medical facilities** **Hospital Britanico**, R Saraiva de Carvalho, has English-speaking doctors or ask at the *turismo* for one. **Police** 24-hr tourist police in the Foz Cultura at Praça dos Restauradores. **Post office** Praça do Comércio, with internet access. **Tourist information** Praça do Comércio, www.visitlisboa.com.

CARLA TOME

2 Ferrel Beaches.

Costa da Caparica

Cross the Ponte 25 de Abril and come face to face with Jesus – well, a 28-m high statue of him (think Rio de Janeiro). Costa da Caparica itself is a huge beach backed by numerous campsites. In the summer and at weekends the northern end of the stretch is packed with holidaymakers, *Lisboetas* and surfers, loosing the crowds as you head south.

Sleeping

Camping Orbitur Costa da Caparica Campisimo, T221-901366, is well located just north of the town, open year round with the option of cabins to rent.

Just south at Fonte da Telha is camping **Costa Nova**, T21-2903078, open Jan-Nov. Another site worth checking includes **Campismo da Praia da Saude**, by the beach of the same name, T21-2902941, open year round.

Directory

Shapers **Polen Surfboards**, R Infante D. Henriques, São João, T21-2914083, www.polensurf.com and www.polensurfgirls.com, established in 1988, shape for some of Portugal's most exciting riders including Ruben Gonzales. Also in São João are **Fusion Surfboards**, R. Alexandre Carvalho, T966-329235, and **Lufi Surfboards**, R. Fernão Magalhães, T91-904 1556, www.lufi.online.pt.

Algarve

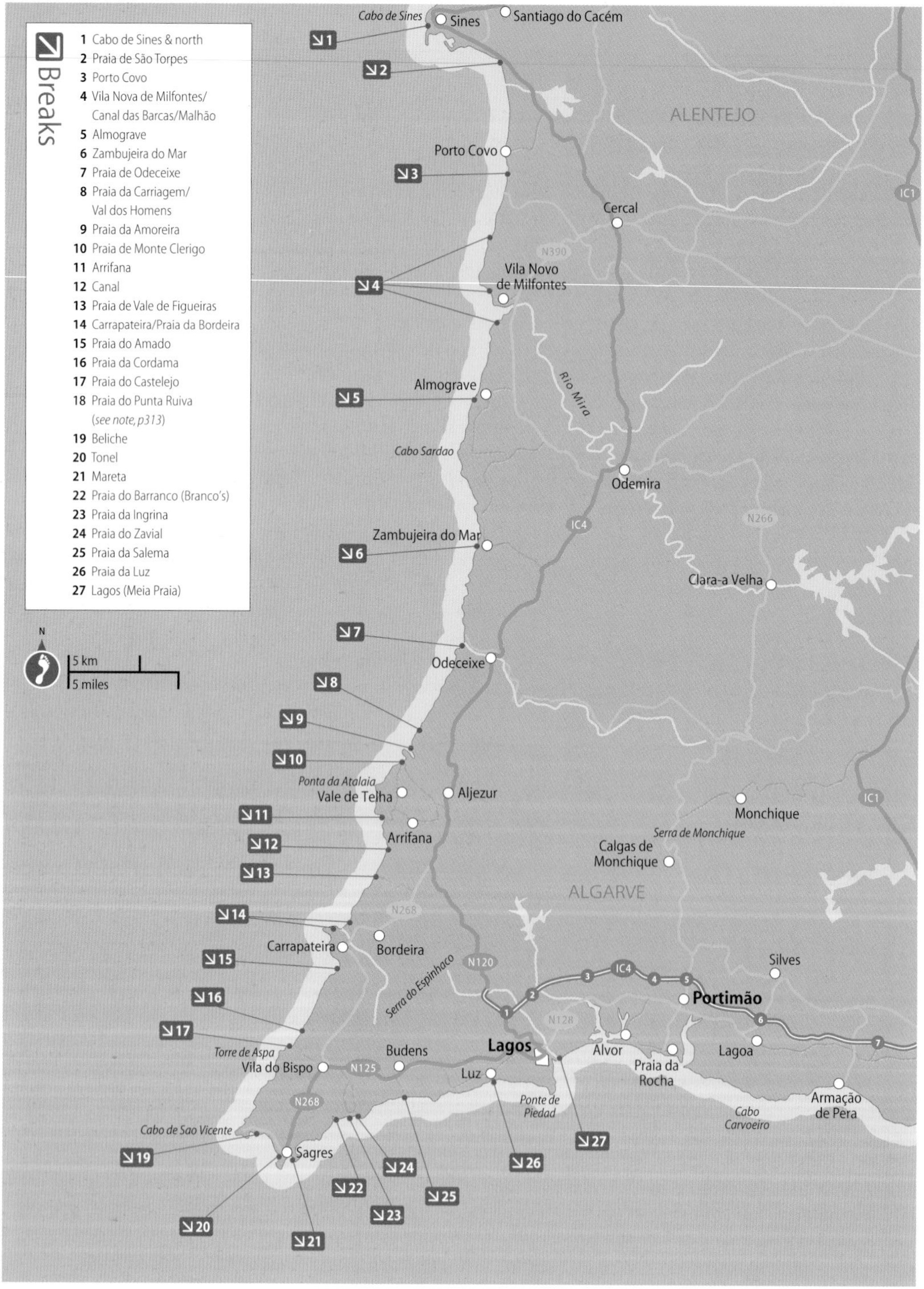

Spring
Air 17°C 63°F
Water 16°C 61°F
3/2mm Wetsuit

Summer
Air 24°C 75°F
Water 20°C 68°F
Shortie

Autumn
Air 19°C 66°F
Water 18°C 64°F
3/2mm Wetsuit

Winter
Air 13°C 55°F
Water 15°C 59°F
3/2mm Wetsuit

Overview

The Algarve is not longer the preserve of the sunseekers, the golfers and the greys. It just had too much to offer the travelling surfer, and it was just too perfect a proposition to resist. The bottom right-hand corner of Europe is probably the most flexible surfing destination on the whole continent. Just look at its résumé. Move away from the eastern Algarve, with the greasy spoons and high-rise blocks and it's not long before you're driving through whitewashed villages, fringed by flower filled pastures which in turn overlook empty, golden beaches. Beaches spread across not one but two coastlines. The west coast is a veritable swell magnet. It's not often you rock up and find it flat. In fact it probably picks up more swell that anywhere else in mainland Europe. If anything, often the swell here is just too big. The wind can also put the thumb-screws on out and out perfection, those frustrating on-shores that often put in an appearance when the day heats up and you're considering session number 3. Luckily the south coast can often come to the rescue with beaches and coves offering wrap around swell potential and offshore winds.

It didn't take long for the surf schools and media to discover just what was on offer here. The weather, the warm water, the consistent swell patterns, the something-for-everyone feast of points, beachies and reefs, all brought to you at a very reasonable price – although the introduction of the Euro has seen prices rise a little. But despite all the coverage, the visitors, the camps, the magazine spreads and a growing local surfing population, there are still plenty of empty breaks out there to be surfed. And not just secret spots, but breaks listed here in this chapter. Put in a bit of time getting to know the region, check on the swells and the winds, and you could be sharing empty, azure walls with a just a few friends. Isn't that what a surf trip is all about after all?

Coastline

The western coastline from the industrial port of Sines down to Arrifana is a mixture of rocky coastline interspersed with small bays and attractive beaches. The potential of this area is incredible, with secret points and heavy beach breaks that have somehow never made it onto the surfing map. From Arrifana south to Torre de Aspa, two huge expanses of sandy beach are exposed to the full onslaught of the Atlantic Ocean. These are some of the most powerful breaks in Europe and, due to their aspect are only worth checking in small to medium swells.

Sagres, on the southwest toe of Portugal, has an amazing seafaring history and is home to a sometimes overly protective surf community. The increasingly popular breaks here are sandy bays nestled below sheltering cliffs, watched over by an impressive fortress.

The south coast between Ponta de Sagres and Lagos is, again, an impressive series of beaches and points, some fronting picturesque villages, many hidden away down dirt tracks. The water is warm, clean and crystal clear and the sun seems to shine every day. Sitting in the line-up here, you can see why more and more people are attracted here in search of winter paradise.

6'3" Channel Islands Flyer II

Shaper: Al Merrick

6'3" x $18\frac{3}{4}$" x $2\frac{3}{8}$"

Built with Surftech's proven TUFLITE construction.

One of the most versatile boards on earth, features full rails for better floatation in small waves while swallow tail keeps it solid in overhead surf. If you can only have one board for all types of waves, this is your board.

Single to double concave with FCS GAM fins.

6'1" Byrne Maca

Shaper: Phil Byrne

6'1" x $18\frac{3}{8}$" x $2\frac{3}{8}$"

Surftech's lively, responsive TL2 composite technology.

Designed by Phil Byrne for WCT title contender Phil Macdonald for a variety of surf conditions around the world. A high-performance shortboard ideally suited for waves in the waist to slightly overhead range.

Single to double concave with FCS fins.

Boards by **Surftech**
www.surftech.com info@surftech.com

Local environment

The local environment around southwest Portugal is mostly excellent water quality, but around villages and towns there can be some localised issues with sewage outfalls. Mostly good water quality though. The biggest blot on the region is Sines and the vast petro-chemical industry that watches over coastline just south of the city. There used to be a history of localism in Sagres, but that seems to have cooled off somewhat. It's still worth bearing in mind if you are surfing near the town try to avoid turning up in large groups and remain chilled in the water and you should have no problems. Bear in mind that the Portuguese are competitive in the line-up but don't mistake this for aggression.

Getting around

The N125 is a modern highway that runs just inland from Lagos to Vila de Bispo and allows quick access to the south coast. The N268 heads north to Arrifana and is a good quality road, but it is worth topping up with petrol as there are no filling stations on this section of the west coast until you get to Aljezur. Some of the breaks are hard to access with rough *pistes*, potholes and muddy slopes to negotiate. Signs to beaches are routinely removed. A bit of exploring can pay dividends.

Breaks

BEACH BREAK

↘1 Cabo de Sines and north

- **Conditions** Small to medium NW to SW swells, offshore in light E winds
- **Hazards/tips** Access to sections of the beach can be difficult
- **Sleeping** Porto Covo » p316

Sines was once a pretty port town that is now dominated by surrounding petrochemical plants and a large harbour complex. Cabo de Sines is a very smelly rock point with spectacular waves crashing on the rocks. North of this point starts a huge crescent-shaped beach that runs north all the way to the Peninsula de Troia, just south of Setubal. The further north you travel, the more Cabo Espichel cuts out the swell. The beaches here are virtually unsurfed and fully exposed to wind and swell. At high tide the waves tend to turn into shore dump. This stretch of coastline is one of Europe's last real unexplored areas.

BEACH BREAK

↘2 Praia de São Torpes

- **Conditions** Medium to big NW to SW swells, offshore in E to NE winds
- **Hazards/tips** Pollution
- **Sleeping** Porto Covo » p316

To the south of Sines stretches a long sandy beach that picks up more swell as you head further south. This area is offshore in northeasterly winds and offers some protection from big northwesterly swells. A good spot to check are the jetties in front of the power plant (not nuclear!) on the N120 just south of Sines. Sand builds up next to the jetties producing some quality waves. The piers are usually uncrowded, as are the beaches nearby. The water quality here can be poor due to the huge petrochemical plants in Sines.

BEACH AND REEF BREAK

↘3 Porto Covo

- **Conditions** Medium NW to SW swells, offshore in E winds
- **Hazards/tips** Rocky reef
- **Sleeping** Porto Covo » p316

This is a very pretty fishing settlement that has metamorphozed into a holiday village of white painted cottages and small cafés. Around the village are numerous coves and reefs, some of which may only come to life a couple of times a year. The most famous break in Porto Covo is a sheltered mid tide reef break with rights and lefts, found in the shadow of **Ilha Do Pessegueiro** (Peach Tree Island). This peak needs a decent swell to break and is offshore in easterly winds. There are also peaks to be found on the beaches to the north and south of this spot. Time spent exploring could be rewarding. A quiet spot with campsites and free-camping possibilities. Busy with tourists in the summer but quiet off season.

RIVERMOUTH, BEACH AND POINT BREAK

↘4 Vila Nova de Milfontes/Canal das Barcas/Malhão

- **Conditions** All NW to SW swells, offshore in E winds
- **Hazards/tips** Great waves off the beaten track
- **Sleeping** Vila Nova de Milfontes » p316

South of the Rio Mira is a beach break accessible via the road to Furnas, which leads to dune parking. There are shifting peaks around the beachfront café. The rivermouth has a left, of variable quality depending on the swell and tidal flow. There are also a couple of further breaks in front of the town north of the river which can be checked from the seafront at the rivermouth.

Leaving town via the small coastal road, follow the signs north to the harbour for **Canal das Barcas**. This right-hand rocky point can produce long, quality waves. These peel in front of a huge rock and when a big, clean swell combines with easterly winds, it will fire. This is one of the area's class waves so respect is needed in the line-up. **Praia do Malhão** is a long, popular beach that works at all tides and picks up a lot of swell. Follow the *piste* off the main road north of the town.

ROCKY BEACH BREAK

↘5 Almograve

- **Conditions** Small to medium SW to NW swells, offshore in E winds
- **Hazards/tips** Fickle and rocky bay but usually very quiet
- **Sleeping** Vila Nova de Milfontes/Zambujeira do Mar » p316

This rocky beach break has a number of peaks worth checking in different swells and tides. There can be a left to the south near the Restaurant de Pescador and a rocky right towards the middle of the bay. It's worth checking the point to the north.

BEACH BREAK

↘6 Zambujeira do Mar

- **Conditions** Small to medium NW to SW swells, offshore in an E wind
- **Hazards/tips** Campsite in village
- **Sleeping** Zambujeira do Mar » p317

This beach is the last of the Alentejo breaks. It's a protected beach within rocky outcrops. A left breaks off the cliff to the south and can produce some quality waves, and dependent on the sandbar there can also be a peak in the middle of the bay. Headlands provide some protection from Northerly and southerly winds. The village is not unattractive and has all the usual amenities. Some vans free-camp on the cliff-top car park south of the beach. There are beaches north and south worth checking.

RIVERMOUTH BEACH BREAK

↘7 Praia de Odeceixe

- **Conditions** Small to medium NW to SW swells, offshore in E winds
- **Hazards/tips** Fickle break, rips in bigger swells
- **Sleeping** Odeceixe » p317

Turn off the N120 onto the new road south of the river to Praia de Odeceixe and park up overlooking the break in the village. The beach here is sheltered by cliffs at the northern end and offshore in an easterly wind. Peaks work best at low tide on the push and tend to shift about almost daily. This pretty beach is usually uncrowded making it a nice spot to escape the crowds both in and out the water.

BEACH BREAKS

↘8 Praia da Carriagem/ Val dos Homens

- **Conditions** Small to medium NW to SW swells, offshore in E winds
- **Hazards/tips** Long drive on rough *piste*.
- **Sleeping** Odeceixe » p317

Turn off the N120 at Rogil and follow the *piste* track to these two breaks. **Carriagem** works on all tides but is exposed to the wind. **Val dos Homens** is a rocky beach with a scar where the waves break. Park at the top of the cliff. Susceptible to winds unless from the east.

RIVERMOUTH BEACH BREAK

↘9 Praia da Amoreira

- **Conditions** Small to medium NW to SW swells, offshore in E winds
- **Hazards/tips** Safe beach for learners on small days. Vans sometimes free-camp in car park
- **Sleeping** Arrifana » p317

Amoreira is a beach break with a left-hand sandbar at the mouth of the river under the headland and a reef in the middle of the bay. The left can work in big, clean swells peeling for up to 100 m. On clean, small days any number of peaks can pop up in the bay. Can be empty and rippy when big but popular with local surfers when small.

BEACH AND REEF BREAK

↘10 Praia de Monte Clerigo

- **Conditions** Small to medium NW to SW swells, offshore in E winds
- **Hazards/tips** Quiet break, rips in large swells
- **Sleeping** Arrifana » p317

Take the right turn at the top of the hill coming up from Aljezur to Arrifana and follow the road to the small village of Monte Clerigo. It has cafés and a beautiful, quiet beach. There is an assortment of waves here from reefs to sandbars, so on a clean swell with light easterlies you could be spoilt for choice. At the south end of the beach at low tide is a reef with lefts and rights. On the beach are a number of banks, good from low up to high, and at the north end of the beach breaks another right. This beach is exposed and unfavourable winds are a problem.

BEACH AND POINT BREAK

↘11 Arrifana

- **Conditions** Medium to big NW to SW swells, offshore in easterly winds.
- **Hazards/tips** Rocks on the point. On the peak, problems are from other surfers
- **Sleeping** Arrifana » p317

This crescent shaped, cliff lined bay is probably the area's best known wave. In an area that gets so much swell, it is one of the few places that offers shelter. With a good beach café, it is a favourite with local surf schools, travellers and locals, it's therefore usually crowded. The undemanding beach break often sees hassling over waves. Works

DEMI TAYLOR

8 Val dos Homens.

DEMI TAYLOR

10 In a small swell and light winds this exposed spot can offer several quality waves.

DAMIAN POULLENOT

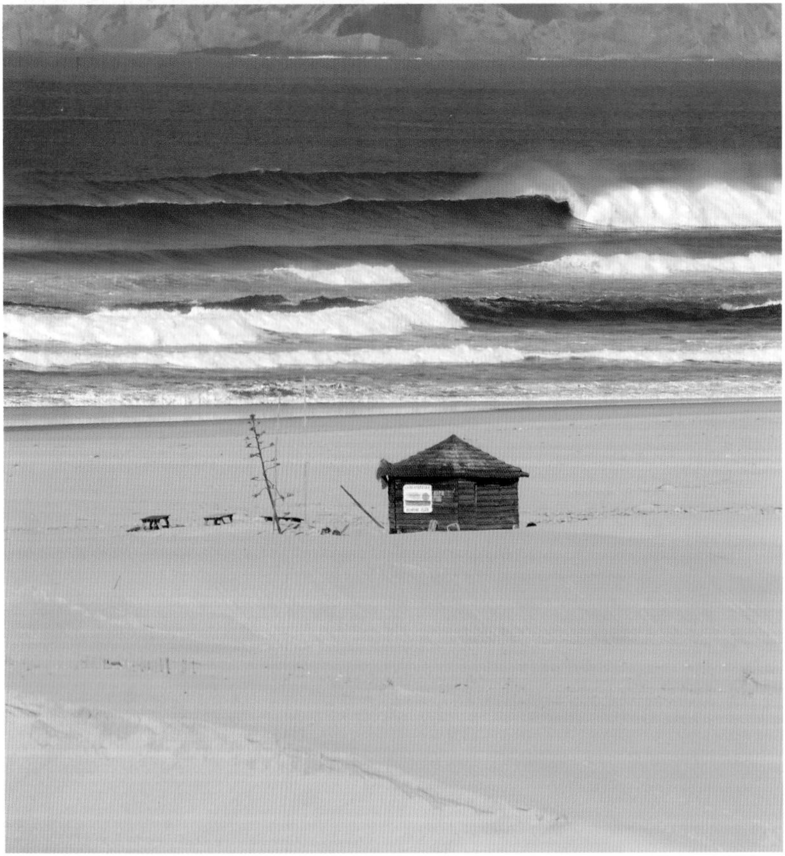

GREG MARTIN/FINDYOURWAVE

Top: Germany's Melvin Lipke at home in the Algarve.
Above: **14** Carrapateira.

at all states of tide and is sheltered in everything but direct onshore winds. The point is a different proposition altogether. It's a big, chunky right that produces long walls with occasional hollow section breaking over rocks and boulders in massive swells. Doesn't start working until the waves get over 6 ft on the point. One huge rock sits right in the line of the wave, so the bigger the swell, the more chance of making it around the rock. A wave for experienced surfers only.

BEACH WITH RIGHT POINT BREAK

↘12 Canal

- **Conditions** Small to medium NW to SW swells, offshore in E winds
- **Hazards/tips** Rips when big
- **Sleeping** Arrifana ›› *p317*

Sheltered under the cliffs to the south of Arrifana, Canal can be home to some quality waves. There is an outside right that breaks under the cliffs and an inside right that breaks over rocks and sand. Need medium, clean northwesterly swells. Access is via a piste road from just outside Arrifana. The beach runs from here all the way to Vale de Figueiras to the south.

BEACH AND SAND-COVERED REEF BREAK

↘13 Praia de Vale de Figueiras

- **Conditions** Small to medium NW to SW swells, offshore in E winds
- **Hazards/tips** Rips when big, Isolated so never surf alone
- **Sleeping** Arrifana ›› *p317*

Take the turning off the N268 for Monte Novo and follow the long, rough *piste*. Can be a mission to find but the tricky access does keep crowds down to virtually zero. Can have quality lefts and rights at low tide. This spot gives access to a huge expanse of beach where you can walk and find a peak. Works best on a small to medium swell. Waves break over sand or sand-covered reef and are offshore in easterly winds.

LEFT POINT AND BEACH BREAK

↘14 Carrapateira/Praia da Bordeira

- **Conditions** Small to medium NW to SW swells, offshore in E winds
- **Hazards/tips** Powerful waves and strong rips, not for inexperienced surfers
- **Sleeping** Carrapateira » p318

At the southern end of the beach the clifftop car park overlooks the left point of Carrapateira. The wave peels over sand in front of rocks and the cliff towards the rivermouth and is best from low on the push. It can produce some excellent, long rides in small to large swells. Heading north from the headland is a long sandy beach that is usually virtually empty. At the rivermouth, a hollow, punchy right breaks, producing excellent board-breaking waves in clean swells. Looking north there are sandbanks along the length of the beach in light, easterly, offshore winds and clean, northwesterly swells. The beach is, however, exposed and frustratingly susceptible to winds. Overall one of the region's top spots. There are rips near the river and rocks on the point. Easy access from the village.

BEACH BREAK

↘15 Praia do Amado

- **Conditions** Small to medium NW to SW swells, offshore in E winds
- **Hazards/tips** Crowds
- **Sleeping** Carrapateira » p318

Just to the south of the village of Carrapateira lies this surprisingly busy beach. Amado is home to a surf school and café and in the summer is packed with surfers of all nationalities. The wave quality here varies a lot with shifting sandbars. Picks up less swell than Carrapateira to the north, and the sandbars are usually not as good. The headland offers some protection from northerly winds. Works best on small swells. Peaks near car park get very busy. Overly popular for its wave quality. Popular free-camping area with motorhomes and vans.

DAMIAN POULLENOT

GREG MARTIN/FINDYOURWAVE

Top: 15 Arthur Bourbon, Amado.
Above: 15 Amado.

BEACH BREAK

↘16 Praia da Cordama

- **Conditions** Small to medium NW to SW swells, offshore in E winds
- **Hazards/tips** Rips when big, rocks
- **Sleeping** Carrapateira/Sagres » p318

This huge stretch of coastline sits beneath cliffs with access points scattered evenly along its length heading north from Cordama. Nearly all work at low to mid tide with some working through until high. Currents and rocks sculpt regular sandbars with the occasional reef. Best checked in small to medium, clean swells. They also need slack or offshore easterly winds as they are easily blown out. Access is via a series of *piste* roads north. Most beaches are quite isolated so never surf alone. Can have rips when big.

LEFT-HAND POINT BREAK

↘17 Praia do Castelejo

- **Conditions** Small to medium NW to SW swells, offshore in E winds
- **Hazards/tips** Cliff top between here and Cordama gives views of the whole coastline
- **Sleeping** Carrapateira/Sagres » p318

Below the headland on the southern edge of this bay lies a long, shallow, rocky left point break. Needs small to medium clean swells to turn on but can be classic. Towards the northern end, a right-hand sandbar can produce good waves. Access via road from Vila do Bispo.

POINT BREAK

↘18 Praia do Punta Ruiva

- **Conditions** All NW to W swells, offshore in S winds
- **Hazards/tips** Hidden down miles of rutted *piste*
- **Sleeping** Carrapateira/Sagres » p318

An exposed point break that picks up loads of swell but is susceptible to wind. Signs are switched round, missing etc so it can be a mission to find. Respect the locals if you do. It is not marked on our map.

GREG MARTIN/FINDYOURWAVE

GREG MARTIN/FINDYOURWAVE

GREG MARTIN/FINDYOURWAVE

Top: 19 Beliche.
Above and top right: 20 Tonel.

BEACH BREAK

↘19 Beliche

- **Conditions** Big NW to all SW swells, offshore in N to NE winds
- **Hazards/tips** Crowds and localism
- **Sleeping** Sagres ›› *p318*

This small, sandy southerly facing cove is classed as one of the Sagres breaks. The peak here can be very good, producing hollow waves, but consequently gets very crowded depending on the time of day (lunch and evenings). Picks up less swell than Tonel, beach can disappear at high tide and it. Parking above the break.

BEACH BREAK

↘20 Tonel

- **Conditions** Medium NW and W and all SW swells, offshore in E winds
- **Hazards/tips** Localism and crowds
- **Sleeping** Sagres ›› *p318*

This westerly facing, cliff lined cove is home to some excellent sandbars along the length of its beach. Best at low to three quarter tide as much disappears at high. Sheltered from winds and northwesterly swells will be smaller here than on the west coast so a good place to check in big swells. As a result it can get busy and there are lots of local bodyboarders. Peaks nearest the parking are always the busiest so check out the far end if you want some waves to yourself. Overlooked by an imposing fortress.

BEACH BREAK

↘21 Mareta

- **Conditions** Medium SW to big W or NW swells, offshore in NW winds
- **Hazards/tips** Crowds
- **Sleeping** Sagres ›› *p318*

Mareta is a good spot to check in a big northwesterly swell when the west coast is blown out and onshore. The swell will wrap into the southeasterly facing bay and be offshore. The sandy beach has peaks along its length, which break in medium southwesterly or big northwesterly swells. As a result it can be busy, especially during holidays and at weekends. Cafés on the beachfront and cliff top overlook the breaks with parking and showers beachside.

RIGHT-HAND POINT BREAK

↘22 Praia do Barranco (Branco's)

- **Conditions** All SW and big NW swells, offshore in N winds
- **Hazards/tips** Access along a rutted track, can be a problem in wet weather
- **Sleeping** Sagres/Luz/Lagos ›› *p318*

Popular mid to high tide beach with a right hander breaking over pebbles. Can get crowded as people will head here when the west coast is big or when a good southwesterly swell is running. Popular as a free-camping area as it is a trek to get to.

LEFT REEF BREAK

↘23 Praia da Ingrina

- **Conditions** All SW and big NW swells, offshore in N winds
- **Hazards/tips** For experienced surfers only, bar overlooks break
- **Sleeping** Sagres/Luz/Lagos ›› *p318*

This is a short left that breaks in front of a large rock and peels into a small cove. Popular with boogers in small swells, as they can take off on the backwash off the rock. Better for surfers when a bit bigger and clean.

RIGHT POINT AND BEACH BREAK

↘24 Praia do Zavial

- **Conditions** All SW and big NW swells, offshore in N winds
- **Hazards/tips** Popular beach which gets crowded
- **Sleeping** Sagres/Luz/Lagos » p318

Sandy cove that opens up at low tide with right point at the western edge, which can produce some quality waves. Waves peel from headland towards beach along this sand-covered reef. Peaks in the bay tend to close out in bigger swells. The best spot on the south coast when west coast gets too big. Café overlooks beach with parking. Walk out onto the rocks to check the point, which is obscured from the car park.

BEACH BREAK

↘25 Praia da Salema

- **Conditions** All SW and big NW swells, offshore in N winds
- **Hazards/tips** Car park on seafront in small village
- **Sleeping** Luz/Lagos » p319

Small village with sheltered beach. Peaks on seafront can be good depending on banks. Picks up less swell than Zavial.

LEFT POINT, BEACH AND RIGHT POINT BREAKS

↘26 Praia da Luz

- **Conditions** All SW and big NW swells, offshore in N winds
- **Hazards/tips** Rocky point best left to experienced surfers
- **Sleeping** Luz/Lagos » p318

Luz is a whitewashed holiday village just outside Lagos off the N125. The beach break can have nice peaks shaped by a small rivermouth. The sloping right reef on the western edge and long, rocky left point on the eastern end both work in big, clean, southwesterly swells. Parking on the seafront.

BEACH BREAK

↘27 Lagos (Meia Praia)

- **Conditions** All SW and huge NW swells, offshore in N winds
- Hazards/tips Fairly safe beach for beginners
- **Sleeping** Lagos » p318

Across the river from Lagos sits the huge, curved sandy beach. At the western end sandbars can be found near the harbour/rivermouth where the sea wall can provide protection in big westerlies. Further along, the horseshoe-shaped beach picks up more swell. Better on a low to mid tide. Beach is packed with tourists in summer (but it's flat then), but off season it's quiet. A good place to check if big northerlies are battering the west coast. Not worth heading east of here.

Bottom: 17 Castelejo. **Below:** 20 Josh Hughes.

GREG MARTIN/FINDYOURWAVE

GREG MARTIN/FINDYOURWAVE

Practicalities

Porto Covo

South of the petrochemical blight that is Sines, Porto Covo is a pretty whitewashed fishing village. Although it is becoming a tourist resort with good amenities, modern housing and developments springing up on the edge of the village, it has retained most of its charm and has plenty of accommodation.

Sleeping

€ Porto Covo Hotel ApartamentoR Vitalina da Silva, T269-959140, www.hotelportocovo.com, apartment complex with pool sleeping 1-4 with very reasonable off-season rates – apts for 4 from €66-97 per night. Slightly more upmarket than the basic **€ Pensão Boa Esperança**, R Conde Bandeira, T269-905109.

Camping **Camping Porto Covo**, T269-905136, at the south end of the village is open year round and has cabins for rent. **Ilha do Pessegueiro Camping**, T269-905178, open year round, overlooks the island south of Porto Covo and has wooden chalets and apartments available to rent.

Eating

O Balneario, at Baia dos Pescadores is a serves up good, well priced pizzas against the backdrop of the fishing port.

Restaurant O Rosas, R Vasco da Gama, is a very popular spot for seafood and fish dishes.

Directory

Tourist information on Praça Mercado Municipal (the main square www.costa-azul.rts.pt).

Flat spells

Bikes Portugal has a right to roam policy which means hours of off-road fun and barely a restriction in sight. The new Algarve Ecovia – 214 km of cycle paths – starts at Cabo Sao Vicente and winds west along the coast towards Spain, concluding at Vila Real do Sto. Check out www.ecoviasalgarve.org. For bike hire try **Motoride**, R Jose Alfonso, Lagos, T282-761720, or for guided rides check out the excellent Lagos based **The Mountain Bike Adventure**, T918-502663/T091-6137082, www.themountainbikeadventure.com, who offer something for all levels from technical cross country to coastal café cruises from €335 including bike hire.

Cabo Sao Vicente Just west of Beliche, continental Europe's most south westerly point is a wild and beautiful place and the ultimate spot to watch the sun go down on another perfect day. The Cape is topped by a lighthouse however the nearby fortifications were ravaged by Sir Francis drake in the 1500s and totalled by the Lisbon earthquake in 1755. Just 6 km from Sagres, it's an excellent cliff-side walk out and you never know what secrets may be revealed.

Dolphins If it's too flat to surf, it's going to be pretty perfect weather to spot dolphins. **Algarve Dolphins**, Lagos, www.algarvedolphins.com, working with a captain and onboard marine biologist, are so confident of their ability to find dolphins, that they'll offer you another trip on their RIB for free if yours is fruitless. From €30/90 mins, T282-087587.

Fortaleza de Sagres Has a dramatic setting perched on cliff top Ponta de Sagres and is worth a quick look but there is little here to warrant a longer visit.

Horses On horseback is a great way to experience the rugged landscapes of this corner of Europe. **Tiffany's Riding Centre**, Vale Grifo, Almadena, T282-697395, offers 1-hr country treks from €30 and beginners rides from €40.

Vila Nova de Milfontes

The N390 heads towards the coast where it hits the Rio Mira at this popular coastal town. On the north bank of the estuary, Vila Nova makes a good base with excellent waves close to the town and plenty of accommodation and facilities to hand. The resort is popular with Portuguese holidaymakers but is off the travelling surfer's European trail and out of season manages to keep the feeling of a normal, pleasant working town.

Sleeping

€€ Casa do Adro, R Diario de Noticas, T283-997102, in the town centre has light, pretty rooms mostly with balconies as well as internet access. Good value outside peak Jul-Aug.

€ Casa Azul, Alagoachos lotte 229, T917-848 269, has 4 double rooms each with their own theme – sea, dunes etc and also offer surf packages with equipment and lessons from €350 per week.

€ Pensão do Cais, R do Cais, T283-996268, is busy in the summer so book ahead. It's cheaper off-season with good, clean rooms and is one of the best options in town.

€ Casa Dos Arcos, also on R do Cais up from the Jardin do Cais, T283-996264, is slightly more expensive but offers B&B with pretty rooms.

Camping **Parques de Milfontes**, T283-996104, is the larger of the 2 campsites with excellent facilities, electric hook-ups mobile homes available to hire, while nearby **Campiferias**, T283-996409, is smaller but similarly priced also with mobiles available to rent. Vans free-camp off season south of the river, near the seafront, and are serviced by a mobile shop/van that can supply most basic requirements, from water to tinned foods and fruit.

Eating and drinking

A Choupana, on Av Marginal, is a popular spot specializing in good value, local seafood.
Churrasqueira A Telha on R da Pinhal, try this for a post-surf binge of grilled chicken and chips.
O Pescador, on Largo da Praça, is a very good seafood restaurant popular with locals – a bit pricey, but worth it, especially for the seafood stew.
The town has plenty of nightlife coming to life at the weekends.
Café Azul, on Rossio, plays good music, is popular with local surfers and stays open until the early hours, as does the busy **Pacifica Bar**, on R Dr Barbosa.

Directory

Tourist information R Antonio Mantas.

Zambujeira do Mar

While busy in the summer, this cliff top coastal resort – which has supermarkets, public toilets and a bank with ATM – can be extremely quiet off season. **Parque de Campismo da Zambujeira**, on the edge of town is open Apr-Nov, T283-961172.

Odeceixe

The River Seixe, marks the Alentejo /Algarve border, south of which is this popular summer holiday retreat. The village, a couple of kilometres inland, is pretty mellow and has shops, a bank, a post office plus **Lokko Surf Shop**, R dos Correiros. For a reasonable but fairy basic place to stay try **€ Hospedaria Firmino Bernardino**, on R Praia, T282-947362.
Satellite village **Praia de Odeceixe** sits at the mouth of the river. It has a couple of cafés, including **Dorita**, with views over the beach. It also has several double and family rooms available to let T282-947581. There are also showers, toilets and changing areas on the cliff top.

Agrigento

The village is a regional centre and sits on the busy N120 where the road squeezes over the small, shady bridge across the River Cerca. The picturesque older parts of Aljezur are set back up the hill leading to the Moorish castle. There is a great daily indoor market by the river that sells local produce and fresh seafood as well as couple of *multibancos* on the main road through town. As there is a bit of a gas station drought in the area, it's worth filling up at one of petrol stations here.

Sleeping

The *turismo* provides a list of available rooms – there are always plenty of places to stay at very reasonable rates.
€€-€ Carpe Vita, have 4 small 1 bedroom pads available to rent sleeping 2. They are clean and pretty in a simple rustico way. Prices hike for Jul-Aug but very reasonable outside these months (from €60 for 2).
€ Hospedaria S. Sebastião, on the busy main road, T933-264943, has decent rooms with ensuite bathrooms and is conveniently placed.
Camping Parque de Campismo do Serrao, north of Aljezur off the N120, T282-990220, is very quiet off season with pitches in among the rows of eucalyptus trees. It also has good apartments available sleeping 2-4.

GREG MARTIN/FINDYOURWAVE

Sam Smart against the fractured Algarve coastline.

Eating and drinking

There are plenty of cafés and restaurants here.
Restaurante Ruth, on R 25 de Abril near the bridge, does good seafood.
Primavera, just to the south on the main road, does excellent *frango* (grilled chicken) ribs and seafood.

Directory

SW Surf Shop, on the main road, stocks boards, wetsuits and clothing. The *turismo* is just off on the main road near the market.

Arrifana

This is a small cliff-top village of whitewashed cottages and holiday homes, some hugging the cobbled road that winds down to the beach. There are cafés, some villas for rent, cliff top parking overlooking the break but not alot else. The beach is very popular and if it's working will be crowded.
Café de Praia, has the ultimate position at the bottom of the hill overlooking the sea. It's a great place to grab a post-surf beer and snack – the savoury pancakes are recommended.
Café Restaurant Fortaleza, serves fresh seafood overlooking the sea and has apartments for rent.
The **Brisamar Café**, at the top of the cliff may also have rooms available.
€€-€ Mission to Surf, is close to the action in Arrifana, T282-997431. The modern surf house that offers the usual package including chill-out area, internet access or

accommodation only options with a bed in a shared room from €175 and doubles from €245 per week they also offer camping in the garden.(prices hike Jul-Aug) http://missiontosurf.com.

Carrapateira

Just inland on the N120, this is a great place to be based for access to the main beaches, Bordeira and Amado.

Sleeping

€ Pensão das Dunas, on R da Padaria, T282-973118, is comfortable yet basic and has a number of rooms available but if you ask around in the cafés there are sure to be rooms available in the village. For a post-surf eat, **Restaurant do Cabrita**, on the road to Bordeira, does good seafood and grilled chicken. On the beach at Bordeira, **O Sitio do Rio** restaurant has a wide menu including vegetarian options. **Surf Planet Surf Shop**, on Praca do Commercial in the village is well stocked with all the essentials.

Sagres

This settlement on the southwest tip of Portugal dates back to pre-Roman times and was used as a base by Prince Henry the Navigator, who built the Fortaleza on the headland. This fortress was sacked by Sir Francis Drake in 1587 and damaged in the earthquake of 1755, which destroyed much of the town. Sagres isn't the prettiest of towns but does have some good basic amenities like banks, cafes and shops.

Sleeping

€€-€ Alojamento Particular, Praca de Republica, T282-624096, doesn't look particulary inspiring from the outside but has a good vibe and decent rooms available – some of which look as though they may have escaped from the set of a 1970s film. Small apartments also available to rent. The huge plus is the balconies. Also try **€ Pensão Navegante II**, T282-624 442. **Villa Martinhal**, T+0044 (0)20-8673 1027, is a beautiful, stylish contemporary self-catering villa overlooking the beach with a pool and spa bath, sleeping 8 from £900 per week (almost doubling in peak season).
Camping There is a good campsite on the EN268 between Beliche and Tonel, **Orbitur Parque de Campismo Sagres**, T282-624371, also with mobile homes available sleeping up to 4 from €50 per night. There are a couple of areas where vans free-camp including the car park for Fortaleza.

Eating and drinking

Bossa Nova, R da Mareta, does good pizzas and pastas as well as a number of vegetarian options.
Bubble Lounge, with it's contemporary meets Moroccan interior and Wi-Fi access is the place to go whether for breakie (there's a good choice but the pancakes are where it's at), a smoothie, a bite to eat, cocktails, dancing to DJs 'til 2 in the morning or to catch a surf movie.

Directory

Surf Shops With a thriving surf community, there are several good resources here including a couple of **Surf Planet**, shops – on the main route into town, and in the Praca Republica. **Banks** R Comandante Matoso. **Tourist information** R Comandante Matoso.

GREG MARTIN/FINDYOURWAVE

Luz

This is purely a resort town in the typical western Algarve style of whitewashed apartments and plenty of cafés and bars. If that's what you're looking for, Lagos has more to offer and is a better bet for an extended stay.

Sleeping

Camping Coming into town, **Orbitur Camping Valverde**, T282-789211, is a large, shady site about 1.5 km from the beach. Cabins also available. **Camping Turismo**, on the main N125 just east of Espiche, T282-789265, is a large site with some shaded pitches and wooden bungalows sleeping 2-8 people. You may find vans free-camping near the seafront west of Luz.

Eating and drinking

The **Bull**, just off the main square, does steak and kidney pie, steaks and home made puddings and has Sky sports and a balcony. The flip side is **Lazuli Bar** which has

GREG MARTIN/FINDYOURWAVE

GREG MARTIN/FINDYOURWAVE

Opposite: With two coastlines, there are always waves on offer in the Algarve. **Right**: Red Point. **Bottom right**: Cordama coastline.

a beachside terrace with internet access and does a good line in toasties.

Directory

Surf Shops With a thriving surf community, there are several good resources here including a couple of **Surf Planet**, shops – on the main route into town, and in the Praca Republica. **Banks** R Comandante Matoso. **Tourist information** R Comandante Matoso.

Lagos

When looking at a map of the Algarve, the ancient town of Lagos doesn't appear to be the ideal base for a surf trip, but this place is the complete package. It combines pretty cobbled back streets, Moorish-influenced white-washed architecture with contemporary bars, cool clubs, awesome eateries and cheap accommodation. Most importantly is has easy access to both the west and south coast breaks. Lagos was founded around its natural harbour and has been both a Phoenician and Moorish trading post. Today it is a thriving tourist destination, heaving in the summer and comfortably lively off season.

Sleeping

Surf camp **The Surf Experience**, T282-761943, www.surf-experience.com, is the centrally based Lagos surf camp. Their whole ethos is geared towards fun and good times and after more than 10 years at it, their enthusiasm and stoke shows no signs of waining. As well as comfortable accommodation with Wifi access and transfers, they offer daily 4WD transport to the best breaks.

€€-€ Pensão Lagos-Mar, R Dr Faria e Silva, T282-763523, en suite, TV, some have balconies.

€ Pensão Caravela, R 25 de Abril, T282-763361, good, centrally based basic accommodation at reasonable prices.

Self Catering For couples or groups after a mellow/ family friendly experience **Motel Marsol**, T282-702031, has 3 apartments available, sleeping 2-6 people in a complex with a pool and mini-golf course. Studio for 2 from €35-70 per night.

Camping Limited options. **Parque de Campismo da Trindade**, T282-763893, is a shabby, walled, shaded site on the western side of town by the Sagres road, next to the football stadium. In the winter there is usually a corral of vans free-camping in the car park behind Meia Praia, but the police do come and move them on occasionally.

Eating and drinking

Mullen's, R Cândido dos Reis near the cinema, is the showcase – it has an excellent menu with plenty for fish lovers and true carnivores alike. But it's really the atmosphere and personality that makes the place -it's certainly not prissy and almost has the feeling of a medieval banqueting hall with communal-style tables. When the eating's done, it turns into a great drinking hole.
Fools and Horses, just north of the square, do great evening meals and Sunday roast. There are also several good *churrasqueiras* dotted around the new and old town – perfect fast food fall backs.
Eddies Bar, on R 25 de Abril and **3 Monkeys**, Rua Lançarote de Freitasare, are a couple of good bars but the town certainly isn't lacking in nightlife.

Directory

Surf Shops There are a couple including the well stocked, boutiquey **Adrenalina**, R1 Malo. **Banks** Praça Gil Eanes.
Internet Access available at **Lançerote Bar**, R Lançerote de Freitas as well as the **Irish Rover**, R do Ferrador. **Post office** On Praça Gil Eanes. **Pharmacy** There are several including **Neves**, R Ponte Pequena and **Silva**, on main drag R 25 Abril. **Tourist information** Centrally located on Largo Marques de Pombal.

DEMI TAYLOR

Surfers' tales

Fairy tale gone foul by Will Henry

My first trip to Madeira remains etched upon my memory with such lucidity that I remember almost every single minute of the experience. From the moment I stepped off the airplane into the humid, drizzly night air, I had a strange feeling that this voyage would somehow alter the course of my life. Looking back on that evening, which seems so long ago, I realize how much can change in just a few years time. The year was 1995 – not long ago, really – yet the Madeira of today is a far different place than it was back then.

My first morning in Jardim do Mar, I awoke to a scene that took my breath away. Cliffs of multicolored rock towering overhead, azure water, flowered gardens and grape vines surrounding a small cluster of red-roofed houses. The surf was flat but I didn't care. I felt as though I had woken up in a fairy tale. I spent the next two weeks exploring the island with the only two other surfers there, and finding waves around every corner. We were all staying with Cecilia, the matron of surfing on the island, in rooms with a view of three classic surf spots.

I returned every year after that, as though satisfying an addiction. On my third trip to the island, I unfortunately arrived with no luggage at all – board, wetsuit, and clothing all lost by the airlines. For three days I waited with only the shirt on my back. Thankfully, the waves were small. I still hadn't caught a good day at Ponta Jardim, and was hoping that it would happen on this trip. On the fourth morning of my stay I awoke to the sound of thundering swell. I looked out the window and saw giant lines stacked to the horizon and not a breath of wind. It was the day I had always dreamed of – finally I would taste Jardim at her best. But wait – I had no equipment! I ran around the village searching for my surfer friends, only to discover they were all out in the line-up already. Where could I find a board? I lamented my poor luck to Cecilia, who grabbed my hand and led me up to her attic, where a cache of boards was stashed. I selected a clean 8-foot gun and thanked her profusely.

WILL HENRY

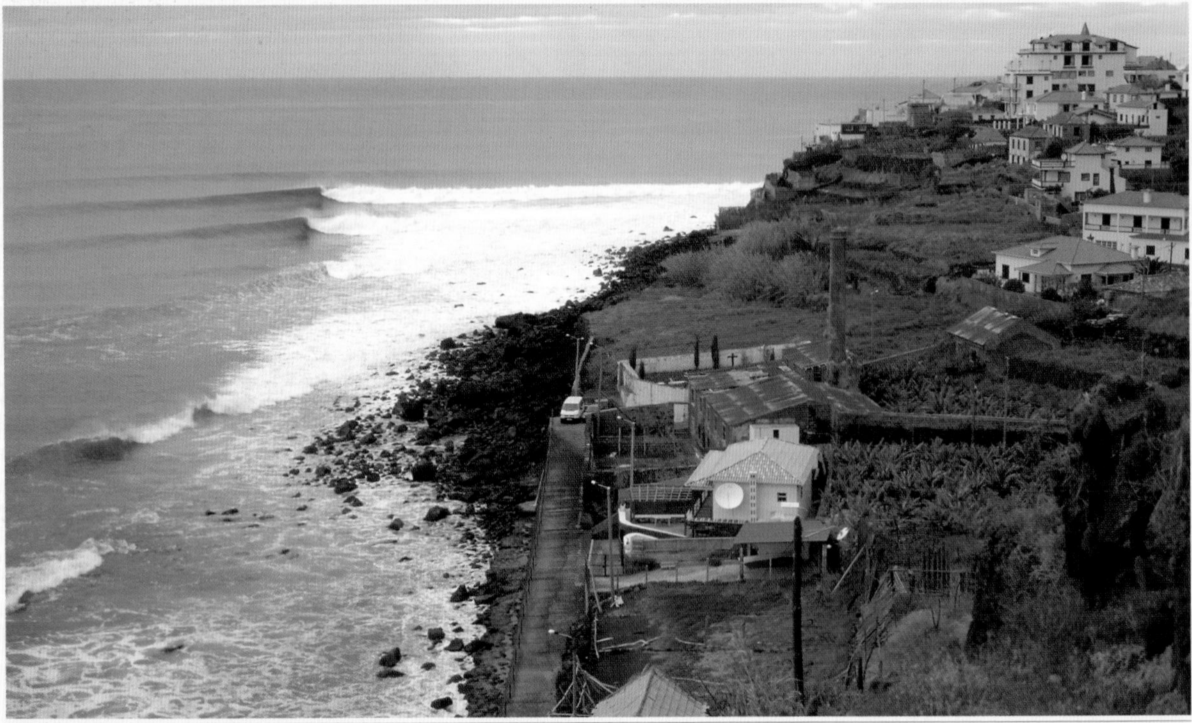

Jardim do Mar.

WILL HENRY

Cas Collier dropping in.

I paddled out in my underwear. The waves were solid double overhead and utterly perfect. I caught a big set wave and pulled into a wide-open blue tube, as my friend Matt watched from the shoulder. I kicked out next to him and he laughed. "Calvin Klein would pay a million bucks for a photo of that!" he proclaimed.

Some people say that all good things must come to an end. In the case of Madeira, we always feared that crowds would be the decisive factor, but we were wrong about that. In 2001, during a surf session at Lugar de Baixo, two giant excavators rumbled down to the water's edge and started removing boulders from the inside section. Lugar de Baixo was a phenomenal, barreling right point break that favoured high tide. The water turned a muddy brown, and the excavators piled the rocks higher up on the shore, as though building a seawall. We were witnessing the destruction of a surf spot before our very eyes.

I subsequently learned that this was to be the future site for a marina. At this point in time, Madeira had about 50 or so local surfers, most of whom were quite young. I spoke with many of them about the marina, but they didn't think there was even a remote possibility that a group of surfers could stop a project of this magnitude. At that point in my life, everything changed. I realized that what was considered priceless to a surfer meant nothing in the eyes of most others. I was determined to do everything I could to stop this natural wonder from being destroyed.

Hence Save the Waves Coalition was formed, and eventually we succeeded in convincing the government to move the marina to a different location, which spared the wave in Lugar de Baixo further damage. But the battle raged on. Next on the government's hit list was Jardim do Mar, where a massive seawall and promenade was proposed that would all but bury the wave. We fought long and hard against this project, but in the end a seawall was built. The huge concrete structure now riddles the once-perfect line-up with backwash and turbulence.

My experiences in Madeira taught me many things. I learned that we must never be complacent when a natural resource is in jeopardy, because it cannot ever be replaced. I learned that a marriage exists between money and politics that can, at times, destroy something that is valuable to many people, just for the profit of a few. I also learned that, as surfers, we must continue to educate the world about the value of a good wave. A good surf spot is worth a lot of money, but nothing is more valuable than the smiles it puts on peoples' faces.

Will Henry is the executive director of Save the Waves Coalition, www.savethewaves.org.

veltra
RIP CURL

Italy

Dealing with a spot of Bova watched over by Mount Etna.

ROCCO CARTISANO

Star breaks

1 Varazze La Secca The Mecca of Italian surfing, this A-star A-frame turns on in SW swells, but watch out for the crowds and Gozzilla! ▶▶ *p336*.

EMILIANO CATALDI

On east coast Calabria a few Ionian secrets still remain.

Hit the coast, park up, out the car, study the bay while engaged in much chin-rubbing and fevered debate. Then, back in the car, down the road, along the coast, down the track, park up, out of the car, study the bay, debate, chin-rubbing, studying. Not quite. Back in the car. Options checked, winds cursed, mobile phones buzzing as information spreads across the airwaves between small cohorts of friends. To surf in the Mediterranean you need commitment, energy, passion. Luckily, Italian surfers have these qualities in spades. Chasing swells that sometimes fail to turn up, dropping everything at a moments notice when an unexpected classic day materializes. Scanning the charts and trying to predict the complex weather patterns that sweep across this underestimated body of water. The chase; always the chase. Hours in the car, checking the breaks, following swell from coast to coast, from north to south, from west to east. There are few places in Europe where surfing and travel are so interrelated as in Italy, where hard miles have to be put in for every resulting wave ridden. But does the chase make the final outcome more rewarding? How can you measure the feeling when you pull into the car park to be greeted by offshores fanning an azure peak, reeling head high walls regailed in ruler topped perfection? Ask any surfer then if the journey was worth the end result and you'll only get one answer – a resounding "Si!"

Surfing Italy

"Nowadays catching good waves has become easy for all. We all have five days accurate wave forecasts, web-cams and on the spot shops to ring. Once you manage to understand the weather patterns of Mistral and Scirocco, you have a huge playground to roam board-in-hand. From the big peaks of Liguria to the long left points of Puglia in the south, there's so many surf gems in Italy. And everywhere is different. It is like "The Morning of the Earth" but with an olive oil scent!" Nik Zanella, SurfNews Editor, Surf Explorer

Pros

- Incredible mix of surfing and culture.
- Good quality points and reefs.
- Easily predictable weather patterns.
- Warm, sunny climate and mild water temperatures.
- Room for exploration.
- Fantastic food.

Cons

- Short fetch swells with windy/choppy conditions.
- Pollution in urban areas.
- Main breaks can be very busy.
- A lot of driving needed.
- There are some big great whites out there.

Troy. Mythical Troy. The legend, new lands conquered, boundaries redefined. In the Mediterranean region it's so easy to conjure up images of great ancient civilizations now buried under eons of history and rubble. But no, we are not talking of Helen, the wooden horse and the great siege; we are referring to Peter Troy, world traveller, surf explorer, discoverer of the mighty Nias. In AD 1963,Troy paddled out into the Azure of the Mediterranean and brought the ancient sport of kings to these historic shores. Or so legend has it. It's easy to say that history was changed, but with benefit of hindsight, it's clear nothing can stop the surfing virus from entering marine environments – especially one as inviting as this. What is without doubt is that the first generations of Italian surfers established their citadels of waveriding between 1978 and 1982, when several small communities erupted around the coastline. Viareggio in Tuscany, was the epicentre back then, fired up by pioneer Alessandro Dini.

EMILIANO CATALDI

EMILIANO CATALDI

Above: With 7,600 km of coastline, Italian surfers are great travellers. With Puglian gems like this on offer, it's easy to see why.
Below left: 2 Fabio Giusto ready to weave down the line at Varazze, one of Italy's most popular spots.

It's here that the first club (Italia Wave Surf Team), the first shop (Natural Surf) and the first contests were established. Bimonthly magazine SurfNews was started in '94 and has become the lifeblood of the Italian surf community. In the last 15 years surfing has literally exploded as a lifestyle and as a marketplace, with Italy attracting the attention of all the major surf companies. Now, there are over 300 surf shops, 40,000 surfers and 320 known surf spots in this Mediterranean paradise. Who would have predicted that, over 40 years ago when Troy caught his first Italian wave in Genova?

Climate

Italy may not be the most consistent surfing environment on the planet, but it is a more reliable destination than many people think. Atlantic, African and Continental weather fronts sweep through regularly turning on many parts of the 7600 km of west, east and south facing coastline. It's just a matter of knowing where the swell is heading. Italian surfers tune into the elements and stay up to the minute on their forecasts, plus they always have a good back-up plan.

Best seasons to go

Autumn, Winter and Spring, thanks to the dominant Mistral winds (northwest) are the best seasons surf-wise, with the Azores high pressure (flat surf) rarely lasting more than a few days. Summers are generally flat, hot and expensive (Italy literally lives on summer tourism when prices go up drastically in most coastal locations), except in the eastern regions where northeast wind can ease the summer blues with choppy but rideable conditions. Of course occasional lows can enter the Mediterranean at any time of the year, as they did in 2005 when several consecutive Mistral swells hit Sardinia between June and August creating prime point surf conditions on a daily basis.

Italy is often described as the land of the sun. As an average, air temps rarely fall below 10°C (50°F) along west and south coasts and water stays between 12°C-15°C in winter (53-59°F) and 26°C (78°F) in summer. On the east coast expect more of a variation, with winter enjoying freezing northeast trade winds the particularly shallow sea gets much colder with water temps as low as 7C° (44°F) in February, and as high as 30°C (86°F) in summer. 4.3 mm and boots is all you need in the

EMILIANO CATALDI

6 Edoardo Gorreri, Il Pontile, Toscana.

cold months of November to mid April. You'll only need gloves and hood along the northeast coast at this time. 3.2 mm will be more than enough for May-June and September-October everywhere. The big bonus is that no rubber is needed from July to September.

So where to go? Sardinia and Sicily, with around 200 surfable days/year are the safest bet. They both sit right in the middle of the northwest to southeast track followed by the Atlantic lows, so they receive waves from 360 degrees. The continental west coast from Genova to Naples is another interesting area to roam, board in hand. Quality spots like Varazze, Levanto (in Liguria), Rosignano (in Tuscany) and also Santa Marinella (north of Rome) receive surf from the southeast to northwest angle at an average of around 100 days/year. All spots along this coast are connected through the National Road SS1 and by the efficient Florence–Rome–Naples Highway, making a sight-seeing and surfing trip here very easy. The Southern Italy regions of Puglia and Calabria are some of the richest surf areas under the rare southeast swells in October to April. Wave quality is at the top of Mediterranean possibilities but the poor condition of the Highway Salerno–Reggio Calabria and the low frequency of the swells (less than 50 days per year) make the long drive south a move to be considered carefully. The Italian east coast (from Ravenna to Pescara) is also popular as it receives rare southeast swells and frequent northeast storms when most of other areas are flat.

Boards

With all these possibilities a few thing are mandatory. First is a good car, but remember that unleaded costs €1.20 per litre. Your quiver of boards should include a high performance board in the 6.0-6.6 range for when the surf pumps and a 20 in + wide fun board of your choice for the many mushy days. Last but not least, internet access to keep track of the weather situation and plan side visits when the swell simply does not show up. With over 300 recognized surf spots and 3,000 years of history and art to roam through, Italy can keep you entertained for a lifetime.

Good charts for surf

Windswells can spring up along the coastline at most times of the year, but Italy gets its fair share of solid swells too. Although the Mediterranean looks like a small body of water, certain weather patterns can, and do, produce winds with a good fetch, or at least one long enough to produce a decent ground swell. Low pressure systems tracking through the basin, and strong trade winds can turn on the west, south and east coastlines, but their duration is usually short lived. The advantage this region has is that it sits at the boundary between continental Europe and Africa. The resulting complex weather patterns have turned Italian surfers into keen meteorologists. If there's a swell, they need to be on it because by the afternoon it may be gone.

Geography and the breaks

Italy is a land where geology isn't about boring rocks formations or dusty million year old samples sitting in museums. Here geology is living and breathing. It's an active, fluid and exciting process. Not convinced? Just look at what happened in Pompeii when Mount Vesuvius vapourized the population of the whole city in one fell swoop of pyroclastic flows. Italians live with an evolving landscape. Earthquakes, flooding, landslides and volcanic eruptions are all part of the active geological process and make for an interesting coastal morphology. New rock is created and old rock eroded by the force of the ocean. This is a varied surfing environment where sharp jagged laval reefs and huge open tracts of sand can sit side by side. There is also an endless choice of sleeping rocky, boulder or sandy points, forged beneath a once raging volcanic peak and angled in such a way that will only wake on specific swell directions. Here, Italian surfers have truly become accustomed to the ways of "The Search".

In the northwest of the country, breaks are predominantly beaches, either sandy or a sandy rock combination with the occasional reef ledge. Liguria's gently curving coastline bustles with dark sandy

Italy: a brief surf history

1963 → Peter Troy, legendary surf traveller, surfs at Genova kick starting the Italian surf scene. **1978-1982** → Several small surf communities spring up inspired by the rise in surfing's media profile. Alessandro Dini in Viareggio spearheads the new movement. Surfers travel to France for inspiration and equipment. **1980s** → Natural Surf becomes Italy's first surf shop and Italia Wave Surf Team becomes the first surf club. **1994** → SurfNews is launched and becomes Italy's premiere surf magazine. **2007** → Italy finishes 7th in Eurosurf 2007 ahead of more established surf nations such as England and Ireland. **Today** → Italy has over 40,000 surfers and over 300 surf shops. About 320 surf breaks are known.

Low Pressure Chart for Italy

While the Mediterranean does not have the size and fetch of the Atlantic, it still generates regular swells from strong wind patterns. **Mistral winds** are cold, strong northerly and northwesterlies common in the winter and spring. Air masses move off the Massive Central **L1** or Alps **L2** blowing south towards Sardinia, or down the Adriatic, igniting breaks on Sardinia, NW Sicily and on the SE fringe of Adriatic Italy. **Sirocco winds** are formed mostly in Autumn and Spring, when low pressure systems **L3** move eastward along the Mediterranean, the spinning depression drawing dry, warm air from the Sahara towards the NW seaboard of Italy and SW fringes of Sardinia. A Ghibli **L4** may blow north off the Libyan deserts generating swell on the S Italian mainland, S Sicily as well as pushing up the Adriatic. **Poniente winds** occur when a low pressure **L5** tracks off the Atlantic, with W winds pushing swell along the Med. Western facing breaks turn on from Liguria and Sardinia down to Sicily. There are other conditions under which Italy can see rideable waves including occasional swells generated by easterly winds in the eastern Med. Monitor charts like a hawk.

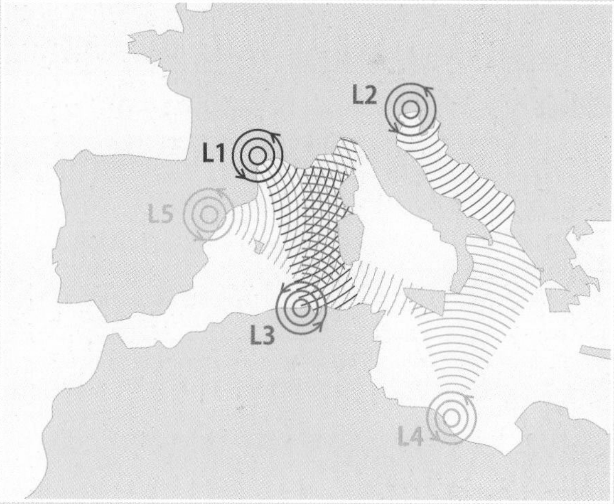

private beaches with occasional public access, broken by intermittent rocky headlands. The port cities of Savona and Genova signal a change as the coastal fringe takes on a more rocky feel. The occasional sandy sanctuary can be found on the run down from Portofino, a haven for the rich and stylish, to the picturesque headland protecting Portovenere, before the curving bay meets the tourist haven of Tuscany. From here the coastal geology morphs into a huge sandy beach that spreads south to the port of Livorno. Tuscany is famous for its tourist beaches, and these are only broken by the occasional headland or arcing bay.

Lazio is home to the Roman legions, a weekend playground for the city hordes and a stylish and buzzing hub of activity. While the reef at Banzai attracts huge crowds, the pools and private beaches mark out beach breaks such as Lido di Ostia. Each beach a huge rectangle of colour co-ordinated sun loungers and umbrellas, as the seemingly endless sandy margin heads south in a concerted effort to reach Anzio unapposed. From here on the beach links a series of graceful arcs until it runs into the pincer shaped bay that grasps Napoli firmly in its clasp. The city is watched over by the brooding hulk of Vesuvius, a potentially deadly neighbour on the fringes of the packed suburbs, while the mountain ridges to the south are snowcapped in the winter, a stark contrast to the jet black sand and azure ocean.

Italy's toe may be fringed by cliffs for long sections, but their bases are often accessible and offer a number of pointbreak options. The 'sole' is a huge open expanse, where points and beaches break in a number of swell combinations, before arcing round onto the less explored, rocky heel south of Taranto.

The east coast could be described as one huge beach break, broken only by the occasional bulging headland or sprawling port – such as Ancona. From here the coastline continues its northwesterly bearing, often held firmly in place by strategic boulder groynes and breakwaters such as north of Rimini, until the sea finally invades the land at Venice.

Surfing and environment

With 20% of the world's oil passing through the narrows of the Med, it's no surprise the quality of water in Italy is generally poor. The Italian Minister of Health has declared that nearly 5% of the Italian coastline is not suitable for bathing. The worst conditions are reported to be the beaches near Rome, Naples and in certain areas of Sicily.

Italy is probably the only country mentioned in Surfing Europe where there is a shark factor to be taken into account. The Mediterranean is home to a community of 15 potentially dangerous species of sharks including great whites and there have been 60 documented attacks in the last century. In 1987, a great white reputedly 23 ft (7 m) long was caught off Malta, and large specimens are often caught in tuna nets off Sicily. Scientists point out there have been surprisingly few attacks in relation to the number of water users, and hardly any have involved surfers.

The surf community

Localism is generally not a problem even if some unpleasant situations have been reported over the years in Varazze, Capo Mannu and in some well kept secrets to the south. Just be nice, travel in small numbers and you will experience the proverbial Italian hospitality!

Resources

Italy top surfing magazine is *SurfNews*, a bi-monthly founded in 1994. The country's other surfing publication is *Revolt* founded in 1997. Italy's surfing authorities' website can be found at www.surfingitalia.org.

Essentials

Position

Boot-shaped Italy extends in a southeasterly direction into the Mediterranean Sea. It borders France, Switzerland, Austria and Slovenia and is the fifth largest country in Western Europe.

Language

Italian is the dominant language but there are some dialects are still in use, including a form of Catalan (found in northwest Alghero region of Sardinia), Liguian, Lombard, Sardinian and Sicilian. A basic grasp of Italian is required for visitors, especially away from tourist centres.

Crime/safety

Italy has a fairly moderate crime rate and for tourists the main threats are petty crime and car crime. Pickpockets operate in crowded city centres, airports and stations. Car crime is common in cities and near beaches. Never leave anything valuable in a car, and never leave anything on show. Watch surfboards and equipment. If you need to report anything lost or stolen the **Polizia di Stato** deal with most crime, motoring offences etc. The **Carabinieri** are the paramilitary police and deal with drugs, public order and security matters. They also act as military police and overseas peacekeepers. There are some local police forces and there is a degree of overlap between all these forces, but most tourist crimes would come under the jurisdiction of the Polizia. Recreational drugs are definitely not tolerated and offenders can expect harsh treatment from the police.

Fact file

Capital: → Rome
Time zone: → +1hr GMT
Currency: → Euro (€)
Coastline: → 7,600 km
Emergency Numbers:
→ Fire: 115
→ Police: 113
→ Ambulance: 118
→ International Operator: 176
Country code: → +39
Electricity: → 220v continental dual pin
Visa: → None required for EU citizens, or tourists from North America, Australia and NZ
Tourist Board: → www.italiantouristboard.co.uk

Health

In towns at least one *Farmacia* will be open on Sundays and at night. In minor cases of illness or injury the pharmacists may be able to prescribe the required drugs. See also page 19.

Opening hours

Opening hours are pretty flexible but generally Monday-Saturday 0900-1300 and 1630-1930. Some shops remain closed on Monday morning, or Wednesday or Saturday afternoon. During August some businesses close for 1-2 weeks holiday.

Sleeping

There are plenty of accommodation options. **Hotels** have rates fixed with the local tourist board, and prices include taxes and service. They operate on a 1-5 star system. Prices vary massively so shop around on the internet and it's usually best to book ahead, especially in the summer. Bring a printed confirmation as occasionally bookings are 'lost'. The term *pensione* is being replaced and now refers to some smaller 1-2 star hotels. B&Bs are also usually smaller hotels that offer bed and breakfast only. There are a range of farmhouses and cottages that offer accommodation under the banner '*Agroturismo*' which helps raise the profile of local produce and environment as well as supplementing farmers' incomes. These can prove a popular and affordable option but may not be near many amenities. Check out www.agriturist.it and www.agriturismo.net. Private rooms may be available through the local tourist office.

Camping is popular and sites are found all along the coastline. In July and August they will be buzzing and can be a lot of fun. There are over 1700 official sites to choose from; check out www.camping.it. Freecamping is less easy here than in countries like Portugal. There are some freecamping areas by motorways and in some coastal areas. Best bet is to talk to Italian motorhomers who will pass on the best places to park up and where the police will move you on.

Eating and drinking

Food is something the Italians take great pride in. The ingredients are usually good quality, fresh and seasonal and the flavours and dishes differ hugely from region to region. The basics are also familiar, fast, filling and affordable. The carb-rich diet ensures that a good refueling will stave off muscle fatigue during long surf sessions. Breakfast is a low-key affair of *brioche* – sweet, buttery bread or *cornetti* washed down with a cappuccino (one of the only times of the day when ordering this milky, frothy coffee is tolerated by waiters and polite society). Lunch (served 1200-1500) is traditionally the most important meal of the day, with businesses closing for the period. Trattoria were traditionally simpler and cheaper places to eat than more upmarket *ristorante* but with the growing love affair with all things 'real' and 'rustic' the two classifications are virtually interchangeable. Lunch can roll through antipasto, a pasta course, a meat or fish course, a cheese course and dessert but you can also order just a pasta dish for around €6-12. *Tavola Calda* are like self-service cafés where simple, reasonably priced and often regional dishes are available. Be aware you will often be charged a cover price per person on top of your bill – this is not the same as a tip! For around a couple of euros you can pick up a panini at a paninoteca or stop by a bread shop which often sell slices of pizza or *focaccae* – delicious thick bread topped with oil, salt, rosemary and tomatoes, olives or cheese. Dinner, from around 1930 onwards, is usually a more limited affair. Italian wine is excellent and should definitely be sampled with your meal – *vino della casa* should be perfectly drinkable. If you want to try local Italian beer (light lager) ask for *una birra alla spina* – on tap – the cheapest way to enjoy it. An after-dinner grappa is an acquired taste – a *digestivo* made of grape stalks, skins and other cast offs from wine making. Aniseed sambucca and almond-based amaretto are other popular and more drinkable liqueurs although it's worth remembering that Italians only really drink with food. After dinner head to a *gelateria* for an ice cream or *gelato*. Coffee in Italy is worlds away from the milky varieties peddled by international chains: cappuccino may be fine with breakfast but after that espresso is the norm and is ordered by simply requesting 'un caffe'. If that's too hardcore try a macchiato – an espresso stained with a dash of milk. Note that it's always cheaper to drink at the bar.

Getting there

Road Entering Italy by road is never boring. The run from the north comes over or under the towering Alps and the coastal hugging route in from the west runs along the Riviera. From Innsbruck in Austria the fastest route is via the A13 and A22 to Verona. This takes about 2½ hours for the 270 km. Tolls are about €16 and there is a €7.60 road tax payable in Austria. From Geneva there is the famous Mont Blanc tunnel route along the A40 and A5 to Genoa (Genova). This 4-hour 380-km run is expensive with a total of €57 payable in tolls (including €32 for the tunnel) and a further €27 for Swiss road tax. The Nice to Genoa crossing via motorway is via the A8 and A10 to Genoa. At €16 the 2 ½-hour run is probably the cheapest and the 200 km hugs the Mediterranean. There are non-motorway, non toll roads but these tend to be busy, slower and longer. Minor passes through the Alps may be closed during the winter.

Sea Ferry crossings to Sardinia and Sicily are operated by a number of companies. For Sardinia, check out www.sardiniatourism.com for up-to-date times and operators. These include **Enermar** (www.enermar.it), **Grimaldi** (www1.gnv.it), **Linea dei Golfi** (www.lineadeigolfi.it/uk), **MobyLines** (www.mobylines.it) and **Tirrenia** (www.gruppotirrenia.it). September crossing from Genoa to Olbia for 2 people and a car costs from approx €230 when booked in advance. This route is a 9 ½-hour crossing. For Sicily check www.italiantourism.com. There are many routes and operators including **Grimaldi**, **Tirrenia**, **SNAV** (www.snav.it) and **TTT Lines**.

Air Rome and Milan are the main international airports although there are many routes into regional airports with low cost airlines. **Alitalia** (www.alitalia.com) flies to all major European capitals and national airlines such as **Lufthansa** (www.lufthansa.com) , **TAP** (www.flytap.com) and **Air France** (www.airfrance.com) all operate scheduled flights into major airports. Budget airlines such as **Jet2**, www.jet2.com, **easyJet** (www.easyjet.com), **BMI** (www.flybmi.com) and **Ryanair** (www.ryanair.com) operate out of major UK cities into the main Italian cities. Return flights can be booked from €50 depending on time of year and availability plus board carriage. Avoid **Iberia** who have ridiculously excessive board carriage charges.

Rail From London you can take the Eurostar to Paris, then 'The Palatino' sleeper to Milan, Florence and Rome. Leave London at midday and arrive in Rome for breakfast. Check out the excellent www.seat61.com . **Rail Europe** (www.raileurope.com) also has a route map and booking facility for journeys right across Europe.

Getting around

Driving (right-hand side) A full driving licence (photo type or IDP) is required plus liability insurance (bring it with you). You also need to carry a warning triangle and spare set of bulbs. On the spot fines are levied for speeding/traffic offences (get a receipt). Blood/alcohol limits are lower than the UK at 0.5 mg. Italy has an excellent motorway (*autostrada*; speed limit 130 kph) system that covers nearly 4000 miles. Note that Italian drivers are notoriously impatient. The speed limit is 50 kph on urban roads (*strade communali*). These are vigorously enforced with on-the-spot fines. *Strada statali* are main arterial roads and dual carriageways (speed limit 110 kph).

Car hire Shopping around should see some good deals on car hire – from about €400 for two weeks. All the major companies operate in Italy though fly/drives may offer better deals. You usually need to be over 21 and pay by credit card. If you've booked ahead prepare yourself for other charges they'll try to slip in such as extra insurance.

Public transport

There is an extensive public transport system and if you decide to visit major cities, it is easier to leave the car and take the train into town. **Rail Trenitalia** (www.trenitalia.com) operates the national rail network with over 3500 m of track. They offer highspeed Eurostar Italia (ES) between major cities – reservations are required with these services. They also operate Intercity (IC) connections between major cities and towns (both domestic and international) as well as the nighttime Intercity Night (ICN) that have both seats and sleeping compartments. There is also a network of commuter and local trains.

Surfers' tales
Azurri seas by John S Callahan

Italy is thought of as a nice place for a holiday, but surfing? Where? For many surfers the Meditteranean is not considered a surfing zone, but despite being relatively small it can produce sizeable waves from several swell directions during different times of the year. This delivers a wide variety of waves, from hollow beach break to long point waves.

The Med wasn't surfed much until well into the 1970s. Today, though, it's home to waveriders from Israel to the desert coasts of Egypt and Tunisia, as well as the mainland and offshore islands of France and Spain. But nowhere in the Mediterranean is more heavily surfed than Italy. There are thousands of Italian surfers along the north to south geography of the Italian mainland; and the rugged and indented coastline ensures a variety of coastal and underwater topography, making for great waves in many areas when there is swell.

When there is swell. Remember those words, because surfing in the Med is similar yet different to anywhere else in the world, and the difference is consistency. It can be consistent, but most of the time it is not, and entire sections of coast can see weeks or even months of complete unsurfable flatness. The key to being a successful surfer here is surf forecasting. In other parts of the surfing world, the established pattern is to be a local at one particular beach, like Fistral in Cornwall, or Malibu in California, and wait for waves at your home break where you have local knowledge and priority. That pattern won't work in Italy, or anywhere else in the Mediterranean, as surfable waves can be so infrequent you may not surf for months.

Modern surf forecasting has had a more positive impact on the Mediterranean than perhaps any other surfing region, for several reasons – the main one being wind fetches; and therefore surfable swells, are short; as short as three hours of waves, then flat again. Fetches are also highly directional, as the area of the Mediterranean is too small for swells to spread, so only one narrow area of the coast will receive a swell. As consequence of these factors, Italian surfers have become expert forecast watchers and interpreters, regularly monitoring several sites for

JS CALLAHAN/TROPICALPIX

Above: Davide Pulvirenti, Sicily. **Opposite page**: Sam Bleakley eeking out enjoyment from every drop of Mediterranean swell.

JS CALLAHAN/TROPICALPIX

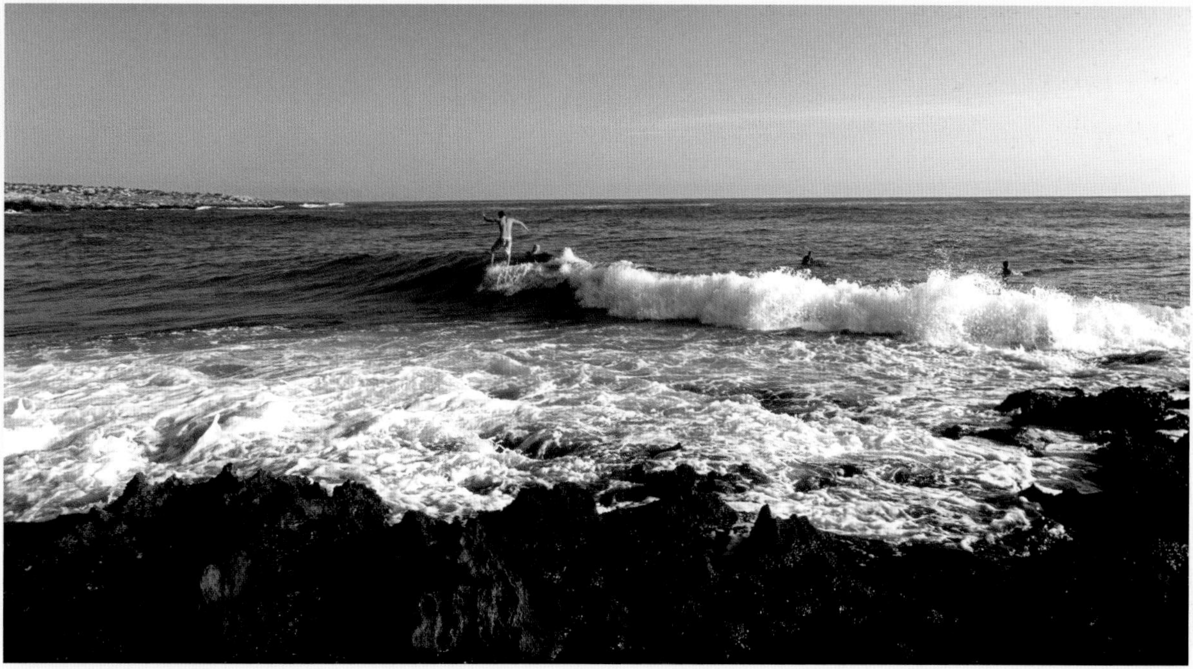

wind, weather, and surf information, and dropping everything to drive six, eight, or even 10 hours for a swell; sometimes for just a few hours of rideable waves. A decade ago, such forecasting simply did not exist, making Mediterranean and Italian surfing a marginal proposition.

Perhaps the most reliable swell generator for Italy is the Mistral, the dry offshore wind of southern France, which can make for solid swell on the west coast of the Italian island of Sardinia. Sardinia can get up to 10 feet of swell from a stiff Mistral, and is well-known in Italy and Europe in general as a reliable surfing location in the winter months.

For our Italy Project, we took the advice of Emiliano Cataldi, one of Italy's best surfers and an expert forecaster, not to make any plans beyond flying in to Rome and staying at his place for the first night. "We'll make the plan based on the forecast," was his advice. While we had hopes for Sardinia and the big wave magnet of Cabo Manu, a forecast review after our arrival said no. Instead, a rare long easterly fetch was setting up from Israel to Tunisia, and Emi's advice was to drop everything and head for the southern island of Sicily. "We don't see this fetch very often, and there are some great waves in Sicily – some good points". We were sold, and left that night for the 10-hour drive to catch the ferry to Sicily the next morning.

Once in Sicily, we drove to southernmost point of the island, where there is a concentration of points and several good beachbreaks, completely devoid of any surfers in the warm October sun. The swell arrived as forecast, and we were fortunate enough to get two days of waves as the dormant points came to life. As the swell dropped quickly to almost flat, the forecast showed a new fetch; this time from the south, with the wind field moving across the Mediterranean in the direction of Puglia, the region at the heel of the Italian boot. The decision was made to pack up and follow the forecast, and we crossed the strait between Sicily and the mainland on the first ferry the next morning, and were checking the line-up in Puglia that evening. Wind and rain had followed the wind field, but the next morning was clear and sunny, with 1-2 m of swell at the high-quality reef breaks in this area. Several of the local crew joined Sam and Emi in the line-up at a long and tapered left point, looking like an Indonesian reef wave transported to Europe.

Getting two good yet unrelated swells in two separate areas of Italy in the space of less than a week showed us what is possible in the Mediterranean, with knowledgeable local surfers who can interpret a modern wind and swell forecast – and are willing to drive to be in the right place at the right time!

John Callahan is one of the world's top surf photographers and one of the most widely travelled. His pioneering trips to the Philippines and coastal fringes from Africa to Asia are the stuff of legend.

Overview

There are already many, many good reasons to go to Italy. The culture, countryside, climate, history and food are all good enough on their own, but now there appears to be an added extra dimension in the equation. The profile of Italian surfing has risen to new heights and with it has come an understanding and acknowledgement that the quality of surf here can rival anywhere in Europe – on a classic day that is. And as the likes of Slater, Occy, Pat O'Connell, Joel Tudor, Beau Young and Joel Fitzgerald have all returned home with tales of epic adventure and classy waves, the media have been hot to pick up the story. Their sessions, along Italian breaks, have been portrayed in magazines such as Surf Session, Transworld Surf, Surfing, and in videos like Fuel TV's 'On Surfary', 'Drive Thru Europe' and Taylor Steele's recent masterpiece 'Sipping Jet-Streams'. It's no longer a secret that Italy has quality waves.

"Of course, if you are looking for consistent reliable 10 ft+ groundswells you should book a flight to somewhere else," says SurfNews editor Nik Zanella. "The surf in the Med is often weak but still the offshore and glassy days, when clean points are breaking at the foot of postcard-like landscapes not far from cultural sites like Florence, Rome or Palermo, are moments bound to last in a surfer's memories for a lifetime. True that these sweet moments rarely last more than three days in the same area, but if you are patient and willing to hop from coast to coast, as most Italian surfers do, you can follow the swell as it spins through the basin and keep surfing good conditions for days. In fact the 1,500 km long peninsula sits in the middle of three huge weather systems. Atlantic, African and Continental fronts continuously struggle with each other and, alternatively, deliver swells to west, east and south exposed coasts. It's all a matter of tuning with the elements, checking the forecasts and having a good sightseeing side program if the swell simply fades from the forecasts."

Coastline

The northeastern coastline around Liguria, south through Tuscany is where Italian waves were first ridden and home to some of the most famous breaks in the country. The beaches and reefs that curve around the fringe of the Ligurian Sea attract waveriders from cities such as Milan and Bologna to add to the crowds at spots like Varazze. There's easy access to these breaks from the coastal A roads. The west coast is a series of bays and reefs offering flexible angles to the

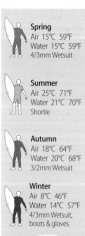

Spring
Air 15°C 59°F
Water 15°C 59°F
4/3mm Wetsuit

Summer
Air 25°C 71°F
Water 21°C 70°F
Shortie

Autumn
Air 18°C 64°F
Water 20°C 68°F
3/2mm Wetsuit

Winter
Air 8°C 46°F
Water 14°C 57°F
4/3mm Wetsuit, boots & gloves

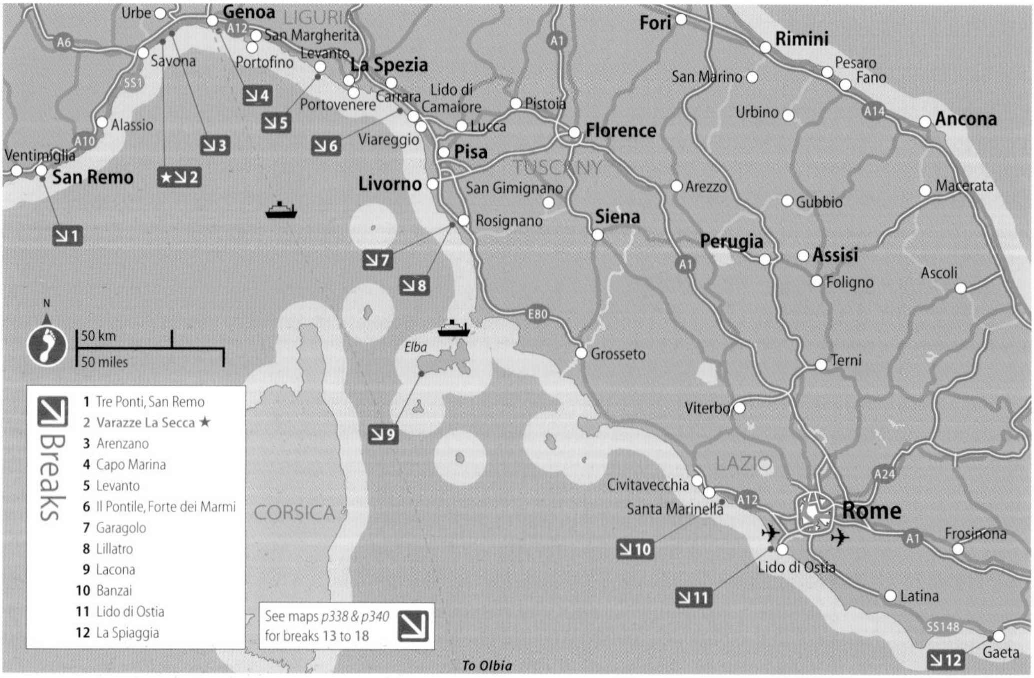

ACHILLE PIOTROWICZ

Rocky Montanari, Lillatro Primo Picco, Tuscany.

bustling spots popular with the '*surfisti*' from Rome to Napoli. Those keen to escape the crowds head south, where the southern region offers opportunity to find hidden rocky points and quiet reefs. The east coast looks like it would offer little to entice the travelling surfer, but it is as tranquil as a debate about Italian football. In southeasterly and northeasterly swells the Adriatic can deliver surprisingly fun surf to this varied and diverse coastline, even providing some light relief during the height of summer. It's all a question of keeping an eye on those charts, and then checking out the maps for the perfect foil for the impending swell.

5'10" Xanadu Rocky Model

Shaper: Stretch

5'10" x 19$\frac{3}{4}$" x 2$\frac{1}{16}$"
Built with Surftech's proven TUFLITE construction.
Flatter entry rocker with rounder outline, "wider nose, wider tail". Should be 6" shorter than shortboard. Flatter deck makes rails fuller for more buoyancy, better performance in smaller waves. Can be a tri-fin, twin fin, or with small trailer fin, making it adaptable.
FCS YU fins.

9'2" Takayama DT-2 Noserider

Shaper: Donald Takayama

9'2" x 22$\frac{1}{4}$" x 2$\frac{5}{16}$"
Built with Surftech's proven TUFLITE construction.
Built with more focus on nose riding, however very VERSATILE. Drop in, draw a clean line off the bottom, set-up that high line, and take a walk on the Takayama side. Rounded pintail and tri-fin are perfect for any turn. From ankle high to well overhead.
2+1 with FCS side fins.

Boards by **Surftech**
www.surftech.com info@surftech.com

Local environment

Water quality along the mainland coast varies greatly. You may come across everything from pristine crystal clear through to heavy pollution. There is industrial discharge from factories and at rivermouths as well as sewage discharges from towns where the infrastructure has not kept up to population growth. City beaches are sometimes closed due to poor water quality.

Many of the most popular breaks get very busy when the swells kick in. Travelling in small numbers, chatting with the locals and not dropping in ensures there should be no problems, even if you stumble across a closely guarded secret spot. Italian surfers are generally very friendly to respectful visitors.

Getting around

All Autostrada (motorways) are toll roads. City driving is a somewhat exciting experience and city centres are probably best avoided. Coastal access is generally good although you may find petrol stations closed from 1230 to 1500 for lunch. Never leave valuables in the car.

BEACH BREAK

↘1 Tre Ponti, San Remo

- **Conditions** Small to medium SW to SE swells, offshore in N winds
- **Hazards/tips** Can get busy
- **Sleeping** Savona » *p341*

Tre Ponti is a popular, long, dark sandy beach where you'll find a consistent and powerful beach break to the west of San Remo near the border city of Ventimiglia. It needs any southeasterly to southwesterly swell to turn on but will close out over 6 ft. Benefits from the fact that it still provides surfable conditions in moderate onshore winds. If busy try other banks.

Every year in Feb the town hosts the famous Festival di Sanremo music festival attended by many international stars. It sucks!

A-FRAME BREAK

↘2 Varazze La Secca

- **Swell** SW, SE
- **Wind** N
- **Tide** All tides
- **Size** 2-8 ft
- **Length** 50-100 m
- **Bottom** Man made sharp reef
- **Ability level** Intermediate-advanced
- **Best months** Winter, Spring
- **Board** Performance Thruster
- **Access** Channel off the beach
- **Hazards/tips** Crowds, locals, rocks
- **Sleeping** Savona » *p341*

This A-frame is one of the best known breaks in the whole of Italy and has been surfed since the early '80s. It constitutes a true surfing Mecca for the many Italians who want to take on serious quality waves. "La secca" (the Bank) as the locals call it, needs a SW to SE swell to turn on or alternatively a strong Poniente swell. The peak splits into a long and powerful right-hander with serious tube-time available along its two sections. The left is shorter but still intense as it bends on the reef in a U shaped bowl. Varazze is still surfable with onshore winds but with still or offshore conditions it will truly fire. Access to the peak is easy, simply paddle through the channel on the left but do not forget that this is a wave of consequence where sufers are sometimes injured hitting the sharp bottom. The "star" of the line-up is 'Gozzilla', a big rock lurking below the take-off spot. Because of the proximity of the densely inhabited towns of northern Italy (such as Genoa and Milan), Varazze can get very crowded. Many stories of localism circulate in Italy but, if you show respect and travel in small numbers, you'll be fine.

If you like Varazze La Secca, try Fistral in England *(see page 79)*.

Bottom left: 5 Il Pontile – winter pier pressure.
Top left: 5 Carlo Pilotti, Levanto. **Below:** 2 Luca Guglielmino tucks into a sundown helping of Varazze.
Opposite page: 9 Paddling out at Isola d'Elba which lies 10 km off the mainland.

COURTESY SALOMON

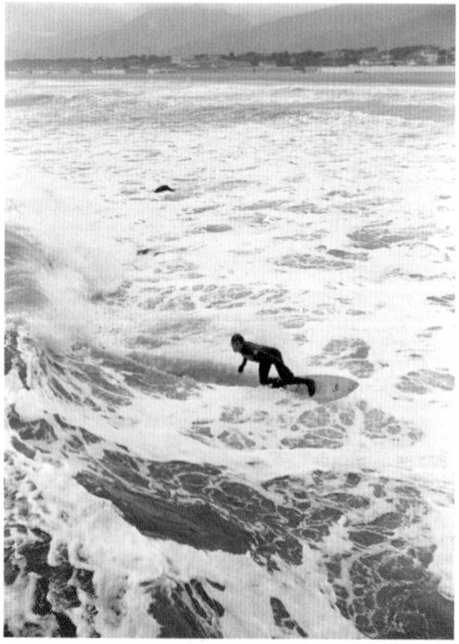

EMILIANO MAZZONI

GHIGLIO.COM

RIGHT REEF BREAK

↘3 Arenzano

- **Conditions** Big SW swell, offshore in N winds
- **Hazards/tips** Rocks, rips
- **Sleeping** Savona » *p341*

Arenzano is home to a long, sectiony right-hander that peels over a sand and rock bottom. If a good southwesterly swell hits, this is a good spot to escape the crowds at Varazze. To avoid the rocks and the strong rips, best to paddle out between the second and third pier. The granite blocks stick out perpendicularly from the coast for about 50 m. As everywhere in Italy, piers like these were meant to reduce erosion but, in reality, they made it worse. The little sand left on the beach is very dark. This break is home to a small but dedicated surf community, but the water quality is poor. To find the wave, head for the football field.

BEACH BREAK

↘4 Capo Marina

- **Conditions** Big S to SW swells, offshore in N winds
- **Hazards/tips** Popular with bodyboarders
- **Sleeping** Savona/Levanto » *p341*

This spot is located along Genova's central Corso Italia in front of the Capo Marina beach bar and is the only wave in the big noisy city of Genova. The wave itself is a thick shore dump that breaks over a sand and rock bottom, regardless of the wind direction. Water quality is not good.

BEACH BREAK

↘5 Levanto

- **Conditions** Big W to S swell, offshore in NW to NE winds
- **Hazards/tips** Big bay with big waves
- **Sleeping** Levanto » *p341*

This pretty, crescent-shaped bay is known as one of the regions best spots when big swells kick in. Its sheltered aspect means it's surfable when pretty much everywhere else is blown out, and it can break in even the biggest swells but drops off soon after the brunt of the storm has passed. There are three defined peaks, the central one always being the biggest. The harbour breakwater at the southern end of the bay allows easy access to the line-up, even in big swells. The bay is popular and can get crowded, but has the space to hold a crowd (100+ surfers). Friendly local vibe. Its clean waters are overlooked by green hills and picturesque villas. Check out Forte dei Marmi in Tuscany (1 hour drive south) when the waves get too small.

BEACH BREAK

↘6 Il Pontile, Forte dei Marmi

- **Conditions** All NW to SW swells, offshore in NE winds
- **Hazards/tips**Fun beach break
- **Sleeping** Viareggio » *p341*

Heading to the seafront in the popular tourist town of Forte dei Marmi, you'll find the popular beach break known as Il Pontile. This is a massive stretch of featureless golden sand, but at Il Pontile, the pier has caused the currents to deposit sandbanks 50 m either side and these have become consistent swell catchers. Three generations of surfers have grown up on these hollow peaks. This is one of the original spots where the fledgling Italian surf community took off, but the atmosphere in the water is generally pretty friendly, even if it is pretty crowded at weekends. On good days the swell sucks on the bank creating thick, overhead walls. When big swells kick in, you'll find the locals accessing the line-up from the pier. There are other waves down the beach, but not as good. Water quality is pretty poor.

REEF BREAK

↘7 Garagolo

- **Conditions** Medium to big W to SW swells, offshore in NE winds
- **Hazards/tips** Heavy, shallow reef
- **Sleeping** Viareggio » *p341*

When a swell of a metre or more is running, head to the north of Rosignano harbour and you'll find one of the heaviest waves in Italy. This thick right-hander breaks on a recently created reef, the wave really sucking out on take off, then leading into a dark barrel that speeds over the rock bottom. It was accidentally created by a wrecked ship, and it has become very popular among west coast

EMILIANO MAZZONI

surfers because it is one of the few 'waves-of-consequence' in Italy. People can get worked badly on its jagged rocks, like the Italian version of Australia's 'The Box'. This is the place to check when all the other spots are blown out. Definitely for experienced surfers only. Poor water quality.

REEF BREAK

↘8 Lillatro

- **Conditions** Small to medium SW to NW swells, offshore in NE winds
- **Hazards/tips** Busy, localism, poor water quality
- **Sleeping** Viareggio » *p341*

Just 2 km south of Rosignano, Lillatro Bay is the first to turn on during a small to medium swell. There are three peaks here that produce clean and very ripable right-handers on a shallow rock bottom. Lillatro stays surfable with a moderate onshore breeze, but favours glassy conditions when 100 m long rides are possible. The central peak is popular with local surfers and has a reputation for localism. Gets crowded on weekends.

EMILIANO MAZZONI

9 Fantasy Island – overhead and undersurfed.

BEACH AND POINT BREAKS

↘9 Lacona

- **Conditions** All SE to SW swells, offshore in N to NE winds
- **Hazards/tips** Beautiful spot, clean water
- **Sleeping** Viareggio » *p341*

Elba is a beautiful, green island floating an hour's boat trip off the Tuscan coastline. It is the third biggest Italian island and home to over 10 km of beaches and 3 km of reefs. Lacona, on the south side of the island, is the main surf area. It is a big, golden sandy bay over a kilometre long, backed by fine dunes and flanked by lush headlands. There are a number of peaks here in rare southeasterly and more frequent southwesterly swells. The best wave in the area is a left, rock bottom, point break located on the eastern side of nearby Margidore Bay. The beach itself is a quiet spot covered with smooth, dark pebbles, but the point comes to life when the southeasterly swells kick in. There are also fun peaks at Laconella Bay. Water quality on the island is excellent.

REEF BREAK

↘10 Banzai

- **Conditions** All SE to NW swells, offshore in NE winds
- **Hazards/tips** Crowded, urchins
- **Sleeping** Lido di Ostia » *p342*

This spot lies only an hour away from the Italian capital, so Banzia beach is infamous for

GIUSEPPE ARIONI

A rose between two thorns – Lazio.

> There's nothing I love better than an overhead day at my home spot. "Il Ponte" is a fast, sucky and violent wave on its days… on the other hand it can go flat for weeks if the swell does not materialize. Surfing in Italy is a matter of faith … and patience!
>
> *Francesco Palattella, 2x Italian champion and Forte dei Marmi local*

its wild crowds. It's no surprise as this spot works on any and all swells from a rare southeasterly to a more common northwesterly, providing a rideable peak under any given conditions. The reef produces long, easy right-handers with west and southwesterly swells and speedy left trains under the infrequent south-easterly swells. Be careful of the sharp and urchin infested rock bottom. The wave lies just south of Santa Marinella. The water quality here is decent and there are other waves to check out just to the north and south that break under similar westerly conditions.

BEACH BREAK

11 Lido di Ostia

- **Conditions** Small to medium SW to NW swells, offshore in NE winds
- **Hazards/tips** Some parts are private beaches
- **Sleeping** Lido di Ostia » *p342*

There are several peaks that break along Rome's most popular beach, producing average waves in small swells. Most of the beach is private so ask bar owner's permission before entering the dirty, crowded waters.

BEACH BREAK

12 La Spiaggia

- **Conditions** All S to SE swells, offshore with N winds
- **Hazards/tips** Quiet beach with clean water
- **Sleeping** Lido di Ostia » *p342*

With its more open southerly aspect, Sant Agostina is the place to try when the Rome region has gone flat. This long sandy beach offers fast lefthanders towards the south of the bay in southerly or southeasterly swells. These swells are short lived but can be surprisingly good quality. The beach is just north of Gaeta along national route SS Flacca.

RIVERMOUTH BREAK

13 Bova

- **Conditions** All SE and E swells, offshore in NW winds
- **Hazards/tips** Can be crowded
- **Sleeping** Ionian Coast » *p343*

Sitting on the toe of Italy, this is a long, rivermouth break that lies in the bay by Bova village. It is considered one of Italy's best left points when any decent southeasterly or easterly swell kicks in. There is a fun take-off with occasional back-doorable tube sections that lead, in prime conditions, into two different sections for rides that can be as long as 200 m. Thanks to the high mountains at its back, Bova never receives the brunt of the wind. Can be crowded and watch out for cross-shore drift in bigger swells.

LEFT POINT BREAK

14 Capo Spartivento

- **Conditions** All S to E swells, offshore in NW winds
- **Hazards/tips** Shallow rock bottom
- **Sleeping** Ionian Coast » *p343*

This is the spot to check if Bova is too small as it is more open to southern swells. The wave itself is a deepwater left point breaking over a shallow bottom composed of smooth rocks, but it does offer the prospect of some rippable walls and the occasional cover up. The shoreline is a pretty easy hop over pebbles, round stones and dark boulders. Check off the SS 106 south of Brancaleone Marina.

REEF BREAK

15 Il Parcheggio

- **Conditions** Medium to big S to SE swell, SE winds
- **Hazards/tips**
- **Sleeping** Lecce » *p343*

Follow the coast road south of Pulsano in a good south or southeasterly swell and you'll see the long left-hand point break of Il Parcheggio peeling. Has the advantage of being a very flexible spot, working even in a southeasterly wind. Needs a medium to big southeasterly swell with following wind as the wave wraps in on a long ledge meaning the southeasterly wind is nearly offshore. Also, this wind direction just does not get

EMILIANO MAZZONI

Golfo di Taranto, Puglia.

EMILIANO MAZZONI

ACHILLE PIOTROWICZ

Above: 17 Andrea Di Pietro, reaping the rewards of patience in the Adriatic. **Right: 16** This sheltered right point is a big draw for the Ancona surf community.

very intense in this area. (As with Bova, windy conditions do not affect the wave much). Breaks over a rock bottom. Main spot for the growing scene in nearby Taranto. Several other reefs and beach breaks can be found along this same road.

A-FRAME REEF BREAK

↘16 Acquabella

Conditions All N swells, offshore in SW winds
Hazards/tips Fairly consistent spot
Sleeping Pescara » *p344*

This A-frame reef is probably the most consistent wave in the area and breaks under the quite frequent northeasterly to northwesterly swells funnelling down the Adriatic. Long, sectiony right-handers are popular as are the mellower lefts, and there is also an occasional fast left south of the main peak. Picturesque Acquabella is a very small ghost village (maybe 10 houses, all empty in winter) right behind the shoreline. No beach here, only small stones and jagged rocks. Just minutes south of Ortona city centre on route SS16.

RIGHT POINT BREAK

↘17 La Nave, Portonovo

Conditions Big SE swells, Offshore in SW to SE winds
Hazards/tips Main surf spot for the Ancona surf community
Sleeping Ancona » *p344*

This right-hand break is located in Portonovo Bay, on the sheltered side of Mount Conero, just to the south of Ancona. The long right point breaks over a rocky bottom and needs a big southeasterly swell pushing up the Adriatic, it can also still be surfed in strong onshore winds. This is the main surf spot for the Ancona surf community so it can get crowded, but water quality is good. Check Sassi Neri beach on the south side of Mount Conero (in Sirolo village) when La Nave gets too small.

BEACH BREAK

↘18 Adria, Casal Borsetti

Conditions Any SE swell, offshore in W winds
Hazards/tips Crowded, car crime
Sleeping Rimini » *p344*

Head north from Ravenna on route 309 towards Venice and you'll find this beach break in front of the Adria Beach Bar. When a southeasterly swell pushes up the Adriatic it hits the sandbar out in front of the block jetty, producing surprisingly good right hand walls. The wave peaks out front into a slowish section before speeding through to the inside, providing several workable sections and even the occasional cover-up. Considered the best spot in the area. Can also work with an onshore, as long as it isn't from the northeast. Other spots are in Marina Romea to the south.

Practicalities

Savona

Heading east along the Riviera di Ponente from the French border you can follow the Autostrada, which speeds above the coastline giving panoramic views across the sea, or choose to follow the coast hugging P1. The eastern stretch of coastline is lined with resorts but the port town of Savona can make a good base allowing access to the coastline east of Genova, and for day trips to the city, without the hassle of being based in a big city.

Sleeping

€ **Priamar Hostel**, on Corso Guiseppe Mazzini, T019-812653, priamarhostel@iol.it, is based in the Fortezza Priamar fort. Open year round.
Camping **Buggi International**, T019-860120/804573, is just back from the beach and has excellent facilities but is only open Apr-Sep.

Eating

Telecaffe, on Colletta di Castelbianco, is a café that also offers Internet access and Wi-Fi, as well as food and drink.

Directory

Surf Shops In Savona there's **Maresport**, at Via Montenotte 52, which stocks a range of hardware. They also have a branch in nearby Varazze, at 15 Piazza Dante. Centre of the local scene is **Varazze Surf Shop**, can be found at Via Campana 44, www.vsssurf.com, opened in Apr 1998. **Tourist Office** Corso Italia 157, open year round.

Levanto

This picturesque village is known as the gateway to Cinque Terre, the national park with wonderful walks into the hills and down to beaches. The buildings wrap around the pebbly beach and the green hills provide a lovely backdrop. A popular resort out of season.

EMILIANO MAZZONI

Shayne McIntyre floats his boat on the west coast.

Sleeping

€ **Hotel Europa**, Via Dante 41, T0187-808126, www.europalevanto.com, offers comfortable and clean en suite rooms with decent priced B&B accommodation in this 22-room hotel with roof terrace.
€ **Ospitalia del Mare**, Via S. Nicolò, T0187-802562, www.ospitaliadelmare.it, is a modern, clean hostel that offers good value accommodation as well as internet access.
Camping **Camping Aqua Dolce**, T0187-808465, www.campingacquadolce.com, has 100 plots with electric hook-ups, many of which also have water and waste hook-ups as well. There is an on-site pizzeria, satellite TV room as well as surfboard hire.

Eating

On the main street Corsa Italia you could dine out at **Antica Trattoria Centro** or grab a pizza at **Le Palme**. Levanto has eateries to suit all pockets. For seafood check out **Osteria Tumelin**, where you can sit on the terrace and enjoy spaghetti with clam sauce.

Directory

Surf shops **Area 51**, at Via Rimembranza 14, T0187-808764, offers hardware and clothing as well as lessons. Drop by for the lowdown on the local breaks. The bay also hosts a Quiksilver sponsored contest. **Post office** Jacopo Da Levanto, 31. **Tourist Information Office** At Piazza Mazzini 3.

Viareggio

North of Pisa sits this beach resort town, home to Italy's first real surf scene. The huge sandy beach is divided into parceled off sections of sun loungers and umbrellas. It isn't the picturesque Tuscan village that most holiday makers think of when envisaging this region, but it does offer good access to the coastline to the north and south, and plenty of good value accommodation. It runs north into Lido di Camaiore.

Sleeping

€ Hotel Eros, Via del Fortino 50, in nearby Lido di Camaiore, T0584-650173, www.hoteleros.it, may sound like something from the red light district, but is infact a 2-star beach front hotel with links to the local surf school and shop.

€ Hotel Ornella, also in Lido di Camaiore, T0584-617598, stevencr@tiscalinet.it. If you want to get away from the surf crowd this hotel is open year round with comfortable accommodation.

Camping There are plenty of camping options, but most seem to be seasonal only. **Camping La Pineta**, found on Via dei Lecci, Viareggio, T0584-383397, www.campinglapineta.com, open from Apr to the end of Sep.

Eating

The town has plenty of good eateries and cafés including **La Mela** on Via Regio, that does simple vegetarian food for around €15. There's even a **Flannery's Bar** and a couple of pubs.

Directory

Surf shops **Inside Surf Shop**, at Viale Colombo 257, in Lido di Camaiore, T0584-66204, www.insideboardshop.it, which stocks surf and skate hardware and clothing. The famous **Natural Surf Shop**, can be found in Via Coppino in Viareggio, T0584-395215, www.naturalsurf.it. Italy's first, opened in 1983 and provides a wide selection of boards, wetsuits and clothing. **Tourist Information Office** Viale Carducci 10 and is open all week.

Flat spells

Italy has so much culture and history that we've only room to focus on just a few cultural days out for when the chart looks hopeless.

Genoa, Italy's largest port, is a warren of narrow medieval streets, alleys and piazzas, which make a great day out exploring the cafés and museums. The Aquario di Genova, www.acquario digenova.it, is the largest in Europe, reproducing marine environments from across the globe and home to sharks, seals, penguins and dolphins.

Pisa is famed for its leaning tower, the Torre Pendente but this architectural blunder is just one of the jewels to be found at the Piazza dei Miracoli, one of the country's most celebrated squares. Set within open lawns there is the Romanesque cathedral, baptistery and tower. If you want to be one of the limited number allowed up the tower each day it pays to book ahead on the website www.opapisa.it/boxoffice or get there early.

Florence is more than a day trip. This is the place to spend a few days when the chart says no, the sheer splendor of the city will make up for the lack of surf. Invest in a good city guide and find out all about the Renaissance, Machiavelli and Michelangelo. Check out the view from Piazzale Michelangelo out over the

JS CALLAHAN/TRPOCIALPIX

Rome's Colosseum.

roof tops. Don't miss the following: Ponte Vecchio, Piazza del Duomo, Piazza della Signoria, the Uffizi Gallery and Michelangelo's statue of David in the Galleria dell'Accademia.

Rome is one of the world's great cities. From the Vatican to the Colosseum, this is a place weighed down by history and one that takes time to fully explore. The Pantheon is a spectacular building and one of Rome's most impressive. Dating from 27 BC and rebuilt by Hadrian in 125 AD, the domed roof casts a shaft of light into what would have been a richly decorated interior. The ruined Roman Forum and the villas of Palatine Hill were once the centre of the huge empire and shouldn't be missed.

The eastern town of **Urbino** is beautifully draped over a hill top and was once the cultural centre for the renaissance, being home to some wonderful examples of this style of architecture with a sprinkling of medieval buildings.

Lido di Ostia

Where Rome comes to the sea, this resort is manic in the summer, but pretty quiet during the week off-season (which is probably when you'll be there). It's a beach resort with miles of private beaches, each with their own colour coded beach furniture. From here you can access the breaks to the north and south easily. There is the local Ostia Surf Club who host social events throughout the year so check out www.ostiasurfclub.it

Sleeping

€€ Hotel Sirenetta, lies right on the beach front at Lungomare Paolo Toscanelli 46-48, T06-5622310, www.hotelsirenetta.com. This clean, modern hotel has friendly staff and provides quick and easy access to and from the airport. Prices are pretty fair, (about €100 per double room), especially this close to Rome.

Eating

There are plenty of good restaurants and pizzerias in town. Try **Blue Fin** on Lugomare Paulo Toscanelli 120 or **Le Azzorre** on Via Delle Azzorre.

Directory

Surf shops **Quiksilver Boardriders**, on Via della Fusoliera 20, www.ostia-quiksilverstore.com, surf shop, stocks a full range of QS hardware and clothing and they host promotional events and surf evenings at local nightclubs.
Chemist **Farmacia dei Promontori**, Via Genoese Zerbi 47. **DB Surf Shop**, Via C Marenco di Moriondo 107, T0656-73072, www.dbsurfshop.com. **Pura Vida Surf Shop**, Via dei Velieri 138, T0656-46144, www.puravida-surfshop.it.

Ionian Coast

Most of the surf in this area is found on the south and southeasterly facing Ionian coast, which is dotted with small villages and towns. There is a surf contest held in Bova during the late autumn. Reggio di Calabria is the port town and point of access across to Sicily, but isn't the most picturesque location in the region. Follow the coast road south and you'll find a more raw Italian experience.

Sleeping

€ Hotel Restorante Costa Blu, lies down the coast in Locri, 300 m from the sea, at Contrada Mandorleta 19, T0964-390106. This is a basic hotel with reasonably priced rooms, speaks English and is open year round. Internet access point.
€ Agroturismo Poala, Via Giardini 101, Marina di Gioiosa Jonica, T0964-51495. The built up beach resort is close by, but this is a pretty farmhouse B&B set just back from the coast.
Camping In Riace there is the **Villagio Camping Calypso**, Via Nazionale, Marina di Caulonia, T0964-82028, which offers camping and bungalows. Open Apr to end of Sep.

Directory

Surf shops There are a few surf shops scattered through Calabria, but for any hardware needs check out **Chilipepper Surf Shop**, in Reggio di Calabria.

EMILIANO CATALDI

Toe surfing.

Chemists **Farmacia Lazzaro**, via Nazionale 11, Reggio Calabria, T0965-542368. **Tourist Office** **Reggio di Calabria Tourist Office**, Via Tripepi 72, Reggio di Calabria.

Lecce

The geology and geography of the southeastern tip of the Italian peninsula means that it is dotted with out of the way surf spots for the keen explorer. Either find a coastal B&B or the town of Lecce – famous for its Baroque architecture – is a good place to base yourself, with access to all the coastlines. From here you can strike out south on the S101, southeast on the S16 or northeast on the S543.

Sleeping

€€-€ Villa de Giorgi, Via San Filo 110, Monteroni di Lecce, T0832-327065, www.villagiorgi.it. This wonderful sandstone B&B is topped by battlements, and sits to the southwest of Lecce, ideal for those who want to avoid the hustle and bustle of the town. They also speak English and Spanish.
€ Hotel Cappello, Via Montegrappa 4, T0832-308881, www.hotelcappello.it. Offers very good value B&B in a grand building with clean, comfortable rooms. In a good location to access the centre by foot and also has garage parking.
€ Centro Storicco, Via Vignes 2b, T0832-242727, is a very pretty B&B that also has an apartment available. Lovely rooms and a roof terrace. Staff will provide a permit for parking in the centre.
Camping 15 km north of Lecce on the coast sits **Camping Torre Rinalda**, Marina di Lecca, Litoranea Salentina, T0832-382161, www.torrerinalda.it. It's open year round and offers 750 camping places, bungalows and apartments.

Eating

The centre of town is full of wonderful bars and cafes on the piazzas and tucked away down side streets. **Café Letterario**, on Via Paladini 46, is a quirky café that offers coffee, light food and jazz and opens late night. **Villa della Monica**, on Via Giacomo e Filippo, offers wonderful Italian cuisine and regional specialities with an outside courtyard for warm summer evenings.

Directory

Surf shops Surf shops here tend to offer a combination of surf, kitesurf and windsurf equipment to maximize conditions available for getting out on the water. In Lecce check

out **Crazy Sport** at Villa Zanardelli 19 and **Buriana** at Via Cesar Batistes 7. Both stock a good range of hardware and clothing and are open year round. There's also **Jaws Surf Shop** in Otranto to the southeast on the coast, at Via S. Francesco di Pada 2a, www.jawssurfshop.com, which stocks mostly windsurf gear but also some surfboards and accessories.
Chemist **Famacia Gugliemi** at Piazza S. Oronzo 18, or **Famacia Migali** at Viale Leopardi Giacomo 74. **Internet** There's an internet café on Piazza D'Italia E-Book Libreria Multimediale. **Tourist Office** Via Vittorio Emanuele.

Pescara

This is the region's biggest town with a population of 120,000 that swells annually as this beach resort expands under the summer onslaught of tourists. As you'll probably be here off-season, the key in most resort towns is finding places that are still open, but Pescara has a large enough local population that it shouldn't present too much of a problem finding eateries and hotels open year round. The old town has plenty of good bars and restaurants, especially along Via delle Caserme and Corso Manthone, with everything from jazz cafés and nightclubs to family run eateries. Ryanair runs low cost flights into Pescara airport.

Sleeping

€€-€ Hotel Bellariva, Viale Riviera 213, T085-4710606. This beachfront hotel is modern and comfortable offering balconies overlooking the sea. Also has free wi-fi and is open all year. Rooms sleeping 1 to 4 people so can be a cheap option, especially offseason.
€ Albergo Marisa, Viale Regina Margherita 39, T085-4217466. Small family run B&B with just 2 double rooms but centrally located.
Camping All the camping around Pescara seems to be seasonal, with the **Eurocamping**, Via Lungomare, Trieste Sud, T085-8993179, www.eurocamping.it, being open from the beginning of Apr through to the end of Oct. It is situated about 25 km north and offers bungalow accommodation.

Eating

Restaurants and cafes abound in the centre of town. If you want to grab a good pizza try **Pinguino** at Corso Manthone 36 where you'll be spoilt for choice, with some weird and wonderful pizza combinations.

Directory

Surf shops **White Shark**, at Via Ugo Foscolo 41, T085-4225380, is a surf/wind/snow shop. **Chemist** Farmacia Moderna, Corso Vittorio Emanuele II, 56 **Internet** Webzone, Via Trento 62. **Tourist Office** Corso Vittorio Emanuele II 301.

Ancona

This port town was built on the two hills that form an amphitheatre around the harbour, and was settled by the Greeks and the Romans due to its strategic importance. However the last century has been less than kind with the town, ravaged by bombing during the Second World War, and then by a massive earthquake in 1972. It has traditionally been the exit and entry point for ferries heading to and from Greece and Croatia and has a functional appearance but a certain charm as it goes about its business in the warmth of an Italian autumn afternoon. You may find this a good port of entry for a fly drive exploration of the east (on a good chart) as Ryanair operates flights into Ancona Airport.

Sleeping

€€-€ Hotel Il Giglio, Via del Corso 8, Cornaldo, T071-7976324 www.hotelilgiglio.it. It's worth the 15 km drive into the hills to stay at this converted monastery with a beautiful walled village. The rooms have vaulted ceilings and there is a roof terrace for breakfast that overlooks the surrounding hills.
€ Hotel Fortuna, Piazza Rosselli 15, T071-42663, www.hotelfortuna.it, is newly

EMILIANO MAZZONI

17 Acquabella – crossing the line.

refurbished, clean and comfortable and conveniently located by the railway station. For the budget minded there is a hostel close to the railway station at Via Lamaticci 7.

Eating

Trattoria Clarice di Amico, at Via del Traffico 6, T071-202926, has a great local reputation and produces some wonderful seafood dishes. **Passetto**, Piazza IV Novembre 1, T071-33214, is said to be the town's best, serving up seafood with great sea view.

Directory

Surf shops **Surf Maniacs Surf Shop**, on Via Flaminia 222, T071-2181600, offers a full range of hardware and clothing. Drop by for a chat and get the low down on the local breaks or a surf forecast. Just up the coast at Senigallia is **Jan Surf Shop**, Lungomare Alighieri Dante 14, T071-7922382.
Chemist **Farmacia Centrale**, Corso Mazzinin 1. **Internet** **World Wide Media Centre**, at Piazza Roselli 5a opposite the Train Station. **Tourist Office** Via Thaon de Revel 4

Rimini

This town seems to juggle many identities. Heavily bombed during the war it's a modern looking classic Italian beach resort

STEFANO VIOLA

11 Matteo Corvaia, Sant' Agostino.

with miles of beaches filled with holiday makers through August, everything from groups of young attracted by the vibrant club scene, through to families on a more traditional break. The nightlife here is regarded as some of the best in the country and offers something for everyone, including raging clubs and chilled late night bars, but be aware of the slightly seedy fringe. With so many attracted here, and easy access from cities like Bologna, the surf scene is growing quickly. Is much quieter out of season.

Sleeping

€ Hotel Villa Lalla, Viale Vittorio Vento 22, T0541-55155, is a clean, modern 3-star hotel that is very reasonable during the off-season and medium season which is the best time to score surf. Only a short distance from the seafront in the Marine District.

€ Hotel Donau, Via Alfieri 12, T0541-381302. www.hoteldonau.it, is another year round option that's not quite as nice as Villa Lalla but slightly cheaper.

Camping In Rimini most campsites are a summer only affair – when they are packed out with families. The only year round option is up the coast slightly in Bellaria at the **Happy Camping Village**, Via Panzini 228, T0541-346102, www.happycamping.it. As camping goes it's not the cheapest, with a large pitch for 2 adults about €20 per night. It's beach side but you'll still need to drive to the surf – there are stone groynes protecting the beach.

Eating and drinking

The bar and club scene here attracts top club DJs from across Europe. One spot that's been at the centre of the scene for years now is **Club Paradiso**, Via Covignano 260, a superclub in the hills outside the town, overlooking the sea and traditionally attracting celebs and the beautiful people. This hedonistic hotspot may be worth getting dressed up for. **Pic-Nic**, at Via Tempo Malatestiano 30, this friendly restaurant offers some great seafood dishes as well as reasonably priced pizza and pasta dishes. For a quick hit of caffeine and a pastry try **Caffe Cavour**, at Piazza Cavour 13.

Directory

Surf shops A couple of surf shops in Rimini are **Vintage Surf Shop**, on Via Colett 190, T0541-23957, or there is also **Wave Pro**, at Via le Vespucci 75. In nearby Riccione there is **Surfparadise**, at Viali Cimarosa 14. Rimini has an active surf scene centred around the **Marasma Surf Club**, marasmasurfclub.com. Check out their website to see if they have any social nights on when you're in town.
Chemist Via IV Novembre 39.
Internet **Email Beach** at Via le Vespucci 29.
Tourist Office: Parco Federico Fellini 3.

Overview

Just as Italy sits at the centre of competing weather patterns sweeping in from Europe, Africa and Asia, so it has been at the centre of a geopolitical maelstrom that has blown across the country for millennia. Through conquests, reconquests, invasions and wars, new cultures and civilizations have gained footholds and new trading hubs have sprung up. The islands have proven to be particularly exposed and their rich heritage has left an indelible mark on the people, the landscapes and the architecture of these rugged outposts. Sicily is the largest island in the Mediterranean and sits just off the toe of Italy, the western flank dominated by the smouldering, menacing hulk of Mount Etna. To the north, Sardinia, the slightly smaller cousin, is famed for its white sandy beaches, cliffs and rocky points that draw tourists in increasing number year on year.

JS CALLAHAN/TROPICALPIX

Sam Bleakley, Sicily, making the most of a small, warm water waves.

Surf wise, these two islands are the most consistent regions in the whole of Italy and offer the travelling surfer a surprisingly high quality diet of long reeling points and grunty, hollow reefs. Their very island nature leaves them open to any swell direction. But even if the swell doesn't materialize, you can immerse yourself in some of Europe's most amazing architectural sites, followed by a late night fiesta where local wine and seafood are the order of the day. There's always tomorrow and the promise that the battling continental weather patterns may send in yet more swell to storm the beaches of Italy's offshore bastions.

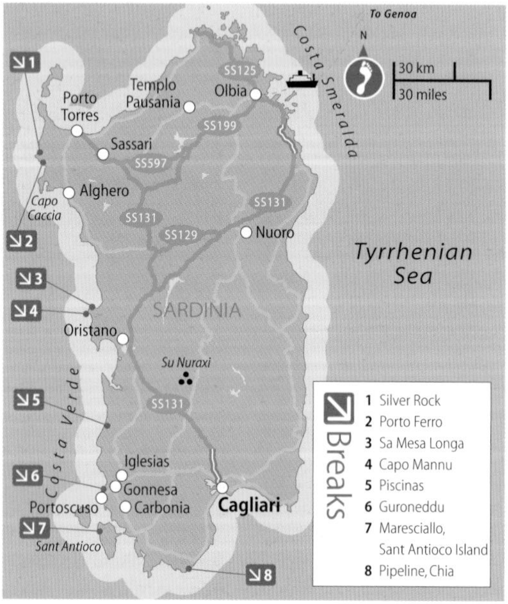

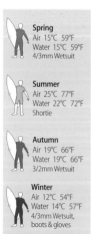

Spring
Air 15°C 59°F
Water 15°C 59°F
4/3mm Wetsuit

Summer
Air 25°C 77°F
Water 22°C 72°F
Shortie

Autumn
Air 19°C 66°F
Water 19°C 66°F
3/2mm Wetsuit

Winter
Air 12°C 54°F
Water 14°C 57°F
4/3mm Wetsuit, boots & gloves

Coastline

From the tiny coves of Costa Smeralda, that draw the super-rich from across Europe, to the famed Costa Verde with its miles of luscious beaches, the ocean environment is Sardinia's biggest selling point. The combo of crystal blue waters under a scorching summer sun means people flock to enjoy the fine sandy coasts and expensive boutiques. Out of season the consistent swells find a whole smorgesbord of waiting breaks. In onshore conditions, sandy beaches are forgiving while sheltered points offer protection from the shadowing winds. In clean swells there are some excellent reefs carved from sandstone or schists (deposits of igneous rocks rich in minerals). Sicily has a similarly cosmopolitan coastline, offering a spectrum of beaches (from white sand to dark laval deposits), pebble strewn coves, to long points and rocky reefs. Towering peaks make spectacular backdrops as they meet the turbulent sea. With so many swell directions, the coastal morphology offers any number of options for the arriving swells. The locals have put in the miles, scouring the varied breaks to find just where to head on each swell and wind combo. Brush up on your Italian and make sure you're nice to the locals. A bit of local knowledge goes a long way in 'the islands'.

EMILIANO MAZZONI

Surfing the Med requires a totally different approach from the ocean. You don't just get there and wait, you have to keep an eye on the Net all the time and be ready to hit the road. During our many Med trips we commonly arrive on spot 12 hours before the swell starts, set base, check the reefs then surf a couple of days under onshore conditions before the one good offshore day. Than pack things and go home or follow the swell to the next stop. It can be exhausting!

Emiliano Cataldi, Bear teamrider, Surf Explorer and surf reporter

Above: Capo Mannu, Sardinia – one of the Med's main draws.

5'10" Xanadu Rocky Model

Shaper: Stretch

5'10" x 19¾" x 2¹/₁₆"

Built with Surftech's proven TUFLITE construction.

Flatter entry rocker with rounder outline, "wider nose, wider tail". Should be 6" shorter than shortboard. Flatter deck makes rails fuller for more buoyancy, better performance in smaller waves. Can be a tri-fin, twin fin, or with small trailer fin, making it adaptable.

FCS YU fins.

9'2" Takayama DT-2 Noserider

Shaper: Donald Takayama

9'2" x 22¼" x 2⁵/₁₆"

Built with Surftech's proven TUFLITE construction.

Built with more focus on nose riding, however very VERSATILE. Drop in, draw a clean line off the bottom, set-up that high line, and take a walk on the Takayama side. Rounded pintail and tri-fin are perfect for any turn. From ankle high to well overhead.

2+1 with FCS side fins.

ⓘ Boards by **Surftech**
www.surftech.com info@surftech.com

Breaks

9 Lungomare
10 Isola Delle Femmine
11 Ciammarita
12 San Marco
13 La Playa, Catania

Stromboli

Aeolian Islands

Salina
Lipari
Vulcano

Tyrrhenian Sea

Messina

Reggio di Calabria

↘ 9

↘ 10

↘ 11

Palermo · Cefalù

A20

Taormina

Trapani

A19

Etna ▲

A18

A29D

A29

SICILY

Catania

↘ 13

Marsala

SS121

SS189

Caltanissetta

A19

Siracusa

Sciacca

SS640

SS417

SS194

↘ 12

Agrigento

SS115

A18

Gela

Ragusa

N

30 km
30 miles

Mediterranean Sea

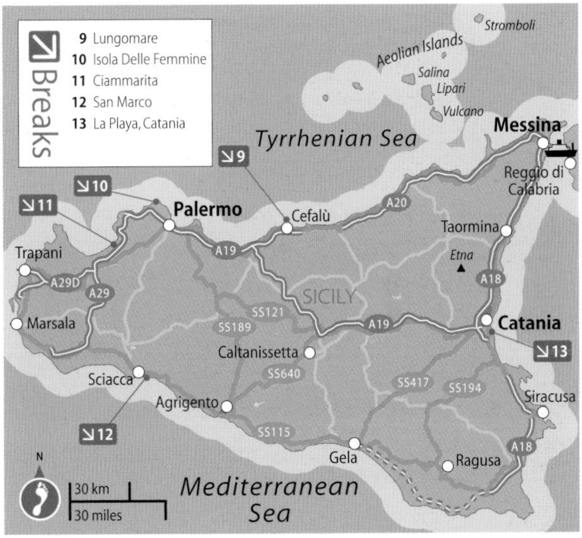

Local environment

These two islands are home to some of the most pristine coves and bays in Europe, away from villages and tourists. A landscape dominated by olive and citrus groves, fields of grain and vineyards. There is some pollution in towns where infrastructure may not be able to cope with the summer influx of thousands of extra tourists. Around ports, oil and diesel rainbows are visible and occasional discharges from passing tankers can occur.

Italian surfers are keen and enthusiastic, and with a short swell window and a boom in numbers you can imagine that popular spots can get a little crowded and frenetic. Patience and politeness go a long way, as does exploration. There are still many breaks off the radar and if you do find them, don't go mob handed. Chat with the local surfers and you'll find them friendly and tolerant of travellers.

Getting around

It's all about the car! Hire cars are available in major cities and at airports. Sicilian autostrada link the major cities and some stretches are toll roads. Most roads are single lane Strade statali (state roads) or country lanes that feed the more remote stretches of coastline. In Sardinia there is a spine of fast roads linking the north and south of the island, but coastal access is via a network of smaller, single track roads or even rough tracks.

Sardinia

A-FRAME REEF BREAK

↘1 Silver Rock

- **Conditions** Small to medium NW to SW swells, offshore in NE winds
- **Hazards/tips** Clear, clean water
- **Sleeping** Alghero » p351

Silver Rock is a powerful A-frame reef with long rights and fast lefts, named after the many silver mines that once operated in the area. It is partly sheltered from northwesterly winds and works in any swell from a westerly direction, but really fires in medium to big Mistral swells, during which it remains surfable even with strong winds. Doesn't get too crowded but the smooth, urchin covered rock bottom means it's best left to experienced surfers. Follow the road from Porto Palmas to Argentiera and then turn after the caravan park.

BEACH BREAK

↘2 Porto Ferro

- **Conditions** All N to SW swells, offshore in E winds
- **Hazards/tips** Strong currents
- **Sleeping** Alghero » p351

This bay is one of the most consistent spots in Sardinia and hosts several peaks breaking over a sand and rock bottom. They turn on in any swell from a northerly, northwesterly, westerly or southwesterly direction. Winds from an east or northeasterly direction blow offshore, but this is a flexible spot where it remains surfable under big windy southwesterlies when it can easily throw up long walls at double overhead. The water quality here is excellent but watch out for rips when big.

ANTONIO MUGLA

EMILIANO MAZZONI

Above: 2 Paddling out at the beautiful, consistent Porto Ferro. **Top: 3** Sa Mesa Longa.

A-FRAME REEF BREAK

↘3 Sa Mesa Longa

- **Conditions** Small to medium SW to NW swells, offshore in SE winds
- **Hazards/tips** Sharp reef with urchins
- **Sleeping** Oristano » p351

Found in incredible scenery on the northerly edge of Capo Mannu just north of Mandriola, this jagged reef is a classic A-frame breaking in front of a little island just off an enclosed lagoon. Needs a southeasterly, westerly or windless northwesterly to fire but this is the place to check when the Mistral has subsided and the swell is clean. The left closes out over 2.5 m. Access to the line-up is from the channel on the left of the little island. Shallow with urchins.

RIGHT POINT BREAK

↘4 Capo Mannu

- **Conditions** Small to medium N to SW swells, offshore in NE winds
- **Hazards/tips** Quality but crowded
- **Sleeping** Oristano » p351

North from Oristano, close to the village of Mandriola. Arguably the most consistent, famous and crowded surf area in the Med, Capo Mannu's long right point-break peels for over 200 m along the peninsula, making it totally sheltered from the Mistral. The easy take-off and the many workable walls make this wave a real crowd pleaser. Breaks over sharp lava rocks with urchins and lots of them. Enter from up the point on small days (up to 2.5 m), otherwise it's a paddle up the point from the inside to where the line-up breaks, which is way out the back on those big days. Two other points can be seen further down the peninsula: Medicapo, a long mellow and super localized right, and Minicapo, a beautiful A-frame peak breaking at the foot of the peninsula.

ALESSANDRO DINI

4 Graziano Lai taking the high line at one of Italy's big wave spots.

BEACH BREAK

↘5 Piscinas

- **Conditions** All SW to NW swells, offshore in E winds
- **Hazards/tips** Consistent beach
- **Sleeping** Oristano/Portoscuso » *p351*

Along the beautiful Costa Verde, south of Marina di Arbus, Piscinas is a golden sandy beach that offers the perfect sandbanks for small windless NW, W and SW swells. Waves have travelled half the length of the Med before breaking here so they are thick and juicy, good for all levels of hot-dogging. This area does miracles when Capo Mannu and Sa Mesa are flat. Clear water. Not crowded.

REEF BREAK

↘6 Guroneddu

- **Conditions** All NW swells, offshore in E winds
- **Hazards/tips** Shallow, heavy, urchins
- **Sleeping** Portoscuso » *p351*

This heavy, hollow reef was a long kept secret among SW Sardinia locals. "Guro", as the locals call it, works on any NW swell and likes it up to 3 m + but is unsurfable with onshore Mistral. Bowly, hollow take off leads to the inside, which is a fast wall breaking on a shallow slab of urchin covered rocks. Can be crowded. Very clear water. This spot is located along the Gonnesa-Portoscuso coastal road. Turn right at the second road you find after the Fontanamare-Masua crossroad. As soon as you see the water, park the car on the right side of the street and walk down.

RIGHT POINT BREAK

↘7 Maresciallo, Sant Antioco Island

- **Conditions** All W to SW swells, offshore in N winds
- **Hazards/tips** Rocks and urchins
- **Sleeping** Portoscuso » *p351*

Sant Antioco is a small Punic island located off the southwestern tip of Sardegna. The main wave is located 1 km north of main village Calasetta and has the perfect aspect to hoover up any west to southwesterly swells as it peels around the north side of the bay. Maresciallo's right-hander point is one of the longest waves in Italy with 200 m rides not uncommon on good days. Breaks over round rocks, but there are urchins. There are also many other high quality waves on this island.

BEACH BREAK

↘8 Pipeline, Chia

- **Conditions** All NW to SW swells, offshore in N winds
- **Hazards/tips** Crowded
- **Sleeping** Portoscuso » *p351*

Chia is a great place to check when big W swells kick in. There is a peak at the beach called Pipeline that is a long, sand and rock bottomed right-hander that breaks on the outside bank. Several other peaks form along the beach. Often crowded because of proximity with Cagliari.

Sicily

BEACH BREAK

↘9 Lungomare

- **Conditions** Small to medium NW to N swells, offshore in SE winds
- **Hazards/tips** Beautiful town
- **Sleeping** Palermo » *p352*

The medieval town of Cefalù sits 75 km east of Palermo on the north coast of Sicily on the Messina-Palermo highway. The picturesque town is a wonderful maze of winding, narrow streets overlooked by a towering Norman/Romanesque cathedral. When a swell kicks in from a northerly direction, check out Lungomare beach, which is located along the sea promenade. You'll find several peaks on sand bottom kicking in with either a north, northwesterly or northeasterly swell, though the beach is pretty much unsurfable when it's onshore.

BEACH BREAK

↘10 Isola Delle Femmine

- **Conditions** Any NW to NE swells, offshore in SE winds
- **Hazards/tips** Crystal clear waters
- **Sleeping** Palermo » p352

Several good peaks can be found near this town when a good northwesterly swell hits. Check the bay and you should find several waves breaking over the sand and rock bottom. It's also worth checking the right-hander that peels on sharp rocks to the east of the bay, just after the village. Can be crowded as it attracts the many surfers from Sicilian capital town Palermo. Legend has it that the town takes its name from the small island that lies just off the coast that supposedly housed a woman's prison in the 1500s. "Isola" is perched on a rocky headland and has about 6,000 inhabitants. Exit at Capaci on the Palermo-Trapani highway and follow signs for Isola delle Femmine. Check the pier in Magaggiari (5 km west) if Isola is blown out.

JS CALLAHAN/TROPICALPIX

JS CALLAHAN/TROPICALPIX

JS CALLAHAN/TROPICALPIX

Above: Sweet Sicilian sundown secret.
Top: Valentina Dazzeo, east coast Sicily.
Top right: Emiliano Cataldi, one of Italy's leading lensmen, enjoying his work in Sicilly.

BEACH BREAK

↘11 Ciammarita

- **Conditions** Small to medium N to NW swells, offshore in SE winds
- **Hazards/tips** Popular beach
- **Sleeping** Palermo » p352

This long, golden sandy beach is the place to be when small to medium northwesterly swells are running. Check the many peaks along the big bay. This spot is popular as it remains surfable under moderate on-shore conditions, so can be crowded. Follow signs to Trapetto village and then to Spiaggia di Ciammarita. Beachfront parking.

POINT BREAK

↘12 San Marco

- **Conditions** Small to medium SW to SE swells, offshore in N winds
- **Hazards/tips** Rips
- **Sleeping** Agrigento » p352

The coast around Sciacca is particularly exposed to southeasterly and southwesterly swells. Here at San Marco there's a fun left point that breaks over rocks and sand, wrapping through to a steeper inside. It needs a medium to big southeasterly swell to come to life. This spot is capable of turning a windy swell into clean lines. The water here is clean but beware of side-shore currents. Follow signs to Contrada Foggia than to Spiaggia di San Marco. More spots along the coast heading west.

BEACH BREAK

↘13 La Playa, Catania

- **Conditions** Any E to SE swells, offshore in W winds
- **Hazards/tips** Popular beach for hanging out
- **Sleeping** Catania » p353

Several A-frame peaks can be found here breaking on hard sand along the city's long bay. The quality depends on the angle of the swell and the shifting positions of the banks. The break in front of Lido Capannine usually offers the best rides. Walk along the beach 'til you find a peak you like. Needs an easterly swell with offshore wind to work properly. Main spot for the growing community of Catania. Many Lidos (beaches) are private in the summer and cost a few euros to enter, but have bars and showers. In winter you have to find an open access to the beach.

Practicalities

ANTONIO MUGLIA

Sardinia

Alghero

This picturesque walled town, on the northwestern edge of the island, makes a great base for exploring this part of the Sardinian coastline. The region was conquered by Spanish invaders in the 14th century and still harbours strong links – you can often hear Catalan spoken around the town. The old part juts out into the Med, defended by walls and towers, the winding network of streets a haven for great cafés and restaurants where excellent seafood is on offer. The bustling harbour just to the north is another spot worth checking out.

Sleeping

€€-€ Hotel San Francesco, located at Via Ambrogio Machin 2, T079-980330, www.sanfrancescohotel.com, this 3-star hotel is a converted 14th-century church featuring basic but comfortable rooms set around a wonderful cloistered courtyard.
€€-€ Mamajuana B&B, Vicolo Adami 12, T079-930489. www.mamajuana.it, overlooks a small piazza. Breakfast is served in the café on the square.
€ Catalan B and B, Via Manzoni 41, T079-981909, www.algherocasavacanze.it. Basic, clean, if slightly dated B&B. Also has an apartment for rent which sleeps up to 4.
Camping Camping La Mariposa, Via Lido 22, T079-950360, www.lamariposa.it, is just to the north of the town and directly on the beach. It has the longest opening period of the local sites, starting 1 Apr and closing 31 Oct. It also has bungalows and caravans for rent.

Eating

Obviously seafood is big here with some great restaurants offering fresh delicacies. **Al Vecchio Mulino**, Via Don Derma 3, gives a range of both seafood, meat and pasta dishes. For a good value pizza there's **Casablanca**, Via Principe Umberto 76.

Directory

Chemist Farmacia Bulla, Via Garbaldi 13. **Internet Bar Miramare**, Via Gramsci 2. **Tourist Office** Piazza Porta 9.

Oristano

This town makes a very appealing base for west coast exploration with bustling streets and a laid back atmosphere.

Sleeping

€ Albergo Duomo, Via Vittorio Emanuele 34, T0783-778061, www.hotelduomo.net. This 16th-century building has been modernized into a crisp, smart hotel offering very comfortable accommodation set around a central courtyard.
€ Eleonora Bed and Breakfast, overlooks Piazza Eleonora d'Arborea, T0783-70435, www.eleonora-bed-and-breakfast.com, a popular choice, the pretty 3-story building combining old skool charm with comfortable rooms.
Camping Campegggio Villagio Spinnaker, Strade Torregrande, Pontile, T0783-22074, www.campingspinnaker.com. This beach side campsite is open year round and also has bungalows/chalets.

Directory

Surf shops Ono Surf Shop, Viale San Martino 9a, T078-3300453, www.onosurf.it, offers a wide range of clothing as well as some hardware and boards.
Chemist Farmacia Bresciani Achenza, Corso Umberto 51. **Internet Bar Miramare**, Via Gramsci 2, has Internet access (not Wi-Fi) and is open until 0200.
Tourist Office Piazza Elenora d'Arborea 19.

Portoscuso

This small fishing town is pretty much off the tourist map. The small harbour is most famous for its tuna fishing, when huge nets are laid to catch the massive fish. Occasionally large great whites get snarled up. Nice. Beautiful beaches and coastline, but few accommodation options.

Sleeping

€€-€ Hotel Panorama, Via Giulio Cesare 40, T0781-508077. This 3-star hotel has balconies that overlook the harbour and has a real 70's charm about it.
€€-€ Hotel Don Pedro, Via Vespucci 19, T0781-510219, is also a 3-star option.
Camping Limited options around here. To the north there's **Camping Ortus de Mari**, Ortus de Mari, Buggerru, T0781-54964, which is open from May to end of Sep. On San Antioco you can stay at **Campeggi Sardi Le Saline**, Le Saline, Calasetta, T0781-88615, www.campinglesaline.com, open seasonally from 1 May to 31 Oct.

RICCARDO GHILARDI

Top left: North shore Sardinia delights.
Right: Isola di Sant' Antioco.

Flat spells

Sardinia is relaxed with little pressure to tick off any 'must-see' sights. Instead, take your time to sample the food and drink in the scenery.

Cagliari, the capital, has an impressive old district which makes for good exploring. The city walls are flanked by two 14th-century limestone towers, Torre di San Pancrazio and Torre dell'Elefante, which can be climbed for views towards the port and over the city. Offering impressive vistas across the city and towards the Golfo degli Angeli, the Bastion di San Remy fortress is definitely worth the climb. If you like museums, then you'll love the Cittadella dei Musei, a group of four museums housing important items from Sardinia's past. The Museo Archeologico (Tue-Sun €4) includes Roman artefacts and a collection of pieces from the Bronze Age Nuraghic civilization.

Grotta di Nettuno, at the limestone headland, Capo Caccia, on the north-western coast is just a 20-min drive from nearby Alghero and is home to the most fabulous collection of stalactites and stalagmites (€10 for the 45-min tour). The cave system housing them is best reached by car or bus – a scenic drive followed by a walk down more than 650 steps cut into the hillside. They can also be reached by boat.

Su Nuraxi, 50 km north of Cagliari, is a 1500BC settlement – complete with fortress and coned stone structures – is the largest and most impressive Nuraghe complex to have been revealed on the island, entry €5. The native Sardinian Nuraghic civilization littered the landscape with their round stone constructions – approximately 7,000 structures dating from 1500-500 BC are still standing in Sardinia.

Sicily

Palermo

The capital city of Sicily and home to over 600,000 people is a vibrant and buzzing area, which reverberates to the sound of razzing scooters and car horns. Overlooked by the peak of Monte Pellegrino, it sits at the western end of a sweeping bay and its strategic importance has made it home to Phoenicians, Carthaginians, Saracens and Normans over the centuries. The architecture and flavours of the city reflect this with everything from Spanish to North African influences.

Sleeping

As with any city accommodation, be prepared to have to schlep your board up flights of stairs to get to your room or B&B, as some smaller accommodation options are apartments set on the 2nd or 3rd floors.
€€ Alla Kala Hotel, Corso Vittorio Emanuele 71, T091-7434763, www.allakala.it. If you want a couple of nights of luxury, then check out this boutique hotel that overlooks the marina.
€ Giorgio's House B&B, Via A Mongitore, T091-525057, www.giorgioshouse.com. Great location, clean, comfy and homely 3-room B&B, very friendly. Recommended.
€ Harmony B&B, Via Lungarini 48, T091 6177944, www.harmonyhotel.it. Modern B&B, tastefully renovated and offers hotel style, air-conditioned rooms. Has a computer hooked up to broadband.
Camping On the western side of the headland outside Palermo you'll find **Camping Trinacria**, on Via Barcarello, T091-530590, www.campingtrinacria.it. This small site sits on the seafront and is open year round with some covered pitches for tents as well as hook-ups for caravans and motorhomes.

Eating and drinking

Il Garage, Vicolo San Nicolo Albergheria 4, serves up wonderful good value meals with a North African influence. If you've not had enough pizza yet, check out **Pizzeria Italia** at Via del Orologio 54. **I Candelai**, Via dei Candelai 65, www.candelai.it, is a nightclub and bar housed in a converted warehouse. Check out their website as they have a programme of live bands and exhibitions.

Directory

Surf shops **Surfside Board Shop** that has hardware, accessories and clothing at Via Ugdulena 26, T091-7302984. Down the street there's **Surfside Girl**, via Ugdulena 5, T091-6259048, and then there's **Surfside Classic** at Via Liberta 181, T091-7308575, www.surfside.it. There's also **Extreme Surf Shop**, Via Sciuti Giuseppe 74, T091 343035. **Chemist** **Farmacia da Naro**, Via Roma 207. **Internet** **Internet Point**, Corso Vittorio Emanuele. Open until 2200. **Post Office** Palazzo delle Poste, Via Roma 322. Surfside has 3 shops in the city. **Tourist Office** Piazza Castelnuovo 35.

Agrigento

This is a wonderful, historic town set back slightly from the coast and close to some of the island's finest architectural sites. There is the Archaeological Park with the ruins of ancient temples as well as a museum. Driving in the old town is difficult as large parts are pedestrianised although there is metered parking at the station. It's just a short car journey down to the sea.

Sleeping

€€-€ Hotel Costazzurra, Via delle Viole 2, San Leone, T0922-411222, www.costa zzurra.it. This is a modern, clean and comfortable hotel that offers good value accommodation. Run by a friendly, English speaking family, with parking.
€ Camere a Sud, Via Ficani 6, T0349-6384424, www.camereasud.it. Fresh and modern B&B situated in the heart of the old town, just off Via Atenea.
€ Villa Amico, Via delle Azalee 6, San Leone, T0349-8346639. Modern, good value B&B in San Leone not far from the sea.
Camping **Camping Internazionale Lido**

Oasi, Viale delle Dune 5a, Spiaggia San Leone, T0922-416096. Beachside site, open year round. **Camping Internazionale Nettuno**, Via Lacco Ameno 3, San Leone. T0922-416268.

Eating
La Forchetta, Piazza San Francesco 9, offers great value meals and is reassuringly popular with the locals. For something a bit more up market try **Leon d'Oro** at Viale Emporium102, offering regional specialties.

Directory
Surf shops **Surfstore Sicily** can be found on Via Atenea 28, T092-221520.
Chemist **Farmacia Minacori**, Via Atenea 91, T092-225089. **Internet** **Internet Train**, Cortile Contarini 7. Open until 2300. **Tourist Office** Via Cesare Battisti 15.

Catania

Sicily's second city sits in the shadow of imposing Mt Etna, which has helped shape its history and physical make-up over the centuries. The volcano is still relatively active to this day and you can walk up to the summit but extreme care is advised, as an observatory set up to monitor the volcano was recently destroyed!

Sleeping
€€€-€€ Una Hotel Palace, Via Etna 218, T095-2505111, www.unahotels.it. Only worth doing if you book ahead and get the great off season discounts, but a luxurious boutique hotel with rooftop terrace with views over to Mt Etna.
€ Agora Hostel at Piazza Curro 6, T095-7233010, www.agorahostel.com. Popular hostel open year round with dorms and doubles, as well as Internet access with the bonus of an underground bar in a cave. You can also enjoy the warm evenings outside in the Piazza.
€ Pensione Rubens, Via Etna 196, T095-317073. Best to book ahead with this popular B&B with a friendly owner and comfortable rooms.

Flat spells

Sicily bears the architectural and cultural influences of her invaders (Greeks, Romans, Arabs, Normans and Spanish).

Palermo The labyrinthine, bustling streets of the capital are always worth losing yourself in, especially La Vucciria, a souk-like market where the you can find excellent seafood and spices. Don't miss the 12th-century Norman Cattedrale, Corso Vittorio Emanuele, whose tall spires emerge stealth-like from its narrow surrounds. Entry €2.50, daily 0930-1730. Another beautiful site is the mosaic-encrusted, medieval, Monreale Cattedrale, 7 km southwest of Palermo.

Mountain biking On the east coat is Rent Bike, www.rentbike.it, based in Acireale, just north of Catania offers mountain and road bikes to hire from around €13/day. They also offer itineraries or guided rides. Also Sole & Bike (www.solebike.it) from €60/day.

Etna Driving south along the eastern coast road it is virtually impossible to miss this active volcano whose peak is often snow covered during the winter. There are many excursions on offer to the 3315-m summit. You can take a cable car and 4WD to 2900 m and then trek. Check latest conditions at www.volcanotrek.com.

The Aeolian Islands This cluster of volcanic islands lie just off the north eastern tip of Sicily and have had a varied background; they have been a former keeping place of the wind for Greek God Aeolus, mined for their minerals, overrun by pirates and been home to the exiled. Today they are a UNESCO site attracting tourists to their raw, untamed, beauty. In summer, the islands are busy and pricey but in the early autumn can be a real treat. Jump on a ferry or the faster hydrofoil from Milazzo on the north coast of Sicily mainland to any of the seven islands: check out www.usticalines.it for info. Vulcano is the nearest island taking around 45 mins to reach by hydrofoil. Highlights include exploring the Gran Cratere which last exploded in 1890. It offers great views into the heart of the volcano and across the archipelago. Other highlights include the sulphurous mud baths open Easter-Oct. Stromboli, the farthest island, is all about making the trek to the active volcanic peak – rising 2400 m from the seabed – which has a constant lava flow and regularly flashes, reminding all that it is still very active. Seeing the volcano by moonlight is most spectacular. Check out www.magmatrek.it for information on guided walks.

Camping **Campining Jonio** sits on the northern fringe of the city on the coastline at Via Villini a Mare 2, Ognina, T095-491139. It's open all year, has bungalows as well as tent pitches and space for campervans.

Eating
Note that some restaurants don't take credit cards. **Osteria Antica Marina** near the fish market on Via Pardo, is best for seafood. Always busy so worth booking ahead. If you fancy good value food in a great location check out **I Sale Art Café** at Via S Filomena 10, a popular converted art gallery.

Directory
Surf shops **Spin Out Action**, at Via F, Riso 40, T095-7167518, who stock a range of hardware including boards. There is also **W Point**, at Via V, Emanuele Orlando 15A, T095-381636. **Chemist** **Del Centro Farmacia**, Via Etna 107. **Internet** **Internet Caffetteria**, Via Penninello 44. **Tourist Office** Via Cimarosa 10.

TIM NUNN

Morocco

Llewelyn Whittaker – high times in Morocco's little-explored deep south.

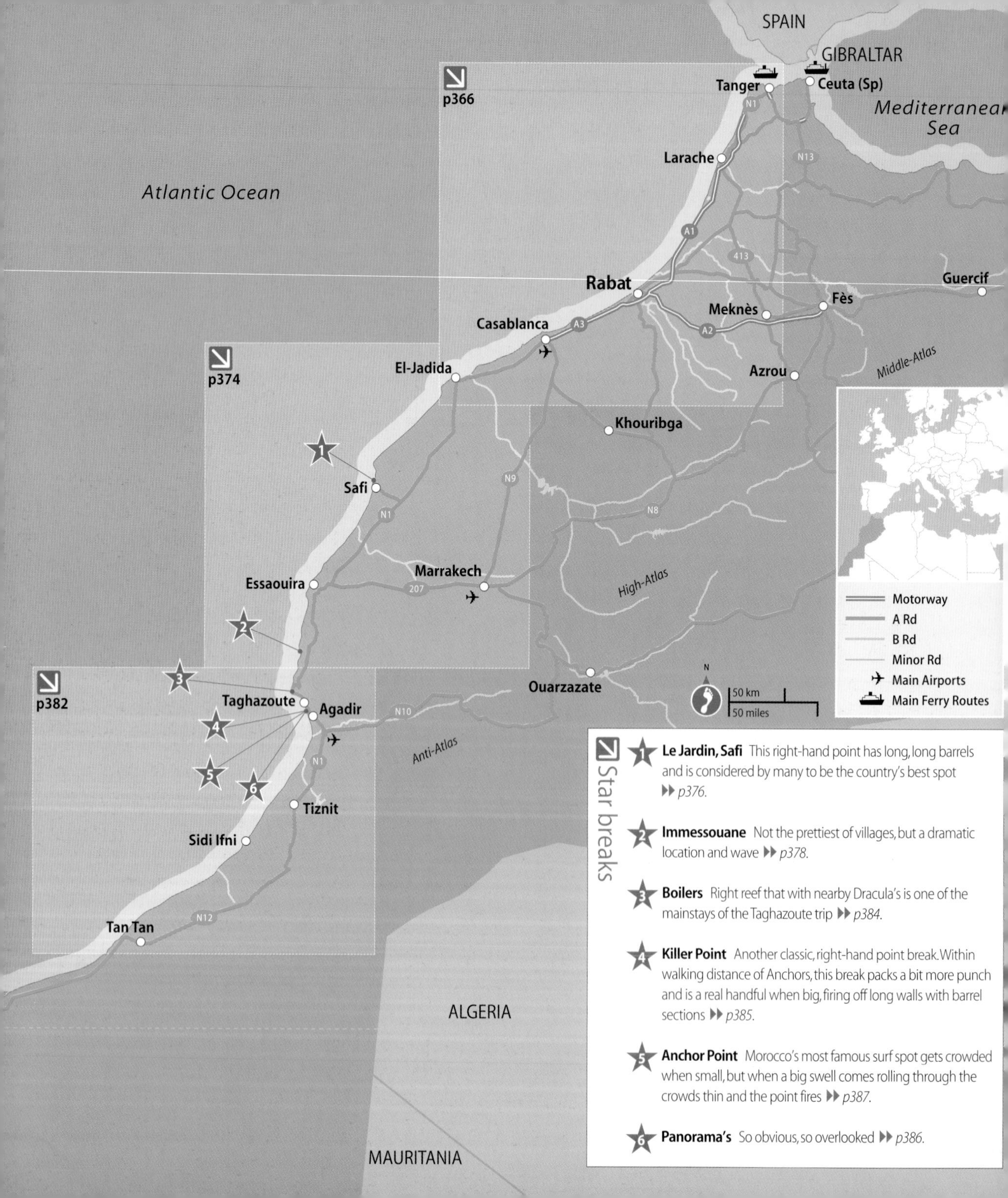

Star breaks

1. **Le Jardin, Safi** This right-hand point has long, long barrels and is considered by many to be the country's best spot ▸▸ *p376*.

2. **Immessouane** Not the prettiest of villages, but a dramatic location and wave ▸▸ *p378*.

3. **Boilers** Right reef that with nearby Dracula's is one of the mainstays of the Taghazoute trip ▸▸ *p384*.

4. **Killer Point** Another classic, right-hand point break. Within walking distance of Anchors, this break packs a bit more punch and is a real handful when big, firing off long walls with barrel sections ▸▸ *p385*.

5. **Anchor Point** Morocco's most famous surf spot gets crowded when small, but when a big swell comes rolling through the crowds thin and the point fires ▸▸ *p387*.

6. **Panorama's** So obvious, so overlooked ▸▸ *p386*.

TIM NUNN

The Central coast's Immessouane, with its sandy bottom and long peeling walls, has become a hugely popular proposition for all levels of surfers.

Morocco is a land shrouded in a dusty veil, her true identity sometimes glimpsed but never fully revealed. Dry, windblown Saharan particles cast a fine haze over line-ups; classic days shot soft focus, teasing and shy like the coy centerfold from an upmarket 1970's top shelf magazine. Corduroy swell lines feather as they reach the burnt red point, then reel away from the photographer, casting a modest glance back over their shoulders. It's only from the emerald line-up that the true perspective is revealed, staring down the mesmerizing production line as it spins ever onward down the headland. Photos cannot communicate the energy crackling off a crowded Souk, where people jostle, rhythmic voices rise and fall and the aroma of spices drifts through the air. An image can never capture the true vast expanse of the desert south, the rocky headlands, blazing sun, cool waters and towering dunes. Colours on the page can never interpret precisely the glorious and subtle hues of reds, yellows, browns and greens that make up the Moroccan countryside, or the stunning blue of Berber eyes expressing the emotions of animated conversation. No description can encapsulate how it feels to sit in the line-up on a big day at one of the world class point breaks, paddling up the face of an outside set and watching as the neoprene clad figure to your right drops down the feathering jade face, rail biting and angling into an arcing bottom turn, knowing that the next one's yours. The only way to get a true sense of what Morocco is like, is to go there for yourself. It may not all be classic days on the point, but it will be an experience that cannot easily be described to your mates back home, and can never be truly captured on the screen of your digital camera. Only the memory can do the whole experience justice.

Surfing Morocco

"Well, I took my longboard, my shortboard and my fish and rode them all. That's the thing about Morocco, although it's know for its cranking right points, it has something for every occasion – from grinding reefs to fun beaches. Absolutely classic." Dan Harris, Welsh Champion

The dazzling emerald crystal walls leave a rainbow vapour trail in their wake as they thunder along the fringe of this burnt-red rocky point. The only other witnesses are gnarled and twisted Argan trees, the only sounds that accompany the background bass is the frenetic clatter and childlike wailing of the nearby foraging goats. Even in splendid isolation Morocco provides an intense sensory onslaught. But this is no flashback to the Freeride era, this is the reality of modern Morocco. It may no longer bear any similarity to the daily scenes played out at Anchors or Killers, but it is more than a distinct possibility – for those willing to push out beyond the boundaries and away from the crowds. Modern day Morocco is a land undergoing a massive sea change. From season to season, this dynamic country is transformed. For a brief time, towns like Taghazoute offered uncrowded perfection, rich culture, cheap accommodation, all within a short drive from a major airport serviced by budget flights. Over the last five years the region around Taghazoute has become busier, the line-ups more crowded and an eruption of concrete has sprung from the ground to accommodate.

Modern Morocco is striding forward as a progressive nation. Tourism is high on the agenda with six upmarket tourist centres planned along the coastline as part of the government's 'Vision 2010' strategy to attract affluent holidaymakers including resorts at Mazagan–El Jadida, Mogador–Essaouira and the pristine Plage Blanche south of Sidi Ifni. According to Travel Weekly, Taghazoute has also been earmarked for a US$2 billion facelift. This redevelopment of 5½ km of Taghazoute coastline will include seven hotels and two golf courses. The impact this will have on the people, environment and world-class waves in the area is yet to be determined. But one thing is for sure, things are going to change.

To find the true spirit of Moroccan surfing means getting on the road a heading out towards unfamiliar places with unfamiliar names. Those classic points are still out there, harder to get to, without the luxury of apartments and surf camps. Some hide in plane view in the busy northern reaches of the country – urban breaks with bustling city realism. Others in the vast expanse to the south, where there are risks, long hard hours on dusty roads and the chance of disappointment at the end of the drive is pitted against a chance at enlightenment. But then think back to the earliest pioneers of Tagahzoute, before flights to Agadir, Internet, mobile phones and surf camps. It's a long drive from the ferry at Tangiers – even longer when it's a drive into the unknown as it was then. Perhaps it's time to load up the van, embrace the spirit of *In Shallah*, and break away from the confines of modern Morocco, in search of the new Morocco.

Climate

Morocco is a land of contradictions – towards the desert south, hot days convert into cold nights; dry riverbeds can be brought back to life during flash floods, and just as quickly disappear. Regions that are geographically close can experience massive seasonal differences. While the tourist haven of Marrakech can top 40°C, the snow-capped High Atlas mountains that overlook it boast a number of good ski resorts with boarding possibilities. While the northern plains are lush and green in their mild winter months, the south opens into the spectacular harsh surroundings of the Sahara Desert. From Casablanca, north, the country receives almost double the rainfall in comparison with the area around Agadir.

The coastal regions, tempered by the cooling Canaries current are less extreme and benefit from an almost endless supply of sun, with the huge mass of the North Atlantic acting as a heat sink, helping to keep temperatures extremely comfortable. The Canaries current also means that the sea temperature is often cooler than expected, making, a 3/2 wettie necessary in the popular winter months. Agadir has become a popular winter destination for holidaying Europeans due to the warm winter days and cool evening temperatures, while in the summer this coastal region is a popular draw for locals looking for a little respite from the intense inland temperatures.

Best seasons to go

The prime time to hit Morocco in terms of consistent swells, favourable winds and temperatures are autumn and winter. Summer temperatures are high and Atlantic swells are inconsistent. The

✓ Pros	✗ Cons
Long and rugged coastline that picks up loads of swell from Atlantic low pressures.	Breaks around Taghazoute are now very busy.
Seemingly endless surfing possibilities with classic right-hand points as good as any in the world.	Food hygiene can be poor at some restaurants.
Scope to explore rugged and deserted surf spots.	Some breaks polluted by industrial and sewage waste.
Warm, sunny winter climate and mild water temperatures.	
Relaxed pace of life.	
Cheap cost of living.

DAMIEN POULLENOT

Thumbs up to Taghazoute and the land of the right point.

HILTON DAWE

Taj burrows out of another Moroccan Surf Adventure.

predominantly onshore wind can also be tortuous at times, ripping up any surf that does filter through. Your best chance of scoring some waves is to head to the more exposed stretch of coastline to the north of Safi – water temperatures are at their warmest so pack a shortie. Autumn means the hot nights start to cool and the waves in the central regions begin to pump. Low pressures tracking through the North Atlantic are far enough away to deliver well-spaced swells of a long period. This can be a consistent time for Immessouane and the surrounding region whereas from mid-Autumn onwards, the fabled points of Safi and Taghazoute begin to come to life. The air and water temperatures on the central coast hover around 19°C, meaning a 3/2 is best. In terms of crowds, Autumn can be a quieter season than the winter months. Winter As northern Europe freezes, January and February sees central and southern Morocco enjoying warm days and the peak of the swell season. Air temperature around Taghazoute hovers around 17°C, as does the water meaning a decent 3/2 is ideal for making the most out of some seriously long sessions. The swells can seem never ending and the sun seems to shine every day. Long, clean walls reel with glassy waves anywhere between 3-10 ft as deep depressions off Europe turn up here as groomed lines. The NE-NW winds are also at their lightest. With larger swells reaching more sheltered points, this is the most consistent time to score in the Taghazoute region, and everyone knows it. This can be a great time to head out and explore the quieter breaks towards the desert south. Cooler daytime temperatures mean that frustrating onshore sea breezes that usually threaten this stretch are at their lightest and the larger, more consistent swells can unearth some gems. Spring As March starts to melt into April, the winds kick in again and the surf quality decreases, heralding the departure of the few remaining campers straggling around Taghazoute.

Boards

A thruster and a longer pintail would be the mainstays of any Moroccan adventure. A good, rounded squash tail or swallow tailed thruster, about 18½" wide, will give plenty of range. For the big days, or for when the points fire, a good semi-gun will definitely be a help, something between a 6'4" to 7'0" pin tail.

Geography and the breaks

In general, northern Morocco consists of a series of beach breaks interspersed with a few rocky points and reefs and, around the larger cities and towns, man-made jetties and groynes that marshal the sand. This region is generally overlooked by travelling surfers as it is colder and wetter than breaks further south, but it does hold a few gems. From Tangier down to Bouznika, huge stretches of sand see few surfers until the urban breaks of Rabat – home to one of Morocco's largest surf clubs as well as the rivermouth left that can reel on and on. At Mohamedia, the points and reefs are popular with local bodyboarders and surfers with only the occasional traveller stopping for a few waves. Casablanca is a huge urban sprawl with some polluted breaks but once past the shanty towns and crazy driving, the countryside opens up again and the undulating rocky coastline offers incredible opportunities. Many unknown spots break between the points at El Jadida, Safi and Immessouane.

From the now busy line-ups at Immessouane the landscape changes. The rugged coastline here is home to the thorny Argan trees, whose nuts are harvested to produce a versatile, but expensive cooking oil. Goats climb into these trees to eat the nuts which are actually harvested from their droppings – a flavour, some say, that stays with the oil. It is among the Argan trees that Morocco's most famous waves break, at spots like Anchor Point and Killers.

Below Agadir the desert south beckons. Beaches expand, temperatures rise and the numbers of surfers drops off to virtually zero. Pistes lead to dried-up rivermouths while long expanses of beach breaks, some backed by cliffs, are only broken by the occasional points and reefs. Here a couple of Morocco's premium points live a hermit like existence. You won't find them listed in this guide, but they are out there for the adventurous to find.

Low Pressure Chart for Morocco

In all instances we assume the depressions are deep enough to produce classic swells (say 986 to 992mb). Most charts that are good for Europe will be good for Morocco, from a long distance westerly swell emanating in **L1**, to a northwesterly from **L2**. By the time they reach the points of Taghazoute and Safi, if the low is deep enough, they will produce very long period, clean groundswells. Morocco has the added bonus of being far enough away from the trajectory of the tracking lows that even those that bring stormy, unsettled weather to Europe should have swells that have cleaned up into classic lines by the time they break on Moroccan shores. **L3** hovering off Portugal pushes swell down the seaboard wrapping into the bays and igniting the more exposed points like Killers and Immessouane.

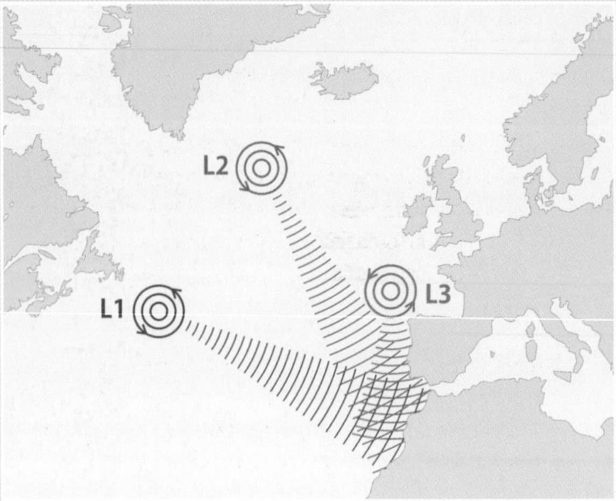

Surfing and environment

Morocco is a developing country and as such lacks a lot of the infrastructure many take for granted. Water purification and sewage treatment are basic at best. Morocco's water table is extremely low meaning that all fresh water is a precious commodity. Tap water is not safe to drink – bottled water is not a luxury but a necessity.

In a lot of areas sewage and industrial waste is discharged straight into the sea, so urban breaks can be badly polluted – especially rivermouths. Many large villages and towns right along the coastline have outfalls near the line-ups and are best avoided, especially after heavy rains, while waves further away from urban centres are usually as clean as you'll find anywhere. However make sure you are up to date on your jabs before you leave home.

Localism and surf communities

Moroccans are generally very friendly and hospitable, but also fairly determined, and this extends into the line-up. It would be unusual to experience localism here from local surfers, unless it is at one of the very busy urban breaks near Casablanca or Safi. In fact you are more likely to be dropped in on by a travelling surfer, some of whom take on the role of 'honorary local' after a few weeks in town.

Crowding around Taghazoute has exploded over the last five years or so. Anchor Point, Killers and The Source will be packed whenever they break and this level of crowding is now spreading out to the north. At breaks that were traditionally quieter, like Immessouane, it's not uncommon to now find over fifty surfers in the water. It's vital that surfing etiquette is followed otherwise these breaks will become blighted by hassles and tension in the line-up. There are plenty of other breaks around, just strike out and do some exploring.

Surf directory

Morocco has yet to develop a large surf industry infrastructure of magazines, shapers and brands. It does have a number board repair businesses, many regional surf clubs and an increasing number of surf shops. Morocco's main surf website is www.surfaumaroc.com.

Morocco: a brief surf history

1950s → US soldiers based in Kénitra begin to explore the surf potential of Morocco. **1969** → Paul Witzig's seminal film *Evolution* presents Morocco as a place of untapped surf potential and sees the country firmly placed on the surf explorers' itinerary. **1988** → National surf contests are held in Rabat, Mohammedia and Casablanca.
1990 → Association Marocaine de Surf established. **1991** → Cap Surf Morocco is founded and Morocco participates in EPSA contest. **1991** → The first Moroccan surf camp, Surfland, opens in Oualidia. **1997** → Agadir surf club is founded. **1999** → King Mohammed VI becomes president of Oudayas surf club in Rabat. **2005** → Abdel El Harim becomes the first Moroccan professional surfer to compete in a WCT event when he wins a wildcard for the Rip Curl Search Reunion Pro in July 2005. **2007** → Abdel El Harim competes in selected WQS events.

Essentials

Position
Separated from Europe by just 14 km of water, Morocco lies on the northwestern edge of Africa, fringed by the Mediterranean to the north, the Atlantic to the west and bordered by the less hospitable Algeria and Mauritania to the east and south. Spiritually it forms the westernmost pillar of Islam and has a long tradition of religious tolerance.

Language
Arabic is the official language of Morocco, and French is also taught in the schools. In cities, towns and tourist zones, French is generally understood. In the mountains, Amazizh is spoken and the Berber languages are also an influence. Spanish is generally understood in the north.

Currency
Dirham (dh), divided into 100 centimes. There are 1, 5 and 10dh coins and 10, 20, 50, 100 and 200dh notes – study them hard as it is easy to mistake a 20dh note for a 100dh note. A dirham is split into 5, 10, 20 and 50 centime coins. As the currency is restricted, it's pretty hard to get hold of currency before you enter Morocco and you're not allowed to take it out of the country again but you can change Euros on the ferry or hit a hole in the wall (*guichet automatiques*) once in Morocco. There are plenty of ATMs in the cities and main towns and this is probably the easiest way to get hold of cash in Morocco. €1 will get you about 10dh. Keep a supply of small coins to hand for doling out tips for services (from waiters to garduanns who keep watch over your car) or the giving of alms to elderly beggars.

Crime/safety
Violent crime isn't a serious problem but you do need to be take care in major towns and cities especially around ATMs or in poorly lit areas. Main hassles usually involve pickpockets, con artists and non-official 'guides'. May 2003 saw Casablanca targeted by extremist suicide bombers killing more than 40 people, and targeted again in April 2007. It pays to travel respectfully, keep an eye on the media and avoid being in and around political demonstrations and rallies.

If you are travelling in a van, break-ins are a frequent occurrence and carried out with an artful dodger style of skill and opportunism. While the majority of break-ins are non violent, do not assume that because you're asleep in your van, it will put off potential burglars – thieves have become very adept at removing seals from windows and creeping in. Be aware, despite its availability, marijuana is illegal in Morocco and if caught with it, you could face a fine or jail time

Women travelling alone, or even separated from friends by a few feet, can quickly attract a lot of attention. Moroccan women are rarely seen out alone and the majority of local ladies in nightclubs are pay to play. Be firm but fair and wearing a 'wedding band' can be useful. Dress modestly (topless is not an option here) and try to be discreet when getting into or out of your wetsuit.

Health
Before entering Morocco, make sure you are up to date with your jabs: tetanus, typhoid, hepatitis A/B and MMR are all recommended. If you're driving in from Europe, a good idea is to pick up some antibiotics or similar from the pharmacist as a fallback.

The general standard of health care is not as high or widely available as in Europe, especially outside major cities. If you take regular medication, take enough with you to see you through your trip (plus a note from your doctor). In larger cities, pharmacists are generally well trained and can dispense both advice and drugs and if you know what you need they should be able to sell it to you. If not, the majority will be able to give you the contact details for a good *médecin généraliste* (GP). Most major cities have access to good private healthcare. Tap water needs to be boiled/sterilized before use. The best bet though is to buy bottled water (about 5dh/litre). The most common complaint in Morocco is food poisoning/diarrhoea caused by bad food hygiene or surfing in sewage-contaminated water (common around urban breaks). Rehydration and rest is the key but generally if it goes on for more than three days or if you're passing blood, go see a doctor.

Opening hours
Everyone stops for lunch. Banks and post offices are generally open Monday-Friday 0830-1130 and 1430-1700; shops 0900-1200 and 1500-1900. Saturdays are half days. During Ramadan working hours are shortened and many restaurants close during the day.

Sleeping
Levels and prices of accommodation vary wildly, from 5-star riads and Kasbahs in achingly hip Essaouira to basic scrubland freecamping areas watched over by local guardians. In between, there are plenty of low cost apartments and **hotels** that can easily be sourced through word of mouth for as little as 100dh a night. The standards vary from 'room with a view' to 'prisoner cell block H', so check it out before you agree to anything. At the lower end – don't expect ensuite bathroom facilities. There are plenty of official **campsites** along the Moroccan coastline – popular with foreign tourists during the winter and locals throughout the summer months. Generally, the standards are basic – hole in the ground toilets, limited shower facilities (if any). Many resemble whitewashed military encampments. They are comparatively pricey (around 25dh per person and per campervan with electricity and showers usually on top) however it's usually worth the extra just for the fact that they are much more secure than freecamping. The police have little sympathy for those who get ripped off freecamping.

Eating and drinking

A hangover from the days of French rule, breakfast is usually bread and jam. Bigger towns boast patisseries while smaller villages have spawned entrepreneurial kids who do a mean trade in doughnuts. Moroccan cooking is all about spices and for the most part lunch is a bigger affair than dinner. A popular staple of cafés are kebabs or *kefta* (non-specific meat on sticks) usually served with couscous or chips. Another cheap and popular choice (especially during Ramadan) is the *harira* soup, which can take pretty much any form but usually contains lentils, veg and meaty bits. For a more substantial lunch or dinner opt for a tagine. This Moroccan style casserole – usually chicken, meat (non-specific) or fish with vegetables and spices – is cooked in a conical clay pot over embers for a couple of hours. They are shared straight from the pot using hunks of bread held in the right hand only (the left is reserved for bathroom business). In a café, a tagine costs about 40-50dh. If you're self-catering you can buy a tagine for about 15-20dh in most markets. The climate ensures that the fruit and vegetables you eat are both tasty and cheap – and usually pesticide free. The month of **Ramadan** sees Muslims fasting during daylight hours (and abstaining from things like smoking). Cafés close, the roads become even more dangerous, but by night the cities come alive.

Tea is the lifeblood of Morocco. Made with a palmfull of gunpowder green tea, a fist full of mint and enough sugar to make your teeth dissolve, it is poured from a height and enjoys the local name 'Berber whisky'. Although an Islamic state, alcohol is not actually banned and is available from supermarkets such as **Marjane**, as well as in top-end hotels, tourist bars and a select few discreet off-licences. Local lagers include *Flag* and *Castel*.

Getting there

Air **Casablanca**'s Mohammed V Airport, T022-539040, 30 km outside the city, is one of the main gateways to Morocco. National airline **Royal Air Maroc**, www.royalairmaroc.com, offers regular, direct routes from Montreal and New York (6½ hr flight). Better deals can sometimes be found flying to Europe and booking onward journeys from there (London and Paris offer great connection options). There are no direct flights from Australia or NZ. **Marrakech's** Menara Airport, T024-447910, has become a hub of cheap flight activity and is only about 175 km from Essaouira and 275 km from Agadir. Check out the national budget airline, **Atlas Blue**, www.atlas-blue.com, for prices and details of routes right across Europe. Al Massira airport, 22 km south of **Agadir**, is the most convenient for exploring the breaks of Taghazoute and is serviced by **RAM**, and **Thomson**, www.thomson.co.uk, who offer flights from Gatwick. Other major airlines servicing Morocco include **Air France**, www.airfrance.com, **KLM**, www.klm.com, and **Lufthansa**, www.lufthansa.com.

Flights from the UK take about 3-4 hours. The budget sector serve Marrakech well: aside from Atlas Blue try **easyJet** and **Ryanair**. Prices can vary wildly between about €140-500 depending on when you go so shop around. A cheaper option might be to look at charter flights or package holidays to Agadir with accommodation thrown in. Try **First Choice**, www.firstchoice.com, or **Airtours**, www.airtours.co.uk.

Sea The intercontinental journey from Europe to Morocco crosses the busy Straits of Gibraltar. There are plenty of routes, the best with a van being Algeciras, Spain. Among others, **Trasmediterranea**, www.trasmediterranea.es, make regular crossings. Tickets can be bought in the UK from **Southern Ferries**, T0870-4991305, via **Direct Ferries**, www.directferries.co.uk, or at the ferry terminal up to the day of travel from one of the various kiosks.

Algeciras to Tanger is the busier of the two crossings, takes twice as long and is more expensive. A car and two people start at around €150 per return and go up to about €350 for two plus a large camper van. Foot passengers can travel for about €30. An open return costs the same as two singles The crossing takes 1½- 2½ hours and there are up to 10 crossings a day. The ships are quite basic with cafés and lounge areas. Ferry departures are usually late so take this into account when planning your onward journey. Before getting off, you'll need to fill in a disembarkation form and have your passport stamped by the police official onboard. The onboard bureau de change will open during the journey but details are vague so be prepared to loiter.

Disembarkation and Moroccan customs is an experience. Allow 60-90 minutes to get yourself and your vehicle through the unique system of paperwork and a queue of people expecting a tip for their services (see Red tape, below18). The ferry terminal has a bureau de change with a bank outside.

Algeciras to Ceuta is the most popular crossing with seasoned surf travellers. The 45-minute crossing to the Spanish enclave of Ceuta is a bit cheaper than the Tanger run with up to nine services a day. There are no customs to go through on disembarkation as you're still

Fact file

Capital city: → Rabat
Time zone: → GMT
Currency: → Dirham (dh)
Length of coastline: → 1,835 km
Emergency Numbers:
→ Police: 19
→ International Operator: 12
Country code: → +212
Electricity: → 240v continental style dual pin
Visa: None required for citizens of EU countries, or tourists from the US, Canada, Australia and New Zealand. Stay limited to 3 months, but can be extended. For all up to date info check: www.morocco.com/essentials/visas-passports.
Tourist Board: www.visitmorocco.org

officially in Spain, but you will have to fill in the same paperwork when you reach the inland border (see below).

Red tape Citizens of the UK, USA, Canada, Australia, NZ and most EU countries don't need a visa. At the border you'll need to hand in a green entry form with your details and destination. Passports are also checked and stamped. You can enter Morocco for up to three months after which you must either leave and re-enter, or apply for an extension at the Immigration or Bureau des Etrangers department in larger towns. Check you have been allocated your full three-month stay when your passport is stamped.

If you are driving, you need to fill in a D16 form for the temporary importation of your vehicle – valid for a maximum of six months per year. You'll also need to present your ownership documents and a green card showing valid insurance cover for Morocco. If your insurance doesn't stretch that far, you can always get cover at the port or border crossing. The registration number and details of the vehicle will be logged in the owner's passport and checked on departure to ensure the vehicle has not been sold without the full taxes being paid. Check the correct registration number has been recorded to ensure a hassle-free return. Alternatively you can register the import of your vehicle in advance; see www.douane.gov.ma for details (in French).

Getting around

Driving (right-hand side) in Morocco is like running the gauntlet – according the Moroccan Ministry for Equipment and Transport there were around 56,000 accidents on the roads in 2006 resulting in more than 12,000 serious injuries and 3,600 deaths. Driving at night should be avoided at all costs as there can be various hidden obstacles lurking around the next bend – people in *djellabas*, animals, carts, boulders, trucks etc. You need a full licence plus liability insurance which is checked at the border. The standard of roads varies from a high quality toll *autopista* to thousands of kilometres of *pistes* or unsurfaced tracks – useful for exploring more out-of-the-way-breaks. Speed limits are enforced and tourist can be hit with on-the-spot fines.

Motorways *(autopista)* **Speed limit 120 kph**. The motorway, stretching along the west coast from north of Larache south to Casablanca, is shared by cars, the odd cart, and truck drivers with suicidal tendencies and regularly crossed by families of kamikaze pedestrians. For details of tolls check out www.adm.co.ma.

Other roads Speed limit 100 kph/40 kph urban areas. P roads are major trunk roads of a fair standard, generally single track, and can take you direct to Agadir from Casablanca. **S** (secondary) roads of varying quality hug the coast south from Casablanca to Essaouira.

KRISTEN PELOU

The camel trail

Parking In towns a guardian, looking like a bus conductor, will watch your vehicle for you day and night in lieu of metered parking: 5-10dh for a couple of hours overnight should cover it.

Car hire This is not a problem here although it is pretty pricey. About €300-450 for two weeks will hire a standard issue white Fiat Uno, although a bit of haggling might get the price down. It pays to book ahead to guarantee availability through big companies like **Hertz**, www.hertz.com, and **Europcar**, www.europcar.com. Smaller companies are more open to negotiation but may be all out at busy times such as Christmas and New Year.

Public transport Morocco has a good rail network run by **ONCF**, www.oncf.org.ma (poor website), but only runs as far south as Marrakech. A journey from Casablanca to Marrakech takes about 3½ hours and costs around 90dh. From Marrakech, a bus network – **Supratours** or **CTM** – links you to most major destinations. Luggage (ie your board) will generally be stowed on the roof or in a luggage locker – at their discretion – so travel off peak and remember to tip the baggage man to avoid breakages. Taking the local bus is like taking your life in your hands but can be a cheap way to hit the town to pick up supplies – Taghazoute to Agadir sets you back 3-4dh and is an adrenaline rush the whole way. **Petits taxis** (little painted hatchbacks; orange in Agadir, red in Casablanca and beige in Marrakech) are metered, licensed to carry three passengers and can get you around town. **Grands taxis** (old Merc saloons) are long distance vehicles, licensed to carry six cramped passengers at a reasonable price, that travel between set destinations – agree the price and pick them up from the taxi ranks in town.

Surfers' tales

Carry on Camping by Denny Tolley

A surf camp experience can be one of the best weeks of your life, or a living nightmare. And there are so many to choose from these days. But what makes someone want to leave home and set up a camp in a far off country, and what drives them to find great surf for other people?

The path that lead me to this corner of the Moroccan coastline started when my family emigrated to Australia when I was just 11 years of age – one of the most traumatic experiences I have ever had to face. We hit the beach on the first day, trying to put the memories of crying relatives and good old Blighty out of our minds. I was already a very good swimmer so after seeing some strange looking guys with long blonde hair and shell necklaces out on the water, riding lines of white water to the beach on strange looking flying saucers, I decided to ask my mother for some money to hire my very own saucer. I hit the local surf shop in my union jack swimming trunks and asked for some advice. The shop assistant and his mates took one look at my trunks and handed me a foamie and a good ribbing. I spent the next two hours getting trashed on my polystyrene stick but absolutely loving it, even if I did end up with a rather large red rash from my knees to my nose. "You should have wore a t-shirt you silly little pom" said the less than sympathetic surf shop owner. This was enough. I knew that I would master this strange new craft. It was the start of my travelling surfing career. We returned to the UK five years later with me kicking and screaming, but my father promised that there was actually surf in the UK. This I found was true but soon, warmer climes and powerful waves were calling me. I travelled to various countries searching for the perfect wave but knew that a vocation working on and around the beach was for me.

I first travelled to Morocco in the winter months with a group of friends, staying for a blissful five weeks of reasonably uncrowded, perfect surf without a cloud in sight. I vowed to return – and did, nearly seven years ago, to set up the first surfcamp in the Taghazoute region. After a few very hard seasons picturing my house full of happy surfers, the camp finally took off.

I always knew the surf camp would work, as Morocco's southern shores are a surfer's dream. A coastline so diverse, with so many different setups, that everyone from total beginners to top pros would be able to have their fill. This all combines with the fantastic people and culture that Morocco has to offer. I truly fell in love with the place.

I suppose that you really have to love somewhere you are going to make a new life, otherwise things will not work. I say this as starting a business two weeks after 9/11 in a Muslim country did have its problems. Many friends and family were calling me crazy. This, with all the usual trials and tribulations of initially setting up the business, and having no guests at all, at times I did ponder on their advice. Those moments didn't last too long. I was surfing perfect point waves and catching the odd 3 kg bass, which not only provided my wife and I with a good meal, but also an excuse to really explore the coastline with all its nooks and crannies. I now knew the coastal fringe better than many locals, who were quite happy to just surf Anchors. When my first guests did arrive, I knew I could get them un-crowded surf and they could catch all the waves that they paddled for. Better than hassling with the masses, after all this is a land with great consistency and quality conditions. With the arrival of my first guests and some serious money spent on advertising, word soon spread.

It seems as though Morocco has now become very trendy for travelling surfers. This I think all came about with the photo-shoots and then film projects. I hosted most of these and met all kinds of professionals in the world of surfing. Taylor Steele came over with a group of pros including my all time idol, Shane Dorian. They arrived just after a week of terrible weather and all time bad surf. When Taylor mentioned that they wanted to sleep for their first day I secretly counted my blessings. The next morning I awoke to find the skies blue and the swell clean, with all indications pointing to a secret spot my good buddy Skunk and I had found a couple of years earlier. The guys scored big time at all the spots and Taylor said at the end of his stay that it was the best trip he had been on since he started as a surf filmmaker. Hence, his idea for 'Sippin' Jetstreams' was born. What an honour and what a pleasure it was to surf with my idol, especially one that

DEN TOLLEY

The daily search.

CARLA TOME/MOROCSURF

Den Tolley working hard to explore the region's best breaks.

would surf for eight hours straight, even if the waves were bad.

I have been lucky enough to meet more of my idols since then and it's a pleasure to see the stoke on their faces when they find Morocco far exceeds their expectations, both in the water and on Morocco far exceeds their expectations, both in the water and on the land. Legends like Taj Burrow, who has travelled the globe many times over and also from intermediate surfers, who often say "you've scored me the best waves of my life" and "thanks for taking me out somewhere I would not normally have surfed on my own." This is real job satisfaction.

Things have changed a little in this area since the old days, with the arrival of solid investment, the building of hotels and apartments. Even the free camping that attracted travelling surfers from Europe every winter is no longer allowed. New apartments have been built at The Source, an area just north of Anchors where there was a natural spring This was used by locals, campers, goats and the odd camel. Just in front of the source was the wave of the same name. You could sit in the spring and watch guys shred in front of you, it really was a cool spot. These days it seems people want and can afford more comfort, so the Moroccan Government has made sure to cater for their needs with new developments. Even Taghazoute is about to get a face lift with investment coming from all over the world – places such as Hawaii, Dubai and the US. There has also been a sharp increase in new surf camps over the past couple of years, some run pretty well, others run very badly – it seems like some people jump on the band wagon without giving the area or its locals any thought at all. Hopefully this should all be addressed now the local council is taking a firm interest in quality and control. On the whole this expansion in business is a great thing as tourism is important, especially to an area that has boomed since the tourists first came. It is giving the locals more sustainable, consistent incomes and the opportunity to develop their businesses to a much higher level. It also brings the rate of pay up for those who work in more menial jobs. I know many young kids who are now studying hard in hotel management, languages, accounting and all other aspects of the public sector, so surely this is a positive aspect to growth in certain areas. They are the future of a once very poor region of Morocco.

Speaking personally, the standard of service I strive to achieve at Moroccan Surf Adventures should hopefully keep me up and running in Morocco, ensuring my family and I a future here. I run a five star business but charge two star prices. I have a local guy who works for me and is the absolute best with the beginners, leaving me to take the better surfers to surf. We often go to great lengths, covering many kilometres to get myself and my guests uncrowded surf. I now have a three-year-old-son who I hope one day will not only speak French, but also Arabic and more importantly Berber, the local dialect. I hope he will have a future in this up and coming country as well as enjoying the surf with kids from all over the world – and of course his local grom mates.

Denny Tolley, Moroccan Surf Adventures, morocsurf.com

Northern Morocco

Overview

"Northern Morocco has even more consistent waves than down south and it doesn't suffer from the crowds. Beach, reefs and point breaks for all levels of surfer, plus great time out in Morocco's cultural capital Rabat."
Marcus Waters, Pure Blue Surf Adventures, North Morocco.

Morocco has seen a huge explosion in popularity over the last 10 years. In Taghazoute and the surrounding regions the crowd factor and the hassles are starting to negate the reason for going there in the first place – that unique experience of the culture, quiet waves and a laid-back and friendly atmosphere. However, the myopic focus on the Taghazoute region has meant that there are still huge swaithes of this coastline where the real Moroccan surf experience still exists. One such region is actually, strangely, the easiest to reach. Northern Morocco still offers the chilled line-ups, consistent waves and distinct culture that draws surfers further south, but has avoided the Euro crowds and associated price hikes. This is the region bypassed by the legions heading for Anchor Point, but why have so few made it their destinations of choice?

In the winter months while many are drawn to the dry,

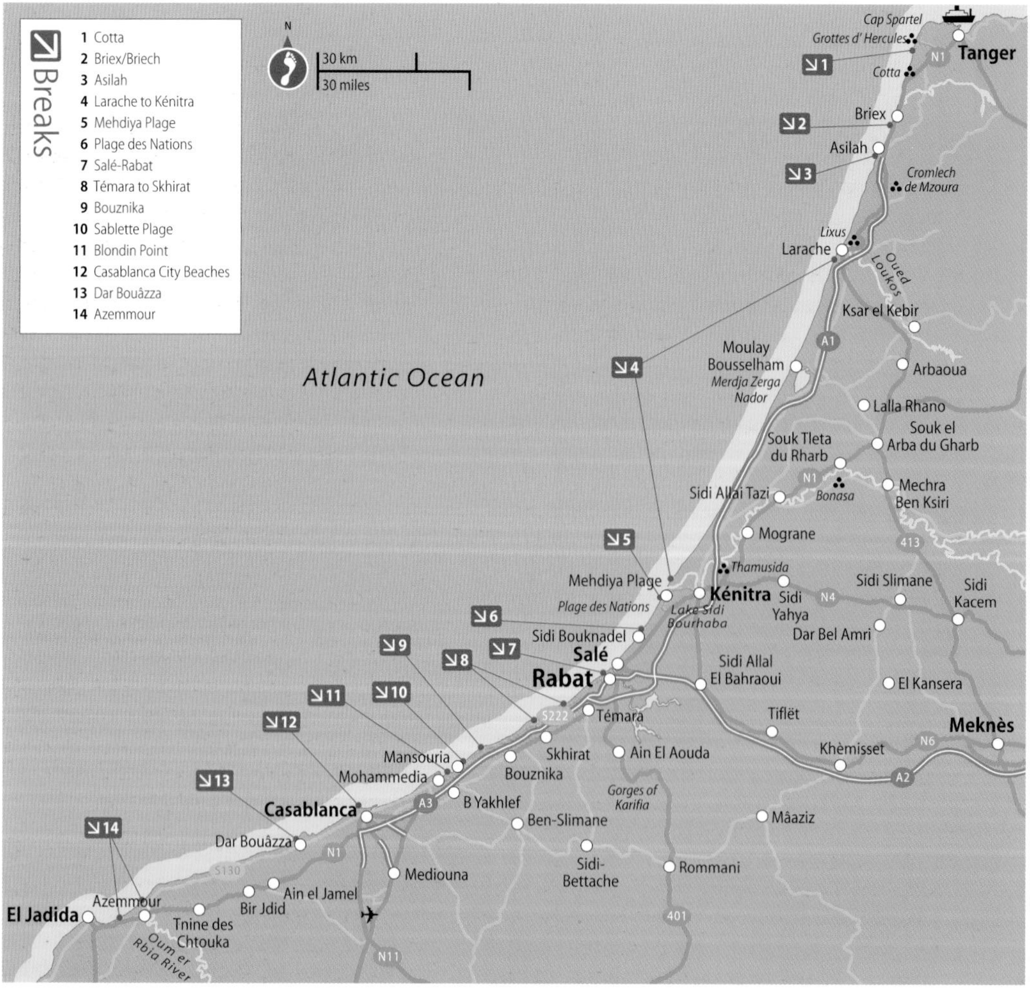

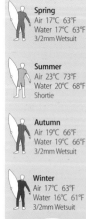

Spring
Air 17°C 63°F
Water 17°C 63°F
3/2mm Wetsuit

Summer
Air 23°C 73°F
Water 20°C 68°F
Shortie

Autumn
Air 19°C 66°F
Water 19°C 66°F
3/2mm Wetsuit

Winter
Air 17°C 63°F
Water 16°C 61°F
3/2mm Wetsuit

DAMIEN POULLENOT

7 City surfing, Rabat.

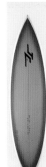

dusty warmth of southern Morocco, the north is greener (read wetter – about double the rainfall of Agadir) and a few degrees cooler. The irony is that this region can offer the surf traveller a more varied experience. While the points to the south may suit the more experienced waverider, this coastline offers every possible surfing terrain to suit every possible ability level. The exposed beaches to the north are ideal for those traveling either side of the classic Morocco surf window but can easily close out in large winter swells. From Rabat south the coastline is more varied, punctuated by groynes, rivermouths and points which better serve the winter season. The Northern regions also retain some of the feel of the Morocco that attracted surfers back in the 1970s. The towns and cities are crazy, hectic, wild, pulsing, frantic, frenzied, exciting, chaotic, confusing and frenetic. So much condensed energy is waiting to greet the traveller, with a pocket full of freshly changed dirham, that the onslaught of sales pitches hits before vehicles have even cleared customs. These busy and bustling environments can seem daunting to the first time visitor, but you can quickly get used to the energy and vibe. It's also easy to get away from it all, finding yourself surfing quality breaks that are yet to adorn the pages of the surf media with locals who are enthusiastic and friendly to visitors. Travellers still swap tips and advice, and miles of golden sand and ledgy point breaks are there for the finding. If the swell dies, delve into the wonders of Rabat or Casablanca with their bustling souks and amazing culture.

Coastline

The northern coastline in Morocco is a beach lovers dream. Endless miles of sandbanks and rivermouth breaks makes for a surfing experience that combines the quality of France and exotic essence of Africa all in one. This region is less of a swell catcher than the Casablanca region, but is still fairly consistent, and crowd numbers are pretty low. Once around the Rabat region, the coastline curves to a more northwesterly aspect, with sandy bays interspersed but rocky and ledgy headlands, some of which form good quality point breaks. The sandstone reefs and bouldery points can test the best surfers, and the beaches provide a great environment for all abilities. Some of the rivermouths and groynes are truly world class, such as Mehdiya and Doura, although the water quality can be anything but pristine.

Local environment

The water quality at the northern beaches is generally good. Rivermouths tend to have dubious waters, especially after rains and there are localized problems with oils pollution from harbours and dumping of pollutants into watercourses. To the southern end of this coastline the city breaks can be very poor, especially around Mohammedia and the other industrialized areas such as near ports. There are few pollution safeguards, but the government is becoming increasingly aware of the problems caused by water contamination.

More and more local surfers are taking to the water every year with strong communities emerging around Rabat and Casablanca and certain breaks are already pretty crowded. In general the atmosphere is good, especially if you go with a relaxed and friendly attitude. Bouznika, Sablette and Dar Bouâzza can get very busy at weekends but, although there may be the odd drop in, there is not the level of localism found in certain regions in Europe.

Getting around

An excellent toll motorway runs from Asilah south to Casablanca. It has regular service stations, which can be a good place for vans to overnight on the journey down. Any Moroccan veteran will advise against driving at night. Watch out for things in the road – people, donkeys, rocks and dogs. Driving in central Casablanca is best avoided. Hire cars are available at Casablanca airport for those flying in, but it is always advisable to book in advance. Compared to the general prices of things in Morocco, fuel prices are relatively expensive – on a par with those in Europe. Getting around by bus and train is really best left to those unencumbered by a surfboard. In this region access to breaks is usually via piste roads leading off the coast road. It's sometimes worth exploring tracks used by fishermen that allow coastal access to some of the more out of the way spots.

Breaks

BEACH BREAK

↘1 Cotta

- **Conditions** Small to medium NW to SW swells, offshore in E winds
- **Hazards/tips** Rips when big, major sand excavation from beach
- **Sleeping** Tanger ›› *p371*

Take the P2 south out of Tanger and take a right turn for Grottes d'Hercules and follow the road to the coast. It will bring you out to the south of Grottes d'Hercules at a long stretch of sandy beach, similar to the kind you get in southern Spain. Pretty featureless, it works on all tides and has a good exposure to northwesterly swells. Can have some nice peaks on clean swells and is pretty quiet.

BEACH BREAK

↘2 Briex/Briech

- **Conditions** Small to medium NW to SW swells, offshore in E winds
- **Hazards/tips** Rips when big
- **Sleeping** Asilah ›› *p371*

A good beach break north of Asilah that runs parallel to the main road south. Variable banks that work through the tides but its open exposure makes it susceptible to afternoon onshores. Always quiet.

BEACH BREAK

↘3 Asilah

- **Conditions** Small to medium NW to W swells, offshore in E winds
- **Hazards/tips** Access difficult to breaks to the south of the town
- **Sleeping** ›› Asilah *p371*

The picturesque whitewashed walled town of Asilah sits on a rocky outcrop but has a huge stretch of deserted beach breaks stretching away to the north, with easy access from the P2. Again works on all tides. Popular tourist destination but quiet in the line-up.

Below: Nestled in the rivermouth, the Charatane only comes to life in big swells, but when it does can be a regional classic.

KRISTEN PELOU

BEACH, RIVERMOUTHS AND REEF BREAKS

↘4 Larache to Kénitra

- **Conditions** All NW to W swells and E to SE winds
- **Hazards/tips** Access via pistes to breaks
- **Sleeping** Larache/Moulay Bousselham ›› *p371*

This huge stretch of coastline offers a mass of exploration opportunities. There can be a good wave inside the rivermouth at Larache if you fancy braving the rips and pollution. There is also a consistent, good quality left that is visible from the seafront. Bring a good map and a sturdy car and you'll have the opportunity to really get away from it all. Moulay Bousselham has a consistent, hollow beach that works in all swells and a lagoon rivermouth. To the south, Kénitra has a grinding left inside the Mehdiya rivermouth groynes on huge swells, but although it looks inviting it is also polluted.

RIGHT-HAND SANDBANK BREAK

↘5 Mehdiya Plage

- **Conditions** All NW swells, offshore in an easterly/southeasterly wind
- **Hazards/tips** Access via S212 to the coast near Kénitra
- **Sleeping** Salé-Rabat ›› *p372*

Mehdiya Plage is home to one of northern Morocco's best quality waves. A clean northwesterly swell wraps around the breakwater here and fires off as long, hollow right-handers. These work through the tidal range. Although best in overhead swells, in the smaller range there's still fun walls to be had. The beach gets busy in the summer but classic conditions kick in during the autumn. The beach can also be worth a look. Not many local surfers and very quiet in the winter. Great place to check on the way south. The birth place of Moroccan surfing in the 1960s.

BEACH BREAK

↘6 Plage des Nations

- **Conditions** Small to medium NW swells, offshore in southeasterly wind
- **Hazards/tips** Busy tourist beach in summer
- **Sleeping** Salé-Rabat » *p372*

This popular beach north of Rabat has fun waves that work on all tides. Turn off the P2 to Sidi Bouknadel halfway between Kénitra and Rabat.

BEACH BREAKS

↘7 Salé-Rabat

- **Conditions** Medium to big swells, offshore in E to SE winds
- **Hazards/tips** Busy city breaks with poor water quality, especially after rains
- **Sleeping** Salé-Rabat » *p372*

There is a series of rocky groynes with waves peeling off sandbanks formed alongside them and beach breaks in between. Doura is probably the most famous spot here with a right point style sandbank firing off fast hollow barrels, especially at low tide. There are popular surf clubs based in both Rabat and Salé. These urban breaks throng with a large population of surfers and bodyboarders. The water quality can be poor though especially after the rains.

BEACH BREAKS

↘8 Témara to Skhirat

- **Conditions** Small to medium NW swells, offshore in SE winds
- **Hazards/tips** Access via the S222 south of Rabat.
- **Sleeping** Témara » *p372*

A stretch of beach break with banks that work through the tides. Skhirat has a jetty with a long left that is best at low to mid tide.

DAMIEN POULLENOT

DAMIEN POULLENOT

Top: 5 Classic Mehdiya. **Above**: Rabat is home to one of Morocco's fastest growing surf communities.

RIGHT-HAND POINT BREAK

↘9 Bouznika

- **Conditions** Medium to big NW swells, Offshore in E winds
- **Hazards/tips** Water quality not great, rocks, can get crowded, urchins
- **Sleeping** Mohammedia » *p373*

Popular and well known, this low to mid tide flat rock point attracts plenty of local surfers and bodyboarders. Walling right-handers wrap along the sharp, urchin-covered reef and around the rock platform. Access is from the beach or off the point. Motorway exit sign posted Bouznika.

BEACH BREAK

↘10 Sablette Plage

- **Conditions** All NW swells, offshore in SE wind
- **Hazards/tips** Very busy break with a large local crew
- **Sleeping** Mohammedia » p373

Just north of Mohammedia lies this popular and consistent break, one that works on all tides. "Sablette Bay is suitable for beginners and good surfers," says Amine Afal of Mohammedia Surf Association (FAST). "Both left- and right-hand waves can be hollow, but the current is sometimes strong. Moreover, the waves change dramatically from low to high tide." There is a strong surfing tradition here – top French WQS surfer Micky Picon was born in Casablanca and learned to surf here.

DAMIEN POULLENOT

RIGHT-POINT BREAK

↘11 Blondin Point

- **Conditions** All NW swells, offshore in S to SE wind
- **Hazards/tips** Mohammedia has a large petroleum refinery, so the water quality is not good
- **Sleeping** Mohammedia » p373

A popular right-hand point wraps around a flat urchin covered reef at the northern end of the bay. Works best at low and can get busy with bodyboarders. The beaches here and at Sablette are popular weekend and holiday destinations, so can get very busy, especially in the summer. There are lots of campsites around Mansouria.

BEACH BREAKS

↘12 Casablanca City Beaches

- **Conditions** All NW swells, offshore in S winds
- **Hazards/tips** Rips when big, pollution and crowds
- **Sleeping** Casablanca » p373

A series of rock jetties delineate the various beaches here and help to create decent sandbars that work at various states of tide. The city beaches are very competitive and quickly become crowded with bodyboarders. As you'd imagine, the water quality isn't the best. Casablanca is Morocco's surf capital, home to the Cap Surf Association, with no shortage of surf shops.

LEFT POINT BREAK

↘13 Dar Bouâzza

- **Conditions** Medium to big NW swells, offshore in southerly winds
- **Hazards/tips** Gets crowded, especially at weekends
- **Sleeping** Casablanca » p373

Long, low tide lefts peel along this ledgy point in clean swells. One of the north's best-known waves but watch out for the sharp reef and the omnipresent urchins. A good place to hook into some long and walling lefts in the land of the rights. Another spot worth checking is Jack's. Carry on along the S130 south until you hit **Jack's Beach**, a good beach break that hosts the occasional surf competition.

BEACH BREAK

↘14 Azemmour

- **Conditions** All NW swells, offshore in southeasterly winds
- **Hazards/tips** Rips when big
- **Sleeping** Azemmour » p373

Haouzia beach stretches south with the mouth of the Oum er Rbia River to the north. Works on all tides. About 1 km from Azemmour, follow the coast road or face a half hour walk from the town.

Top: 7 Doura is famed for its rivermouth rights and can offer protection when large swells batter the exposed northern coastline. **Below: 13** South of Dar Bouazza, the northwesterly orientated Jack Beach is a consistent but exposed spot. **Below right: 5** The rock groyne at Mehdiya trains the sand into quality banks to produce long, hollow waves.

DAMIEN POULLENOT

DAMIEN POULLENOT

Practicalities

Tanger

Cosmopolitan Tanger, the gateway to Morocco, has always been a lure for those drawn to the wilder side of life – from international playboys, to counter culturalists to artists, among them Oscar Wilde, Ian Fleming, Matisse, Jack Kerouac and William Burroughs. As a busy intercontinental port, flooded by a steady stream of tourists and trippers it's also home to a high concentration of hasslers and hustlers, but there are plenty of places to soak up the atmosphere. Head up the main Av Mohammed V/Blvd Pasteur and on up the R de la Liberté north towards the Grand Socco and on to the médina or city centre and fortified Kasbah that watches over he city.

Sleeping

Accommodation in the medina can be pretty basic and it is often better to find accommodation outside the city walls.
For the experience, the pick of the medina pack is € **Hotel Continental** on Dar El-Baroud, T039-931024. It combines a faded grandeur shabby chic-ness with port views. Doubles around 400dh including breakfast. The € **youth hostel**, on R Antaki off Pl des Nations, T039-946127, is clean, basic and about 40dh a night – showers around 5dh, HI affiliated. There are plenty of cheap but very basic pensions on R de la Plage running up towards the Grand Socco.
€ **El-Djenina**, is just a couple of doors up from the hostel on R Antaki, T039-942244, with clean, ensuite doubles around 300dh. **Camping Miramonte**, about 3 km west of the town centre, T039-937133, is fine if basic. **Achakar**, 12 km west towards Cap Spartel, T039-333840, is more handy for exploring the northern beaches. The toilet block is pretty basic and as with most sites, feels pricey for what you get. NB Sand from this northwest strip is regularly excavated by building contractors.

Eating and drinking

Africa, on R de la Plage is a reasonable and fairly reliable place to grab a simple taste of Morocco. If you're still hungry, head to one of the many cafés on Blvd Pasteur. Grab a coffee and watch the world go by at these former artists' haunts: **Café de France** on Pl de France or **Café Central** in the Petit Socco.

Directory

South of the Grand Socco, around Blv Pasteur and Mohammed V, is where most amenities are based. **Internet Cybercafé Adam**, R ibn Rochd (just off Blvd Pasteur/MohammedV jct) is handy, doubles as a café and has access for around10dh/hr. **Banks** Av Mohammed V and Blvd Pasteur have several banks and ATMs the BMCE on Pasteur has a good bureau de change. **Car hire** Av Mohammed V/Pasteur are home to the biggies. **Pharmacy** Av Mohammed V. **Post office** Av Mohammed V. **Tourist office** Blvd Pasteur, Mon-Fri 0830-1200, 1430-1800.

Asilah

This pretty whitewashed fishing port was a former Portuguese outpost and is now an increasingly popular summer resort town with wealthy Europeans and Moroccans. The ramparts were built by the Portuguese in the 15th century while the whitewashed walls inside the medina are adorned with new murals every August during the **International Cultural Festival of Asilah** when the town is heaving (www.c-assilah.com for festival pictures and information). There are good amenities here such as banks at Place Mohammed V as well as cafes and a range of accommodation.

Sleeping

€ **Marhaba**, close to the médina on Place Zelaka, has clean, basic (if slightly shabby) rooms for around 80dh – one of the cheapest hotels in town.
€ **Hotel Patio de la Luna**, this whitewashed hotel, also on Place Zelaka, T039-416074, is small, simple, charming and packed with plenty of character. Double and triple rooms with ensuites available from 450dh.
Camping There are a couple of options just north of the town **Camping Echrigui**, T039-417182, and the slightly better **Camping As Sada**, T039-417317, person/campervan 12/20dh, hot showers 10dh. Both close to the beach with limited facilities and summertime mossies. Off season check out the harbour where a guardian will watch your van overnight for 10dh.

Larache

Formeryl occupied, Larache still has a certain Iberian influence, most notably in the vibe and cooking. This pretty white and blue port town is quiet off season. Banks on the main Av Mohammed V leading down from Place de la Liberation. The autoroute continues south to Casablanca – around 100dh in van tolls.

Sleeping

€ **Pension Atlas**, in the médina, T039-912014, and the welcoming
€ **Pension Amal**, Ave Abdallah ben Yassin, T039-912014, are basic but some of the best budget options in town.
Crossing the Loukos estuary to the north, the beach road yields a **camping** area.

Eating

There are plenty of good, cheap eats to be had south of the medina around Bab el Khemis.

Moulay Bousselham

Lovely low-key summer beach resort/fishing

Flat spells

Birds The vast **Merdja Zerga Park** southeast of Moulay Bousselham is twitcher heaven, attracting birds from flamingos to falcons Dec-Mar. Boat trips out to the birds can be organized for between 200-300dh. Just inland from Mehdiya Plage, the forest-ringed nature reserve of **Lac de Sidi Bourhaba** is another fantastic place to experience the international migration of birds between Africa and Europe from Oct-Apr.

Caves West of Tanger on the S701, **Grottes d'Hercules** was once a party venue for the rich, famous and decadent and is now known for its inverted Africa-shaped portal through which you can look out over the sea. A nominal charge will get you entry to the caves – sunset is the showcase.

Cinema In Rabat, catch the latest Bollywood epic at one of the cinemas on Av Mohammed V.

Hammam In Casablanca, go for the old skool traditional experience for less than 10dh at **Ancienne Medina Hammam**, Pl Ahmed el Bidaoui within the medina (men until midday, women from 1300). Remember to take a towel and something to sit on.

Sights 5 km northeast of Larache lies **Lixus**, a site of partially excavated ancient Roman ruins and legendary Garden of Hesperides where Hercules is said to have killed a local dragon and picked golden apples. Entry and access to the site is free and worth the trip. The **Kasbah des Oudaias** set into the walls of the médina in Rabat on the banks of the river affords awesome views down the coast. **Hassan II Mosque** overlooking the ocean, is the crowning glory of Casa and one of the few mosques open to non-Muslims. To see inside you have to take a tour – 1 hr around 150dh, not Fri.

village. To the south, the Merdja Zerga (blue lagoon) stretches over 30 km and is an important place for wintering birds. The main street running to the beach and lake divides the town and is filled with grill cafés.

Sleeping

Camping Moulay Bousselham, is summer opening only, basic and a real mozzie haven. A better (and free) bet is a motorway stopover – try the coastal stretch to the south.

Eating and drinking

Eat at one of the little restaurants such as **L'Ocean** for fresh fish snacks and grab a drink at the lagoon-edged **Hotel le Lagon**.

Salé/Rabat

Twin towns of Salé and Rabat are separated by the Oued Bou Regreg. Rabat is the hardworking political capital to Salé's old walled city. Although fairly cosmopolitan, Rabat is no party town. The main road, Av Mohammed V, packed with stores, banks and hotels runs north from the new town, past the train station and impressive 18th-century As-Sunna Mosque to the walls of the médina.

Sleeping

Sleeping is centred around Av Mohammed V while the médina has plenty of cheap but dodgy options.

€ Hotel Dorhmi, just inside the médina off Mohamed V, T037-723898, is clean, welcoming and one of the best affordable choices. Doubles around 140dh, hot showers extra. Close to good eating options. The **€ youth hostel**, R Marassa, just inside the southwest corner of the médina, T037-725769, is very basic but offers dorm beds from about 50dh.

Eating

Mohammed V has more pâtisseries and crémeries offering juices and sandwiches than you can possibly sample. For good old home-cooked pizza or pasta, head to **La Mamma**, R Tanta, mains around 100dh or less. If you prefer home-cooked, traditional Moroccan fare, try **Restaurant El Bahia** in the médina wall, where set lunches are tasty, filling and good value.

Directory

Surf Shops There is a **Quiksilver Boardriders** store on R de Madagascar Diour Djamma as well as a **Rip Curl** store on Ave D'Atlas. **Banks** Mohammed V has a steady supply of cashpoints. **Internet Zerrad Net**, Av al-Amir Fal Ould Omar, Agdal has a reasonable connection. **Post office** Mohammed V. **Tourist information** R Oued El Makhazine and R Zalaka, Agdal district southwest of the Medina, Av d'Alger near Pl de Golan, www.visitrabat.com.

Témara

South along the S222, this is a popular weekend beach stop with Rabat residents. There are a couple of **campsites** here including, **Camping La Palmeraie** 100 m from the beach T037-749251, **Camping Gambusias**. South towards Skhirat, near the mouth of the Oued Yquem by Plage Jawhara is **Camping Rose-Marie**, T037 749251. For a more comfortable option, continue south to Skhirat where **Pure Blue**, www.purebluewater.com/moroc, have a surf camp operating Oct-Apr, maximising on the region's optimum swell window. For comfort, the beachfront, authentic Moroccan-style accommodation is set out in twin rooms. Prices from around £250 per week which includes bed, breakfast and lunch, 4WD surfaris to the best breaks every day and transfers from Casablanca. Yoga classes are also available as an optional extra. Also available are selected beginners and improvers weeks during the season where you can learn with the pros. Head south to Skhirat for the souk on Sun.

Mohammedia

After Skhirat, the coastal road to Mohammedia is less developed with simple sandy tracks running down to Bouznika and Dahomey Plages. Mohammedia however is not so simple. Port Blondin at the mouth of the Oued Nefifikh marks the start of the 3-km stretch of Mohammedia sands. Although a popular and pretty summer retreat from Casablanca, a thriving petrochemical industry and oil refinery shadows the town.

Sleeping

Camping There are several camping options here and just to the north at Mansouria however the hygiene standards and facilities are not generally brilliant. The best choice is the year round **Camping Mimosa**, at Mansouria with shaded parking and chalets available. If you ask nicely, you can have a hot shower in the chalets when they're quiet (read winter!).

Directory

Banks R Rachidi.
Post office Av Mohammed Zerktouni.
Tourist information R Al Jahid.

Casablanca

Casablanca – the 'white house' – grew from a trading port into a sprawling, hustling, traffic-filled, cosmopolitan metropolis. South of the port, the walled médina stretches out towards the main square, Pl Mohammed V, from which the rest of the city radiates. To the west, the Hassan II Mosque watches over the Atlantic. West along the seafront

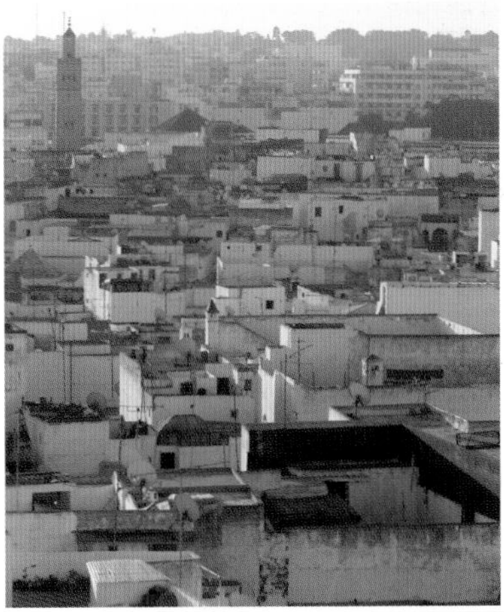

KRISTEN PELOU

Rabat medina.

Blvd Corniche you hit Plage Ain Diab and the significant nightlife district. The sprawling *bidonvilles* (shanty towns) surround the city, while above pollution hangs like a fog. Circumnavigating Casa is like entering a Mad-Max style road race: cars exit and enter where there are no slip roads, people run across the lanes, dodging traffic, and that's just the beginning – so it's best negotiated in daylight. The Mohammed V Airport is to the south of the city at Nouasseur. The train journey to Casa-Port in the city centre takes about 40 mins, costing around 25dh. A *grand taxi* in the evening after the trains stop running should cost about 320dh.

Sleeping

Head to R Allal Ben Abdallah at the south eastern edge of the médina and try: **€ Hotel Touring**, T022-310216, or **€ Hotel des Negociants**, T022-314023, basic but decent rooms in the centre of town and well placed for cheap eating options.
The **€ youth hostel**, Place Ahmed el-Bidaoui on the eastern edge of the médina is another OK bet – clean, good showers with beds from 45dh a night.
Camping Not a practical option in the city.
Camping International, T022-330060, is about 15 km south of the city, 100 m from beach, and popular in the summer.
Camping Tamaris is further along the 1122 at Hajra Khala, handy for Jack's Beach.

Eating

Café Anwal, on Allal Ben Abdallah, does a good, affordable traditional set menu while **Snack Amine** on R Chaouia is the place for vast quantities of good value fried fish. For some outstanding ice creams take a stroll on the Corniche above Ain Diab beach to **Palais des Glaces**.

Directory

Surf shops with a thriving surf community, there are plenty here including a **Quiksilver** and a **Rip Curl** store as well as the **Malibu** surf shop on R el Fourat, **Balibongo** on Daoud Dahiri, **Pipeline** on Blvd Rahal el Meskini and **Moby Dick** on R de l'Atlas Maarif. **Banks** There are plenty including Credit Maroc on Mohammed V.
Chemist 24-hr chemist on Mohammed V.
Internet Several cafes have Wi-Fi access including **Rick's Café**, Blvd Sour Jdid (which also has Sunday jazz – nice). Also try Euronet R Tata south of the Medina. **Post office** and **Tourist information** Mohammed V.

Azemmour

The white Portuguese médina of Azemmour sits on the banks of the river Oum er Rbia. The main road Mohammed V runs up to the central Pl de Souk and the médina. The ramparts surrounding the médina offer great views north up the coast to Casablanca while to the south the popular, long sandy beach is about half an hour's walk through eucalyptus trees.

Sleeping

There are a couple of hotels here:
€ Hotel de la Poste, as the name suggests, is by the post office, and **€ Hotel Victoire**, by the mosque, both just off the main Mohammed V thoroughfare.

Eating

There are a couple of good cafés by Pl de Souk including **El Manzah**.

Overview

"Even compared to Mundaka, the speed is higher. The base of the wave is so perfect and impressive, but you have the sand filling in the holes, which can only add some degrees to the perfection of the wave." *Laurent Miramont on Safi.*

The Central Moroccan coastline has become a real media darling in recent years. She has starred in many mainstream travel features, splashed across the pages of magazines and national newspapers, probably more than any other part of the country's diverse and alluring coastal fringe. The focus of nearly all this attention has been the picturesque walled enclave of Essaouira, a town that has become *the* jet-set destination. The whitewashed medina, bustling souk and frantic harbour have become a snapshot of the archetypal Moroccan experience. For surfers, the culture of the narrow streets and a walk to Henrix's Castle in the Sand is all it really offers, for unlike the majority of this waverich coastline, the surfing here is pretty limited – unless you like your boards with a huge sail attached. For real world class action you must strike out to the north or to the south of this tourist Mecca, to destinations that are much less of a traveller's heaven, but much more of a surfer's paradise.

Safi is an urbanized, industrialized port town that also happens to harbour one of surfing's great unkept secrets. The truth about this monstrous, reeling right hand point has been out of the bag for a while now, long enough for the

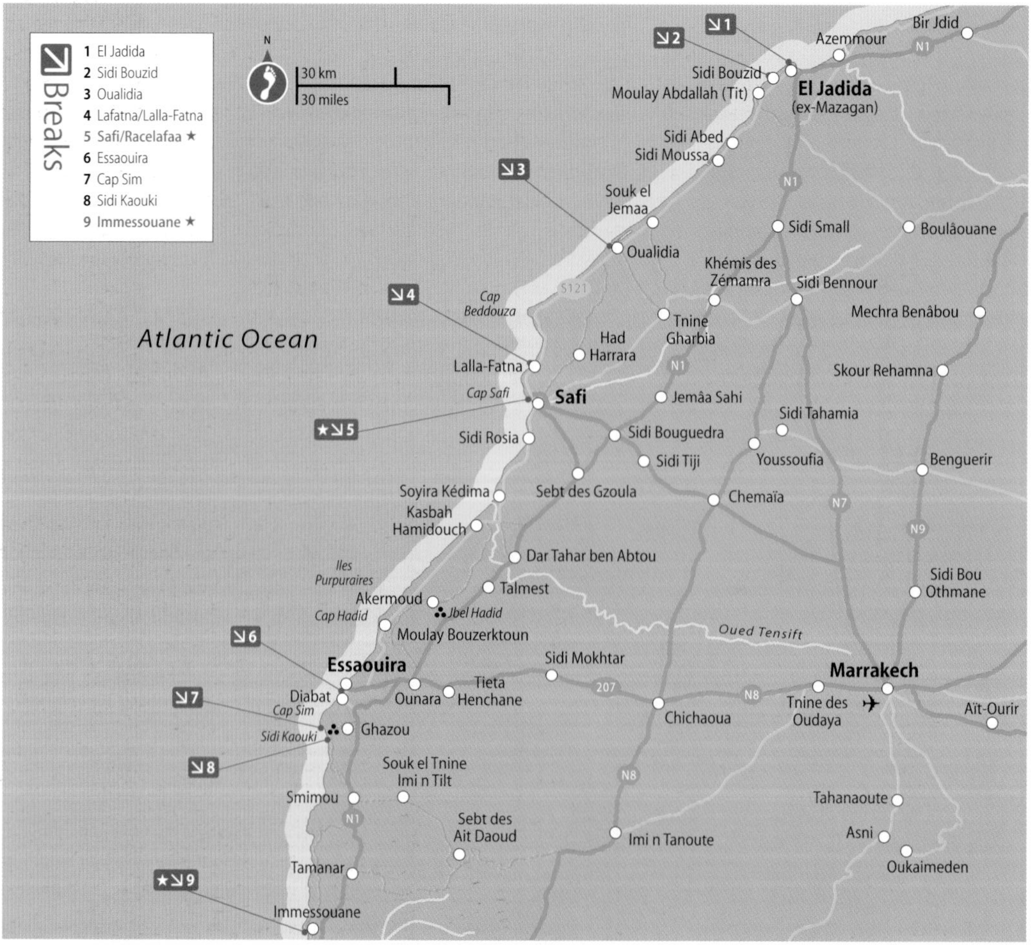

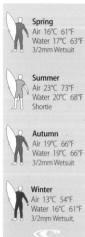

Spring
Air 16°C 61°F
Water 17°C 63°F
3/2mm Wetsuit

Summer
Air 23°C 73°F
Water 20°C 68°F
Shortie

Autumn
Air 19°C 66°F
Water 19°C 66°F
3/2mm Wetsuit

Winter
Air 13°C 54°F
Water 16°C 61°F
3/2mm Wetsuit,

localism to die down, for travelling and local surfers to get down to the serious business of taking on this serious wave and for Ministry of Tourism to officially classify the site as a surf park. To the southern edge of the central region lies another awesome surfing challenge. At Immessouane, there's no town to speak of, just a small dusty village huddled around a small, hard working harbour and three reeling righthanders. Once a getaway from all the hustle and bustle of the waves to the south, this spot is now packed with all manner of wave riding vehicles whenever the swell hits. While Essaouira may be the darling of the travel press, the crowded line-ups at Immessouane have come to truly symbolize the changes that have taken place along this once empty stretch of coastline. Hendrix predicted that all castles made of sand slip into the sea eventually but surfing is a dream whose very foundations are built on shifting sands. We know that where one castle is washed away on the falling tide, another is being built grain by grain, just around the next headland.

Coastline

The Central Moroccan coastline south of El Jadida is composed of long stretches of exposed beaches broken by rocky outcrops and cliffs. The beaches are powerful and usually facing northwest so they pick up plenty of swell, but the quality of the banks is very variable. Between the 30 km headland at Cap Beddouza and Safi the rocky coastline is much more sheltered and many swells march past the southwesterly facing shore. Bigger NW and W swells are needed to work here. South of Safi the rocky coastline heads southwest again and is home to a mixture of rarely surfed spots broken by occasional points. Below the bay at Essaouira the coastline turns and heads south into a region where many unridden, quality waves break along difficult, rocky points. Here access to the coastline becomes tough. A 4WD, a good map and local knowledge become invaluable. Local surfers may offer advice and tips to respectful travellers.

Local environment

There is certainly pollution around the industrialized and urban areas along this stretch of coastline. Safi, with its large population, lack of adequate sewage infrastructure and busy port, definitely has water pollution issues. Between towns the water may be polluted by agricultural runoff. Safi was Morocco's most notorious wave with a reputation as one of the most localized spots in the country. The right hand point had become somewhat controversial but the boom in number visiting the wave and a general rise in tolerance all round has helped with the vibe. This is a pretty heavy wave: be patient and the atmosphere should be pretty chilled. Don't drop litter or freecamp in a disrespectful way. Immessouane has changed massively over the last five years or so. Numbers have increased and so has the hassle factor. Morocco is pretty chilled and that's why most surfers go there. Try not to bring Euro-style hassling into the line-up.

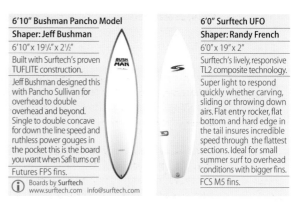

Getting around

Access to the breaks in central Morocco is pretty straightforward. The coastal roads are of good quality and allow easy access to many spots along the Central Moroccan fringes. However there are breaks where access is limited to piste roads and a few where hiking in may be the only option. Make sure you leave your vehicle in a safe place or with a guardian. Don't leave any valuables visible.

6'10" Bushman Pancho Model
Shaper: Jeff Bushman
6'10" x 19¼" x 2½"
Built with Surftech's proven TUFLITE construction.
Jeff Bushman designed this with Pancho Sullivan for overhead to double overhead and beyond. Single to double concave for down the line speed and ruthless power gouges in the pocket this is the board you want when Safi turns on!
Futures FPS fins.

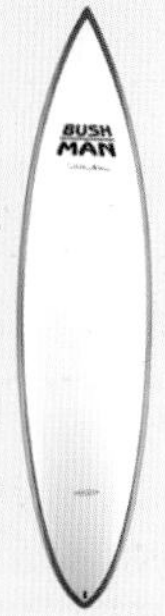

Boards by **Surftech**
www.surftech.com info@surftech.com

6'0" Surftech UFO
Shaper: Randy French
6'0" x 19" x 2"
Surftech's lively, responsive TL2 composite technology.
Super light to respond quickly whether carving, sliding or throwing down airs. Flat entry rocker, flat bottom and hard edge in the tail insures incredible speed through the flattest sections. Ideal for small summer surf to overhead conditions with bigger fins.
FCS M5 fins.

Left: Nick Tiscoe enjoying a fun session at increasingly popular Immessouane.
Below: This freight-training wave is not something to underestimate.

GREG MARTIN/FINDYOURWAVE.COM

KRISHA SOWINSKI/PUREBLUE.COM

Breaks

DAMIEN POULLENOT

5 A trawler powers out avoiding the thundering lines wrapping, for up to 300 m, along the point at Safi.

BEACH BREAK

1 El Jadida

- **Conditions** Medium NW swells, offshore in S winds
- **Hazards/tips** El Jadida can suffer from pollution from the nearby port
- **Sleeping** El Jadida » p379

Northeast-facing beach with decent waves and a right that breaks off a sandbar alongside the jetty. Popular holiday spot in the summer with Moroccan families.

POINT AND BEACH BREAK

2 Sidi Bouzid

- **Conditions** Medium NW swells, offshore in SE winds
- **Hazards/tips** Pollution
- **Sleeping** El Jadida » p379

This curved sandy beach stretches for 3 km. Overlooked by an endless line of whitewashed homes the beach throngs in the summer when it's a popular resort. Autumn sees serious swells kick in and the point at the northern end comes to life. Like others in the region it's a rock platform with a fringing sandbar. Limited sewage facilities means the water can be polluted with household waste.

BEACH BREAK

3 Oualidia

- **Conditions** Small to big NW swells, offshore in SE winds
- **Hazards/tips** Location of Surfland surf camp
- **Sleeping** Oualidia » p379

This is a powerful, exposed stretch of beaches with heavy waves working on all tides. Beaches front a very sheltered lagoon that has reform waves suitable for beginners in a big swell. Beautiful location with dolphins and flamingos.

BEACH BREAK

4 Lafatna/Lalla-Fatna

- **Conditions** Big NW swells, E winds
- **Hazards/tips** Rips and rocks
- **Sleeping** Safi » p380

South from Cap Beddouza, the rocky headland protects a series of cliff-backed sandy coves. Lalla-Fatna is a 2-km descent from the coast road. Westerly facing beach that needs a big swell to work as it is sheltered by the headland. Produces mainly right-hand sandbanks. If camping on the beach, be aware of tidal range.

RIGHT POINT BREAK

5 Le Jardin, Safi

- **Swell** NW
- **Wind** Offshore in NE and E winds
- **Tide** Low to mid
- **Size** 4-12 ft plus
- **Length** 300-600 m
- **Bottom** Sand and rock
- **Ability level** Advanced
- **Best months**Sept to March
- **Board** Semi-gun
- **Access** Good timing off the rocks
- **Hazards/tips** Access, rocks, localism, heavy wave, advanced surfers only
- **Sleeping** Safi » p380

Just on the northern fringe of the town of Safi lies one of the world's most enigmatic, yet terrifyingly perfect point breaks. Call a hollow reef Pipe-like, call a thumping hollow beach Hossegor-like, but ride a 600 m long, 10 ft reeling point offering endless barrel sections and where do you look for comparisons? "It's like a mix of Kirra and J-Bay," says top French surfer Didier Piter. "It's like a reverse Mundaka," says British pro Gabe Davies. "Like Burleigh only longer and more hollow," says Tom Carroll. One man who knows the wave well is Laurent Miramont. "Even compared to Mundaka, the speed is higher. The base of the wave is so perfect and impressive, but you also have the sand filling the holes, which can only add to the degrees of perfection."

Le Jardin has gone from a jealously guarded secret, to a well known semi-secret spot famous for its Quiksilver training camps, to a world wide star since the 1990s. But what makes this wave so special? Looking across to the harbour at Safi, this long headland curves away to the northwest, acting as a foil to the huge swells that angle in from the north Atlantic. This is a wave that can work from 4 ft through to over 12. Breaking over a rock reef covered with a smooth deposit of Saharan sands, the swell jacks as it reaches the outside edge of 'The Garden' and throws into a fast hollow, reeling barrel. This outside section is particularly treacherous and difficult, breaking close to the rocks. "That's a dangerous place, specially at the top" says Larent. "There's a 200 m section, which is at a very close angle to the cliff, and the scheme of the rocks is very bad. The very first one to take-off there was Ross Clarke-Jones. He opened the door. We had to wait for such an experienced surfer."

Once through the outside section the wave wraps into the middle and inside sections, both of which can be big and hollow, before breaking onto the beach on the inside. Luckily for the traveling surfer, its reputation as a localized spot has now eased and respectful surfers can enjoy some of the longest, hollowest waves in the whole of the country. Like all great and challenging waves, watch the locals for a while, and then sit further down the line. With such long waves, a bit of patience will bring its rewards.

***If you like Safi**, try **Killer Point** (see page 385) or **La Santa Right** in Lanzarote (see page 265).*

BEACH BREAK

↘6 Essaouira

Conditions Medium to big NW to W swells, offshore in E winds
Hazards/tips Surfboards (Bics) available for hire on northern end the beach
Sleeping Essaouira ⏩ *p380*

This long, crescent-shaped beach stretches away from the walled Medina and harbour at the northern end. It works on all tides but an offshore island cuts out a lot of swell. The southern end towards Diabat is where you'll see the 'Castle in the Sand' that inspired Hendrix, as well as the most consistent and well formed banks. This is a famous windsurfing spot so don't expect too many glassy days. Best in the winter, when there is less wind. There is a local crew of surfers worth talking to about other spots around the town.

RIGHT-HAND POINT BREAK

↘7 Cap Sim

Conditions Medium to big swell, offshore in E to SE winds
Hazards/tips Access is difficult. Store valuables somewhere safe
Sleeping Sidi Kaouki ⏩ *p380*

Cap Sim needs a decent sized swell to get going but produces long, walling rights over a sand-covered rock bottom. Works on all

DAMIEN POULLENOT

KRISTEN PELOU

Top: 5 The view from the lineup – taking off in front of cliffs isn't for everyone. **Above: 6** The beach at Essaouira may be a windsurfers' playground but other, better options lie nearby.

Top: 9 Immessouane serves up a series of quality right points. **Above:** 9 Toby Donachie finds a bashable lip.

tides but best on low. Access is from the road to Sidi Kaouki. Turn right onto the *piste* road towards the point, then the final part is on foot. Quality waves. Be friendly to the locals and you will be received well. Don't leave valuables.

BEACH BREAK

8 Sidi Kaouki

- **Conditions** All swells, offshore in easterly winds
- **Hazards/tips** Exposed, few facilities
- **Sleeping** Sidi Kaouki ›› *p380*

This long beach, which works on all tides, can produce some good banks but is exposed to the wind. Can have excellent waves with rights at the northern end and peaks along the length. Parking, with a guardian, at the northern end of the beach by the cafes. Check the wind direction before making the long drive from Essaouira. Keep an eye on your belongings.

BEACH AND POINT BREAKS

9 Immessouane

- **Swell** NW
- **Wind** SE to E
- **Tide** All tides except high
- **Size** 3-10 ft
- **Length** 50 to 300 m plus
- **Bottom** Sand/reef
- **Ability level** Intermediate
- **Best months** Nov to March
- **Board** Performance Thruster
- **Access** Off the rocks/from the harbour
- **Hazards/tips** Rarely crowded.
- **Sleeping** Immessouane ›› *p381*

When you first arrive in Immessouane it looks like the village has been beamed up, snatched into outer space or has just decided this dusty headland isn't really the place to be and has up and relocated to greener pastures. The grid of roads cris-crosses the headland leading down to the actual village that sits clustered around the large harbour. First impressions aren't favourable. There's a great view down the coastline, but not much else here. No bustling village centre like Taghazoute, no walled medina like Essaouira. No, the reason you come to such an out of the way place is for the wave.

Or should I say waves, for this headland boasts at least three waves that will tempt you to pitch up on the dusty, God forsaken campsite or to book into a local auberge. The first wave fills your view from the basic campground, walls wrapping off the end of the rocky headland through to the inside of the bay. This in itself is nice fun point wave offering enough on a good day to make up for the hot and dusty drive from the main coastal road, but there is more. A few hundred metres to the south a stark tower stands guard over a concrete harbour wall that protects the wooden fishing fleet, laid up inside the reach of its reassuring arm. Were it not for this defensive wall, the reeling barrel that's firing across in front would be making short work of the matchwood remains of the resting fleet. This second right is a hollow and powerful wave with a steep take off that offers adrenaline fueled barrels. Winds from the east or southeast are offshore and it works in big swells at mid to high tide. For experienced surfers only, the harbour wall wave is one of the heaviest in this region.

Inside the bay lies the most popular and longest of the three right-handers. It starts to break at the southern end of the harbour mouth and peels through to the beach at low tide. Suitable for all surfers, this is an excellent, long walling wave breaking over sand and rocks. Sheltered from northerly and northeasterly winds by cliffs, it is also the most sheltered from swell. The days of catching Immessouane to yourself are long gone, the line-ups are now crowded whenever the swells kick in and even when it doesn't.

*If you like **Immessouane**, try **Inch Reef** in Ireland (see page 143) or **The Gare** in England (see page 65).*

Practicalities

El Jadida

This relaxed port town is still protected by the ramparts of the Portuguese médina built in the 1500s. Quiet off-season, it is popular spot with holidaying Moroccans who set up summertime makeshift tented villages along the beaches. The bus station is south of the town; No 2 serves Sidi-Bouzid Plage a few km south. Just 15 km south is the industrial port Jorf Lasfar and a phosphate processing plant, resulting in often dubious water quality.

Sleeping

There are a couple of decent cheap options:
€ Hotel Bordeaux, R Moulay Ahmed Tahiri, in the medina is small but well formed and friendly.
€ Hotel Suisse, on the main R Zerktouni, has rooms with showers.
Camping Camping International, T023-342755, about 15 mins from El Jadida on the road into town not far from the beach, also has cabins.

Eating

For cheap eats head to Pl El Hansali and try the popular **La Broche** for simple Moroccan and basic dishes or **Cousteau** on Bvd Suez for platters of fried fish, both just south of Pl Mohammed V.

KRISTEN PELOU

Meat market.

Directory

Banks Ave Mohammed V. **Post office** Ave Mohammed V. **Tourist information** Pl Mohammed V.

Oualidia

Travelling south, the coastal S121 passes a series of quiet dune backed beaches and rocky outcrops; around Sidi Moussa, the scenery is a gastronomic marriage of saltpans and hot houses ripening tomatoes. The mellow town of Oualidia hugs the edges of a tidal lagoon, which fills through two gaps in the spit of land separating it from the ocean. Beyond this stretches miles of empty beach. Famous for its oysters and flanked by a 17th-century kasbah, Oualidia is also slowly becoming an upmarket holiday resort – building work is afoot and prices are beginning to rise.

El Jadida to Safi

Sleeping

€ Thalassa, T023-366050, on the main strip, with large rooms is a good budget choice with a restaurant downstairs cooking up

Flat spells

Essaouira The heart of Essaouira, the 18th-century fortified medina is UNESCO listed and a wonderful maze of streets and shops in which to loose yourself for several hours. At the south end of the beach, across the River Ksob a ruined ancient fortress is sinking slowly into the sands which, as legend has it, was the inspiration for Hendrix's 'Castles Made of Sand'…worth a stroll and a look.

Marrakech Souks aside there is plenty to see in this walled city including Djemaa el-Fna – the huge square and beating heart of Marrakech that literally crackles with energy as snake charmers compete with a plethora of distractions from musicians and street theatre to story tellers and vendors for attention. Other sights include the impressive 16th-century theological school Ali Ben Youssef Medersa just north of square – the intricate designs and stucco plasterwork are simply beautiful, entry around 40dh.

Souks This central stretch of Morocco is home to several fantastic souks or markets including those in Essaouira and Marrakech that are definitely worth exploring whether just to soak up the ambience or to invest in slippers, spices, carpets, jewelry or any other treasures that may take your fancy. If you are looking to buy, get ready to haggle – a good-natured theatrical tango of guile, wit and cunning between vendor and vendee as a mutually agreeable price is reached. It's a lengthy affair so just take your time, don't loose your patience (or your temper) and try to enjoy the whole process – it's all part of the Moroccan experience.

Snowboarding OK, so we're not talking bluebird powder days (more of a snow and rock affair) but the High Atlas resort of **Oukaimeden**, 1½-hr drive south of Marrakech on the S513, can deliver just enough snowfall during the short Jan-Mar season for a fun day or 2... Check out CAF Refuge www.caf-maroc.com for a good, cheap dorm-style accommodation option.

cheap eats from pizzas to tagines.
€ Hotel Restaurant l'Initial, T023-366246, is small, clean, comfortable, well placed with some pretty rooms and an onsite licensed restaurant – one of the best mid-priced choices in town around 400dh per double.
Camping Les Sables d'Or heading down towards the beach, the site is pretty basic but clean and well placed – around 40dh van and 2 people.

Safi

Winding along the road south, the sea and stretches of deserted beach are intermittently hidden by sand dunes. Cap Beddouza with its lighthouse offers views along the coast, as well as a protective rocky headland, sheltering small sandy coves southwards to Cap Safi. Safi itself is a fairly industrialized, working port town with phosphate factories and sardine-canning plants – the surrounding coast is unsurprisingly fairly polluted. However Fort Dar el Bahar offers good views of the coast towards Essaouira while the seafront médina is the place to pick up pottery. Outside of the médina, life centres around two main squares – Pl de l'Independence near the seafront bustling with shops, cafés, cheap accommodation and banks and the more sensible Pl Mohammed V to the south of the médina with the post office and tourist office leading off it. A small surf shop stocking basics was also recently opened on the beach here.

Sleeping
The cheapest places to sleep are squeezed between the médina and the seafront but are not necessarily great.
€ Hotel de Paris, T044-462149, is one of the best with big clean double rooms.
Camping International a couple of kilometres north at Sidi Bouzid has good facilities including a pool and pay hot showers.

Eating
Café M'Zoughan, on Pl de l'Independence, is a good pâtisserie and a nice place to get breakfast while **Café El Bahia** is the place to grab a snack and watch the world go by.

Essaouira

Travelling via the coastal road or the faster P8, arty Essaouira makes a great stopover for atmosphere alone. The bustling, craft filled, white walled médina, is all about ambience and has been a bohemian lure since Jimi Hendrix stayed here in the 1960s. Next to the médina the busy fishing port is also an old boats rehab zone where wooden hulls are ripped apart and rebuilt. From the kasbah a wide beach – popular with footie fanatics – follows the main road south towards Cap Sim. Offshore the Îles Purpuraires, named for their ancient production of purple dye, are home to a colony of falcons. Essaouira is Africa's windy city (the wind known locally as the *alizée*) so if you're into windsurfing then this place is your kind of heaven.

Sleeping
Essaouira is attracting an increasingly chic crowd so a lot of accommodation is geared to the higher end. There are however a number of good options that won't break the bank but be aware that in June the town is taken over by the **Gnaoua & World music festival** when accommodation can get booked up.
€ Hotel Smara, inside the ramparts on R Skala, has a roof terrace and clean double rooms from around 100dh (the best have a sea view around 160dh) – as with all rooms see it before you agree to it.
€ Dar Afram, R Sidi Magdoul at the western end of the médina by Bab al-Bahr entrance, T024-785657, www.dar-afram.com, is a fusion of modern Moroccan and relaxed European the result is a clean, friendly guesthouse with roof terrace and mini hammam. Rooms around 300dh.
Camping southbound on the road out of town, about 2 km from the medina is a small, walled site with good showers and toilets (even if it does feel a bit like a prison complex) and a good place to stop overnight (around 40dh van and 2 people) . Alternatively, you can overnight in the carpark near the harbour front, watched over by guardians for about 20dh – a popular spot.

Eating and drinking
Unquestionably the best place to eat here is at one of the fish grills set up between the port and the médina. Sitting at a communal table at midday or early evening, eat fresh fish off the boats from about 30dh (agree the price first) and watch the world fly by. On Moulay Hassan head to **Restaurant Essalam** for a cheap 3-course set menu of *harira*, couscous and fruit. **Restaurant Les Alizes** R la Skala is an atmospheric spot serving up generous portions of tasty, traditional Moroccan dishes. Set menu around 80dh.

Directory
Surf Shops There are a couple of wind/surfing shops here including **L'Ocean Vagabond** on the seafront and **Palais d'Ocean**, where you can pick up basics like wax etc. **Banks** Pl Moulay Hassan. **Internet** Av l'Istiqual – the main drag through the médina. **Pharmacies** Av l'Istiqual. **Tourist information** Av du Caire.

Sidi Kaouki

Some 25 km south of Essaouria, Sidi Kaouki is transforming from one-horse town to windsurfing beach resort, but luckily the metamorphosis seems to be slow. There are several snack-shacks here including the surf-inspired **Point Break**.
€ The established, simple **Residence Le Kaouki**, T024-783206, near the beach offers B&B from around 260-300dh and is popular with German windsurfers, www.sidikaouki.com.
€ Auberge de la Plage, T024-476600, www.kaouki.com, has simple, elegant and modern doubles (plus rooms sleeping 3 or 4) with ensuites or shared bathrooms B&B from 380-450dh. Evening meals also available.

Marrakech

From world leaders to leading creatives, the city of the south, has always had a hypnotic pull and for many Marrakech, with its wild and exotic médina, is their first introduction to Morocco.

The skyscape is dominated by the High Atlas mountains while the spiritual and physical heart of Marrakech is the Jemaâ el Fna or 'assembly of the dead' – 'La Place'. Once the site of public executions the market square, bursting with the weird and the wonderful, has an almost filmic quality; grill cafés rub shoulders with snake charmers and watersellers, while 'dentists' with molars piled high on rugs by their feet compete with storytellers, fire breathers and the musicians. The sensory overload is awesome and intoxicating so as with any busy city be aware of your wallet (although security has much improved in recent years). Watching over the square is the 12th-century Koutoubia minaret which, legend has it, bled its spirit into the city, giving Marrakech its colour. North of the square are a series of souks for every occasion – you probably won't need a 'guide' – just go with the flow – the hussle and haggle are all part of the experience. Surrounding the city, the ramparts stretch for 16 km defending Marrakech from the encroaching desert.

Marrakech-Menara **airport** is about 5 km southwest of the city – around a 60dh cab ride. The **train station** is on the edge of Guéliz, the new town – west of the médina. A *petit taxi* ride into the médina should cost about 15dh. Just outside the ramparts, the **bus station** on Bab Doukkala can offer long-distance solutions south to Agadir.

Sleeping

There are good cheap places to find around R Bab Agnaou south of Jemaâ el Fna but places do get packed out so try to book in advance.

€ **Hotel Central Place** , off Bab Agnaou on Deb Sidi Bouloukat is a good and popular cheap choice with rooms centred around a courtyard.

€ **Afriqua**, off Bab Agnaou, T024-442403, is another budget option with a roof terrace.

€ **Hotel Sherzade** , Derb Djama, south of La Place is a popular and more quality spot with riad –style accommodation and rooms leading off from a central courtyard that won't break the bank. Doubles from 220-660dh.

East off the square are a couple of good, cheapy choices including the clean, clinical € **Mimosa**, R des Banques, T024-426385.

DAMIEN POULLENOT

Cover up south of Cap Safi.

Eating

For atmosphere, eat at one of the open-air grills on the Jemaâ el Fna – the standards are pretty safe but if you're worried, choose something cooked to order. Or head to Chez Chegrouni on the square – a popular spot for excellent tagines for around 45dh and a bit of people watching. Former *Tracks* editor, Phil Jarratt, recommends: "**Stylo** in the souk. It's not too expensive and is an amazing experience. **Café Argana** on the square – you can't miss it – has great views especially at sunset and reasonable snacks. Just off Mohammed V, **L'Escale** does a great chicken 'n' chips – you can even get a beer here!"

Directory

Banks in the Ville Nouvelle there are plenty around the main Av Mohammed V while in the heart of the médina you can find them just off the main square including R Bab Agnaou. **Pharmacy** **Pharmacie Unite**, Ave des Nations Unies, off Pl du 16 Novembre open late. **Internet** There are plenty in the city including the conveniently placed **Hanan Internet** and **Cyber Koutoubia** on R Bab Agnaou. **Post office** R Bab Agnaou south of Jemaâ el Fna plus the main Pl du 16 Novembre office. **Tourist information** Av Mohammed V.

Immessouane

This sleepy one-horse town, has also begun to wake up over the past few years due to the huge numbers of surfers visiting. Despite the makeover of the Kahina into a surf camp and school, there is still little here other than a Japanese fishing company, a couple of basic shops and small cafés, an exposed and dusty **campsite** with limited facilities on the headland, but this may be set to change. If you're coming to stay, come prepared.

€ **Kahina Hostel**, T028-826032, www.kahinasurfschool.com, has a terrace overlooking the bay plus a comfortable Moroccan lounge as well as singles, doubles and rooms sleeping up to 5 – doubles from around €18, full board around €26. Board and suits available to hire.

Overview

When the vanguard of the freewheelin' 'Freeride Generation' rolled into this small coastal village at the dawn of the seventies, Taghazoute was a very different place to the one modern surfers jet into today. The blue and white patchwork of square houses, split by the main road, had yet to start its creeping migration out onto the point. To the villagers, the headland provided protection for the fishing boats, but the shaggy haired interlopers immediately recognised its quality. This collection of Aussies, Brits and Yanks formed a motley crew, carving Anchor Point on their single fins by day, smoking themselves to sleep by night. No communication with the outside world. No Internet surf checks or calls from home. The local community embraced these laid back visitors and soon an annual migration was underway, supplemented by those on the hippy trail.

For the next two decades, the 'Freecamp Generation' took up residence on the dusty, hazy points. The Source became base camp for the summiteers, a veritable united nations of colours, with orange VW Kombis, faded white Bedford ambulances and matt green ex-German army vans. Village buildings were transformed into the uniform terracotta we see today and the village high street grew as the local service sector expanded. The drone of Mohammed V's moped making its daily run with bread and provisions became a welcome sound and phone booths did a brisk trade as surfers queued to call home, hands filled with silver dhirams, making their weekly communication with the outside world. Line-ups were getting busier but there was a certain etiquette in the water, a nodded understanding. If you came to Morocco you came for the same reasons – to leave the hustle and bustle behind and just share some waves with new friends.

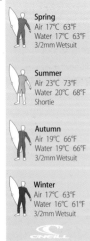

Spring
Air 17°C 63°F
Water 17°C 63°F
3/2mm Wetsuit

Summer
Air 23°C 73°F
Water 20°C 68°F
Shortie

Autumn
Air 19°C 66°F
Water 19°C 66°F
3/2mm Wetsuit

Winter
Air 17°C 63°F
Water 16°C 61°F
3/2mm Wetsuit

Breaks

1 Tamri Plage	14 Taghazoute Plage
2 KM 128 or Hicks'	15 Devil's Rock/Devil's Point
3 Cap Rhir	16 Banana Village
4 Boilers ★	17 The Left
5 Dracula's	18 Cement Factory
6 Hotel Point	19 Agadir Beach
7 Camel Point	20 Royal Groynes
8 Killer Point ★	21 Inezgane to Tifnite
9 The Source	22 Tifnite
10 Mysteries	23 Aglou Plage
11 Anchor Point ★	24 Mirhleft
12 Hash Point	25 Sidi Ifni
13 Panorama's ★	26 Saharan South

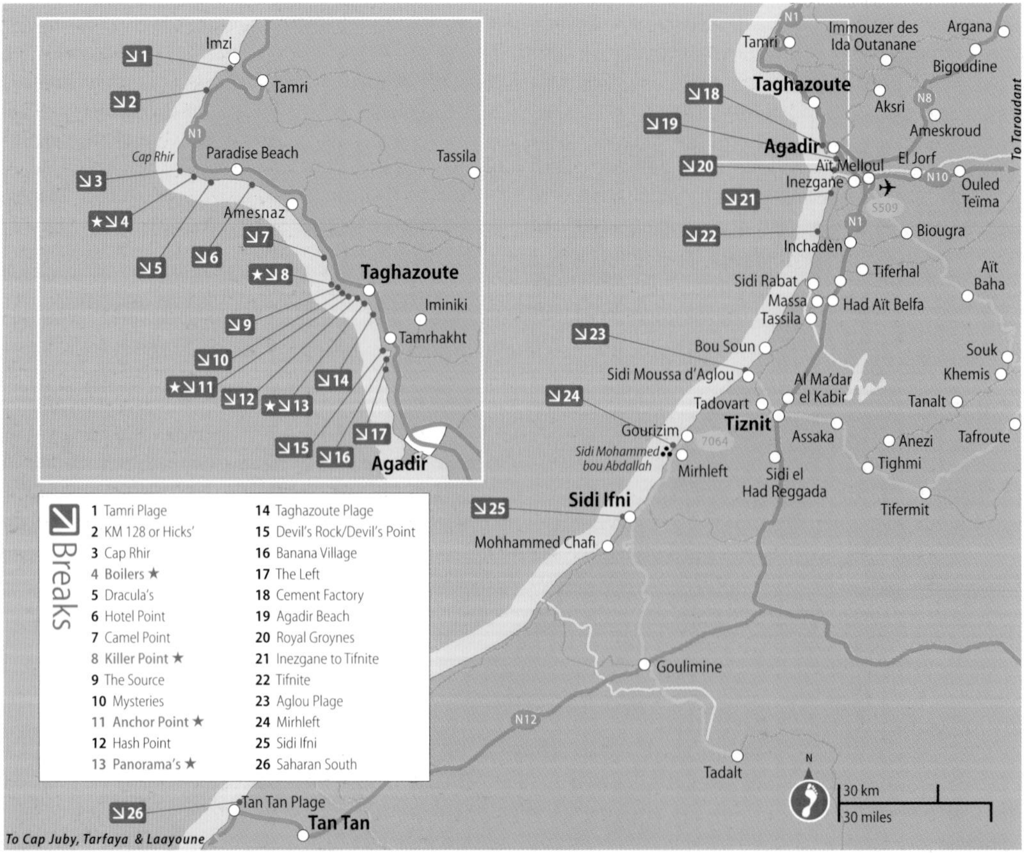

6'1" Rusty Pro-Ject

Shaper: Rusty Presiendorfer

6'1" x 18¼" x 2$^{1}/_{16}$"

Built with Surftech's proven TUFLITE construction.

Full round tail, low tail rocker with single concave into a tail that's pulled in through the last six inches to handle the lift from the deep concave. Low tail rocker and single concave creates a ride that is fast and drivey ideal for the long walls of Anchor Point.

Futures VFR3 fins.

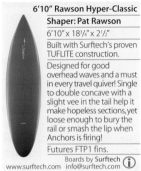

6'10" Rawson Hyper-Classic

Shaper: Pat Rawson

6'10" x 18¾" x 2½"

Built with Surftech's proven TUFLITE construction.

Designed for good overhead waves and a must in every travel quiver! Single to double concave with a slight vee in the tail help it make hopeless sections, yet loose enough to bury the rail or smash the lip when Anchors is firing!

Futures FTP1 fins.

Boards by **Surftech**
www.surftech.com info@surftech.com

Today, your morning bliss can be shattered by the harsh trill of mobile ringtones while checking Anchors, the internet café offers the opportunity for daily surf checks and email updates from 'back in the world'. The Government hasn't been slow to recognise the potential that Taghazoute offers, the region quietly earmarked for a big tourist development. New apartments already overlook The Source and Killers on the site of the old freecamp area, but bigger proposals have been outlined including a massive new complex that will stretch along the empty beachfront from Panoramas south towards Banana Village. There are even hushed discussions about a marina. Many now complain that the crowd and hassle factor in Morocco has got as bad as everywhere else, diminishing one of the major reasons that drew people here. So are we in danger of becoming the 'Free-for-all Generation'?

Just to the south of Agadir the coastline opens out into a huge expanse of points and beaches where few surfers bother to venture. Here you can surf alone with your travel companions, enjoy the arid scenery and a sense of adventure. In these villages the sight of visiting surfers can still illicit the offer of mint tea from the friendly locals.

Coastline

The geography of this coastline conspires to deliver a seemingly endless selection of sand bottomed points with a cluster of rocky reefs to the north. There are also huge open stretches of sandy beach running south of Agadir for anyone with a spirit of adventure to explore. Rounding Cap Rhir there lies a series of reefs and a beach that receive the full force of any northwesterly swell, but south of the cape, around Taghazoute, the coastline undulates with a series of points, each with slightly different characteristics. Their fickle nature is determined by the fact that sand builds up on the rocks and gives rise to changing characteristics that can vary greatly year to year, or even within the same swell season. A point that failed to break one year, may fire the next. With 5½ km of Taghazoute beachfront earmarked for a US$2 billion dollar development, including luxury hotels and golf courses, expect the coastline to change. Effects may include changes in sand deposition patterns and water run off.

Agadir shelters in the lee of Cap Rhir which means the huge, crescent-shaped sandy bay is an ideal tourist beach for those who descend upon the town looking for some winter sun. Heading south, the coastline opens out from the swell shadow into a series of beaches, rivermouths and points that pick up masses of swell. The point at Tifnite can be double overhead when Anchor Point is 3 ft. Sidi Ifni is a town that some intrepid surfers head for, with its relaxed line-up and excellent surf potential. But from here on, the only limit is time and road access. With a 4WD and a spare can of petrol, a whole world of possibilities open up. **NB** Plage Blanche south of Sidi Ifni is the proposed site of another luxury resort.

Local environment

The villages around Agadir have no waste water infrastructure so raw sewage ends up in the ocean. Bigger the village, bigger the sewage outflows. The groundwater can also become contaminated from farm chemicals such as fertilizer. The water delivered to the campsite and the houses comes from a local aquifer at Banana Village, so it isn't advisable to drink, even if boiled first. Stick to sealed bottled water. Also bear in mind that eating out is somewhat of a lottery. Food hygiene standards are very different here.

The vibe in the water has changed as the crowds have got bigger and bigger. Unfortunately the culprits are generally Europeans and Australians. Toby from *The Surf Experience* has been running camps there for years and says "When we first went there with some crews there was only Surf Sans Frontieres, very laid-back and a bunch of space and cordiality on every point. Recently I saw 90 surfers on Anchors as the sun came up! This is only Taghazoute, there is a whole bunch of spots along the entire Northern and Southern sections of the coast."

Getting around

Taghazoute is one of the few places in Morocco where you can happily exist without a car, if you don't mind being limited to the breaks around the village. Anchors, Killers and Mysteries are all within walking distance. However they are crowded and a will allow access to the many other breaks in the area. The roads around Taghazoute are generally very good and the P8 allows access to all the major breaks. Those without a car can take one of the regular buses from the village square to either Aourir to the south or to Boilers and Tamri Plage to the north. Tickets are cheap and the buses run every 30 minutes.

DAMIEN POULLENOT

Freeriding Taghazoute – the ethereal moment captured.

Breaks

BEACH BREAK

↘1 Tamri Plage

- **Conditions** Small NW to W swell, offshore in E winds
- **Hazards/tips** Crowded, lacks power
- **Sleeping** Taghazoute » p390

This is a beach that often flatters to deceive. Overall Tamri Plage is disappointing, although on first impressions from the cliff top lay-by it looks like a promising beach break. This is the place everyone seems to head for when there's no swell in the Taghazoute to Boilers region, so expect it to be crowded. Works on all tides but better nearer low tide, it easily maxes out in bigger swells. Waves begin to break out from the rocks to the south of the beach as the tide drops and there may also be a right-hander in front of the rivermouth. The waves are great for beginners, but often lack any real power or drive.

Park in the lay-by on top of the cliffs at the southern end of the beach, just off the main road (but be prepared to be hassled by local kids for dihram – have a couple of stickers or pens instead). Best peaks usually form in front of the cliffs.

RIGHT-HAND REEF BREAK

↘2 KM 128 or Hicks'

- **Conditions** Small NW swells, offshore in light E winds
- **Hazards/tips** Rocky reef, shallow, urchins and difficult access
- **Sleeping** Taghazoute » p390

Low tide reef that needs a small clean swell and glassy conditions to work. Sits out in a very exposed spot so easily maxes out and is easily blown out. Access by jumping off the rocks; come in over the shelf just to the south of the break. Always wear boots as the reef and shelf are both urchin infested. The expression "Three's a crowd" was invented for this break. If people are already in, try somewhere else – there are other reefs in the area. When heading north from Taghazoute, turn left at the 'Essaouira 128 km' sign. Park on the cliff top and you should see a right-hand reef breaking at low tide.

RIGHT-HAND POINT BREAK

↘3 Cap Rhir

- **Conditions** Medium and big swells, offshore in southeasterly and easterly winds.
- **Hazards/tips** Big powerful waves, tricky access, rocks.
- **Sleeping** Taghazoute » p390

Out along the exposed end section of Cap Rhir north of Boilers sits a long, right, point break wave. Not for the faint-hearted and rarely surfed. It's a good place to escape the crowds and produces some epic waves in big swells. Access is best by 4WD or sturdy hire car. Explore north from Boilers or south from the lighthouse. Sharp, urchin-infested reef – access to the break is tricky, as is entry and exit from the water. Tides depend on swell size. Gets big.

RIGHT-HAND REEF BREAK

↘4 Boilers

- **Swell** N to W
- **Wind** NE to E
- **Tide** All tides
- **Size** 3-8 ft
- **Length** 50-100 m plus
- **Bottom** Rocky reef
- **Ability level** Intermediate to advanced
- **Best months** Sep-Mar
- **Board** Performance Thruster
- **Access** Paddle out between huge rock and boiler, in over rocks
- **Hazards/tips** Sharp reef, urchins, difficult exit in big swells, crowds.
- **Sleeping** Taghazoute » p390

Although Anchor Point gets all the plaudits, Boilers has been the saviour of many a Moroccan surf trip. This right-hander is probably the most consistent point in the region, and while not exactly the longest, it certainly is a rewarding wave. Named after the huge ship's boiler that sits next to the peak, this spot is a great indicator reef and is clearly visible from the coast road. If Boilers is maxed out, head for Taghazoute; if too small, head for

ALEX LAUREL

4 Boilers.

Morocco Taghazoute & the south Breaks

Tamri. If the wind is calm and a 6-ft swell is running, it can reel off perfect wave after perfect wave. Works at all tides but better nearer low when it can throw up the odd hollow section. If the swell picks up, the wave can section and exiting the water can be a real challenge, high tailing it over the jagged, urchin infested reef between sets. Getting into the line-up is a simpler prospect, a short paddle to the right of the boiler, but time it well in big swells. You won't be doing yourself any favours here by not wearing boots.

Boilers can have a weather system all of its own so is always worth a check. Due to the effect of the surrounding hills it can be onshore everywhere else, yet offshore here but it does have an ability to switch wind directions at the drop of a hat – or the flip of a board as it blows away down the point. The main downside is the crowds. At times the line-up is packed and can get hassley. Seems silly when there are so many other prospects around to seek out.

*If you like **Boilers**, try **Punta dos Picos** in Spain (see page 253) or **Easkey Right** in Ireland (see page 131).*

RIGHT-HAND REEF BREAK

5 Dracula's

- **Conditions** Medium NW swells, offshore in E to NE winds
- **Hazards/tips** Tricky access, shallow with urchins, experienced surfers only
- **Sleeping** Taghazoute ›› *p390*

Here is a spot that for years was overlooked but has suddenly become a lot more in vogue. This could be due to the fact that crowding at Boilers has pushed numbers onto this neighbouring break, or it could be due to a change in the type of waves we surf. The tricky access and exit used to put many off this fast, hollow right but this seems to be less of a disincentive when the reef is empty and firing. Park just south of the break in the small fishermen's car park.

TIM NUNN

5 A tricker, suckier, punchier proposition than its more popular neighbour.

RIGHT-HAND POINT BREAK

6 Hotel Point

- **Conditions** Big NW swell, E to NE winds
- **Hazards/tips** Rips when big, sheltered from winds, rocks
- **Sleeping** Taghazoute ›› *p390*

Hotel Point is a mid to low tide, right point located where the road bends out along the point towards Boilers. It needs a big swell to break, but it can be calm and glassy even on the windiest of days due to the sheltering hills. Breaks in front of the small village. On a big swell, long barrels are there for the taking but beware of rips. It is rarely surfed as it works when many other points are firing.

RIGHT-HAND POINT BREAK

7 Camel Point

- **Conditions** Small to medium NW swells, offshore in E winds
- **Hazards/tips** Suitable for all surfers
- **Sleeping** Taghazoute ›› *p390*

If the crowds of Taghazoute are getting too much then head round the corner from Killers into the next bay and check out the headland at the northern edge. Camel Point is named after a rock that looks like a camel reclining next to the beach. This right-hand point works well on a low to mid tide in small to medium swells. The take-off point is out level with the end of the headland and, although the wave is often sectiony, it can be ridden through to the beach on good days. Not a world-class wave, but a great place to leave the crowds behind. Good spot for intermediate surfers as it has a sand bottom and easy access from the beach.

RIGHT-HAND POINT BREAK

8 Killer Point

- **Swell** N, NW, W
- **Wind** E
- **Tide** All tides
- **Size** 2-10 ft
- **Length** 50-300 m
- **Bottom** Sand-covered reef
- **Ability level** Intermediate to advanced
- **Best months** Oct-Mar
- **Board** Thruster to semi-gun
- **Access** Paddle off the beach at the Source, not from the cliffs
- **Hazards/tips** Crowds, rips when big, heavy wave
- **Sleeping** Taghazoute ›› *p390*

The points around the Taghazoute region all have a similar geological make-up. The flat rock reefs have a deposit of sand that builds up over them during the quiet of the summer, which is then groomed by the season's early swells into long sandbars. Some years these can be epic, and in others a wave may not break at all. Killer Point is one such place. Catch it good and you'll be rewarded with the best wave in the whole of

DAMIEN POULLENOT

8 Killers

the region, outclassing Anchor Point and all other contenders. At other times it will be sectiony, rippy and frustrating. It is certainly the most flexible of the waves within walking distance of Taghazoute. In small swells the outside section can Hoover up the passing lines and produce fun, short rides way out from the beach. But it's in medium to big swells that it really comes alive. The take off is steep and challenging, the wave then bowls and zippers down the reef. Unlike the big walls of Anchors, Killers opens up into hollow sections and is a real challenge. The pack often pushes too deep in an effort to pick off the cherries, so keep an eye on the line-up points and stay patient. There is a huge channel that runs out to the peak, but in big swells there is a nasty rip pushing down towards Mysteries. This is a wave for competent surfers only. You're taking off in front of cliffs (with caves) and it's a long swim in if you lose your board. Best at low to three quarter tide, but often has surfable waves at high in the right swell. Legend has it that Killer Point is named after the killer whales that are occasionally seen here.

ⓘ ***If you like** Killer Point, try **Safi** (see page 376) or **Roca Puta** in Euskadi (see page 213).*

A FRAME REEF BREAK

↘9 The Source

- **Conditions** Small to medium NW swells, offshore in E to NE winds
- **Hazards/tips** Crowded, suitable for all surfers
- **Sleeping** Taghazoute » *p390*

This sand-covered reef works in small to medium swells at low to mid tides and gets its name from the natural spring that emerges on the shore nearby. Breaking both left and right, the Source can be one of the few places where goofy footers may pick up a few front-side waves. A sign of the big changes in Morocco as surfing destination is that that the ancient freecamping area that used to overlook these breaks is now buried beneath a new luxury apartment block.

RIGHT-HAND REEF BREAK

↘10 Mysteries

- **Conditions** All N, NW and W swells, offshore in E to NE winds
- **Hazards/tips** Crowded, inconsistent
- **Sleeping** Taghazoute » *p390*

In the years that the sand deposition has worked in our favour, Mysteries can be an amazing wave. In other years, it's a short fun wall. Needs some water on the reef to work, so best surfed from mid to high tide. The take-off zone here is notoriously small and it gets crowded. Can be a bit of a zoo.

RIGHT-HAND POINT BREAK

↘12 Hash Point

- **Conditions** Medium NW swells, E winds
- **Hazards/tips** Pollution from village, but an easy-going atmosphere
- **Sleeping** Taghazoute » *p390*

Hash Point sits in the heart of Taghazoute village by the picturesque beach where the local fishermen keep their multicoloured boats. A wave of variable quality, usually a short wall in front of rocks. Usually uncrowded and can be a great place for an evening session for those staying in the village. On good years it may even join up with Panorama's.

RIGHT-HAND POINT BREAK

↘13 Panorama's

- **Swell** NW to W
- **Wind** NE
- **Tide** Low to mid
- **Size** 3-8 ft
- **Length** 50-150 m
- **Bottom** Sand-covered reef
- **Ability level** Intermediate to Adavanced
- **Best Months** Oct-Mar
- **Board** Thruster to semi-gun
- **Access** Paddle off beach or jump off rocks in front of apartments
- **Hazards/tips** Not usually crowded, rips pushing south when big
- **Sleeping** Taghazoute » *p390*

A real Jekyll and Hyde this wave, one that's often overlooked in favour of its more glamorous siblings. This point break can be a speeding, hollow Indo style gem, a slow frustrating wall or a closeout depending on the combination of swell, tide and sand banks. Catch it good and Panorama's can deliver

Right-hand point break

↘11 Anchor Point

- **Swell** N, NW, W
- **Wind** E to NE
- **Tide** Low to three-quarter tide
- **Size** 2-12 ft
- **Length** 50-200 m
- **Bottom** Sand-covered reef
- **Ability level** Intermediate to advanced
- **Best months** Oct-Mar
- **Board** Thruster to semi-gun
- **Access** Jump off the big rock near the end of the point
- **Hazards/tips** Crowds, rips when big, access and exit
- **Sleeping** Taghazoute » *p390*

LUCIA GRIGGI

DAMIEN POULLENOT

Top: 11 Johnny Fryer enjoying classic Anchors. **Above:** Anchor point isn't all glassy walls and soul arches – when the sand banks and the pressure systems conspire it can show its mean, moody side. And it sucks.

Anchor Point (Anchors/Ankas) is a wave of world renown. It conjures up images of soul surfers, arcing bottom turns on single fins in the heady days of the seventies, Vee-Dub campers parked up on the point in a makeshift encampment. Over three decades later the encampments have gone and so has much of the relaxed vibe. Expect the line-up to be packed every time the wave breaks and surfers don't so much soul arch, as weave through the flotilla littering the shoulder. But the wave is still the same. Offering that big, green wall, those long leg aching rides and at 8 ft plus, when the wave really comes into it's own, a world-class challenge.

Stretching north from the edge of Taghazoute, this rocky ledge of a point leads out to the old anchor factory that gives the place its' name. How long before this prime piece of real estate is developed into a spa or hotel complete with infinity pool? When the huge winter storms roll through the north Atlantic, it'll only be a matter of days before the waiting point comes to life. Anchors works best from low to three-quarter tide and picks up less swell than the other waves in the Taghazoute area. It doesn't really get going until it's over 4 ft, and if it's small it will be packed. The bigger it gets, the more the crowds will thin out. Anchor Point at 6 ft plus is great, at 8-10 ft even better. Wait for a lull and jump off the rock at the end of the point and make for the line-up, but watch out for big rips. Waves start breaking way out beyond the point and can fire through to Hash Point in the village. Don't expect many barrels as this wave is all about big walls. To exit the water in a big swell, aim for the small beach near Taghazoute.

ⓘ ***If you like*** *Anchor Point, try* ***Doolin Point*** *in Ireland (see page 134) or* ***Skaill Bay*** *in Orkney (see page 52).*

some of the most exciting waves in the area.

The Panorama Café once overlooked this right-hand point break, lending the spot its name, but sadly is there no more. Currents and swell conspire to deposit sand around the point where the rocky headland meets the long, flat expanse of Taghazoute beach. This stretch of sand is popular with holidaymakers and has a seemingly endless soccer game in progress. If Anchor Point is firing, Panorama's should be too which helps keep crowds down. A low tide break where barrel after barrel spins off the point, but at size it is not for the faint-hearted. A rip pushes away from the take-off point by the apartments and a difficult, steep take-off leads into a fast, driving section. Blow the take-off on a big day and you'll have a nightmare paddle all the way round again from the inside. Make the drop, pull in and you'll be rewarded with a barrel to rival any in the region. Choose between a well-timed paddle off the rocks or the safer, but arm taxing route from the beach.

ⓘ ***If you like*** *Panorama's, try* ***Devil's Rock*** *(see page 388)* *or* ***Lafitenia*** *in France* *(see page 194)**.*

ALEX LAUREL

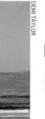

DEMI TAYLOR

Above: 13 Pete Mendia sampling Taghazoute's Panoramic pleasures. **Left: 20** Royal Groynes.

BEACH BREAK

↘14 Taghazoute Plage

- **Conditions** Small to medium NW swells, offshore in E to SE winds
- **Hazards/tips** Poor water quality
- **Sleeping** Taghazoute » *p390*

Taghazoute beach is probably the least glamorous of all the surfing options in the area. It starts at Panorama's and runs all the way to Devil's Rock. If everywhere else is flat you might get a few short waves here between low and mid tide. Water quality here may be affected by the run-off from the campsite toilets, but having said that there is probably less pollution than comes from Taghazoute itself. Banks can be found in front of the cafés and the campsite.

RIGHT-HAND POINT BREAK

↘15 Devil's Rock/Devil's Point

- **Conditions** All N, NW and W swells, offshore in E winds
- **Hazards/tips** Crowds, outer section shallow reef
- **Sleeping** Taghazoute » *p390*

Look out onto the northern point at the market village of Aourir, or Banana Village as it is known locally, and you'll see the long, right hand point of Devil's Rock. The wave has two sections, a faster more hollow outside section that bowls around a reef, and a long, walling inside section that runs from the edge of the headland through to the beach. This inside section is the most popular, consistent and attracts intermediate surfers as it breaks over sand. The outside section can offer heavy, fast barrels and is really best left to the experienced. This quality point works on all states of tide, but the outside section is at its most hollow at low. The headland provides a great vantage point to view the action and access to the water is down a cliff track. It can get pretty crowded, especially the inside section.

A-FRAME REEF BREAK

↘16 Banana Village

- **Conditions** Small to medium NW swells, offshore in an E to NE wind
- **Hazards/tips** Can get crowded
- **Sleeping** Taghazoute » *p390*

On the opposite side of the bay to Devil's Rock sits an A-frame reef that produces a good left and short right. A fun wave that works well in small and medium swells, providing a change of scenery from the many right points. Named after the Village, which has banana stalls lining the main road. The reef can be checked from the main coast road south towards Agadir just as you leave the village heading south. Parking is possible right in front of the break, accessed through the market/car park at the roundabout.

LEFT-HAND REEF BREAK

↘17 The Left

- **Conditions** Small to medium NW swells, offshore in E winds
- **Hazards/tips** Wednesday is Souk day!
- **Sleeping** Taghazoute » *p390*

Look to the south of Banana Village reef and you should see this short, powerful left hand barrel. A popular wave with local bodyboarding grommets and one of only a few true barreling left-handers on this stretch of coastline. Wednesday afternoons are packed as the kids from the local school have surfing as part of their school sports.

RIGHT-HAND POINT BREAK

↘18 Cement Factory

- **Conditions** Medium to big N to NW swells, offshore in E winds
- **Hazards/tips** Pollution and access
- **Sleeping** Agadir » *p392*

If you happen to be heading into Agadir when a decent swell is running you may notice white water breaking out on the point in front of the cement factory and Camping Gaz works that make such a picturesque backdrop to the coastal road. This is home to one of the areas most obvious, yet least-surfed waves. Beyond the shantytown lies a sand-covered rock point tapering in from the northern fringe. It can throw up endless J-Bay like barrels and reeling walls. The fact that the bay is fringed by shipwrecks is testament to the power of the swells that hit here making The Cement Factory a pretty consistent break. It works in all tides and is offshore in southerly through to easterly winds. The down side? Due to the bay's position in a rundown part of town and its proximity to these industrial plants, this wave is rarely surfed. Water quality is what you'd expect but those who've braved the line-up claim it's the best wave on this whole stretch of coastline. See it in full flow and you'll be tempted.

BEACH BREAK

↘19 Agadir Beach

- **Conditions** Big NW to W swell, offshore in NE winds
- **Hazards/tips** Pretty poor, flat beach
- **Sleeping** Agadir » *p392*

You can pretty much right this place off as a surf spot. It's a flat, sheltered, crescent-shaped beach that gets little swell or closes out. You may see local grommets out.

GROYNE AND BEACH BREAK

↘20 Royal Groynes

- **Conditions** Small to medium NW swells, offshore in E winds
- **Hazards/tips** Access by car, depends on whether the King is in residence
- **Sleeping** Agadir » *p392*

A little bit of exploration will bring you to this high quality beach break. Sandbanks form alongside huge stone breakwaters, producing classic lefts and rights. Works through the tides and picks up plenty of swell. The first wave is a right-hander that peels off the most southerly groyne and can produce excellent hollow waves. The other side of the breakwater sees a fast, barrelling left and across the channel peels another barrelling right. This break picks up more swell than the breaks around Taghazoute. If the King is in residence, you may have to park and walk 20 mins.

BEACH BREAK

↘21 Inezgane to Tifnite

- **Conditions** Small to medium NW swells, offshore in E to SE winds
- **Hazards/tips** Isolated spots, don't surf alone
- **Sleeping** Agadir » *p392*

A stretch of exposed beaches that work on all tides and pick up heaps of swell. This is a huge stretch of beach break that is very rarely surfed. Access is via rough *piste* roads off the main P30 south from Agadir.

RIGHT POINT AND REEF BREAK

↘22 Tifnite

- **Conditions** Small to big NW swells, offshore in E to SE winds
- **Hazards/tips** Isolated waves that can be powerful
- **Sleeping** Agadir » *p392*

Turn right off the P30 at Inchadèn, head west and you come to a large, crescent-shaped, dune-backed bay. There is a rocky ledge point at the northern fringe on which the village of Tifnite sits, but access is by 4WD or on foot across the beach. The main break is a long right hand point that peaks outside the bay and wraps all the way through to the beach on the inside. Waves here can be over 10 ft in a decent swell although the crowd factor is always pretty low. Not as perfect as Anchor Point, but still very good and more hollow. A wave for more advanced surfers.

A second break known as **Outsides** sits, strange as it may seem, outside the northern edge of the bay, on the exposed shoreline in front of the village. This is a fast, hollow, set of waves that hold swell up to 8 ft, breaking over a sand covered rock shelf that produces a couple of reef waves. They pick up a huge amount of swell, the main break being a right but there is also a left and a peak there as well. These waves work from 3 ft up to 8 ft plus, with easy access off the rocks. On big days, watch out for 'outside' sneaker sets. This spot is very rarely surfed and just checking the spot usually attracts a few villagers keen to pass the time of day. Also check in front of the army post at the southern end of the bay, where a more intermediate friendly left wraps through to the beach. The hour drive down from Taghazoute puts many off, making it a great place to escape the crowds.

BEACH AND RIVERMOUTH BREAK

↘23 Aglou Plage

- **Conditions** Small to medium NW swells, offshore in SE winds
- **Hazards/tips** Very quiet break
- **Sleeping** Tiznit » *p393*

Aglou is worth checking on the trip south. It works through all tides and the rivermouth can have some excellent waves depending on the banks. Access from Tiznit on the 7062.

BEACH BREAK

↘24 Mirhleft

- **Conditions** Small to medium N to W swells, offshore in SE winds
- **Hazards/tips** Picks up heaps of swell, usually pretty quiet
- **Sleeping** Tiznit/Sidi Ifni » *p393*

More and more people are heading out to explore the southern breaks and the coast road to Sidi Ifni uncovers plenty of surfing potential. Spots like Mirleft – which, with its cliff-lined bays has more than a passing resemblance to breaks around north coast Cornwall – pick up loads of swell and, depending on the banks, can produce excellent, hollow waves. Mirleft is home to a surf school, small surf shop and a number of local surfers. The small, low-key village is expanding with some upmarket coastal redevelopment but for now retains its mellow atmosphere.

BEACH AND REEF BREAK

↘25 Sidi Ifni

Conditions Small to medium N to W swells, offshore in SE winds
Hazards/tips Pollution, access.
Sleeping Sidi Ifni » *p393*

This collection of breaks around the southern town of Sidi Ifni are predominantly offshore in southeasterly winds but gets mixed reviews from many who go there. The village has laid-back attitude and relaxed line-up overlooked by the cliff-top settlement. There is a long righthander and across the channel you'll find a shorter left. Breaks around this area can be a good place to escape the crowds, but it's a harsh environment to surf on your own.

ALL TYPES

↘26 Saharan South

Conditions All swells, offshore in southeasterly or southerly winds.
Hazards/tips Isolation, go with other surfers for safety.
Sleeping South of Sidi Ifni » *p393*

If you're going to hit the south of the country, go well prepared. Don't go alone, if you're not in a 4WD then go with at least one other van, plenty of food, water and spare fuel. Do your research and get some good advice from people you meet who've already done it. Access to much of the coast is limited and there are huge stretches of cliffs. Still, there are plenty of virgin breaks out there...

Practicalities

Taghazoute

Travelling along the P8, Taghazoute is about 150 km south of Essaouira and 15 km north of Agadir. The hippies and surfers that have headed to this unremarkable looking village since the 1970s, have created a unique and relaxed micro-community where men in *djellabas* share a table with salt-crusted crews in boardies. It is a fully contained neighborhood (in fact the only thing lacking is an ATM) with cafés, general stores, a mosque, (basic) surf shop and (good) surf repair shop, internet café and launderette centred around the main drag that bisects the village. There's also a small market on the main square selling fish – wares vary daily depending on the catch but there are always a few good deals. Get there by midday and smell check it for freshness. The village has long been earmarked for 'improvements' and the face and feeling of Taghazoute is changing – freecamping at Mysteries is out and chic new apartments at La Source are in. To get out and about, a regular bus runs to Tamri from around the mosque about every half hour while a bus to Agadir departs from by to the main square.

Sleeping

There are apartments in Taghazoute overlooking the sea at Panorama's and Anchors for around 1600-2500dh a week for 2 (higher prices during Christmas week when demand is greater). The apartments overlooking La Source are high quality, well finished and furnished and come with a private pool. Many of the surf tour operators advertise this complex with 8 of the 9 s/c apts sleeping 4. Some of the best deals can be found with Errant, www.errantsurf holidays.co.uk – around €900 per week for plus hire car. There are also cheap rooms available in private houses – check how secure your room will be. Don't worry if you are stuck for somewhere to stay, there are plenty of local agents vying for business.
€ Hotel Atlantique, is clean, can supply you with breakfast and a good instant base for a night.
Surf camps Many surf camps have sprung up in and around Taghazoute offering a variety of services from guiding to tutoring at varying levels. Check what is included in the price (most importantly daily transport to the best breaks for your ability as well as food and accommodation) before handing

ALEX LAUREL

4 Jason Apparicio turning up the dial for a rapid boil.

over your precious holiday time and cash. Recommended are UK-based **Moroccan Surf Adventures**, www.morocsurf.com based in Tamrhakht, 2 km south of Taghazoute. They offer a great, personal service including daily transport to the best breaks, video analysis, comfortable (not dorm) accommodation, airport transfers and half board (with optional fantastic dinner) from €400 per week.
Dynamic Loisirs also in Tamrhakht, T028-314655, www.surf-morocco.com, is a popular camp with French surfers.

Camping

Freecamping at Mysteries and around Taghazoute has been stamped out as the wheel of development rolls on. Where campers once pitched up for months on end, apartment complexes now stand.
Camping Taghazoute, south of the village, overlooks Taghazoute Plage. Vast, dusty and featureless, facilities are extremely basic but it is cheap and does offer protection against break-ins so it gets packed out. You also get the daily rounds from locals touting everything from carpets and rugs to fruit and fish. About 25dh per night for a van and 2 people, although in the face of development, the life of the site is limited.
Atlantica Parc, T028-820805, www.atlanticaparc.com, 7 km north of the village, is a modern French style campsite complete with a pool, bungalows and mobile homes to rent (from around 3000dh per week). Camping from around 80 dh per day for 2 people and a van (longer stays of 30 days or more yield better rates). The beach is a 5-min stroll away. Although English is spoken, a better reception is usually received when French is used.

Eating and drinking

There are plenty of cheap cafés and restaurants lining the main drag in the village selling the usuals like tagines and omletes, though with variable hygiene standards eating out can be a bit of a wheel of fortune – dine out in Taghazoute often enough and eventually your number should come up.
Brahim's Café, at Devil's Rock is a great spot to have a post surf mint tea or "calamari to die for", as recommended by Denny of Moroccan Surf Adventures.

Self catering is a great option here. Head a couple of kilometres south to **Aourir** (Banana Village) on a Wed for the **seafront souk** where you can pick up fresh fruit, veg and spices as well as a tagine to cook it all in and other essentials.

Directory

Surf Shop The **Ankor Surf Shop**, opposite Café Florida on the main road, is basic (a lot is second-hand) and a bit pricey but has wax, boards, leashes and boardies as well as basic camping equipment. The board repair shops that spring up each season are normally pretty good and reasonable – about 500dh will fix a clean break.
Internet On the main road, connection isn't that fast but it's always full
Chemist South end of the village just off the main road it's well stocked with all the basic essentials. **Police** Just off the main square. **Petrol Afriqua** main street Aourir.
Van repairs If you're in a van that needs some TLC, get it done here at one of the mechanics on the road south to Tamrhakht – welding, roof racks, resprays and repairs are extremely cheap.

Flat spells

Close shave Smarten up your act for customs for the return journey – get a cut-throat shave and a haircut at the barber in Taghazoute just off the main square – about 20dh for a shave, 40dh for a haircut.

Golf There are several courses in and around Agadir: The **Royal Club de Golf**, about 12 km outside Agadir, T028-248551, is updating from a 9 to 18 hole course and is the most reasonably priced (around 300dh per 18 holes). There are also the pricier **Golf les Dunes**, Chemin Oued Souss, on the road to Inezgane, T028-834690, with 3 9-hole courses and the newly opened **Golf du Soleil**, Chemin des Dunes, T028-337229, www.golfdusoleil.com. Both around 600dh per 18 holes and compulsory caddies.

Hammam For a luxury hammam experience, stop by the Sofitel Hotel, Agadir, Baie des Palmiers, T028-820088, which is reasonably priced for non-residents.

Inland oasis Just south of Taghazoute, head 50 km into the hills on the road between Aourir and Tamrhakht to **Imouzzer des Ida Outanane** – the seasonal waterfalls and plunge pool that are usually be tempted into life between Feb and Jul. Even in the dry season, it is lovely and worth a trip out for a different perspective of the Moroccan landscape. Thursday is market day when there is a bit of a buzz about the place – it's also the easiest time to organise transport with locals keen to split the cost of a grand taxi. On the way you'll pass the palm fringed gorge **Paradise Valley** which is also a great mini trip out.

Souk Agadir's souk on the southern edge of town is open every day but Monday and does play towards the tourist. This walled, covered market is half fruit and veg and half tat, among which there are few bargins to be had.

DEMI TAYLOR

13 The view from the line-up may have changed but the wave is still a fast, hollow underestimated pleasure.

Agadir

20 min south of Taghazoute, the port town and beach resort of Agadir is the royal choice (though not necessarily the best surf choice unless you've scored a great package deal). The King of Morocco, Mohammed VI, has his summer palace just south of the town, while the Saudi royal family favours northern Agadir – so much so that they had the road rebuilt, connecting their palace to the town. A huge earthquake in 1960 destroyed the town and much of its history, killing more than 15,000 of the inhabitants. In the fairly charmless rebuild the entire town shifted south and, with a 9-km beach out front, was constructed with tourism in mind. With its coastal climate and relaxed drinking laws, it's a hotspot for visiting Arabs and over-wintering Europeans alike and with casinos, nightlife and attached sex industry, plus ubiquitous McDonald's is the 'sin city' of the Muslim world.

If you're using it as a jumping off point, you can get to most destinations via **bus/taxi** from Pl Salam at the bottom end of R Fes on the southern edge of the town. For Taghazoute, jump on 12 or 14 (about 5dh). The main **car hire** companies are based at the other end of town, centred around the north end of Mohammed V – get ready to haggle. **Al Massira Airport**, T028-839112, 25 km southeast of Agadir, is a popular entry point given its proximity to Taghazoute (about a 50-min drive) and has the essentials – bureau de change, ATM, car hire etc. A *grand taxi* into Agadir should cost about 200dh – more at night. Some will accommodate boards (for a fee) remember board straps. They're licensed to take 6 people and won't leave until it's full or you agree to pay for the empty spaces.

Sleeping

Package deals to Agadir with **First Choice**, **Thomson**, **Air Tours** or the rest of the gang usually come with a fair standard of room and can be the cheapest option for a 2-week stay. Given the choice, this is not the ideal place to base yourself for a surf trip to the region, however, if you want a room for the night there are plenty of choices, some of the cheapest being in the Talborjt area. Some of the best include:

€ Hotel El Bahia, R El Mehdi Bin Toumert, T028-822724, clean, tidy room with a courtyard you can chill out in and the cheaper, more simple.

€ Hotel Canaria, T028-846727, Place Lahcen Tamri on the opposite side of the square from El Bahia with rooms around 100dh.

Camping **Camping International d'Agadir**, on north end of Av Mohammed V, is not a bad bet for a night. It's got good facilities, great showers, is near the town but gets pretty cramped.

Eating and drinking

For good cheap eats, head to the fish cafés by the port at the north end of town. Menus are based on the day's catch and the restaurants, set up back to back on long plastic covered trestle tables, compete for business. Open midday to early evening, 50dh should get you a good meal.

Mickey Burger, Hassan II, is the best burger and chips in town and possibly the world. They mince the meat for each burger as you place your order and the potatoes are freshly chipped and fried. The daddy of burgers comes complete with a slice of melted cheese and a fried egg on top.

Restaurant Mille et Une Nuits (1001 nights), R 29 de Fevrier, is a good place to head for affordable but authentic Moroccan fare including tagines and couscous. If you're looking to shake your money-maker at one of the big hotel's nightclubs, be aware that a number of the ladies there are literally that and could be 'pay to play'! No town is complete without the mandatory 'Irish Bar' just off Av 20 Août.

Directory

Surf shops There are a couple of spots to pick up basics including **Marine and Sport** on the seafront. **Internet** There are several handily placed internet cafes on the main Hassan II and Mohammed V – connection around 10dh per hr. **Chemist** 24-hr pharmacy near the post office on Prince Moulay Abdallah also check the door of the tourist office for updates and other pharmacies. **Police** R 18 Novembre. **Post office** Cnr Av Prince Moulay Abdallah and Av Sidi Mohammed. **Tourist information** Av Mohammed V, T028-840307. **Supermarkets** **Uniprix**, Hassan II is a good place to stock up on food (booze also). **Marjane**, Mohammed V, heading south out of town towards the airport, this French style supermarket is full of home comforts including alcohol.

Tiznit

South of Agadir the N1 runs inland to Tiznit, a walled market town known for its silver jewellery; head to the souk at Pl el Mechouar just inside the main entrance. It's also the main focal point for the region and a good place to stock up before pushing south; just outside the main medina entrance, key amenities centre around Ave 20 Aout.

Sleeping

There are plenty of cheap placed to crash on Pl Mechouar.

€ **Hotel des Tourists**, is clean, relaxed and a good choice with hot showers – doubles around 90dh.

€ **Aglou Beach Hotel**, Aglou Plage, T028-866196, www.agloubeach.com, is in a great spot offering comfortable beach side accommodation with bathrooms 250dh plus the optional extra of balconies. Breakfast 20dh plus international restaurant serving lunch and dinner.

There is also a **campsite** just south of the médina which is basic but fine for a night or two. About 15 km northwest of the town.

Mirleft

The relaxed, bohemian town of Mirleft, around 40 km south of Tiznit is an easy and happy place to loose yourself for a few days. It has life's essentials including daily market, post office, basic surf shop and surf school, **Aftas Trip**, www.aftastrip.com, plus internet. Unfortunately there is no bank here so make sure you've filled up your wallet in Tiznit. The charm of the village is beginning to attract developers looking to build upmarket riads.

Sleeping

There are plenty of cheap placed to crash on Pl Mechouar.

€ **Hotel Café Restaurant Atlas**, T028-719309, www.atlas-mirleft.com, is a real gem. This vibrant yet relaxed hotel is a champion of the modern Moroccan vibe – fusing bright colours with simple yet chic traditional furnishings. Nice chill-out areas including a roof terrace with seating and covered balcony area. B&B from 240dh or 300dh with bathroom.

€ **Hotel Abertih**, T028-710304, www.abertih.com, is another fantastic, eclectic small hotel with 11 simple yet pretty rooms plus a roof terrace bang in the centre of the village. B&B from 240dh or 300dh with bathroom.

Sidi Ifni

Spanish controlled until 1969 Sidi Ifni is now a quiet, crumbling, fishing town with a port 2 km to the south. There is a bank here as well as a post office and internet access.

Sleeping

There are several cheap places to stay.

€ **Hotel Suerta Loca**, just off Plaza de la Marina, T028-875350, blue and white fronted, one of the best with doubles around 110dh. It's clean, comfortable and friendly and does good food – just give them a bit of advance notice.

Alternatively swing by the chilled **Café Nomad** by the mosque on Moulay Youssef for some tasty fare and chat. There is a also a basic **campsite** just south of the town.

South of Sidi Ifni

South of Sidi Ifni, heading towards Plage Blanche the coast road turns to rough *piste* which is fairly inaccessible without a 4WD. Travelling just inland along the main N1, the next major town south of Sidi Ifni is, Tan Tan, formerly the southernmost town in Morocco before the integration of the Western Sahara (still a disputed territory). Tan Tan is pretty uninspiring but has handy banks, food stores, cafés and accommodation. Tan Tan plage is around 25 km from the town and home to the

€ **Auberge Villa Ocean**, T028-879660, a mellow spot on the sea front and popular with bikers heading south. Rooms around 200dh, restaurant also available.

Over 200 km west along the wild, sand-blown N1, the dune-backed **Tarfaya** at Cap Juby is just 72 nautical miles from Lanzarote and has its own 'castle' melting into the sands but little else: a few stores, basic cafés and very simple accommodation.

Continuing 100 km south is **Laayoune**, the main town in Western Sahara, complete with banks, post office, police, internet, cafés, accommodation from 4-star to basic, as well as it's very own weird vibe. Built by the Spanish, it is now very much Moroccan (following huge investment and resettlement). The most noticeable benefit to transiting surfers being cheaper fuel. However due to ongoing disputes over the ownership of the territory, there is a noticeable police and UN presence here.

Dakhla is a serious commitment – around a 500 km drive south from Laayoune but if you make the trek there are banks and even a tourist office here as well as plenty of places to stay and a couple of cafes. If the thought of the drive north is too much, fear not you could always hop on the daily bus to Agadir – around a 20-hr trip!

LUCIA GRIGGI

11 The old anchor factory watches over the point.

KRISTEN PELOU

Fishermen riding out the waves in Taghazoute.

PENICHE PORTUGAL
SURFCAMP
SURF SCHOOL
BEDS
SURF TOURS
RENTALS
BIKES
INTERNET
BBQ
WWW.PENICHESURFCAMP.COM

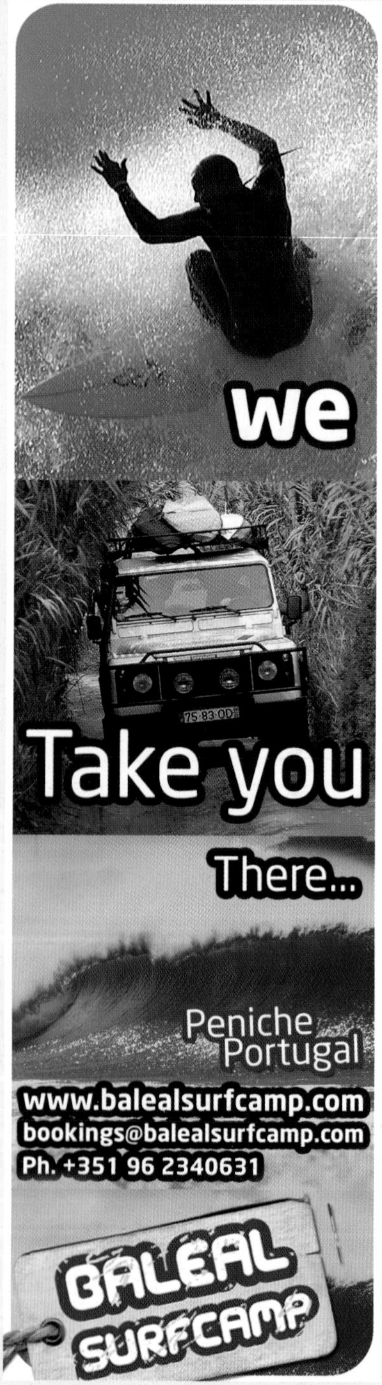
we
Take you
There...
Peniche
Portugal
www.balealsurfcamp.com
bookings@balealsurfcamp.com
Ph. +351 96 2340631
BALEAL
SURFCAMP

Surf Adventures

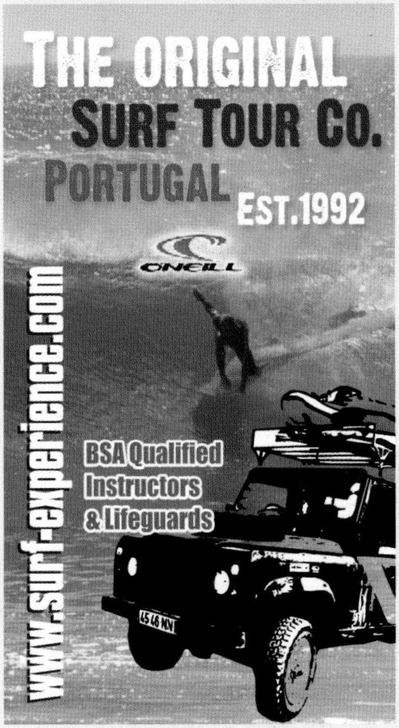

Surf Shops

Surf Shops

Lahinch Surf Shop
Old Promenade, Lahinch, Co. Clare, Eire
☎00 353 65708 1543 Fax 00 353 65708 1684
Surf report on 00 353 (0)818 365 180
Email: bear@iol.ie www.lahinchsurfshop.com

Lahinch Surf Shop was the first surf shop to open in Ireland. It is also closer to the surf than any surf shop anywhere according to visitors who have been in surf shops all over the world. At times it is too close as the storm waves try to come in the door. We are open all year round.

puro nectar is located in the seaside town of Dunbar with a wide selection of all your surfing needs stockists of john carper (jc) almeric, saltrock, oshea, and nsp boards there is something for every one, also surf hire £20.00 per full day. Wide range of surf wear and accesories.

opening times
mon- wed 10am -5pm
thurs-fri 10am-6pm
sat 10am 5pm
sun12-5pm
or by arrangment by calling
07900617740

puro nectar surf
High Street, Dunbar, East Lothian
EH42 1JJ
tel 01368 869 810
Fax 01368 869 810
web www.puronectarsurf.com

SURF & SNOW HOLIDAYS
IN THE UK & ABROAD
SURFERS
WORLD
www.surfersworld.co.uk
+44 (0) 1271 871224

CROYDE'S FAMOUS
FREEHOUSE
GOOD FOOD
The Thatch
Since 85
& DRINK COMPANY
Great Food, Superb Bar
& Friendly Service Since 1985
Bed & Breakfast from £30pp
www.thethatch-croyde.com
Tel. 01271 890349
The Thatched Barn Inn
14 Hobbs Hill, Croyde, North Devon, Ex33 1LZ

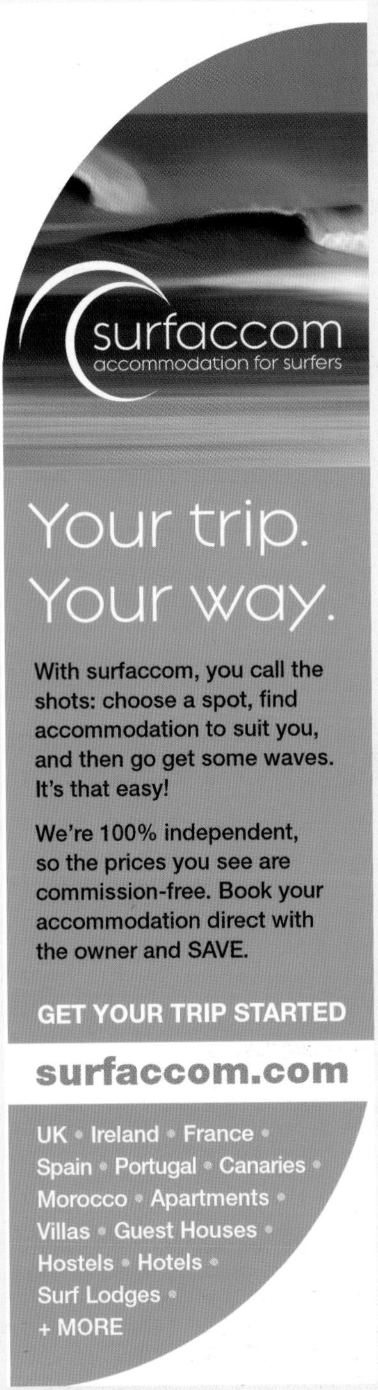
surfaccom
accommodation for surfers
Your trip.
Your way.
With surfaccom, you call the shots: choose a spot, find accommodation to suit you, and then go get some waves. It's that easy!
We're 100% independent, so the prices you see are commission-free. Book your accommodation direct with the owner and SAVE.
GET YOUR TRIP STARTED
surfaccom.com
UK • Ireland • France •
Spain • Portugal • Canaries •
Morocco • Apartments •
Villas • Guest Houses •
Hostels • Hotels •
Surf Lodges •
+ MORE

Out
now!
Footprint
Snowboarding the World
Matt Barr, Chris Moran & Ewan Wallace
ISBN: 9781904777786 £19.99
An endless source of reference...
Ed Leigh,
snowboarder
& broadcaster
Footprint
Travel guides

Credits

Footprint credits
Editor: Alan Murphy
Map editor: Sarah Sorensen
Layout and production: Patrick Dawson, Angus Dawson, Emma Bryers

Managing Director: Andy Riddle
Publisher: Patrick Dawson
Editorial: Felicity Laughton, Nicola Gibbs, Jo Williams, Sophie Blacksell, Sara Chare
Cartography: Robert Lunn, Kevin Feeney
Design: Mytton Williams
Sales and marketing: Hannah Bonnell
Advertising: Renu Sibal
Business Development: Zoë Jackson
Finance and administration: Elizabeth Taylor

Photography credits
Front cover: Sharpy
Back cover: Laurent Masurel

Print
Manufactured in Italy by Printer Trento
Pulp from sustainable forests

The colour maps are not intended to have any political significance.

Every effort has been made to ensure that the facts in this guidebook are accurate. However, travellers should note that places change, owners move on and properties close or are sold. Travellers should also obtain advice from consulates, airlines etc about travel and visa requirements before travelling. The authors and publishers cannot accept responsibility for any loss, injury or inconvenience however caused.

Publishing information
Surfing Europe
2nd edition

March 2008

ISBN 978-1-904777-95-3
CIP DATA: A catalogue record for this book is available from the British Library

Published by Footprint
6 Riverside Court
Lower Bristol Road
Bath BA2 3DZ, UK
T +44 (0)1225 469141
F +44 (0)1225 469461
discover@footprintbooks.com
www.footprintbooks.com

Footprint feedback
We try as hard as we can to make each Footprint guide as up to date as possible but, of course, things always change. If you want to let us know about your experiences – good, bad or ugly – then don't delay, go to www.footprintbooks.com and send in your comments.